RENEWALS 458-4574

THE NEW BLACKWELL COMPANION TO SOCIAL THEORY

BLACKWELL COMPANIONS TO SOCIOLOGY

The *Blackwell Companions to Sociology* provide introductions to emerging topics and theoretical orientations in sociology as well as presenting the scope and quality of the discipline as it is currently configured. Essays in the Companions tackle broad themes or central puzzles within the field and are authored by key scholars who have spent considerable time in research and reflection on the questions and controversies that have activated interest in their area. This authoritative series will interest those studying sociology at advanced undergraduate or graduate level as well as scholars in the social sciences and informed readers in applied disciplines.

Series List:

The New Blackwell Companion to Social Theory
Edited by Bryan S. Turner

The Blackwell Companion to Major Social Theorists
Edited by George Ritzer

The Blackwell Companion to Law and Society
Edited by Austin Sarat

The Blackwell Companion to the Sociology of Culture
Edited by Mark Jacobs and Nancy Hanrahan

The Blackwell Companion to Social Inequalities
Edited by Mary Romero and Eric Margolis

Available in paperback

The Blackwell Companion to Political Sociology
Edited by Kate Nash and Alan Scott

The Blackwell Companion to Medical Sociology
Edited by William C. Cockerham

The Blackwell Companion to Sociology
Edited by Judith R. Błau

The Blackwell Companion to Major Classical Social Theorists
Edited by George Ritzer

The Blackwell Companion to Major Contemporary Social Theorists
Edited by George Ritzer

The Blackwell Companion to Criminology
Edited by Colin Sumner

The Blackwell Companion to the Sociology of Families
Edited by Jacqueline Scott, Judith Treas, and Martin Richards

The Blackwell Companion to Social Movements
Edited by David A. Snow, Sarah A. Soule, and Hanspeter Kriesi

THE NEW BLACKWELL COMPANION TO

Social Theory

EDITED BY

BRYAN S. TURNER

WILEY-BLACKWELL
A John Wiley & Sons, Ltd., Publication

This edition first published 2009
© 2009 Blackwell Publishing Ltd

Blackwell Publishing was acquired by John Wiley & Sons in February 2007. Blackwell's publishing program has been merged with Wiley's global Scientific, Technical, and Medical business to form Wiley-Blackwell.

Registered Office
John Wiley & Sons Ltd, The Atrium, Southern Gate, Chichester, West Sussex, PO19 8SQ, United Kingdom

Editorial Offices
350 Main Street, Malden, MA 02148-5020, USA
9600 Garsington Road, Oxford, OX4 2DQ, UK
The Atrium, Southern Gate, Chichester, West Sussex, PO19 8SQ, UK

For details of our global editorial offices, for customer services, and for information about how to apply for permission to reuse the copyright material in this book please see our website at www.wiley.com/wiley-blackwell.

The right of Bryan S. Turner to be identified as the author of the editorial material in this work has been asserted in accordance with the Copyright, Designs and Patents Act 1988.

Wiley also publishes its books in a variety of electronic formats. Some content that appears in print may not be available in electronic books.

Designations used by companies to distinguish their products are often claimed as trademarks. All brand names and product names used in this book are trade names, service marks, trademarks or registered trademarks of their respective owners. The publisher is not associated with any product or vendor mentioned in this book. This publication is designed to provide accurate and authoritative information in regard to the subject matter covered. It is sold on the understanding that the publisher is not engaged in rendering professional services. If professional advice or other expert assistance is required, the services of a competent professional should be sought.

Library of Congress Cataloging-in-Publication Data has been applied for

ISBN: 978-1-4051-6900-4 (hardback)

A catalogue record for this book is available from the British Library.

Set in 10 on 12.5 pt Sabon by SNP Best-set Typesetter Ltd., Hong Kong

Printed in Singapore by Markono Print Media Pte Ltd

1   2009

Contents

List of Contributors

Jeffrey C. Alexander is the Lillian Chavenson Saden Professor of Sociology and Co-director of the Center for Cultural Sociology at Yale University. He is the author of *The Meanings of Social Life: A Cultural Sociology* (2003) and *The Civil Sphere* (2006), co-author of *Cultural Trauma and Collective Identity* (2004), and co-editor of *Social Performance: Symbolic Action, Cultural Pragmatics, and Ritual* (2006) and *The Cambridge Companion to Durkheim* (2005).

Patrick Baert is University Senior Lecturer in Sociology at the University of Cambridge. He is also Fellow and Director of Studies in Social and Political Sciences at Selwyn College, Cambridge. He is interested in social theory, the philosophy of social science, and the sociology of culture. Amongst his publications are *Philosophy of the Social Sciences: Towards Pragmatism* (2005), *Social Theory in the 20th Century* (1998), *Time, Self and Social Being* (1992), and the edited volumes *Pragmatism and European Social Theory* (with B. S. Turner, 2007) and *Time in Contemporary Intellectual Thought* (2000). He studied at the universities of Brussels and Oxford, where he obtained his DPhil. He has held various visiting posts, for instance at Amiens, Aix-en-Provence, Berlin, Brussels, Cape Town, Concepcion, London, Paris, Rome, and Vancouver. He has been Vice-President for Publications of the European Sociological Association and Coordinator of the Social Theory Research Network of the ESA. He holds editorial positions at *European Societies*, the *Journal for Classical Sociology*, the *European Journal of Social Theory*, and the *International Journal of the Humanities*.

Jack Barbalet is Foundation Professor of Sociology at the University of Western Sydney. Previously he was Professor of Sociology at the University of Leicester (1999–2008), and he has held positions in sociology at the Australian National University, in political science at the University of Adelaide, and in economics at the University of Papua New Guinea. In 2007 he was Scholar-in-Residence at the Max Planck Institute for the Study of Societies, in Cologne, Germany. He has researched and published widely in sociological theory, political sociology, economic sociology, and, more recently, the sociology of emotions. Among his recent publications are *Emotion, Social Theory, and Social Structure: A Macrosociological Approach* (1998 and 2001), *Emotions and Sociology* (2002), and *Weber, Passion and Profits: "The Protestant Ethic and the Spirit of Capitalism" in Context* (2008). He is currently writing another book, *The Constitution of Markets: Rationality, Power and Interests*, to be published by Oxford University Press. Current research is concerned with the interface between economic science and sociological themes, and especially the benefits to sociological theorizing of critical engagement with recent developments in economic science.

Judith Blau is Professor of Sociology at the University of North Carolina, Chapel Hill, where she chairs the university's Social and Economic Justice Undergraduate Program. Blau is president of the US chapter of Sociologists without Borders/ Sociólogos sin Fronteras, an NGO that advances an epistemic rooted in three premises: the universality of human rights, the importance of collective goods over private goods, and the merits of participatory democracy. Her recent books include a trilogy with Alberto Moncada.

John Boli is Professor of Sociology at Emory University. He has held visiting appointments at Lund University, Sweden, the University of Copenhagen, Denmark, and the University of Santa Clara, California. A native Californian and graduate of Stanford University, he has published extensively on the topics of globalization, world culture, international nongovernmental organizations, education, citizenship, and state power and authority in the world polity. Recent books include *World Culture: Origins and Consequences* and *The Globalization Reader* (third edition), both with Frank Lechner, as well as *Constructing World Culture: International Nongovernmental Organizations since 1875*, with George Thomas. His current research concerns the origins and development of world culture and transnational structuration since the twelfth century, with a special focus on Christendom and the Roman Catholic Church. He is also studying the impact of world culture on transnational corporations over the past several decades.

Raymond Boudon is Professor Emeritus at the University of Paris–Sorbonne, and has worked on education, social mobility, beliefs, values, sociological theory, and the philosophy of the social sciences. He is member of the Institut de France (Académie des Sciences Morales et Politiques), the Academia Europaea, the British Academy, the American Academy of Arts and Sciences, the Royal Society of Canada, the Central European Academy of Arts and Sciences, the International Academy of the Human Sciences of St. Petersburg, and the Academy of the Social Sciences of Argentina. He has been a Fellow at the Stanford Center for Advanced Study in the Behavioural Sciences, and invited professor, notably at the universities of Geneva, Harvard, Oxford, Chicago, Stockholm, and Trent. His publications include *Education, Opportunity and Social Inequality* (1974); *The Logic of Social Action* (1981); *Theories of Social Change* (1986); *The Analysis of Ideology* (1989); *A Critical Dictionary of Sociology* (1989; with F. Bourricaud); *The Art of Self Persuasion* (1994); *The Origin of Values* (2001); *The Poverty of Relativism* (2004); *Tocqueville* *for Today* (2006); and *The Virtue of Common Sense* (forthcoming). He is on the board of the *Année sociologique* and *Rationality and Society* and has been on the board of the *American Journal of Sociology*. He has been the editor for sociology of the *International Encyclopedia of the Social and Behavioral Sciences*.

Daniel Chaffee is an Associate Lecturer and PhD student at Flinders University, Australia. He studied social theory and philosophy at Wesleyan University, USA. He received his MA by research in sociology from University of Kent at Canterbury, UK. He is currently writing his PhD dissertation, provisionally entitled "Social Theory after Society: A Comparative Critique of Anthony Giddens and Manuel Castells." He is currently editing, with Sam Han, *The Charles Lemert Reader* (forthcoming from Paradigm Press).

Daniel Chernilo graduated in sociology from the University of Chile and obtained his PhD at the University of Warwick, where he was also a lecturer in sociology. He is currently an associate professor of sociology at the University of Alberto Hurtado in Chile, where he is the director of its doctoral program. He is a member of the International Advisory Board of the *European Journal of Social Theory* and a Fellow of the Warwick Centre for Social Theory. He has published a number of articles, in both English and Spanish, on classical and contemporary social theory, and is the author of *A Social Theory of the Nation-State: The Political Forms of Modernity beyond Methodological Nationalism* (2007). He is now writing on the normative foundations of modern social theory in connection with the tradition of natural law.

Oonagh Corrigan is Senior Lecturer in Clinical Education Research at the Peninsula Medical School, University of Plymouth. She has previously held lectureships in sociology at the universities of Cambridge and Plymouth as well as a Leverhulme Visiting Fellowship at the W. Maurice Young Centre for Applied Ethics, University of British Columbia. Her main areas of interest are in medical sociology, specifically genetics, bioethics, and, more recently, medical education. She has published widely on these topics. Her work on informed consent has made a noteworthy contribution to an understanding of this concept in the context of biomedical research, and with Richard Tutton she edited *Genetic Databases: Socio-ethical Issues in the Collection and Use of DNA* (2004).

Gerard Delanty is Professor of Sociology and Social and Political Thought at the University of Sussex, where he is Director of the Centre of Critical Social Theory and convener of the MA in Social and Political Thought. He was previously Professor of Sociology, University of Liverpool. In 2006 he was a visiting professor at Deakin University, Melbourne, and has previously held visiting professorships at Doshisha University, Kyoto, and York University, Toronto. He is the editor of the *European Journal of Social Theory*. He has written on various issues in social and political theory, European identity, and the cultural and historical sociology of modernity. His books include *Social Theory in a Changing World* (1999), *Modernity and Postmodernity* (2000), *Community* (2003), and, with C. Rumford) *Rethinking Europe: Social Theory and the Implications of Europeanization* (2005). He has edited the *Handbook of Contemporary European Social Theory* (2005), *Europe and Asia Beyond East and West* (2006), (with Piet Strydom) *Philosophies of Social Science: The Classic and Contemporary Readings* (2003), and (with Krishan Kumar) *The Handbook of Nations and Nationalism* (2006). His main current research concerns cosmopolitanism theory and with an application to issues of Europeanization and modernity in comparative perspective.

Julio Pérez Díaz is a research fellow in the Demography Department of the Spanish Council for Scientific Research (CSIC) in Madrid and previously worked at the Centre d'Estudis Demogràfics, Universitat Autònoma de Barcelona. He is a specialist in population policies and demographic aging, and member of the International Union for the Scientific Study of Population. He edits a portal on the internet on population aging (<http://www.ced.uab.es/jperez>) and advises the Colegio de Médicos de Barcelona on the subject. Recent publications include *La Madurez de Masas* (Observatorio de las Personas Mayores-IMSERSO, 2003) which received a Fundació La Caixa Prize; 'Consecuencias sociales del envejecimiento demográfico', in *Papeles de Economía Española* (2005), and 'Feminización de la vejez y estado del bienestar en España', in *Revista Española de Investigaciones Sociológicas* (2003).

Michele Dillon is a native of Ireland, where she graduated with a bachelor's degree in social science and a master's degree in sociology from University College Dublin. She subsequently received her PhD in sociology from the University of California at Berkeley. Currently, Dillon is Professor of Sociology at the University of New Hampshire, president-elect of the Association for the Sociology of Religion, and past chair of the American Sociological Association section for the sociology of religion. Her research and writing focuses on religion broadly defined to engage important questions in culture, politics, identity, the life course, and sociological theory. Dillon's publications include *In the Course of a Lifetime: Tracing Religious Belief, Practice, and Change* (2007; with Paul Wink), *Catholic Identity: Balancing Reason, Faith, and Power* (1999), and *Debating Divorce: Moral Conflict in Ireland* (1993). She has also published many research articles, and edited the Cambridge *Handbook of the Sociology of Religion* (2003).

Mary Evans taught sociology and women's studies at the University of Kent from 1971 to 2007 and was part of the group which established the MA in women's studies. She has written on various literary figures (most particularly Jane Austen and Simone de Beauvoir), and on various aspects of feminism and social theory, and was an editor of the *European Journal of Women's Studies* for 15 years. At present she is a Visiting Professorial Fellow at the Gender Institute of the London School of Economics, and is working on studies of detective fiction and the literature of twenty-first-century pessimism.

Michael G. Flaherty is Professor of Sociology at Eckerd College. His areas of interest include social psychology, qualitative methods, and the sociology of time. He is the author of *A Watched Pot: How We Experience Time* (1999). His current research concerns the relationship between agency and various forms of temporal experience.

He was the editor of *Symbolic Interaction* from 1996 to 1999. With Carolyn Ellis, he is the co-editor of *Investigating Subjectivity: Research on Lived Experience* (1992) and *Social Perspectives on Emotions*, volume 3 (1995). Recent publications include "Variation in the Perceived Passage of Time: A Cross-National Study," with Betina Freidin and Ruth Sautu, in *Social Psychology Quarterly* (2005); "Sociotemporal Rhythms in E-mail: A Case Study," with Lucas Seipp-Williams, in *Time and Society* (2005); "Time Work: Customizing Temporal Experience," in *Social Psychology Quarterly* (2003); and "Making Time: Agency and the Construction of Temporal Experience," in *Symbolic Interaction* (2002).

John Heritage is Professor of Sociology, at UCLA. His primary research field is conversation analysis, together with its applications in the fields of mass communication and medicine. He is the author of *Garfinkel and Ethnomethodology* (1984) and, with Steven Clayman, *The News Interview: Journalists and Public Figures on the Air* (2002). He is the editor of *Structures of Social Action* (1984, with Max Atkinson), *Talk at Work* (1992, with Paul Drew), *Communication in Medical Care* (2006, with Douglas Maynard), and *Conversation Analysis* (2006, with Paul Drew). He is currently working on a range of topics in physician–patient interaction, and on US presidential press conferences (with Steven Clayman).

Richard A. Hilbert received his PhD at the University of California, Santa Barbara, and is Professor of Sociology at Gustavus Adolphus College. He has studied teacher education, chronic pain, role theory, bureaucracy, and anomie, as well as classical sociology and ethnomethodology. His is currently examining how people report dreams to one another.

John Holmwood is Professor of Sociology at the University of Birmingham. His first academic post was at the University of Tasmania before taking up a position at the University of Edinburgh. He has held professorships at the University of Edinburgh and at the University of Sussex, where he was also Dean of the School of Social Sciences and Cultural Studies. His main research interests are the relation between social theory and explanation and social stratification and inequality. His current research addresses the challenge of global social inquiry and the role of pragmatism in the construction of public sociology. He is the author of *Social Theory and Explanation* (1991; with A. Stewart) and *Founding Sociology? Talcott Parsons and the Idea of General Theory* (1996), as well as other edited books and articles.

Krishan Kumar is University Professor and William R. Kenan, Jr., Professor of Sociology at the University of Virginia. He was previously Professor of Social and Political Thought at the University of Kent at Canterbury, England. He has been a Visiting Professor at the universities of Harvard, Colorado, Bergen, and Bristol, and at the Ecole des Hautes Etudes en Sciences Sociales, Paris. In 2004–5 he was a member of the Institute for Advanced Study, Princeton. Among his publications are *Utopia and Anti-Utopia in Modern Times* (1987), *1989: Revolutionary Ideas and Ideals* (2001), *The Making of English National Identity* (2003), and *From Post-Industrial to Post-Modern Society*, 2nd edition (2003). He is currently working on empires.

John Law is a Professor of Sociology at Lancaster University and at the Centre for Science Studies. With a background in both sociology and science, technology, and society (STS), he is interested in disorder, multiple orderings, materialities, and methods. He works primarily on nature and culture, agriculture, animal welfare, spatiality, and catastrophes, and he is currently exploring the 2001 UK foot and mouth epizootic. His books include *Organizing Modernity* (1994), *Aircraft Stories* (2002), and, most recently, *After Method* (2004), which is on methodologies for knowing disorderly phenomena, and brings together humanities and social science insights to propose a more generous, distributed, and inclusive understanding of research method that is able to deal with "mess." His website is at <http://www.lancs.ac.uk/fass/sociology/staff/law/law.htm>.

Frank J. Lechner is Professor of Sociology at Emory University in Atlanta. A native of the Netherlands, he obtained his PhD from the University of Pittsburgh before joining the Emory faculty. His interest in the cultural dimensions of globalization is reflected in two recent books, *World Culture: Origins and Consequences* (2005; with John Boli) and *The Netherlands: Globalization and National Identity* (2008). With Boli he also edited *The Globalization Reader* (Blackwell, several editions). He continues to contribute to the sociology of religion, for example with a paper on "Rational Choice and Religious Economies" in the forthcoming Sage *Handbook of the Sociology of Religion*, and is also branching out into the sociology of sports, as illustrated by a paper on "Imagined Communities in the Global Game" in *Global Networks* (2007). He is working on a text, *Globalization: The Making of World Society*, that addresses recent controversies in the field in an empirically focused manner.

Charles Lemert is the John C. Andrus Professor of Sociology at Wesleyan University in Connecticut. He is the author, most recently, of *Durkheim's Ghosts: Cultural Logics and Social Things*, and *Thinking the Unthinkable: The Riddles of Classical Social Theories*. Lemert is currently at work on *Queer Things Abounding: The Force of Small Clues in Marx and Freud*, as well as the fourth editions of his popular textbooks, *Social Things: An Introduction to the Sociological Life* and *Social Theory: The Classic and Multicultural Readings*.

John MacInnes is Professor of the Sociology of Europe at the University of Edinburgh, and Investigador Associado at the Centre d'Estudis Demogràfics, Universitat Autònoma de Barcelona. Previously he was a research fellow and then lecturer at the University of Glasgow (1978–95) and has also worked or been a visiting fellow at the universities of Lyon II and Pompeu Fabra (Barcelona). With Julio Pérez Diaz he is completing a reinterpretation of the nature of the demographic transition, *The Reproductive Revolution*, to be published by Routledge. Previous books include *The End of Masculinity* (1998) and *Thatcherism at Work* (1987), both published by Open University Press, and the jointly authored *Stateless Nations in the 21st Century* (2001), *For Sociology: Legacies and Prospects* (2000), *Industrial Sociology and Economic Crisis* (1991), and *Just Managing: Authority and Democracy in Industry* (1985). His interests range from the integration of demography and sociology, and in particular the relationship between families and the labor market, through to the study of "identity" in its various dimensions: gender, national, ethnic, and class. He is currently writing a monograph on national identity and constitutional change in the UK and Spain.

Alberto Moncada is currently vice-president of UNESCO's Valencia Center and president of Sociologists without Borders/Sociólogos sin Fronteras, an NGO that advances an understanding of human rights and promotes alliances between academicians and human rights advocates. Moncada has a PhD in public law from Madrid University, and in studies in sociology and education from London University. He has taught at several universities – Madrid, Stanford, Florida International, Lima, and Alcalá – and was the first rector of the University of Piura, Peru. He has served as consultant to the Organization of American States, UNESCO, and the Council of Europe, and is a founding member of various associations, including the European Association for University Education, the Sociological Association of Madrid, the Association of Friendship with Latinos, and the Moncada Kajon Foundation for Social Research. The most recent of his 12 major research projects is an investigation of the complex links between American and Spanish culture. Besides his collaborative books with Judith Blau on human rights, Moncada is the author of articles in academic and general journals and of 30 books, the most recent of which is *Para Entender la Globalización* (2006). He is regularly consulted by Spanish media.

Jan Pakulski (PhD ANU, MA Warsaw) is Professor of Sociology and Dean of Arts at the University of Tasmania, Hobart. He writes on social change, social inequality, elites, social movements, and post-communism. He is author of *Globalising Inequality* (2004), co-editor of *Postcommunist Elites and Democracy in Eastern Europe* (1998), and co-author of *The Death of Class* (1996) and *Postmodernization* (1992).

Isaac Reed is Assistant Professor of Sociology at the University of Colorado. He has published articles in *Sociological Theory* and *Cultural Sociology*, and is the co-editor of *Culture, Society, and Democracy: The Interpretive Approach* (2007) and *Meaning and Method: The Cultural Approach to Sociology* (forthcoming).

Sophia Roosth is a graduate student in the Science, Technology and Society Program at MIT, and her research focuses on the anthropology of the experimental life sciences, specifically the emerging field of synthetic biology. In studying the construction of biotic systems de novo, Roosth is most interested in examining how biological materials are designed, fabricated, and standardized, how engineering idioms are imported into biological practice, and how the free software movement affects bioengineering research. She is also currently writing about the use of acoustic technologies to listen to cells.

Fernando Domínguez Rubio is a doctoral candidate in the Department of Sociology at the University of Cambridge, UK. He has been a visiting scholar at the University of Berkeley (EEUU), at Lancaster University, and at the Centre de Sociologie de l'Innovation in France. His research interests include social theory, cultural sociology and the sociology of the arts. He has recently published "The Politics of Nature Cultures: Republican Constitutions and Animal Manifestos" in *European Societies* (2005).

Giuseppe Sciortino (PhD Bologna) is Associate Professor of Sociology at the University of Trento, Italy. He is a Faculty Fellow of Yale's Center for Cultural Sociology as well as serving on the editorial board of *Sociological Theory*. He has experience in ethnographic fieldwork in Southeast Asia, particularly in rural Cambodia. Besides sociological theory, his research interests are in migration studies and ethnic relations. Recent work includes a critical edition of Talcott Parsons' last major manuscript, *American Society: Toward a Theory of Societal Community* (2007). Recent articles in English include "How Different Can We Be? Talcott Parsons, the Societal Community and the Multicultural Debate," in R. C. Fox, V. M. Lidz, and H. J. Berhshady (eds.), *After Parsons* (2005), and "From Homogeneity to Difference? Comparing Multiculturalism as a Description and as a Field for Claim-Making," in *Comparative Social Research*, 22 (2003). He is currently involved in two projects: an empirical study of irregular migratory systems in western Europe and an analytic reconstruction of the classical roots of a sociology of human sexuality.

Susan Silbey received her PhD in political science from the University of Chicago and did her postgraduate training in ethnography in the Sociology Department of Brandeis University. She has written about the social organization of law in diverse institutional and informal settings, including attorney general's offices, courts, schools, private homes, businesses, and scientific laboratories; she has also studied alternative forms of dispute resolution, including negotiation and mediation. She edited *Studies in Law, Politics and Society* (1990–7) and the *Law & Society Review* (1998–2000). In 1998 she published, with Patricia Ewick, *The Common Place of Law: Stories from Everyday Life*, describing the ways in which Americans imagine, use, and construct the rule of law, and in 2003 co-edited *In Litigation: Do the "Haves" Still Come Out Ahead?* with Herbert Kritzer. Her current research looks at the role and conceptions of law in scientific laboratories, comparing the place of law in expert communities and popular culture. She is supervising an experiment in ethnographic fieldwork, as well as research on the development of new safety regimes in research labs and the effects of laboratory organization on gender hierarchies in science. In addition, she is conducting a six-year longitudinal study of engineering education, following a cohort of students through four different engineering schools. Professor Silbey is past president of the Law & Society Association, and a fellow of the American Academy of Political and Social Science, and in November 2006 received a Doctor Honoris Causa from the Ecole Normale Supérieure Cachan in Paris.

Rob Stones is Professor in Sociology at the University of Essex, and was head of department there from 2004 to 2007. He is the editor of two book series for Palgrave Macmillan, *Traditions in Social Theory* and the forthcoming *Themes in Social Theory*. His research interests lie in the development of structuration theory; the ways in which social theory can inform empirical case studies; documentary and feature films' representations of modernity and postmodernity; and the deepening of links between moral and political philosophy and sociological theory. His books include the second edition of the edited volume *Key Sociological Thinkers* (2008), *Structuration Theory* (2005), and *Sociological Reasoning: Towards a PAst-modern Sociology* (1996). Recent articles include "Power and Structuration Theory," in S. Clegg and M. Haugaard (eds.), *Handbook of Power* (2008); "Film, Postmodernism and the Sociological Imagination," in J. Powell and T. Owen (eds.), *Reconstructing Postmodernism* (2007; with Sung Kyung Kim); and "Rights, Social Theory and Political Philosophy: A Framework for Case Study Research," in Lydia Morris (ed.), *Rights: Sociological Perspectives* (2006).

Richard Swedberg is Professor of Sociology at Cornell University. His specialties are economic sociology, including economy and law, and sociological theory, especially the classics. His degrees are in law (Stockholm University) and in sociology (Boston College). Before going to Cornell he worked at the Department of Sociology at Stockholm University as Professor of Sociology, especially economic sociology. His books include *Interest* (2005), *A Max Weber Dictionary* (2005; with the assistance of Ola Agevall), *Principles of Economic Sociology* (2003), *Max Weber and the Idea of Economic Sociology* (1998), and *Joseph A. Schumpeter: His Life and Work* (1991). He is also the editor of various volumes, most recently *On Capitalism* (2007; with Victor Nee), but also, with Neil Smelser, *The Handbook of Economic Sociology* (first edition 1994; second edition 2005). Swedberg is currently working on two topics: Alexis de Tocqueville and entrepreneurship.

Bryan S. Turner was Professor of Sociology at the University of Cambridge (1998–2005) and Professor of Sociology in the Asia Research Institute, National University of Singapore (2005–9). He is currently the Alona Evans Distinguished Professor of Sociology at Wellesley College Boston, and Professor of Social and Political Thought at the University of Western Sydney. His current research is on religion and politics in Asia, the growth of piety in the Asian middle classes, and the problems of citizenship and human rights. Professor Turner's long-term research interest concerns the human body and vulnerability with special reference to religion, medicine, and law. He has published *Vulnerability and Human Rights* (2006) with Penn State University Press, and has edited the *Cambridge Dictionary of Sociology* (2006). Other recent publications include *Classical Sociology* (1999) and *The New Medical Sociology* (2004). With Chris Rojek, he has published *Society & Culture: Principles of Scarcity and Solidarity* (2001), and he has edited, with Engin Isin, the *Handbook of Citizenship Studies* (2002), and, with Craig Calhoun and Chris Rojek, *The Sage Handbook of Sociology* (2005).

Stephen Turner is Graduate Research Professor in Philosophy at the University of South Florida. His writings on social theory include books on explanation, such as *Sociological Explanation as Translation* (1980), Weber, and Durkheim, and on such topics as practice (*The Social Theory of Practices*, 1994), and politics (*Liberal Democracy 3.0: Civil Society in an Age of Experts*, 2003), as well as articles and chapters on charisma, rationality, agency theory, fascism, organizational culture, and normativity. He has also written extensively on the history and philosophy of social science and on the politics of science.

John Urry is Professor of Sociology at Lancaster University. He was educated at Cambridge, with a BA/MA (double first) in economics and a PhD in sociology. He has since worked at Lancaster University, where he has been Head of Department, Founding Dean of the Social Sciences Faculty, and University Dean of Research. He is also a Fellow of the Royal Society of Arts, Founding Academician, UK Academy of Social Sciences, and Member (1992) and Chair, RAE Panels (1996, 2001), and has an honorary doctorate from Roskilde University. He has received recent research funding from the DTI Foresight Programme, the Department for Transport (twice), EPSRC, ESRC, and the Forestry Commission. He has published more than 35 books and special issues, 100 refereed articles and 80 chapters in books. His work is translated into 11 languages, and he has lectured in more than 30 countries. His is currently Director of the Centre for Mobilities Research at Lancaster, which has extensive links throughout the world relating to the study of physical movement and its interconnections with the "virtual" and the "imaginative" (see <http://www. lancs.ac.uk/fss/sociology/cemore/index.htm>, and <http://www.cemore.blogspot. com/>). Some recent books include *Sociology beyond Societies* (2000), *The Tourist Gaze* (second edition 2002), *Tourism Mobilities: Places to Play, Places in Play* (2004), *Performing Tourist Places* (2004), *Automobilities* (2005), *Mobile Technologies of the City* (2006), *Mobilities, Networks, Geographies* (2006), and *Mobilities* (2007).

Darin Weinberg studied social philosophy at the London School of Economics and sociology at UCLA, where he received his PhD in 1998. After teaching sociological theory at the University of Florida for three years he went to Cambridge in 2000, where he is currently University Senior Lecturer in the Department of Sociology and a Fellow of King's College. His research has focused primarily on two related projects. The first has been to articulate, and defend, a perspective on social research methods that reconciles the insights of the sociology of scientific practice regarding the social structural embeddedness of scientific research with a resolute commitment to scientific objectivity. The second project has been to critique, and provide an analytic alternative to, the longstanding antinomy between naturalism and social constructionism in the sociology of mental health, the addictions, and learning disability. This research considers the practical purposes to which concepts of addiction, mental disorder, and learning disability are applied in various historical and contemporary contexts. He is particularly interested in how these concepts figure in state-sponsored campaigns of social welfare and social control, and in what their uses reveal about how and why people distinguish the social and natural forces held to govern human behavior. His books include *Of Others Inside: Insanity, Addiction, and Belonging in America* (2005), *Talk and Interaction in Social Research Methods* (2006; edited with Paul Drew and Geoffrey Raymond), and *Qualitative Research Methods* (2002).

Introduction

A New Agenda for Social Theory?

BRYAN S. TURNER

PRELIMINARY REMARKS

Social theory provides the necessary analytical and philosophical framework within which the social sciences can develop. Social theory both sustains the achievements of the past, notes the needs and limitations of the present, and points the way to future research issues and questions.

Any attempt to offer a generic definition of social theory is confronted immediately by the important differences between various sociological traditions. In considering social theory within a broad international framework, we need to recognize that sociology is inevitably colored by different local, national, or civilizational circumstances. Polish sociology is obviously very different from American sociology. The growth of nationalism and the nation-state had a profound effect on the early development of social theory in Europe in the nineteenth century, and World War I brought to a tragic conclusion the enormous developments in sociology in both Germany and France. In the late twentieth century, social theory has also been responding to the specific national or regional manifestations of information technology and cultural consumption in new theories of globalization. In developing this *New Companion*, I have therefore been conscious of the fact that there has been an important cultural and intellectual gap between American and European social theory. While Europeans tend to look towards Émile Durkheim, Georg Simmel, and Max Weber to define the foundational contents of classical sociology, American sociologists are more likely to consider John Dewey and G. H. Mead as crucial figures (see CHAPTER 10). This hiatus between American and European traditions, for example by reference to pragmatism, can often be exaggerated, but the division is nevertheless real (Baert and Turner 2007).

While there are important local and national contexts for the growth of social theory, the *New Companion* attempts to recognize a range of generic issues that inform its analytical content and substantive direction. There are a number of basic presuppositions to any sociological theory that we need to take into account

(Alexander 1987). Let us take four illustrations. First, there are basic questions about the epistemological and philosophical underpinnings of social theory that have a general relevance. These include fundamental questions about the relationship between social action, social practice, and social structure. Secondly, there are generic issues about the rationality of action, the difference between behavior and action, and the question about intentionality and unintended consequences of social action (see CHAPTER 9). Thirdly there are also general features of social systems that remain relevant to theoretical inquiry, regardless of specific or local concerns. There are also important debates about the relationship between ethical issues, political power, and the social functions of social theory. These debates shape the responsibility of intellectuals towards public life. Finally, there are systematic questions and problems relating to the intellectual relationships, for instance between anthropology, political science, and economics as components of social theory. These questions relate to the structure and boundaries of the social sciences as methods of understanding social phenomena.

WHAT IS SOCIAL THEORY?

Why should we take social theory seriously? Before we can answer this question, we need to grasp what is meant by "social theory." As a preliminary distinction, let us say simply that "sociological theory" is a sub-set of this more general characterization of "social theory." Answering this question about what constitutes social theory is complicated, but the task may be rendered easier by looking at some historical examples. Defining social theory apparently used to be an easy matter. Let us take two early accounts of social theory before looking at some contemporary approaches. Writing in the revised edition in 1970 to *A Reader's Guide to the Social Sciences*, Peter Blau and Joan Moore felt it sufficient simply to distinguish between grand theories of large-scale change and middle-range theories that were more closely tied to empirical data. Encompassing theories of social institutions in general were still undertaken by sociologists like Pitrim Sorokin and Talcott Parsons, but they noticed that "[i]ncreasing numbers of empirical studies are theoretically oriented, addressing themselves to problems posed by social theory and seeking to refine theoretical principles on the basis of empirical findings" (Blau and Moore 1970: 20). As leading examples, they cited the work of Seymour Martin Lipset, Michael Trow, and James Coleman (1956) on union democracy and George Homans (1950) on *The Human Group*.

In making this distinction, they were of course reflecting on the notion of "middle-range theory" that had been developed by Robert K. Merton in his *Social Theory and Social Structure* (1963) as a response to criticisms of general theories that were deemed to be too abstract and general. Merton, probably the most influential American social theorist of his generation, noted that various types of academic work were frequently lumped together under the notion of sociological theory – methodology; general sociological orientations; analysis of sociological concepts; *post factum* sociological interpretations; empirical generalizations, and finally sociological theory itself. Lamenting the all too frequent disjunction between empirical research and systematic theorizing, Merton developed the idea of theories of the middle range as illustrated in his own development of reference group theory. The problem of connecting social theory to empirical work and vice versa has, however, remained an endemic problem in sociology.

Let us take another early attempt to define theory, namely Leon Bramson's essay on "Social Theory" in *A Guide to the Social Sciences* (1966). Bramson usefully distinguished between three fundamental meanings of social theory. In the first it simply means any attempt to understand the nature and workings of society. In sociology "social theory has meant the effort to try to explain social phenomena in the same way in which the facts of the physical world were explained by the burgeoning natural sciences" (Bramson 1966: 185). In short, social theory comprises the attempt of the social sciences such as economics, sociology, and demography to explain social phenomena or "the social." But Bramson noted a second meaning, namely the development of normative theories of what would or should constitute a "good society." In this sense a social theory is not simply descriptive and explanatory but normative and prescriptive, possibly establishing strategies to create a better world. This second meaning has been highly contested since it is held that any *scientific* theory of society should be value-free and value-neutral. This defense of a scientific view of social investigation which is sometimes referred to as a positivistic orientation has been characteristically legitimized by reference to Max Weber's famous essays on objectivity in the social sciences edited by Shils and Finch (1949). Finally, Bramson noted that social theories were often part and parcel of political ideologies such as fascism and communism in the sense that, for example, Lenin's theory of the party is a "social theory" of how politics works and how to organize revolutionary activity. Bramson usefully thereby brought to attention that social theory, however overtly value-free, is necessarily bound up with actual social movements and social classes. One example would be the fact that Weber's own theories of leadership became a fundamental aspect of German politics partly through the influence of the jurist Carl Schmitt.

What might one say about contemporary attempts to define social theory? Most textbooks of modern sociology have an introductory section on either sociological theory or social theory. One influential account of sociological theory was offered by Walter Wallace, who argued persuasively that theory was simply part of the general process of sociological inquiry involving methods, observations, empirical generalizations, hypotheses, and theories. In particular he noted that theory has two crucial roles. It specifies the factors that the researcher should be able to measure *before* an inquiry and, secondly, "theory serves, *after* the research is done, as a common language (i.e. the empirical generalizations) may be translated for purposes of comparison and logical integration with the results of other researchers" (Wallace 1969: x). One good example is Richard Jenkins's *Foundations of Sociology* in which under the subheading "The Necessity of Theory" he apologetically notes that the question "what is the *point* of theory?" is among the "most common questions asked by non-sociologists and students" (Jenkins 2002: 31). He goes on nevertheless to assert that broadly defined "sociological theorizing involves the creation of abstract models of those observable realities in order to aid our better understanding of what goes on in the world of humans," and furthermore theory is at "the core of sociology's distinctive perspective" on the world of humans.

From this brief and incomplete survey, we might note that the major issues in social theory are related to: (1) the relationship between theory and empirical research, or, more naively, between concepts and facts; (2) the relationship between theory and values or between scientific inquiry and (moral) judgment; and (3) the relationship between academic work (within universities and research institutes) and the wider society, or between theory and politics. These issues have to some extent always between prominent in modern social theory – consider Karl Marx's attempt to overthrow the alleged idealism of Hegel and to proclaim that the real point of philosophy was to change the world and not merely to understand it.

Two Metaphors for Theorizing

We can shift the emphasis of this introduction by thinking less about what social theory is and thinking more about how social theory gets done by reference to two metaphors. First, we might think metaphorically of social theory as a scaffold that helps us explore data and move around social reality rather like workmen moving about the outside surface of an office block. Theoretical scaffolding permits us to examine social data from many angles, and in particular as a normative exercise to detect major faults in the social fabric – such as a condition of anomie – that might require repair. The relationship between scaffolding and buildings is interactive and mutually supportive. We cannot get around the face of the building without the support of the building itself. This metaphor may help us to encapsulate the view that theory without empirical work is empty, but empirical data without theory are blind. Theory helps us to build an edifice of concepts and explanations to understand social reality.

Of course, metaphors are always limited. The idea of scaffolding might suggest a relatively neutral and universal system of concepts, by implying a passive relationship between data and theory. To move to a second metaphor, possibly the best short definition of social theory has been proposed by Barry Markovsky (2005: 834) in the second volume of the *Encyclopedia of Social Theory* as an "argument" in which the "author of the theory offers the argument in an attempt to convince readers that one or more *conclusions* must follow from a series of assumptions or *premises*." I will modify Markovsky's definition to say that a theory is like a legal argument where a lawyer (researcher) attempts to convince a jury (an academic audience) that something is the case by reference to evidence (often incomplete and contested), narratives about agents (that attribute motives, reasons, and causes) as to why and how something took place (a person was murdered for example). A theory is an argument in which the social theorist strives to convince others about the nature of social reality by the use of evidence, narratives, hunches, concepts, and even material objects as "exhibits." The legal decision is then open to further inspection by legal philosophers as well as by convicted criminals.

In short, theories are rhetorical devices, and this preliminary conclusion suggests that this way of viewing theory is consistent with pragmatism (Baert 2005). Theories survive or fail depending on their rhetorical force in convincing other social scientists that their accounts of social reality are plausible, if not definitive. The plausibility of a social theory will depend on its scope, its precision, and its capacity to guide us through empirical findings. A good social theory, like a good legal argument, tends to be persuasive, plausible, and parsimonious. Finally we might extend the metaphor to say that, in English common law, legal cases are won or lost in part by reference to case law, that is, to a legal tradition. Good social theories can be cumulative rather than simply discontinuous and fashionable. The problem with modern social theory is that there is more disruption than continuity, and the rhetorical force of sociological argument has lost much of its public plausibility. This *New Companion* attempts to restore some the argumentative force of sociology as an aspect of public culture.

THE CONTEMPORARY CRISIS

Contemporary social theory can therefore be said to be in a crisis. The context and character of social theory since the 1980s (to select a decade somewhat arbitrarily) have become increasingly uncertain and difficult. As Stephen Turner points out in the final chapter of this volume (CHAPTER 28, these problems are in part related to significant changes in modern philosophy which have in large measure influenced the ways in which sociologists now think about social theory. We can connect this crisis in social theory with the rise of postmodernism, the collapse of world communism, the globalization of neoliberal economics, and the attendant transformations of social life. The postmodern era – which is explored fully by Jan Pakulski in CHAPTER 13 – can be said to have been announced with the publication in French of Jean-François Lyotard's *The Postmodern Condition*, which was translated into English in 1984.

The basic assumption of this *New Companion* is that social theory is in an intellectual crisis, and furthermore this intellectual crisis has important consequences for sociology as an academic discipline as a whole. To care about the future of sociology as an academic practice means that we need to attend to the difficulties of contemporary social theory. This crisis of sociology is in fact part of a larger issue within the social sciences and the humanities. One aspect of this crisis has been a revolution in the philosophy of the social sciences and epistemology whereby the certainties of positivism, empiricism, and objectivism have waned before the insistence that there are no theory-neutral observations of reality, that all theory is context-dependent, and that the pretension of scientific neutrality is just that – a pretension. The problems facing theory were recognized for example in Anthony Giddens and Jonathan H. Turner's *Social Theory Today*, where they observed that theory-neutral assumptions about research had been repudiated, and more "importantly science is presumed to be an interpretative endeavor, such that problems of meaning, communication and translation are immediately relevant to scientific theories" (Giddens and Turner 1987: 2). The consequence was an "increasing disillusionment" with the assumptions of mainstream social science.

What is the nature of this crisis? In fact we can speak of a double crisis, namely a crisis of the social and a crisis of its theory. The crisis in social theory can be summarized easily. It involves (1) the fragmentation of social theory into cultural theory, film theory, critical theory, feminist theory, queer theory, and so forth; (2) the widespread abandonment of or skepticism towards classical theory; (3) an increasing dependency on (continental) philosophy, literature, and humanities for inspiration; (4) a deepening divorce between theory and research; (5) an inability to provide much insight into major modern issues such as environmental pollution, low-intensity warfare and civil unrest, terrorism, famine, and global slavery; and finally (6) a tendency for social theory to become narcissistic, thereby leading to theory about theory or theory about theorists. In this final issue, we can register a distinction between first-order and second-order social theory. In first-order theorizing, there is a concentration on creating an original conceptual framework that is addressed to something. We can take almost any example. The church-sect typology attempts to explain why over time evangelical sectarian movements tend to become denominations with a bureaucracy and professional ministry (Wilson 1961). By contrast a textbook about the sociology of religion such as Richard Fenn's *The Blackwell Companion to Sociology of Religion* (2001) is a book about sociological theories and obviously not as such a theory of religious organizations. There is clearly a place for exegesis and interpretation, but these activities do not, however brilliant, amount to theories of social phenomena.

In more detail, the crisis can be illustrated by reference to the influence of post-modernism, poststructuralism (see CHAPTER 6) and the skeptical pragmatic philosophy of Richard Rorty. His reputation was originally built on his philosophy of science, namely *Philosophy and the Mirror of Nature* (1979), in which he argued that philosophers should give up the fantasy that philosophical truths could be simply a mirror of (or to) nature. If there are any philosophical truths, they are not simply mirrors of an objective reality. Because Rorty holds that all observations of nature are theory-dependent and that a correspondence theory of truth is untenable, he rejects realism as a plausible scientific position. Rorty has argued that professional philosophy has ignored the relevance of history to an understanding of philosophical concepts, mainly because philosophers have rejected the view that concepts are context-dependent. For Rorty, the task of philosophers is essentially modest, namely to help their readers abandon outdated ideas and to find more rewarding ways of thinking about society and their lives. As such, philosophy is a product of specific times and places rather than a grand narrative.

This approach to truth claims owes a great deal to John Dewey and Ludwig Wittgenstein, for whom the ability to assert truth claims is a function of language, and language is best seen as a set of social practices. The result of Dewey's pragmatism is to demolish the Cartesian tradition that Truth can be grasped by a Mind Apart, thereby introducing the social into the heart of any debate about truth and reality. Finally, truth does not occur at the level of facts but only at the level of propositions, and objectivity simply means an inter-subjective consensus.

While Rorty's notion of consensus looks rather like the idea that social theory is an argument, there is an important issue that a sociological argument or first-order theory must appeal to some notion of the independence of evidence. In the scaffold metaphor, Rorty might be forced to argue that there is no building beyond the scaffolding; there is only scaffolding. One consequence of Rorty-type arguments is that too much of what passes for "social theory" is simply a reflection on social theory rather than the issues that lie behind it; in other words, it assumes a second-order status. Put simply, I want to claim that theory has to be an argument about *something* and not just an argument about an argument.

What are the elements of the solution to what I perceive as a crisis in modern social theory? These can be enumerated simply as: a defense of classical sociology and the idea of a vital sociological tradition; the attempt to connect and in some cases reconnect sociology with its sister disciplines such as demography (see CHAPTER 22) and economics (see CHAPTER 18); the need to have a strong grasp of historical sociology (see CHAPTER 20); the development of a sociology of human rights and justice (see CHAPTER 25; the importance of attending to major social and political issues; and the avoidance of any artificial choice between sociological arguments and ethical judgments.

DEFENDING A CLASSICAL TRADITION

When sociologists question the value of social theory, they are often skeptical about "classical sociology" in particular, and hence there is an encompassing question that we must confront: why read the sociological classics at all? In this *New Companion*, CHAPTER 1, and CHAPTER 2, are concerned to explore and defend the "classical foundations" of sociology and its legacy. Another major criticism of classical sociology is that it was dominated by the patriarchal assumptions of the period in which it was inaugurated. Feminism and feminist theory have subsequently had major consequences for the ways in which we conceptualize the social and hence for the ways in which we may wish to think about the legacy of sociology (see CHAPTER 12).

There are several preliminary justifications that one might offer for reading the texts of classical sociology. Any pedagogy demands a discipline, and hence the training of sociology students requires the practice of confronting major texts. One cannot properly come to terms with social theory without paying regard to its context, history, and major works. If social theory is an argument, then the actual "textuality" of classical sociological theory needs to be addressed by any serious student of the subject. Furthermore, the sociological imagination has been shaped and continues to be shaped by themes and issues that were established by and within these classical texts – for example imperialism, capitalism, modernity, alienation, and social class. The classics continue to inspire research. One modern example of such an application would be George Ritzer's use of Weber's rationalization theory to explain the McDonaldization process (Ritzer 2000).

To reject the legacy of classical sociology often means that students will inevitably have an eclectic, partial, and ad hoc relationship to sociological theory, and as a result they are denied the opportunity to experience the accumulation of both theoretical and empirical research. The result is unfortunately that postmodern readings of sociological texts tend to suggest that anything can pass as "sociology." Critical responses to the very idea of a canon of sociology leave us with a weak and passive version of disciplinarity. While interdisciplinarity has become a fashionable orientation towards the undergraduate curriculum, there can be no interdisciplinarity without disciplines. If there is in an argument in favor of interdisciplinarity, it should be made primarily at the research level and not by reference to undergraduate teaching. Once more it is the classical texts such as Weber's *Economy and Society* (1968) that provide the model of interdisciplinarity with its capacity to integrate sociology, economics, jurisprudence, and politics.

The defense of classical texts as a basis for discipline is not therefore simply a conservative or narrow exercise, but merely recognition of the cumulative steps that are necessary in any defensible pedagogy. However, my final defense of the classics rests on the substantive argument that they help us to understand the social world and they establish the foundations for critical and effective interventions into modern politics. If the classics fail in this regard, then they are merely museum pieces.

What we might recognize as the strong program of classical sociology was an attempt to defend the notion of "the social" as an autonomous field of social forces. In practice this defense of "the social" amounted to the study of social institutions or patterns of social action and interaction involving social norms, social constraints, and power. John Heritage (CHAPTER 15) gives a good account of how we can regard conversational practice as a system of institutions such as queues in conversations. Broadly speaking these social institutions are the social forces that bind and unbind communities. "The social" is thus characterized by a dynamic between solidarity (processes that bind us together into communities) and scarcity (processes that divide and break communities). In practical terms, classical sociology involves, on the one hand, the study of the values, cultural patterns, trust, and normative arrangements that underpin institutions and, on the other, the systems of social stratification that express scarcity.

By contrast, in my view the weak program of sociology is the study of the meanings of social actions for individuals in their social relations. The strong program insists that, in the majority of cases, the social forces that determine social life are not recognized or understood by social actors themselves. Indeed there is a sense in which social actors in their everyday lives are not interested in such questions; their orientation to everyday life is pragmatic and practical rather than reflective and theoretical. There is therefore an important difference between the motives and reasons for action in the everyday world and the models of explanation of social science.

Classical sociology as the quest to define "the social" was very closely connected with Durkheim's attempt to understand "the social" in *The Rules of Sociological Method* (1958), in which sociology avoids reference to psychological variables in its explanations of social phenomena or social facts. In more precise terms, the *locus classicus* of this tradition was initially presented in *Primitive Classification* (1963), where Durkheim and Mauss understood the general schema of logical classification as manifestations of social structure. Classical sociological explanations are sociological in the strong sense, because they do not refer to individual intentions as causes of action; sociological explanations are simply indifferent to human psychology. The obvious problem with this definition is that it may appear to exclude Weber from the strong program precisely because he developed a notion of social action that was a response to economics, thereby treating notions of social structure as reified concepts. In response to this problem, it can be argued that Weber's sociological explanations rested on the notion of "unintended consequences" rather than self-conscious actions of individuals. The idea of unintended consequences in Weber or of ambiguity in Merton's sociology points to the ways in which the social structure works "behind the backs" of the social actors. More importantly, not all sociological explanations adhere to Durkheim's *Rules*. Insofar as sociological explanations do not employ references to social structure or social facts in Durkheim's sense, they are not examples of the strong program of classical sociology, but they may nevertheless be explanations that one can regard as sociologically useful and persuasive.

It is also important to grasp the fact that classical sociology is a critical discipline, because it represents typically an attack on the taken-for-granted assumptions of bourgeois, utilitarian liberalism. This critical tradition is conventionally associated with Marxism, but here again Durkheim offers the definitive critique of utilitarian individualism. Both *Suicide* (1951) and *Professional Ethics and Civic Morals* (1992) were political attacks on (English) economic individualism and the sociology of Herbert Spencer, and thus Durkheim's professional or academic sociology was constructed as an attack on a particular trend in society that was seen to be destructive of the social. Durkheim's attack on the corrosive consequences of the ideology of egoistic individualism is in this respect the precursor of recent French sociology (Boltanski and Thevenot 2006; Bourdieu 1998).

The double crisis of social theory involves the notion that the social in the modern world is being eroded. Because I have already discussed this issue in the second edition of the *Companion to Social Theory*, there is no need to repeat that argument here. Suffice it to say that the neoliberal revolution in economics has produced societies that depend increasingly on market mechanisms rather than social capital and trust, and give pronounced emphasis to individualism and choice over collective solutions to social issues. Many public institutions are in decline – state universities, public libraries, public broadcasting, public health systems, public transport, and so forth – leading to societies that depend more on voluntary agencies and charities rather than states. The social is being eroded along with social citizenship as the social glue of civil society (Turner 2001). In modern societies more and more social activities are deregulated, outsourced, or privatized, leaving little scope for accountability and little hope of universalism in provision. Even military activities, for example in Iraq, are outsourced to private agencies, with the result that citizens are at risk from military actions for which these private companies are not wholly accountable.

A sociological understanding of the social is also being eroded by the fact that public opinion and public policy are increasingly influenced by genetic rather than social explanations of human behavior. The great revolution in modern biology has produced a number of major breakthroughs in genetics, leading to the quest for genetic explanations of social deviance, individual disorders, and behavior patterns. The notion that, to quote Durkheim, social facts are required to explain social facts is constantly challenged in the media (even when natural scientists themselves may be far more cautious about the scope of explanations of human behavior by reference to genes). Although there is much utopian aspiration associated with modern genetics and much fantasy about for example "living forever" (Appleyard 2007), the ideological power of modern medicine does represent a challenge to the sociologist as a public intellectual. Many of these important issues are discussed by Oonagh Corrigan in CHAPTER 17, and to some extent by Darin Weinberg in CHAPTER 14.

Although I have emphasized the importance of early versions of classical sociology (especially Durkheim and Weber) as the foundation of social theory, this defense implies no conservative stance towards modern social theory. On the contrary, a robust sociological tradition must be open to new ideas and perspectives such as actor network theory (CHAPTER 7), the sociology of the body (CHAPTER 26) or theories of mobility (CHAPTER 24). There is in any case an intellectual depth to sociology that we must not neglect or underestimate. In this *New Companion* I have felt it important to include such traditions as ethnomethodology (see CHAPTER 8), and phenomenology (see CHAPTER 11), which offer creative ways of looking at social structures and appropriate methodologies for sociology.

THE SOCIAL AND THE POLITICAL

While the social and social theory have been deeply challenged by postmodernism, by the changing nature of the social, and by the rise of genetic theories of social behavior, there is some evidence to suggest that the fortunes of political theory have been more encouraging than those of sociology. In this introduction I want to consider what "social theory" might learn from the recent history of "political theory."

In 1962 Isaiah Berlin published an article on the question "Does Political Theory Still Exist?" (Berlin 1962). This article alone did much to reverse the uncertain fortunes of political philosophy in British universities, to establish a program of what political theory was about, and distinguished political philosophy from political science. Berlin and his students did much to steer British political studies in the direction of political theory rather than political science. The article outlined his objections to historical determinism in the social sciences, which included both American political science and, more importantly, Marxist historical determinism. The intellectual background to this essay was the impact of linguistic philosophy on the idea of "political principles," which had led Peter Laslett (1956: vii) to claim provocatively that "For the moment, anyway, political philosophy is dead."

The political background to Berlin's liberalism was communist authoritarianism and the Cold War, and the ensuing struggle to defend liberalism and individual rights against authoritarian governments. His overt aim was to defend the idea of philosophical inquiry into the causes and nature of politics, and hence the need for political philosophy in the first place. Berlin consequently regarded sociology with some degree of suspicion. For him, "sociology" sounded too much like "socialism," appeared to embrace deterministic arguments, and claimed with too much presumption to be a science. A Jewish refugee from the Soviet system, Berlin came to intellectual maturity against the background of European fascism. His commitment to liberal political theory and his antagonism to sociology were hardly surprising. At least in Britain, sociology in the 1950s and 1960s had strong affiliations with Marxism and developed the analysis of social class as one its principal research objectives. Berlin's suspicions about the intellectual association of sociology with socialism were not entirely unfounded.

In the 1950s there was a sense of malaise in political philosophy, at least as it was taught in British universities. As I have indicated, there is also a sense of contemporary malaise in social theory in which the impact of posthumanism, poststructuralism, and postmodernism have brought many to assume that, with the "cultural turn," there was little to distinguish literary theory from social theory (see CHAPTER 28). In European universities, social theory is increasingly subsumed under cultural studies or cultural theory (see, however, CHAPTER 19, by Jeffrey Alexander and Isaac Reed, who develop a robust defense of the program of cultural sociology).

I propose immodestly that to revive sociology today we need an argument that will answer the hypothetical question "Does sociological theory still exist?" with the same decisiveness that Berlin answered Laslett's accusation that political theory was comatose. The current challenge to social theory remains closely connected with the traditional issues of social action theory (see CHAPTER 4). It is clear that the conundrum of institution and action is yet another way of describing the debate about agency and structure, or structuration in Anthony Giddens's theory of the constitution of society (Giddens 1984). However, in retrospect it seems to me that the real point of the debate was lost in theories that became too abstract to be useful. If social structure is over-emphasized, one moves towards a highly determin- istic theory of action. If individual agency is over-emphasized, then one has an individualistic, not a sociological, theory of the social. But what is the real point of this contrast between agency and social structure?

If modern sociology wants to be relevant to modern society, especially in a period of globalization, it has to develop a sociology of rights, an understanding of how the rule of law functions, and an objective theory of justice (see CHAPTER 25). To do this, it needs to go beyond a general cultural relativism (Turner 2006). People can only have rights if they have moral autonomy – that is, if they are moral agents. This moral autonomy cannot work if we assert a mechanistic theory of causality. This is the classical liberal Berlin-type argument, and it is correct. However, if people have rights, in the strong sense, then they must also have duties. Where does a sense of duty come from? Moral duties are typically inscribed in what we as sociologists call "culture" – an umbrella term that includes morality, values, and religion. In a largely implicit way, sociology is the study of the duties (mores, morals, norms, and values) that are important in creating the social. The separation between sociology and law in the modern university has had severely negative consequences for sociol- ogy, because the sociological study of norms, institutions, and social action now takes place quite separately from jurisprudence. This institutional division between legal and sociological reasoning was not characteristic for example of the intellectual context of classical sociology. In a related field, the study of rights has become largely the concern of jurisprudence and political philosophy; the study of duties – or normative institutions – has been the task of sociology, but you cannot have rights without duties and vice versa, and you cannot have political philosophy without sociology.

JUSTICE AND EQUALITY

Sociology has also been impoverished by its separation from political theory for at least one obvious reason. Political theory has been especially concerned with ques- tions of rights and justice. But sociology rarely considers justice; its major concern has been inequality (that is, the sociology of stratification), not injustice as such. When sociology comes to study justice, it is often simply concerned with the individual and the subjective apprehension of justice. The examples are few and far between: Barrington Moore on *Injustice* (1978), Morris Ginsberg *On Justice in Society* (1965) and Garry Runciman on *Relative Deprivation and Social Justice* (1963). Sociological relativism means that it is difficult to formulate critical theories about gross inequality. Relativism means that we cannot, as sociologists, criticize modern-day crises in capitalist societies, only describe and account for their ideologies.

For social theory to exist in some sense as a vibrant and important part of sociology as a discipline, it has to throw light on problems of major contemporary concern. A relevant social theory should not be a theory about theorizing, that is, it must be something more than a metatheory. In my estimation the major contemporary problems are the changing nature of warfare, the impact of bio-technology on human expectations (see CHAPTER 17 and CHAPTER 26), the growth of cosmopolitanism (see CHAPTER 27), the relationship between technology, science, and society (see CHAPTER 23), the degradation of the environment, globalization (see CHAPTER 16 and CHAPTER 24), and the growing incivility of the public sphere. In all of these situations, the assertion of and claims for rights are central issues.

An important distinction between sociology and politics is that political philosophy has been primarily concerned with the question of justice, and hence the analysis of rights arises necessarily from a concern with the justice and legitimacy of political regimes. By contrast, sociology often portrays itself as "value-neutral," and hence it does not raise normative questions about justice or rights. Sociology approaches these normative issues indirectly, for example from the study of inequality. The paradoxical consequence of this concentration on empirical studies of income inequality is that sociology typically does not study equality directly. Equality is merely the absence of inequality, and not, as it were, an independent phenomenon. Normative debates about equality and justice are buried under empirical and descriptive analysis of inequality and injustice. For mainstream sociology, injustice is translated into a value-neutral study of social stratification as simply an empirically given hierarchy of different income levels. Because anthropologists and sociologists have typically been either positivists or relativists, they have not developed an analysis of justice and rights, and therefore they have failed to engage with the most significant institutional revolution of the twentieth century – the growth of universal human rights. Because sociology has withdrawn from the issues covered by international relations as a subject area, it does not have much to say about many macro political issues: regime change, international intervention, international wars, famine relief, and so forth.

AGENCY AND STRUCTURE AS A FRAMEWORK

An intellectually exciting sociology can never be merely the study of significant contemporary problems; it has to make a lasting contribution to sociological theory. What examples do we have from British sociology, given my focus on Isaiah Berlin and British liberalism, that might be instructive with respect to the analysis of political problems? One example might be taken from the research of John Rex, who makes a major contribution to the study of race relations, but has also made critical contributions to social theory. *Key Problems in Sociological Theory* (Rex 1961) was a key text of post-war British sociology. For example, there is an important relationship between his empirical research on social class and race and his interpretation of Weber's sociology as a theory of social action. In the 1960s Rex's sociological theory and his political analysis of apartheid provided students with a critical perspective on society and politics. Another example might be taken from the sociological theory of Alan Dawe, who in "The Two Sociologies" (1970) played a significant role in shaping the sociological imagination In the British political and intellectual context, Dawe stressed the connection between certain forms of sociological theory, social action, political responsibility, and sociological theories of action, arguing against functionalism (see CHAPTER 5) that action theory in Weberian sociology provided insights into contemporary issues (such as nuclear disarmament) but also at another level fostered motives for political action.

In short, the debate about agency and structure is constitutive of sociology itself, but the implications of this distinction have not always been adequately and clearly understood. Much of the debate in sociology about structure and agency is in fact parasitic on the moral philosophy of Immanuel Kant, who defined enlightenment as freedom from any self-imposed tutelage. We might include social determinism in the notion of tutelage. It is necessary to retain a vision of human autonomy and agency (against behavior) if we are to regard social actors as moral agents capable of choice. The sociology of Talcott Parsons retained this distinction in the theory of voluntary action in *The Structure of Social Action* – a theory that is distinctively Kantian. Sociological theory needs to retain a clear notion of the voluntary character of social action and hence the possibility that humans can be held accountable for their actions. The role of "social structure" is to draw attention to the limitations and constraints on social action, and hence on human autonomy. In retaining a notion of "structuration," it does not follow that social theory supports a (theological) notion of free will, but it also means that it does not accept a positivist version of determinism.

If social theory is to have any positive role in modern society, then I want to follow Hannah Arendt (2003) in *Responsibility and Judgment* to argue that things can always be otherwise. Sociologists, for example Erving Goffman, have often been concerned to understand the roles we play and the masks we acquire to perform socially. Arendt said that these are necessary if society is to function, but she reminded us of the Roman legal distinction between *persona* (somebody who possess civil rights) and *homo* (somebody who is nothing but a member of the species). In order for social theory to continue to exist, it needs to retain this legacy of a critical theory the purpose of which is to uncover the constraints that prevent the moral action (of people with rights) as opposed to the conditioned behavior of members of *homo sapiens*.

What are the conditions necessary for a revival of social theory? One condition would be a better integration of social and political theory. These two disciplines are regrettably often separated institutionally in modern universities. Social theory may, however, often assume a negative relationship to politics in the public sphere. As the handmaiden of politics, its role may be negative in exploring those conditions of social life – in fact the conditions of civil society – that make the achievement of moral autonomy and responsibility difficult if not impossible. As a critical theory the role of sociology is to consider those circumstances that artificially constrain the voluntary character of social action and interaction. By taking this moral issue seriously, of course, sociology needs to maintain the idea that the isolated existence of the individual is a fiction. On a more positive note, social theory does not have to choose between the social rights of citizens living in a moral community and the civil liberties of liberalism. The role of sociology might be to explore the historically variable role for example of property rights in either promoting the exploitation of the poor and homeless (Victorian Britain) or defending peasants from arbitrary eviction (as in modern capitalist China). Finally, I have argued that the conventional relativism of traditional sociology may prove an impoverished basis for contemporary sociology that needs to go beyond Marx's rhetorical pamphlets and Weber's pessimistic vision of the night of polar darkness.

THE NEW COMPANION TO SOCIAL THEORY

The *New Companion* was assembled in a period of extraordinary international crisis, with growing evidence of global warming and its political consequences for wars over water; the spread of infectious diseases such as avian flu that can have devastating consequences for economic growth and social stability; the conflicts in Iraq, Afghanistan, and the Middle East; the genocide in Darfur; the crisis in the global financial markets, and growing tension between the major powers over basic resources. In some respects all of these issues are bound up with globalization (CHAPTER 16), technological changes (CHAPTER 23), demographic changes (CHAPTER 22), and fundamentalist religious movements (CHAPTER 21). In short, I have sought to develop a *New Companion* that provides a guide to the sociological tradition and also attempts to show how sociology can address fundamental social and political issues. I have defended traditional sociology but have also addressed the concerns of modern sociologists over conversation analysis (CHAPTER 15), cultural theory (CHAPTER 19) and actor network theory (CHAPTER 7). I have also recognized the need to develop critical theories relating, for example, to gender (CHAPTER 12) and to postmodernism (CHAPTER 13).

Finally in this introduction I have referred frequently to the crisis of modern social theory, but a crisis can also be, as in the case of a threatening illness, a turning point where there is a resolution of existing dangers and the emergence of new opportunities for growth and development. The intention in publishing this *New Companion* has been to answer this challenge, thereby contributing to the growth and renewal of a sociological vision of the social world.

Bibliography

Alexander, J. C. (1987) *Twenty Lectures: Sociological Theory since World War II*. New York: Columbia University Press.

Appleyard, B. (2007) *How to Live Forever or Die Trying: On the New Immortality*. New York.

Arendt, H. (2003) *Responsibility and Judgment*. New York: Schocken Books.

Baert, P. (2005) *Philosophy of the Social Sciences*. Cambridge: Polity.

Baert, P., and Turner, B. S. (eds.) (2007) *Pragmatism and European Social Theory*. Oxford: Bardwell.

Berlin, I. (1962) "Does Political Theory Still Exist?," in P. Laslett and W. G. Runciman (eds.), *Philosophy Politics and Society*. Oxford: Blackwell.

Berlin, I. (1978) *Karl Marx*. Oxford: Oxford University Press.

Blau, P. M., and Moore, J. W. (1970) "Sociology," in B. F. Hoselitz (ed.), *A Reader's Guide to the Social Sciences*. New York: Free Press.

Boltanski, L., and Thevenot, L. (2006) *On Justification. Economies of Worth*. Princeton and Oxford: Princeton University Press.

Bourdieu, P. (1998) *Acts of Resistance*. Cambridge: Polity.

Bramson, L. (1966) "Social Theory," in N. MacKenzie (ed.), *A Guide to the Social Sciences*. London: Weidenfeld & Nicolson.

Dawe, Alan. (1970) "The Two Sociologies." *British Journal of Sociology* 21(2): 207–18.

Durkheim, É. (1951) *Suicide. A Study in Sociology*. Glencoe: Free Press.

Durkheim, É. (1958) *The Rules of Sociological Method*. Glencoe: Free Press.

Durkheim, É. (1992) *Professional Ethics and Civic Morals*. London: Routledge.

Durkheim, É., and Mauss, M. (1963) *Primitive Classification*. Chicago: University of Chicago Press.

Fenn, R. K. (ed.) (2001) *The Blackwell Companion to Sociology of Religion*. Oxford: Blackwell.

Giddens, A. (1984) *The Constitution of Society*. Cambridge: Polity.

Giddens, A., and Turner, J. (eds.) (1987) *Social Theory Today*. Cambridge: Polity.

Ginsberg, M. (1965) *On Justice in Society*. Harmondsworth: Penguin Books.

Homans, G. (1950) *The Human Group*. New York: Harcourt Brace.

Jenkins, R. (2002) *Foundations of Sociology*. Houndmills: Palgrave.

Laslett, P. (1956) "Introduction," in *Philosophy Politics and Society*. Oxford: Blackwell.

Lipset, S. M., Trow, M., and Coleman, J. (1956) *Union Democracy: The Inside Politics of the International Typographical Union*. Glencoe, IL: Free Press.

Lyotard, J.-F. (1984) *The Postmodern Condition: A Report on Knowledge*. Manchester: Manchester University Press.

Markovsky, B. (2005) "Theory Construction," in G. Ritzer (ed.), *Encyclopedia of Social Theory*. Thousand Oaks: Sage.

Merton, R. K. (1963) *Social Theory and Social Structure*. New York: Free Press.

Moore, B. (1978) *Injustice: The Social Bases of Obedience and Revolt*. London: Macmillan.

Neumann, F. (1957) *The Democratic and the Authoritarian State*. New York: Free Press.

Parsons, T. (1937) *The Structure of Social Action*. New York: McGraw-Hill.

Rex, J. (1961) *Key Problems in Sociological Theory*. London: Routledge & Kegan Paul.

Ritzer, G. (2000) *The McDonaldization of Society*. Thousand Oaks: Sage.

Rorty, R. (1979) *Philosophy and the Mirror of Nature*. Princeton: Princeton University Press.

Runciman, G. W. (1963) *Relative Deprivation and Social Justice*. London: Routledge & Kegan Paul.

Shils, E. A., and Finch, H. A. (eds.) (1949) *The Methodology of the Social Sciences: Max Weber*. New York: Free Press.

Turner, B. S. (2001) "The Erosion of Citizenship." *British Journal of Sociology* 52(2): 189–209.

Turner, B. S. (2006) *Vulnerability and Human Rights*. University Park, PA: Penn State University Press,

Wallace, W. L. (ed.) (1969) *Sociological Theory*. London: Heinemann.

Weber, M. (1949) *The Methodology of the Social Sciences*. New York: Free Press.

Weber, M. (1968) *Economy and Society*. Berkeley: University of California Press.

Wilson, B. (1961) *Sects and Society*. London: Heinemann.

Part I
Foundations

1

The Foundations of Social Theory

GERARD DELANTY

INTRODUCTION

The emergence of social theory coincides with the emergence of modernity.[1] It can be seen in the most general sense to be a reflection on the nature of modern society. Social theory aims to provide a general interpretation of the social forces that have shaped the modern world. The classical tradition in social theory, the focus of this chapter, was one of the great attempts in modern thought to understand the totality of forces at work in the making of modern society. Classical social theory was both a product of modernity and at the same time an attempt to reflect critically on its problems.

Although it is more accurate to speak of classical traditions, for there was not one single one, underlying all approaches was a sense of modernity entailing a social crisis. All the major social theories were responses to the experience of crisis within modernity. The various epochal shifts in modernity from the eighteenth century to the present day have all been accompanied by different crises and this has varied depending on the national context. The view from early nineteenth-century France was very different from that in early twentieth-century Germany.

But modernity was not only experienced in terms of crisis, it was also experienced as a promise of new freedoms, and for many contained within it a utopian impulse. This tension between crisis and future possibility encapsulates both the spirit of modernity and the responses of social theorists to the predicament of modern society. On the one side, modernity offered the vision of a social order that has been variously understood in terms of human autonomy or freedom and, on the other, modern society has unleashed forces that have the tendency to destroy the future possibilities contained within it. As will be demonstrated in this chapter, the classical social theorists attempted in their different ways to make sense of modern society in terms of this dual conflict. Where social theorists have differed it has been in their responses to what has been often called the central conflict of modernity.[2]

   This chapter provides an assessment of the era of classical social theory from its
origins in the Enlightenment to the post-World War II period.[3] The central theme
in this story is the fate of the Enlightenment in face of the reality of modern society.
The chapter begins with a look at the rise of social theory in the Enlightenment
period, roughly from the end of the seventeenth century in the first half of the
nineteenth century. The next section concerns the legacy of the social thought of
the Enlightenment in the formative period of modern social theory in the second
half of the nineteenth century, beginning with Marx and including Spencer, Weber,
and Durkheim and concluding with Simmel. The third section takes the aftermath
of World War I as the point of departure to look at European social theory in the
first half of the twentieth century, when disenchantment with modernity becomes
particularly pronounced. The final section concerns the reorientation of the classical
tradition in American social theory culminating in Parsons's attempt to establish a
general social theory of modern society in all its complexity.

THE RISE OF THE SOCIAL AND ENLIGHTENMENT
SOCIAL THEORY

While the origins of political theory go back to ancient thought, social theory is a
product of modernity. The rise of social theory can be related to the emergence of
the social as a specific domain separate from the sphere of the state and the realm
of the household or private sphere. Early social theory was a response to the rise
of "civil society" and the recognition that society was an artifact produced by
human action as opposed to being part of the preordained nature of the world. The
word "society" initially signified a pact or contract between the citizen and ruler,
but increasingly lost its juridical meaning and acquired a social meaning as community, suggesting normative integration or a notion of solidarity in which social
interaction was seen to entail symbolic relations. According to Talcott Parsons, in
his first major work, published in 1937, *The Structure of Social Action*, modern
sociology is essentially an attempt to find an answer to the problem posed by
Thomas Hobbes (1588–1697) and John Locke (1632–1704), namely how social
order is possible. While Hobbes and Locke conceived of this in political terms as a
social contract, social theory properly begins only with the recognition that society
is a reality in itself. The eighteenth-century Enlightenment thinkers were the first to
give systematic consideration to the reality of the social. Émile Durkheim regarded
Rousseau and Montesquieu as the founders of sociology. Rousseau's *The Social
Contract*, published in 1762, introduced the notion of the "general will" as the
symbolic basis of social subjectivity, which he linked to the importance of citizenship. Although he tended to view social institutions as corrupting the human spirit
of freedom, he articulated a notion of society that was a departure from the earlier
contractarian philosophies of the liberal thinkers. For instance, in the earlier *Discourse on the Origin of Inequality*, he argued that inequality is a product of society
as opposed to being natural. But there is no doubt that it was Montesquieu in 1748,
in *The Spirit of the Laws*, who advanced the first sociological conception of society.
He demonstrated how social control operates through what he called social mores
which were conditioned by geographic factors. One of his great themes was that of

the variability of human societies and the importance of social context. This work had a lasting influence on social theory in the idea it articulated that societies have inner logics of development and that the social is always more than the sum of its parts. Durkheim's notion of social representations or Weber's thesis of the spirit of capitalism all recall motifs in the work of Rousseau and Montesquieu, who drew attention in different ways to the symbolic structure of social relations, the idea of a spirit of will that transcends the sum of the parts.

Enlightenment social theory was most advanced in Scotland, where the so-called moral philosophers – Adam Ferguson and John Millar in particular – wrote about the rise of civil society (Strydom 2000). This was an age in which the older "court society" was being challenged by the rise of a new conception of society, known variously as bourgeois society or civil society. The realization that the social field was opening up forced the recognition that social thought had to address a wider sphere of interpretation than that of the domain of the state. Ferguson's *Essay on the History of Civil Society*, published in 1767, was one of the most advanced interpretations of civil society and exerted an important influence on Hegel. In *The Origins of the Distinction of Ranks*, in 1771, Millar developed an influential argument about the nature of social stratification in terms of the organization of society into classes, or "ranks." Although he did not use the term social science, a term that did not come into currency until the end of the eighteenth century, he held that beneath the diversity of society is a structure of causality that can be known by science. What we have in these early works of modern social thought is the first attempt to develop a theory of society, that is an interpretation of the social as a distinctive reality. Pervading these Enlightenment theories of society was a sense of the emergence of modernity as the promise of a new principle of social integration. With this came a consciousness of a rupture of past and present. This sense of a fundamental discord at the heart of modernity was reflected in a range of dichotomies that were to define some of the core concerns of classical sociology: community and society, tradition and modernity, status and contract, differentiation and integration, solidarity and scarcity. Social theory from the beginning was greatly preoccupied with the search for a principle of social integration which could be capable of reconciling the contradictions of modernity and imposing unity on a disordered and fragmented world.

The French Revolution was the event that heralded the new age of social theory as an interpretation of the modern age, for no other episode encapsulated modernity more than 1789 and its aftermath, when entirely new visions of social and political order emerged. Post-revolutionary social theory was a product of the Enlightenment's quest for intellectual mastery, but it was also a response to the realization that the state alone was incapable of establishing social order. Enlightenment social theory was encapsulated in the work of two major thinkers whose work has exercised considerable influence on the subsequent history of social theory: Kant and Hegel (see Rundel 1987).

Immanuel Kant (1724–1804) was not a social theorist in the conventional sense of the term, but his work has been important in establishing a foundation for much of modern social and political thought. In his major philosophical works he demolished the older notion of natural law and in its place he put human freedom and the autonomy of the individual. In this respect his work encapsulated the spirit of modernity as one founded on the principle of freedom and a spirit of universalism that was based on what human beings could create for themselves rather than deriving from a preordained structure. The significance of his philosophical system – as outlined in *The Critique of Pure Reason*, published in 1781 – was that it separated the claims of reason from those of faith, and moreover aimed to clarify the condition of the possibility of knowledge in order to limit knowledge to the domain of the empirical. This critical endeavor was hugely consequential in that it led to a differentiation of reason into different spheres, each with different truth claims. From Kant onwards – as is reflected in the work of Weber and Habermas for instance – relativism and universalism could no longer be considered as alternatives. After Kant the different spheres of knowledge – moral, religious, aesthetic, scientific – were differentiated, each with its own form of reason (Habermas 1987). In this way Kant demonstrated for social theory the relevance of a universalistic perspective, but one that had had to be reconciled to the particular.

Kant's 1784 essay "What Is Enlightenment?" has often been considered to be the defining text of the idea of modernity. For Kant, Enlightenment does not refer to an age but to a condition or attitude in which knowledge as self-critical reason becomes a means of emancipation. In works such as *The Idea of Universal History from a Cosmopolitan Perspective* and the later and more important *Eternal Peace*, published in 1795, Kant outlined one of the first, and certainly the most influential, notion of a cosmopolitan political order. A supporter of Rousseau's republican political philosophy, Kant sought to extend the idea of a republican polity to the international context. In this respect Kant was the founder of modern cosmopolitanism understood in terms of a normative transnational order (see CHAPTER 27). In sum, Kant was the Enlightenment thinker who established the foundations of an emancipatory kind of social theory based on a cosmopolitan outlook and a critique of dogmatism.

G. W. F. Hegel (1770–1831) offered a deeper historical contextualization of Kant's philosophy and a conception of morality as a product of society. With Hegel epistemology becomes social theory, since for him the question is to explore how knowledge is constituted in history, a process which can be understood in terms of evolving modes of consciousness. Hegel's philosophy was the principal reference point for the Marxist and critical tradition in modern social thought. For Marx and the tradition he inaugurated, Hegel established the basis of a notion of critical knowledge as a form of consciousness-raising. In his major work, *The Phenomenology of Spirit*, published in 1807, Hegel developed a dialectical conception of knowledge, which replaced Kant's critical philosophy in the view it espoused of the world as self-constituting. Society, nature, consciousness are always the working out of contradictions in a process of continuous self-creation. In *The Philosophy of Right*, published in 1821, his most sociological work, Hegel developed a theory of civil society, which, as remarked above, was influenced by Ferguson. In this work he advanced a notion of "ethical life" (*Sittlichkeit*), which can be related to the notion of community, or "life-world," and which is realized in the spheres of the private, civil society or the public realm, and the state. But civil society destroys ethical life because the "system of needs" is realized under the conditions of capitalism: "ethical life is split into its extremes and lost." The modern consciousness, as a result, is "an unhappy consciousness." For Hegel, the state is a higher expression of community than civil society and has the function of compensating for the shortcomings of civil society. The theme of Hegel's social theory is that of the fragmentation and alienation of consciousness in civil society and the search for a political solution for the realization of community. It laid the foundations of social theory by providing a framework to interpret social and epochal change and the search for a viable social and political order.

THE ENLIGHTENMENT LEGACY AND CLASSICAL EUROPEAN SOCIAL THEORY

The social thought of the Enlightenment was characterized by a certain utopianism, which was a reflection of the belief in the promises of modernity to bring about freedom. Unlike earlier social thought, it displayed a great belief in the power of human action to shape the future. The social and political thought of Kant and Hegel displayed that utopianism, but in Hegel the first signs of a disenchantment with modernity are to be found in his thoughts on the "unhappy consciousness" and the destructive forces of civil society. The preoccupation with utopia and the question of social order in an age of revolution was most evident in the work of Auguste Comte (1798–1857) who, along with Karl Marx, effectively replaced philosophical analysis with an advanced social theory of modern society. Comte is generally credited as the founder of sociology, a term he coined in 1838 as a general science of society that was "positive" as opposed to speculative and hence superior to philosophy. His major work, the *Course of Positive Philosophy*, published between 1830 and 1842, is one of the great sociological interpretations of modernity, as well as an attempt to develop a theory and method for a positive sociology. Unlike all previous social theorists, Comte was the first to reflect systematically on the nature of society itself. As a post-revolutionary Enlightenment thinker he was already skeptical of the promises of the Enlightenment to bring about a new age of freedom. The theme that pervades his work is that of the incompleteness of the present. He was acutely aware of the crisis of modernity, for the post-revolutionary era was one of social disorder, terror, and fragmentation. In order to understand the present it was necessary to understand the entire historical process by which societies undergo change. Inspired by Hegel, his sociology was one that stressed change and, as with Hegel, an approach to the history of human societies that saw societies undergoing change accordingly as their systems of knowledge changed. His "law of the three stages" describes the normative process by which societies progress from the "theological stage" (when magical or prereflective kinds of knowledge were dominant), to the "metaphysical stage" (characterized by rational and abstract knowledge, such as conceptions of law and sovereignty), and finally to the "positive stage" (where modern experimental science becomes the dominant mode of knowledge and consciousness). It was not quite clear whether the positive stage had begun or whether it was a utopian projection of the modern condition, but it is evident that Comte saw the positive age as the promise of a new modernity in which the crisis of the age would be overcome.

His contribution to sociology has been significant. He introduced new terms for the analysis of societies, such as the distinction between "social statics" and "social dynamics" – terms that suggest order and change – and a view of sociological analysis as the investigation of structure and functions. Influenced by developments in biology, Comte believed that societies could be analyzed in terms of the functional relationship of the part and the whole. For him modernity is above all a product of the growing power of knowledge. The age that he saw dawning was the era of positivism, by which he meant an age in which knowledge would be fully diffused in society and science would be the new religion.

Comte was the pre-eminent social thinker of the 1830s, and influential beyond France (Heilbron 1995). His work can be seen as establishing the foundation of classical social theory in the sense of a systematic sociological analysis of modern society. However, from the 1850s Comte's sociological positivism received its greatest challenge from the revolutionary tradition, which Karl Marx recovered and recast as a theory of society. At this stage social theory becomes a critique of the Enlightenment whose legacy increasingly would be seen to be inadequate. In place of the Enlightenment's emphasis on knowledge as emancipatory Marx stressed the ideological nature of knowledge, and in place of the individual as the primary agent he put the collective actor. For the utopian impulse that was a feature of the theorists of the first half of the nineteenth century – Auguste Comte and Claude Saint-Simon for instance – Marx posited political action, for he did not see industrial society as the carrier of a new utopia. He was also a critic of the liberal theorists in his argument that rights must be complemented by social justice and that without the emancipation of labor there could be no real kind of freedom. Taking up Hegel's critique of civil society, Marx extended Hegel's account of fragmentation with an analysis of the class structure. Like Hegel, Marx believed that the social world could not be reduced to an essence but was composed of various contradictory forces, and that the aim of theory is to grasp this field of tensions. However, unlike Hegel, he did not see the resolution of these contradictions in a higher order (the state or "absolute mind," as in Hegel). Marx retained the notion of dialectics but gave it a new significance in a more grounded social theory. He was possibly most sympathetic to the political economists of the age, but disagreed with them in their restrictive view of capitalism and their failure to see how capitalism is driven by class relations and the pursuit of profit for private appropriation.

Marx's early work, *The Economic and Philosophical Manuscripts*, written in 1844, was dominated by the Aristotelian notion of "praxis," which he linked to his major theme of alienation, the separation of subject from object. In this case, the separation of human subjectivity from the objectivity of society is analyzed in terms of the alienation of labor. Labor is the primary category of praxis, as human self-realization, creativity, and the actualization of needs. The older epistemological question of the separation of subject and object is now a struggle between capital and labor. In *Capital*, published in three volumes in 1867, 1885, and 1894, he outlined a purely sociological theory of capitalist society that had divested itself of much of the early philosophical language. The dominant theme of *Capital* as far as social theory is concerned is undoubtedly the notion of commodification. Capitalist society is a society that reduces all social relations to commodities, which are not just mere objects but "fetishisms" in that they are made up of distorted relations between subjectivity and objects. His concept of the "fetishism of commodities" demonstrated how structure and cultural production are intertwined and that therefore culture cannot be seen as something that transcends social reality. Now social theory becomes the "critique of political economy," for Marx's work was located in the field of political economy. One of his principal endeavors was to explain the origin and significance of profit, which in his view was one of the driving forces in modern society. Unlike the classical economists (Proudhon, Ricardo, and Smith), Marx succeeded in explaining the origin of profit, outlined in his "labor theory of surplus value." This theory is the basis of his entire theory of capitalism, and enabled Marx to argue that the class structure is the most fundamental structure in capitalist society and that it is based on a contradiction, for profit is generated in the exchange of labor for wages. The products generated by labor are objectified commodities in that they exist for profit which is privately appropriated by the owners of the means of production. So for Marx wage labor is the basis of profit and the source of a structural inequality. The resolution of this contradiction would be the driving force of capitalist society, making it the most dynamic society that has ever existed. In sum, then, for Marx modernity was above all characterized by commodification. The social as object of analysis could not be reduced to civil society and the struggle for rights, but required a critique whose normative standpoint was the struggle for social justice. Marx's social theory was a critical one. Critique does not try to explain or simply interpret society for its own sake, but is inherently critical of the prevailing social order and seeks to reveal the system of domination. Marx established a tradition in social theory around the explanation of the rise and transformation of capitalist society. Attempts to explain the nature of capitalist society were not confined to Marxists, as is evident from such works as Werner Sombart's seminal *Modern Capitalism*, published in 1902.

After Comte and Marx, social theory split into three classical traditions. If anything was common to all of them it was the declining significance of utopia that was a feature of the Enlightenment legacy and present in both Comte and Marx in different ways. The three can be summarized as a tradition that stems directly from Comte, and whose main representatives are Spencer and Durkheim; a heritage that derives from Marx and includes the critical tradition; and a tradition that goes back to Kant and includes Max Weber, Georg Simmel, Karl Mannheim, and Norbert Elias. The first tended towards a view of modernity in terms of a process of differentiation and liberal individualism; the second was a view of modernity in terms of capitalist domination and commodification; the third tradition brought social theory in the direction of a civilizational theory that stressed the role of values and cultural orientations in shaping social relations.

Comte's ideas were taken up in a more systematic way by Herbert Spencer, who heavily influenced modern sociology. He took up Comte's functionalism, which he established as the theoretical basis of sociological explanation. Social statics was to be the analysis of social order, while social dynamics was the analysis of change. His entire writings were based on the conviction that change was at work in the process of what he called differentiation, which arises from the interplay of matter, energy, and movement. His theory of evolution claimed that change was the result of a movement from simplicity to complexity and specialization. This movement – of uniformity and homogeneity to differentiation – was at work in all forms of matter, whether biological or social. The defining characteristic of modern society was the ways in which differentiation worked to make integration possible. In place of the idea of utopia he emphasized progress, which was closer to the liberal philosophy of reformism that he espoused. The emergence of a differentiated modern society was the result of a process of evolutionary progress, in which a modern "industrial society" would replace the "militant society" of the past and bring about greater stability. Although these were ideal types as opposed to being specific kinds of societies, he tended towards a view of the age in which he lived as most closely corresponding to his vision of an organic social entity in which the parts function to maintain the whole.

Émile Durkheim (1858–1917) can be considered to be the first social theorist to establish social theory as a social scientific endeavor. Although both Comte and Spencer used the term sociology to describe their work, they were not professional social scientists, but public intellectuals. Durkheim was the first professor of sociology, and developed in his major early work, *The Division of Labour in Society*, a systemic theory of modern society, which for him was an objective entity. Like Spencer he operated with a dichotomous typology of societies, the traditional and the modern. In the transition from traditional societies to modern societies "mechanical" forms of integration (which are characterized by the collective consciousness with its strong focus on the group and a direct or "mechanical" relationship between value systems and social actors) are replaced by "organic" forms of solidarity (which are characterized by individualism and cooperation, and are expressed in generalized norms as opposed to substantive values). In this work, published in 1893, he argued that modern societies are highly differentiated and products of the "division of labor." Modernity comes about with the shift from social integration through family and religion to integration through membership of occupational groups and the interdependence of these groups, as well as through educational meritocracy. The cultural structures of modern society are restitutive as opposed to being repressive, as in traditional societies, and provide individuals with possibilities for mutual cooperation.

Durkheim was schooled in French philosophy and, like Comte and Hegel, he was greatly concerned with the moral foundations of society. But, like many thinkers of his time, he believed modern society was in crisis. The specter of social and political disorder was foremost in his mind, as reflected in the disaster of the Franco-Prussian war, the Paris Commune, and the Dreyfus Affair. His social theory was an attempt to explain sociologically the modern experience of crisis in way that avoided some of the more speculative diagnoses of the age that were a feature of the culturally pessimistic *fin-de-siècle*. It is in this context that Durkheim's concern with "anomie" can be placed. Modern societies are prone to anomie, the breakdown in social cohesion and the production of social pathologies such as normlessness and suicide. His study on suicide in 1897 can be seen as a comment on the malaise of modernity, and may have been influenced by the German philosopher Arthur Schopenhauer's 1851 essay on suicide. Durkheim was influenced by Schopenhauer's pessimistic thought, which pointed to another side to modernity than that of the Enlightenment and the liberal and positivistic ideas that he generally embraced. For instance, his notion of "collective representations" is directly inspired by Schopenhauer's earlier work *The World as Will and Representation*. But, despite the prevailing popularity of German cultural pessimism, Durkheim was a French positivist, a rationalist, and, most of all, a pragmatist. He hoped for social reform and reconstruction based on moral individualism and political liberalism.

Max Weber (1864–1920) was influenced by Nietzsche, who led him to the idea of the "ethical irrationality" of the world, and was deeply preoccupied with the problem of meaning in an intellectualized and rationalized world. Like Durkheim he was interested in the moral foundations of society, but unlike Durkheim he gave a greater emphasis to meaning, and was especially interested in the ways people give meaning to their material interests. The guiding theme in his work concerned the process of cultural rationalization, by which cultural systems of meaning become increasingly rationalized as a result of their internal dynamics. Weber examined and documented this, from the rationalization of magic to the emergence of world religions to modern materialism. In *The Protestant Ethic and the Spirit of Capitalism*, published in 1904/5, Weber illustrated how religious values, and particularly the quest for salvation, lead to a particular attitude to the profane world of material wealth and work. The uniqueness of the West was that Christianity, particularly in its Calvinistic variant, involved a tension with the material world, and in order to ensure salvation in the next world Christianity, unlike other world religions, required an ethic of world mastery, both intellectual and material. The Protestant Reformation brought about a certain coincidence of values and interests, in that Protestantism entailed a greater emphasis on gaining salvation through the mastery of the material world. In this way, Christianity was a dynamic force in bringing about social change and ultimately in preparing the way for modern science and capitalism. Weber did not operate with a simple model of mono-causality. Rationalization operates in all spheres: law, science, music, economy, religion. It was one of his major claims that the "methodic manner of life" characteristic of capitalism and reformed Christianity had spread into all areas of life, leading to the emergence of a bureaucratic individualism and the loss of meaning in "the iron cage" of modernity.

The key to his interpretation of modernity is the notion of the "paradox of rationalism," namely the thesis that the Western quest for meaning generated a rationalized, meaningful order which destroyed the very possibility of meaning. The more the Protestant ethic rationalized the world for spiritual meaning, the more it eliminated meaning from it and ultimately disenchanted it. This paradox gave rise to two central conflicts. The first was the conflict of modern value systems. The loss of a unified world-view and the emergence of autonomous orders of science, morality, and art leads to a conflict of different value systems none of which can enchant the world but within each meaning can be found. The result of this is the recognition that modernity is based on "ethical irrationality." A second conflict between different orders of rationality can be detected in Weber's social theory of modernity. This is the conflict between value rationality and instrumental rationality, or in other words the conflict between culture in general and the instrumentalized orders of law, economy, and the state which seem to be breaking free from cultural value systems. For Weber, the last traces of enchantment are to be found in charisma (in public life) and the erotic (in private life). In his famous lecture "Science as a Vocation," delivered as the Russian Revolution broke out and as Germany descended into chaos at the end of World War I, there is the suggestion that the modern world has not only lost the certainty of religion but may also be undermining its own presuppositions.

As a social theorist, Weber set out to explain the modern world. He wished to explain the uniqueness of the modern West, where capitalism had become the dominant ethic. What both Durkheim and Weber offered was a general social theory of modern society, and one that was underpinned by new methodological approaches for social science (see CHAPTER 3). The theme of crisis was common to both theorists, as it was with Marx. This was also the case with Ferdinand Tönnies, who in a classic work published in 1887, *Community and Society*, saw the modern world in terms of the demise of community, which signifies the cohesive and organic world of traditional social relations, while "society" signifies the fragmented world of mediated social relations. With the coming of society, there was a danger of a return to the Hobbesian state of nature.

No discussion of classical European social theory can be complete without mention of Georg Simmel (1858–1918). One of his central concepts, the "tragedy of culture," gives expression to the growing pessimism about modernity that was a characteristic of European thought in the early twentieth century. In essays written during World War I, "The Concept and Tragedy of Culture" and "The Conflict in Modern Culture," he looked at modernity as a dualism of "objective" and "subjective" culture. He argued that culture is divided between two forms, the subjective creation of culture – in the sense of emanating from the creative imagination of an individual – and the tendency for culture to take on an objective existence of its own. By the tragedy of culture he meant the separation of these two domains of culture, with the resulting loss of autonomy and creativity as a result of rationalization, which was leading to the objectivation of culture. In an earlier and famous essay, "The Metropolis and Mental Life," Simmel argued that the modern city is where objective culture develops at the cost of subjective culture. One of the distinctive features of the metropolis is the experience of distance between people. In the metropolis the money economy becomes all-dominant and shapes social relations, bringing about the fragmentation of experience. This was the theme of his major work, *The Philosophy of Money*, published in 1907, in which Marx's notion of alienation became the central motif in his account of modernity as one of the fragmentation of human experience. Comparing Simmel to Durkheim, we also find the theme of differentiation, which was the title of a book he published in 1890, *On Social Differentiation*. However, unlike Durkheim, he tended to view the cultural expressions of modernity in terms of fragmentation, and in particular the fragmentation of subjective meaning. Simmel's legacy for social theory was the application of concepts in Marx, Weber, whom he influenced, and Durkheim to the world of social consumption, sociability, and urban life, for in Simmel's sociology consumption is more typical of modern urban life than is production, as in Marx. He extended the analysis of social relations to the micro level of sociability, as in his famous analysis of the dyad and the triad, and made important links with the wider context of modernity. Simmel's influence on social theory has been widely recognized since the so-called cultural turn in the social sciences in the 1980s. However, following his death his ideas exerted a major influence on classical American sociology – in particular the urban sociology of the Chicago School – for the Americans were more receptive to his work, and that of Weber, than they were to that of either Marx or Durkheim.

In conclusion, we can say that modernity, conceived of in terms of the crisis of the Enlightenment project of the emancipation of the individual, was the context for the emergence of classical social theory, which can be seen as an attempt to explore the continuity and rupture that modernity has brought. The three great founders of social theory – Marx, Durkheim, and Weber – built on earlier Enlightenment social thought to produce systematic socia scientific analyses of the condition of modernity. The themes that dominated their work were, respectively, differentiation/anomie, rationalization/disenchantment, and commodification/alienation. Their works, which have shaped the sociological heritage, were both diagnostic and explanatory.

SOCIAL THEORY AND THE DISENCHANTMENT WITH MODERNITY

As noted in the foregoing account of social theory, the theme of crisis and a certain cultural pessimism was present in the work of many theorists. This was to take on an enhanced momentum after the end of World War I, which marked a watershed in European social theory. Durkheim died in 1917, Simmel in 1918, and Weber in 1920. The tone of pessimism that was present in their work was balanced by their concern with a systematic analysis of modernity and an attempt to develop a theory of society. Unfortunately, Simmel succumbed to the pathology of war and, influenced like many thinkers of the age by nationalism and aestheticism, he welcomed the war as a liberating event capable of overcoming the "tragedy of culture" and creating a new "form." Both Weber and Durkheim became identified with national policy. Early twentieth-century European social theory, unlike American social theory, which will be considered in the next section, was influenced by three anti-Enlightenment thinkers, Friedrich Nietzsche (1844–1900), Sigmund Freud (1856–1939) and Martin Heidegger (1889–1976). In their work the theme of disenchantment with modernity led to a redirection of social theory away from the classical tradition as represented by Marx, Weber, and Durkheim to one that took more the form of a pessimistic diagnosis of the age in which cultural and psychological factors played a significant role.

Nietzsche was influential in the rejection of the very premises of the Enlightenment as an emancipatory project, namely the certainty of knowledge and the possibility of a rationally organized political order. Rejecting the collectivist ideologies of Marxism and nationalism, he argued for a personal ethics of resistance – often called nihilism – which rejects all absolute values. Although less intentionally anti-Enlightenment, Freud demonstrated that beneath the unity and coherence of personality there are the deep irrational forces of the unconscious, where the prehistorical conflicts of civilization are played out. One of his central insights was that human beings have a tendency to love the object of aggression and that all of civilization is based on a primordial act of violence. However, Freud's legacy for social theory ultimately went beyond the pessimistic cultural criticism that was a feature of his later work, and he was a major figure in influencing the interpretive or hermeneutical tradition in later social theory. The significance of Heidegger for social theory was his emphasis on language, not reason, as the foundation or ontology of human society. His philosophy, as outlined in his major work *Being and Time* (1927), resulted in a return to Presocratic Greek thinking, as well as an interest in the works of Nietzsche and a critique of technology, leading to a rejection of the Enlightenment heritage. All three thinkers displayed a strong emphasis on subjectivity and a general suspicion of collective action, as well as a liberal political ideology. It is possible to speak of a turn to subjectivity in social theory. However, none of these theorists attempted to enter into a constructive debate with classical sociologists.

It was the main achievement of the so-called Frankfurt School to make precisely the connection between the turn to subjectivity and the objective analysis of modernity from the perspective of a theory of society that was broadly in line with the emancipatory project of a normatively grounded social theory of human emancipation. The Frankfurt School theorists, who can be considered to be methodologically Marxists, represented an important strand within Western Marxism and modern German philosophy (Held 1980; Jay 1996). They continued the sociological tradition by linking it with psychology and the cultural and philosophical analysis of modernity, to lay the foundations for a new approach that would bring social theory towards a new kind of critical interpretation of the symbolic structure of power in modernity. Theodor Adorno, Max Horkheimer, Walter Benjamin, and Herbert Marcuse, the principal representatives of what was to become known as critical theory, sought to reconcile Marxism with the approaches of Freud, Weber, and more generally the emerging discipline of sociology. The thesis of Adorno and Horkheimer's *Dialectic of Enlightenment*, originally published in 1944 in response to the Holocaust, was that human history is the story of the struggle between nature and myth. Enlightenment, which they project back to the beginning of civilization, is the expression of the mastery of nature which is also the mastery of fear, but it is achieved through instrumental reason, which becomes a new kind of domination. Accordingly, as society gains more and more mastery over nature, it must exercise new forms of domination over subjectivity: the price of mastery over nature is domination over the self. This is the "dialectic of Enlightenment": the internalization of domination. The ultimate expression of civilization was totalitarianism in its Nazi as well as in its Soviet manifestations and, in their view, modern mass society. Popular culture, entertainment, or the "culture industry" were explained as the continuation of authoritarianism by other means. For Adorno and Horkheimer, the gas chamber, not Weber's "iron cage," is the motif modernity.

While the Frankfurt School did establish the foundations of a critical social theory of society and re-established a link between sociology and psychology, which Weber had opposed, the particular approach they adopted had its limits. The tendency to reduce modern society to its negative dimensions limited the wider application of their insights. The Holocaust was the central preoccupation of their theory of society, which they saw in terms of a total system of power in which emancipation could only be contemplative and largely embodied in its aesthetic expressions beyond direct political application.

With the Frankfurt School the cultural turn in social theory is most vividly apparent. Western Marxism, more generally, also reflected a turn away from an exclusive preoccupation with political economy to a concern with culture. This is evident in the work of Antonio Gramsci, Georg Lukács, Karl Korsch, and Ernst Bloch and the later generation of western Marxists, such as Henri Lefebvre, Lucien Goldmann, and Louis Althusser. Western Marxism, which marked a return to Hegel and has often been called Hegelian Marxism, was a response to the failure of proletarian revolution and the aftermath of the Russian Revolution of 1918. If Marx's writings were a response to the aftermath of the French Revolution of 1789, twentieth-century Marxism was a reflection of the fate of revolution in the wake of 1918 and, in western Europe, the rise of nationalism and fascism, developments which called into question the emancipatory project of modernity.

The attention given here to Western Marxism and the project of a critical theory of society should not detract from the conservative tradition in early to mid-twentieth-century social theory as well as to other kinds of social theory, such as those of thinkers as diverse as Karl Mannheim, Karl Jaspers, Norbert Elias, and Hannah Arendt, who in their different ways all attempted to offer an interpretation of the modern world. European social thought in the period from 1918 to 1945 was dominated by a sense of the decline of the political, to use Arendt's expression, and the disappearance of the ideas and ideals of the Enlightenment in the rising mass society. Common to many of the critiques from both the right and the left was the critique of mass society. This was as much apparent in the writings of the Frankfurt School as it was in books such as José Ortega y Gasset's *The Revolt of the Elites* in 1930 and in Oswald Spengler's work of 1918, *The Decline of the West*. In general, this was a period in which European social theory underwent a process of disorientation in which the visions of the classical sociologists were lost amidst a variety of culturally oriented diagnoses of the age. It was in the United States during this period that the foundations were laid for the revival of social theory. Indeed, many American theorists had studied in Germany, and when they returned to the United States the classical tradition become wedded to American intellectual tradition to produce new approaches.

Two classical Italian social theorists of this period, Pareto and Mosca, became important transmitters of European social thought in the United States and influencing sociologists as diverse as Talcott Parsons and C. Wright Mills in their studies on power and elites in American society. Vilfredo Pareto (1848–1923) and Gaetano Mosca (1858–1941) shared the disenchantment with modernity and contempt for mass society that was a feature of European social thought in the early twentieth century.

CLASSICAL AMERICAN SOCIAL THEORY

The dominant influence in American social thought was pragmatism. The main representatives of American pragmatism were Charles Sanders Peirce (1839–1914), who can be credited with introducing the term, William James (1842–1910), and Charles Dewey (1859–1952). None of these was a social theorist as such; they were primarily philosophers whose impact on American social theory has been considerable. Other sources of American social theory were American liberal theory – in particular the constitutional theory of Madison, Hamilton, and Jefferson – and German idealism, including both neo-Kantian idealism and Hegelianism. The constitutional theorists provided the basis of a political conception of society in terms of a liberal polity based on a shared morality, while the pragmatists established an alternative to a purely liberal conception of society that entailed a rejection of utilitarianism. Pragmatism had a huge influence on sociology and social theory, not only in the United States but also in Europe. Indeed, Weber, for all his skepticism of the United States, was influenced by pragmatism, as Jack Barbalet has argued (see CHAPTER 10). Barbalet is also correct to claim that pragmatism is not exhausted by George Herbert Mead's particular symbolic interactionism, but has a far more extensive reach. Pragmatism in sociology can be seen as an attempt to develop a specifically social theory that avoids many of the assumptions of political theory, with its utilitarian and liberal assumptions. The central aim of pragmatism was to link ideas to action.

Peirce was the founder of pragmatism, a term he coined in 1877, but it was William James who can be credited with developing pragmatism, which he did in a strongly psychological direction. Along with Freud, he was the most important psychologist of the period. His work, more than Peirce's, lent itself to social scientific applications since it made a connection with the emotions (Barbalet 2001). It was his theory of emotions that was of particular relevance to social theorists. This figured in his work on religion, as in *Varieties of Religious Experience* (1905). Both Weber and Durkheim, in their own writings on religion, were aware of, and influenced by, his work on emotions. The influence of pragmatism is especially apparent in Durkheim.[4] However, Weber was opposed to what they regarded as the individualistic orientation of psychology and preferred to emphasize the cognitive and functional aspects of culture against its emotional aspects. Yet the sociological approach they adopted, which entailed the analysis of religious ideas in terms of particular forms of action, reflected one of the core premises of pragmatist theory. James's influence on American social thought had a more positive impact than the social psychology of Freud, whose influence tended to focus on destructive forces. He was also a major influence on George Herbert Mead and numerous other American sociologists, such as Thorstein Veblen and Charles Cooley. Later American pragmatists, such as Richard Rorty and Richard Bernstein, have relied on the early pragmatists. John Dewey, for instance, was a source of inspiration for Rorty's anti-foundationalism.

Of the classical American sociologists it was George Herbert Mead (1863–1931) who was the most significant in taking up the pragmatist heritage. Mead studied in Germany, where he worked with one of the leading neo-Kantian philosophers, Wilhelm Dilthey, and sought to link German social thought to American pragmatism. This was the basis of symbolic interactionism, which offered an entirely new understanding of subjectivity as socially constituted. In his best-known work, *Mind, Self and Society*, published in 1934, Mead advocated an understanding of the Self as intersubjective, constructed in interaction with others through such mechanisms as social control, roles, and the generalized Other. The significance of Mead's approach was that it made interaction more central to sociological analysis than action. It also pointed to an alternative to consciousness and experience as the basis of social analysis. The interactionist conception of the self broke from the individualist self in liberal theory as well as the collectivist self in Marxism, and opened sociology to new ways of looking at social relations in terms of a social subjectivity.

The pragmatist influence in his sociological theory is reflected in the concern, central to his work, with a universalistic morality with which society could be better equipped to deal with its problems. This aspiration toward a public morality, sometimes called a "civil religion," was a distinctive feature of American social theory which, unlike European social theory, was less concerned with the declining significance of the Enlightenment.

American social theory, originally shaped by the humanistic and liberal ethos of pragmatism as in Mead's symbolic interactionism, became more and more influenced by the structural functionalism of Talcott Parsons (1902–79), who dominated social theory in the United States and world-wide after 1945. Parsons was the first major social theorist to provide a synthesis of classical social theory, which had fragmented into the traditions represented by Marx, Durkheim, and Weber. The task that Parsons set himself in his first major work, *The Structure of Social Action*, published in 1937, was to develop precisely such a synthesis of classical social theory. Indeed with Parsons the very notion of a classical sociological tradition begins. It was his thesis that classical social theory can be read as a convergence of theoretical traditions leading from economic theory to sociological theory. In this work, Parsons sought to integrate the approaches of Weber and Durkheim with what he called the voluntaristic theories, such as those of Vilfredo Pareto and Alfred Marshall. The problem for Parsons was to see how values, as in Durkheim's sociology, and action, as represented by Weber, can be linked to interests. Marx did not figure in this theory. The economic theories that Parsons drew from were those of Pareto and Marshall. The work was significant in establishing the recognition of sociological theory as having a contribution distinct from that of economic theory.

The central theme in all of Parsons's work was the question: how is social order possible? In his early work, which was heavily influenced by economic theory, the question of social order was posed in terms of the limitations of restraint and choice. Unlike many of the European sociologists he did not have a background in philosophy and was less preoccupied with the legacy of history. The twin figures of Marx and Freud that were so much present in twentieth-century European social theory were absent from his work. However, Parsons did acknowledge the significance of Freud in the second edition of *The Structure of Social Action*. For Parsons, the most basic questions of human society were those of Hobbes, but the answer had to be more normative than utilitarian. His mature works – *The Social System* and *Towards a General Theory of Action*, both published in 1951 – were much more Durkheimian in the emphasis that they gave to normative integration. In these works from the early 1950s, Parsons abandoned voluntarism in favor of functionalism. While European social theorists – as is best illustrated by some of Weber's ideas and those of the Frankfurt School – believed that normative integration was being undermined by ideological distortions and instrumental rationalization by an all-powerful capitalism, Parsons – as an American liberal, and optimistic about the future of society – was convinced that the functional differentiation brought about by modernity was firmly regulated by normative mechanisms, and that a kind of functional unity existed that guaranteed the reproducibility of society. This can be seen as the expression of "American exceptionalism," the view that America's path to modernity was able to avoid the disasters that befell Europe.

Parsons's vision of modernity was one that recast the classical European notion of modernity in terms of a theory of modernization, the essence of which was a view of the progressive unfolding of the structures of a functionally integrated society. Thus, while European social theory culminated in a certain resignation to dissensus, Parsons had established a social theory based on a belief in consensual integration. Mention can be made in this context of another leading American social theorist, Daniel Bell, whose book *The End of Ideology*, published in 1962, epitomized the ideological assumptions of Parsonian theory, namely the view that postwar American society had eliminated conflict in the creation of a political culture based on the relatively stable values of liberal democracy and personal achievement. Functional structuralism provided sociology with what it needed to gain recognition as a social science, namely an elaborate conceptual system as well as a general theory of society. None of the other classical sociologists quite succeeded in this, and their various approaches only gained partisan supporters. Parsons, by contrast, commanded almost world-wide influence in the post-1945 period. Undoubtedly structural functionalism was a reflection of the political context of the period in which the US was able to project its vision of society onto the rest of the world. The models of society present in European social theory were generally judged to be less pertinent to an age that had witnessed two European wars.

The Parsonian synthesis of classical social theory was not to last, despite Robert Merton's revision of some of its central concepts. Merton (1910–2003) aimed to correct some of the shortcomings of structural functionalism, for instance the absence of conflict and dysfunctionality. One of his most important contributions was the introduction of the notion of dysfunction. Lewis Coser (1913–2003) developed conflict theory, which was also an important corrective of structural functionalism's concern with macro-level analysis. The sociology of knowledge, associated with Peter Berger and Thomas Luckmann's *The Social Construction of Knowledge*, published in 1966, presented a challenge to the Parsonian orthodoxy and opened the way for an approach which rehabilitated the neglected figure of Karl Mannheim, as well as an more hermeneutic and phenomenologically oriented sociological theory deriving from Alfred Schutz. Symbolic interactionism ceased to be a marginal preoccupation, and its resurgence signaled a general shift from macrosociological theorizing towards microtheorizing within American sociology.

By the mid-1960s, Parsons's influence had waned, challenged by the resurgence of Marxist thinking and critics of modernization theory, attentive to the multiple paths to modernity. In the United States, C. Wright Mills – inspired by both the Frankfurt School in exile and pragmatism – had introduced Marxist theory, and in 1970 Alvin Gouldner, in *The Coming Crisis of Western Sociology*, had declared the need for a new radical sociology to replace the Parsonian orthodoxy. Critics of Parsonian functionalism, ranging from Alvin Gouldner to Western Marxists such as Herbert Marcuse, did much to undermine its dominance. Moreover, the ideological presuppositions of the theory – the idea of a society based on consensual values and functional unity – was no longer credible in an age that was entering cultural revolution. The student rebellion, Vietnam, the civil rights movement, the counterculture and feminism, and nationalist liberation movements in the developing world all questioned the assumptions of structural functionalism, which was further challenged by the global crisis of capitalism in the early 1970s. When Parsons came to write one of his last works, *The American University*, published in 1973, structural functionalism had become an outmoded system of thought, unable to deal with social protest.

With the decline of Parsonian structural functionalism American social theory began to lose its influence. Merton brought social theory in the direction of grounded theorizing around, what he called, "middle-range theories," which were addressed to empirical social research. This move away from "Grand Theory" was enhanced by the influence of neo-positivist theory in social science, such as the school of thought represented by Carl Hempel. While Jeffrey Alexander developed a socio-logical theory that claimed to be neo-functionalism and Randall Collins advanced conflict theory, much of what was to become American social theory came from outside sociology. Hannah Arendt, for instance, while operating from the wider context of social and political thought, is clearly one of the central figures in modern social theory. This is also the case with regard to other influential theorists such as Barrington Moore. Developments in political theory, around the liberal com-munitarian debate, as well as in cultural theory, offered new reference points for social theory. However, what has remained as the distinctive feature of the classical tradition in the United States is a grounded kind of sociological theorizing that abandons the attempt to develop a comprehensive theory of society. This is in contrast to the diagnostic tradition in European social theory. However, both European and American classical social theory were both decidedly Western in that they presupposed a Western conception of the world and, with hardly any excep-tions, did not subject that view of the world to much critical scrutiny. Indeed, the critical tradition was mostly confined to the concerns of the modern Western world.

CONCLUSION

From the late 1960s, social theory in Europe enjoyed a resurgence and the plurality of traditions that it generated challenged the very possibility of a theoretical ortho-doxy; for instance, the structuralism of Claude Lévi-Strauss and Louis Althusser, Raymond Aron's sociology of industrial society, the work of historically oriented thinkers such as Michel Foucault and Norbert Elias, varieties of post-structuralism and hermeneutics, as well as the work of Giddens, Castoriadis, Touraine, Bourdieu, and Habermas. A feature of these developments was the growth of social theory outside sociology.

Within sociology in the post-1945 period there were important developments that can be seen as establishing a new phase in the classical tradition. In the US phenomenology became increasingly influential as a result of the work of Alfred Schutz, a philosopher of social science who emigrated to the United States. In Britain the philosopher Peter Winch published his influential *The Idea of a Social Science* in 1958, introducing a combination of Weber and Wittgenstein to sociology. Also in Britain, T. H. Marshall published his seminal essay "Citizenship and Social Class" in 1950, which provided a theoretical framework for citizenship theory. In France, Raymond Aron revised the older theories of capitalism in his work on industrial society.

From the 1950s Weberian sociology enjoyed widespread appeal, as is evident in the work of Lewis Coser, S. N. Eisenstadt, and W. G. Runciman. Coser linked structural functionalism with conflict theory, while Eisenstadt introduced cultural issues into modernization and Runciman's selectionist paradigm offered an alternative to the evolutionist assumptions of modernization theory. However, the major developments in social theory that were to shape post-classical social theory came largely from continental Europe in the 1970s: the social theories of Habermas, Touraine, Bourdieu, Luhmann, and Foucault to mention some of the most significant ones.

Notes

1 This chapter is a revised and more concise version of chapter 1 in the 2nd edn. of B. S. Turner (ed.), *The Blackwell Companion to Social Theory*.
2 On the concept of modernity in social theory, see Delanty (1999), Wagner (1994).
3 For some useful historical surveys see Abraham (1973), Aron (1965, 1967), Bottomore and Nisbet (1978), Callinicos (1999), Camic (1997), Coser (1977), Craib (1997), Levine (1994), Nisbet (1970), Ritzer (1996), Swidgewood (1991), and Szacbi (1979).
4 See the volume edited by Allcock (Durkheim 1983).

Bibliography

Abraham, J. H. (1973) *Origins and Growth of Sociology*. Harmondsworth: Penguin Books.

Aron, R. (1965, 1967) *Main Currents in Sociological Theory*, vols. 1 and 2. New York: Basic Books.

Barbalet, J. (2001) *Emotion, Social Theory, and Social Structure*. Cambridge: Cambridge University Press.

Bottomore, T., and Nisbet, R. (eds.) (1978) *History of Sociological Analysis*. London: Heinemann.

Callinicos, A. (1999) *Social Theory: A Historical Introduction*. Cambridge: Polity.

Camic, C. (ed.) (1997) *Reclaiming the Sociological Classics*. Oxford: Blackwell.

Coser, L. A. (1977) *Masters of Sociological Thought*, 2nd edn. New York: Harcourt Brace Jovanovich.

Craib, I. (1997) *Classical Social Theory*. Oxford: Oxford University Press.

Delanty, G. (1999) *Social Theory in a Changing World*. Cambridge: Polity.

Durkheim, É. (1983) *Pragmatism and Sociology*, ed. J. Allcock. Cambridge: Cambridge: Cambridge University Press.

Gane, M. (2003) *French Social Theory*. London: Sage.

Habermas, J. (1987) *The Philosophical Discourse of Modernity*. Cambridge, MA: MIT Press.

Held, D. (1980) *Introduction to Critical Theory*. Berkeley: University of California Press.

Heilbron, J. (1995) *The Rise of Social Theory*. Cambridge: Polity.

Jay, M. (1996) *The Dialectical Imagination: A History of the Frankfurt School and the Institute of Social Research, 1923–1950*. Berkeley: University of California Press.

Levine, D. (1994) *Visions of the Sociological Tradition*. Chicago: University of Chicago Press.

Nisbet, R. (1970) *The Sociological Tradition*. London: Heinemann.

Ritzer, G. (1996) *Classical Sociological Theory*. 2nd edn. New York: McGraw-Hill.

Rundel, J. (1987) *The Origins of Social Theory*. Cambridge: Polity.

Strydom, P. (2000) *Discourse and Knowledge: The Making of Enlightenment Sociology*. Liverpool: Liverpool University Press.

Swidgewood, A. (1991) *A Short History of Sociological Theory*, 2nd edn. London: Macmillan.

Szacbi, J. (1979) *A History of Sociological Thought*. London: Aldwych.

Wagner, P. (1994) *A Sociology of Modernity*. London: Routledge.

2

Contemporary Sociological Theory: Post-Parsonian Developments

John Holmwood

Talcott Parsons is a pivotal figure in the development of contemporary sociology. He defined what might be called a "high modernist" moment when *sociological theory* was attached to a collective project of disciplinary formation and was clearly demarcated from its "shadow," *social theory*. This was a moment when it was believed that secure and consensual foundations for sociology could be established, distinguishing scientific from ideological or normative expressions. Increasingly since the 1950s, this idea of a foundational project has been under criticism and few have associated themselves with it, at least not in its Parsonian form. Yet, if its moment has passed, Parsons remains a significant figure, such that it makes sense to refer to contemporary sociological theory as post-Parsonian. His work has remained as a critical reference point for many subsequent theorists. As Jürgen Habermas put it, "any theoretical work in sociology today that failed to take account of Talcott Parsons could not be taken seriously" (1981: 174). While, for Bryan Turner, the seemingly radical critiques that emerged in the 1960s and 1970s represented merely "shifts in theoretical dialect rather than fundamental changes in discourse" (1986: 200). More recently, however, as we shall see, some more fundamental changes of discourse can be discerned.

PROFESSIONAL ORDER AND DISORDERLY OTHERS

Parsons famously began his monumental work, *The Structure of Social Action* (1937), with the rhetorical question "Who now reads Spencer?" His intention was to indicate the nature of progress in science. Figures who once dominated the scene can fade away and what brings that about is evolution in the scientific field itself, an evolution that is frequently marked by major shifts in its conceptualization. Parsons intended his own study also to inaugurate such a shift and to provide a set of analytic concepts – those associated with a theory of action – that would set sociology on the same footing as economics and psychology and would serve to articulate the relations between the disciplines and their respective explanatory domains.

For Parsons, the most significant problem facing sociology as a discipline in the USA was "empiricism" and a tendency to engage with pressing practical problems in an ad hoc rather than a systematic way. The latter would require their proper expression within the terms of a general theory. Parsons's target was, in part, the American tradition of pragmatism and, while he shared some of their criticisms of laissez-faire economics, he felt that they introduced "sociological elements" into the application of economic theory in an "empiricist" way (Parsons 1935). In consequence, sociology lacked systematic development and presented itself in the critical terms of "institutionalist economics" – what we might say today, in "heterodox" terms (Lawson 2003) – rather than as the complement of economic theory.

In contrast, European social thought was more engaged with theoretical issues, but tended to interpret these through the lens of ideological concerns, primarily those associated with the "social(ism) question." For Parsons, however, this question was essentially associated with early capitalism and, as capitalism matured, so the problems of its emergence receded to be replaced by new concerns. In this sense, Parsons was an early proponent of the "end of ideology" thesis, in the specific sense that he proposed the end of the ideological conflict between rigid liberal individualism (of the sort propounded by Spencer) and socialist collectivism (of the sort propounded by Marx) that had characterized nineteenth-century debates. Mature capitalism would confront problems of affluence, rather than problems of scarcity.

His account in *The Structure of Social Action* of the "1890–1920 generation" of social theorists of economy and society – primarily, Durkheim, Weber, Pareto, and Marshall – saw it as a transitional generation presaging a synthesis that would be the basis of future scientific endeavors. This was also underpinned by a sociological analysis of the changing social context for sociology itself. It was a transitional generation, in part, because it was also located in a transition in the institutional development of capitalism. The particular authors were also selected because they bore upon the relation between sociology and economics, which was crucial to the emerging discipline and what Parsons saw as its necessary formation. According to Parsons, their writings converged on the perception of a necessary role for general theory and its form as a general theory of action beyond the limitations of utilitarian, instrumental action. However, while they went beyond other work in the period, the full realization of their achievement was to be the systematic representation of the categories implicit in their work in a synthetic general frame of reference, and that achievement was to be Parsons's own (Holmwood 1996).

Parsons remained true to this vision of social theory throughout his career. Indeed, from his earliest writings through to the publication of *The Social System* in 1951, which is where my chapter begins, he promoted it with great vigor, frequently conflating "the current state of sociological theory" or "its prospects" with the latest development of his own theory. At the same time, he was rising to prominence in the profession and held the office of President of the American Sociological Society (shortly to change its name to the American Sociological Association) in 1949. His vision of sociological theory was accompanied by a vision of the corporate organization of sociology itself as a profession.

In his presidential address, he set out recent developments in the evolution of his own theory as establishing the integration of the field of sociology. In effect, he proposed that sociology was finally entering the phase of development presaged in *The Structure of Social Action*, in which the "pragmatic empiricism" of an earlier phase was giving way in recognition of the role of "general theory," interpreted as "the theory of the social system in its sociologically relevant aspect" (1954 [1950]: 5). General theory was argued to be important because problems of objectivity and value-bias are confronted by social scientists to a much higher degree than is the case for natural scientists, and there is a greater "problem of selection among an enormous number of variables" (1954 [1950]: 3). It would also help to insulate sociology from ideological influences and provide principles for the selection of research problems. It would also facilitate the cumulative development of knowledge insofar as the latter is "a function of the degree of generality of implications by which it is possible to relate findings, interpretations, and hypotheses on different levels and in different specific empirical fields to each other" (1954 [1950]: 5). Finally, it provided "a common conceptual scheme which makes the work of different investigators in a specific sub-field and those in different sub-fields commensurable" (1954 [1950]: 6).

Ten years later, in an article commissioned for discussion at the 1960 ASA conference, Parsons was asked to consider "some problems confronting sociology as a profession" (1959). Here he suggested that the ideological pressures on sociology were greater than hitherto recognized and growing, even if capitalism had matured such to make the nineteenth century ideological conflict over the "individualism–socialism" dilemma increasingly redundant. Social structural changes to capitalism had made the sociological dimension of social problems more evident, but this also meant an increase in the popular consumption of sociology.

It is now a commonplace that sociological ideas can become part of everyday understandings under conditions of late modernity (Giddens 1991), but Parsons also identified that "the term sociology is coming increasingly to be a central symbol in the popular ideological preoccupations of our time" (1959: 553). While the earlier ideological primacy of the "economic" found expression in terms of the problem of "productivity" versus "equality," the ideological primacy of the "sociological" tends to be the problem of "conformity" (or, as it might now be put, the problem of "identity"). For Parsons. these "ideological preoccupations" tend to predominate in undergraduate teaching programs, where an earlier concern with "social problems" has given way to a more general intellectual preoccupation with the nature of society and its direction. In this context, Parsons believed the profession would come under increasing pressure from being more in the public eye: "it will be exposed to more distortion and misunderstanding than before" (1959: 559). It is a fundamental responsibility of the sociological profession, he argued, "to maintain high standards of scientific competence and objectivity" (1959: 559), though this must interpreted in a non-empiricist way.

This has been rather a lengthy introduction to set the scene for the irruption of new conceptions of the sociological task. Parsons's career, that had waxed so brilliantly, rapidly began to wane, despite his continued prolific rate of publication until his death in 1979. Indeed, it is significant that Parsons's article on the problems facing the profession was written in the same year as C. Wright Mills's *The*

Sociological Imagination (1959). The latter criticized the "grand theory" of Parsons, as well as arid, but technically sophisticated, "abstract empiricism," in the name of a sociology engaged with "private troubles and public problems." It might have been possible, initially, to dismiss Mills's critique as a throwback to the "pragmatism" of an earlier period, but it soon became evident that a major shift in sensibility was under way.

What lay behind this shift, and grew in momentum, was the rise of new social movements to challenge the prevailing status quo, in particular the civil rights movement in America and, waiting in the wings, second-wave feminism and the gay liberation movement. Moreover, the USA – what Parsons (1966) called the new "lead society" – was embroiled in the Vietnam war and opposition to it was growing, while, in Europe, the events of 1968 seemed to be a dramatic harbinger of radical social change. It seemed that after a period of social conformity and conservatism in the 1950s, Western societies were entering a new "noisy ideological age" (Baltzell 1972). Elsewhere, movements of independence from colonial rule were similarly bringing forth critical ideas and challenging "Eurocentric" conceptions of social theory, especially those with pretensions to universalism (Hall 1992).

To its critics, "positivist" (or "empiricist" – the terms were frequently used interchangeably) sociology had become obsessed with trivial issues when compared with those that had motivated "classical" social theory. Moreover, Parsons's structural-functional theory of society seemed to offer no real alternative and, indeed, in the way in which it seemed to set the "system" over the "actor" (see CHAPTER 5), came itself to be designated as a form of positivism. It was the major social theory of the time with pretensions to grasp large-scale social processes, yet it, too, seemed fundamentally flawed. With its emphasis upon processes of social integration and the role of common values, it seemed too much a part of what had given way, too determined by the assumptions of an "end of ideology" and, therefore, ill equipped to give insight into the social conflict and disorder which increasingly seemed so evident.

As a consequence of these radical critiques, sociology began to enter a crisis of self-confidence, where its current offerings – even when gathered collectively – hardly seemed to fulfill the promise of progress and, indeed, looked insignificant when placed against those of its founding period. For many, the proponents of modern professional social science, far from dwarfing the achievements of the founding giants, had, it seems, subverted their undertakings and trivialized their concerns. As Wardell and Turner put it, "the 'advantages of the division of labour' of which Weber so casually speaks in 'Science as a vocation' gradually have evolved into a cage of iron" (1986: 16).

With these criticisms of the fruits of sociology came an attack upon the professional claims of sociologists. Rather than being the embodiment of neutral inquiry, or the disinterested mediation of competing public claims, professional sociology was increasingly seen to represent particular interests. In Germany, Habermas (1970 [1968], 1989 [1962]) powerfully identified the role of the social sciences in the decline of the public sphere. Habermas suggested that the idea of value-freedom was a covert commitment to values. This was not merely in the sense that value-freedom entailed a commitment to the cognitive ideals of science, as Parsons clearly allowed. Habermas argued further that those cognitive ideals involve a commitment to technical mastery and control which, when applied in social inquiry, gave rise to the "depoliticization" of the public sphere and, hence, meant that a sociology, so defined, would favor the status quo, whatever the formal commitment of its practitioners to value-freedom.

In France, the work of Michel Foucault, with its Nietzschean conception of a "power–knowledge" nexus, was less directly engaged with sociological concerns, but it, too, came to have a major influence on social theory. Indeed, when Foucault (1970 [1966]) addressed epistemological issues it was precisely to identify the conditions necessary for science and to identify the emergence of three proper human sciences associated with the "quasi-transcendentals" of labor, life, and language. This, in turn, entailed a critique of "humanisms," which do not achieve the status of sciences, that is, forms of inquiry that fail to define objects of study separate from the social practices that produce and reproduce them. In other words, "bourgeois sociology" was condemned to a non-scientific status, or to (ideological) "discourse." Alain Touraine (1973 [1969]), for his part, identified the emergence of a new post-industrial society, not with the end of ideology, but with the emergence of new collective actors associated with role of knowledge. While old collective actors, such as the proletariat, had become absorbed to the system, and sociology itself had come to reflect the "point of view of the system," new social movements offered the possibility of a different point of view, that of historicity and change (Touraine 1977 [1973]), and sociologists might identify themselves as the "eye" and the "voice" of such movements and their transformative possibilities (Touraine 1981 [1978]).

For many North American sociologists, however, it was Alvin Gouldner's *Coming Crisis of Western Sociology* (1970) that was the culmination of the criticisms and their definitive statement. Sociologists, he argued, had "swallowed" – indeed, had helped to form – the "ideology" by which the professions sought to promote their own private interests at the cost of the interests of their clients or a wider public. Yet, as Parsons had observed, sociologists themselves were professionals, espousing the cognitive claims of science, objectivity, and a broad social utility. At best, the disinterested inquiries of "professional positivism" seemed irrelevant to the pressing social and political issues, but Gouldner's criticism was yet more severe. Professional sociology was partisan and not just in the sense of implicitly supporting the status quo. It was, Gouldner argued, part of the modern "military–industrial–welfare complex," sponsored by government agencies, including the military, on an increasingly large scale. Sociology had become absorbed into the management of the advanced state, and had become part of the apparatus of social control.

All these social theorists looked to building connections between sociology and wider communities of interest outside the academy. Sociology must necessarily engage not simply with issues of public relevance, but with new *publics*. From now on, it would be possible to see that a sociology that had emerged as a separate discipline from within a more broadly engaged social theory (Heilbron 1995) could not be sustained independently of it. Sociology was seen to be inextricably bound up with social theory, and it was precisely the latter that had a diminished role in Parsons's approach. Indeed, the role of social theory as means of expressing the public significance of sociology to diverse audiences is evident in Michael Burawoy's (2005) presidential address, "For Public Sociology." It covers the same themes as

Parsons's own address (1954 [1950]), but it represents a wholly different sensibility, one deeply informed by Mills and Gouldner.

FROM PARSONS TO MARX (AND OTHERS) AND BACK AGAIN

With this shift in sensibilities in the 1970s, it appeared that Parsons's moment had indeed irrevocably passed. His own epigram at the start of *The Structure of Social Action* returned to haunt him: "Who now reads Parsons?" And yet, ironically, this proved to be false; if many purported to disagree fundamentally with him, many more now read him, and especially those working within the European tradition of social theory. When *The Structure of Social Action* was first published it was in an edition of less than 500. Reviewers of the book thought it powerful, but distinctly odd, for it was neither straightforwardly history of sociology, nor exposition of systematic theory (House 1939; Kirkpatrick 1938; Wirth 1939). Moreover, it purported to be a systematic study of the concept of social action in sociology, yet it neglected to mention the American tradition of pragmatism. This tradition had a developed theory of action and had gone on to influence symbolic interactionism, a movement that had come to be seen to provide an alternative conceptualization of action to that of Parsons (see CHAPTER 10).

The Structure of Social Action was first published in a paperback edition in 1967 at the height of criticisms directed at *The Social System*, which had led to a reappraisal of the earlier volume. Paradoxically, engagement with its convergence thesis served also to establish the very mode of sociological argument that earlier critics had found puzzling, where foundations of sociological theory are to be sought in a critical exegesis of selected sociological classics rather than in substantive engagement with the social world. Thus, major critics of the 1960s and 1970s, such as Lockwood (1992) and Habermas (1984 [1981], 1987 [1981]), went on to produce their own interpretations of the classics and, through that, to propose a reordering of the field. The trend has continued since then with notable contributions to the genre from Alexander (1982a, 1982b, 1983, 1984), Münch (1987), and Joas (1996 [1992]), among others.

For many commentators, the primary failure of the book was its lack of engagement with the "pessimistic" side of European thought, especially Marx and Freud. Indeed, each of these writers was conspicuous by his absence, while Freud, at least, might have been considered a member of the 1890–1920 generation, albeit one active until 1939. Parsons had repaired this omission in a series of articles on the personality and its relation to the social system (Parsons 1964b). Although Parsons found Freud's distinction between the id, ego, and super-ego, to be useful, they were put at the service of a theory of integration. As Dennis Wrong (1959) argued, Parsons presented an "over-socialized" view of the human personality. There can be little doubt that Parsons seriously downplayed the tensions between the three "elements" of personality, but he also neglected the tensions between the complexity of a modern social system (or civilization) and the needs of the personality found in Freud's later cultural criticism (Freud 1961 [1930]). The latter was something taken up by Philip Rieff (1959), demonstrating that the criticism of Parsons's essentially optimistic account of modern life was not restricted to the "cultural left" that was to grow in influence during the 1960s, allying Freud with Marx (see Marcuse 1955).

Marx was also seen to have contributed to those areas where Parsons's theory was perceived as deficient, that is, to power, conflict, contradiction, and change. Yet, on closer examination, this response also frequently conceded the same point that Parsons (1949) had made, and that had led to his dismissal of Marx, namely, that Weber incorporated the important insights of Marx, but did so in a way more appropriate to the development of systematic sociological theory (Habermas 1987 [1981]; Lockwood 1964; Rex 1961). Not the least of the reasons for this preference for a Weber-inflected version of Marx is that Parsons was seen to have shifted from an action frame of reference to a systems approach in which "external structures" dominated over actors. Weber, for his part, was seen to be the superior to Marx, just insofar as he addressed action as a fundamental category of social theory. At the same time, he seemed to share Marx's concern with power and social change.

None of this is to deny the importance of more orthodox Marxist, approaches, to which I shall return after briefly tracing the convergence with Parsons in Lockwood and Habermas. Lockwood's critique of Parsons emerged in the context of the conflict theory espoused by Dahrendorf (1958) and Rex (1961), which identified a separate conflict approach to be set alongside Parsons's consensus model of society, regarding each to be "polar theoretical cases." These criticisms were resonant, but they were unstable. It was difficult to argue issues of conflict and consensus should be kept apart theoretically when it was also argued that most empirical cases lay between the two poles. Rather than proposing two separate models of conflict and consensus, Lockwood (1964) argued that it was necessary to consider the question of cooperation, conflict, and social change in terms of two distinct, but interrelated, sets of processes. One set concerned normative processes of *social integration*, the other concerned material processes of *system integration*. The problem with Parsons's model, for Lockwood, was that he conflated the two and emphasized the mutual compatibility of both sets of processes, with the normative having priority in a cybernetic hierarchy. The issue for Lockwood was be more aware of contradictions within a system and how they break through to the level of social integration to bring about potentiality for change.

Lockwood's article was highly influential. However, it was not clear what he thought should follow from his analysis. He used Marx's account of the contradiction between forces and relations of production in capitalism as an example of a problem at the level of system integration, but he did not fully endorse the example as one that was correct in its own terms. Its purpose was to show a type of sociological argument that was outside the confines of Parsons's own account. However, the example could be turned around. If Marx were correct in his analysis of a system contradiction inherent to capitalism, its consequences had yet to be realized. It would seem that the weakness of Marx's approach was to be insufficiently aware of how contradictions at the level of the system could be contained by processes of social integration.

If Marx potentially provided the answer to the problems of Parsons's analysis, the latter could be seen to contain the answer to the problems in that of Marx, though the parallel was not usually posed so starkly (Holmwood 1996). Significantly, Habermas reversed the emphasis found in Lockwood, arguing that Parsons and Marx, alike, overemphasized the dimension of the system to the neglect of that of social integration (or, as he termed it, the lifeworld). Thus, Habermas (1981) argued that what was missing in Parsons was precisely what other critics found to be overemphasized, namely the normative dimensions of culture and the lifeworld. This was a useful corrective to Marx, too. Unsurprisingly perhaps, Habermas's general theory of communicative action ended up with a conception of coordinating mechanisms of action that is remarkably similar to that of Parsons. As greater generality of analysis was achieved, so the substance of Marx's critique of capitalism fell away in the name of "society in general" and with that the specific substance of contradiction. Habermas writes that, "naturally even the simplest action systems cannot function without a certain amount of *generalized* action assumptions. Every society has to face the basic problem of coordinating action: how does ego get alter to continue action in the desired way? How does he avoid conflicts that interrupt the sequence of action?" (1987 [1981]: 179). This is the problem of order, no less.

Similar developments are found in more orthodox Marxist approaches that also emerged in the 1960s, such as that of Althusser (1969 [1962]). The substantial problem for any Marxist is to explain why capitalist development has not followed the path laid out by Marx. Given that the aim is to conserve the Marxist concept of the (economic) mode of production, the issue quickly became the identification of factors additional to the economic that operate interdependently with it, but also independently of it; that is, relatively autonomously. The outcome is similar to that found in Lockwood and Habermas. Supposedly contradictory processes of the economic can be annulled by the countervailing operation of the political and the ideological. What remains is a scheme of less generality than that proposed by Parsons, but mirroring its features. To be sure, the "overdetermined" totality emphasized by structuralist Marxists, is held to be different from the "expressive" totality found in Parsons. In truth, the "overdetermined totality" is simply an expression of a totality underdetermined by the economic, where "the lonely hour of the last instance [of the economic] never comes" (Althusser 1969 [1962]: 113). The role of contradiction in the production of change is fundamentally diminished.

In fact, the development in this critical strand of Marx-inspired theory mirrored developments in Parsons's own theory. He applied his theory to the evolutionary development of societies to identify stages in development through "primitive," "intermediate," and "modern" forms (Parsons 1964a, 1966). The critical developments for the emergence of modernity were the conjunction of administrative bureaucracy, the expansion of money and markets, and universalized norms and democratic association. Moreover, given that stratification was an "evolutionary universal" associated with the rise of intermediate societies, the critique of stratification in radical left-wing thought presaged structural de-differentiation, or the dominance of collectivist political structures over democratic associations and markets as occurred in Soviet-type societies. Evolution culminated in modernity, and the USA had become the "new lead society" (Parsons 1966).

Parsons's account was highly schematic and theoretically derived, but it gave rise to important empirical studies of the most significant transitions he had identified. Seymour Martin Lipset (1960), for example, examined the conditions of democratic associations and the relation between democracy and modernity. He also took issue with Parsons's simple account of the significance of the US by examining its status as "exception" (Lipset 1963). Shmuel Eisenstadt, for his part, provided a comparative historical and sociological account of "intermediate societies" in his study of the *Political Systems of Empires* (1963) in which different paths to modernity (and different forms of modernity itself) were identified. However, it was not until the collapse of communism in the late 1980s that the subtlety of Eisenstadt's earlier work was recognized and he became the doyen of a new approach to "multiple modernities" (Eisenstadt 2000) in which a Parsonian approach to structural differentiation was proposed, albeit inflected through a Weberian sensibility for the paradoxes of modernity.

Other critics, more directly inspired by Weber, had begun their critiques of Parsons from the concept of action. In the development of his scheme, Parsons had seemed to move from action to system (or structure). "Action" is represented analytically in the reproduction of (perfectly integrated) systems where it is specified as conformity, or it is identified as *concrete* deviance, unlocated in systems. What seemed to be missing is a sufficiently rich concept of action, one derived from the interpretive tradition inaugurated by Weber. Giddens expresses the problem well, "there is no action in Parsons' '*action frame of reference*', only behaviour which is propelled by need-dispositions or role expectations. The stage is set, but the actors only perform according to scripts which have been written out for them" (1976: 16). The implication of the critique is that Parsons had adopted a behaviorist conception of action, where external factors dominate, whether these are conceived instrumentally (as rational calculations of "environmental" constraints, including other actors) or normatively (as need dispositions).[1] Giddens allows that external factors are important; the interpretive tradition is also to be criticized for its inadequate treatment of structure. A dualism of structure and action is found in Parsons and the interpretive tradition alike, with "creative action" a residual category (deviance) in the former and "structure" a residual category in the latter.

Giddens proposed a theory of structuration to replace a dualism of structure and action with a concept of "duality," which will explain "how it comes about that structures are constituted through action, and reciprocally how actions is constituted structurally" (1976: 161). Yet the development of his scheme moved quickly to a position where a dualism appears between two points of view, one the "structural" point of view, where "strategic action" is bracketed, the other the point of view of "strategic action" where "structure" is bracketed. Systematic sociological theory – structuration theory – is associated with the development of the structural point of view and is expressed in a manner very similar to that of Parsons: Giddens writes that "what from the structural point of view – where strategic conduct is bracketed – appears as a normatively co-ordinated legitimate order, in which rights and obligations are merely two aspects of norms, from the point of view of strategic conduct represents claims whose realisation is contingent upon the successful mobilization of obligations through the medium of the responses of other actors" (1979: 86).[2]

At best, the differences among schemes hinge around particular theoretical expressions and emphases. Does the scheme manifest duality or dualism? Margaret Archer (1988) prefers a dualistic scheme that retains the distinction between "structure" and "agency" in contrast to its "conflation" in Giddens. Yet Giddens does produce a dualism of the form advocated by Archer, at the same time as he emphasizes duality. The dualisms promoted by Archer have the same distinctions among levels of personality, social interaction, and culture that are also found in Giddens (and in Habermas, too). Similarly, Pierre Bourdieu (1977 [1972]) distinguishes between a "logic of structures" and "practices." Structures bear upon practices and are reproduced through them, but there is a residue to practices that is to be understood independently of structures. While Bourdieu, unlike Parsons or Giddens, produced a series of major empirical studies of lasting value, his attempt to derive a set of formal concepts gave rise to similar problems.

In all the schemes, the issue is that structures are perceived as self-reproducing while agency is understood also to include the possibility of their transformation. This is a problem that has beset general theory over the last generations. Touraine, for example, identified functional processes that serve to maintain systems, alongside action which can produce transformative social change. Similarly, Alberoni (1984) wrote of a dialectic between "institution" and "movement." In each case, what is identified are processes toward self-reproduction, alongside the possibility of transformative social change identified with some form of creative agency that resists capture to structural processes. More recently, this has been expressed in Hans Joas's (1996 [1992]) articulation of a theory of creative action that will overcome problems of normative action in Parsons. Yet he also endorses "structural differentiation" as an appropriate object of sociological concern, one that is adequately formulated in Giddens's structuration theory (notwithstanding its similarity to the functionalist scheme of Parsons). Whether or not differentiation is extended or reduced is an empirical matter that is contingent upon action.

Indeed, it is even possible to interpret Foucault's incorporation into sociological discourses in this way. His arguments about power have been recommended as transcending the limitations of other approaches (Flyvbjerg 2001; Hindess 1996). He is commended for recognizing that power is positive and productive and cannot be assigned simply to relations of superordination and subordination. At best, however, this would be a critique of those approaches to power that seem to associate it necessarily with conflict and the opposition of interests, and a confirmation, at least, of one strand of Parsons's general theory. Quite simply, what Foucault proposes is a version of the latter's understanding of the "system" as the joint capacity of the collectivity, where its realization has to occur in the activities it governs and, therefore, against potential deviance (or, as Foucault would term it, resistance). What is distinctive in Foucault is the "valorization" of deviance and transgressive projects. Where Parsons identifies with the "system," Foucault identifies with "resistance," just as Giddens lays stress on "strategic action."

Perhaps the most rigorous attempt to develop a systems approach that would avoid the problem of an emergent dualism of structure and agency is that by the German sociologist and student of Parsons, Niklas Luhmann, though, by that token, most critics regard its rejection of a theory of action to be precisely what is most problematic.[3] He used the concept of *autopoiesis* (coined by Chilean biologists Humberto Maturana and Francisco Varela to describe the self-regulation of living systems) to develop a constructivist, or self-referential, account of systems (Luhmann 1995 [1984]). Unlike Habermas, with whom he was engaged in debate, Luhmann argued that the structure/agency, system/lifeworld divisions were false ones. The divisions can be appropriately conflated within a systems theory based on the communicative coupling of actors and systems. Communication among systems, not actors, should be the core concept of sociology; modern societies, or social systems, are too complex to be reducible to actors' reasons for acting, which can be many. According to Luhmann, autopoietic social systems construct themselves self-referentially as social relationships made up of differentiated sub-systems. These sub-systems interact, but have their own relatively autonomous logics, and are not limited by a pre-given set of functions.

Differentiation increases communication and the scale and complexity of society. Luhmann argues that this form of system theory avoids the priority given to integration in the Parsonian scheme. His theory is not about the re-establishment of equilibrium in the face of contingent disturbances from the environment, but about the renewal of system elements; all elements must pass away in time, and reproduction is a matter of "dynamic stability." Disintegration and reproduction are intertwined: "systems with temporalized complexity depend on constant disintegration. Continuous disintegration creates, as it were, a place and a need for succeeding elements; it is a necessary, contributing cause of reproduction" (1995 [1984]: 48).

Unsurprisingly, given the way in which these different theoretical arguments have echoed many of the themes found in Parsons, even if it is the counter-melody that has prominence, some have seen in this the basis for a new synthesis or syntheses (Ritzer 1990). Prominent among these is Jeffrey Alexander's argument for a higher level of metatheoretical resolution than that achieved by Parsons. According to him (Alexander 1988), there is a "new theoretical movement" that, after the clamor of the 1970s and 1980s, is converging upon the categories of a genuinely multidimensional theory. Sociological analysis, for Alexander, necessarily presupposes categories of "action" and "order" and these are further distinguished in terms of the role of rational and non-rational aspects of action, and material and ideal elements of order.

Alexander (1984) suggests that Parsons had developed the elements of a satisfactory "multidimensional" scheme, but that, for much of its subsequent development, his solution remained caught up in his statement of the problem. In consequence, critics were right to identify weaknesses, but in taking the "partiality" of their criticisms as establishing a new way forward, these led to a series of approaches that are also unbalanced. Alexander, then, also presents a new version of Parsons's original convergence thesis, one that is now applied both to him and to his critics. Within each of the proposed successor paradigms, there is a convergence on synthetic theory. However, recognition of this requires an understanding of the role of metatheory in the social sciences. Unlike the natural sciences, the social sciences are characterized by "discourse" as well as "explanation." In consequence, the social sciences will not be unified by the rigorous application of method as the positivists had supposed, but by the *presuppositions* that govern discourse. As Alexander puts it, "generalized discourse is central and theory is inherently multivalent" (1988: 80).

Although this makes controversy endemic in the social sciences, because every social scientific statement has to be justified by reference to general principles, this opens up a domain in which those general principles can be thematized. In effect, Alexander suggests that the different one-dimensional paradigms have each stretched beyond their self-conscious limitation to identify the role of factors additional to their own self-conscious justification – for example, agency within structuralist approaches and vice versa, value-rational action within rational actor approaches, and so on. The "new theoretical movement," then, is represented by attempts to achieve different kinds of synthesis beyond the separate paradigms. Post-Parsonian theory is brought centre-stage in this movement precisely because, according to Alexander, this is how Parsons had conceived of general theory. In this perspective, the fundamental discourse of sociological theory is little changed since Parsons. As Turner commented, "Parsonian sociology is the dominant *episteme* . . . and the promise of a new domain of concepts is yet to be realised" (1986: 200).

OUTSIDE THE LOOP?

If Alexander is correct, no new domain of concepts *could be realized*. Yet there is something hubristic about his claim. On the one hand, he recognizes that the dominant view of sociological theory is that it is fragmented and that this has reinforced postmodern claims that disciplinary consensus is impossible (not to mention suspect). Although he argues that this is relativistic and nihilistic (Alexander 1995a), the fact that he would prefer it not to be so could not be sufficient to establish that it is not so. On the other hand, there are those who accept methodological strictures as a constraint on inquires, but do not accept his theoretical logic as appropriate. I shall discuss the latter set of arguments in this section of the article, before turning to more fundamental criticisms in the final section.

Perhaps the two most significant currents of sociological theory to challenge the claims of a generalized action frame of reference are those associated with rational actor theory (or "exchange theory," as it was initially termed) and those from within the "interpretivist tradition," symbolic interactionism and ethnomethodology. The former argued for an analytical framework of rational action common to economics, sociology, and political science as the building blocks of explanatory theory. The latter eschewed Parsons's theoretical abstractions, while also criticizing the abstraction of "rational actors" from contexts of interaction.

In an influential article, "Bringing Men Back In," George Homans (1964) expressed the common concern that there was a problem of action in the Parsonian action frame of reference, but he was equally scathing about his idea of theory. Where Parsons had challenged the dominant conception of scientific explanation, namely the "hypothetic-deductive" or "covering law" model of explanation, Homans responded that Parsons was not offering a *theory* – that is, something that can be empirically specified and tested – but a mere orienting framework. In addition, although Parsons identified processes of systems that depend upon individual action, he seemed to ignore any explanation of *why* individuals act in the way that the theory sets out. The only way this can be done, Homans argued, is through the direct examination of social interaction in terms of real, concrete individuals, their dispositions, motives, and calculations, and not in terms of abstracted roles of a generalized social system. These attributes of individuals can be derived from the studies of economists and psychologists and can be given a general axiomatic form to be applied to the field of sociology. In essence, then, Homans's critique was a powerful restatement of the utilitarian and methodologically individualist position that Parsons had criticized and so, in turn, it attracted the standard sociological criticism of the utilitarian conception of action derived from Parsons (see Turk and Simpson 1971).

Peter Blau (1964) acknowledged the criticism that exchange theory was frequently narrowly utilitarian, and sought to elaborate normative principles of reciprocity and justice alongside instrumental rationality and marginal utility in order to understand both conflict and integration within social relationships. Randall Collins (1975), for his part, accepted Homans's conception of theory and explanation and, connecting it to Weber, set out to produce a compilation of causal principles that would constitute "conflict sociology" as an explanatory science, though the number of such principles that he would regard as satisfactorily established would diminish dramatically over time (Collins 1989).[4]

However, perhaps the most ambitious of developments within rational actor theory was that by James Coleman, who built upon his early criticism of Parsons (Coleman 1971) to produce at the end of his career a major treatise of social theory that set out rational actor foundations of social theory (Coleman 1991). This sought to develop the explanatory theory proposed by Homans and to present it in mathematical form. It also set out a much more subtle critique of theories of systems. For Coleman, the object of sociological interest is indeed social systems, but this must be approached from a methodological perspective of individualism precisely because the data collected by social scientists are data about individuals, their behavior and their opinions. Social systems cannot be observed, only inferred. In this situation, the risk, according to Coleman, is a split between theory and research: "social theory continues to be about the functioning of social systems of behaviour, but empirical research is often concerned with explaining empirical behaviour" (1991: 1).

Although concrete social systems are what sociologists want to explain, Coleman argued that they are not best approached via an analytical theory of systems, conceived as perfectly integrated. Rather, it is rational actor theory that offers the best means with which to construct an explanatory theory that is directly supported by empirical evidence. For example, while trust may be important in maintaining stable social relationships, as Parsons argued, it is vulnerable to actors defaulting upon it and so, rather than constructing an analytical theory that makes trust a central presupposition of social order, it would be better to examine the different circumstances that serve to sustain or undermine it. This will be facilitated by the use of models that describe dilemmas that rational actors face in behaving altruistically when confronted with the possibility that other actors may default or free-ride.

Over the years, the dispute between functionalist action theory and rational choice theory has been a continuous feature of sociological debates. For many critics of rational actor models, then, even if they do not endorse his final scheme, Parsons provided the definitive critique of the utilitarian concept of action on which the models are based (Gould 1989; Lockwood 1992; Scott 1995). Although there are strong advocates of rational actor approaches (see CHAPTER 9), there is considerable suspicion among many sociologists that it is a reductionist position that misrepresents the specificity of *social* action. Moreover, it has had little resonance within the wider field of social theory, as a consequence of its embrace of a scientific model of explanation. The dominant view is that the emphasis upon rational, self-interested actors is too narrow, lacking a sufficiently strong concept of the reflexive actor who self-monitors his or her preferences (Bohman 1991). Notwithstanding Blau's attempt to do so, it cannot adequately account for social conventions and norms which seem to be constitutive of action, rather than being simply their outcome.

Within the interpretive tradition of sociology, there has also been a critique of highly generalized theories of both action and system. Where Homans emphasized the requirements of sociology as a science of observable behavior, Alfred Schutz emphatically endorsed Parsons's concern with action *as necessarily a subjective phenomenon*, something that had meaning to actors and that must be addressed in those terms. Action, for Schutz, was to be distinguished from mere behavior by virtue of it being "determined by a project which precedes it in time" (1978 [1940]: 33). However, the "meaning" of this "project" is not straightforward and varies with the moment at which reflection is occurring (for example, whether during or after its completion), or, given that reflection is not a continuous feature of acting, according to what has prompted it.

Once the process by which actors come to be self-conscious about their actions and the "typifications" they use to characterize their own actions and those of others is understood, we can ground social scientific representations of action and, at the same time, understand "objectivity" as a special kind of "third party" understanding. However, while categories grounded in subjective meanings of actors are the appropriate basis of sociological theories, they are "fictions" from the point of view of a phenomenology of concrete action and the risk is that they can become detached from what ultimately gives them meaning. Parsons's elaborated theory of social systems and sub-systems stands as a warning about this problem of a possible reification of categories. In Schutz's view, his failure to carry through a phenomenological analysis of the categories of his action frame of reference gave rise to a kind of residual, "objectivist" bias, evident in the way in which systems came to be seen as having priority over actors.

Schutz's arguments were taken up by symbolic interactionists (see CHAPTER 10) and by ethnomethodologists (see CHAPTER 8). Each took to heart the arguments against an analytical general theory of systems. The former – for example, Becker (1963) and Goffman (1959) – developed an argument similar to that of Coleman, albeit one that also criticized the abstraction of individual actors from their contexts of action, such as occurs within rational actor approaches. What existed concretely was networks, or systems, of interaction, and interaction should be understood in terms of negotiated meanings. Significantly, given the way in which Parsons's theory had seemed to devolve into a statement of a general system realized in circumstances of potential deviance by individual actors, "deviance" was a major focus of interest for symbolic interactionists. For example, juvenile delinquency was examined from the point of view of how deviant behavior was labeled as such, and who had the power to make their label stick (Lemert 1951). "Deviance" was a complex phenomenon of social interaction, poorly represented in terms of socialized need dispositions and systems of collective sanctions. Howard Becker (1953) developed this position further to show that "socialization" – for example, into becoming a marijuana user – was an ongoing process of interaction in which "deviant" roles were not simply a matter of definition by powerful others, but were also sustained by interaction processes within the sub-group.

In a series of landmark studies, Goffman utilized a dramaturgical analogy, which also showed the complexity of "interaction orders" across a range of phenomena, from "total institutions" (1961) to "fleeting" interactions, such as running a successful con (1952). Here actors perform for each other on a stage, engage in the management of impressions as well as the pursuit of strategic ends, and go "backstage" to adjust their performances. While Goffman was much more concerned with a bravura ethnographic performance than with the systematic development of the theoretical implications of his studies (but see Goffman 1974), it was not difficult for others to draw out the implications. It was the very *sociability* of social interaction that was lost in generalized theories of social action. At the same time, the representation of action in rational actor models was equally deficient; the "free-rider" is no simple self-interested actor, but also has to be socially aware and manage breaches of trust with their requirement of "cooling the mark out."

The post-Parsonian response, perhaps unsurprisingly, was to suggest that these studies were concerned with the micro-foundations of social life, but there was also a significant domain of social life that was missing, namely the macro-sociology of institutions and their interrelationships. As Alexander and Giesen (1987) put it, if macro-sociology had micro-foundations, their interrelationship would require theoretical expression. However, it was precisely this kind of easy claim of complementarity that was challenged by the ethnomethodological approach developed by Garfinkel and his colleagues (Garfinkel 1967; Garfinkel and Sacks 1970). Garfinkel was a former student and research associate of Parsons, but he was also influenced by Schutz. He became interested in order not as a theoretical assumption, but as a practical and contingent achievement of actors. He came to identify a fundamental disjunction between the two concerns. In order to construct its theoretical models, sociology had to make assumptions about the rationality of actors. "Man-in-sociologists-society," as Garfinkel (1967: 68) put it, was assumed to be a "cultural dope," that is, assumed to have the "dope" about society and to be equipped with the knowledge and motivations necessary to reproduce it. In this way, sociology used as a "resource" (or unexamined assumption) for its inquiries, what ought to be its "topic," namely rationality as a practical accomplishment. Macro-sociology could not be built on micro-foundations, because those were shifting sands. Ultimately, Garfinkel and Sacks (1970) convinced themselves of the incoherence of the sociological project and declared themselves "ethnomethodologically indifferent" to it.

BEYOND GENERAL THEORY?

The foregoing reveals deep tensions in sociological theory. On the one hand, it is possible to argue, as do Alexander (1988) and Ritzer (1990), that there are areas of complementarity between different positions such that some kind of synthesis might be achieved. On the other hand, the different positions also seem to be making mutually contradictory claims that make any argument for synthesis appear facile.

There is also the potential problem that synthesis appears to be achieved only by increased abstraction from more immediate issues of explanation. Very often this move is justified by arguing for the "relative autonomy" of theory and reflection on the fact that, over the period, a dominant positivist model of explanation has given way in the face of the rise of post-positivist philosophies of science (see CHAPTER 3). However, the latter understand the historical development of the natural sciences in terms of the paradigmatic reconstruction of their objects and theoretical categories. If this is accepted, it must also call into question any foundational representation of science, precisely because the sciences reconstruct their "foundations" in their development. The claim for post-Parsonian, or synthetic, general theory in sociology is, however, a claim for metatheoretical foundations, namely for categories of action and order that are the condition of sociological inquiries and not at issue in those inquiries.

This, in turn, gives rise to a rather odd position and a contrast between natural and social science. In the former, differences in approach are regarded as problems to be solved in the practical activities of science through which its capacities are advanced. In the social sciences, it is argued that engagement with practical issues of explanation will not produce the temporary and provisional agreements found in the natural sciences, where foundational agreement is unnecessary. However, precisely because the social world provides a weak constraint on explanations, foundational argument is necessary; sociology, it is argued, can cohere by "discourse" rather than "explanation." Thus, Alexander writes, "it is precisely the perspectival quality of social science that makes its own version of foundationalism, its more or less continuous strain of general theorizing, so necessary and often so compelling. It is natural science that does not exhibit foundationalism, for the very reason that its access to external truth has become increasingly secure. Commensurability and realism delegitimate foundationalism, not increase its plausibility" (1995b: 123). In the absence of a "mirror of society," society is to be understood in the "mirror of theory," but what seems to be reflected is theoretical contradiction!

Indeed, in practice, the "foundational" character of "discourse" looks much less like the provision of a general framework for the collective activities of sociology, and much more like its individuation. I began this essay with a discussion of Parsons's presidential address to the ASA. Unsurprisingly, given his general orientation, he perceived sociology to be a collective undertaking and theory to be its expression. However, increasingly, social theory is understood in terms of the contributions of individual *theorists*. As Wolfe (1992) puts it, "strong theory" has given way to "strong theorists." Put another way, *sociological* theory has given way to *social* theory.

Wolfe does not lament the situation, but it is surely unstable. After all, there is something paradoxical about any theorist's claims to unify the field through a new synthesis, only for another theorist to respond with a counterclaim for a different synthesis. If "recognition" is not to be constrained by the production of agreement, but by the coining of new categories and the sharp differentiation of a position from another one close to it in conception, then the idea of a general framework for sociological theory looks increasingly strained (and itself just another position among competing positions).

In this context, Alexander's account of foundational "discourse" is, at best, a set of categories by which different traditions can be located and their differences expressed. Yet these different "traditions" have their own sets of problems and develop in relation to those problems. Why should we suppose that generalized discourse has any particular role, in contrast to specific problems at issue in the intersection of different traditions? For example, it would be relatively easy to demonstrate that debates in the area of social inequality conducted among Weberians, Marxists, feminists, and others have produced transformations in understandings of inequalities, even if those transformations are not captured in general categories.

In fact, from the perspective of the "universal" claims of general theory, we might say that the theoretical achievements of sociology are more "provincial." I use the term advisedly, to capture something more than the more localized nature of problems that enables engagement across different traditions and allows development in each. The claim of general theory was also to insulate sociology from ideological "distortion." Yet I have shown that one of the significant developments in social theory has been the recognition of the importance of extra-academic influences, even if a dominant trope has also been to convert that back into the form of general theory. Indeed, one significant recent development has been a return to pragmatist thinking (Baert 2005; Rorty 1992).

My survey of post-Parsonian sociological theory has also been deficient precisely insofar as it has not engaged with forms of "theoretical community" where the contribution has been "collective" but not "professional" in the way that Parsons understood. For example, feminism has made one of the most substantial contributions to social theory over the last decades, and it has also transformed research agendas across all the sub-fields of sociology producing significantly new knowledge about the gendered nature of a range of social phenomena. Yet this substantial contribution apparently leaves general "discourse" untouched (see Sayer 2000). Moreover, feminism must be understood as formed in relation to ideological concerns, yet these seem not have been an obstacle to knowledge production, but precisely what has encouraged mutual engagement, both among feminists and between feminists and those they have wished to challenge.

In this way, recognition of the "particularism" inherent in all forms of knowledge claims need not be regarded as giving rise to the "dangerous" and debilitating relativism that Alexander fears. If the example of feminism is correct, rather than being the obstacle to critical engagement, "particularism" might be its very condition. Of course, feminism is not the only social movement that has performed this "disruptive" role across the last decades. Movements for gay rights, for civil rights and the dissolution of racialized divisions, for decolonization and postcolonial reconstruction, have all had a major impact on social theory outside its "post-Parsonian" construction. Indeed, the major contribution of postcolonial theory (Hall 1992; Said 1978) has barely been registered within sociology (Bhambra 2007).

At a time when Western social science and Western publics perceive the world to be increasingly globalized – a feature of the world already known by previously colonized "others" – the impact of other centers of knowledge on conceptions of social theory is likely to be profound. In this context, we are likely to understand the construction of Western forms of social theory differently, to provincialize them

(Chakrabarty 2000), and to find them opened them to other kinds of engagement. Among the hierarchies that may currently be under challenge are those hitherto produced in understanding the activity of social theory itself.

Notes

1   The criticism is similar to that made by Habermas. The interpretive tradition is associated with the development of a concept of the lifeworld and so it is linked to the idea that what is missing in Parsons is sufficient linkages between subjective and intersubjective aspects of the lifeworld, that is, between personality, social system, and cultural system. Thus, Habermas writes, "under the functional aspect of *mutual understanding*, communicative action serves to transmit and renew cultural knowledge; under the aspect of *coordinating action*, it serves social integration and the establishment of solidarity; finally under the aspect of *socialization*, communicative action serves the formation of personal identities" (1987 [1981]: 137).

2   As Giddens develops his "structural analysis" (the structural point of view, while bracketing strategic action) its Parsonian features become clear. For example, he also outlines four structural principles – signification, legitimation, authorization, and allocation (1981: 47; see also Giddens 1984). Not only do these have the same referents as Parsons's functional imperatives, they prescribe two forms of articulation, where "one is how far a society contains distinct spheres of 'specialism' in respect of institutional orders: differentiated forms of symbolic order . . . a differentiated 'polity', 'economy' and 'legal/repressive' apparatus'. The second is how modes of institutional articulation are organized in terms of overall properties of societal reproduction: that is to say, 'structural principles' " (1981: 47–8).

3   Habermas's problems in the interpretation of Parsons's theory arise, at least in part, because he conflates Luhmann and Parsons, such that the former's rejection of the theory of action is read back onto Parsons as the substance of his position. See Habermas (1987 [1985]).

4   Collins (1975) proposed many hundreds of higher-level postulates and derived propositions and generalizations, but the later article (Collins 1989) presents just three valid propositions!

Bibliography

Alberoni, F. (1984) *Movement and Institution*. New York: Columbia University Press.

Alexander, J. C. (1982a) *Theoretical Logic in Sociology*, vol. 1, *Positivism, Presuppositions and Current Controversies*. London: Routledge & Kegan Paul.

Alexander, J. C. (1982b) *Theoretical Logic in Sociology*, vol. 2, *The Antinomies of Classical Thought, Marx and Durkheim*. London: Routledge & Kegan Paul.

Alexander, J. C. (1983) *Theoretical Logic in Sociology*, vol. 3, *The Classical Attempt at Synthesis, Max Weber*. London: Routledge & Kegan Paul.

Alexander, J. C. (1984) *Theoretical Logic in Sociology*, vol. 4, *The Modern Reconstruction of Classical Thought: Talcott Parsons*. London: Routledge & Kegan Paul.

Alexander, J. C. (1988) "The New Theoretical Movement," in N. J. Smelser (ed.), *Handbook of Sociology*. London: Sage.

Alexander, J. C. (1995a) "Modern, Anti, Post, and Neo: How Intellectuals Have Coded, Narrated, and Explained the 'New World of Our Time,'" in *Fin de Siècle Social Theory: Relativism, Reduction, and the Problem of Reason*. London: Verso.

Alexander, J. C. (1995b) "General Theory in the Postpositivist Mode: The "Epistemological Dilemma" and the Search for Present Reason," in *Fin de Siècle Social Theory: Relativism, Reduction, and the Problem of Reason*. London: Verso.

Alexander, J. C., and Giesen, B. (1987) "From Reduction to Linkage: The Long View of the Micro-Macro Link," in J. C. Alexander, B. Giesen, R. Munch, and N. J. Smelser (eds.), *The Micro-Macro Link*. Berkeley and Los Angeles: University of California Press.

Archer, M. S. (1988) *Culture and Agency: The Place of Culture in Social Theory*. Cambridge: Cambridge University Press.

Althusser, L. (1969 [1962]) "Contradiction and Overdetermination," in *For Marx*. London: New Left Books.

Baert, P. (2005) *Philosophy of the Social Sciences: Towards Pragmatism*. Cambridge: Polity.

Baltzell, E. D. (1972) "To be a Phoenix: Reflections on Two Noisy Ages of Prose." *American Journal of Sociology* 78: 211–29.

Becker, H. S. (1953) "Becoming a Marihuana User." *American Journal of Sociology*, 59: 235–42.

Becker, H. S. (1963) *Outsiders: Studies in the Sociology of Deviance*. New York: Free Press.

Bhambra, G. K. (2007) *Rethinking Modernity: Postcolonialism and the Sociological Imagination*. Houndmills: Palgrave Macmillan.

Blau, P. (1964) *Exchange and Power in Social Life*. New York: Wiley.

Bohman, J. (1991) "The Limits of Rational Choice Explanation," in J. S. Coleman and T. J. Fararo (eds.), *Rational Choice Theory: Advocacy and Critique*. London: Sage.

Bourdieu, P. (1977 [1972]) *Outline of a Theory of Practice* Cambridge: Cambridge University Press.

Burawoy, M. (2005) "For Public Sociology." *American Sociological Review* 70: 4–28.

Chakrabarty, D. (2000) *Provincializing Europe: Postcolonial Thought and Historical Difference*. Princeton: Princeton University Press.

Coleman, J. S. (1971) "Collective Decisions," in H. Turk and R. L. Simpson (eds.), *Institutions and Exchange: The Sociologies of Talcott Parsons and George Caspar Homans*. New York: Bobbs-Merrill.

Coleman, J. S. (1991) *Foundations of Social Theory*. Cambridge, MA: Harvard University Press.

Collins, R. (1975) *Conflict Sociology: Toward an Explanatory Science*. New York: Academic Press.

Collins, R. (1989) "Sociology: Proscience or Antiscience?" *American Sociological Review* 54: 124–39.

Dahrendorf, R. (1958) "Out of Utopia: Toward a Reorientation of Sociological Analysis." *American Journal of Sociology* 64: 115–27.

Eisenstadt, S. E. (1963) *The Political System of Empires*. New York: Free Press.

Eisenstadt, S. E. (2000) "Multiple Modernities." *Daedalus*, Winter, 129: 1–29.

Freud, S. (1961 [1930]) *Civilization and its Discontents*. New York: W.W. Norton.

Flyvbjerg, B. (2001) *Making Social Science Matter: Why Social Inquiry Fails and How It Can Succeed Again*. Cambridge: Cambridge University Press.

Foucault, M. (1970 [1966]) *The Order of Things: An Archaeology of the Human Sciences*. New York: Pantheon.

Garfinkel, H. (1967) *Studies in Ethnomethodology*. Englewood Cliffs, NJ: Prentice Hall.

Garfinkel, H., and Sacks, H. (1970) "On Formal Structures of Practical Actions," in J. McKinney and E. Tiryakian (eds.), *Theoretical Sociology: Perspectives and Developments*. New York: Meredith.

Giddens, A. (1976) *New Rules of Sociological Method*. London: Hutchinson.

Giddens, A. (1979) *Central Problems in Social Theory: Action, Structure and Contradiction in Social Analysis*. London: Macmillan.

Giddens, A. (1981) *A Contemporary Critique of Historical Materialism*. London: Macmillan.

Giddens, A. (1984) *The Constitution of Society*. Cambridge: Polity.

Giddens, A. (1991) *The Consequences of Modernity*. Cambridge: Polity.

Goffman, E. (1952) "On Cooling the Mark Out: Some Adaptations to Failure." *Psychiatry* 15: 451–63.

Goffman, E. (1959) *The Presentation of Self in Everyday Life*. New York: Doubleday.

Goffman, E. (1961) *Asylums. Essays on the Social Situation of Mental Patients and Other Inmates*. Chicago: Aldine.

Goffman, E. (1974) *Frame Analysis: An Essay on the Organization of Experience*. New York: Harper & Row.

Gould, M. (1989) "Voluntarism versus Utilitarianism: A Critique of Camic's History of Ideas." *Theory, Culture and Society* 6: 637–54.

Gouldner, A. W. (1970) *The Coming Crisis of Western Sociology*, London: Heinemann.

Habermas, J. (1970 [1968]) "Technology and Sciences as Ideology," in *Toward a Rational Society: Student Protest, Science and Politics*. Boston: Beacon.

Habermas, J. (1981) "Talcott Parsons: Problems of Theory Construction." *Sociological Inquiry* 51: 173–96.

Habermas, J. (1984 [1981]) *The Theory of Communicative Action*, vol. 1, *Reason and the Rationalisation of Society*. London: Heinemann.

Habermas, J. (1987 [1981]) *The Theory of Communicative Action*, vol. 2, *Lifeworld and System*. Cambridge: Polity.

Habermas, J. (1987 [1985]) "Excursus on Luhmann's Appropriation of the Philosophy of the Subject through Systems Theory," in *The Philosophical Discourse of Modernity: Twelve Lectures*. Cambridge, MA: MIT Press.

Habermas, J. (1989 [1962]) *The Structural Transformation of the Public Sphere: An Inquiry into a Category of Bourgeois Society*. Boston: MIT Press.

Hall, S. (1992) "The West and the Rest: Discourse and Power," in S. Hall and B. Gieben (eds.), *Formations of Modernity* Cambridge: Polity/Open University.

Heilbron, J. (1995) *The Rise of Social Theory*. Cambridge: Polity.

Hindess, B. (1996) *Discourses of Power: From Hobbes to Foucault*. Oxford: Blackwell.

Holmwood, J. (1996) *Founding Sociology? Talcott Parsons and the Idea of General Theory*. London: Longman.

Homans, G. C. (1964) "Bringing Men Back In." *American Sociological Review* 29: 809–18.

House, F. W. (1939) "Review of 'The Structure of Social Action.'" *American Journal of Sociology* 45: 129–30.

Joas, H. (1996 [1992]) *The Creativity of Action*, trans. J. Gaines and P. Keast. Cambridge: Polity.

Kirkpatrick, C. (1938) "Review of 'The Structure of Social Action.'" *Journal of Political Economy* 46: 588–9.

Lawson, T. (2003) *Reorienting Economics*. London: Routledge.

Lemert, E. S. (1951) *Social Pathology: A Systematic Approach to the Theory of Sociopathic Behavior*. New York: McGraw-Hill.

Lipset, Seymour Martin (1960) *Political Man: The Social Bases of Politics*. New York: Doubleday.

Lipset, S. M. (1963) *The First New Nation: The United States in Historical and Comparative Perspective*. New York: Basic Books.

Lockwood, D. (1964) "System Integration and Social Integration," in G. Zollschan and W. Hirsch (eds.), *Explorations in Social Change*. London: Routledge & Kegan Paul.

Lockwood, D. (1992) *Solidarity and Schism: "The Problem of Disorder" in Durkheimian and Marxist Sociology*. Oxford: Clarendon Press.

Luhmann, N. (1995 [1984]) *Social Systems*. Stanford: Stanford University Press.

Marcuse, H. (1955) *Eros and Civilization*. Boston: Beacon Press.

Mills, C. W. (1959) *The Sociological Imagination*. New York: Oxford University Press.

Münch, R. (1987) *Theory of Action: Towards a New Synthesis Going Beyond Parsons*. London: Routledge.

Parsons, T. (1935) "Sociological Elements in Economic Thought." *Quarterly Journal of Economics* 49: 415–53.

Parsons, T. (1937) *The Structure of Social Action*. New York: Free Press.

Parsons, T. (1949) "Social Classes and Class Conflict in the Light of Recent Sociological Theory." *The American Economic Review* 39: 16–26.

Parsons, T. (1951) *The Social System*. London: Routledge & Kegan Paul.

Parsons, T. (1954 [1950]) "The Prospects of Sociological Theory," in *Essays in Sociological Theory*. New York: Free Press.

Parsons, T. (1959) "Some Problems Confronting Sociology as a Profession." *American Sociological Review* 24: 547–58.

Parsons, T. (1964a) "Evolutionary Universals in Society." *American Sociological Review* 29: 339–57.

Parsons, T. (1964b) *Social Structure and Personality*. New York: Free Press.

Parsons, T. (1966) *Societies: Evolutionary and Comparative Perspectives*. Englewood Cliffs, NJ: Prentice Hall.

Rex, J. (1961) *Key Problems of Sociological Theory*. London: Routledge & Kegan Paul.

Rieff, P. (1959) *Freud: The Mind of the Moralist*. Chicago: University of Chicago Press.

Ritzer, G. (ed.) (1990) *Frontiers of Social Theory: The New Syntheses*. New York: Columbia University Press.

Rorty, R. (1992) *Consequences of Pragmatism*. Minneapolis: University of Minnesota Press.

Said, E. W. (1978) *Orientalism: Western Conceptions of the Orient*. London: Routledge & Kegan Paul.

Sayer, A. (2000) "System, Lifeworld and Gender: Associational Versus Counterfactual Thinking." *Sociology* 34: 707–25.

Schutz, A. (1978 [1940]) "Parsons' Theory of Social Action," in R. Grathoff (ed.), *The Theory of Social Action: The Correspondence of Alfred Schutz and Talcott Parsons*. Indiana: Indiana University Press.

Scott, J.A. (1995) *Sociological Theory: Contemporary Debates*. Cheltenham: Edward Elgar.

Touraine, A. (1971(1969]) *The Post-Industrial Society: Tomorrow's Social History: Classes, Conflicts and Culture in the Programmed Society*. New York: Random House.

Touraine, A. (1977 [1973]) *The Self-Production of Society*. Chicago: University of Chicago Press.

Touraine, A. (1981 [1978]) *The Voice and the Eye: An Analysis of Social Movements*. Cambridge: Cambridge University Press.

Turk, H., and Simpson, R. L. (eds.) (1971) *Institutions and Exchange: The Sociologies of Talcott Parsons and George Caspar Homans*. New York: Bobbs-Merrill.

Turner, B. S. (1986) "Parsons and his Critics: On the Ubiquity of Functionalism," in R. J. Holton and B. S. Turner (eds.), *Talcott Parsons on Economy and Society*. London: Routledge & Kegan Paul.

Wardell, M., and Turner, S. P. (1986) "The Dissolution of the Classical Project," in M. Wardell and S. P. Turner (eds.), *Sociological Theory in Transition*, London: Allen & Unwin.

Wirth, L. 1939) "Review of 'The Structure of Social Action.'" *American Sociological Review* 4: 399–404.

Wolfe, A. (1992) "Weak Sociology/Strong Sociologists: Consequences and Contradictions of a Field in Turmoil." *Social Research* 59: 759–79.

Wrong, D. H. (1959) "The Over-Socialized Conception of Man in Modern Sociology." *American Sociological Review* 26: 183–93.

3

Philosophy of the Social Sciences

PATRICK BAERT AND FERNANDO DOMÍNGUEZ RUBIO

INTRODUCTION

Compared to other subdivisions within philosophy (such as philosophy of mind and indeed philosophy of science), philosophy of the social sciences occupies a distinctive, and perhaps idiosyncratic, position. Unlike most other strands, it does not enjoy a long heritage. Although a number of questions posed by philosophers of the social sciences clearly pre-date the modern era, the discipline as such cannot be traced back further than the nineteenth century, with its origins closely tied to the emergence and establishment of the social sciences themselves. Before then, philosophers might have reflected on the nature of social inquiry, but there was not a clearly distinguishable area of philosophy of the social sciences as such, nor was the need felt by philosophers or anyone else to carve one out.

The appearance and formation of the social sciences within academic institutions during the nineteenth century led to widespread concerns (not just amongst philosophers and practicing social researchers but also amongst other academicians) about the methodology and scientific legitimacy of these newly founded disciplines, which seemed to find themselves at the crossroads "between science and literature" (Lepenies 1988). The new disciplines, regarded with a mixture of enthusiasm, hope, and suspicion, were in serious need of both academic recognition and methodological guidance. Hence a growing interest amongst philosophers and social scientists in metatheoretical questions, ranging from the "right" kind of method for the social sciences to the differences and similarities with the natural sciences. Those nineteenth-century anxieties about method are neatly exemplified in the *Methodenstreit*, a prolonged and well-documented debate within the German Academy between hermeneutic and positivist accounts of history: about the nature of method in history and about whether or not this method is identical to that of the natural sciences.

Whereas philosophers of mind or moral philosophers seem to exercise an exclusive right to the questions they tackle, philosophers of the social sciences face stiff competition from practicing social scientists. Indeed, from the very beginning, social researchers asked metatheoretical questions which, by all accounts, fall under the heading of philosophy of the social sciences. For instance, Émile Durkheim's *Rules of Sociological Method* includes not only tips about how to conduct sociological research but also sophisticated philosophical claims about social explanation and causality (Durkheim 1982: 31–163). Likewise, Max Weber wrote extensively on the methodology of historical analysis, including the role of intentional explanations, counterfactuals, and ideal types (for instance, Weber 1948, 1949: 1–47, 49–112, 113–88, 1964: 85–157, 1975). Although issues of scientific legitimacy and methodology are possibly less pressing now than they used to be, it is not uncommon for contemporary social scientists to reflect on philosophical issues connected to their work and discipline. If there is any dividing line between the activities of social and natural scientists, it is that the former often accompany their research with philosophical ruminations and the latter rarely do so, leaving this to specialists who are often at the margins of the discipline. To the extent that social disciplines adopt the formal techniques of the natural sciences, they tend in this direction; sociology, for instance, exhibiting strong philosophical inclinations and economics very little. The more diverse the methodological strategies, theories, and general orientations are within a discipline, the more practitioners feel the need to defend their position and encroach on philosophy to do so. The recent ascendancy of social theory and its impact on whole generations of social scientists has made contemporary philosophy of the social sciences a particularly crowded, contested, and hybrid domain, with different traditions and genres inevitably arriving at very different conclusions. The idea that philosophy of the social sciences consists of a limited and well-defined set of questions was held only sporadically by a minority of scholars, and it seems particularly untenable today when the social sciences are so heavily entangled with theoretical and metatheoretical debates.

In addition, while in principle philosophy of the social sciences should pay due respect to each of the social sciences, in practice this has never been the case, and the number of social sciences covered has been rather limited. It is striking how little attention has been given to disciplines like, for instance, geography and political science, which after all occupy an important role within the modern academy. It is even more striking how, at different times, different social sciences take center stage. Initially, the core questions in the philosophy of the social sciences were closely tied to the emergence and establishment of sociology as an autonomous and legitimate science. History and its debate about the nature of historical explanation came a close second. In the course of the twentieth century, sociology remained a central discipline within philosophy of the social sciences, although this connection loosened somewhat and the questions were certainly no longer tied so closely to the search for justification and authority within the academic establishment. In the last couple of decades, philosophers of the social sciences have drawn their attention increasingly towards economics, not just as a field of inquiry, but also as a model of thinking about the social world in general. It is in this light that a number of textbooks appeared which take the centrality of rational choice theory (and game theory) as a given and which tackle a number of sociological and philosophical problems (for example, how to explain the emergence and stability of norms) from this perspective (for instance, Elster 1989; Hollis 2002). This trend within philosophy of the social sciences mirrors developments in, for instance, sociology and politics, in which methodological individualism and in particular rational choice theory have become more prominent and in the case of political science may even acquire a quasi-paradigmatic status.

NATURALIST AND FOUNDATIONALIST MODELS

Positivist promises

Since the 1960s the label "positivism" has acquired strong pejorative connotations. During this period very few social researchers or philosophers subscribed to the doctrine, and the term was increasingly used to caricature and denigrate intellectual opponents. By positivism was, then, meant an amalgam of stances such as scientism (the assumption that the scientific method is the only valuable source of knowledge), naturalism (the presupposition that there is a unity of method across the social and the natural sciences), a regularity notion of causality (the assumption that the regular association of x and y is both necessary and sufficient to talk about causality), an assumption that explanation entails prediction (and vice versa), a rejection of explanations in terms of mental or subjective states (like intentions or motives), a predilection for quantification and sophisticated statistical analysis, and finally a sharp distinction between facts and values. Not only did this cavalier reconstruction of positivism ignore the plurality within the history of the doctrine, it also meant that some significant authors like Max Weber and Karl Popper who explicitly opposed the positivism of their times were wrongly labeled as positivist. There are at least three key phases in the history of positivism, the first referring to the nineteenth-century positivism of Saint-Simon, Auguste Comte, and their followers, the second to the logical positivism as developed in Vienna and Cambridge during the early twentieth century, and finally the deductive-nomological model of Ernest Nagel and Carl Hempel of the mid-twentieth century. Nineteenth-century positivism was strongly associated with the emergence and establishment of sociology as an autonomous scientific discipline and as such preoccupied with questions about the nature of the scientific method and the distinctiveness of the sociological enterprise. J. S. Mill, Herbert Spencer, and Durkheim count amongst those nineteenth-century intellectuals who were sympathetic towards central features of Comte's project whilst keeping a critical distance towards Comte's execution of it. Most nineteenth-century positivists believed that a non-speculative, scientific account of the social world would help accomplish a more ordered and just society. Like early positivism, one of the main concerns of the positivism that emerged in early twentieth-century Vienna and Cambridge was to free philosophy from metaphysics, but, unlike its predecessors, it tried to do so with the help of sophisticated logical analysis. Most logical positivists subscribed to a phenomenalist theory of knowledge, according to which the basis of science lies in sensory observations. Whereas nineteenth-century positivism was intimately linked to sociology, the logical positivism that emerged in the early twentieth century in Vienna and in Cambridge had hardly any such connection. Amongst the Vienna Circle, only Otto Neurath paid particular attention to the social sciences, and his commitment to "physicalism" (according to which various social or psychological phenomena are ultimately to be redescribed in the language of physics) led to such an eccentric view of sociology (as merely the study of behavior) and of social explanations (as excluding any references to mental or subjective states) that Neurath's impact on the social sciences remained limited (Neurath 1944, 1973, 1983: 58–90). Nagel and Hempel's deductive-nomological model had a more significant effect on the social sciences, presenting as it did a neat, straightforward view of scientific theory formation and testing, applicable to both social and natural sciences. Like their contemporary Karl Popper (but unlike early positivism), scientific theories are seen as deductive endeavors, whereby empirical hypotheses are inferred from general laws and initial conditions (for instance, Hempel 1965).

Falsificationism

Aware of the philosophical "problem of induction" and the theory-laden nature of observations, Popper was equally committed to deductivism, but he is particularly remembered for his intellectual efforts round the demarcation between science and non-science. As early as 1934, Popper argued that science differs from non-science (for instance, ideology and religion) in that it produces falsifiable hypotheses, i.e. hypotheses that can be empirically refuted (Popper 1959). Precisely because of the production of refutable knowledge, science can progress through an endless process of trial and error, whereby bold theoretical conjectures are assessed empirically, and, if found wanting, replaced by superior ones. Whilst Popper's knowledge of the social sciences was limited, he became particularly known for his scathing attacks on followers of Marx, Freud, and Adler, who, according to him, developed non-falsifiable theories, i.e. immunized against empirical refutation (Popper 1971, 1991a, 1991b). In the course of the 1960s, Popper's falsificationism came under considerable attack, not least because of the publication of Kuhn's *Structure of Scientific Revolutions*, a study in the history of science which demonstrated that most of the time scientists did not attempt to refute the "paradigm" which they employed, and that even when confronted with anomalous results they rarely blamed the paradigm (Kuhn 1970). Inspired by Kuhn's insights into the history of science, Imre Lakatos fine-tuned Popper's critical rationalism: scientists are considered rational in holding on to their "research program" even if confronted with some empirical refutations, as long as the overall picture of the research program is one that is progressive. In Lakatosian parlance, a research program is progressive (as opposed to degenerating) if it allows for a considerable amount of accurate predictions and new applications (Lakatos 1970). However, Lakatos's "sophisticated falsificationism" was not without blemish either, because it remains unclear how many empirical falsifications are needed for a research program to be labeled as degenerative, and a research program which appears as degenerative might re-emerge as a progressive in the future. In contrast with the publicity around both Popper's debate with Kuhn and Lakatos and his critique of Marxism and psychoanalysis, Popper's own positive prescriptions (about how to carry out social research) did not have much effect until the 1980s, when rational choice theory emerged as an important intellectual force (for instance, Popper 1983). It is important to turn to this perspective as it shows the significance of Popperian social science today.

In the course of the 1980s, sociologists, and in particular political scientists, became progressively more disenchanted with holistic theories such as structuralism and functionalism, partly because of the perceived lack of conceptual clarity or the circularity of the explanations provided. These social scientists were drawn to the intellectual tradition of methodological individualism (which was associated with the writings of a diverse group of people, including Hobbes, Tocqueville, Weber, and Popper), which had remained dormant for a long time because of the dominance of holistic, structural-functional analysis in the mid-twentieth century. Increasingly, social scientists looked towards the discipline of economics for answers to questions regarding general methodological orientation, partly because of the development of game theory and its useful applications in economics, and also because economists like Gary Becker (1976) managed to use their models to supply economic explanations for phenomena like crime, fertility, and marriage that were previously the province of other disciplines. Indicative of this trend towards methodological individualism and economics was a new group of "analytical Marxists" who purposefully broke with the Hegelian tradition and who attempted to reconcile Marx with an individualist starting-point and rational choice theory (for instance, Elster 1986). Rational choice explanations account for people's actions and choice by assuming that they act not only intentionally but also rationally and that they produce a number of effects, some of which are unintended and unanticipated. Most rational choice theorists agree that action is "rational" if it is consistent with and guided by "rational beliefs," but there is less of a consensus about what makes a belief truly rational. There is also disagreement amongst rational choice theorists as to whether the people discussed make conscious calculations or whether they simply act as if they do. Whilst the former position is short of empirical evidence, the latter (sometimes referred to as "externalism") lacks explanatory power and is not easily distinguishable from rival theories. Although rational choice theorists situate themselves within the tradition of falsificationism, in practice they tend to adjust their theories to accommodate behavior that does not fit their models, reconciling "anomalies" with the rational choice paradigm rather than considering this to be empirically challenged.

Critical realism

Positivist and falsificationist philosophies of social sciences were not the only attempts to develop a naturalist agenda for the social sciences. Half a century ago, structuralist authors, like Claude Lévi-Strauss (1972), also attempted to develop a "science" of society, but their notion of science was diametrically opposed to the positivist one. In contrast with the atomism and phenomenalism of logical positivism, structuralists proposed not only a holistic theory of society, but also a two-level world-view, whereby the fast-moving observational level hides the more stable "real" structural level. This position put social scientists in a remarkably privileged position, able as they were supposed to be to detect the structures or mechanisms which were often invisible to laypeople, though structuralists could not really account for why social scientists were allegedly so much better placed than others to gain this level of objectivity and insight. During the 1970s, structuralist Marxism inspired early versions of critical realism, especially Roy Bhaskar's writings, which, like structuralism, exhibited a two-level world-view and a naturalist, non-positivist philosophy (Bhaskar 1997, 1998). Bhaskar's realism distinguishes between three levels: the actual (the events which actually take place), the empirical (people's observations of the events), and the deep (the underlying structures or powers which cause the events). Bhaskar emphasizes the lack of synchrony between the different realms: for instance, there might be a discrepancy between people's observations and what actually happened due to the theory-laden nature and fallibility of those observations. For critical realists, it is especially the lack of synchrony between the empirical and the deep that is crucial. Most, if not all, systems are open, meaning it is impossible to isolate all other variables so as to observe the causal impact of one (as in a closed system), and observable events are "emergent" phenomena that cannot be precisely traced to underlying events. So a particular power or structure that is in operation might not be visible to the observer because other generative mechanisms and powers interfere. From the openness of systems, critical realists infer that the "positivist" or "Humean" notion of causality (by which they mean the view that the observation of regular conjunctions between two discrete events is both necessary and sufficient to claim that there is a causal relationship between the two) is flawed. Once the openness of systems is acknowledged, so they argue, the observation of regularities is neither sufficient nor necessary to talk about causality. It follows that causal explanation does not necessarily entail prediction and vice versa. Causal explanations ought to refer to mechanisms, structures, or powers, which are situated at the deep level, and which are therefore not necessarily accessible to observation. Initially a purely philosophical endeavor, critical realism gained a significant number of followers in a wide variety of social sciences, including sociology, history, economics, and social psychology. Although the critical realist view of science was a laudable attempt to escape the excesses of empiricist social research, it remained unclear how the notion of openness of systems could be reconciled with their belief that social scientists can use empirical research to test and validate their statements about the precise nature of the underlying mechanisms and their effects. Once the lack of synchrony between the actual and the deep is acknowledged (as critical realists do), it seems no longer viable to argue that theories can be tested in a straightforward fashion with the help of empirical research.

MEANING, LANGUAGE, AND CRITIQUE

In the course of the twentieth century, naturalist philosophy of social science has been challenged by three intellectual strands: hermeneutics, Wittgensteinian philosophy, and critical theory.

Hermeneutics

Hermeneutics has a long history and was originally concerned with the art of interpreting and understanding the meaning of the Scriptures, but commentators locate the birth of modern hermeneutics in the nineteenth century and associated it with Friedrich Schleiermacher's writings. Schleiermacher widened the scope of the discipline and contended that the problems of "interpretation" and "understanding" were not confined to the exegesis of sacred texts but were relevant to any human document. Inspired by Schleiermacher, Wilhelm Dilthey argued for the autonomy of the *Geisteswissenschaften*, and contrasted them with the established *Naturwissenschaften*: whereas the latter deal with the *explanation* of sensory experience, the former aim at *understanding* inner experience (Dilthey 1996: chs. 1 and 3, 1988). This opposition between "explanation" and "understanding" became central to the *Methodenstreit*, which raged in Germany for several decades from the 1870s onwards, and which involved two opposing camps: Carl Menger's Austrian School of Economics and Gustav von Schmoller's German Historical School. Arguably, the work of Max Weber was the most fundamental attempt at incorporating the hermeneutical method into the nascent field of the social sciences, and of all hermeneutic authors Heinrich Rickert had the greatest impact on Max Weber's methodological writings. Influenced by Kant and Dilthey, Rickert (1986) argued that the interpretive dimension of the social sciences called into question the objectivity of these sciences because any interpretation is necessarily dependent on a specific viewpoint and system of values. Following Dilthey, Weber (1949, 1968) held that the methodological separation between the natural and the social sciences was a logical consequence from the different nature of their respective objects of study: in contrast with the causal explanation of natural phenomena, making sense of social action requires social scientists to employ the method of *Verstehen*, which captures the subjective meanings of the individuals involved. Although Weber thought that, with the help of ideal-typical constructions, social scientists can develop a causal account of social phenomena, he shared Rickert's belief that social scientists are inherently constrained by the historical system of values through which they interpret and understand social reality.

Whereas nineteenth-century anti-positivist authors were still concerned with the quest for a scientific method, Hans-Georg Gadamer's *Truth and Method* (1975) argued for a hermeneutics that is dissociated from a nineteenth-century preoccupation with method. In contrast with Dilthey, Rickert, and Weber, who conceived of historical context, tradition, and prejudice as external factors limiting and biasing understanding and rationality, Gadamer saw those factors as the very elements that make understanding possible. For him, there is no point in searching for an interpretive "method" that would eradicate values and presuppositions; it is precisely because people are embedded in a specific tradition, with certain values and prejudices, that they are able to make sense of the world at all. Each specific historical context discloses a "horizon" of understanding, and the hermeneutical task of the social sciences is to achieve a "fusion of horizons" whereby the interpreters and interpreted enter a hermeneutical dialog.

The liberation of meaning from the yoke of logics resulted in a myriad of developments which brought into focus the relations between meaning, practices and language. In some cases, these developments have been re-elaborations of the basic tenets of the hermeneutical tradition. For example, Clifford Geertz's (1973) interpretive anthropology applied the notion of *Verstehen* to the ethnographic method. Geertz proposed to understand cultures as symbolic texts: they have to be interpreted through "thick descriptions" that unearth the deep meanings underlying the observable and behavioral elements of culture. In other cases, the attention to meaning, language, and practices has resulted in novel contributions to the hermeneutical tradition. One such contribution was Charles Taylor's (1985) definition of hermeneutics as self-description. According to Taylor, the traditional hermeneutical goal to account for social reality through interpretation has tended to obscure the fact that our interpretations not only depict reality but, in so doing, also serve to depict ourselves. If we pay attention to this element of self-description, Taylor argued, hermeneutics no longer appears as a method to understand and explain the world, but as one of the practices through which we define and make sense of ourselves.

The renewed interest in meaning that arose in late twentieth-century social sciences also led to a rediscovery of the phenomenological tradition, and in particular of Alfred Schutz's work. Quite distinct from the hermeneutic school and influenced by Edmond Husserl, Schutz (1962, 1964) focused on how people make sense of their surroundings by using "typifications" of the "common-sense world." Different from scientific rationality, which centers on doubt and questioning, common-sense rationality operates within a taken-for-granted world where people suspend disbelief. Some commentators see Schutz and Thomas Luckmann (1973) as precursors of constructionist research, emphasizing as they do the way that the categories, through which people interpret the social realm they inhabit also help to create that world (see also Weinberg 2008). Schutz's work, together with Ludwig Wittgenstein's, influenced Harold Garfinkel's ethnomethodological studies of the micro-mechanisms of trust and social order (Garfinkel 1984). The influence of both hermeneutics and ethnomethodology loomed large in Anthony Giddens's structuration theory, which explores the various ways in which people's sense-making practices contribute to the making of social order (Giddens 1984, 1993).

Wittgensteinian philosophy

Ludwig Wittgenstein's *Philosophical Investigations* (1968) implied that the production of meaning is irreducible to any rule-following logic or method. For Wittgenstein, meaning is contingently established through the use of language within what he called a "language-game," and to give an account of the meaning of an utterance we do not need to invoke logical rules but we need to describe how the utterance is used within a specific language-game. The agreement reached by using a language, by playing a specific language-game, is not merely an agreement in opinions but an agreement reached by sharing a specific form of life. In other words, the relationship between the word "red" and a specific event in the world, a specific color, is not established according to logical rules but according to the conventional agreement reached within a specific language-game, within a specific form of life. Wittgenstein's *Philosophical Investigations* constituted a major blow to the positivist endeavor insofar as it showed the logical insufficiency of the positivist attempt to employ logical rules to explain reality. The philosophical bankruptcy of positivism was rapidly employed to defend the irreducibility of the social sciences to the natural sciences. This was the main thesis of Peter Winch's

influential *Idea of Social Science* (1958). In this book, Winch employed Wittgenstein's arguments to rebut the prevailing idea that the social sciences were still in
their infancy, attempting to emulate and draw level with the more advanced natural
sciences.

Over the last couple of decades, Wittgenstein's philosophy has had a huge impact
on the social sciences. First, the Wittgensteinian notion of practice has become
increasingly important for social theorists. It has led to different theories: it has been
crucial for the development of Pierre Bourdieu's (1977, 1990) theory of practice
and Giddens's (1984) structuration theory. In recent years, the increasing centrality
of this notion has even led some authors to talk about the "practice turn" in the
social sciences, by which they mean a social science perspective in which practices
are conceived as "primary generic social things" (Schatzki 2001: 1). This practice
turn has been so prominent that some authors have felt it necessary to warn against
the excessive weight given to practices: for instance, Stephen Turner (1994) criticized the reification of the notion of "practice" and argued strongly against the view
that practices are discrete natural objects with causal powers.

Secondly, stronger emphasis on meaning and language has given rise to different
forms of relativism, some of which call into question the very status of the social
sciences. For instance, Jean-François Lyotard's theory of postmodernity (1984) drew
on Wittgensteinian concepts to promote an uncompromising relativist position, and
the constructivist school also referred to Wittgenstein to argue against the possibility
of establishing universal and objective knowledge claims. For constructivist authors,
our knowledge claims are embedded in the conventions, agreements, and negotiations established by a given community of language, and even "objectivity" and
"truth" are no longer to be seen as rational or logical categories but as socially
constituted (Bloor 1983; Gergen 1999). Lyotard's postmodernist outlook and
constructivism fit into a broader intellectual development which involves both dis-
quiet with traditional philosophy of the social sciences and a move towards
anti-foundationalism.

Critical theory

We have discussed a number of philosophical traditions that conceive of social
research primarily as an explanatory enterprise. Positivists and falsificationists might
have differed in their prescriptions about how to achieve this explanation, but they
had little doubt that, like the natural sciences, the social sciences are in the business
of explaining. Gradually, there has been growing discontent with this restrictive
view of the social sciences and, related to this, an emerging interest in other objectives that may motivate them. Indeed, central to the work of critical theorists is the
idea that social research can also tie in with other "cognitive interests," in particular
critique and emancipation. Proponents of "conventional" research might argue
that it helps to establish the falsehood and incompleteness of many widely held
views and that therefore it is already critical or emancipatory (in the broad sense
of the word). However, critical theorists would reply that they have a particular
notion of critique and emancipation in mind, which ties in very strongly with the
philosophical notions of human needs and interests. Therefore, questions about
philosophy of the social sciences tie in with questions about what makes us full

human beings. Independent of their contributions to the widely publicized *Positivismusstreit* (Adorno et al. 1976), members of the Frankfurt School, in particular Theodor Adorno and Max Horkheimer, criticized extensively the orthodoxy of positivist sociology because of its total disregard for other modes of knowledge, its extreme focus on facts and observations at the expense of theoretical reflection, its excessive emphasis on technical sophistication and quantification, its problematic notion of value-neutrality, and its implicit complicity with the status quo. As an antidote to the prevalence of a particular type of social research at the time, Adorno and Horkheimer's criticisms were poignant (for instance, Horkheimer 1972: 132–87, 188–243), but their own proposals were less clear and, surprisingly, Adorno's one serious venture into empirical research exhibited a strong empiricist, quantitative outlook which seemed very much at odds with his own philosophical position (Adorno et al. 1950).

In contrast with this first wave of critical theory, Jürgen Habermas (1987, 1991a, 1991b) made a significant attempt at a more constructive approach to the philosophy of the social sciences. Arguing that knowledge ought to be placed within the context of "the natural history of the human species," he drew on Peirce's pragmatist philosophy to demonstrate the intricate relationship between "logical-methodological rules" and "knowledge-constitutive interests," arriving at three modes of knowledge, each related to a particular means of social organization. Whereas the "empirical-analytical" sciences tie in with the realm of work and aim at nomological knowledge and predictive power, "historical-hermeneutic" sciences are strongly connected with the domain of language and aim at understanding. Combining the methodologies of both, "critically orientated" sciences are intertwined with the world of power and are ultimately directed towards people's emancipation. One of his favorite examples is psychoanalysis which, according to him, combines in-depth understanding and knowledge of causal mechanisms to help people lift psychological barriers and to enable them to lead a more fulfilling life. Subsequently Habermas felt that his scheme treated the individual too much as an isolated entity, and his theory of communicative action attempted to rectify this problem. With this "communicative turn" Habermas developed a "consensus theory" of truth: that is, truth comes down to an agreement obtained amongst equal participants in an open debate. Surprisingly, this unashamedly non-realist position did not deter a significant number of adherents of critical realism from portraying Habermas as a major ally. Despite Habermas's theory of communicative action receiving this breadth of support and managing to overcome the weaknesses which he identified in his earlier framework, its key concepts of "ideal speech situation" and *Verständigung* have been shown to be problematic. Not surprisingly, a closer look at the work of most practicing social scientists who associate themselves with critical theory and Habermas (Calhoun 1995) shows that they use the notion of critical theory in a loose sense and draw very little on Habermas's theory of universal pragmatics, leaving them open to criticisms that the outcome is not particularly different from the much-derided "conventional" research. In this context, Michael Burawoy (2004, 2005) made a useful distinction between "critical sociology" and "public sociology": both develop reflexive, critical knowledge, but whereas the former addresses an academic audience, the latter actively engages with society and speaks to a non-academic audience.

FURTHER MOVES AWAY FROM NATURALISM AND FOUNDATIONALISM

We have seen so far that, in the course of the twentieth century, hermeneutic and Wittgensteinian perspectives and critical theory challenged the hegemony of positivist epistemology. Recently two new philosophical and theoretical developments – notably anti-foundationalism and actor network theory – further questioned naturalist views and, crucially, managed to take philosophy of the social sciences in a very different direction.

In order to make sense of those new intellectual currents, it is worth recalling that traditional philosophers of social science relied on a number of presuppositions. They tended to see philosophy as a foundational project, securing the basis for reliable knowledge claims; and they presupposed that the notion of the social was unproblematic and could easily be defined in opposition to the natural. More recently, those two assumptions have been questioned, in ways that call for a radical reshaping of the intellectual landscape.

Philosophy and anti-foundationalism

Traditionally, philosophers of science embarked upon foundationalist enterprises, seeking to find a neutral algorithm that underscores successful scientific knowledge. The likes of Carnap or Popper might have disagreed as to the precise nature of this neutral algorithm, but they would not have questioned that it existed, nor would they have denied that it was worth pursuing. Earlier we mentioned Habermas's use of Peirce, which was indicative of the gradual ascendancy of American pragmatism in the second half of the twentieth century. This "pragmatist turn" in philosophy is important for our discussion because contemporary pragmatism threatens to undermine the very foundationalism that is inherent in traditional philosophy of science (see also Weinberg 2008). With the rise of analytical philosophy in the mid-twentieth century, the interest in pragmatism had somewhat waned, but this trend has been reversed in the last two or three decades. Pragmatism is a broad church, with significant differences within it, and there is even controversy as to whether Rorty and Bernstein's neo-pragmatism can legitimately be linked to earlier forms of pragmatism. Nevertheless, it is possible to identify key characteristics which most pragmatists share. There is a common opposition to what John Dewey aptly called "the spectator theory of knowledge," which conceives of scientific knowledge as representing the inner nature of the external world completely and accurately (Dewey 1930). It follows from this that pragmatists are keen to abandon metaphors of vision: knowledge should no longer be seen as mirroring or representing the world "as it really is." Instead, knowledge acquisition is seen as active, as one of the tools people have to cope with and adjust to the demands of life. Most importantly, pragmatists are also skeptical about foundationalist projects that purport to "step outside history" and supposedly ground aesthetic, ethical, or cognitive claims, arguing instead for the primacy of the "agent's point of view" and recognizing people's inability to escape the conceptual framework, language, or cultural setting in which they are situated. However, this does not imply that people's knowledge is merely subjective if by "subjective" is meant that it fails to mirror the inner nature of reality, because, as pointed out before, pragmatists abandon this spectator theory of knowledge (Rorty 1980, 1982). With this critique of foundationalism comes a rejection of any philosophical attempt to capture the scientific method which, it was previously assumed, all successful scientific enterprises have in common. Contrary to the dominance of epistemology in philosophy of science, neo-pragmatists argue for the importance of a hermeneutically inspired dialogical model, which promotes conversation amongst a plurality of voices, without assuming that there is a common ground prior to the conversation. In practice, this perspective promotes research aimed at "self-referential" knowledge acquisition, whereby the confrontation with difference is seen as an opportunity to reconsider our central presuppositions (Baert 2005; Bernstein 1991).

American neo-pragmatists like Rorty have often been linked to continental-European strands of postmodernism and poststructuralism. Rorty himself argued that Dewey had a lot in common with Jacques Derrida and Michel Foucault, eroding as they all did the premises of foundationalist philosophy and the quest for method. He later distanced himself from the excesses of French poststructuralism in the American academy with his vitriolic attacks on the "Cultural Left" (Rorty 1998). In general, philosophers of social science resisted the poststructuralist bandwagon of the 1980s and 1990s. This was partly because they tended to be trained and steeped in the analytical tradition and felt uncomfortable with the elusive writing style that characterized this generation of French intellectuals, but also because this new work threatened to undermine central premises of the philosophical orthodoxy of the day. Interestingly, of all poststructuralists, philosophers of social sciences were most receptive to the writings of Foucault, who made his name initially as a historian, not as a philosopher. The two Foucauldian insights which drew their attention – the notion of a genealogical history and the relationship between power and knowledge – happened to be Nietzsche's. Firstly, genealogical history aimed to demonstrate the historical variability of those entities that appear to be fixed and the role of contingencies and power struggles in how they come to be what they are. Foucault (1977) described this approach as a "history of the present," meaning that its ultimate aim is not to describe or explain the past but to use it as a medium to rearticulate and reconsider what now exists. Secondly, contrary to the view that knowledge is neutral to power relations or enables people to transcend them, Foucault (1980) argued that knowledge and power are very much intertwined: knowledge can be, and often is, used to dominate, curtail, or domesticate others. This was not just a theoretical argument: for instance, Foucault showed that the emerging social sciences in the nineteenth century were central to the implementation of a new, more sophisticated, system of social control. More generally, Foucault's view about knowledge led to growing skepticism towards claims about objectivity and paved the way for alternative perspectives such as standpoint theory (for instance, Harding 1991).

However, anti-foundational theories do not necessarily lead to skepticism towards knowledge. Pierre Bourdieu's "reflexive sociology" (Bourdieu and Wacquant 1992) provides an example of an attempt to wed anti-foundationalist postulates with a vigorous defense of objectivity. For Bourdieu, acknowledging that there is no ultimate foundation for our knowledge claims does not necessarily imply that we are condemned to relativism and subjectivism. Indeed, Bourdieu argued, it is possible to avoid arbitrariness and relativism by becoming aware of the social and historical conditions under which our knowledge is produced. By reflecting on these conditions, Bourdieu contended, we not only gain an objective knowledge about them, but also the possibility to master and neutralize their effects (Bourdieu and Wacquant 1992: 44). Hence, even if we cannot escape our sociohistorical conditions to attain a pure objective knowledge of reality, we can nonetheless gain a greater degree of objectivity by becoming aware of how these conditions influence the way in which we perceive and know the world.

Empirical studies of science and anti-foundationalism

The discontent with naturalist and foundationalist projects was not just expressed by neo-pragmatists like Rorty and Bernstein and poststructuralists like Derrida, but also by the increasing popularity of Kuhn's work and the growing field of sociology of science and science studies. For sociologists, Kuhn's writings demonstrated that scientists' refusal or keenness to substitute new paradigms for old ones did not rely exclusively on rational factors such as the simplicity or predictive power of the paradigm, but also to quite a considerable extent on "non-rational" factors, in particular sociological dynamics intrinsic to the communities in which scientists work. Whether this is precisely what Kuhn wanted to say is a different matter. Paul Feyerabend's *Against Method* was certainly more clear-cut in propagating the view that renowned scientists, like Galileo, did not merely rely on rational arguments to support their claims, and that they regularly employed devices such as rhetoric and persuasion which we normally do not associate with science (Feyerabend 1975). Whatever the author's intention, it was Kuhn's work (rather than Feyerabend's) that spurred a whole generation of social scientists to investigate the "extra-rational" factors that influenced the production of scientific knowledge. Initially centered round the work of David Bloor and Barry Barnes at the "Science Studies Unit" of the University of Edinburgh, the "Strong Program" was the first to approach the sociology of scientific knowledge (also known as SSK) using the "principle of symmetry" (Barnes 1974,1977; Bloor 1976, 1983). According to Bloor (1976), previous sociological attempts to study knowledge abided by the "principle of asymmetry," according to which true statements are explained by reference to reality and false statements by reference to the distorting influence of social forces. In contrast, the principle of symmetry implies that both falsehood and truth have social origins, meaning that they are both collectively produced and held. No longer designating a correspondence between scientific statements and reality, truth comes down to an agreement within a community. Hence the flurry of studies into the various practices through which scientific knowledge is produced, including crucially Bruno Latour and Steven Woolgar's *Laboratory Life*, which occupied an iconic status amongst SSK-practitioners as it was the first ethnographic study into the most sacred chamber of science: the laboratory (Latour and Woolgar 1979) These studies demonstrated not only that the production of scientific knowledge is influenced by a myriad of sociological factors, ranging from the interests of competing groups to broader political and philosophical debates and gender, but also that experimental results are often ambiguous and open to various interpretations and negotiations.

The emergence of SSK implied a critique of the traditional image of natural sciences as objective and neutral enterprises detached from sociohistorical contingencies, and crucially it implied a subversion of the relationship between the social and natural sciences: if the social sciences were hitherto supposed to model themselves on the natural sciences, with the advent of SSK the former could be explained by and thus subsumed to the latter. The more radical proponents of SSK even went as far as arguing that key concepts used by scientists to report their findings or defend their views (like "objectivity," "facts," or "quarks") were mere social constructions, and this radicalization of SSK eventually provoked the "science wars" of the 1990s, in which natural scientists, spurred on by the "Sokal Affair," made a concerted effort to defend publicly their rationality and integrity against the perceived assault of the social sciences (Gross and Levitt 1994; Sokal and Bricmont 1998). For better or worse, the science wars left the feeling that some claims of SSK were unfounded or exaggerated, notably those about the social construction of scientific findings, and this growing unease with SSK partly contributed to the emergence of Science and Technology Studies (STS). STS was no longer concerned with unmasking the social basis of scientific knowledge, but with describing how this knowledge is produced through different material apparatuses (Galison, 1997, 2003; Galison and Thompson 1999), practices (Knorr-Cetina 1999; Pickering 1993, 1995, 2002), political institutions (Jasanoff 1995, 2004, 2005), or (in the terminology of actor network theory) different "networks" of human and nonhuman agents (Latour 1987, 1988, 1999). However, like SSK, STS continued to show that the natural sciences do not evolve according to a fixed set of methodological criteria (see CHAPTER 23). Whether under the heading of SSK or STS, numerous empirical investigations have shown that there is a variety of methods, practices and materials in the sciences, depending not only on the field of inquiry, but also on the historical and social context in which the scientists work. There is no point is searching for a neutral algorithm of scientific success; it does not exist.

Over the last couple of decades, the feminist critique of science emerged as a continuation and extension of the critique of scientific universality and objectivity initially carried out by the sociology of scientific knowledge. Feminist critics argued that the purported neutrality and universality of scientific laws not only veiled the importance of sociohistorical factors but also the fact that science has been produced by men (Harding 1991; Keller 1985; Longino 1989). In this sense, although SSK has been crucial to unveil the social factors underpinning scientific practice, feminist authors argued that it had tended to overlook the fact that the selection and definition of problems has "clearly been skewed toward men's perception of what they find puzzling" (Harding 1986: 22). According to feminist authors, the traditional exclusion of women from science has been far from coincidental. Whilst masculinity has been traditionally identified with the values of objectivity and knowledge, women have been traditionally associated with emotionality and irrationality. In this sense, the feminist critique of science aimed not only to achieve the inclusion of women in scientific practice but also to reclaim "those domains of human experience that have relegated to women: namely, the personal, the emotional, and the sexual." (Keller 1985: 9) The feminist critique of science proposed a new object of study, women and their experiences, and also attempted to elaborate a new feminist epistemology built upon women's standpoints. These theories, known as "standpoint theories," followed the old Hegelian master–slave dialectic to argue that the subjugated position of women provided a potential grounding for more complete and less distorted knowledge (Haraway 1991; Harding 1987: 184–5, 1993).

During the 1990s, the critique of scientific universality and objectivity developed by SSK and "standpoint theories" rapidly expanded beyond the limits of science studies. Postmodern authors saw in these critiques the ultimate proof that science could no longer play its modern role as the guarantor of truth and objectivity (Seidman 1994). Furthermore, in revealing the ideological assumptions, and political agendas, operating in scientific research, these critiques showed that scientific knowledge can be politically contested. This possibility has been instrumental to the development of different critical social movements over the last decade. One such case is queer theory which, building on the feminist critiques of science, has contested scientific discourses on sexual and gender identities by showing that homosexual or heterosexual identities are not fixed biological identities, but "effects" resulting from different social practices and power relations (Butler 1993; Harding 1998; Sedgwick 1990).

Actor network theory

Over the last two decades the traditional notion of philosophy of the social sciences has had to face yet another challenge: it concerns the very notion of the social itself. In traditional philosophy of the social sciences, the notion of the social is taken for granted, referring as it does to the relations between individuals. We tend to forget that this notion of the social is intimately connected with a particular division of labor which became established at the end of the nineteenth century: whereas the natural sciences were assigned the study of "nature" (that is, the world of objects and their relations), the social sciences were supposed to study the "social" (that is, the domain of humans and their relations). However, recent intellectual developments have called into question the very idea of the social as a distinct domain of inquiry, separate from the natural realm. Not surprisingly, the first criticisms came from STS researchers because, given their field of inquiry, traditional "social" explanations (which referred to people's intentions or interests but excluded references to "natural" elements such as cells, viruses, or objects) lacked explanatory power and drew on an artificial distinction between the "social" and the "natural" which was difficult to maintain (Callon 1986a, 1986b; Latour 1983). Various attempts have been made to develop theoretical frameworks that overcome the dualism between the "social" and the "natural," the most systematic one being "actor network theory" (ANT) (see CHAPTER 7). This theory first emerged in the 1980s within the sociology of science as a reaction to the excesses of the Strong Program and its attempt to explain scientific knowledge by reference to social variables. Instead, ANT suggested that we treat the production of scientific knowledge as a complex network of associations between different "human" elements (for instance, the career interests of the individual scientists) and "nonhuman" elements (for instance, computers and machinery).

Subsequently, advocates of ANT argued that these networks of "humans" and "nonhumans" are not restricted to the domain of science, and indeed they have extended their analyses to diverse non-scientific objects, ranging from addictions

(Gomart and Hennion 1999) and the market (Callon 1997) to underground systems (Latour 1996) and even whole empires (Law 1986). Following a similar line of thought, the sociologist of science Andrew Pickering has argued that, in order to deal with the technological nature of society today, social sciences need to forsake their traditional definition of the social as the domain of human interaction. He argued in favor of a "posthumanist social theory" in which the human subject no longer plays a central role and in which the social is conceived in terms of a dialectical relation between human and material agencies. A more radical version of this posthumanist theory can be found in the work of the feminist and science studies scholar Donna Haraway (1991), who argued that the notion of human beings as sociocultural beings is a myth invented by the social sciences. Against this view that the social can be defined in opposition to nature, Haraway insisted that human beings are by necessity "cyborgs" insofar as they are always a mixture of nature, culture, science, and technology. Although initially limited to science studies, this radical critique of the notion of the social has permeated other fields of inquiry, including psychology and anthropology. For example in psychology, proponents of the "distributed cognition paradigm" claim that cognition should be understood as an embedded process that takes place at the intersection between the mind and different material elements in the world (e.g. Clark 2003). Likewise, the notion of embeddedness has been employed in anthropology to criticize the traditional understanding of culture as a detached web of meaning that hovers over the material world (Ingold 2000). Increasingly, anthropologists talk about "material cultures," referring to sets of relations involving human and nonhuman agencies (Gell 1999; Miller 1997; Strathern 1991, 1999). In sum, despite the disparity of these contemporary developments, they have all contributed to the questioning of the definition of the social as the world of "human interaction, human institutions, human rationality, human life." These new currents have forced us to rethink earlier approaches to the philosophy of the social sciences, relying as they did on a firm distinction between the social and the natural.

SOME CONCLUDING REMARKS

Philosophy of the social sciences has come a long way. Initially tied to the emergence and institutionalization of the social sciences and preoccupied with establishing their scientific foundations, the discipline has acquired a remarkable level of reflexivity and managed to question its core assumptions. However, this short survey of philosophy of the social sciences also indicates that, over the last couple of decades, most innovative contributions have come from practicing social scientists like Latour or Strathern rather than professional philosophers of the social sciences. The reasons for this paradoxical development are twofold. Whereas the social sciences are increasingly drawing on social theory and philosophy and engaging with metatheoretical and methodological questions, professional philosophers of the social sciences sometimes lose touch with the actual practice of social science, thereby missing the opportunity to contribute innovatively to the disciplines which they are supposed to cover.

It could be argued that philosophy of the social sciences has become a victim of its own success – establishing itself as a separate discipline at a time of increasing disciplinary subdivision which disqualifies specialists in one area of study from commenting authoritatively on other areas. Take, for example, the recent debate around "public sociology" in American sociology. Public sociology is intended to move beyond the safe contours of the ivory tower, developing a dialog between sociology and its audiences whereby the issues of each partner are brought to the attention to the other, and each adjusts or responds accordingly (Burawoy 2004). One reason for academic social scientists' reluctance to involve, address, or write for the wider public is the fear of their "accessible" work being viewed by peers as dumbed-down and non-academic, a prejudice reinforced by research assessment exercises that discount articles appearing in non-reviewed "practitioner" or popular journals. This caution is reinforced by the observation that various natural scientists (such as James Lovelock, Rupert Sheldrake, Stephen Wolfram, Nigel Calder, and Fritjof Capra) have successfully propagated their radical critiques of mainstream method – and secured the economic means to pursue them outside mainstream academic institutions – by harnessing a large public audience for their popular writing, but have in the process become marginalized from academic debate within their original disciplines.

Whereas the arguments by practicing sociologists in favor of or against a public sociology have a direct bearing on the philosophy of the social sciences, the response by the philosophical community has been relatively muted. With a few exceptions (for instance, Turner 2008), philosophers seem to have missed the opportunity to tackle this issue that is so central to the discipline of philosophy of the social sciences. In short, one of the challenges which philosophers of the social sciences now face is to keep abreast of the rapidly changing developments in the different social sciences and to incorporate those developments in their work. Without this active and ongoing engagement, philosophers of the social sciences are at risk of dealing with issues that are no longer relevant to social research. Interestingly, the philosophers of the social sciences who have been most successful at interacting with and commenting on actual research tend to be the ones who focus their intellectual efforts on one specific discipline. One example is Alison Wylie (2002), whose research contributes to feminist philosophy of social sciences by keeping a close scrutiny of the trials and tribulations of the discipline of archeology. Keeping a peer-respected grounding in one particular social discipline may be the only way in which those wishing to address the general philosophy of social sciences can engage successfully with the disciplines they are supposed to cover.

Bibliography

Adorno, T., et al. (1950) *The Authoritarian Personality*. New York: Harper & Row.

Adorno, T., et al. (1976) *The Positivist Dispute in German Sociology*. London: Heinemann.

Baert, P. (2005) *Philosophy of the Social Sciences: Towards Pragmatism*. Cambridge: Polity.

Barnes, B. (1974) *Scientific Knowledge and Sociological Theory*. London: Routledge & Kegan Paul.

Barnes, B. (1977) *Interests and the Growth of Knowledge*. London: Routledge & Kegan Paul.

Becker, G. (1976) *The Economic Approach to Human Behavior*. Chicago: University of Chicago Press.

Bernstein, R. J. (1991) *The New Constellation: The Ethical-Political Horizons of Modernity/Postmodernity*. Cambridge: Polity.

Bhaskar, R. (1997) *A Realist Theory of Science*. London: Verso.

Bhaskar, R. (1998) *The Possibility of Naturalism; A Philosophical Critique of the Contemporary Human Sciences*. London: Routledge.

Bloor, D. (1976) *Knowledge and Social Imagery*. London: Routledge & Kegan Paul.

Bloor, D. (1983) *Wittgenstein: A Social Theory of Knowledge*. London: Macmillan.

Bourdieu, Pierre (1977) *Outline of a Theory of Practice*. Cambridge: Cambridge University Press.

Bourdieu, P. (1990) *The Logic of Practice*. Cambridge: Polity.

Bourdieu, P., and Wacquant, L. (1992) *Invitation to Reflexive Sociology*. Cambridge: Polity.

Burawoy, M. (2004) "Public Sociologies: A Symposium from Boston College." *Social Problems* 51(1): 103–30.

Burawoy, M. (2005) "For Public Sociology." *American Sociological Review* 70: 4–28.

Butler, J. (1993) *Bodies that Matter: On the Discursive Limits of "Sex"*. London: Routledge.

Calhoun, C. (1995) *Critical Social Theory: Culture, History, and the Challenge of Difference*. Oxford: Blackwell.

Callon, M. (1986a) "The Sociology of an Actor-Network: The Case of the Electric Vehicle," in M. Callon, J. Law and A. Rip (eds.), *Mapping the Dynamics of Science and Technology: Sociology of Science in the Real World*. Basingstoke: Macmillan.

Callon, M. (1986b) "Some Elements of a Sociology of Translation: Domestication of the Scallops and the Fishermen of St Brieuc Bay," in *Power, Action and Belief: A New Sociology of Knowledge?* London: Routledge & Kegan Paul.

Callon, M. (1987) *The Laws of the Market*. Oxford: Blackwell.

Clark, A. (2003) *Natural-Born Cyborgs: Why Minds and Technologies are Made to Merge*. Oxford: Oxford University Press.

Dewey, J. (1930) *The Quest for Certainty: A Study of the Relationship between Knowledge and Action*. London: Allen & Unwin.

Dilthey, W. (1988) *Introduction to the Human Sciences: An Attempt to Lay a Foundation for the Study of Society and History*. Detroit: Wayne State University Press.

Dilthey, W. (1996) *Hermeneutics and the Study of History*. Princeton: Princeton University Press.

Durkheim, É. (1982) *The Rules of Sociological Method and Selected Texts on Sociology and its Method*. London: Macmillan.

Elster, J. (1986) *Making Sense of Marx*. Cambridge: Cambridge University Press.

Elster, J. (1989) *Nuts and Bolts for the Social Sciences*. Cambridge: Cambridge University Press.

Feyerabend, P. (1975) *Against Method: Outline of an Anarchist Theory of Knowledge*. London: Verso.

Foucault, M. (1977) "Nietzsche, Genealogy, History," in *Language, Counter-Memory, Practice*. Ithaca, NY: Cornell University Press.

Foucault, M. (1980) *Power/Knowledge: Selected Interviews and Other Writings 1972–1977*, (ed.) C. Gordon. New York: Pantheon Books.

Gadamer, H.-G. (1975) *Truth and Method*. London: Sheed & Ward.

Galison, P. (1997) *Image and Logic: A Material Culture of Microphysics*. Chicago: University of Chicago Press.

Galison, P. (2003) *Einstein's Clocks and Poincaré's Maps: Empires of Time*. New York: W. W. Norton.

Galison, P., and Thompson, E. (1999) *The Architecture of Science*. Cambridge, MA: MIT Press.

Garfinkel, H. (1984) *Studies in Ethnomethodology*. Cambridge: Polity.

Geertz, C. (1973) *The Interpretation of Cultures: Selected Essays*. New York: Basic Books.

Gell, A. (1999) *The Art of Anthropology: Essay and Diagrams*. London: Athlone Press.

Gergen, K. (1999) *An Invitation to Social Construction*. London: Sage.

Giddens, A. (1984) *The Constitution of Society: Outline of the Theory of Structuration*. Cambridge: Polity.

Giddens, A. (1993) *New Rules of Sociological Method*. Cambridge: Polity.

Gomart, E., and Hennion, A. (1999) "A Sociology of Attachment: Music Amateurs, Drug Users," in J. Law and J. Hassard (eds.), *Actor Network Theory and After*. Oxford: Blackwell.

Gross, and Levitt, N. (1994) *Higher Superstition: The Academic Left and its Quarrels with Science*. Baltimore: Johns Hopkins University Press.

Habermas, J. (1987) *Knowledge and Human Interests*. Cambridge: Polity.

Habermas, J. (1991a) *The Theory of Communicative Action*, vol. 1, *Reason and Rationalization of Society*. Cambridge: Polity.

Habermas, J. (1991b) *The Theory of Communicative Action*, vol. 2, *Lifeworld and System: A Critique of Functionalist Reason*. Cambridge: Polity.

Haraway, D. (1991) *Simians, Cyborgs and Women: The Reinvention of Nature*, London: Free Association.

Harding, S. (1986) *The Science Question in Feminism*. Ithaca, NY: Cornell University Press.

Harding, S. (1987) *Feminism and Methodology: Social Science Issues*. Bloomington: Indiana University Press.

Harding, S. (1991) *Whose Science, whose Knowledge? Thinking from Women's Lives*. Ithaca, NY: Cornell University Press.

Harding, S. (1998) *Sex Acts: Practices of Femininity and Masculinity*. London: Sage.

Hempel, C. G. (1965) *Aspects of Scientific Explanation, and Other Essays in the Philosophy of Science*. New York: Free Press.

Hollis, M. (2002) *The Philosophy of Social Science: An Introduction*. Cambridge: Cambridge University Press.

Horkheimer, M. (1972) *Critical Theory; Selected Essays*. New York: Seabury Press.

Ingold, T. (2000) *The Perception of the Environment: Essays on Livelihood, Dwelling and Skill*. London: Routledge.

Jasanoff, S. (1995) *Science at the Bar: Law, Science, and Technology in America*. Cambridge, MA: Harvard University Press.

Jasanoff, S. (ed.) (2004) *States of Knowledge: The Co-Production of Science and the Social Order*. London: Routledge.

Jasanoff, S. (2005) *Designs on Nature: Science and Democracy in Europe and the United States*. Princeton: Princeton University Press.

Keller, E. F. (1985) *Reflections on Gender and Science*. New Haven: Yale University Press.

Knorr-Cetina, K. (1999) *Epistemic Cultures: How the Sciences Make Knowledge*. Cambridge, MA: Harvard University Press.

Kuhn, T. (1970) *The Structure of Scientific Revolutions*, Chicago: University of Chicago Press.

Lakatos, I. (1970) "Falsification and the Methodology of Scientific Research Programmes," in I. Lakatos and A. Musgrave (eds.), *Criticism and the Growth of Knowledge*. Cambridge: Cambridge University Press.

Latour, B. (1983) "Give me a Laboratory and I will Raise the World," in K. Knorr-Cetina (ed.), *Science Observed: Perspectives on the Social Study of Science*. London: Sage.

Latour, B. (1987) *Science in Action: How to Follow Scientists and Engineers through Society*. Milton Keynes: Open University Press.

Latour, B. (1988) *The Pasteurization of France*. Cambridge, MA: Harvard University Press.

Latour, B. (1996) *Pandora's Hope: Essays on the Reality of Science Studies*. Cambridge, MA: Harvard University Press.

Latour, B., and Woolgar, S. (1979) *Laboratory Life: The Social Construction of Scientific Facts*. London: Sage.

Law, J. (1986) "On the Methods of Long-Distance Control: Vessels, Navigation, and the Portuguese Route to India," in J. Law (ed.), *Power, Action and Belief: A New Sociology of Knowledge?* London: Routledge & Kegan Paul.

Lepenies, W. (1988) *Between Literature and Science: The Rise of Sociology*. Cambridge: Cambridge University Press.

Lévi-Strauss, C. (1972) *Structural Anthropology*. Harmondsworth: Penguin.

Longino, H. (1989) "Can There Be a Feminist Science?," in A. Garry and M. Pearsall (eds.), *Women, Knowledge, and Reality: Explorations in Feminist Philosophy*. London: Unwin Hyman.

Lyotard, J.-F. (1984) *The Postmodern Condition: A Report on Knowledge*. Minneapolis: University of Minnesota Press.

Miller, D. (1997) *Material Cultures: Why Some Things Matter*. London: UCL Press.

Neurath, O. (1944) *Foundations of the Social Sciences*. Cambridge: Cambridge University Press.

Neurath, O. (1973) *Empiricism and Sociology*. Dordrecht: Reidel.

Neurath, O. (1983) *Philosophical Papers 1913–1946*. Dordrecht: Reidel.

Pickering, A. (1993) "The Mangle of Practice: Agency and Emergence in the Sociology of Science." *The American Journal of Sociology* 99: 559–89.

Pickering, A. (1995) *The Mangle of Practice: Time, Agency and Science*. Chicago: University of Chicago Press.

Pickering, A. (2002) "Cybernetics and the Mangle: Ashby, Beer and Pask." *Social Studies of Science* 14: 399–441.

Popper, K. (1959) *The Logic of Scientific Discovery*. London: Hutchinson.

Popper, K. (1971) *The Open Society and its Enemies*, vol. 2, *The High Tide of Prophecy: Hegel, Marx, and the Aftermath*. Princeton: Princeton University Press.

Popper, K. (1983) "The Rationality Principle," in D. Miller (ed.), *A Pocket Popper*. London: Fontana.

Popper, K. (1991a) *Conjectures and Refutations*. London: Routledge.

Popper, K. (1991b) *The Poverty of Historicism*. London: Routledge.

Rickert, H. (1986) *The Limits of Concept Formation in the Natural Sciences: A Logical Introduction to the Historical Sciences*. Cambridge: Cambridge University Press.

Rorty, R. (1980) *Philosophy and the Mirror of Nature*. Oxford: Blackwell.

Rorty, R. (1982) *Consequences of Pragmatism.* New York: University of Minnesota Press.

Rorty, R. (1998) *Achieving our Country.* Cambridge MA: Harvard University Press.

Schatzki, T. (2001) "Introduction: Practice Theory," in K. Knorr-Cetina and E. V. Savigny (eds.), *The Practice Turn in Contemporary Theory.* New York: Routledge.

Schutz, A. (1962) *Collected Papers I: The Problem of Social Reality.* The Hague: Martinus Nijhoff.

Schutz, A. (1964) *Collected Papers II: Studies in Social Theory.* The Hague: Martinus Nijhoff.

Schutz, A., and Luckmann, T. (1973) *The Structures of the Life-World.* London: Heinemann.

Sedgwick, E. K. (1990) *Epistemology of the Closet.* Berkeley: University of California Press.

Seidman, S. (1994) *Contested Knowledge: Social Theory in the Postmodern Era.* Oxford: Blackwell.

Sokal, A., and Bricmont, J. (1998) *Intellectual Imposters: Postmodern Philosophers' Abuse of Science.* London: Profile Books.

Strathern, M. (1991) *Partial Connections.* London: Rowman & Littlefield.

Strathern, M. (1999) *Property, Substance and Effect: Anthropological Essays on Persons and Things.* London: Athlone.

Taylor, C. (1985) *Philosophy and the Human Sciences.* Cambridge: Cambridge University Press.

Turner, S. (1994) *The Social Theory of Practices: Tradition, Tacit Knowledge, and Presuppositions.* Chicago: Chicago University Press.

Turner, S. (2008) "Public Sociology and Democratic Theory." *Sociology* 41(5): 785–98.

Weber, M. (1948) *From Max Weber: Essays in Sociology.* London: Routledge.

Weber, M. (1949) *The Methodology of the Social Sciences.* New York: Macmillan.

Weber, M. (1964) *The Theory of Social and Economic Organization.* New York: Free Press.

Weber, M. (1975) *Roscher and Knies: The Logical Problems of Historical Economics.* New York: Free Press.

Weinberg, D. (2008) "The Philosophical Foundations of Constructionist Research," in J. K. Holstein and J. Gubrium (eds.), *The Handbook of Constructionist Research.* New York: Guilford Press.

Winch, P. (1958) *The Idea of a Social Science and its Relation to Philosophy.* London: Routledge & Kegan Paul.

Wittgenstein, L. (1968) *Philosophical Investigations.* Oxford: Blackwell.

Wylie, A. (2002) *Thinking from Things: Essays in the Philosophy of Archaeology.* Berkeley: University of California Press.

Part II
Actions, Actors, and Systems

4

Theories of Social Action

ROB STONES

It is impossible to go very far in any direction within the world of social theory without having to confront serious questions thrown up by one or other dimension of social action. Weber explicitly singled out social action as the "central subject matter" of his sociology (Weber 1968: 24), and whilst Marx is often crudely characterized as the master of structure and determinism, any serious engagement with his work will soon come across long passages and telling statements which convey sustained and complex reflections on the role of social action both in itself and in its relationship to social structures. Two of the telling statements I refer to will provide core themes for this chapter: the first is his famous saying that "it is not the consciousness of men that determines their being, but, on the contrary, their social being determines their consciousness" (Marx 1962: 363; see Avineri 1968: 75–6); the second is the eleventh thesis on Feuerbach: "The philosophers have only interpreted the world, in various ways; the point is to change it" (Marx, quoted in McLellan 1977: 158). By thematizing these statements I want to allow a closer scrutiny of their substance and implications, but also to provide a frame within which to acknowledge both the various refinements and advances in conceptualization and approach accrued by subsequent theoretical developments and the continuing influence of classical thinkers.

The first of Marx's statements, on social being and consciousness, is a causal claim about the weight of influence which social context has on the ideas, values, and sentiments of individuals. It not only denies the image of uniquely foundational individuals who are the origin and the source of all that they think and feel about the world in which they act, it also pushes the emphasis very much the other way. It suggests that it is usually the social conditions in which an individual grows up, works, and lives which are the major source of what and how individuals think and feel. By a simple extension, the implication is that it isn't primarily individuals who author what they quaintly refer to as their own actions, but, rather, the primary authors of these actions are a variety of more or less powerful social influences which constitute individuals' "being," and hence their consciousness and the actions it contributes to. Marx's statement here has more than a passing family resemblance to the message sent out by Philip Zimbardo's Stanford prison experiment (Haney et al. 1973) in which volunteer students recruited to spend two weeks as guards of prisoners who were, likewise, volunteers, were very soon exhibiting fiercely aggressive and vindictive behavior towards their charges. This was a stunning commentary on the almost immediate power of socially sanctioned positions, even within role-play, to infiltrate and overwhelm the pre-existing ideas, values, and sentiments of individuals. Zimbardo has recently revisited this terrain in his book *The Lucifer Effect: How Good People Turn Evil* (2007), which focuses on the parallel issues that emerged in the behavior of sections of the US Army Reserve Military Police in carrying out atrocities on civilian prisoners at Abu Ghraib prison in Iraq. Whilst Zimbardo's work is primarily about the effects of immediate social circumstances, roles, and related peer pressure on the individual's consciousness and actions, other work in the history of social theory has focused more on the long-term effects of social being on the consciousness of people. This is the meaning of Simone de Beauvoir's famous statement in *The Second Sex*, written in the late 1940s, that "one is not born, but rather becomes, a woman," and it is the desire to fully convey the massive force of a lifetime's social being on the consciousness of women which lies behind her additional comments that "it is civilization as a whole that produces this creature, intermediate between male and eunuch, which is described as feminine" (de Beauvoir 1964: 249, cited in Evans 1998: 126).

The second statement is an injunction, a call to action. Marx is reversing the emphasis here, suggesting now that social being doesn't entirely determine action; that the actions of actors are, after all, in some sense their own, however limited a sense this may be. Within this gesture towards actors and action, however, he emphasizes the importance of praxis – purposive actions in the world – over reflection and thought, however complex, in truly making a difference. Just as social being heavily influences consciousness, which in turn shapes actions in the world, so, we need to understand, those actions have the ability to shape and reshape the conditions of social being. It was always important to Marx, however, that plans and intentions to change the world should not be "voluntaristic." That is, they shouldn't be based more on wishful thinking than on a realistic appraisal of the material, social, and political distribution of possibilities at a given point in time. Equally, however, real possibilities for change should not be defeated at the first hurdle by a misguided sense of reification or fatalism. Critical here in avoiding both voluntarism and misguided fatalism is the intellectual capacity to accurately appraise the strategic terrain, the real constraints it presents, and the extent of one's power to influence decisive aspects of it.

These two issues concerning social action – the relation between social conditions, consciousness, and action and the ability of purposive actions to make a difference in the world – belong to a core of concerns that have been ever present, in one form or another, throughout the history of social theory. Social theory has gradually refined, developed, and deepened its conceptualization of enduring concerns, whilst also broadening its field of vision. In exploring this history I will emphasize the various ways in which theorists have refined the conceptualization of the individual actor, internally differentiating constituent aspects of the actor; the very closely attendant differentiation of ways in which the actor is linked to the external terrain they inhabit and act within; and advances in the way that external terrain of action is itself conceptualized. A development which is closely related to these refinements, one which has gathered pace over the last 20 years or so, has been a greater differentiation within social theory itself, whereby there is now a plurality of specializations in which a greater proportion of books and journals are now devoted to specific aspects of social ontology, or social being. These specialisms include the body, time, space, speed, emotions, phenomenology and consciousness, values, culture, identities, significations and discourses, power, strategies, and so on. Each of these themes, abstracted from the combination of elements found in the "real concrete," has the potential to be fruitfully reintegrated into a synthetic conception of theories of social action – which would be rejuvenated and revitalized accordingly – and I will try to reflect some of this in what follows.

Starting with the first emphasis, Weber's contributions to thought about social action help to refine our understanding of the nature and capacities of the individual social actor through a typology of different ways in which she can act within the external terrain. Thus, Weber distinguished between four different types of social action which an actor may engage in: *instrumentally rational action* geared towards "the attainment of the actor's own rationally pursued and calculated ends"; *value-rational action* which is pursued for reasons of personally held values irrespective of the prospects for success of that action; *affective action*, determined by the actor's emotional states and orientations; and *traditional action*, "determined by ingrained habituation" (Weber 1968: 24–5). Concrete, in situ, forms of action would tend to combine these types. These types of orientation to action are consistent with Weber's idea of social action as behavior that is oriented to the behavior of others and to which the actor attaches subjective meanings (Weber 1968: 22–4; Swedberg 2005: 246). The types tell us something about the nature of the actor herself as they indicate the possibility of different internal moods and states, and their concrete enactments tell us that actors have the ability to combine these in complex internal formations which manifest themselves in a hybrid orientation to action. The emphasis on meaning and understanding (*Verstehen*) invokes and presages the importance of hermeneutics and phenomenology within social action theory. Ira J. Cohen rightly insists on the importance of placing these insights within the context of Weber's definition of a social relationship (Weber 1968: 26–8), in which "several actors mutually orient the meaning of their actions so that each, to some extent, takes account of the behaviour of the others . . . [who] may or may not reciprocally agree on their interpretations of one another's behaviour" (Cohen 1996: 144).

Weber's insights begin the process of adding more complexity, and the promise of more precision, to the framework of understanding we can bring to the core concerns signaled by Marx's iconic statements. They do this, not least, through the precision of the emphasis placed on social conditions, in the shape of others, impinging on the consciousness, moods, states of mind, and orientations of the actor in focus. These, in turn, constrain and influence her perception as to how she can act within and upon the world, to sustain or to change it. Simmel's concept of *Wechselwirkung*, interaction, through its commitment to studying sociation, the relations *between* actors, deepens further not only how we think about the links between actors and the external terrain, but also how we think about the external terrain itself. Thus, actors will face external circumstances populated by groups and social units with varying degrees of cohesiveness. This level of integration will, in turn, be continually influenced by the dynamic processes of sociation its members are engaged in, whether this is through the bonding and solidarity engendered through the relational forms of mutual struggle against an enemy or competitor, the loyalty provoked by mutual secrets, the relations of deference and superordination reproduced in institutional hierarchies, or the camaraderie and intimacy that results from meals shared or liaisons honored. In socially differentiated modern societies actors will face situations populated by a range of these variously affiliated actors, each themselves involved in a plurality of ongoing, overlapping, and intersecting sets of relations (Simmel 1950; Watier 2008).

As already intimated with respect to Marx and social being, action and agency are typically related to "structure" in the sociological literature. Conventional understandings of structure are deeply problematized by the relational and processual understanding of social action advocated by Weber and elaborated upon more extensively and subtly by Simmel. Conventional understandings tend to present structures, or the social conditions in which actors act, as hard, fixed, and stable, unyielding in themselves to the will of actors. Actors, on this model, work within the spaces left to them by the social structures. Relational, interactional, and processual views of social conditions, however, compel us to review the meaning and the role we give to structures in social explanation. One possibility is to combine both emphases so that the interactional and the processual are nominally acknowledged but are effectively subsumed by the fixed and unyielding. Thus, in an influential account of "Theories of Social Action" towards the end of the 1970s, Alan Dawe argued that to account for the reproduction of relatively stable social circumstances major theorists such as Talcott Parsons ultimately allowed their concern with action and agency to be drowned out by more structural concerns with the power of social norms, sanctions, and regulations. In some ways this was ironic as one of Parsons's most fruitful contributions was his attempt to build on the sociological insights of Weber, Émile Durkheim, and Vilfredo Pareto, and on the work of the economist Alfred Marshall, to construct a "voluntaristic theory of action." This rested on an elaboration of what he called "the unit act," a refined notion of the constituents which were said to be involved together, in combination, in all instances of meaningful human behavior. It included: the actor; the future-oriented *ends* or goals geared, in Weber's terms, towards "the attainment of the actor's own rationally pursued and calculated ends"; the *means* which would be required to pursue those ends, which included the parts of both the external terrain and of his or her own body over which the actor has control; those *conditions* within the external environment and his or her own body "over which the actor has no control, that is which he cannot alter, or prevent from being altered" (Parsons 1968: 43–51, and *passim*; Parsons 1949 cited in Hamilton 1985: 74); and, finally, central to Parsons's concerns, there would be a "normative orientation" of action through which the actor brings all these dimensions together in a determinate manner which informs both the ends and the means chosen.

It was Parsons's interest in the role played by values and norms within the unit act which set him on the path towards what many saw as an overly fixed and stable view of structural conditions. He became increasingly interested in how values (actors' ideals) and norms (rules of conduct in social interaction) become institutionalized so that the goals of actors and the means they choose to pursue those goals are regulated by the same normative standards of conduct. It was a small step from this sustained focus on the place of socialized values and regulative normative standards, both within the agent and within the external terrain, to a creeping sense of them as *conditions* "over which the actor has no control, that is which he cannot alter, or prevent from being altered" (Parsons 1949 cited in Hamilton 1985: 74). Dennis Wrong famously criticized this Parsonian emphasis on the structural force of values and norms by labeling it an "oversocialized conception" of actors which denied their relative autonomy (Wrong 1961). Debate still continues over the extent to which this is really a fair characterization of Parsons's work (see e.g. Clegg 1989: 129–37; Turner 1986: 179–206). Whatever the answer to this, it is clear to me that there are valuable insights to take from Parsons when thinking in terms of conceptual development and synthesis. These include the various elements of the unit act; the importance, following Weber, given to the actor's point of view implicit in the emphasis on values and "normative orientations"; the clear differentiation between the values lodged within the actor and the norms which are a feature of the external terrain, and the substance accorded to each; the attention given to the body, both as part of the means of action and, in the form of conditions, as dimensions of the actor which cannot be altered or controlled; the emphasis on time, with a reference to the future, to a state which is not yet in existence, contained within the idea of goals; and the explicit critique of utilitarians, behaviorists, and positivists contained within the central role accorded to normative orientations.

It is quite striking how all these elements are valuable components, more or less qualified and refined, of the synthesis which has since emerged within contemporary theories of social action. The emphasis on the body, for example, provides a point of articulation with pioneering contemporary explorations of this area of ontology (see CHAPTER 26). It is easy, for example, to see how the problematic of the unit act is directly affected by recent debates over what it means to be an individual actor. The introduction of the notion of "actants," for example, signals a reaction against thinking of individual actors as bounded by the human body. Writers such as Donna Haraway (1985) and Bruno Latour (2005) have insisted that machines and technological aids, from automobiles and e-mails to robotic parts and computer networks, are vital and significant functioning parts of actors, and increasingly so, hence the coining of "actants" to capture this. Actors, it is said, are "not all us." Extending this notion, John Urry (2000; see also Thrift 1996) has suggested that one needs increasingly to conceptualize individuals as already embedded within human–machine networks and social flows, of communication, money, energy, fluids, and so on, in ways which radically qualify what it means to be an actor.

As a means of thinking through the relationship between Parsons's writings and more contemporary work within a refinement and synthesis, and as a link to what is to come, I want to look briefly at some comments on the role of normative expectations and social order in Parsons's work made by one of his former students, Victor Lidz. He writes:

> Actors who share normative standards are able to develop reciprocal expectations of one another. Concrete expectations often differ according to specialized roles, but actors in different roles and pursuing different ends may yet agree on the expectations

appropriate to each of the parties engaged in common relationships. By focusing on the shared elements of normative order and common grounds of expectation, Parsons was able to analyze the *integration* of social action. (Lidz 2003: 384; original emphasis)

Lidz brings out well the mechanisms by which actors could possibly be constrained, limited, and channeled by normative expectations embedded within the external societal terrain and internalized in their own action orientations. He also conveys the socially positive dimension of this, captured in the idea of integration. However, the reference to the potential disruption contained within the differentiation of roles is not followed up at all satisfactorily. Lidz simply makes a loose distinction between concrete expectations, that often differ, and shared expectations, that "may yet" transcend the specific exigencies of the concrete roles. This begs a number of significant questions about the interplay between concrete roles and fairly generalized ideals and values. For there is no a priori reason why generalized norms should override the more localized norms and expectations associated with a particular role or set of roles. Zimbardo's work showed clearly the power of at least some particular roles to quickly override previously inculcated generalized values. Answering the question as to the part played by generalized as opposed to more particular, local, norms, or by norms of either kind as opposed to other factors, is something which requires an empirical investigation of particular instances of social action. It also requires a richer array of concepts than those we have built up thus far.

In taking this further I will first introduce additional refinements in the conceptualization of the agent herself, her relations with the external terrain, and how these allow the possibility for far more contingency than Lidz suggests. I will then discuss concepts which develop our grasp of the external terrain which confronts and influences *in situ*, concrete, actions undertaken from within specific roles. Both sets of refinements suggest that case-by-case analysis of concrete circumstances of social action may or may not reveal situations of social integration, and, in the instances where some kind of social integration is indeed found, the extent of it will clearly be variable, and this will be dependent upon a number of analytically distinguishable and empirically variable features.

The founder of ethnomethodology, Harold Garfinkel, who had also been a student of Parsons at Harvard in the 1940s and into the 1950s, felt that the work of his teacher neglected the common-sense lifeworld and contingency of everyday decisionmaking and action. He felt that Parsons's abstractions were cut off from the "gritty texture of reasonable actions in terms of which the mundane world is constituted, produced and reproduced" (Heritage 1984: 36). Garfinkel insisted that for norms, values, and social institutions to exist at all, actors needed to have a skilled and complex grasp of their own actions; an understanding and awareness of what they "do." The understandings which "doing" required were understandings of a quite intricate and not unproblematic nature. Action was typically joint action, in one way or another, and it required an understanding not only of one's own actions but also of the understandings, expectations, and actions of others. This necessary background knowledge and understanding of people and circumstances is built up over time, and draws on what the phenomenologist Alfred Schutz (1962) refers to as background "typifications" – of people, places, and so on, but also of kinds of action and how to competently carry them out. The aspiration to competence brings with it an acceptance of *accountability* on the part of actors, a tacit commitment to have good, intelligible reasons for doing what they do. The skillful and competent production of actions also requires an ability to match and adapt this background, taken-for-granted knowledge, built up over time, to the exigencies of new situations and the sense-data that come along with them. Garfinkel referred to this latter process as the "documentary method of interpretation" (Garfinkel 1967: 77–9), and this is a method used all the time by ordinary people as they go about everyday life, involving themselves in sense-making *in situ*, handling unfolding sequences of social interactions with others.

Thus, Garfinkel reports a conversation between a husband and wife in which explicit statements, that which was said, are distinguished from what was communicated, which was much more. So, when the wife says out loud: "Did you take him to the record store?" she is drawing on background knowledge she knows is shared with her husband – knowledge gleaned both from the immediately preceding conversation and from other times in the history of their time together – to ask a question in a shorthand and simplified manner. She expects her husband to do the work of combining what she has actually said with aspects of their mutual knowledge that have gone unsaid but which need to be invoked in order to understand the meaning of her utterance. When Garfinkel *spells out in longhand* the full content of the question actually communicated to the husband by the very short spoken phrase ("Did you take him to the record store?") he reveals just how much the efficient brevity of our everyday conversation relies on the busy, skillful work we do in incorporating our background knowledge into our complex handling of spoken interchanges:

> "Since he put a penny in a meter that means that you stopped while he was with you. I know that you stopped at the record store either on the way to get him or on the way back. Was it on the way back, so that he was with you or did you stop there on the way to get him and somewhere else on the way back?" (Garfinkel 1967: 25)

The extent to which we expect other people to energetically and respectfully perform this work for us, just as we perform it for them, in everyday interaction, is revealed by the "breaching experiments" carried out by Garfinkel's students. They breached the routine expectations of others by simply abstaining from the usual extra work required in order to make sense of what others were saying to them. So, when someone says: "How is your girl friend feeling?" the experimenter replied: "What do you mean, 'How is she feeling?' Do you mean physical or mental?" Or, when a friend says "Hurry or we will be late," the experimenter asked what he meant by late, and with reference to what point of view he was taking (Garfinkel 1967: 42–4). At one and the same time the experimenters refused to do the usual work expected of them and called for their disconcerted interlocutors to do the extra work instead. These and similar experiments provoked immediate responses of perplexity, emotion, acute irritation, and moral outrage on the part of the subjects of the experiments, revealing, again, just how much we rely on others' "motivated compliance with these background expectancies" (Garfinkel 1967: 53), on them routinely understanding the "texture of relevancies" and unquestioningly performing the necessary work to pull off the interaction smoothly and seamlessly. Using other devices, and in almost all his books, but perhaps most acutely in *Interaction Ritual: Essays on Face-to-Face Behavior*, Erving Goffman also emphasized the chronic role played by tacit knowledge in the production of social practices. Like Garfinkel he drew attention to the reflexive awareness of actors, but also to their skillful capacity for adjustment and adaptation within the unfolding course of an interaction in response to warning signs and cues, from subtle signs of embarrassment or unease to those of open ridicule and silent but visible contempt (Goffman 1967).

Without the existence of these shared methods (ethno-methods), society as we know it could not exist, but central to Garfinkel's approach is also the recognition that their successful deployment is highly contingent. They are employed, performed, in conditions of uncertainty, of contingent mutual adjustments, and the extent to which particular actors are indeed skillful and accomplished will naturally vary to a considerable degree, and will require all kinds of accommodations to changing times. The contingencies of unfolding sequences of action have also been fruitfully explored within the symbolic interactionist tradition, in ways which rarely now reach the theoretical commentaries for the reason that their lessons have simply been integrated into the received wisdom of sociological theory, a point argued recently by Atkinson and Housley (2003). Nicos Mouzelis, whose open-minded and inclusive approach to theoretical problems has made him one of the most important synthesizers within the domain of theories of social action, refers to these aspects of actors and their actions as the unfolding "situational-interactional" dimension. He gives the mundane but telling example of his own classroom interactions to clearly exemplify this dimension and to differentiate it from other dimensions of action and agency we will come to below, such as his *positional role* as a university teacher or his more general *dispositions*:

> when I interact in a particular classroom with particular students, a set of constraints and possibilities emerges that is more directly linked to the actual configuration of the interrelated, interacting participants in that situation. Within such an interaction, specific cleavages between class members, say, or specific teacher–student interchanges, can enhance or sabotage my teaching performance in ways that cannot be primarily derived from or understood by mere reference to role expectations or social dispositions. (Mouzelis 1991: 199; see also 1995)

Garfinkel's intervention is usefully located within one of the two overlapping approaches to the dynamism, creativity, and relative autonomy of actors which emerged in the late 1960s and the 1970s as critical responses to the excessive emphasis which theorists such as Parsons had placed on order. Both of these two approaches helped to flesh out the nature of actors and agency and their links with the external terrain. Ethnomethodology is best grouped within the perspective which had its lineage in those writings of Weber and Simmel we touched upon earlier, and which included Schutz, and Peter Berger and Thomas Luckmann (1966), all broadly within the neo-Kantian and phenomenological traditions. The second broad approach was that of pragmatism and symbolic interactionism, which again we have already alluded to, and this grouping included William James, George Herbert

Mead, Herbert Blumer, and Goffman. These theorists, too, emphasized the reflection, reflexivity, the meanings and the creativity inherent in the very process of interaction itself, but they also directed more explicit attention to two other dimensions of action, both related to each other. The first of these, emphasized by Mead, is on the making of individual selves, through all of the above processes but also through these selves seeing themselves through the eyes of others, and presenting and molding themselves over time, gradually, incrementally, in performances and interactions with these others (Mead 1934). Language, symbolism, and communication are central to this process. The second, closely related, process, central to all within the symbolic interactionist tradition, is precisely the significance of others – present, absent, concrete, and generalized – in the actor's shaping not only of self, but also of all their actions and interactions (see Plummer 1991).

Both of these influences can be profitably looked for in Anthony Giddens's formulation of structuration theory, which was highly significant in the historical development of theories of social action in the latter part of the twentieth century. Giddens attempted to conceptualize actors and action in a way that could account both for those hard, unyielding dimensions of social life which pressured and constrained action and for the relative autonomy of actors and their creative, dynamic capabilities. Garfinkel's work was one of the most important of the various ingredients brought together within early structuration theory, and it was explicitly acknowledged as such by Giddens, who echoed his source in presenting structuration's actors as skilled and knowledgeable practitioners and performers (Giddens 1979, 1984, *passim*; Bryant and Jary 1991: 11). Giddens is less inclined to acknowledge the influence of pragmatism and symbolic interactionism on his approach, but the influence of Mead's generalized and concrete others can be seen, I believe, in his central conception of *external social structures* – the external contextual conditions of action – as also inhabiting the actors-in-focus and providing *the medium of action* upon which, mediated through knowledge and memory traces, these actors draw when they engage in social practices. Goffman's emphasis on the skilled and accomplished presentations and performances of selves to others in tacitly rule-bound everyday interactions (e.g. Goffman 1959, 1963) is also surely a paradigm case of agents drawing on what they "know (believe) about the circumstances of their action and that of others . . . in the production and reproduction of that action" (Giddens 1984: 375). It is clearly the case that structuralism's notion of the paradigmatic axis of language (*langue*), a virtual resource, or pool, drawn upon by speaking agents (*parole*), is also a significant source for Giddens's structures, and one which provides more sophisticated tools with which to explore the influence of processes of signification and discourses on the world-views lodged within actors' dispositions (see below). However, the emphasis of the pragmatist and symbolic interactionist traditions, from Mead to Goffman, is surely significant too in providing a more embedded, contextual sense of how actors respond in practical ways to what others expect them to do, or to be. These are responses to perceived external others who, in their manifestation as internalized and phenomenologically inflected reference points, have great causal powers.

Giddens's approach attempts to avoid the kind of reductionism which places too much weight, by conceptual fiat, on norms and normative expectations (a charge leveled at Parsons), or a similar kind of reductionism of action and subjectivity to signification or meaning, typical of structuralist and poststructuralist approaches. He insists that there are three analytically significant dimensions of social structure (or social being): the structures of domination (power), signification (meaning), and legitimation (norms) which all need to be considered in order to understand actors and their actions (e.g. Giddens 1979: 82). All are inevitably intertwined within the external conditions of action in the midst of which actors are formed and within which they act. They reside, in turn, within the knowledgeability of agents, phenomenologically framed and inflected. The great strength of this conception's emphasis on "internalized structures" is that the agents are thus grounded in, anchored in, their social milieu at the same time as the agents' own internal complexity means that they are not entirely subsumed by this milieu. The three dimensions of structure are, in reality, closely intertwined, and so assessments of, for example, the causal significance of norms and mutual expectations in a sequence of action will inevitably also involve interlinked judgments about power and meanings. Hence, structures-within-knowledgeability involve phenomenologically inflected "stocks of knowledge" about the external context and conditions of action. This is knowledgeability about the distributions and configurations of norms, power, and meaning within the terrain of action. An "external critique" (Giddens 1984: 374) of an actor's view of the terrain of action must take into account this process of mediation as well as the unacknowledged conditions of action and unintended consequences of action. Alongside its strengths, it is important to register the significant weaknesses within Giddens's thinking about structures and action. Most important, it remained at a very generalized and abstract level (Stones 2005) and, as a result, his conception of external structures facing particular actors remained underdeveloped and vague (see Archer 1995; Mouzelis 1991). A further consequence was that the quality of conceptualization of the various ways in which the actor is grounded in, and linked to, the external terrain, also remained highly underdeveloped. Nevertheless, his analytical distinction between the three types of structure provides the basis for more empirically oriented researchers to focus on any one of the structures independently and, in principle, to examine the particular ways in which they are combined. Sometimes, norms may indeed be decisive as the primary structural force within the constitution of an action, sometimes it will be a configuration of power, and at other times it will be a particular regime of signification. Moreover, when combined with the contingencies of understanding, goodwill, energy, skill, and performance involved in the unfolding of situated interactions, this suggests a great deal of indeterminacy, and hence variability, regarding the part played by generalized normative expectations in the performance of tasks associated with specialized concrete roles.

This conceptualization of structures and action has been significantly developed in the "strong" version of structuration oriented to *in situ* studies that has emerged through a process of critique, counter-critique, synthesis, and diverse empirical applications over the last decade or so (see Stones 2005). Strong structuration provides the basis for a more refined conception of the axes along which actors can be linked to their immediate external and strategic terrain. The complexity and richness of the emerging picture is added to by Pierre Bourdieu's notion of *habitus*, which provides the means to think about a further significant aspect of both the internal constitution of the actor herself, and also a further aspect of the links between the actor and the external terrain. By habitus Bourdieu denotes certain properties that are embedded within the minds and bodies of human beings, but instead of the emphasis being on the perception, knowledge, and decisive influence of immediate circumstances, or particular times, places, and practices, as it tends to be in Giddens's work, and as it is in the type of insight associated with Zimbardo, the emphasis here is on more enduring qualities embedded within the actor, and built up over time through socialization and experience. This is an emphasis more in line with, and offering to refine, Mead's writings on the making of selves, and de Beauvoir's insistence that one is not born but, gradually and socially, *becomes* a woman. Habitus should be seen as:

> a system of lasting transposable dispositions which, integrating past experiences, functions at every moment as a *matrix of perceptions, appreciations, and actions* and makes possible the achievements of infinitely diversified tasks, thanks to analogical transfers of schemes permitting the solution of similarly shaped problems. (Bourdieu 1977: 83; emphasis in original)

This conception draws from the phenomenological tradition, with its clear borrowing of notions of typifications and background knowledge. It is indebted also to Marcel Mauss's focus on bodily habits and has affinities with Norbert Elias's use of the term to emphasize the socially embedded psychology of actors. Bourdieu sees the embodied, internal, dispositions of actors as coming about through what he calls the "internalization of externality," whereby individuals develop "know-how" about their external social and material milieu in order to engage successfully in a broad range of social practices. This "know-how," these dispositions, become so deeply ingrained that they become "second nature." They provide a pool of latent resources, in the form of what Bourdieu calls "generative schemes" that can be drawn upon whenever circumstances require.

It is clear from Bourdieu's discussion of habitus in the closing chapters of an *Outline of a Theory of Practice*, and elsewhere, that he wants to include general cultural discourses and world-views within its ambit (Bourdieu 1977: 159–71), and this is something usefully amplified by the social theorist and historian William Sewell Jr. in an influential article on structure, agency, and historical transformations.[1] Sewell refers to the resources of habitus as involving "cultural schemas" which include the deep binary oppositions that structuralism and poststructuralism emphasize, in addition to "the various conventions, recipes, scenarios, principles of action, and habits of speech and gesture built up with these fundamental tools" (Sewell 1992: 7–8). Much of habitus exists as *doxa*, as unquestioned and taken for granted, below the level of conscious reflection, although there is no repressive bar, as with the unconscious, to aspects of habitus emerging into consciousness and becoming the object of critical reflection. This is as true for the formations of culture and discourse within habitus as it is for the embodied motor and practical skills and dispositions such as bodily capacities, deportment, speech, and gesture.

Habitus thus denotes a site in which theories of actors and action can lodge relatively enduring and sedimented characteristics and capacities at both the practical and the more transcendental cultural levels. There is a meeting and interaction here between the relatively enduring and embodied skills, dispositions, and orientations adapted and drawn on in a range of immediate practical settings, and the broader cultural dispositions that inform such actions, dispositions derived from the various "ways in which the social world is constructed for the actor by previous interpretations and collective languages" (Reed and Alexander 2006: 114). There is a process of, primarily pre-reflective, interpretation and transmission whereby the general cultural discourses and constructions inform and color those background understandings and typifications, illuminated by ethnomethodology, that themselves inform practical actions *in situ*. This is an argument pursued by the innovative American social sociologist Jeffrey Alexander who, in a series of articles and in books such as *Durkheimian Sociology: Cultural Studies* (1987) and *Action and its Environments* (1988) which combined theory with specific studies of the discourses of American civil society, including a seminal analysis of "Watergate," probably did more than any other theorist in the latter decades of the twentieth century to emphasize and elaborate upon the *sui generis* characteristics of the cultural level. We will return to these points below, and in doing so it is important to remember that both the transposable skills and dispositions drawn on variably in a range of different practical encounters and also the broader cultural discourses and worldviews which are contained within the agent will have been internalized in more or less complex fashions from the external world and that the two aspects of general dispositions will inform one another.

Bourdieu leaves himself open to the charge of determinism (e.g. Alexander 1995: 128ff; Honneth 1986; Lukes 2005) through his tendency to overemphasize the inherited and enduring dispositions (habitus) at the expense of their contingent and potentially creative articulation with the relatively autonomous, variable, concerns an actor has with the specific contours of the immediate situation. Alexander has criticized Bourdieu along these lines, and a major strand of his recent work (Alexander and Smith 2003; Alexander et al. 2006), in which he has argued for a "strong program in cultural sociology," is an insistence that more attention be given to the precise processes through which actions themselves are the product of the interpretation of received cultural logics of meaning and identities: "a strong program tries to anchor causality in proximate actors and agencies, specifying in detail just how culture interferes with and directs what really happens" (Alexander and Smith 2003: 14). This moment of articulation needs more theorization than Alexander provides, however, and to remedy this it is necessary to make a further firm distinction. This is between, on the one hand, the general and dispositional internalizations of the external world (habitus) we have just been discussing – embracing both general cultural discourses *and* practical skills and dispositions that are enduring and transposable such that they transcend their particular application in any specific setting or situation – and, on the other, the type of emphasis Giddens places on more contingent and conjunctural aspects of knowledge and awareness about immediate and specific situations – on what we might call the "conjuncturally specific structures" within the actor (see Stones 2005: 87–94).

We thus have two main types of internalized structures, each with a different kind of history and different kinds of functions and capacities. There will, however, be a complex, and more or less dynamic, interplay between the two types of "internal structure." For example, any strategic conception of – or practical engagement with – the immediate conjunctural terrain will be mediated by the culturally informed phenomenology embedded within the actor's transposable habitus, but is not reducible to that habitus. There will also be conjuncturally specific elements of the immediate terrain to take into account, with the nexus of norms, power, and meaning that will impact on the consequences of any action. Nicos Mouzelis is making an overlapping, but not identical, point when he distinguishes between the situational-interactional, the positional, and the dispositional (habitus) (see Mouzelis 1991: 194–200, 1995). The recognition that the cultural dispositions located within habitus are in a dynamic and mutually influencing relationship with an actor's experience of her immediate and more enduring social positioning – with all its pressures, demands, and patterned relationships (see the discussion of "position-practice relations," below, and the points made in relation to Lidz and Parsons, above) – is also how I interpret Gregor McLennan's considerable unease (McLennan 2006: 120–38) with Alexander's "sharp analytical uncoupling of culture from social structure [which] is the most important quality of a strong program" (Alexander and Smith 2003: 13). There is a persuasive argument for some degree of analytical autonomy – which would involve the " 'thick description' of the codes, narratives, and symbols that create the textured webs of social meaning" (2003: 13), and Alexander's cultural sociology has done much to enrich our understanding of the cultural formation of actors, but the mutual imbrications between the cultural and the social that are ever present at the level of actuality, and the necessity for ongoing articulation between the two at the analytical level, also need to be thoroughly recognized and conceptualized.

Careful synthesis is required here in order to retain what is of value in the writings of these various theorists, and much remains to be done. The distinctions between the two aspects of the internalization of the external (the general-dispositional and the conjuncturally specific), together with the greater specification and exploration of their various components, enhance our ability to theorize social action, as do the allied concepts crystallized by Mouzelis. They allow a more adequate grasp of complexity and offer the possibility, through synthesis, of bringing greater precision to the emphases of Weber, Parsons, and other writers, on values, norms, means, interests and goals, and the ways in which they influence unfolding interactions.

Andrew Sayer's powerful recent volume *The Moral Significance of Class* (2005) adds yet another important register to the conception of the social actor, arguing that values and emotions should be included much more vigorously within our conceptualizations, and that a more developed notion of habitus should be the primary site for this. He shows just how powerful emotions and mixed feelings such as "envy, pride, resentment, anger and – in extreme situations as a consequence – consternation" can be, arguing that they "are not to be counterposed to reason but are evaluative judgements about circumstances beyond people's control which are likely to affect their well-being and their commitments" (Sayer 2005: 133). Sayer argues persuasively, and through sustained systematic argumentation, that emotional values, cares, concerns, and commitments need to be connected to gender, class, and cultural logics, but that both complexes then need to be reconnected to concrete circumstances, to what we have called the conjuncturally specific. The decisive point is that, unless we can grasp what circumstances these cares are about, and how exactly they affect the actor's well-being, we will not genuinely be able to understand why and how specific inequalities of class, gender, and so on, matter to the people they affect (Sayer 2005: 51).

There is an important point of contact here to the literature on rights and human rights, and to how these fit in to the care and value frames of the people they would affect (see CHAPTER 25). For example, in a chapter discussing what the conditions might be for reaching a non-coerced consensus on human rights in the countries of East Asia, the political philosopher Charles Taylor (1999: 124–44), in the process of arguing for a version of John Rawls's "overlapping consensus" (Rawls 1993), similarly highlights the importance of grasping and taking seriously others' background values, justifications, and beliefs. Writing about societies whose religious heritages are marked by one or more of Islam, Buddhism, Christianity, Confucianism, and various forms of folk religion, to name just some, his point is that an agreement to abide by mutual norms in spite of very different fundamental beliefs – which is the point and the goal of the overlapping consensus – is more likely to be brought about if it has its basis in a prior, and profound, *mutual* grasp and understanding of the other groups' very different cultural world-views, religions, metaphysics, understandings of human nature, and so on. This hermeneutic moment in Taylor's argument – focused on the interpretation of the other's habitus – is designed to counter the ethnocentrism of an overly disengaged and monologic imputation of interests and rights to others, imputations it would be clear they would reject if one understood something about their background traditions and understandings; about what they care about, how much they care about it, and why. Such hermeneutic sensitivity in the multicultural conditions Taylor is writing about can pose a significant challenge to already held, relatively self-contained, systems of values and principles. Such could well be the case, for example, with existing liberal political conceptions of rights which place individual autonomy – the ability of an individual to choose, within reason, the way they live their life, to choose their own conception of the good life (see Kymlicka 1989: 9–20) – at the center of their universe. For it is quite possible that notions of belonging and obeisance to a traditional communal ethos will be more important than the capacity for agency and choice for actors whose habitus has, say, been influenced more by Confucianism than by liberalism.

Significant work has been done on a further important dimension of the internal constitution of the actor, and this is the dimension of active agency. This relates to the ability of the actor not to be consumed and overwhelmed by the immediate circumstances of their social being – whether this be within the confines of Abu Ghraib, in other situations in which social injuries are inflicted on the basis of ethnicity, race, gender, class, or other social markers of discrimination, or in the context of less overtly conflictual social pressures. Active agency can cover a number of different things, from resistance, improvisation, innovation, creativity, and play through the varying degrees of critical distance and reflection which an agent brings to bear on her circumstances (Mouzelis 1991: 27–31), to the process of value commitments through which an actor sorts out her various concerns, more or less clearly, into some kind of hierarchy of purposes or matrix of mutually compatible pursuits (Stones 2005: 103–4, 111–13). Recent work on Simmel has argued that there is a valuable aspect of dynamic and active agency in his writings that is insufficiently spelt out in contemporary theories of action. Thus, in a move reminiscent of structuration, Birgitta Nedelmann identifies key moments of "internalization," moments in which actors are the receivers or the addressees of the effects of previous or concurrent interaction sequences. These moments are to be contrasted with "externalization," those moments in which acting (*tun*) actors produce effects in the external world. Within internalization the receivers are said to experience or "suffer" (*leiden*) these effects; however, there is no necessary imputation of passivity to them in the part they play in this moment of the interactional sequence (Nedelmann 2001: 70). There can be a range of strategies and orientations taken up towards "receiving," and the normative texture of such responses can also vary. The latter, it is clear, could range across a spectrum of responses as disparate as an emotional and normative embracing of the effects or pressures of social being, as one kind of extreme, through to a cold and resentful, yet subtly calculated, restraint or submission, as another. The manner of receiving can have implications both for the cumulative formation of habitus and for strategic orientations to one's more or less flexible positional duties and obligations.

A further factor which bears on all of these is the necessary ability of actors to shift their horizons of action depending upon the motivated, purposive action in hand. This horizon affects the "contexts of relevance" which influence which particular aspects of the latent internal structures will be animated (cf. Schutz 1962; Habermas 1987: 122–3). The importance of shifting horizons, and the nuanced and fine-grained specification of what is involved in this, can be seen in recent work on social action in the respective domains of morality and time.[2] Thus, in relation to morality, Luc Boltanski and Laurent Thévenot have shown how actors, in a series of phenomenological gestalt shifts, can switch between different normative frameworks and *principles of justice* within different social settings, or sometimes the very same social setting, depending upon how a given situation is defined (Boltanski and Thévenot 1991/2006; 1999: 359–77). These shifts rely on background understandings of the appropriate "elementary relations" between actors involved in different types of sociation. The elementary relation will, for example, be *exchange* in a market situation, *solidarity* in a civic environment, adequate *functional links* in an industrial situation, *passion* in an artistic environment, and *trust* in a domestic one. These, in turn, are linked to a range of conceptions of justice or "orders of worth" which are typically felt to be appropriate generically to these different institutional settings, but which can change depending upon the specific nature of the dispute within that institution. Thus, different horizons and types of justification are typically invoked in daily life depending upon the nature of the institution – polling stations, shop floors, media, artistic shows, and family ceremonies (Boltanski and Thévenot 1999: 366) – and situation. Boltanski and Thévenot wish not only to interpret their finely textured world but also, modestly and incrementally, to have an impact upon it. Accordingly, they suggest that these types of routine justification invoked within people's own everyday phenomenological worlds parallel, albeit approximately, a number of political philosophies, including Rousseau's *The Social Contract* (the civic world), Adam Smith's *The Wealth of Nations* (the market world), and St Augustine's *City of God* (the world of inspiration and creativity), each of which can potentially further enrich debate, judgment, and practice within the respective everyday domains. The order of worth legitimately evoked in an artistic situation will be different than that invoked in a situation defined by the moral rules of the market, for example. The order of worth associated with the artistic situation will be based on grace, nonconformity, and creativity, whilst that invoked by the market will be based simply on price. Whilst the human qualities invoked in the first horizon will be creativity and ingenuity, those invoked in the second will be desire and purchasing power (Boltanski and Thévenot 1999: 368–73).

Mustafa Emirbayer and Ann Mische's highly influential "What Is Agency?," which appeared in the *American Journal of Sociology* in 1998, is a synthesis that draws on a combination of pragmatism, phenomenology, and a wide range of empirical studies to distinguish three major *temporal orientations* of situated actors. These are: (1) the *iterational* orientation of agency, in which the actor draws primarily on elements which are very close to Bourdieu's notion of habitus, in which past patterns of thought and action are selectively and tacitly reactivated in relevant circumstances and are routinely incorporated into practical activity; (2)) the *projective* orientation, which encompasses actors' use of creativity and invention to imagine a range of possible future trajectories of action (extending the work of Hans Joas and Alexander, who themselves draw from Mead 1932); and (3) the *practical-evaluative* orientation, which involves situationally based judgments about how to act "in response to emerging demands, dilemmas, and ambiguities of presently evolving situations" (Emirbayer and Mische 1998: 971). Emirbayer and Mische make a further series of valuable conceptual discriminations within each of these categories. Within the last category of the practical-evaluative, for example, they distinguish "three dominant tones within its internal chordal structure" (1998: 997). The first of these is *problematization*: the "recognition that the concrete particular situation at hand is somehow ambiguous, unsettled or unresolved" (1998: 998). There are two secondary tones, in turn, within this category. These are "the *characterization* of a given situation against the background of past patterns of experience" and the "*deliberation* over possible trajectories of action, in which actors consider alternative hypothetical scenarios by critically evaluating the consequences of implementing these within real-world situations" (1998: 997–8). The final two dominant tones are the self-explanatory ones of *decision*, which marks a resolution to move towards concrete action, and *execution*, which is the translation of resolution and capacity into concrete empirical intervention (1998: 999–1000).

All three of these major temporal orientations – the iterational, the projective and the practical-evaluative – will necessarily be combined in any concrete action, but one of them will typically be dominant at any particular time within the horizon of action. It is clear that each of them will have to draw on varying combinations of dispositional and conjunctural internal structures with, for example, the balance being towards the dispositional within the iterational horizon and towards the conjunctural and the strategic within the practical-evaluative horizon. The precise combination will depend on the action at hand, and one's focus as an investigator will depend, as ever, upon the particular explanatory purposes one has in mind. At the end of their accounts of each analytical category of temporal orientation, Emirbayer and Mische make reference to a number of empirical case studies in which that category may be elicited. These are useful in loosely illustrative ways, revealing the particular value of the category itself, and also pointing towards its connection with other categories. Thus, an example they give under the heading "Practical

Evaluation in Empirical Research" is that of Charles Tilly's work (1986, 1994) on the stance of individuals and groups in the implementation of "repertoires of contention." Their focus is on the "shrewdness, tact and situational awareness" of these actors as they adapt and improvise their previously learned roles and scripts to new unfolding situations (Emirbayer and Mische 1998: 1001). At one and the same time this reveals both the practical-evaluative temporal orientations within what Mouzelis call the "situational-interactional," and also the reliance of this moment on the predispositions of habitus, on the previously learned roles – on them knowing "their approximate parts" – as a necessary condition of its existence.

It is most productive to think of all the developments in the theorization of social action covered so far within a broader external frame of networks or social relations into which the actors have been thrown, and without which one cannot make sense of them or what they do. For network analysts themselves the focus is on regularities in how people and collectivities behave and on patterns of ties linking the members of social structures together (Scott 2000). The essential wider point, however, is that all actors are caught up in a web of relationships which can be influencing, molding, facilitating, or constraining depending on circumstances. Action takes place in the midst of ongoing social relations, practices, and structures. This meso-level of the institutionalized relationships from within which individuals confront the strategic terrain of possibilities and constraints has been developed in various ways by a number of theorists and writers. Each of them emphasizes the specialization of roles and tasks, mutual interdependencies, and relational structuring. This work includes the conceptual elaboration by symbolic interactionists of interactive webs of people "doing things" and Norbert Elias's general idea of figurations of mutual interdependencies. More precisely, in addition to distinguishing between the dispositional (habitus/the iterational element) and the situational-interactional (the practical-evaluative arena) in conceptualizing actors and action, Mouzelis separates out a further category, "the positional," which is extremely productive in this context.

The positional is akin to the classical conception of role within social theory but without any unwelcome connotations of excessive rigidity or total subsumption of the actor within the role or position. It remains useful because it provides a sociological point of reference by which to situate the actor within the ambient institutional nexus, allowing us, for example, to ground the abstractions of norms, meaning, and power within a definable empirical context, and so to translate the abstractions into the recognizable pressures and influences associated with particular hierarchies, duties, prerogatives, obligations, and relationships. It is within a definable position that dispositional and conjunctural orientations and understandings become focused on particular tasks and unfolding interactional performances. The nature of the positional is best understood by returning to Robert K. Merton's by now overly neglected account of the notion of roles and role relationships. Merton's notion of role-sets directs one to the number of different roles which are attached to any one "status" or position such as lawyer, police officer, medical doctor, politician, film director, wife, mother, professor, schoolteacher, and so on. The position of schoolteacher will bring with it a diversity of different tasks to carry out daily or from time to time, and each of these tasks will bring the teacher into a "role relationship" with others whose own positions bring them into contact, likewise, with the teacher. Illustrating the status and task-oriented specifics and relational quality of this external terrain of action, Merton notes that schoolteachers thus relate "not only to the correlative status, pupil, but also to colleagues, the school principal and superintendent, the Board of Education, professional associations and, in the United States, local patriotic organizations" (Merton 1957: 42).

Drawing today on Merton's example, taken from the US in the 1950s and 1960s, has the added virtue of directing attention to the specifics of time, place, and organizational culture within which any set of role relationships will be carried out. One of the most systematic theoretical treatments of this meso-level of social action has been provided by Ira J. Cohen; influenced by Merton and developing the tradition of structuration theory, Cohen is keen to avoid any sense that roles and role relationships somehow subsume agency, a charge that was leveled at Parsons, as we have seen. As a consequence he insists that roles have to be continually sustained through practices or active "position-taking." This is informed by an ontological emphasis on the pivotal significance of praxis, relationality, and process in the constitution of social life. In this vein Cohen describes position-practices and position-practice relations as involving the following elements:

- vertical and horizontal sets of power relationships and interdependencies;
- positional identities defined in terms of identifying criteria such as documented qualifications and observable attributes;
- clusters of practices through which identifying criteria, prerogatives, and obligations are made manifest in ways that are generally acknowledged by others;
- a range of other position-practices that must be, or can be, interrelated with a given position-practice;
- a range of institutionalized reciprocities, including asymmetrical power relations, through which position-practice relations occur (Cohen 1989: 210).

Parallel explorations of the structures of meso-level relations and practices have been developed in various ways in a number of more substantive and concrete sociological studies, each of them tracing their lineage to classical sources such as Durkheim on the division of labor and Weber's account of bureaucracy. The most concrete manifestations of such emphases have been in sub-specialisms of the social sciences, such as organizational and industrial sociology, studies of social movements and collective action, and in the field of policy networks within political science. In industrial sociology, to take just one example, the well-known comparative study of work organizations carried out by the Industrial Administration Research Unit at Aston University, Birmingham, UK, distinguished between six primary dimensions of organizational structure (Pugh et al. 1963; Pugh and Hickson 1976), which included the specialization of activities; the standardization of procedures; the formalization of documentation; the centralization of authority; the configuration of positions/roles, and the degree of flexibility within the organizational structure, including the speed of possible changes in the shape of role relationships and expectations (Brown 1992: 105–6). Critics have pointed out that the danger with such taxonomies is that they abstract from complex processes and become little more than reified reference points for the sake of comparisons with an ideal type (Clegg 2007). Ideally, they should be explored *in situ*, with actors embedded within relational circumstances in which the various dimensions of organizational structure will be hybridized and evolving. There is also much to be gained by starting to think through the relationship of meso-level configurations to macro-level periodizations of the social such as those of modernity – in which actors are typically and chronically located within the social technology of several large, and cross-cutting, concentrated systems (Kallinikos 2004, 2006) – and postmodernity.

The more concrete approaches make up in substance and empirical reference points for what they can sometimes lack in conceptual refinement. Further developments in refining our grasp of how the meso-level – within which social actors are inevitably situated – impacts upon social being and actors' ability to make a difference will require the bringing together of the systematic conceptual work with the more substantive literature. This would provide a more refined sense of the pressures to act in particular ways which are felt by social actors *in situ*. A combination of these two levels of analysis, however, needs to keep sight of two simple but highly consequential truths. The first is that the meso-level, which provides the external or structural terrain for any one given actor, is itself full of other social actors. The second is that any adequate approach to the institutional meso-level, including the theorization of collective actors and action, must therefore include within it as sophisticated an approach to individual social actors and social (inter)action as has been elaborated here. We can return now to the second of the two statements from Marx that we started out with. For the problem of fathoming what the possibilities and constraints are which face any particular *in situ* social actor – fathoming what the configuration of external structures will effectively yield to or forbid – needs to be placed within an exploration of these parameters. The possibility of actors making a difference relies, quite simply, not only on the relation between social being and consciousness but also upon whether the relationally constituted external structures they face – and the actors within these – will be impermeable or malleable to their attempts not only to interpret them, but also to change them.

Theories of social action have been gradually, incrementally, and sometimes radically, developed and refined over the last century or so. Major themes of social being, transformative action, and external constraint have remained, whilst our ability to address them, both conceptually and empirically, has been greatly enhanced. There have been complex and careful differentiations within the conceptualization of the individual actor, and with respect to her relations with the external world, and also a curiously slow, but thankfully persistent, dawning awareness that external structures cannot be conceptualized adequately without the existence of actors at their heart. There is still much work left to do. However, invigorated both by an explosion of specializations in a plurality of ontological themes and a contrasting but complementary movement towards systematic synthesis, theories of social action as we approach the second decade of the twenty-first century have never been better equipped to confront the plurality of questions – old, new, and mixtures of the two – they continue to be called upon to address.

Notes

1   I have argued elsewhere (Stones 2005: 67–74) that the article has shortcomings in its conceptualization of the relationship between cultural schemas and resources. However, there is much that is rich within the account, and the shortcomings do not affect its positive insights with respect to cultural schemas per se.
2   Also see Martina Löw (forthcoming), for an illuminating account of the active and contingent procedures of phenomenological synthesis employed by actors as they move between different spatial horizons of action.

Bibliography

Alexander, J. C. (1987) *Durkheimian Sociology: Cultural Studies*. Cambridge: Cambridge University Press.

Alexander, J. C. (1988) *Action and its Environments*. New York: Colombia University Press.

Alexander, J. C. (1995) *Fin-de-siècle Social Theory*. London: Verso.

Alexander, J. C., and Smith. P. (2003) "The Strong Program in Cultural Sociology: Elements of a Structural Hermeneutics," in J. Alexander, *The Meanings of Social Life: A Cultural Sociology*. Oxford: Oxford University Press.

Alexander, J., Giesen, B., and Mast, J (eds.) (2006) *Social Performance: Symbolic Action, Cultural Pragmatics, and Ritual*. Cambridge: Cambridge University Press.

Archer, M. (1995) *Realist Social Theory: The Morphogenetic Approach*. Cambridge: Cambridge University Press.

Atkinson, P., and Housley, W. (2003) *Interactionism*. London: Sage.

Avineri, S. (1968) *The Social and Political Thought of Karl Marx*. Cambridge: Cambridge University Press.

Berger, P., and Luckmann, T. (1966) *The Social Construction of Reality*. Garden City, NY: Doubleday.

Boltanski, L., and Thévenot, L. (1991/2006) *On Justification: Economies of Worth*, trans. C. Worth. Princeton: Princeton University Press.

Boltanski, L., and Thévenot, L. (1999) The Sociology of Critical Capacity. *European Journal of Social Theory* 2(3): 359–77.

Bourdieu, P. (1977) *Outline of a Theory of Practice*, trans. R. Nice. Cambridge: Cambridge University Press.

Brown, R. (1992) *Understanding Industrial Organizations: Theoretical Perspectives in Industrial Sociology*. London: Routledge.

Bryant, C. G. A., and Jary, D. (eds.) (1991) *Giddens' Theory of Structuration: A Critical Appreciation*. London: Routledge.

Clegg, S. (1989) *Frameworks of Power*. London: Sage.

Clegg, S. (2007) "Something Is Happening, but You Don't Know What It Is, Do You Mister Jones?," keynote paper, Workshop on Post-Bureaucracy and Organizational Change in the Knowledge Society, School of Accounting, Finance and Management, University of Essex, September 12–14.

Cohen, I. J. (1989) *Structuration Theory: Anthony Giddens and the Constitution of Social Life*. London: Macmillan.

Cohen, I. J. (1996) "Theories of Action and Praxis," in B. S. Turner (ed.), *The Blackwell Companion to Social Theory*. Oxford: Blackwell.

Dawe, A. "Theories of Social Action," in T. Bottomore and R. Nisbet (eds.), *A History of Sociological Analysis*. New York: Basic Books.

De Beauvoir, S. (1964) *The Second Sex*. Toronto: Bantam Books.

Emirbayer, M., and Mische, A. (1998) "What Is Agency?" *American Journal of Sociology* 103(4): 962–1023.

Evans, M. (1998) "Simone de Beauvoir," in R. Stones (ed.), *Key Sociological Thinkers*, 1st edn. London: Palgrave Macmillan.

Garfinkel, H. (1967) *Studies in Ethnomethodology*. Englewood Cliffs, NJ: Prentice Hall.

Giddens, A. (1976) *New Rules of Sociological Method: A Positive Critique of Interpretative Sociologies*. London: Macmillan; 2nd edn. (1993) Cambridge: Polity.

Giddens, A. (1979) *Central Problems in Social Theory: Action, Structure and Contradiction in Social Analysis*. London: Macmillan.

Giddens, A. (1984) *The Constitution of Society: Outline of the Theory of Structuration*. Cambridge: Polity.

Goffman, E. (1959) *The Presentation of Self in Everyday Life*. Garden City, NY: Anchor Books.

Goffman, E. (1963) *Behavior in Public Places: Notes on the Social Organisation of Gatherings*. Glencoe, IL: Free Press.

Goffman, E. (1967) *Interaction Ritual: Essay on Face-to-Face Behavior*. Garden City, NY: Anchor Books.

Habermas, J. (1987) *The Theory of Communicative Action*, vol. 2, *Lifeworld and System: A Critique of Functionalist Reason*, trans. T. McCarthy. Cambridge: Polity.

Hamilton, P. (1985) *Readings from Talcott Parsons*, ed. P. Hamilton. Chichester and London: Ellis Horwood/Tavistock Publications.

Haney, C., Banks, C., and Zimbardo, P. (1973) "Interpersonal Dynamics in a Simulated Prison." *International Journal of Criminology and Penology* 1: 69–97.

Haraway, D. (1985) "Manifesto for Cyborgs: Science, Technology and Socialist Feminism in the 1980s." *Socialist Review* 80, 65–108.

Heritage, J. (1984) *Garfinkel and Ethnomethodology*. Cambridge, Polity.

Honneth, A. (1986) "The Fragmented World of Symbolic Forms." *Theory, Culture & Society* 3: 55–66.

Kallinikos, J. (2004) "The Social Foundations of the Bureaucratic Order." *Organization* 11(1): 13–36.

Kallinikos, J. (2006) "The Institution of Bureaucracy: Administration, Pluralism, Democracy." *Economy and Society* 35(4): 611–27.

Kymlicka, W. (1989) *Liberalism, Community and Culture*. Oxford: Clarendon Press.

Latour, B. (2005) *Reassembling the Social: An Introduction to Actor-Network Theory*. Oxford: Oxford University Press.

Lidz, V. (2003) "Talcott Parsons," in G. Ritzer (ed.), *The Blackwell Companion to Major Classical Social Theorists*. Oxford: Blackwell.

Löw, M. (forthcoming) "The Constitution of Space." *European Journal of Social Theory*.

Lukes, S. (2005) *Power: A Radical View*, expanded 2nd edn. London: Palgrave Macmillan.

Marx, K. (1962) *Selected Works, 1*. Moscow.

Marx, K., and Engels, F. (1956) *Werke*, vol. 3. Berlin: Dietz Verlag.

McLellan, D. (1977) *Karl Marx: Selected Writings*. Oxford: Oxford University Press.

McLennan, G. (2006) *Sociological Cultural Studies: Reflexivity and Positivity in the Human Sciences*. London: Palgrave Macmillan.

Mead, G. H. (1932) *The Philosophy of the Present*, ed. and introd. A. E. Murphy. Chicago: Chicago University Press.

Mead, G. H. (1934) *Mind, Self and Society*, ed. and introd. C. Morris. Chicago: Chicago University Press.

Merton, R. K. (1957) "The Role-Set: Problems in Sociological Theory." *The British Journal of Sociology* 8: 106–20.

Merton, R. K. (1968) *Social Theory and Social Structure*. New York: The Free Press.

Mouzelis, N. (1991) *Back to Sociological Theory: The Construction of Social Orders*. London: Macmillan.

Mouzelis, N. (1995) *Sociological Theory: What Went Wrong? Diagnoses and Remedies*. London: Routledge.

Nedelmann, B. (2001) "The Continuing Relevance of Georg Simmel: Staking Out Anew the Field of Sociology," in G. Ritzer and B. Smart (eds.), *Handbook of Social Theory*. London: Sage.

Parsons, T. (1968) *The Structure of Social Action*, vol. 1, *Marshall, Pareto, Durkheim*. New York: The Free Press. 1st pub. 1937, New York: McGraw-Hill; repr. 1949 Glencoe: The Free Press.

Plummer, K. (ed.) (1991) *Symbolic Interactionism*, 2 vols. Aldershot: Edward Elgar.

Pugh, D. S., and Hickson, D. J. (eds.) (1976) *Organizational Structure in its Context: The Aston Programme 1*. Farnborough: Saxon House.

Pugh, D. S., Hickson, D. J., Hinings, C. R., Macdonald, K. M., Turner C., and Lupton, T. (1963) "A Conceptual Scheme for Organizational Analysis." *Administrative Science Quarterly* 8(3): 291–315.

Rawls, J. (1993) *Political Liberalism*. New York: Colombia University Press.

Reed, I., and Alexander, J. (2006) "Culture," in B. S. Turner (ed.), *The Cambridge Dictionary of Sociology*. Cambridge: Cambridge University Press.

Sayer, A. (2005) *The Moral Significance of Class*. Cambridge: Cambridge University Press.

Schutz, A. (1962) "Commonsense and Scientific Interpretations of Human Action," in *Collected Papers*, vol. 1. The Hague: Martinus Nijhoff.

Scott, J. (2000) *Social Network Analysis*, 2nd edn. London: Sage.

Sewell, W. (1992) "A Theory of Structure: Duality, Agency and Transformations." *American Journal of Sociology* 98: 1–29.

Simmel, G. (1950) *The Sociology of Georg Simmel*, ed. K. H. Wolff. Glencoe, IL: The Free Press.

Stones, R. (2005) *Structuration Theory*. London: Palgrave Macmillan.

Swedberg, R. (2005) *The Max Weber Dictionary: Key Words and Concepts*. Stanford: Stanford University Press.

Taylor, C. (1999) "Conditions of an Unforced Consensus on Human Rights," in J. R. Bauer and D. Bell (eds.), *The East Asian Challenge for Human Rights*. Cambridge: Cambridge University Press.

Thrift, N. (1996) *Spatial Formations*. London: Sage.

Tilly, C. (1986) *The Contentious French*. Cambridge, MA: Harvard University Press.

Tilly, C. (1994) "History and Sociological Imagining." *Tocqueville Review* 15: 57–74.

Turner, B. (1986) "Parsons and his Critics: On the Ubiquity of Functionalism," in R. J. Holton and B. S. Turner (eds.), *Talcott Parsons on Economy and Society*. London: Routledge & Kegan Paul.

Urry, J. (2000) *Sociology Beyond Societies: Mobilities for the Twenty-First Century*. London: Routledge.

Watier, P. (2008) "Georg Simmel," in R. Stones (ed.), *Key Sociological Thinkers*, 2nd edn. London: Palgrave Macmillan.

Weber, M. (1968 [1921]). *Economy and Society: An Outline of Interpretive Sociology*, ed. G. Roth and C. Wittich. New York: Bedminster Press.

Wrong, D. (1961) "The Oversocialised Conception of Man in Modern Sociology." *American Sociological Review* 26: 183–93.

Zimbardo, P. (2007) *The Lucifer Effect: How Good People Turn Evil*. New York: Random House.

5

Functionalism and Social Systems Theory

GIUSEPPE SCIORTINO

THE FOUNDATIONS OF FUNCTIONAL ANALYSIS

Functionalism has been defined mainly as a methodological stance, by its supporters and critics alike. It can be much better understood, however, as a loose tradition, as a network of intellectual influences kept together by some (broadly defined) theoretical interests as well as by a shared attribution of intellectual significance to some analytical problems. Functionalism has evolved historically as a kind of generalized sensibility for certain dimensions of social inquiry, both methodological (functionalism) and substantive (social systems theory).

At its most basic level, functionalism may be defined as any approach that tries to assess an action or social process in terms of its consequences for the social unit deemed relevant. The intellectual roots are usually traced to Herbert Spencer's decision to follow the biological usage of calling function the consequences of the various organs for the life of an organism. Another often-mentioned ancestor is Vilfredo Pareto, for his insistence on the centrality of mechanisms able to keep or restore a social system to a state of (dynamic) equilibrium as well as for his sharp distinction between subjective goals and objective outcomes. Functionalism's roots may be traced also further back, to Leibniz's theodicy or to the tradition of natural law. As the methodological debate on functionalism has produced more than the usual share of technicalities, abstruse terms, and dialogs among the deaf, it seems better in this context to provide a minimal and step-by-step survey of the options that have defined the various stances in the debate. This will help in highlighting how such methodological debates have been shaped by a variety of sociological concerns.

A good starting point is provided by Bronislaw Malinowski in his classic analysis of the Kula ring in the western Pacific:

> Yet it must be remembered that what appears to us an extensive, complicated, and yet
> well ordered institution is the outcome of so many doings and pursuits, carried on by

savages, who have no laws or aims or charters definitively laid down. They have no knowledge of the *total outline* of any of their social structure. They know their own motives, know the purpose of individual actions and the rules which apply to them, but how, out of these, the whole collective institution shapes, this is beyond their mental range. Not even the most intelligent native has any clear idea of the Kula as a big, organized social construction, still less of its sociological function and implication s.... The integration of all the details observed, the achievement of a sociological synthesis of all the various, relevant symptoms, is the task of the Ethnographer. First of all he has to find out that certain activities, which at first sight might appear incoherent and not correlated, have a meaning. He then has to find out what is constant and relevant in these activities, and what accidental and inessential, that is to find out the laws and rules of all the transactions. Again, the Ethnographer has to *construct* the picture of the big institution, very much as the physicist constructs his theory from the experimental data, which always have been within reach of everybody, but needed a consistent interpretation. (Malinowski 1984: 83–4)

As this passage makes clear, functionalism is primarily defined by the assumption that institutional analysis cannot (and should not) be carried out on the basis of the member's accounts of those very same institutions. Functional analysis is a tool reserved to the observer (the *ethnographer*). Such a stance must, however, be properly understood. Functionalists did not deny that members (the *native*) had opinions about these institutions and ways of describing their functioning. Malinowski never assumed that members were participating because some hidden mechanism forced them "behind their backs"; on the contrary, he argued that self-interest, maneuvering, manipulation, and competition were everyday occurrences. He argued quite forcefully that members have interests served by participating in these institutions and strong reasons to enter into the obligations prescribed by such arrangements. What Malinowski, and all subsequent functionalists, claimed was that the reconstruction of the members' lifeworlds and knowledge belonged to a different analytical level than institutional analysis. The latter is concerned with the ways and mechanisms that keep social action coordinated, not with the motivation for the action themselves (Luhmann 1962).

The observer, however, is bound by a specific frame of reference. The consequences of any action or process are endless, and their impacts may be simultaneously significant on a variety of levels. Any functional analysis has to identify the units whose functioning, adaptation, or adjustment is evaluated as an outcome of the actions and processes observed. Here the crucial link between functional analysis and system theory is established. In the beginning, on this point there were two sharply divergent options. One line of thought – particularly developed by Herbert Spencer and Bronislaw Malinowski – advocated a generalized anthropology – a set of stable needs and dispositions – as the proper structural reference for the functional analysis of behavior. The analysis of whatever social process was analyzed was to be considered complete only when its contribution to the satisfaction of one or more anthropological needs had been fully reconstructed (Malinowski 1936). This line of analysis never succeed in becoming influential: it ran quickly into the oscillation between catalogs of "needs" too generic to be of use and ad hoc reasoning. Its critics, moreover, were ready to point out that linking social practices to

cultural systems and cultural systems to biological needs made it difficult to explain
the several occasions where what is functional for the group is actually dysfunctional
for the individual.[1] Victory was attained by the strict sociological alternative, claiming that the key question of any functional analysis of a social action or process
was to identify the contribution played by it in the maintenance and change of a
given *social* structure (Durkheim 1950; Merton 1949). The line was consequently
drawn not between the actor and the organism, but between the actor and the social
system, thus making functionalism the most consistent stronghold of anti-reductionist thinking in the social sciences.

A third line of contention concerned the implications drawn by the observer from
the existence of a functional relationship between the processes observed and its
impact on the social structure taken as a reference point. In other words, *which is
the proper function of functional analysis?* Again, the first generation of functionalists provided two sharply radical alternatives. Some of them, particularly in anthropology, assumed such a relationship was largely unproblematic. No matter how
different they were in other regards, both Malinowski and Radcliffe-Brown seemed
somewhat to accept the idea that all significant institutions had a function that
explained their enduring presence. If certain actions or customs could be shown to
have certain structural consequences, this was often considered enough to explain
their existence. The risk here is the establishment of a vicious circle: as every
observed action is thought to have some functions, everything may be "explained"
in terms of the contribution given to the social whole, and vice versa. According to
others, however, functional analysis was just a descriptive or exploratory tool,
having an ancillary role to the real scientific task, causal analysis. Functional analysis
was to be restricted, in other words, to the description of contexts where some very
special condition would occur: some institutions whose functioning was unintended
by the actors involved; where such functioning was beneficial to at least some of
them and where such benefits were not linked by those who enjoyed the benefit to
the specific behavior enacted (Merton 1936).

A large part of the methodological debate on functionalism has focused precisely
on the discussion of the possibilities for a "third way" between these two alternatives, able to distinguish casual from functional analysis without restricting the latter
to a mere descriptive status. The existence of this "third way" was first argued by
Émile Durkheim, with his distinction between the causes of the development of a
specific institutional pattern and the causes of its survival and reproduction. In his
Rules of the Sociological Method, Durkheim argued forcefully that functional and
causal analysis were completely different kinds of analysis. Functional analysis,
focusing on the interdependencies of social situations, was necessary to make intelligible the autonomous working of collective structures, but it could not explain the
causes of such relationships or their historical origins. At the same time, however,
he argued that, when functional analysis was applied to issues of institutional stability and change, its status was not merely descriptive. To explain such long-term
stability, it was necessary to show how the unintended consequences of actions or
processes – patterned through a given institutional order – could produce a set of
structural conditions where further actions and processes of the same kind will
occur. In these cases, if the existence of a functional relationship could be successfully identified, such analysis would be crucial also to *explain* its persistence or

constrained development. If functional analysis was coupled to issues of structural stability, functionalists could shift their analytic claims from the level of description (and interpretation) to issues of full-fledged explanation, albeit limited to issues related to the persistence in a given set of states or sequences (Levy 1952).

FUNCTIONALISM AS NORMAL SOCIAL SCIENCE

The conceptual developments summarized above defined the basic intellectual coordinates of functional analysis as we still know it: *an observer's tool aimed at the production of institutional accounts based on the unintended consequences of selected actions or processes to the maintenance of some larger structure in which such actions or patterns are included.*

The most sophisticated versions of this basic framework have been developed during the 1930s and 1940s by a brilliant network of young North American intellectuals. While they identified with the classical functionalist program, they were also very critical of the quality of functional debate. They claimed the time was ripe to go beyond the ambiguities and inconsistencies produced – or tolerated – by the generations of founders. They argued in favor of a more systematic development of functionalism able to make it the base for sociology as a normal science. In doing so, however, they worked towards two different goals that, albeit fully complementary in principle, turned out to be somewhat competitive in practice.

For one group, the major figure in which is Talcott Parsons (to be discussed below), the priority was to establish an adequate theory of the social system, able to provide a consistent set of structural references for the analysis. The practical implication of such priority, however, was to tie functional analysis to a set of problems justified independently on theoretical grounds.

Others, who will also be discussed here, argued on the contrary that the most urgent thing to do was to "normalize" functionalism, making functional analysis a standardized tool of analysis available in principle to any researcher, no matter his specific ideological and theoretical persuasions or the empirical issue at hand. This required the decoupling of functional analysis from system theory and the establishment of strictly methodological requirements for the satisfactory development of functional analysis.

The most successful attempt to normalize functional analysis was carried out by Robert King Merton (Merton 1936, 1949). Merton's explicit purpose was to provide the outline of a guide for an adequate and fruitful functional analysis. To do so, he started with a systematic criticism of the previous debate on functional analysis, arguing step by step that the most problematic assumptions that could be found in the previous generations of functionalists – the vision of society as a unitary body, the attitude that every action or process analyzed has to have some functions, the idea of a neat correspondence between certain social phenomena and certain societal functions – were not necessary elements for a functionalist approach but rather stumbling blocks to be abandoned. In parallel, Merton carefully denied that functional analysis was linked to specific theoretical or ideological positions. On the contrary, the existence of a functional relationship, and the consequences of given actions or patterns for social structures, had to be assessed empirically. Merton did not deny that some previous functionalists could be interested in specific ideological or theoretical objectives. But such links were not in any way intrinsic to the method.

Once the ground had been cleared, Merton identified a certain number of requisites an adequate functional analysis had to satisfy. Firstly, he defined as viable for functional analysis only *standardized* social units; secondly, the analysis should account separately for subjective disposition and unintended objective consequences; thirdly, the unintended consequences had to be described as a net balance of various – positive and negative, manifest and latent – consequences; fourthly, the functional consequences should be related to specific structural units, whose requirements should be made object of a separate analysis; eventually, the analysis should provide a satisfactory discussion of the mechanisms through which such requisites are satisfied, of the possible functional alternatives (actions or processes that could provide the same outcome in a different way) and structural constraints (the range of variation in the items acceptable in the given structural conditions). Only after having performed all these tasks, could the analyst safely assess the role played by the functional relationship in the dynamic process (reproduction vs. change) and its ideological implications.

Merton's essay is still one of the best exemplars of intellectual argument in the social sciences. It is consequently no surprise it quickly became a classic. Two implications of his argument need particular attention. Firstly, Merton was quite careful in not entering the discussion on the exact epistemological status of functional analysis. He insisted, rather, that, while functional analysis did not substitute or subsume causal analysis, it had a specific and necessary role to play in an ambiguously defined "interpretation" of sociological data (Elster 1990). This stratagem left open the potentialities of functional analysis without having to depend upon the stability issue predicated by Durkheim. Secondly, in his attempt to decouple functionalism from system theory, Merton changed the kind of structural references used. The earlier generation of functionalists had actually dealt with two different structural references: the relationships between certain patterns of behavior and some given institutions, but also the relationships among the various institutions. Albeit implicitly, Merton's proposal adopted as a structural reference ought to be seen as one that takes into account mostly individuals, groups, and organizations. The contribution of the latent functions was consequently defined as the contribution to the reproduction – or change – of a given structural arrangement between individuals, organizations, and groups, making marginal or absent the earlier insistence on the relationships among institutional patterns. As a consequence, the kind of structural problems functional analysis defined no longer required a specific theoretical justification.

The strategy of normalization was taken again, and further radicalized, by Kingsley Davis in his 1959 ASA presidential address. Davis had previously elaborated, together with Wilbert Moore, an influential theory of social stratification based on the idea that social stratification was the answer to two closely linked functional problems: allocating people to differently appealing roles and motivating the actors to perform the duties attached to such roles (Davis and Moore 1945). Triggering a wide and lively debate, their work attracted a great deal of attention to the possibilities and limits of functional analysis. In 1959 Davis argued even more radically than Merton that functional analysis was just synonymous with non-reductionist social theory. As such, it had no necessary connections to issues of social system stability: the problems functional analysis was used to explore had to be justified independently from the use of the tool as such. The time was ripe to define functional analysis as social research *tout court* (Davis 1959).

Although the specific solutions advocated by Merton and Davis were different in many points, they both shared the loyalty to the sharp distinction between observer and member while at the same time advocating the decoupling from specific theoretical issues. In the short run, their strategy was an extraordinary success: functional analysis obtained or reached a level of centrality in the social science debate hard to imagine even in the current climate. Although never fully hegemonic, for a few years it really seemed as if sociology and anthropology were on the verge of becoming "normal sciences." Such success may be seen in the endemic presence of Merton's framework in nearly all significant readers, textbooks, and theoretical summaries of the 1950s and 1960s, in the great popularity of functional ideas in the work of a vast majority of the sociologists active in those years, and, above all, in the fact that functional analysis was also developed and appropriated by researchers not working with, or even strongly opposed to, system theory.

As the entry for "functionalism" in Wikipedia informs us, functionalism was "a popular idea until the 1970s when it came under criticism from new ideas." In many ways, this is precisely what happened. In a very short span of time, the functionalist centrality collapsed: if in 1964 the large majority of North American sociologists had agreed with the great value of functionalism for their work (Sprehe 1967), little more than a decade later a panelist at a session of the ASA conference in 1975 could easily claim that "there were no functionalists under 30 years old." Contrary to the positivist expectation about the development of social theory, functionalism was not proven false, being substituted by stricter methodological standards and by more logically tight theoretical frameworks. Rather, the functionalist collapse may be better described as a relatively short period where the functionalist framework was under fierce attack from a variety of standpoints, no matter how incompatible they were among themselves. Symbolic interactionists and ethnomethodologists attacked the very same distinction between observer and native, exchange and rational choice theorists challenged the non-reductionist stance, conflict theorists, Marxists, and new-left theorists rejected the very distinction between theoretical, methodological, and political levels, neo-positivists proved that even the most sophisticated version of functional analysis could not qualify as causally adequate, and social critics blamed functionalism for being void of human values and morally suspicious. The attacks were more than successful in making functionalism lose legitimacy and centrality. When the situation cooled down, the context of sociological debate and practice was a very different ecological niche from the one functionalism had expanded in. The death knell of functionalism was not the heat of the contention but the winter of irrelevance: as a theoretical movement, it softly and suddenly vanished away.

SOCIOLOGY'S STRONG PROGRAM: SOCIAL SYSTEMS THEORY

The foregoing pages have sketched a conceptual genealogy of functional analysis. Even if here have been references to the substantive assumptions often made by functionalists, the nature of such references has until now been left implicit. It has been noted that the generation of the founders had nearly always worked with a partly undefined notion of the "social" as a kind of concrete totality, as attested by the frequent mention of an unspecified "society" as a structural whole. Many of the emphases on functional analysis make sense only if we take into account that many of the participants assumed the existence of such a whole was unproblematic enough to be of concern only with regard to the ways in which its parts could be related to it. Even Durkheim, the most sophisticated member of the founder genera-tion, did not precisely define the factors and dynamics accounting for the unity of the society, focusing most of his efforts in drawing a clear distinction between the social – taken as a whole – and the non-social (biological and psychological) ele-ments. As has been discussed in the previous paragraph, this kind of difficulty led to Merton's attempt to decouple functional analysis from any substantive theory.

A different path was taken by Talcott Parsons with his attempt to break away from the very same difficulties on strictly conceptual grounds, through the develop-ment of a theoretical framework able to move sociological analysis beyond the search for social "wholes," the construction of epochal dichotomies, and the attempt to identify "first movers" for societal processes. Parsons argued that the develop-ment of such a conceptual framework implied the capacity to identify some *theoreti-cal* problems that could be treated only focusing on the unintended consequences of intentional social action. The identification of these problems, however, could not be left to external pressures or idiosyncratic preferences. It had to be derived from the constraints placed by the conceptual framework itself.

According to Parsons, any satisfactory framework for the social sciences has to account at the same time for the autonomy of purposeful actors and the autonomy of a complex institutional order. Contrary to conventional wisdom, Parsons's work shows a remarkable consistency in taking seriously the autonomy and freedom of individual actors. The center of his initial analysis is the means–end schema implying that actors strive to attain goals within social situations that do not determine them. He defined his analytic scheme as *voluntaristic* precisely because it implied that actors pay an active, and not only adaptive, role: they live in a social world where there is a structural gap between the actual and the desirable (and between the desirable and the desired). Social action has to be seen as a tension oriented to reduce such a gap (Parsons 1937, 2007).

To acknowledge this degree of structural autonomy and actors' freedom implies, however, acknowledging a corresponding level of indeterminacy in their reciprocal interactions. Leaving individual action to its own devices, Parsons argues, implies a level of indeterminacy and instability both theoretically useless and empirically wrong. A voluntaristic vision of action requires a structural theory of the social order, an explanation of the ways in which a plurality of independent actors is able to understand and coordinate their reciprocal actions. In his first major work, *The Structure of Social Action*, Parsons stressed, however, another important element of the puzzle: such coordination mechanisms cannot be derived from (or be sus-tained by) intentional individual action. The very same purposeful nature of human actors would otherwise activate – via widespread recourse to force and fraud – a situation where no meaningful life could be carried out. To explain how the exis-tence of a set of (analytically) autonomous actors requires the functioning of an unintentionally generated (and sustained) social structure is the key intellectual puzzle that kept Parsons busy in his long and prolific career.

Parsonian theories have lived in a state of structural change. For more than 50 years, Parsons constantly revised and modified his positions, language, and insights. Although it is not possible here to account satisfactorily for the rich legacy of his work,[2] some key elements of his argument may provide a satisfactory index for its enduring relevance in contemporary social theory. The theoretical direction of Parsons's effort has in fact been quite stable: in all his phases, Parsons argued that the solution to problems of social order has to be looked for in the existence and functions of the normative elements of social life.

The best and most concise statement of Parsons's position may be found in his analysis of double contingency interaction (Parsons 1968). His starting point is that interacting actors have a double problem: to understand the other partner's actual goals and preferences and to coordinate with him or her in ways that are practically effective. To do so, however, requires the actor not only to decide which the best course of action is, but also to anticipate how the partners will react to such selection. In short:

> The actor is knower and object of cognition, utilizer of instrumental means and himself a means, emotionally attached to others and an object of attachment, evaluator and object of evaluation, interpreter of symbols and himself a symbol . . . Not only, as for isolated behaving units, animal or human, is a goal outcome contingent on successful cognition and manipulation of environmental objects by the actors, but since the most important objects involved in the interaction act too, it is also contingent on *their* action or intervention in the course of events. (Parsons, 1968:167)

At face value, such a situation does not raise problems in an individualist framework. Individualists may claim that it is enough to stipulate that each actor anticipates all the courses of action the other members of the interaction could choose for each of his possible choices. The problem is that such an option would place an intolerable burden on the computational capabilities of human beings, even at very limited and rudimentary levels of social coordination. Even a minimum level of interactional predictability – and thus of meaningful choice – requires an extra-individual mechanism able to prioritize the possible alternatives in ways consistent with the possible reaction of the interactional partners. According to Parsons, such a function can be performed only by only on the basis of a *shared normative order* embedded in a shared culture and defined by the existence of shared normative elements.

To understand adequately such a stance, it is necessary to ask why a non-normative solution – such as a familiarity born out of repeated interaction – could not provide an equally satisfactory solution. Parsons argues that this is precisely a consequence of the actors' autonomy: nothing in their past can guarantee that they will keep on behaving the same way. Parsons's approach, again contrary to conventional wisdom, takes for granted that social expectations will often fail, that deviance and change are everyday possibilities. This is precisely the reason, Parsons argues, why social expectations cannot be grounded purely in cognitive capabilities. If the actor has *always* to adapt his expectations to the real interactional dynamics – to look

always for behavioral regularities rather than for normative ways of doing things –
the burden on his information-processing capabilities will be intolerable. Plus, as is
the case with cognitive expectations, he will be guilty of credulity and lack of understanding. A purposeful actor in such a situation would do the most rational thing:
keep social interaction to the minimum and, whenever possible, try always to defect
first. To avoid such an outcome, it is necessary to rely on social expectations of a
normative kind, expectations that are to be maintained even in face of uncertainty
and risk. In case of disappointment, the actor will blame the deviant interactional
partner rather than himself, and he will uphold the definition of the situation intact
(in the short run).

   From his earliest work Parsons acknowledged also that the functioning of such
normative expectations cannot be described as a simple system of rules, such as
those accepted by utilitarian thinkers. The complexity of the interaction between
voluntarist actors needs both a shared definition of the situation in terms of significant and broadly defined priorities (*values*) and specific expectations pertaining to
particular identities or roles (*norms*). The first element, he is careful to stress, provides a basic definition of reality that may be taken for granted (a definition of the
desirable, not necessarily of the *desired*), shared by a plurality of differentiated and
diversified actors independently of any specific interaction. The second provides
broad (but interaction-specific) rules of conduct whose implications may be settled,
in case of conflict, through references to more general and shared definitions. From
Ego's point of view, the existence of shared values allows him to anticipate what
Alter presumably wants or requires; the existence of shared norms allows him to
anticipate how Alter Ego will react to his actions and to anticipate the kind of sanction his actions will receive. Through his analysis of the double contingency of
interaction, Parsons made an elegant argument in favor of the necessity of normative
elements for any social relationship that keeps an ongoing minimal degree of social
order.

THE ANALYSIS OF SOCIAL SYSTEMS

The first question opened by such a perspective is of course how such a system
of social expectations is able to function and reproduce itself. Here Parsons
criticized most of previous social theorists for their failure to develop a fully sociological view of the problem, making reference to extra-sociological factors such as
biological heredity or environmental determination. In his view, it was necessary
to face directly the scientific problems concerning the *analytical* independence
between the personality of the actor, the cultural nature of values and norms,
and the requirements of social interaction (Parsons 1951). To do so, Parsons
identified two significant social processes: socialization, through which cultural
patterns become – or fail to become – selectively incorporated in a personality
system (with a particular emphasis on superegos), and institutionalization, through
which the cultural pattern is selectively embedded – or fails to be so – in the system
of actual social rewards (Parsons and Shils 1951). In these analyses Parsons provides a strong argument in favor of what was later known as *institutionalized
individualism*, the argument being that one actor's freedom and autonomy are not
theoretical givens, but rather the outcome of a to-be-investigated socialized growth

process where social relationships and cultural templates play a crucial role (Parsons 2007).

Social analysis, according to Parsons, can thus proceed from the ideal case of a social situation where the dynamics of these two processes are consistent and perfectly tuned. Such an ideal case he called "complete institutional integration of individual motivation": the actors desire socially desirable goals using socially prescribed means, and the structure of the interaction is such that their actions bring positive assessments by the other interactional partners and satisfactory outcomes. Parsons stressed many times that such a definition was not meant as an empirical description. It was an abstract point of reference to be used as a comparative criterion for assessing the relative distance of the various empirical contexts, theoretically analogous to the notion of market equilibrium in economic theory. This notwithstanding, this part of Parsons's analysis has turned out to be the most controversial. Helped by several ambiguous statements available in Parsons's writings, critics have been quick to portray Parsons as a supporter of an oversocialized conception of man (Wrong 1961) and as lacking a sensibility for strains and conflicts (Dahrendorf 1968).

Parsons's analysis of socialization and institutionalization deals with the relationships between social, cultural, and personality systems. Parsons, however, was also interested in the kind of problems the institutional level has to deal with in order to function. Parsons argued that usage by previous functionalists of an indefinite list of functions was at the root of both the methodological difficulties (the proliferation of new functions on an ad hoc basis) and the reduced appeal of functional analysis in theoretical works. The definition of such a list, however, turned out to be far from easy. In *The Social System*, Parsons identified two functional problems that any social system – from a couple to a world society – has to deal with: the allocation of resources among the various units and the compatibility (or integration) of the various institutions, including methods of social control and methods for managing disputes and strains (Parsons 1951). Although *The Social System* is his best-known analysis of the problem, it is far from being the most convincing: as a matter of fact, the book provided only some rudimentary statements. Parsons started to revise his scheme in depth even before the book appeared on the bookshelves. Already in the early 1950s, he devised a different scheme, centered on the identification of four functional problems any social system had to manage. Such new scheme, best known by the acronym AGIL, was to stay at the center of all his subsequent work. Within this framework, any system has to deal with the following systemic problems: *adaptation* (the control and transformation of non-social resources); *goal attainment* (the management of concerted action by the social units involved for collective purposes); *integration* (the adjustment of relationships among the units of the system, the management of conflicts, the settling of disputes); and *pattern maintenance* (the generation of long-term commitment to shared values and identities). Parsons added that no system can satisfy all these requirements at once: as a consequence, there is a level of tension and strain that has constantly to be managed. In other words, any social system has the same built-in tensions between actual and possible, between conditional and normative, that Parsons had previously placed at the center of his analysis of individual action.

When applied to contemporary societies – a term Parsons assumed, albeit with some perplexities, as closely approximated by the nation-state – the AGIL scheme identifies four distinct subsystems. Adaptive exigencies become the focus of a differentiated economic system, specialized in the development and allocation of fluid resources for a variety of goals (Parsons and Smelser 1956); the attainment of collective goals is entrusted to the political system, made of governmental bodies as well as of non-public organizations (Parsons 1969); the integrative functions are managed by the societal community, the abstract definition of social memberships and the management of the rights and duties attached to such a system of statuses, including the settling of disputes (Parsons 2007); the fiduciary system, specialized in the transmission and development of societal culture (Parsons 1978). Contemporary society is consequently described as complex web of conditional and normative elements, where differentiated institutions and systems of complex solidarities are kept together by a network of flexible interdependencies.

It is likely that the main lasting achievement of the AGIL scheme is the substitution of "last-instance" explanations – rooted in structure/superstructure assumptions – with analysis of interdependencies among analytically irreducible elements. System theory has consequently substituted "total" types or wholes with nested levels of analysis; it has avoided reductionism through multidimensional analysis rather than reification. In many ways, systems theory has been an inquiry into the modalities of coordination of the different.

Parsons's later work was dedicated to showing how the functional analysis of social systems was a necessary step for the development of a scientifically viable voluntarism. The best example is perhaps provided by Parsons's analysis of what he called the generalized media of interchange.

In the early 1960s Parsons focused his attention on an analytical classification of the ways in which, given a double contingency interaction, an actor may try to bring about a change in what the actions of other units would otherwise have been (Parsons 1969). In other words, he focused on social coordination of voluntarist actors, within the same framework in which the analysis of socialization and institutionalization evolved. To classify the means available to the actor, Parsons selected two dimensions: the type of sanctions available to Ego in order to obtain Alter Ego compliance (positive versus negative sanctions) and the channel he could use to bring about such compliance (situational versus intentional). Alter Ego's compliance may be looked at in four analytically irreducible ways: inducement, coercion, persuasion, and activation of value commitments (see figure 5.1).

Parsons is careful to stress that Ego's actions inevitably have to have a symbolic element. First of all, Ego's intentions have to be communicated to Alter Ego at a previous moment: even the most brutal coercion is meaningless without a previous communication of a contingent threat. Secondly, the sanction itself may be symbolic, as in the case in which we transfer money or property titles. Parsons's emphasis on this symbolic element serves to bring attention to the fact that the interaction-level sanctions and rewards are interdependent with the four structural dimensions of societal systems. In Parsons's view, this symbolic element allows the use in the interaction of more resources than are actually materially available in the environment at any given point. The capacity to pose a credible threat makes possible the control of many more actions and contexts than would be possible where each threat has to be backed by the actual use of physical force. In the same vein, the ability to take for granted certain symbolically generalized commitments of Alter

		Channel	
		Situation	Intention
	Positive	Inducement	Persuasion
Sanction type			
	Negative	Coercion	Activation of commitments

Figure 5.1 Generalized media of interchange
Source: Adapted from Parsons 1969: 413

Ego makes possible a degree of trust far higher than would be possible if the life of Alter Ego had to be investigated in detail before each interaction. Such expansion of interactional means is made possible by the structural anchoring of such interactional means in social system media – money, power, influence, and value-commitment – each of them related to a functional sub-system (Parsons 1969). In the modern economic order, it is a well known fact that the use of money in any interaction relies on the existence of an institutional order that simultaneously constrains and enables Ego in its choices. At the same time, the aggregate composition of Ego's spending decisions affects the state of the economic system in many ways, notably in determining processes of inflation and deflation. In a complex series of essays Parsons argued that the same applies to all the other sub-systems, through in different ways linked to the different natures of the media involved. The trick here is that what from the point of view of the actor is a means to further his interests, from the point of view of the institutional order is a set of conditions under which processes in it can be carried out stably (Parsons 1969).

AFTER THE COLLAPSE: VICISSITUDES OF A LEGACY

There are few doubts that Talcott Parsons was an extraordinarily central figure in the social science debate in the post-war decades. For many years, whoever was seriously interested in social theory could not help reading and discussing Parsons. Still today, many of the now popular approaches have to make references to his work in accounting for (at least) their origins. As for functionalism, such an extraordinary level of centrality collapsed in a relatively short span of time. This was due to some intrinsic weaknesses in the construction – and even more in communication – of his system theory: his writings were often characterized as a nearly compulsive multiplication of four-squared boxes, that these same critics defined as an endemic tetra mania; there was a relative abundance of arguments by elimination, implication, and analogy as well as occasional dogmatic statements. The very speed with which he revised his own work made it difficult to follow. A second reason for the collapse was the fact that Parsons often did not carry out his work within the multidimensional requirements he himself set as a standard: a variety of idealist biases and conceptual conflations may be found relatively easily in his corpus – and they have been fully exploited by critics (Alexander 1983).

It is likely, however, that the speed and depth of the collapse was more a consequence of the 1960s climate, where many of Parsons's concerns appeared irrelevant,
even more than wrong, for most of the audience. As Alvin Gouldner sarcastically
remarked, the mind boggled at the thought of a Parsonian hippie (Gouldner 1970:
160). More ideologically inclined readers, moreover, soon discovered that his
remarkable willingness to explore and expand the boundaries of liberalism was
matched by an equally remarkable rigid objection to any step outside such boundaries. In the climate of the period, it surely did not help.

For many years, Parsons's work was left in a state of disarray. The criticisms
codified during the 1960s – the arch-conservative theorist devoted to the multiplication of empty, abstruse classifications void of any empirical or political interest –
slowly become the conventional wisdom filling textbooks and undergraduate
courses. Although system thinking developed and ramified in a variety of fields –
under labels such as complexity theory, autopoiesis, second-order cybernetics, emergence theory – this happened in the absence of any visible link with Parsons's project
and within a radically empiricist and anti-agency framework he would not have
approved. As for functionalism in general, it seemed for a while that his work was
basically an archeological relic of a bygone era.

The situation slowly started to change in the early 1980s, when Parsons's works
started to be read again, albeit in a critical and mediated way. Subsequent developments may be seen as providing a full range of strategies to recognize the relevance
of Parsons's concerns, if not of his proposals.

The first way in which Parsons's legacy started to be appropriated is what usually
happens with legacies. Just as drawings or books dispersed after the death of the
original owner end up in a variety of different collections, so there has been a
growing acknowledgment of the Parsonian elements incorporated in traditions
previously defined as strong alternatives to it. This is the case with Erving Goffman's
dramaturgy and Harold Garfinkel's ethnomethodology, both of whom Alvin Gouldner was partly right in blaming for being somewhat covert members of the functionalist tradition. Certain similarities to Parsons's ideas have also appeared in more
unexpected quarters, such as transaction-cost economics, political philosophy, and
even network theory and British cultural studies.

A second strategy of selective appropriation has been focused on the attempts to
show that, whatever the weaknesses of the overall Parsonian framework, his corpus
contains elements or even whole dimensions still unsurpassed and consequently still
having a contemporary significance for dealing with pressing social and intellectual
problems. These critical assessments have given a great deal of attention to Parsons's
vision of modernity, as a stance still useful to orient the contemporary intellectual
debate (Fox, Lidz, and Bershady 2005; Turner 2005).

A third direction of appropriation has been provided by the attempts, during the
1980s, to recognize the existence of a neo-functionalist – but actually more neo-
Parsonian – stance in the contemporary theory debate (Alexander 1985). This
movement was aimed self-consciously at a critical and selective appropriation of
Parsons's broad theoretical orientations, able to answer to the criticism of the 1960s
in a not merely defensive way. The main feature of such a movement has been its
synthetic character, willing for example to cross-fertilize social system theory with
Marxism to provide an adequate theory of societal crisis (Gould 1987), or to go

beyond Parsons's underestimation of the interactional level in the interpretation of the social role of normative elements.

The trajectories outlined above have been successful in making Parsons a fairly normal "classic figure," whose ideas and concepts can be appropriated consciously for a variety of theoretical projects. Since the 1980s, the overall relevance of such a legacy has been acknowledged in proving the truth of Jürgen Habermas's warning that no contemporary social theory can be defined as serious if it ignores Parsons (Habermas 1981). As a consequence, the label of neo-functionalism has become less and less necessary up to the point of being judged no longer useful (Alexander 1998).

RADICALIZING FUNCTIONALISM: NIKLAS LUHMANN'S THEORY OF SOCIAL SYSTEMS

The intellectual projects reviewed above have all in some ways desystematized Parsons, at least in the sense of abandoning the technical requirements of social system theory in favor of a more flexible and ecumenical framework. The same applies to the selective appropriation of the functionalist legacy, only rarely considered nowadays in strictly methodological terms.[3]

For the contemporary social theory scene, however, another, distinctive, option is available, one implemented with particular vigor by the German theorist Niklas Luhmann. In his work, he reacted to the crisis of functional analysis, arguing that such a crisis was rooted in a lack of radicalism not an excess of it. In the same way, he claimed that the only way to produce a viable social system theory was to extend the Parsonian notion of double contingency to the ultimate. The result has been a theory that makes functionalism an observational device that claims to be fully independent of any kind of causal reasoning, and a radically anti-humanist system theory (Luhmann 1962, 1984).

Luhmann critiques previous functionalists as doomed by the implicit acceptance of causal analysis as a normative model. On the contrary, Luhmann argues that the real benefit of functional analysis is to provide a conceptual reference that establishes a comparative range for a variety of alternatives. The main outcome of a functional analysis is not the capacity to establish if a given action or process has really provided a given social structure with a condition for survival but rather the ability to provide a regulative scheme through which a variety of actions and processes – no matter how substantively and intrinsically different – can be seen as functional equivalents *given a specific problem identified by the observer* (Luhmann 1984). He consequently defines functional analysis as the opposite of causal analysis: while the latter has the ultimate goal to exclude the existence of other possibilities, functional analysis wants to show that everything can be done otherwise, that what in social life is considered effective and familiar is a contingent outcome of processes that have a range of possible alternatives. In the context of the previous discussion, two aspects of Luhmann's proposals are worth stressing. First of all, Luhmann radicalizes further the distinction between observer and member so typical for functional analysis: not only is institutional analysis radically different from members' accounts, but the very same experiences of the members may be treated at the same time by a wide range of mutually autonomous systemic problems. The intrinsic nature of social action is dissolved in a grid of functional problems managed by a plurality of systemic codes. In the same vein, the more the observer adopts a functional method, the greater the detachment from any concrete instance becomes, as the trick of the game is just the fact that whatever happens can be done otherwise. Secondly, although Luhmann recognizes the autonomy of the methodological level, a key implication of his treatment is that functional analysis cannot be decoupled from system theory, as the latter is the place where the meaningfulness of a given functional problem can be established and communicated. Once functionalism is defined as a tool for the research of functional equivalents, the selection of the actual action or process observed has to be justified in the light of the existence of other structural problems that take place at the same time. Contrary to Merton and Davis, functional analysis cannot be developed in isolation but only within an understanding of the structural interdependence of functionally differentiated parts.

Such functional analysis requires a very different kind of social system theory. According to Luhmann, the key systemic problem is not stability – in whatever form – but rather the reduction of complexity to manageable levels. The starting point is that the meaning of every social unit – in the case of Luhmann each communication – is given by the fact of having been selected against a background of other possibilities. Each communication acquires its meaning from the web of sequences it is part of, not from the speaker's intentions, the latter being reconstructed through communication, not revealed by it. Such sequences last as long as they last, as their meaning is not driven by an intrinsic purpose but rather by the sequence of selections that both psychic systems (i.e. individual consciousnesses) and social systems make according to their internal functioning (Luhmann 1984). Individuals are consequently part of the environment of the social system and the relationship between social systems and personalities must be seen not as an analytic distinction but as a fully differentiated system–environment relation. The result is the radically diminished importance of both socialization and institutionalization processes, treated as reciprocal autonomous adaptations that may well take place otherwise.

Luhmann radicalizes Parsons also in his definition of social systems. Like Parsons, he sees society as defined primarily by the form of its differentiation, and contemporary society as defined by a functional form of differentiation in a plurality of sub-systems. Contrary to Parsons, however, Luhmann sees these systems as ruled by functional codes, which select the flows of communication according to their meaning for specific purposes. Everything that happens may be processed by the legal system in terms of lawful/unlawful, by the economic system in terms of having or not having the ability to pay, by the aesthetic system in terms of beautiful or ugly, by science as true or false, by religion in terms of immanent or transcendent. Nothing keeps these systems together in any special way and none of these systems may – in contemporary society – claim any special superordinate status. Each of these systems, as matter of fact, treats the rest of society as one of its environments. Consequently Luhmann refuses to grant modern differentiated society any kind of emancipatory potential. As a matter of fact, Luhmann's most controversial stance is that there is no way in which it is possible to develop an emancipatory reading within a functionally differentiated society: such a society is not the embodiment of a value system, and social theory can only repeat endlessly that everything could have been done otherwise. In Luhmann's sarcastic statement, "The person who communicates with reference to values lays claim to a sort of values bonus . . . One does not discuss values, only preferences, interests, prescriptions, programs" (Luhmann 2002).

The fate of Luhmann's system theory is still fairly uncertain. The level of abstraction in which he frames his works is unheard of in the social sciences, thus sharply reducing the potential audience. He himself admits that the development of his theory requires a kind of formal logic quite distinct from the one with which social scientists are more or less acquainted (Esposito 1992). His stances, moreover, run contrary to some of the most cherished holy cows of contemporary social theory: subjectivity, normativity, emancipation, identity, power, the foundational significance of gender, existential meaning. There is no doubt, however, that precisely his level of consistent radicalism provides an intellectual challenge that may be helpful in rethinking much disciplinary common sense (Moeller 2006). And a few readers may have noticed – one example among many – that Luhmann is among the very few theorists taken seriously by Michael Hardt and Toni Negri in their self-defined revolutionary book, *Empire*.

CONCLUSIONS

Functionalism and system theory are related components of a loose tradition with a long history of debate and controversy. Functional analysis established itself as a way of bringing to light the significance of the institutional order and connecting it with the unintentional consequences of social action. System theory has evolved as a conceptual framework dealing with several specific and interconnected problems: the integrated analysis of purposeful individual action and structural mechanisms of social coordination (i.e. social systems), the ways in which a variety of social institutions could operate at the same time with a minimal degree of consistency, the ways in which long-term large-scale social change may be conceptualized. Such specific problems, however, have been shown to be much more difficult than expected. Trying to deal with them, a variety of new issues has been added to the catalog: the relationships between culture and social and personality structures, the role of shared cultural backgrounds in shaping individual and social interests; the nature and future of modern contemporary society; and the meaning of institutionalism as a cultural and social value.

For a few decades of the last century the sometimes uneasy alliance of functionalism and system theory attained an extraordinary degree of centrality in several social science disciplines: anthropology, sociology, and political science (on the contrary, attempts to initiate a dialog with economics and history produced dismal results). Such centrality did not last, however, and in the mid-1960s both functionalism and system theory collapsed. The institutional infrastructure of the movement was marginalized, disappeared, or fragmented, and the same seemed for a while to apply to its ideas.

In subsequent years, however, both functionalist and social system sensibilities and ideas have shown a certain degree of resilience. Although far from getting the kind of centrality enjoyed before the collapse, the tradition is significant for many of the current points of contention in contemporary social theory. If very few would today subscribe to the solutions advocated by functionalists, their way of identifying some problems and some of their ways of dealing with them are still unsurpassed. As has been documented in these pages, they have attained the (only apparently) paradoxical status of being problem-central and solution-marginal for a wide variety of debates in contemporary social theory. Such a tendency may be expected to grow stronger under the influence of two factors. Firstly, demographic change implies the emergence of a new generation of theorists that are emotionally detached from both the era of functionalism's centrality and from the polemical reactions of the 1960s. For many of them, functionalism and system theory will be "just theories," rather than symbols of sanctity or pollution. Secondly, the theoretical agenda again has at its center some issues – such as the cultural dimension of social action, the need to integrate a variety of social coordination mechanisms, the key role played by societal pluralism, the new debate on modernity – in relation to which the functionalist legacy has an enduring significance.

Notes

1 Today, however, developments in biology have triggered a variety of new attempts to explain individual behavior in terms of its function for the reproductive success of specific genetic inheritances.
2 Beside Parsons's many texts, the interested reader may find some of the general introductions to his work useful, such as The *Sociology of Talcott Parsons* by François Bourricaud (1977), a text that has the advantage of having been highly appreciated by Parsons himself. A shorter systematic introduction has been produced by Victor M. Lidz (2000). A selection of Parsons's texts is available in the reader edited by Bryan S. Turner (Turner 1999).
3 The notable exception is Faia (1986).

Bibliography

Alexander, J. C. (1983) *The Modern Reconstruction of Classical Thought: Talcott Parsons.* Berkeley: University of California Press.
Alexander, J. C. (ed.) (1985) *Neofunctionalism.* Beverly Hills: Sage.
Alexander, J. C. (1998) *Neofunctionalism and After.* Oxford: Blackwell.
Bourricaud, F. (1977) *L'Individualisme institutionnel.* Paris: Presses Universitaires de France.
Dahrendorf, R. (1968) *Essays in the Theory of Society.* Stanford: Stanford University Press.
Davis, K. (1959) "The Myth of Functional Analysis as a Special Method in Sociology and Anthropology." *American Sociological Review* 24: 757–72.
Davis, K., and Moore, W. (1945) "Some Principles of Stratification." *American Sociological Review* 10: 242–9.
Durkheim, É. (1950 [1895]) *The Rules of Sociological Method.* New York: The Free Press.
Elster, J. (1990) "Merton's Functionalism and the Unintended Consequences of Action," in J. Clark, C. Modgil, and S. Modgil (eds.), *Robert Merton: Consensus and Controversy.* New York: Falmer Press.

Esposito, E. (1992) *L'operazione di osservazione: costruttivismo e teoria dei sistemi sociali.* Milan: Franco Angeli.

Faia, M. A. (1986) *Dynamic Functionalism: Strategy and Tactics.* Cambridge: Cambridge University Press.

Fox, R., Lidz, V., and Bershady, H. (eds.) (2005) *After Parsons.* New York: Russell Sage.

Gould, M. (1987) *Revolution in the Development of Capitalism.* Berkeley: University of California Press.

Gouldner, A. W. (1970) *The Coming Crisis of Western Sociology.* New York: Basic Books.

Habermas, J. (1981) "Talcott Parsons: Problems of Theory Construction." *Sociological Inquiry* 51: 173–96.

Levy, M. J. (1952) *The Structure of Society.* Princeton: Princeton University Press.

Lidz, V. M. (2000) "Talcott Parsons," in G. Ritzer (ed.), *The Blackwell Companion to Major Social Theorists.* Oxford: Blackwell.

Luhmann, N. (1962) "Funktion und Kausalität." *Kölner Zeitschrift für Soziologie und Sozialpsychologie* 14: 617–44.

Luhmann, N. (1984) *Soziale Systeme.* Frankfurt: Suhrkamp Verlag.

Luhmann, N. (2002) *Theories of Distinction: Redescribing the Descriptions of Modernity.* Stanford: Stanford University Press.

Malinowski, B. (1936) "Anthropology." in *Encyclopaedia Britannica: First Supplementary Volume.*

Malinowski, B. (1984 [1922]) *Argonauts of the Western Pacific.* Long Grove: Waveland Press.

Merton, R. K. (1936) "The Unanticipated Consequences of Purposive Social Action." *American Sociological Review* 1: 894–904.

Merton, R. K. (1949) *Social Theory and Social Structure.* New York: The Free Press.

Moeller, H.-G. (2006) *Luhmann Explained: From Souls to Systems.* Chicago: Open Court.

Parsons, T. (1937) *The Structure of Social Action.* New York: McGraw-Hill.

Parsons, T. (1951) *The Social System.* New York: The Free Press.

Parsons, T. (1968) "Interaction. Social Interaction," in *International Encyclopedia of the Social Sciences.* New York: The Free Press.

Parsons, T. (1969) *Politics and Social Structure.* New York: The Free Press.

Parsons, T. (1978) *Action Theory and the Human Condition.* New York: The Free Press.

Parsons, T. (2007) *American Society: A Theory of the Societal Community.* Boulder: Paradigm Publishers.

Parsons, T., and Shils, E. (1951) "Values, Motives and Systems of Action," in T. Parsons and E. Shils (eds.), *Toward a General Theory of Action.* Cambridge, MA: Harvard University Press.

Parsons, T., and Smelser, N. J. (1956) *Economy and Society: A Study in the Integration of Economic and Social Theory.* New York: The Free Press.

Sprehe, J. T. (1967) *The Climate of Opinion in Sociology: A Study of the Professional Value and Belief Systems of Sociologists.* PhD dissertation, Washington University.

Turner, B. S. (ed.) (1999) *The Talcott Parsons Reader.* Oxford: Blackwell.

Turner, B. S. (2005) "Talcott Parsons's Sociology of Religion and the Expressive Revolution: The Problem of Western Individualism." *Journal of Classical Sociology* 5: 303–18.

Wrong, D. H. (1961) "The Oversocialized Conception of Man in Modern Sociology." *American Sociological Review* 26: 183–93.

6

Structuralism and Poststructuralism

Daniel Chaffee and Charles Lemert

All sciences, including human and cultural sciences, begin with the assumption that the field of objects and events they study is structured. In all fields of empirical study, structure is a formal term stipulating the prior existence of order in the field under investigation. "Structuralism," thereby, is an organized and shared attitude among scholars or experts that takes the structures of any observable field of objects or events with utter seriousness, occasionally to an extreme. It is possible, broadly speaking, to say that all fields of empirical research are structuralist in the sense that, whatever their particular subjects, science, as it has come to be in the modern world, looks for structures that are enduring, organizing, and salient with respect to a field of events and objects.

A "structuralism" can also be understood as a method because the contents of most empirical fields cannot be observed directly because, more often than not, their objects behave in irregular, even arbitrary, ways such that events cannot be located with respect to organizing structures. Thus, in social fields especially, the structures thought to organize events and objects are ultimately instruments of their measurement. In sociology, for example, numeric data used to define the structure of income distributions are also measures of inequality. "Structuralism," thereby, is in effect theories of measurement, even when the structures themselves can only be described weakly.

Still, there are strong structural methods. In a strict sense, civil engineering is an instance of a pure structural science because, for example, a built bridge must obey strict laws of physics with respect to gravitational force and other aspects of weight and stress that may affect the structure's load-bearing capacity. Yet, insofar as the final test of a bridge's adequacy is the extent to which the structure endures over time in the face of many variables – extreme weather conditions, traffic volume and speed, durability and plasticity of construction materials, among others – not all variables can be calculated in the design phase, nor can the quality of workmanship and material supply be assured in construction. Thus, the structure in question remains abstract until such time as the bridge may collapse or be put out of service.

Structural engineers, in principle, want their structures to endure but, since they can neither fully anticipate nor absolutely control all the variables in the construction phase, some bridges fail.

Thus, it is better to say that, with rare exceptions, "structures" are postulates of logical or empirical work that cannot be directly observed and that "structuralisms" are the principles and methods whereby structures are discerned in the absence of pure, perfect observations of events and objects.

Not even structures postulated in fields with relatively observable objects, such as astrophysics, literary criticism, or molecular biology, fully meet the observing eye. Still, the structural assumption is applied with respect to prominent features of the field in question. Interstellar distances, plot resolutions, or subatomic biochemistry are reasonably well warranted by indirect measures accepted by explicit accord among technically certified members of the disciplines. As a result, protocols in these relatively pure sciences are artifacts of their social organization. Sciences could not endure without necessary, if insufficient, evidence that the field investigated is orderly, even when the short-run evidence is unclear on this point. Hence, it could be said that scientific structuralisms require a strong demarcation between professional and lay judgment.

Yet it must be noted that this reliance on the social organization of a scientific field exposes the structural element in fields of investigation to two extreme dangers – orthodoxy and scandal. Orthodoxy arises when a dominant structural principle is reinforced by long-valued beliefs that cause practitioners to resist innovations that would threaten the dominant understanding of the field. Ptolemaic and Newtonian physics are prominent examples. Scandal arises, as in all organized human practices, when defense of a structural principle originates in rank ideological or financial interests – as in extreme elements in environmental science and biochemistry that, historically, have suppressed or distorted evidence with respect to the harmful effects of global warming and tobacco smoking. Fortunately, in the long run, orthodoxies tend to respect good evidence and scandals are short-lived and local. Yet when structures cannot be precisely and definitively observed they will occur, because social organizations – even scientific ones – are themselves structures in which behaviors can be observed only imperfectly.

As a consequence, "structuralisms," as such, are more likely to occur in the human or cultural sciences where the demarcation between lay and professional knowledge is more difficult to certify and maintain. This is because practitioners in these fields rely on their practical understandings which Max Weber, following Immanuel Kant's philosophy of pure practical reason, described as the naturally occurring ability to recognize subjectively adequate meanings. In the cultural and human sciences, professional warrants for the nature of structures are open to challenge by individuals not technically competent in respect of the scientific protocols. In economics, for example, markets are stipulated as definite structures in spite of the evidence that markets, like subatomic particles, are at best observable by means of assays like price or rent fluctuations, demand pressures, inventories, or bank reserves. In the end, even precise measures of the movement of the assay are susceptible to the corruption of practical, often irrational, behaviors – price-fixing, lost leader product dumping, just-in-time failures, and external assaults on bank reserves – that upset the assumption of strong structures.

Thus one surprising feature of all "structuralisms," is that they tend to arise in fields in which consensus as to the definiteness of structures is more vulnerable due to the intrusion of practical distorting behaviors, including both those of the scientist herself and of those she recognizes as fellow members of the structured social field under investigation. Thus, in contrast to civil engineering, structural methods in fields such as cultural anthropology, the sociology of culture, and developmental psychology, among others, must contend with variables ever more resistant to precise calculation than those affecting the durability of a bridge. For one thing, the anthropology of cultures must contend with the inscrutability of exotic societies; for another, sociologies of familiar cultures must work against the ignorance of members of groups as to the contents of the cultures they live by; often, also, members may have their own good reasons for providing investigators with deceptive reports. The culture of street gangs is a notorious instance of both problems. Likewise, developmental psychologies, to their credit, usually recognize the futility of subjecting infants and small children to experimental instruments – thus requiring that the study of cognitive and emotional development must impose a structural scheme on subjects who are unable directly to provide corroborating information. An infant with neurological deficits is not, and cannot be made into, a mouse in a maze. In this respect, all three of the examples have much in common with literary criticism, social history, and other liberal arts where the objects of study are either fictions or are long dead or otherwise unavailable to direct observation.

It is often said that the most important tool of structural methods in all fields is the archive – that is, the discovered (or maintained) residue of mental or cultural events held in libraries and other social forms of memory. The structural method is often referred to as archeological or geological in nature – a systematic reconstruction of evidently dead and buried events and objects.

STRUCTURALISMS IN THE SOCIAL, CULTURAL, AND HUMAN SCIENCES

"Structuralisms," therefore, are found most often in sciences devoted to the study of fields of least certain structural values – political economy, cultural anthropology, social studies, literary theory, and semiotics (or semiology). Though it is tempting to interpret this phenomenon as a perverse reaction to the scientific failures of the fields in question, the more likely explanation is that structuralisms are more robust in those sciences where the field is less open to interpretive certainty. Thus, "structuralisms" are commonly found in fields in which observable events require a strong structural assumption if their sense is to be discerned.

The first serious structuralism of the modern era was Karl Marx's theory of commodity values, which appeared in its strongest form in *Capital*, volume 1 (1867). Marx's structuralism serves as both the inspiration for and the model of a nearly pure structuralism in the social sciences – hence, it is important to understand his thinking well in order to appreciate the strengths and weaknesses of all structuralisms.

Marx understood that there was a structural scandal at work in the modern world. In *Capital*, he asks and answers the ironic question he first posed in "The

Economic and Philosophical Manuscripts of 1844": Why is it that "the worker becomes all the poorer the more wealth he produces" (Marx 1978: 70–9)? His answer was first outlined in the 1848 *Manifesto of the Communist Party* where with Engels, he set forth his basic structural principle in the famous opening line "The history of all hitherto existing society is the history of class struggles" (Marx and Engels 2005: 1). In this remark he and Engels identified the scandal of modern industrial society which professed values of human freedom and progress while, under the surface of a liberal ideology, the capitalist class was as ruthless in its exploitation of the worker as feudal lords were of the peasantry. Hence, as his thinking matured in the first volume of *Capital* into a full-blown historical and social analysis of the capitalist mode of the production, so too did Marx's structuralism.

In essays originally published as *For Marx* (1965), Louis Althusser (2005) proposed a substantial rupture between the younger, more philosophical Marx of the 1840s and the mature, more scientific, Marx of the 1860s. There can be little doubt that Marx's structuralism was more pronounced in volume 1 of *Capital*, but it is hard to justify Althusser's claim of an epistemological break. Already in the 1844 essay "Estranged Labour," where he first identified the scandal of modern capitalism, Marx held the view that the estrangement (or alienation) of the worker begins in the factory system of production wherein the worker no longer owns the means of production (the tools and resources owned and supplied by the capitalist class) and thus is cut off from the value produced by his labor (or labor power). Therein begins the contradiction of capitalism wherein the overt class conflict of other historical forms of production (notably feudalism and slavery) is hidden from view by a cynical ideology of human progress. Thus, estrangement from the value of his labor also alienates the worker from his human nature, from fellow workers, and even from himself. Two decades later, in *Capital*, this structural principle is developed as a comprehensive structural analysis of, in Marx's view, the precise mechanisms whereby the capitalist mode of production systematically exploits the worker through such structural effects as the prolongation of the working day and the suppression of rates of pay – both allowed by essential attributes of the factory system whereby, again, the capitalist class owns the means of production which requires the worker to submit to the conditions set by the factory owner who, in turn, is moved by the structural logic of profit.

One of the most important elements of Marx's mature theory of the structures of capitalism is the way he derives the contradictions of a structural whole – in effect the whole of the modern world's economic system – from the most elementary unit of economic exchange: the commodity. Simply put, a commodity is any thing (literally, *res*, as in reification or thingification), whether material or immaterial, that has exchange value on an open market. That value may or may not be based on the commodity's use-value. In extreme drought, water, which is normally free in nature, can be bought and sold at a price because of its essential use-value to human life. On the other hand, a rare vintage of wine, with little or no use-value, can command a very high price. This strange fact of economic exchange entails a sociology of economic exchange. For any commodity to be exchanged for a value, it must be different in kind but equivalent in value. The modern measure of equivalence between different commodities is the money system, which itself is a structured social convention that must be well understood by the parties to an exchange. The implication is that for the commodity to have exchange value it must, in principle, bear a relation to all other commodities in the economy.

Hence, the exceptional aspect of Marx's structuralism was his ability to link the commodity, which is the smallest object, or unit, in the economy to its most salient, organizing structure, the market. Even more striking is the subtlety by which (though himself a strict materialist for his belief that the economic substructure determines all in a society) Marx located the fate of the human worker in a social theory of human societies.

In his view the general theory of exchange values was the key to capitalism's particularly deceptive but vicious exploitation (or, in the terms of his youth, estrangement). One of the reasons that exchanged commodities must be qualitatively different but quantitatively equivalent is that the qualitative difference is the only way to account for the profit which he defined as surplus value. If all exchanges, even between different commodities, are between precisely equal values, then there is no way to explain surplus value. In another of his famous lines, Marx said that the capitalist (whom he sneeringly called "Mr. Moneybags") "must be so lucky as to find . . . a commodity whose use-value possesses the peculiar property of being a source of value, whose actual consumption . . . is a creation of value" (Marx 1978 [1867]). That commodity is, of course, the labor power of the worker, who in the early factory system is effectively forced to sell his labor to Mr. Moneybags for wages the capitalist recoups in but a few hours of the working day – thereby leaving the balance of his labor time as surplus value for the owner of the means of production. Obviously in most, if not all, forms of mass production wages will be as low as possible, while the working day must be as long as possible – otherwise under capitalism there can be no surplus value, hence no profit.

Though much has changed in capitalist economies since the days of the early factory system, even the introduction of laws protecting some workers and profit-sharing by corporations with workers among other innovations, the worker remains vulnerable to exploitation. Since Marx's day, there have been numerous applications of his ideas, usually in combination with ideas not necessarily derived from Marxism. One of these is Immanuel Wallerstein's (1976) idea of the modern world system which is a method for analyzing the global structure of modern economies and states in respect to a dominant core state that exploits weaker, peripheral regions of the world by extracting cheap labor and resources that are converted into valuable commodities and profit. Britain in the nineteenth century and the United States in the twentieth were, in Wallerstein's terms, the core states of the modern world system that, through military and economic power, extracted precious metals, oil, foodstuffs, and spices, *inter alia*, from colonies or virtual colonies in Africa, the Middle East, and Asia.

Many argue that the principal weakness of all structuralisms in the human and social sciences is that they tend to be deterministic by downplaying or excluding considerations of power and the freedoms of the human individual. This is a fair criticism, but it is often made at the cost of ignoring the fact that Marx meant his structuralism to be a historically based account of the actual conditions of working men and women in a social structure, the very essence of which was the alienation of human individuals. To be a worker under capitalism is to be alienated. This defense is weakened by the evident failure of Marx and Marxism to generate a working theory of just how human individuals, acting alone or collectively, could bring about a revolution that would replace capitalist greed with socialist justice. The failure of actually existing socialisms in the prominent instances of Soviet Union and the People's Republic of China is proof enough of the people. Yet a common mistake among social theorists is to counter an overly strong emphasis on the power of structures by accentuating the agency of the human subject. This approach, however, has its own weakness which is to suggest that human subjects are capable of acting outside of, or at least in resistance to, power-organizing structures like economies, states, and cultures.

Another, seriously deficient, attempt to correct the deterministic principles of structuralisms is a variant of what has been called the macro–micro link. Here the proposal is that there are two independent (or semi-autonomous) spheres of social action – the macro, being structured sectors like the economy; and the micro, being small, local, and presumably more vibrant spheres of social interaction like trade unions or community action groups. It would seem, however, that Marx's thinking on this score was far the suppler, at least on the point of situating the alienated subject (*and* her potential liberation) not in a sphere external to the structured system but directly within it. Thus, whatever its weaknesses, and there are many, Marx's structuralism is a near-perfect illustration of the properties of all structuralisms by illustrating how structures are the salient and organizing features of fields that cannot be directly observed but must be reconstructed historically and analytically. Thus, most famously, for Marx, the key structure is the mode of production which, in contrast to the marketplace, is hidden from view in the sense of the shop floor is private, thus not open to ready inspection.

Curiously, structuralisms subsequent to Marx's have proven themselves able, at least partly, to correct some of the deficiencies of his determinism. Of these, the most important is structural linguistics, which derives from the ideas of the Swiss linguist Ferdinand de Saussure (1857–1913). Though there is little direct evidence that Saussure was closely familiar with Marx's ideas, his theory of linguistic values bears a striking resemblance to Marx's theory of exchange values.

Language, according to Saussure, is a form of social exchange. The word "dog" is commonly assumed to correspond to the animal named by the term. But this correspondence is in fact a structural relation based on social conventions rather than the inherent properties of the class of animals named by the word. "Dog," the word, is no more than an English-language convention as are the German *Hund* or the Korean 개. Words are not natural signs for realities or things. In effect, words operate in spoken languages just as do commodities in economies. Members of the language community, like buyers and sellers in economies, share community-wide conventions that are used to determine values – money (usually) in the case of economies, signs in the case of languages.

Saussure was, thus, the first to recognize and persuasively explain the structural and thereby social nature of language in *Course in General Linguistics* (1916) which was in fact, a compilation of lecture notes by students at the University of Geneva. Here he explains that spoken words are signs exchanged by speakers in a social community. One of the more powerful structuralist ideas in this book is the idea that the principles of structural linguistics could be developed into a general theory of social and economic values he called a semiology (the science of signs; often also called a semiotic).

Saussure's key structural idea could well have been (though it was not) quoted from Marx:

> Even outside language all values are apparently governed by the same paradoxical principle. They are always composed:
> 1. of a *dissimilar* thing that can be *exchanged* for the thing of which the value is to be determined; and
> 2. of *similar* things that can be *compared* with the thing of which the value is to be determined. (Saussure 1974 [1916]: 116–17)

Or, more generally: "Sciences are concerned with *a system for equating things of different orders* – labor and wages in one and a signified and a signifier in the other" (Saussure 1974 [1916]: 116). As in Marx the key to the exchange of values in human communities is different qualities assessed by a system of equivalencies. But what in language is the structuring element?

Here is where Saussure, in many ways, improves upon Marx's scheme by providing for the role of the individual speaker in the structured linguistic community. This involves his famous distinction between *la parole*, speaking, and *la langue*, the language itself in the colloquial sense of "the tongue." Speaking is the work of individuals in producing spoken statements, or signs that are observable (literally, audible). Language, then, is a kind of "collective intelligence" that extends beyond the individual speakers ordering speech into meaningful statements. In this sense language exhibits the most difficult feature of structures – their invisibility.

Just as the mode of production in Marx is a structure that, behind the marketplace, structures the values of commodities, so the countless words and rules of a language form a structure that can only be observed when it is put to use. Yet for the individual speaker competence in *the* language is a given if she is to produce meaningful speech. This entails the social proposition that words (or, more generally, signs), thereby, cannot be based in nature, which is to say that they are arbitrary in the sense that the signs themselves vary from language to language even though they can be compared across languages. "Dog" and *Hund* are different signs for the same meanings. Likewise, within a language, the exchange of meanings in speech depends on the ability of speakers to recognize similarities and differences. "Dog" cannot signify a "cat," just as a new BMW is unlikely to be exchanged for an old Ford. Where Saussure improved on Marx's theory of values was by identifying the speaker as the agent of the structure of language without divorcing the two spheres and without assuming that historically the individual speaker is alienated from and by the structure of his language. Linguistic alienation, when it occurs, is between linguistic communities when a speaker of English is ignorant of the conventions of the German or Korean languages.

As a social theory of structures, Saussure's structuralism is more fluid than Marx's, though at the cost of the critical edge Marx's offers to a diagnosis of human suffering. The foremost criticism of Saussure's structuralism is that of Jacques Derrida (1976 [1967]) who objected to its privileging of spoken language over writing, a subject to which we must return in the consideration of poststructuralism.

At the same time, the implications of Saussure's semiology were not lost on many subsequent social thinkers.

In cultural anthropology, the undisputed father of structuralism is Claude Lévi-Strauss (1908–). Beginning late in the 1940s Lévi-Strauss published a collection of essays that formed the foundation of his structural anthropology. He benefited immensely in his structural thinking from time spent in New York with the Russian linguist Roman Jakobson, who is said to have created the term "structuralism." He also drew on the work of the French sociologist Émile Durkheim (1965 [1912]) and also on his extensive knowledge of field reports by cultural anthropologists such as French anthropologist Marcel Mauss (1924). But the influence of Saussure is most striking in his comparative study of myths, which employs many of Saussure's ideas. Yet the crucial difference is that Lévi-Strauss, in his early and more formalistic essays in *Structural Anthropology* (1958), took as his basic unit the mytheme, roughly the equivalent to the sign in Saussure's scheme. Myths can be broken down into units of meaning which can then, he demonstrated, be compared across time. For example, from Sophocles to Shakespeare to Freud there are numerous versions of the Oedipus myth. By comparing the versions over time he isolated, among others, two recurrent mythemic elements: Oedipus kills his father/Oedipus marries his mother. He then interprets the elements as, in effect, signifiers of a universal human conflict between hate and love toward parents or, more formally, between underattachment to one parent and overattachment to the other. At one point he proposed that his structuralism was meant to be a science of the human mind (by which he meant *esprit*, human spirit or even culture).

The first several of Lévi-Strauss's definitive structuralist essays appeared in France in the years immediately following World War II. They were welcomed by many in Europe who were hungry, after years of war and economic distress, for new sciences that would describe the universal properties of mankind. He applied his principles, with some changes, to numerous subjects – including culinary and musical cultures and kinship systems. His original essays in the 1940s were instrumental in inspiring a structuralist movement in French social thought. Roland Barthes (1915–80), the literary theorist, published an important essay in 1953, *Elements of Semiology*, which introduced Saussure's ideas to a new generation. Just as important was Barthes's famous collection of essays, *Mythologies* (1957) that, like Lévi-Strauss's early essays, applied a structural semiotics to aspects of popular culture such as wrestling.

About the same time that Lévi-Strauss was outlining his structural anthropology, the French psychoanalyst Jacques Lacan (1901–81) applied a structural linguistics to his influential reinterpretations of Freud's theory of the Unconscious. Drawing on Saussure's structural linguistics, Lacan gave us the infamous slogan, "the unconscious is structured like a language" (in "The Agency of the Letter in the Unconscious, or Reason Since Freud" in 1957) Somewhat later, Louis Althusser (1918–90) used Lacan's seminar on the "Mirror Stage" (1949) to refine Marxism's theory of culture by drawing the parallel between the mirror stage, an alleged moment when the infant first sees herself in a mirror thereafter to face the prospect that she is a unity (or a self as some would say) larger and more whole than anyone can be, and culture as an imaginary (in which a culture is presented as if it were a totality bigger and more true than truth itself). The link to Marx is in the retention of Marx's claim that culture is an inversion of the reality. Likewise, the Lacanian notion that mental consciousness is an illusion that the psyche expresses the totality of human understanding to the exclusion of the unconscious mind that actively disorganizes consciousness. Althusser's "Ideology and Ideological State Apparatuses" (1969) is one of the most widely referred to texts in cultural studies.

It could be said that the high-water mark of structuralism was roughly the two decades from 1945 to 1965. Though the movement was originally French, it spread into the rest of European and North American thinking. As it happens, however, the formalism of the early French structuralists proved to be highly unstable. The search for a formal science of structures in language and culture did not translate well from its founders – especially Lévi-Strauss and Barthes, who were brilliant theorists and superb writers – to their followers. In effect, the inherent determinism of strong structuralist programs was exposed by the political and cultural dynamism of the 1960s, when science itself came to be viewed by a younger generation as a cultural arbitrary. Yet the power of Lévi-Strauss's thinking stands, even now, as a road sign along the way of social thought's attempt to resolve the dilemma that Marx first set out between the agency of individuals and the organizing power of social and cultural structures.

It is important to realize that the structuralist period was not a uniquely French affair. In a famous essay, "Social Structure and Anomie" (1938), the American sociologist, Robert K. Merton (1910–2003) outlined a very different kind of structural thinking. Merton is not usually considered a structuralist. Yet, in this and other of his works, he proposed a relatively strong structural theory of social action – that, while culture provides the individual with meaningful goals, social structures may well make the attainment of those goals impossible. In America, to take Merton's example, the salient cultural goal requires the individual to work hard at an institutionally normal occupation in which he earns the income that represents his moral success. Yet if the economy does not provide income-producing jobs for all members of society those without will be unable to achieve the shared cultural goal. One of the essay's most controversial themes was the idea that the individual who wishes to achieve his culture's goals but is unable to find an institutionally normal means (like a job) to do so may innovate by using a deviant means, as when a poor mother steals milk for her baby or an ambitious corporate manager frustrated in his career embezzles to give the appearance of monetary success. Merton's ideas were, thus a strong structuralism, in the sense that he identified the way individuals might be forced to act against their own values and those of the culture.

About the same time, another American sociologist Talcott Parsons was developing a rather more formal structural theory of social action that may have influenced Merton's thinking to a degree. In *The Structure of Social Action* (1937), an enormous two-volume restatement of ideas of selected classical social thinkers, Parsons meant to draw from writers like Émile Durkheim in France and Max Weber in Germany, among others, a formal theory of social action that, as it matured in later writings, suggested that culture, politics, the law, and the economy were the four necessary structural elements in modern societies. Each served a necessary function – culture to maintain cultural patterns, politics to distribute the goods and services needed by social groups, law to adjudicate conflicts where goods are unfairly distributed, and the economy, which provides the dynamic competitive energy that drives individuals to pursue needs and desires in competition up to, perhaps beyond, the point standing down before the laws, rivals, and values that limit his freedom in the action system. This approach has been called structural-functionalist. When applied to modern societies, like that of the United States in the 1950s, Parsons's scheme inclined toward an overly optimistic assessment of the system's ability to resolve differences, and distribute goods and services, to avoid debilitating conflict. Both Parsons and Merton were, obviously affected by the Depression of the 1930s and the global conflict that followed, such that the relative affluence in America after the war combined with naive elements of the American national character to produce a strong structuralism that was overly optimistic as to the ability of the social system to function as smoothly as their theories predicted.

POSTSTRUCTURALISMS AND OTHER CRITIQUES OF STRUCTURALISM

As in the period of the strong structuralisms in the 1940s and 1950s, there were two related but divergent lines of structured thinking – one Francophone, the other Anglophone. The poststructuralisms that developed in the 1960s and 1970s were also of two kinds. Both, however, attempted to resolve the unresolved problems of strong structuralisms that, in being formal and deterministic, were unable to obey the cardinal rule of structural thought – that the structure is a reconstruction based on archives of the events and objects in a field. It is accepted that the structural method will not be able, except in rare instances, to generate strong numeric data that measure the structure's effects with mathematical exactness. What is more troubling about structuralisms is their tendency to overreach the evidence – both to view the structures as neater than any real world can be and to exaggerate their capacity to organize events and objects.

Poststructuralism in France began with a flourish at a gathering of French thinkers in 1966 in, of all places, Johns Hopkins University in Baltimore. The manifesto of the poststructuralism movement is usually considered a paper presented here by the philosopher Jacques Derrida (1930–2004), "Structure, Sign, and Play in the Discourse of the Human Sciences." Though the ostensible purpose was scrupulously to scrutinize Lévi-Strauss's method, Derrida's underlying argument is a critique of the very idea of structure by associating it with all prior structuring elements that undermine the free play of signs in human thought and discourse. "It could be shown that all the names related to fundamentals, to principles, or to the center have always designated an invariable presence – *eidos, archē, telos energia, ousia* (essence, substance, subject), *alēthia*, transcendentality, consciousness, God, man, and so forth" (Derrida 1978: 279–80). Those unable or unwilling to read texts like these assume they are little more than sheer irony and utter abstraction. In fact, Derrida begins this paper with reference to an "event" in the "history of the concept of structure" that provoked a rupture in Western history (Derrida 1978: 278). He does not say exactly what the event is, but it is likely that a Jew born in Algeria had in mind the decolonizing revolutions in his native North African colony that were rupturing the colonial structure of the modern world. In later writings he made his political positions much more explicit. But in this opening salvo of the poststructuralists he was engaged in a method for which he would become famous, if poorly understood: deconstruction.

In truth, deconstruction is not so much a method as a literary attitude that seeks to uncover the silences in the history of philosophical and social thought *and* in effect to create silences of its own. When Derrida first presented his 1966 paper in Baltimore, the world was already moving toward what Wallerstein would call the World Revolution of 1968. No one in France, especially, could have mistaken the event that, in France, had come to a head in Algerian independence in 1962 – a war that had begun in 1954 the year of France's defeat in another of its colonies, Vietnam. Politics were not far from anyone's mind and, among the French, even literature and philosophies are part and parcel of the political scene.

A better word than deconstruction to define Derrida's theoretical approach is the one he used, decentering. At a time when the Eurocentric world was being nudged, and not too gently, from its half-millennium reign as the center of global politics, he and others labeled by observers as poststructuralists were decentering the politics of social and philosophical thought, beginning with the claims of structuralism, to establish, in Lévi-Strauss's expression, a science of the human spirit. Derrida's countless books, over the years, could be described as a systematic rereading of the classic works of modern philosophy by attempting to locate the structural elements that across the long prehistory and history of modern culture led to restrictions on "the free play" of thought and discourse (Derrida 1973, 1976).

Thus, in Derrida's 1966 essay (republished in one of his most important books, *Writing and Difference*, in 1967), he offers a respectful but damning critique of Lévi-Strauss's structuralism. In a word, the argument is similar to his critique of Saussure's structuralism (which appeared prominently in another of Derrida's important books also in 1967 – *Of Grammatology*). As in his attitude toward those he, as some put it, "rereads," Derrida seldom dismissed another thinker out of hand. In fact he appreciated and was influenced by Saussure's structuralism as he was by Lévi-Strauss's. In respect to the former he argues that the flaw in structuralism was not in the idea of structure but the privileging of speech over writing. The problem, so to speak, with speech is that in the modern West the voice is assumed to be the representative of an inner self (or, one might say, the soul of meaning). This idea that meanings can be present in human interaction is the principle of the Center he attacks. Thus, alternatively writing is a form of communication in which the meaning is always deferred – if only by the reality that the written message, even if read to the other in her presence, is always mediated by the distance between the two – notably in books, letters, and even e-mails.

Thus Derrida's idea is that, though there is much to be gained from Saussure's semiology, its theory of the spoken sign as the presence of a meaning participates in the modern centering of social thought, thus limiting the free play of signification. A spoken sign is open to direct challenge, while a written letter can only be interpreted at a distance. In much the same way, in the 1966 paper, Derrida criticizes Lévi-Strauss's overly strong structural theory of myths by insisting that the very idea that the myth or the sign articulates a broad, if not universal, human meaning tends to destroy, as he puts it, "the tension between presence and absence" – that is, between the meanings presented in signs and myths and the structures that generate those meanings which are always absent from the performance of the communication.

In effect, Derrida is here criticizing Saussure and Lévi-Strauss for being unfaithful to Saussure's structuralism. Between speaking, *la parole*, and the language structured by the community, *la langue*, there is always an unavoidable tension created by the fact that no cultural communication communicates if the speaker or the mythmaker tries to bring all of the contents of the structured language into the uttered sentence or articulated myth. Structures are, by their nature, absent. The attempt in the modern West to organize them around a Center is an attempt to tame them, thereby to limit the freedom of communications.

Michel Foucault (1926–84) came to public notice at much the same time as Derrida in a series of books on subjects like the history of madness, the clinic, and the prison. Very probably his most notorious book of the 1960s was *The Order of Things: An Archaeology of the Human Sciences* (1966), which was, by his own tacit admission, a strong structuralist history of the birth of modern social thought. Foucault, still relatively young, was then still somewhat under the influence of his teacher, Louis Althusser. His archeology of social knowledge (as of the birth of modern methods for treating both the mentally and physically ill, as in the rehabilitative prison) aimed to demonstrate that modern thought came into being by, in Althusser's words, an epistemological break – that is, a sudden structural shift occurring late in the eighteenth century when, of course, modern society was coming into its own.

Though Derrida and Foucault worked in quite different fields and lived very different lives, the similarities between them are hard to miss. Where Derrida attacked the idea of the Center, Foucault attacked the ideal of the original Subject. Where Derrida juxtaposed differences and deferrals of meaning to the voice as the presence of meanings, Foucault offered (in *Archaeology of Knowledge* in 1969) the concept of discursive formations which served, among other effects, to identify the power of silences and prohibitions in the history of social discourses as key to understanding how power in the modern world works through the silencing of oppositions.

From this rather formalized theory of the late 1960s, Foucault turned to his influential theory of power as knowledge in *History of Sexuality I* (1976), where he attacked the modern Enlightenment idea that knowledge offered emancipation from the limiting effects of power. On the contrary, Foucault said that, in the modern world, knowledge is the social form of power. Here is another turning point in his own structural theories and in the history of structuralism. As Marx and others after him understood power as a top-down effect – the dominant class exploiting the poor – Foucault said that power is just as much bottom-up. Power is structured by knowledge (or, one might say, culture) that effectively forms the modern individual – subjugates the human subject. Thus, Foucault's interest in the human sciences, including now the practical sciences of sexualities, is the completion of Marx's failed structuralism. A strong materialist theory can never explain the modern method of taming the subjects of the industrial era because, however degraded the worker is, he participates in his own degradation. Foucault left no doubt that top-down domination is at work, but it works not through overt force so much as, one might say, persuasion – the gentle force of practical knowledge taught to schoolchildren, patients, penitents, or university students through the social formation of the modern world.

There were of course many other figures associated with the poststructuralist movement. Barthes, in his later years, was a convert. Lacan was always a precursor of the movement and never a pure structuralist. Foucault, as noted, started as a kind of structuralist, but with very different purposes from Lévi-Strauss's. "Post-structuralism" as a name cannot be taken with too much seriousness. While it is not accurate to say that the poststructuralists, so called, where part of the French structuralist movement, nor should it be assumed that they were a radical departure – and especially not from the principles laid down by Saussure. The best way of understanding the relation of the two movements is that both were beholden to Marx as well as Saussure, and even Freud – a feature particularly evident in another poststructuralist text by Gilles Deleuze and Félix Guattari, *A Thousand Plateaus: Capitalism and Schizophrenia* (1980). The distinction is between taking the ideal of a formal science of signs and meanings too literally and the understanding that cultural meanings, while structured, can never be reduced to abstractions.

BOURDIEU'S HABITUS AND GIDDENS'S STRUCTURATION THEORY

The influence of this long and fruitful structuralist/poststructuralist period of French thought (from roughly 1945 through the 1970s) continues well into our time. Yet even as poststructuralism was emerging in France there were two sociologists who, while aware of this movement, were taking an independent path.

One of course was the prominent French sociologist Pierre Bourdieu (1930–2002), who attempted to straddle the line between his French contemporaries and academic sociology, which until recently had been dominated by Americans. Bourdieu drank from the waters of Paris in the 1960s by joining in the attack on strong structuralisms (objectivisms), on the one hand, and the equally strong sub-jectivisms that claimed that the individual subject is the sole and autonomous source of social action or agency. To this end, in *Outline of a Theory of Practice* (1972), he sketched his now famous distinction between the *champ* (field) of social practices and the *habitus*, or the subjective disposition of actors to balance the demands of structures against the individual's ability to engage in free play with those demands. In one of the more memorable, if obtuse, lines in all of recent social thought, Bourdieu defined the habitus as a system "of durable, transposable dispositions, structured structures, predisposed to function as structuring structures, that is, as principles which generate and organize practices and representations that can be objectively adapted to their outcomes without presupposing a conscious aiming at ends or an express mastery of the operations necessary in order to attain them" (Bourdieu 1977 [1972]: 72). Those willing to meditate even on the opacity of this statement will be rewarded by, at least, the indications that Bourdieu attempted to weld objective structures to subjective dispositions – without allowing either to gain the upper hand. His invention of the neologism "habitus" reflected some of the features of the poststructuralist attitude – that is, to identify the silences in social thought, in this case the powerful silence at the point where determining structures encounter liberating subjects. Bourdieu's empirical studies of this concept were, in a fashion, limited by his preoccupation with Parisian culture as the field of his research. Yet, in both his early and his late writings, Bourdieu was one of the leading proponents of reproduction theory – the idea that culture and education serve to reproduce the dominant structures in modern societies. His genius lay in his ability to mix and match the classic ideas of sociology – nowhere more so than in his reproduction theory, which reflects simultaneously Marx's top-down theory of power as maintaining the prevailing social structures, Durkheim's theory of culture (or knowledge) as the source of the guiding dispositions of the modern individual, and even Weber's notion that the individual subject requires an ethical orientation in order to find her way through the differing spheres of modern society.

British sociologist Anthony Giddens (b. 1938) was influenced by structuralism, but like Bourdieu was not persuaded by the structuralist account of the relationship between social structures and the individual. Giddens writes: "Structuralist and post-structuralist thought alike have consistently failed to generate an account of reference, and it is surely not by chance that these traditions of thought have concentrated their attention so much upon the internal organization of texts, in which they play of signifiers can be analysed as an inside affair" (Giddens 1987: 85). Giddens thus objects to structuralism's distinct lack of a theory of agency. Like Derrida, he is opposed to the inherent determinism of structuralism, but enchanted with the focus on language. One of the strengths of Giddens's structuration theory is that it tries to account for how it is that social structures are both constituted by and changed by social action. In a formulation less obtuse but nearly as charming as Bourdieu's definition of the habitus, Giddens states that social structure is both medium and outcome of social interaction. By this he means that, in going through our daily lives, we draw upon structures as if they were a set of rules and resources, as it were. When we follow these rules, we in a sense create them. In this conception of structure, a social structure is less like the metaphorical girders of a building and more "virtual." Giddens likes to point out that nobody can see social structures. Many would dispute this claim on the grounds the social structures impinge upon the lives of people with great ferocity, as for instance in the terrible inequalities structured around differences of gender, class, race, or economic status.

But to argue that social structure is invisible and virtual, for Giddens, is a guard against saying that we are all cultural dopes. Unlike Derrida's version of poststructuralism, Giddens holds that what is important about social structures is not only the interplay of signs, but the interplay of signs with the production of meaning. Giddens writes, "Meaning is not constructed by the play of signifiers, but by the intersection of the production of signifiers with objects and events in the world, focused and organized via the acting individual" (1987: 91). In this way he tries to maintain an acting subject in the face of the tension around social actors. It is perhaps a vain attempt to maintain subjectivity in the face of objective and cultural domination.

For Giddens, it is not speech, or writing, that is important about language, but talk. Talk is what we do when we use a language (in this he is closer to Foucault's idea of discourse as language in practice). Giddens uses a linguistic metaphor to explain his social theory. He argues that social structures are like the English language. Nobody can literally see "English" (the *langue*), but many people in the world can speak it. And when anybody speaks the English language, they draw upon a set of grammatical rules. Through following those rules, the rules themselves are reinforced, hence "medium and outcome."

Giddens's structuration theory is one of the more innovative attempts at rethinking social structures and how they affect our lives. Structuration theory re-evaluates social structure as something that is less a "fixed" and determined idea of social structure into what he terms "the duality of structure"; a dynamic and active view of social structure as comprised of knowledgeable social agents who recursively draw upon a set of "rules and resources." In short, when acting in social situations social actors draw upon social cues or rules, and, in drawing upon these cues and repeating them, the rule is created. This is the recursive creation of social structure. Much like other structuralisms, social action takes place in specific instances, but there is also a broader system of interaction, namely language, that patterns the specific instances. Except the key different in structuration theory is that the specific instances, in a sense, pattern and create the broader system of language.

CONCLUSION

The lessons offered by structuralism and poststructuralism continue to be taught and studied for the way they help social theorists rethink the still unsolved riddles of social order. In some ways these two joined but opposed movements address, in an original way, the classic question of modern thought that goes back at least to Hobbes's *Leviathan* (1651): why does the individual freely enter into a social contract with others, there to form structures that effectively limit his freedoms? The social sciences, including sociology, were in many ways founded on this riddle which, *mutatis mutandis*, was behind the theories of Marx, Weber, Durkheim, and Freud, as well as the structuralists.

In a most basic way, social science itself is an inherently structuralist enterprise. Markets, minds, nations, globalized societies, cultures are, like much of the natural word, structured things. What structuralism and its aftermath accomplished was to show that social structures cannot be equated with natural ones, if only because social things are by their nature more unruly than molecules, not to mention the starry skies above. Hence the structuralist dilemma: given that social things are structured, how do we account for the eruptions of human invention? To which the corollary: given that human agencies seems to be rooted in the vitality of individuals, whether alone or collectively, how does it happen that there are evident structural features of social life, ones that endure through human time?

In the end, it is sufficient to accept the structuralist movements as the maturation of an ancient conundrum – one that attempted with limited success to discover a science of the contradictory relations between determining structures and liberating agents. To their credit, those associated with the structuralist movements collectively were able to move beyond their founding assumptions. In a rare instance of honest but mutually critical work, they contended with each other's thoughts in ways that a scientific community ought. The result was the setting forth of an ironic principle: social and cultural structures create subjects by means of their determining powers. We, as subjects, cannot *be* (that is, exist) without structured relations with others, which structures cannot adapt to historical change without the freedom of subjects. It is very possible that there is no solution to the puzzle – and that the ultimate contribution of structuralism to social science is to impose a caution upon the urge to over-define the structured variables that move social beings to make and discover what structured meanings they have.

Bibliography

Althusser, L. (1972 [1969]). "Ideology and Ideological State Apparatuses: Notes Toward an Investigation," in *Lenin and Philosophy and Other Essays*, trans. B. Brewster. London: New York: Monthly Review Press.

Althusser, L. (2005 [1965]) *For Marx*, trans. B. Brewster. London: Verso.

Barthes, R. (1968 [1953]) *Elements of Semiology*. New York: Hill & Wang.

Barthes, R. (1972 [1957]) *Mythologies*. New York: Hill & Wang.

Bourdieu, P. (1977 [1972]) *Outline of a Theory of Practice*, trans. R. Nice. Cambridge: Cambridge University Press.

Deleuze, G., and Guattari, F. (1988 [1980]) *A Thousand Plateaus: Capitalism and Schizophrenia*, trans. B. Massumi. London: Athlone Press.

Derrida, J. (1973 [1967]) *Speech and Phenomena and Other Essays on Husserl's Theory of Signs*, trans. D. B. Allison. Evanston: Northwestern University Press.

Derrida, J. (1976 [1967]) *Of Grammatology*, trans. G. C. Spivak. Baltimore: Johns Hopkins University Press.

Derrida, J. (1978) "Structure, Sign and Play in the Discourse of Human Sciences," in *Writing and Difference*, trans. A. Bass. London: Routledge & Kegan Paul.

Derrida, J. (1982) *Margins of Philosophy*, trans. A. Bass. Chicago: University of Chicago Press.

Durkheim, É. (1965 [1912]) *Elementary Forms of Religious Life*. New York: The Free Press.

Foucault, M. (1966) *The Order of Things: An Archaeology of the Human Sciences*. London: Tavistock.

Foucault, M. (1972 [1969]) *The Archaeology of Knowledge*, trans. A. M. Sheridan Smith. London: Tavistock.

Foucault, M. (1981 [1976]) *The History of Sexuality*, vol. 1, trans. R. Hurley. Harmondsworth: Penguin.

Giddens, A. (1979) *Central Problems in Social Theory*. London: Macmillan.

Giddens, A. (1984) *The Constitution of Society: Outline of the Theory of Structuration*. Berkeley: University of California Press.

Giddens, A. (1987) *Social Theory and Modern Sociology*. Cambridge: Polity.

Hobbes, T. (1943 [1651]) *Leviathan*. London: J. M. Dent.

Jakobson, R. (1962–) *Selected Writings*. The Hogue: Mouton/DeGruyter.

Lacan, J. (1977 [1957]) "The Agency of the Letter in the Unconscious or Reason since Freud," in *Écrits: A Selection*, trans. A. Sheridan. London: Tavistock.

Lacan, J. (1977). *Écrits: A Selection*. New York: Norton.

Lévi-Strauss, C. (1963 [1958]). *Structural Anthropology*, trans. C. Jacobson and B. Grundfest Schoepf. London: Penguin.

Lévi-Strauss, C. (1969 [1949]) *The Elementary Structures of Kinship*, rev. edn., trans. J. H. Bell, J. Richard von Sturmer, ed. R. Needham. London: Eyre & Spottiswoode.

Marx, K. (1978 [1844]) "Estranged Labour," in *The Marx–Engels Reader*, ed. R. Tucker. New York: W. W. Norton.

Marx, K. (1978 [1867]) *Capital*, vol. 1, in *The Marx–Engels Reader*, ed. R. Tucker. New York: W. W. Norton.

Marx, K., and Engels, F. (2005 [1848]) *Manifesto of the Communist Party*. New York: Cosimo.

Mauss, M. (1990 [1924]) *The Gift: Forms and Functions of Exchange in Archaic Societies*. London: Routledge.

Merton, R. (1938) "Social Structure and Anomie." *American Sociological Review* 3: 672–82.

Parsons, T. (1967, 1968 [1937]) *The Structure of Social Action*, vols. 1 and 2. New York: The Free Press.

Saussure, F. de (1974 [1916]) *Course in General Linguistics*, ed. C. Bally and A. Sechehaye, with A. Riedlinger; trans. W. Baskin. London: Fontana.

Wallerstein, I. (1976) *The Modern World-System: Capitalist Agriculture and the Origins of the European World-Economy in the Sixteenth Century*. New York: Academic Press.

7

Actor Network Theory and Material Semiotics

John Law

INTRODUCTION

Actor network theory is a disparate family of material-semiotic tools, sensibilities, and methods of analysis that treat everything in the social and natural worlds as a continuously generated effect of the webs of relations within which they are located. It assumes that nothing has reality or form outside the enactment of those relations. Its studies explore and characterize the webs and the practices that carry them. Like other material-semiotic approaches, the actor network approach thus describes the enactment of materially and discursively heterogeneous relations that produce and reshuffle all kinds of actors including objects, subjects, human beings, machines, animals, "nature," ideas, organizations, inequalities, scale and sizes, and geographical arrangements.

In this chapter I explore this definition, expand upon, and qualify it. I start with four qualifications.

First, it is *possible* to describe actor network theory in the abstract. I've just done so, and this is often done in textbooks. But this misses the point because it is not abstract but is grounded in empirical case studies. We can only understand the approach if we have a sense of those case studies and how these work in practice. Some other parts of social theory (for instance symbolic interactionism) work in the same way, and arguably that's how natural science is too: theory is embedded and extended in empirical practice, and practice itself is necessarily theoretical. This means that if this chapter is not to betray the actor network approach it needs to subvert the definition above by translating it into a set of empirically grounded practices.

Second, the actor network approach is not a theory. Theories usually try to explain why something happens, but actor network theory is descriptive rather than foundational in explanatory terms, which means that it is a disappointment for those seeking strong accounts. Instead it tells stories about "how" relations assemble or don't. As a form, one of several, of material semiotics, it is better understood as a toolkit for telling interesting stories about, and interfering in, those relations. More profoundly, it is a sensibility to the messy practices of relationality and materiality of the world. Along with this sensibility comes a wariness of the large-scale claims common in social theory: these usually seem too simple.

Three, I've talked of "it," an actor network theory, but there is no "it." Rather it is a diaspora that overlaps with other intellectual traditions. As I have already hinted, it is better to talk of "material semiotics" rather than "actor network theory." This better catches the openness, uncertainty, revisability, and diversity of the most interesting work. Thus the actor network successor projects are located in many different case studies, practices, and locations done in many different ways, and draw on a range of theoretical resources. How much those studies relate to one another is chronically uncertain, but this is better read as a sign of the strength of material semiotic sensibilities than as a weakness. In short, actor network theory is not a creed or a dogma and at its best a degree of humility is one of its intellectual leitmotifs.

Fourth, if all the world is relational, then so too are texts. They come from somewhere and tell particular stories about particular relations. This implies the need for a health warning. You should beware of this chapter. I hope that it works and is useful, but it comes from somewhere, rather than everywhere or nowhere. It treats the actor network approach and material semiotics in a particular way. It proposes and seeks to enact a particular version of this animal. Beware, then, of this chapter, but beware even more of any text about actor network theory that pretends to the objectivity of an overall view.

In what follows first I offer a particular account of the intellectual origins of the actor network approach. Second, I characterize what I call "actor network theory 1990." This is the version, with all its strengths and weaknesses, that tends to find its way into textbooks. Then I briefly comment on reactions and responses to this animal. And fourth, I explore aspects of its diasporic creativity since 1995.

ORIGIN STORIES

If the actor network approach started at a particular time and place then this was in Paris between 1978 and 1982. The term, devised by Michel Callon, appeared around 1982, but the approach is itself a network that extends out in time and place, so stories of its origins are necessarily in part arbitrary. They lay claim to and include a particular version of the past created for particular purposes. In this section I tell four stories about its origins. My contention is that much of actor network theory 1990 can be understood as a product of their intersection.

Engineers, managers, and systems

It is obvious to most engineers that systems are made not simply of technical bits and pieces but also include people. Managers know this too, and those who study engineers and managers not infrequently end up thinking similarly. All are "system-sensitive" with a strong sense of relationality. An example.

In the late 1970s and early 1980s Thomas Hughes, historian of technology, wrote about Thomas Edison, engineer and manager, and his new New York electricity supply network. Hughes showed that this was an artful combination of transmission lines, generators, coal supplies, voltages, incandescent filaments, legal maneuvers, laboratory calculations, political muscle, financial instruments, technicians, laboratory assistants, and salesmen. In short, it was a system, and it worked because Edison engineered the bits and pieces together. Hughes emphasizes that the *architecture* of the system was the key. Its individual elements, people or objects, were subordinate to the logic of that architecture, created or reshaped in that system (Hughes 1983).

Edison was successful, but the world of engineering is also filled with failures. In 1980 Michel Callon wrote about one of these: the "electric vehicle." The French electricity monopoly utility, EDF, concluded that the age of hydrocarbons was ending and proposed an electric vehicle powered by accumulators or fuel cells. EDF would make the motor, Renault the car body, and consumers would adapt their lifestyles. In fact the electric vehicle was never produced. The catalysts in the fuel cells got contaminated and failed. Renault didn't fancy the technical and economic demotion implied by the plan. And the town councils didn't want to buy the electric-powered buses that were supposed to popularize the new technology. Callon's problem, which was to become the key problem for actor network theory 1990, was: how can we describe socially and materially heterogeneous systems in all their fragility and obduracy (Callon 1980)? This is the first context for actor network theory.

Exemplars and laboratory practices

Long before this Thomas Kuhn's *The Structure of Scientific Revolutions* (Kuhn 1962) was the focus of fierce debate about the character of science. Did scientists use "paradigms," pragmatic sets of intellectual and practical tools for scientific puzzle-solving? This was Kuhn's view. Or was scientific knowledge a representation of reality produced by a special scientific method? Such was the view of epistemology. In the late 1960s sociologists read Kuhn and created a sociology of scientific knowledge. A paradigm can be understood, they said, as a *culture*. Scientists acquire this culture and use it to guide their puzzle-solving practices. Successful puzzle-solving extends the culture, which thus reflects both physical reality and social practices. But success is a practical matter: the issue is, does the paradigm work or not? In this way of thinking the absolute truth of a theory is irrelevant. Indeed, there is no independent way of knowing it. This led to a methodological dictum, the so-called "principle of symmetry": true and false knowledge, it was said, need to be explained in the same terms (Bloor 1976).

Though actor network theory is very different, it borrows from Kuhn and the sociologists of scientific knowledge. I'll return to the principle of symmetry shortly. First a comment on Kuhn. He said that scientists work through cases, exemplars. Knowing the formalisms isn't enough. You need to know what they mean in practice. Kuhn's book, a set of exemplary case studies, exemplifies this. The sociologists of science worked through exemplary case studies too. And the nascent actor network writers, also within the sociology of science and technology, did the same. This is the basic methodological and philosophical principle that I mentioned in the introduction: knowledge lies in exemplars and words are never enough.

The sociologists of science studied scientists' meanings and their exemplary practices. They practiced a version of interpretive sociology: creative actors, they said, use scientific culture to solve puzzles. But there are other ways of thinking about scientific practice. When Bruno Latour went to the Salk Institute in the mid-1970s his preoccupations were different. Drawing on the work of A. J. Greimas and ethnomethodology, he explored the semiotics of the practices that lead to scientific truth-claims. He noted that in the laboratory most claims about the world are vague and promiscuously mix the social and the natural. "Jones told me that his PhD student saw this blip on the graph, and he suspects it might be a sign that . . ." says a post-doc over coffee. A tiny handful of these suggestions subsequently get transmuted into the much harder statements about nature that circulate in scientific papers ("the figures in the table show . . ."). Latour observed that by the time this has happened the social has disappeared, along with almost everything to do with how the new truth was produced. With most of the messy relations gone we are left with nature, a textual account of nature, and a set of more or less formulaic statements about method that purport to explain why the latter reflects the former. The intermediate and heterogeneous relations of production are deleted to generate two quite distinct and separate domains: reality on the one hand and knowledge of reality on the other (Latour 1993; Latour and Woolgar 1986). It is a system of purification that depends on a heterogeneous web of relations that is subsequently effaced.

Latour does not talk of actor network theory here, but many of its elements are present: materially heterogeneous relations analyzed with semiotic tools; a symmetrical indifference to the truth or otherwise of what it is looking at; concern with the productivity of practice; an interest in circulation; and the predisposition to exemplary case studies; all of these are signatures of actor network theory.

Translation, order, and disorder

So how might we study relationality and its productivity? Latour used Greimas, but he and Michel Callon also drew on philosopher of science Michel Serres. Serres writes about order and disorder. In his world there are patches of order in a sea of disorder. The most interesting places lie on the boundaries between order and disorder, or where different orders rub up against one another. Serres generates endless metaphors for imagining the uncertain messengers that pass between different orders or between order and disorder. Angels, parasites, Hermes, the North-West Passage, all of these make precarious links between places that do not belong to the same world. The notion of *translation* is another of his metaphors (Serres 1974).

To translate is to make two words equivalent. But since no two words *are* equivalent, translation also implies betrayal: *traduction, trahison*. So translation is both about making equivalent, and about shifting. It is about moving terms around, about linking and changing them. Michel Callon articulated this in his study of the electric vehicle and his subsequent work on the scallops of St. Brieuc Bay. The latter is another exemplary actor network case study. It is also notorious because Callon analyzes people and scallops in the same terms. His "generalized symmetry" applies not, as in the sociology of science, to truth and falsity, to epistemology, but to ontology, to the different kinds of actors in the world.

Callon describes how a science of scallops is created with its own researchers, a science that leads to an experimental technology for rearing young scallops. He shows that, as a necessary part of the experiment, fishermen are tamed too: they agree not to trawl near the larvae collectors. This, then, is a web of relations that makes and remakes its components. Fishermen, scallops, and scientists are all being domesticated in a process of translation that relates, defines, and orders objects, human and otherwise. Callon adds that they hold themselves together but they do so precariously. All it takes is for one translation to fail and the whole web of reality unravels. And indeed this is what happens. One winter night the fishermen invade the protected areas, trawl the larval grounds, and destroy the collectors (Callon 1986). In short, translation is always insecure, a process susceptible to failure. Disorder – or other orders – are only precariously kept at bay.

Poststructuralist relationality

Precarious relations, the making of the bits and pieces in those relations, a logic of translation, a concern with materials of different kinds, with how it is that everything hangs together if it does, such are the intellectual concerns of the actor network tradition. However, this is a combination of concerns also found in parts of poststructuralism. My final contextual suggestion is that actor network theory can also be understood as an empirical version of poststructuralism. For instance, "actor networks" can be seen as scaled-down versions of Michel Foucault's discourses or epistemes. Foucault asks us to attend to the productively strategic and relational character of epochal epistemes (Foucault 1979). The actor network approach asks us to explore the strategic, relational, and productive character of particular, smaller-scale, heterogeneous actor networks. We've seen this for the Salk laboratory and for the scallops. Here's another example: Latour's account of the Pasteurization of France.

Pasteur, a hero of French science, is said to have revolutionized French agriculture. For instance, he discovered the cause of anthrax and created a vaccine for the disease. But how did this happen? Was he, as Hughes claimed of Edison, a great man? Latour rejects this because in a material-semiotic world all actions, including those of great men, are relational effects. To show this he charts how a network of domesticated farms, technicians, laboratories, veterinarians, statistics, and bacilli was generated. He describes how they were shaped (in some cases created) in this network. And he shows how the result was generative. Farms were turned into laboratories, vaccines made from attenuated bacteria, cattle stopped dying of anthrax, and Pasteur became a great man (Latour 1988b). All of which were the effects of a set of materially heterogeneous relations.

We are offered an historical account of particular translations through time rather than a diagnosis of an epochal epistemic syntax. Even so the logic is not far removed from Foucault's. It can also be understood as an empirical version of Gilles Deleuze's nomadic philosophy (Deleuze and Guattari 1988). Latour has observed that we might talk of "actant rhizomes" rather than "actor networks," and John

Law has argued that there is little difference between Deleuze's *agencement* (awkwardly translated as "assemblage" in English) and the term "actor network" (Law 2004). Both refer to the provisional assembly of productive, heterogeneous, and (this is the crucial point) quite limited forms of ordering located in no larger overall order. This is why it is helpful to see actor network theory as a particular empirical translation of poststructuralism.

ACTOR NETWORK THEORY 1990

Material-semiotic relationality

The date is arbitrary, it could be 1986 or 1994, but I'm trying to catch a moment when actor network theory achieved recognizable form as a distinctive approach to social theory. A moment when the web of different origins described above had been woven together to craft a workable set of tools carried in a persuasive and well-documented set of case studies. A moment when an agenda, a vocabulary, and a set of ambitions became current. So what *was* "actor network theory 1990"? Here is another exemplary case study.

How did the Portuguese reach India? How did they maintain their imperial control? Conventional histories talk of spices, trade, wealth, military power, and Christianity. With some exceptions they treat technology as an essential but ultimately uninteresting infrastructure. Maritime history talks of innovations in shipbuilding and navigation, but is usually little concerned with the politics or economics of imperialism. In 1986 Law brought the two narratives together. He asked how the Portuguese generated a network that allowed them to control half the world. His answer was that ships, sails, mariners, navigators, stores, spices, winds, currents, astrolabes, stars, guns, ephemeredes, gifts, merchants' drafts were all translated into a web. That web, precarious though it was, gave each component a particular shape or form that was to hold together for 150 years. He added that result was a structure of asymmetry. Like Pasteur's lab in Paris, Lisbon became an obligatory point of passage for a whole set of tributaries. Law also argued, following Latour, that the ships became "immutable mobiles" circulating to and fro in space whilst holding their form and shape constant. This, he said was crucial to the success of the system (Law 1986).

This study displays all the ingredients of actor network theory 1990. There is *semiotic relationality* (it's a network whose elements define and shape one another), *heterogeneity* (there are different kinds of actors, human and otherwise), and *materiality* (stuff is there aplenty, not just "the social"). There is an insistence on *process* and its *precariousness* (all elements need to play their part moment by moment or it all comes unstuck). There is attention to *power* as an effect (it is a function of network configuration and in particular the creation of immutable mobiles), to *space* and to *scale* (how it is that networks extend themselves and translate distant actors). New for actor network theory, there is an interest in large-scale political history. And, crucially, it is a study of *how* the Portuguese network worked: how it held together; how it shaped its components; how it made a center and peripheries; in short, of how differences were generated in a semiotic relational logic.

The erosion of foundations

The single-minded commitment to relationality makes it possible to explore strange and heterogeneous links and follow surprising actors to equally surprising places: ships, bacilli, scallops, and scientific texts (Latour 1987). It highlights practices off-limits or uninteresting to non-semiotic approaches: navigational innovations, biological bench work, the habits of larvae, the practices of farmers, food (Mol and Mesman 1996). It does this by eroding distinctions in kind, ontological distinctions. In short, the toolkit can be understood as a powerful set of devices for leveling divisions usually taken to be foundational. These are demoted and treated as the effect of translations. Human and non-human, meaning and materiality, big and small, macro and micro, social and technical, nature and culture – these are just some of the dualisms undone by this relationality. Obviously this posthumanism is intellectually radical and often controversial. Let me, then, talk of some of these disappearing dualisms.

In actor network webs the distinction between *human* and *nonhuman* is of little initial analytical importance: people are relational effects that include both the human and the nonhuman (think, for instance, of "Pasteur") while object webs conversely include people (ephemeredes). Particular networks may end up being labeled "human" or "nonhuman" but this is a secondary matter. Here then, as with Foucault, there is a powerful if controversial nonhumanist relational and semiotic logic at work quite unlike that of humanist sociology. It is obnoxious to those who take people to be morally special, and intellectually flawed for those who frame the social in terms of meaning and intersubjectivity (Collins and Yearley 1992). For the latter a relational semiotics misses out on what it is that constitutes the social. More generally, humanists simply find it difficult to grasp the intellectual single-mindedness of this logic of relationality. Sometimes, for instance, they misunderstand its empirical studies as examples of foundational sociology, assuming that social categories are being used as an explanatory resource. But in the material semiotics of actor network theory the social is also being reworked (Latour 2005).

Again, the distinction between *big* and *small* is a relational effect. Callon and Latour (1981: 229) observe that "[i]t is no more difficult to send tanks into Kabul than to dial 999." Their point is that the same relational logics apply at any scale. Whether we are "big" or "small," the largest part of the webs we draw on and allow us to act are hidden. An actor is always a network of elements that it does not fully recognize or know: simplification or "black boxing" is a necessary part of agency. This implies that the notion of "level" is also a relational effect. To put it differently, and following the Deleuzian logic mentioned above, there is no overall social, natural, or conceptual framework or scale within which events take place: as webs grow they tend to grow their own metrics. But then, without a foundational macro and micro the distinction between macro- and micro-sociologies similarly makes little sense except as a performative effect of those sociologies (Law 2000): class, nation-state, patriarchy become effects rather than explanatory foundations. This is not to say that they are not real – they may indeed be *made* real in practice – but they offer no framework for explanation.

Some of the other disappearing dualisms are less contentious. We have seen that the *social* and the *technical* are embedded in each other. This means that it simply isn't possible to explore the social without at the same time studying the hows of relational materiality. Sociologists sometimes experience this as a diversion from serious social analysis. Why, they wonder, does actor network theory obsess over material minutiae? Why doesn't it look at what is important? The response to this is the counter-complaint that many sociologies have little sense of how the social is done or holds together. They ignore the material practices that generate the social: ships, sailors, currents. They simply move too quickly to a non-material version of the social.

This leads back to another distinction mentioned above. Sociology is usually interested in the *whys* of the social. It grounds its explanations in somewhat stable agents or frameworks. Actor network's material semiotics explore the *hows*. In this non-foundational world nothing is sacred and nothing is necessarily fixed. But this in turn represents a challenge: what might replace the foundations that have been so cheerfully undone? Is it possible to say anything about network-stabilizing regularities, or are we simply left with describing cases, case by case? Actor network theory 1990 responded to this challenge in the only non-foundational way it could, by exploring the logics of network architecture and looking for configurations that might lead to relative stability. Arguably it did this in three different though overlapping ways.

Durability after foundations

Material durability.   There is a straightforward way in which some materials last longer than others. It is easier to imprison people if there are prison walls while, unlike traffic patrols, sleeping policemen are never off duty (Callon and Latour 1992). So the first argument is that social arrangements delegated into non-bodily physical form tend to hold their shape better than those that simply depend on face-to-face interaction. But note the caveat, "tend to": everything is a relational effect. Prison walls work better if they are part of a network including guards and penal bureaucracies, while knotted bedsheets or the sheer passage of time will subvert them. As with Bentham's panopticon, in the end it is the configuration of the web that produces durability. Stability does not inhere in materials themselves.

Strategic durability.   Think again of the Portuguese maritime network. Over a long period the Portuguese experimented with novel designs for vessels suitable for exploration and exploitation. They also, and as a matter of explicit royal policy, created a system of celestial navigation. These were deliberate strategies to create a durable network. Equally important for network stability was the translation of strategies developed in other networks. Examples include the art of growing spices, and the desire of Arab mariners to avoid lethal confrontations. Such strategically durable configurations were translated whole and "black boxed" into the Portuguese web. How they worked was of little direct interest, though mostly indeed they were durable and reliable.

Do these options exhaust the strategic possibilities? The answer is, arguably not. In practice the actor network conception of strategy can be understood more broadly to include teleologically ordered patterns of relations indifferent to human intentions. For the Portuguese examples include the actions of the currents and the winds in the South Atlantic that, year after year, more or less reliably pursued their own telos on an annual pattern. Again, with this third form of durability, the actor network position resonates with that of Foucault, who tells us that strategy is not necessarily located in human deliberation. In short, for a material semiotics teleology may not reside in human intentions.

Discursive stability.   Another case study. How does an organization hold itself together? This was Law's question in 1990 in his ethnography of a large scientific laboratory. He concluded that the managers worked in a series of different logics, four in number. Sometimes they were entrepreneurs, sometimes bureaucrats, sometimes Kuhnian puzzle-solvers, and sometimes they dabbled in charisma. Law argued that this was not a matter of individual character but of different modes of ordering that extended through people to include technologies and organizational arrangements. Enterprise, for instance, generated self-reliant individualism and demands for performance, organizational cost centers, and management accountancy systems. Bureaucracy, quite differently, generated a Weberian respect for administrative due process, organization as a set of competent offices, and an accounting system designed to prevent fraud (Law 1994).

Law was borrowing from Foucault: the modes of ordering are mini-discourses. But what has this to do with stability? The answer comes in two parts. First, as Foucault insists, discourses define conditions of possibility, making some ways of ordering webs of relations easier and others difficult or impossible. In the UK in 1990 "enterprise" and "bureaucracy" were standard ordering strategies easy to enact both because they were known to managers and because they were standard ways of interacting with other organizations. Second, the fact that they are different also contributes to stability. This is because every discourse sets limits to its conditions of possibility so it cannot recognize certain kinds of realities. But those realities exist and they have to be handled. For instance, the laboratory needed bureaucracy but would have been strangled by red tape if this had been the only ordering mode. It likewise depended on enterprise, but would have run the risk of illegality if it had ordered itself in this way alone. It was the multi-discursive ordering of the laboratory that secured its relative stability. When one mode of ordering became problematic others might be more effective. And this was the third non-foundational way for understanding configurational stability developed within actor network 1990, and it foreshadows the move away from centering that characterizes much subsequent material-semiotic work.

RESPONSES AND REACTIONS

I've suggested that actor network theory's refusal of essential foundations was unacceptable to many. Since this, and especially the issue of humanism and nonhumanism, is primarily a metaphysical quarrel perhaps all we can do is to note the difference and move on. But there are other critical stories about actor network 1990. Here are three. First, it was argued that its studies were often centered, managerialist, and even military in character, attending to the powerful, sometimes in functionalist and masculinist mode (Star 1991). Second, it was suggested that the approach effaced whatever could not be translated into network terms, so failing to recognize its own role as an intellectual technology of Othering (Lee and Brown

1994). And third, it was argued that it was not very aware of its own politics, and in particular of the political agendas of its own stories (Haraway 1997).

In response it is possible to offer counter-narratives. First, Latour's work on Pasteur shows the latter to be a network effect rather than a shaping genius. Law's managers are similarly treated not as heroes but products of multiple and decentered discourses. In both studies the authors are trying to deconstruct power by "studying up" rather than down. Second, Latour's laboratory ethnography is an explicit attempt to reject the Othering of French colonial anthropology by applying its techniques (which he originally applied in the classrooms of the Côte d'Ivoire) to high-status scientific knowledge. More studying up rather than down. If there is a difference between the West and the Rest it is, Latour tells us, not because the Rest is radically Other, but because the West has accumulated a series of small and practical techniques that generate cumulative advantage (Latour 1990). Third, it is too simple to say that actor network has no interest in the origins and construction of its own accounts. Steve Woolgar, who cannot quite be claimed for actor network theory though he co-authored the Salk laboratory study (Latour and Woolgar 1979), raised questions of reflexivity for science studies (Woolgar 1991). Amongst others Latour and Law took up his challenge and wrote in reflexive mode (Latour 1988c: 1996; Law 1994), thus exploring what science studies writing does, what it helps to bring into being – a continuing preoccupation to which I return below.

I could go on: there are rebuttals to each of these counter-narratives. But let me ask what we are *doing* if we write like this. One response is that we are assuming that something called "actor network theory" deserves criticism or defense. But do we want to add succor to this assumption? I have argued that the approach is not a single entity but a multiplicity. I have also argued that it is embedded in case studies. If this is right, then general criticisms or defenses of "the approach" are likely to mistranslate its epistemic and practical import. A second answer takes the form of a question. How useful it is to live in an intellectual world defined by criticism, defense, and the desire to "win" arguments? This is a complicated question, but one way of translating it is to ask whether we really think that there is a single intellectual and political space to be "won." Perhaps if we wash away this assumption we might conceive of theoretical intersections differently: as a set of possibly generative partial connections. And this is how I will proceed. My interest is in how the material-semiotic traditions have interfered with one another to articulate new intellectual tools, sensibilities, questions, and versions of politics. The metaphor here is intellectually and politically polytheistic rather than monotheistic: there are, I assume, various truths and various politics. In the final diasporic section of this chapter I articulate a small number of these. Many others, for instance to do with bodies, passions, and spatialities, I exclude purely for reasons of space (Gomart 2002; Gomart and Hennion 1999; Hennion 2001; Law and Mol 2001).

Diaspora

Enactment

Crucial to the new material semiotics is performativity. It is helpful to start with another case study.

How are strawberries bought and sold? Is it possible to drive out inefficiencies and create a perfect market? In Fontaine-en-Sologne in France in 1981 the answer to these questions takes physical and organizational form. In a two-storey building the ground floor is for those selling strawberries, and the first floor for those buying them. Crucial is the fact that buyers and sellers cannot see one another. Equally important is the fact that everyone in both rooms is attending to a single market transaction. This takes the material form of a large electronic display visible to all, which describes the lot being sold, and the level of the current bid. Both buyers and sellers can also see the auctioneer as he sits in his cabin. The prices start high and fall until the lot in question finds a buyer and the price is fixed. If it falls too low the seller can withdraw his strawberries. To repeat, buyers and sellers don't talk with one another directly. They aren't supposed to fix deals in private. The market is intended to be unified and transparent. In short, it is supposed to reproduce the conditions of perfect competition (Garcia 1986; Garcia-Parpet 2007).

This study doesn't belong to actor network: its author was a student of Pierre Bourdieu's. However, it has been assimilated to material semiotics by Callon. Understood in actor network terms it tells of the creation of a heterogeneous, material-semiotic reality that enacts an approximation to a perfect market (Callon 1998a, 2007). This is instructive for a number of reasons: it tells us that "the market" should not be regarded as a state of nature; it suggests, like economic anthropology, that markets will take different forms in different places (Callon 1998b); and, most important for my story, it tells us that neoclassical economics is not real until it is *enacted into being* (MacKenzie, Muniesa, and Siu 2007). In short, we are in the realm of performativity. Economics in theory is all very well, but economics in practice is different. And theory is only translated into practice if it is enacted – in practice. We saw this in the Salk laboratory and for the Pasteurization of France. Now we see it for economics. To understand markets we need to trace how the webs of heterogeneous material and social practices produce them. It is *these* that are performative, that generate realities.

Something seismic is happening here. A vital metaphorical and explanatory shift is taking place. We are no longer dealing with *construction*, social or otherwise: there is no stable prime mover, social or individual, to construct anything, no builder, no puppeteer. Pasteur, we have seen, is an effect rather than a cause. Rather we are dealing with *enactment* or *performance*. In this heterogeneous world everything plays its part, relationally. The shift is easily misunderstood, but it is crucial. The metaphor of construction – and social construction – will no longer serve. Buyers, sellers, noticeboards, strawberries, spatial arrangements, economic theories, and rules of conduct – all of these assemble and together enact a set of practices that make a more or less precarious reality.

Multiplicity

The move to performativity has strange consequences. Here is another case study.

Annemarie Mol's book, *The Body Multiple*, describes diagnostic and treatment practices for lower limb atherosclerosis. The condition turns up in different forms in different places: in the surgery it presents as pain on walking; in radiography as appears as an X-ray photo of narrowed or blocked blood vessels; in the ultrasound department it takes the form of Doppler readings which detect increases in blood speeds at narrowed sections of vessels; and in the operating theater it manifests itself as a white paste scraped out of blood vessels by the surgeon (Mol 2002). It is tempting to say that these are different perspectives on a single disease. This, however, is precisely what Mol rejects. In material-semiotic mode, she argues that each practice generates its *own* material reality. This means that for atherosclerosis there are four actor networks or realities rather than one. Then she says that how these relate together, if they do so at all, is itself a practical matter. Sometimes, and for a time, they may be coordinated into a single reality, but often this does not happen. So Mol's claim is simple but counterintuitive. In theory the body may be *single* but in practice it is *multiple* because there are many body practices and therefore many bodies.

We have seen how the studies of actor network theory 1990 describe the more or less precarious generation of realities. Mol has pushed this logic one step further by washing away a single crucial assumption: that successful translation generates a single coordinated network and a single coherent reality. Any such coherence, if it happens at all, is a momentary achievement. The logic is Serres-like: most of the time and for most purposes practices produce chronic multiplicity. They *may* dovetail together, but equally they may be held apart, contradict, or include one another in complex ways.

How do different realities relate together? How might we think of these partial connections (Strathern 1991)? And then, a new question, how might this patchwork of realities be enacted in better ways? These are the questions that arise if we combine the insistence that realities are enacted with the discovery that they are enacted differently in different places. First the issue of how realities relate.

Fluidity

The answer is: in complex ways. We have encountered this question already in Law's account of the laboratory managers. Is the laboratory organized in a single way? No, says Law: there are multiple modes of ordering, multiple realities, and it works precisely because these are irreducible to one another (see also Law 2002). The idea there are different logics is basic, too, to Latour who has written of different regimes of enunciation including religion (Latour 1999), science, and the law. It takes feminist form in the work of Vicky Singleton on ambivalence in public health programs (Singleton 1998; Singleton and Michael 1993). So this is one way of thinking about it. Realities hold solid by relating though discontinuity, or by Othering one another (Law and Singleton 2005). But perhaps they also hold together because they flow into one another. Madeleine Akrich hints at this in her work on technology transfer: rigid technologies don't translate successfully from the North to the South (Akrich 1992). Another case study builds on her work by exploring a fluid technology.

In the villages of Zimbabwe pure water is a problem. But one kind of effective pump is widely distributed and used in rural areas. Quite simple, it is manufactured in Harare and sold in kit form to village collectives. Before they install it villagers need to drill a borehole with a surrounding concrete apron. Then they attach the base of the pump to the apron and lower the most important working part of the pump, its piston, levers, and plunger, down the borehole on the end of a long rod. Then a handle is attached to the head, and the pump is ready for use (de Laet and Mol 2000).

The pump is a success. It is widespread, and the water that it pumps is cleaner than water from alternative sources. But it is also successful for two further reasons. First, it is very simple. Years of experience have gone into paring it down to a minimum. Second, and more important for my story, it is malleable. When the seals in the pistons fail the leather may be replaced bits of rubber tire. If the rods going down the well are too heavy, they can be replaced with lighter alternatives. If the bolts come loose it is surprisingly tolerant: often it just keeps on working. Mechanically it is malleable. And its success as a source of clean water is malleable too. Sometimes this is measured in bacteria counts, but more often than not the indicator is disease – or relative lack of it.

This is a *fluid technology*. It doesn't work by insisting on rigidity and translating every village into a design created in Harare. Neither does it work by forcing villagers to visit Harare for spare parts. Instead it changes shape – it is a *mutable mobile* rather than the kind of immutable mobile described by Law when he talked of the Portuguese ships. So as we read the study, first we learn something about objects: these may reconfigure themselves. Second, we learn that different realities may be loosely rather than rigidly associated. And third, we learn that material semiotics does not have to imagine a single actor network: that we have moved on from the core preoccupations of actor network 1990. Webs may be partially associated in endless different ways but the need for a center has gone.

Realities and goods

What happens when different enacted realities overlap? Charis Cussins takes us to the Amboseli National Park in Kenya. This is the question: how should the elephants be handled, and how should people relate to them? One of the issues is overgrazing. There are too many elephants in the park. They need to be culled, or they need to be tolerated beyond the boundaries of the park. But beyond those boundaries they damage Maasai agriculture. What to do about this (Thompson 2002)?

There is controversy. On the one hand there are animal behaviorists. They've been studying elephants for a long time and think that these have rights that should be protected. They point to the international scientific journals where they publish their findings, and argue that that the Amboseli elephants are a unique scientific resource for animal behavior studies. They think that culling is appropriate for management purposes, and they also think that while local people should be compensated for damage they shouldn't be allowed to kill elephants in revenge. Indeed, they are generally distrustful of the local people, who they think will act in ways that undermine conservation. For the same reason they are distrustful of economic development: other than safari tourism, conservation and development coexist badly. In practice they want to keep most of the elephants in the park most of the time, but they also want to rent buffer zones to allow some degree of migration.

On the other hand there are conservation biologists. They think that elephants play a key role in conservation: at the right density, neither too high nor too low, they foster biodiversity. They are less interested in knowledge published in international journals than in local ways of witnessing and authenticating links between elephant density and biodiversity. So, for instance, they drive visitors – scientists, tourists, wildlife managers, and locals – from site to site so that they can see the differences in tree density. Then they think that both elephants and local people are stakeholders. Both are actively involved in conservation in practice, and both *need* to be involved and indeed to coexist if long-term conservation is to be achieved. This will involve development and the creation of profitable forms of land use including tourism, some sustainable hunting, and the migration of elephants beyond the park.

This is material semiotics at work. Two realities are counterposed, and those realities are heterogeneous, combining and enacting the natural, the social, and the political. But Thompson breaks "the social" and "the natural" down further. There are *legal* issues to do with rights and responsibilities. There are *land use* questions. There are *economic* concerns about development. There are scientific or *epistemic* tensions about the nature of proper knowledge. And then, finally and most important for my story, there are normative or *moral* issues. How should elephants and the Maasai be treated? What *kinds* of beings are they?

We've seen that material semiotics explores the enactment of realities, the *ontological*. We've also seen that it describes the making of knowledge, the *epistemological*. With Thompson's study this philosophical list grows again, for she shows that practices are also about the doing of *goods*. Goods (or bads), knowledges, and realities, all are being enacted together: this is one of the ways the material-semiotic sensibility leads us into the diaspora.

An ontological politics

There is nowhere to hide beyond the performativity of the webs. But since our own stories weave further webs, it is never the case that they simply describe. They too enact realities and versions of the better and the worse, the right and the wrong, the appealing and the unappealing. There is no innocence. The good is being done as well as the epistemological and the ontological.

Actor network 1990 knew this in theory (Latour 1988a) though it sometimes forgot it in practice. It was forcibly reminded of its non-innocence by Donna Haraway in her own much more explicitly political material semiotics (Haraway 1991a, 1991b). We make realities, she said. They only question is: what kind of difference do we want to make? Material-semiotic writers have responded to this question in different ways. Haraway uses tropes – most famously the cyborg – that interfere with and undermine politically and ethically obnoxious realities. Latour talks of "ontopolitics" (Hinchliffe et al. 2005; Stengers 1997) and of a "parliament of things" where what is real, and how these things might live together, are provisionally determined (Latour 1993, 2004a). Mol talks of "ontological politics" in the specific context of healthcare (Mol 1999). STS feminist writer Moser defends practice-based versions of dementia (Moser 2007). Postcolonial STS writer Helen Verran talks of the ontic softening that would help encounters between the realities of Western technoscience and indigenous knowledge systems (Verran 1998, 2001). And Law, resisting the idea that the different versions of the real can be brought together at a single site of representation, offers methodological tools for partial connection (Law 2004).

There are important differences in the scope and the character of these political visions, but most are specific. Such is what one would expect in the performative, multiple, and partially connected world of material semiotics: there are no general solutions. Latour's non-modern constitution is perhaps an exception, but Haraway's tropic bending leads us to specific Politics with a capital P, both with the cyborg and her subsequent writing on companion species (Haraway 2003). Mol's ontological politics is healthcare located. Walking therapy is cheaper than surgery and often more effective in treating lower limb atherosclerosis. (More recently she has defended "care" against individualist models for practicing diabetes control; Mol 2008). Moser's interventions in dementia are also specific, as are Verran's postcolonial visions which have to do with counting in Yoruba classrooms, and land use and ownership in Australia.

But if the differences between these visions are important, so too are the similarities. This new material semiotics insists that the stories of social theory are performative, not innocent. It also assumes that reality is not destiny. With great difficulty what is real may be remade. And it is with this thought, the possibility and the difficulty of living and doing the real, that I end. The relational semiotic diaspora insists that the good and the bad are embedded in the real, and the real in the good and the bad. To describe the real is always an ethically charged act. But, and this is the crucial point, the two are only partially connected: goods and reals cannot be reduced to each other. An act of political will can never, by itself, overturn the endless and partially connected webs that enact the real. Deconstruction is not enough. Indeed, it is trivial (Latour 2004b). The conclusion is inescapable: as we write we have a simultaneous responsibility both to the real and to the good. Such is the challenge faced by this diasporic material semiotics. To create and recreate ways of working in and on the real while simultaneously working well in and on the good.

Acknowledgment

I am grateful to Annemarie Mol, Ingunn Moser, and Vicky Singleton for sustained intellectual support.

Bibliography

Akrich, M. (1992) "The De-Scription of Technical Objects," in W. E. Bijker and J. Law (eds.), *Shaping Technology, Building Society: Studies in Sociotechnical Change.* Cambridge, MA: MIT Press.

Bloor, D. (1976) *Knowledge and Social Imagery.* London: Routledge & Kegan Paul.

Callon, M. (1980) "Struggles and Negotiations to Define What Is Problematic and What Is Not: The Sociology of Translation," in K. D. Knorr, R. Krohn, and R. D. Whitley (eds.), *The Social Process of Scientific Investigation: Sociology of the Sciences Yearbook,* 4. Dordrecht and Boston: Reidel.

Callon, M. (1986) "Some Elements of a Sociology of Translation: Domestication of the Scallops and the Fishermen of Saint Brieuc Bay," in J. Law (ed.), *Power, Action and Belief: A New Sociology of Knowledge?* Sociological Review Monograph 32. London: Routledge & Kegan Paul.

Callon, M. (1998a) "Introduction: the Embeddedness of Economic Markets in Economics," in M. Callon (ed.), *The Laws of the Markets*. Oxford: Blackwell; Keele: The Sociological Review.

Callon, M. (ed.) (1998b) *The Laws of the Markets*. Oxford: Blackwell; Keele: The Sociological Review.

Callon, M. (2007) "What Does It Mean to Say that Economics Is Performative?," in D. MacKenzie, F. Muniesa, and L. Siu (eds.), *Do Economists Make Markets? On the Performativity of Economics*. Princeton: Princeton University Press.

Callon, M., and Latour, B. (1981) "Unscrewing the Big Leviathan: How Actors Macrostructure Reality and How Sociologists Help Them To Do So," in K. D. Knorr-Cetina and A. V. Cicourel (eds.), *Advances in Social Theory and Methodology: Toward an Integration of Micro- and Macro-Sociologies*. Boston: Routledge & Kegan Paul.

Callon, M., and Latour, B. (1992) "Don't Throw the Baby Out with the Bath School! A Reply to Collins and Yearley," in A. Pickering (ed.), *Science as Practice and Culture*. Chicago: Chicago University Press.

Collins, H. M., and Yearley, S. (1992) "Epistemological Chicken," in A. Pickering (ed.), *Science as Practice and Culture*. Chicago: Chicago University Press.

de Laet, M., and Mol, A. (2000) "The Zimbabwe Bush Pump: Mechanics of a Fluid Technology." *Social Studies of Science* 30(2): 225–63.

Deleuze, G., and Guattari, F. (1988) *A Thousand Plateaus: Capitalism and Schizophrenia*. London: Athlone.

Foucault, M. (1979) *Discipline and Punish: The Birth of the Prison*. Harmondsworth: Penguin.

Garcia, M.-F. (1986) "La Construction sociale d'un marché parfait: Le Marché au cadran de Fontaines en Sologne." *Actes de la Recherche en Sciences Sociales* 65: 2–13.

Garcia-Parpet, M.-F. (2007) "The Social Construction of a Perfect Market: The Strawberry Auction at Fontaines-en-Sologne," in D. MacKenzie, F. Muniesa, and L. Siu (eds.), *Do Economists Make Markets? On the Performativity of Economics*. Princeton: Princeton University Press.

Gomart, E. (2002) "Methadone: Six Effects in Search of a Substance." *Social Studies of Science* 32: 93–135.

Gomart, E., and Hennion, A. (1999) "A Sociology of Attachment: Music Amateurs and Drug Addicts," in J. Law and J. Hassard (eds.), *Actor Network Theory and After*. Oxford: Blackwell; Keele: The Sociological Review.

Haraway, D. J. (1991a) "A Cyborg Manifesto: Science, Technology and Socialist Feminism in the Late Twentieth Century," in D. Haraway (ed.), *Simians, Cyborgs and Women: The Reinvention of Nature*. London: Free Association Books.

Haraway, D. J. (1991b) "Situated Knowledges: The Science Question in Feminism and the Privilege of Partial Perspective," in D. Haraway (ed.), *Simians, Cyborgs and Women: the Reinvention of Nature*. London: Free Association Books.

Haraway, D. J. (1997) *Modest_Witness@Second_Millennium.Female_Man©_Meets_Oncomouse™: Feminism and Technoscience*. New York and London: Routledge.

Haraway, D. J. (2003) *The Companion Species Manifesto: Dogs, People, and Significant Otherness*. Chicago: Prickly Paradigm Press.

Hennion, A. (2001) "Music Lovers: Taste as Performance." *Theory, Culture and Society* 18: 1–22.

Hinchliffe, S., et al. (2005) "Urban Wild Things: A Cosmopolitical Experiment." *Society and Space* 23(5): 643–58.

Hughes, T. P. (1983) *Networks of Power: Electrification in Western Society, 1880–1930*. Baltimore: Johns Hopkins University Press.

Kuhn, T. S. (1962) *The Structure of Scientific Revolutions*. Chicago: Chicago University Press.

Latour, B. (1987) *Science in Action: How to Follow Scientists and Engineers through Society*. Milton Keynes: Open University Press.

Latour, B. (1988a) *Irréductions*, published with *The Pasteurisation of France*. Cambridge, MA: Harvard University Press.

Latour, B. (1988b) *The Pasteurization of France*. Cambridge, MA: Harvard University Press.

Latour, B. (1988c) "The Politics of Explanation: An Alternative," in S. Woolgar (ed.), *Knowledge and Reflexivity: New Frontiers in the Sociology of Knowledge*. London: Sage.

Latour, B. (1990) "Drawing Things Together," in M. Lynch and S. Woolgar (eds.), *Representation in Scientific Practice*. Cambridge, MA: MIT Press.

Latour, B. (1993) *We Have Never Been Modern*. Brighton: Harvester Wheatsheaf.

Latour, B. (1996) *Aramis, or the Love of Technology*. Cambridge, MA: MIT Press.

Latour, B. (1999) " 'Thou Shalt Not Take the Lord's Name in Vain' – Being a Sort of Sermon on the Hesitations of Religious Speech." *Res* 39: 215–34, also available at <www.bruno-latour.fr/articles/article/079.html>.

Latour, B. (2004a) *Politics of Nature: How to Bring the Sciences into Democracy*, Cambridge, MA: Harvard University Press.

Latour, B. (2004b) "Why Has Critique Run out of Steam? From Matters of Fact to Matters of Concern." *Critical Inquiry* 30: 225–48; also available at <http://www.ensmp.fr/~latour/articles/article/089.html>.

Latour, B. (2005) *Reassembling the Social: An Introduction to Actor network theory*. Oxford: Oxford University Press.

Latour, B., and Woolgar, S. (1979) *Laboratory Life: The Social Construction of Scientific Facts*. Beverly Hills: Sage.

Latour, B., and Woolgar, S. (1986) *Laboratory Life: The Construction of Scientific Facts*, 2nd edn. Princeton: Princeton University Press.

Law, J. (1986) "On the Methods of Long Distance Control: Vessels, Navigation and the Portuguese Route to India," in J. Law (ed.), *Power, Action and Belief: A New Sociology of Knowledge?* Sociological Review Monograph 32. London: Routledge & Kegan Paul.

Law, J. (1994) *Organizing Modernity*. Oxford: Blackwell.

Law, J. (2000) "Transitivities." *Society and Space* 18: 133–48.

Law, J. (2002) *Aircraft Stories: Decentering the Object in Technoscience*. Durham, NC: Duke University Press.

Law, J. (2004) *After Method: Mess in Social Science Research*. London: Routledge.

Law, J., and Mol, A. (2001) "Situating Technoscience: An Inquiry into Spatialities." *Society and Space* 19: 609–21.

Law, J., and Singleton, V. (2005) "Object Lessons." *Organization* 12(3): 331–55.

Lee, N., and Brown, S. D. (1994) "Otherness and the Actor Network: The Undiscovered Continent." *American Behavioural Scientist* 36: 772–90.

MacKenzie, D., Muniesa, F., and Siu, L. (eds.) (2007) *Do Economists Make Markets? On the Performativity of Economics*. Princeton: Princeton University Press.

Mol, A. (1999) "Ontological Politics: A Word and Some Questions," in J. Law and J. Hassard (eds.), *Actor Network Theory and After*. Oxford: Blackwell; Keele: The Sociological Review.

Mol, A. (2002) *The Body Multiple: Ontology in Medical Practice*. Durham, NC: Duke University Press.

Mol, A. (2008) "The Logic of Care: Active Patients and the Limits of Choice." Under consideration.

Mol, A., and Mesman, J. (1996) "Neonatal Food and the Politics of Theory: Some Questions of Method." *Social Studies of Science* 26: 419–44.

Moser, I. (2007) "Making Alzheimer's Disease Matter: Enacting, Interfering and Doing Politics of Nature." *Geoforum*.

Serres, M. (1974) *La Traduction: Hermes III*. Paris: Les Éditions de Minuit.

Singleton, V. (1998) "Stabilizing Instabilities: The Role of the Laboratory in the United Kingdom Cervical Screening Programme," in M. Berg and A. Mol (eds.), *Differences in Medicine: Unravelling Practices, Techniques and Bodies*. Durham, NC: Duke University Press.

Singleton, V., and Michael, M. (1993) "Actor-Networks and Ambivalence: General Practitioners in the UK Cervical Screening Programme." *Social Studies of Science* 23: 227–64.

Star, S. L. (1991) "Power, Technologies and the Phenomenology of Conventions: On Being Allergic to Onions," in J. Law (ed.), *A Sociology of Monsters? Essays on Power, Technology and Domination*, Sociological Review Monograph 38, London: Routledge.

Stengers, I. (1997) *Power and Invention: Situating Science*. Minneapolis: University of Minnesota Press.

Strathern, M. (1991) *Partial Connections*. Savage, MD: Rowman & Littlefield.

Thompson, C. (2002) "When Elephants Stand for Competing Models of Nature," in J. Law and Annemarie Mol (eds.), *Complexity in Science, Technology, and Medicine*. Durham, NC: Duke University Press.

Verran, H. (1998) "Re-imagining Land Ownership in Australia." *Postcolonial Studies* 1(2): 237–54.

Verran, H. (2001) *Science and an African Logic*. Chicago: Chicago University Press.

Woolgar, S. (1991) "Configuring the User: The Case of Usability Trials," in J. Law (ed.), *A Sociology of Monsters? Essays on Power, Technology and Domination*, Sociological Review Monograph 38, London: Routledge.

8

Ethnomethodology and Social Theory

RICHARD A. HILBERT

Over the last 40 years, ethnomethodological studies have reported some remarkable discoveries and provided indispensable insights into the workings of society and social systems. At the same time, ethnomethodologists remain ambivalent regarding general conclusions one can properly draw from their studies or how their studies inform general theory. This ambivalence extends not only to how ethnomethodologists might theorize their own empirical investigations but also to what their empirical investigations imply for social theory as practiced by other social scientists. Efforts to resolve the ambivalence are almost always cautious, whether as bold efforts to theorize ethnomethodology or as informed skepticism as to whether ethnomethodology ought to be theorized at all. Thus a perennial question mirroring classical tensions between empiricism and logical reasoning haunts ethnomethodology: when can we make general claims about diverse ethnomethodological studies and when are we making up fictions?

Precise answers to such questions are hard to come by. To begin with, "ethnomethodology" does not name a theoretical perspective or a body of substantive claims. The term derives from a collection of investigations conducted by UCLA sociologist Harold Garfinkel in the 1950s and 1960s published in 1967 under the title *Studies in Ethnomethodology*, universally taken to be ethnomethodology's foundational text. The book makes scarce mention of social theory informing the text, and Garfinkel is often inclined toward defining ethnomethodology as no different than the corpus of those studies, and studies like them, as though the empirical details of the studies speak for themselves (cf. Garfinkel and Wieder 1992: 205). At the same time, however, *Studies* is laden with theoretical vision, lengthy discourses about social phenomenologist Alfred Schutz, and express indebtedness to Aron Gurwitsch and Edmund Husserl, among others.

Subsequent early studies by Garfinkel's students and colleagues promoted methodological orientations to the social world which one might easily read as theoretical, and they often included outright theoretical commentary both challenging and relevant to general sociology (Bittner 1965, 1967; Pollner 1974; Sudnow 1967;

Wieder 1970; Zimmerman and Pollner 1970; Zimmerman and Wieder 1970). However, none of this was systematic or put boldly forward as strong theoretical claims, which no doubt contributed to confusion among non-ethnomethodologists as to what ethnomethodologists could possibly be talking about (see Coser 1975 and Zimmerman's [1976] reply; also Denzin [1969, 1970] and Zimmerman and Wieder's [1970] reply; cf. Maynard 1986). In response to such confusion, some early enthusiasts of the new scholarship stated outright that "No unifying resolution of these disparate 'theories' and 'methods' [within ethnomethodology] need be attempted" (Mehan and Wood 1975: 152). Later, accumulating ethnomethodological studies of the *in situ* character of practical action began to formalize important reasons why such studies could not, and should not, contribute toward general understandings of the substantive matters they investigate (Button 1991; Watson and Seiler 1992). Also, conversation analysis, perhaps ethnomethodology's most important sub-specialty, made great strides in revealing counterintuitive practices in the detailed work of ordinary talk that would not have been possible without a disciplined "indifference" (see Garfinkel and Sacks 1970: 345–6) to whatever general claims one might otherwise be inclined to make about the matters at hand for conversants themselves – roles, statuses, professions, gender, relationships, social organization, structural matters of all sorts, as well as "meaning" and the mind of the actor (Schegloff 1987; Wilson 1991; cf. Sacks, Schegloff, and Jefferson 1974).

More recently Garfinkel (2002) has restated misgivings about general theory, characterizing "the worldwide social science movement" as multiple variations of what he calls Formal Analysis. Their commonality, he says, resides in their unwillingness to see social order in "the concreteness of things." Rather, they find order as outcomes of methodological procedures by which they transform "the concreteness of things" into categorical phenomena legislated by the terms and protocols of their respective disciplines. Thus the "concreteness" of what they study, as well as their own actual real-time methods of transformation, escapes notice. This argument is an extension of one made earlier (Garfinkel 1988), directed specifically at Talcott Parsons, where Garfinkel states that Parsons assumed that "the real and actual society . . . is *not* to be found in the concreteness of things" but only as the product of theorizing and transforming the real society into an accomplished artifact, a stance he calls, in this earlier article, "formal, constructive analysis" (p. 106; cf. Garfinkel and Sacks 1970: 340).

Yet in the same earlier paper critical of Parsons, Garfinkel (1988: 104) attributes the very origins of ethnomethodology to Parsons's *The Structure of Social Action*:

> Ethnomethodology has its origins in this wonderful book. Its earliest initiatives were taken from these texts. Ethnomethodologists have continued to consult its text to understand the practices and the achievements of formal analysis in the work of professional social science.
>
> Inspired by *The Structure of Social Action* ethnomethodology undertook the task of respecifying the production and accountability of immortal, ordinary society.

This in itself came as no surprise to sociologists who knew of Garfinkel's history with Parsons at Harvard University, including the latter's supervision of his PhD dissertation. Ethnomethodology's embeddedness in Parsonian theory had been well known, though hardly well published prior to 1984 (but see Cuff, Sharrock, and Francis 1979: 167–8; Garfinkel 1967: ix). But perhaps a few more readers were taken aback to see Garfinkel, in the same later work where he expresses doubts about general theory and worldwide social science, stating that ethnomethodology fulfills Émile Durkheim's mandate to examine "social facts," that ethnomethodology studies "the phenomena of ordinary society that Durkheim was talking about" (Garfinkel 2002: 92–3), and that his own early studies were "working out Durkheim's aphorism" from the start. Throughout the 1970s and 1980s, it would have been considered an anathema to suggest publicly that ethnomethodology had anything at all to do with Durkheim's sociology except by way of contrast, possibly to discredit it (see Bittner 1965; Wieder 1974). Indeed, efforts were commonly directed to distancing ethnomethodology from everything that had preceded it, even to the point of speaking of ethnomethodology *as opposed* to sociology, as though the former were an independent discipline (Mehan and Wood 1975; Wilson and Zimmerman 1979/80).

The first major statement about ethnomethodology in broad theoretical terms was John Heritage's (1984) *Garfinkel and Ethnomethodology*. Here was a direct challenge to anyone who saw few connecting links between disparate ethnomethodological studies or knew no reasons to articulate them. Heritage reviews Garfinkel's life as a graduate student, specifically his intellectual ties to Parsons and how "he sought to dig still deeper into the basic problems in the theory of action which had been raised, but incompletely dealt with, in *The Structure of Social Action*" (1984: 9). Heritage shows how Garfinkel sought help from phenomenologists Schutz and Gurwitsch, whom he had the good fortune to brush shoulders with at Harvard, to solve the Hobbesean problem of social order, which had been Parsons's major preoccupation. Finding complementary weaknesses in phenomenology, Garfinkel struck out on his own, launching his now famous empirical studies.

By the early 1990s, there was a growing sense in some quarters that ethnomethodology had something general to offer the social sciences on their own terms, not simply as an accumulating set of studies of interest only to ethnomethodologists (see Boden 1990; Maynard and Clayman 1991). In 1992 I published *The Classical Roots of Ethnomethodology*, which sought to supplement Garfinkel's ties to Parsons with the latter's ties to classical theorists Durkheim and Max Weber, particularly the way in which Parsons derived the foundations of functionalist theory ("voluntarism") from the classics. The argument was basically that Parsons's derivations, through logical necessity, included deliberate negations and suppressions of selected classical themes, which, as far as Parsons was concerned, were corrections and diagnosed falsehoods to be supplanted by Parsons's own theory. The result was not only Parsonian theory, but also some uniquely American orthodoxies concerning Durkheim and Weber that cannot be defended by consulting the original texts, a dynamic transparent in detailed review of the texts and of *The Structure of Social Action*. That this was known already, by diverse scholars of the classics including even Parsons's new advocates as expressed in "neo-functionalism," was part of the argument. The argument also re-examined Garfinkel's intervention into the resulting weak spaces in Parsonian theory as described by Heritage (1984). My main offering was how, in negating Parsons, Garfinkel had negated Parsons's negations back to their positive forms, returning us to classical observations which Parsons had expressly driven out of sociology as error. Resonance between lost classical themes and accumulating ethnomethodological discovery seemed, to me, quite striking (see also Hilbert 1986, 1987, 1989). Altogether I found near 20 such themes (1995: 160).

Not all ethnomethodologists were happy to consider even the possibility of historical links between ethnomethodology and classical theory. Informal feedback to *Classical Roots* expressed concern that such arguments would undermine Garfinkel's claim to originality or contribute to an impression that "it had all been done before." Coulter (1993) criticized the book on its face simply for drawing the connections, rhetorically wondering whether Garfinkel ought to be thought of as a sociologist at all. Whatever ethnomethodology is, Coulter suggests, it cannot be reconciled with classical theory except as a sort of self-validating synthesis project or as a "legitimization exercise" on behalf of something that needs no justification.

Then, in the mid-1990s, Anne Rawls published arguments linking detailed readings of Durkheim's sociology of ritual to Garfinkel's studies of social practices (Rawls 1996a, 1996b). Shortly thereafter, she and Garfinkel entered into a collaboration which resulted in some of Garfinkel's most succinct theoretical renderings to date. These include unpublished work from the late 1940s which heretofore have been the province of students and colleagues in the form of mimeographed copies (Garfinkel 2006). They also include new statements and updates concerning ethnomethodological studies since the early 1980s (Garfinkel 2002). It is this latter work that is subtitled *Working Out Durkheim's Aphorism*. This is by no means the final word on the matter, but it does suggest that Garfinkel himself is, for the time being, with appropriate qualifications, satisfied that not all theorizing violates sociology's scientific mandate to be concrete and empirical.

But is he really? One may be forgiven for concluding that Garfinkel waffles on the relationship between studies and theory (see Garfinkel 2002: 97). Yet such a conclusion probably misreads cautious ambivalence as inconsistency. Most ethnomethodological commentaries about this relationship, even those which appear on the surface to be on opposite sides of a debate (Hilbert 1990; Pollner 1991), are nuanced in ways that display finely tuned compatibilities that erase "sides" and move them into a common effort to appreciate matters that are difficult to explicate in so many words. If anything expresses common ethnomethodological attitudes toward theory, including Garfinkel's (2002: 164 n.23), it is, in a manner Weber would appreciate, a determination not to *reify* the topics of sociological study (Hilbert 1987, 1992: 104–60; Maynard and Wilson 1980). In the mid-1970s, students in Garfinkel's seminars were reporting that Garfinkel had "turned against" one of his own most compelling phraseologies, "indexical expressions," because "indexicality," in their rendition of his complaint, had been turned into a *thing*. I have heard him express similar amazement even about the very term "ethnomethodology" – that it has become a thing, something "out there" in the world, an evolving worldwide profession that he can both witness and participate in, much as Erving Goffman used to sit on panels jointly discussing with others what "Goffmanesque sociology" might be. Most disputes internal to ethnomethodology – Does conversation analysis turn up practices central to ethnomethodology or has it reverted to standard canonical social science? Can ethnomethodologists ignore their own participation in what they produce, in the tradition of the natural sciences, or does that compromise the vision of "radical reflexivity" at the heart of ethnomethodology? – revolve around questions of reification.

Suffice it to say that ethnomethodology is endlessly creative and adaptive to circumstances, with an ability to reconstitute what it has been up to for the last 40 years in light of new directions and new studies. Its "central claims" can be expected to remain in dispute among its many practitioners who otherwise recognize merit in one another's concrete findings. Some of these disputes concern the proper relationship between empirical studies and general theoretical claims, but this does not make ethnomethodology itself atheoretical. The problem would be in trying to come to ethnomethodology for the first time through theory as though it were fundamentally a theoretical enterprise. Whatever general statements anyone is inclined to make on behalf of ethnomethodology, none of them are "true" or even intelligible independently of the empirical studies that inspire them.

PARSONS'S ONTOLOGY

Ties between ethnomethodology and Parsonian functionalism are probably the least controversial theoretical entry to ethnomethodology. The ties are plainly biographical and historical (Heritage 1984). Functionalism as a wellspring of ethnomethodological vision was often obliquely referenced by early proponents of the new discipline (for example, Wieder 1974; Wilson 1970; Zimmerman and Wieder 1970). Charles Lemert, also a student of Parsons, describes Garfinkel's unusual qualities as a graduate student this way: "What separates Garfinkel from others is that, unlike me, he was not taken in and, unlike others, like C. Wright Mills, he was not obsessively critical of Parsons" (Lemert 2006: ix). This nicely summarizes Garfinkel's attitude toward Parsons: certainly not hostility, indeed great admiration, but an admiration tempered by a radically empirical attitude in the form of "Well, let's see."

The great Parsons project was solving the "problem of social order" put in the form of a question, "How is society possible?" He conceived the problem as originating in Hobbes, and he conceived existing society in Hobbesean ways: a strictly behavioral order that can be witnessed by any competent observer but one nevertheless difficult to explain or to account for. The order initially on display is non-controversial. Parsons called it "factual order" (Parsons 1968: 91–2) – patterned and repeating behavioral routines that are both structural and predictable by their regularity. Why are they there, he wondered, and how might we account for them as opposed to the randomness that utilitarian actor theory would predict?

Parsons eventually explained social order as caused by a second order, an order he called "normative order" (1968: 91–2), an order he believed is just as empirical as the behavioral order but one which takes special skills to observe. This is the order of "norms and values," the heart of Parsons's voluntaristic theory, which was the subject of so much functionalist elaboration in later decades. This is culture, the "body of rules" (1968, *passim*) which precedes and survives the lives of all societal actors, but which internalizes to the subjectivity of actors during the process of socialization. This is the order that becomes, through internalization, no different than actors' points of view. Thus anyone born into a society already in progress – and that includes virtually everyone – has to adapt to real culture as well as subscribe to it voluntarily. Factual order results from social actors' voluntary compliance with normative order and behavioral conformity to its prescriptive demands. Factual order "mirrors" normative order, in that sense, as though every standardized behavior were deductively linked to a rule that prescribes it (Wilson 1970).

Parsons's solution thus sets up a definite ontology: a factual order, a normative order, and a deductive relationship between them. Of special importance to Parsons was that his solution also account for actors' subjective states, for such was the stated utilitarian problem in the first place. Without subjectivity, actors' patterned behaviors might be written off to biological instinct or environmental conditioning, an objectionable position Parsons calls "radical positivism" (1968: 60–9). Parsons saves actors' subjectivity as internalized culture, a "body of rules," and thus definite mental content. In that actors all internalize the same culture, Parsons's theory also explains intersubjectivity, known historically to philosophers as the problem of other minds. People know each other's subjective orientations because they share the same subjective orientations. This makes communication possible via common language, and it provides for the stability of both face-to-face interaction and higher social organization ultimately known by everyone as the society itself. So we add these additional elements to Parsons's ontology: subjectivity as definite content and intersubjectivity as overlapping subjective material.

Garfinkel's experiments were set up as though he were looking for empirical verification of Parsons's analytically derived theory. His failure to validate Parsons's ontology was Garfinkel's first major achievement, for in the process he turned up "an immense, hitherto unknown domain of social phenomena" (Garfinkel 1967: ix), phenomena he called "members' methods," the study of which, as a topic in their own right, became the basis for his new coinage to name these studies: ethnomethodology. Partly because of the internal ecology of Parsons's theory, and partly because of some natural features of the social world, any of Garfinkel's studies can be seen as addressing Parsons's theory in its entirety. But for explanatory purposes, it is possible to break it down into specifics, which I will do here.

The most counterintuitive of Garfinkel's revelations challenged the very existence of what practically everybody, until then, took for granted as an indisputable given: factual behavioral order, social structure, the society at large in all of its micro and macro manifestations. A good example derives from a study carried out at a mental health clinic, where Garfinkel assigned student researchers the task of discovering the standardized routine whereby patients were processed through various treatment stages (Garfinkel 1967: 18–24). His initial request was not much different than holding students to the highest standards of traditional social research. He asked them to consult files and to code real clinic events to find objective evidence of factual order. In the day-to-day workings of the clinic, both clinic members and coders themselves took the standardized order for granted, could understand it, could see it and appreciate it. Coders were nevertheless unable to document it without grounding their documentations in "loose" knowledge of clinic routines that was itself uncoded. Every effort to capture the uncoded knowledge with precise methodological criteria depended in turn for its adequacy on yet further uncoded knowledge of the clinic for determining that coded versions were coded correctly. When coders were asked to disregard their loose knowledge in order to code clinic events objectively – as though commonsense knowledge corrupts or biases objective renderings – they found the requests incomprehensible. Thus no matter how the objective renderings turned out, the actual work of the clinic (as well as the work of the coders) remained undescribed. It escaped detection even as it was counted on to produce the objective renderings. Garfinkel called this work "ad hoc" practices.

Ad hoc practices were a major focus in Garfinkel's early work, and while he developed other names for them (including "glossing" [Garfinkel and Sacks 1970], "let it pass," "et cetera," "unless," and "factum valet" [1967: 3, 20–1]), they became almost synonymous with "members' methods," or *ethnomethods*, as the designated topic of ethnomethodology. These same practices essential for sustaining a Parsonian factual order were equally implicated in other Parsonian notions. Most commonly cited is Garfinkel's treatment of rule-governed behavior, the very essence of Parsonian explanation. As opposed to clear deductive linkages between rules and behavior, Garfinkel found a chronic incompleteness in rules, in terms of both their number and their clarity. When playing tic-tac-toe, experimenters would erase opponents' marks, replacing them with their own (Garfinkel 1963). Subjects would see that as a rule violation even though nobody could document the rule either as written someplace or as learned sometime in the past. Likewise in chess, replacing an opponent's piece with an identical piece from the box was cited as a violation even though it did not affect the outcome of the game and no proscription could be found in any of the published volumes about chess. Students cited such rules anyway – as "known in the first place" and "there all along" – even though they were producing them for the very first time, in effect making them up, to cover a precise contingency.

Indeed Garfinkel found people can appeal to rules even without the "game" premise that some sort of rules are in play (cf. Bittner 1967). During conversations with others, he would reveal a portable tape recorder in the "record" mode hidden in his pocket (Garfinkel 1967: 75). Here his fellow conversants invoked a sense of there having been a prior "agreement" that the conversation was private and should not be recorded. (This was before the proliferation of small tape recorders and well before Watergate.) It did Garfinkel no good to point out that he had never entered into an agreement at all. At the same time, however, Garfinkel found that people can sometimes violate presumably existing institutional norms with surprisingly little consequence. When bargaining for store merchandise in department stores, in apparent violation of the "institutionalized one price rule" (so named by Parsons), students were surprised to learn that they could secure lower prices and said they planned on engaging their newly acquired skills in the future (Garfinkel 1967: 68–70). Here Garfinkel concludes that standardized society and standardized expectations "could consist of an *attributed* standardization that is supported by the fact that persons avoid the very situations in which they might learn about them." He adds, "the more important the rule, the greater is the likelihood that knowledge [of the nature of rule-governed actions] is based on avoided tests" (1967: 70).

In general, Garfinkel found that people do not so much follow rules as use them, manipulate them, ignore them, invoke them, or invent them whole cloth for practical purposes – to instruct others, to explain behavior in retrospect, to anticipate behavior, to normalize behavior, to restore temporarily disrupted order, to find fault, to repair damaged rapport, or, most generally, simply to describe behavior as the behavior-that-it-is, that is as factual in the first place (see comments on "reflexivity" in Garfinkel 1967: 7–11, and in Wieder 1974). At the same time, people are not patient with others who call forth rules, no matter how deeply respected, that are not seen as relevant to the actual circumstances in which they are invoked, no matter how compellingly one can argue that, in general or from a theoretical standpoint, they *should* be relevant (cf. Garfinkel and Sacks 1970: 363). Hence people appealing to rules that might apply from a disinterested categorical standpoint, but do not apply in the immediate here and now as a practical matter, run risks of being viewed as obstructionist (see Zimmerman 1970, 1974). That people eschew obstructionism may account for how easily Garfinkel's students were able to negotiate ways around apparently institutional rules such as the one-price rule.

Garfinkel's studies also addressed shared understanding, revealing that subjectivity is not definite "content" and neither is intersubjectivity a matter of material in common between two minds (Garfinkel 1967: 24–31). He started off tendentiously assuming that Parsons was correct on this point, and, in that spirit, went looking for shared material. He did this by asking participants in a conversation to write down what they had said in one column, in the manner of a transcript, and what they had "understood they were talking about" in a second column, in the manner of detailed clarification of the transcript. The transcript could then be read as shorthand for what was intended in the actual conversation but unnecessary to delineate in real time. Yet Garfinkel could show conversants that the clarified version required further clarification in order for an independent auditor to know exactly what the conversants originally had in mind, and he asked them to write it as a third column. Predictably, their renditions of the original conversation increased in length with every new clarification. They eventually gave up on the task of "finishing" this ongoing clarification process, complaining that it was impossible. For Garfinkel, the impossibility resided not in the massive complexity of intended material but in the "branching texture" of the experiment itself, the writing, which in each case produced the "more" that needed to be clarified. As he put it, "The very *way* of accomplishing the task multiplied its features" (1967: 26). Garfinkel concludes that intersubjectivity or "shared agreement" is not content or material at all – it is "an operation [a procedure] rather than a common intersection of overlapping sets [mental material or content]" (1967: 30).

Closely related to this study are the experiments in which Garfinkel (1967: 42–4) had students act on the assumption that what is said "refers" to what is meant and that it should be possible to get at the latter by clarifying the former. Hence students would ask people to explain what they meant by such utterances as "I had a flat tire," "How's your girlfriend feeling?" "I'm sick of him," and "How are you?" That students would even seek such clarification was met with confusion and hostility, especially when offered clarification prompted requests for more clarification in kind. It is as though students were violating a background premise of any conversation before its inception: "We *will* know what each other is talking about (unless there are shared, recognizably accountable reasons for breakdown subject to repair through further clarification, which *will* be understood)." Anyone who has found himself nodding to another's talk without a clue as to what the person might be saying will appreciate this tactic, even though it is not restricted to those kind of interactions and is indeed invariant even in the most concerted and vigorous productions of "shared agreement."

ETHNOMETHODOLOGY'S RECEPTIVITY TO AND FROM THE SOCIAL SCIENCES

The last example above brings us to a subtle matter that may have confounded efforts to come to terms with ethnomethodology, especially in its early days, and that is the sense in which ad hoc practices are *productive* of impressions about the social world that social science cannot strictly ratify empirically: that there are standard and repeating behavioral routines (cf. Zimmerman and Pollner 1970), that society is rule-governed (Zimmerman and Wieder 1970), that people "mean" things by what they say (Wieder 1970), and that commonsense knowledge consists of mental content shared between subjective actors (Wieder 1974). These impressions, for societal members, are difficult to "see through" and are experienced almost in the manner of incorrigible axioms (see Pollner 1987) by the very people who are producing them. The subtlety consists in the fact that these commonsense axioms of everyday life are also the axioms of Parsonian sociology. It is a simple matter, then, to demonstrate how functionalist scholars are themselves implicated in the production of the very phenomena they present to the world as objective discovery (Hilbert 1992: 165–87). Nevertheless, unless Garfinkel intended major criticism of human beings for doing what they do and thinking what they think, in what sense did his studies, in reducing Parsons's ontology to social practices, "overthrow" Parsons's theory?

No doubt this little paradox figures into Garfinkel's ability to mix dynamic criticism and deep admiration with respect to his famous teacher. In *Ethnomethodology's Program* (2002), he claims nothing less than enthusiasm for the discoveries and accomplishments of "the worldwide social science movement" even as he characterizes their common unwillingness to see order in the "concreteness of things." His introduction to *Studies* states that "there can be nothing to quarrel with or to correct about practical sociological reasoning" (1967: viii; cf. 2002: 121). Early ethnomethodologists bundled Parsons with all pre-Garfinkel sociology as "traditional sociology," seeming to fault the way it embraces everyday commonsense axioms as resources, as unquestioned premises, for further study – as they put it, "confusing topic and resource" (Zimmerman and Pollner 1970; Zimmerman and Wieder 1970). Even here, though, there is no overt claim that the traditional sociologies have got it, specifically, *wrong*. More to the point, standard social scientists are ignoring something, something perhaps substantively irrelevant to their own work, but nevertheless something essential to the production of their studies as well as the perceived stability of everyday life. Hence the term "folk science," or science-from-within-that-which-it-studies, to describe traditional sociology.

In his seemingly more critical mode, Garfinkel characterizes standard social science as a preoccupation with replacing ad hoc social practices with methodologies and standard vocabularies that lack the natural ambiguities of everyday language, a process he calls the "substitution of objective [context-free] for indexical [context-dependent] expressions" (1967: 4–7). Analogizing this program with tearing the walls of a building down to see what holds the roof up, Garfinkel notes that the long-term project is doomed to failure, because, as he puts it, all expressions are indexical, including the meaning of "context." Members' practices are irremediable, in that sense, and invariant to anyone's recognition of social order, including professional sociologists' efforts to nail down the nature of society scientifically. Social scientists always encounter a familiar "gap" between their general accounts and what they have on hand empirically, a gap they artfully ignore or only acknowledge in anticipation of closing the gap in future studies. This includes efforts to "operationalize" concepts or turn natural categories into variables or scales (cf. Benson and Hughes 1991; Lynch 1991), and it includes footnoted acknowledgments of the gap, or discussions about it in methods appendices, where again a gap appears and is likewise artfully ignored. In other words social scientists have to allow *whatsoever* they have on hand to count as evidence of presupposed patterns or theoretical principles, even while using these same principles as instructed ways of seeing what, exactly, they have on hand. This is a practice they share with everyday members of society, a practice Garfinkel calls, following Karl Mannheim, "the documentary method of interpretation" (1967: 77–9; cf. pp. 101–3). Examples Garfinkel cites in everyday life include recognizing mailmen, friendly gestures, promises, and what somebody is talking about. Examples from professional sociology include recognizing "Goffman's strategies for the management of impressions, Erikson's identity crises, Riesman's types of conformity, Parsons' value systems, Malinowski's magical practices, Bales' interaction counts, Merton's types of deviance, Lazarfeld's latent structure of attitudes, and the U.S. Census' occupational categories" (1967: 78–9).

As surely as Garfinkel makes his case, such commentary surely fed impressions that he "had it in" for the social sciences, that he wanted to discredit the whole enterprise. But just as surely, ethnomethodologists are not out to discredit anyone. If they were, they would have to begin by discrediting the entirety of the human species. By extension, their studies would then seem to undermine and discredit whatever institutionalized ways of acting and knowing have come within their purview, including: the natural sciences (Bjelic and Lynch 1992; Garfinkel 2002: 263–85; Garfinkel, Lynch, and Livingston 1981; Lynch 1985, 1993), police practices (Bittner 1967; Whalen and Zimmerman 1987, 1990; Whalen, Zimmerman, and Whalen 1988; Zimmerman 1992), professional media practices (Clayman and Heritage 2002; Fishman 1980; Jalbert 1999), professional medicine (Atkinson and Drew 1979; Heritage and Maynard 2006; Maynard 2003; Sudnow 1967), deductive logic and other forms of reasoning (Coulter 1991; Livingston forthcoming), mathematics (Livingston 1986), legal argument (Maynard 1984; Pollner 1987; Sudnow 1965), and all manner of professional work (Boden and Zimmerman 1991; Drew and Heritage 1992). In none of these studies, though, have ethnomethodologists sought to discredit (or affirm) the work of practitioners even as their studies reveal how the work of practitioners is made real and accountable in practitioners' own terms. For the most part this much is apparent to any capable reader of ethnomethodological studies. Yet this same transparency is far less obvious where studies reveal the methodogenic foundations of the social sciences. Indeed sociologists have sometimes found themselves under such discrediting assault that they have sought refuge in caricatures of ethnomethodology that make it seem easy to dismiss – trivial, commonsensical, subjectivist, idealist, neo-positivist, reactionary, liberal, relativistic, mentalistic, or ridiculous (see Maynard 1986; cf. Sharrock and Anderson 1991). Why is this?

The answer lies partly in the fact that sociologists' own studies of like settings are competitive with Garfinkel's in that Garfinkel is himself a sociologist. More importantly, a tacit obligation to read ethnomethodology and somehow come to terms with it pervades sociology in ways that it does not pervade other professions, again precisely because Garfinkel is a sociologist. And it is not altogether uncommon for members of a setting undergoing ethnomethodological investigation to suspect hostile intent or some kind of discrediting project, to wit: students asked to behave as guests in their own family homes, to behave deferentially and politely, found family members upset and annoyed, sometimes explosively so, even when the point of the experiment was divulged and the period of experimentation was over (Garfinkel 1967: 47–9). People asked to explain exactly what they mean by what they say generally find such probings rude, annoying, or hostile, and they respond in kind (1967: 42–4). Garfinkel's efforts to get jurors to talk about their actual practices of deliberation, as opposed to the way they describe them in idealized accounts, "rapidly used up interview rapport" (1967: 113). And astronomers, after reading what ethnomethodologists had reported on their work by examining tape recordings of their pulsar discovery (Garfinkel, Lynch, and Livingston 1981), joked that Garfinkel was a dangerous man.

Such outcomes shed light on one of the earliest named properties of social practices, their character as "uninteresting" (Garfinkel 1967: 7–9). One indicator of practical success in any social occasion is the artful cover-up, the active camouflage, of these practices, and that certainly includes not talking about them. They are not proper topics of discussion. Although "known" by virtually everybody, there is almost a taboo against topicalizing them. There are some loosely delimited exceptions, the most obvious being jokes, comedic routines, or settings – such as arguments or political debates – where people are indeed trying to discredit one another, yet even here ad hoc practices are treated not as invariant but as momentary, circumscribed, unusual, cynical, or the antithesis of good faith. Ethnomethodology proposes social practices as a topic in their own right – practices without alternative or remedy. Hence the conundrum for sociologists: while other professions can rightly shrug off these studies as irrelevant to their trade, sociologists find ethnomethodology directly in their midst, commenting on them in every literature review, which seemingly makes them endless subjects of an endless breaching experiment (cf. Hilbert 1989 on Durkheimian anomie and ritual crime production). How to deal with ethnomethodology? Isolate the culprit. Bag it.

For the most part, such marginalization efforts have failed. Exactly why they failed would make a lengthy sociohistorical study in itself. There was nothing foreseen about ethnomethodology's fortunes, nothing forgone on the basis of merit alone. In the early 1970s, informal speculation among graduate students about ethnomethodology's future ran the gamut of possible outcomes – it was a mere flash in the night, better have a backup plan; it would be the hottest thing on the job market in a few years, you can name your salary; under political pressure it would be absorbed by social psychology and lose its identity; it would be institutionalized by prominent universities competing to establish independent Departments of Ethnomethodology. So what happened? As Garfinkel might put it, people just kept doing studies.

Forty years after *Studies* we might still ponder ethnomethodology's future, but "flash in the night" speculation has been put to rest. The number of publications, around 20 in 1972, has proliferated into the thousands, including individual and collected articles, books, and other monographs. Ethnomethodology has inspired generations of diverse research around the world in at least six languages, with special concentrations at various campuses of the University of California, University of Manchester, Boston University, University of Wisconsin, University of London, and the Palo Alto Research Center. Ethnomethodology has influenced virtually every substantive area of sociology as well as cognate disciplines such as communications, education, medicine, law, and cognitive science. Every year it is the focus of professional conferences and workshops all over the world. Ethnomethodology and conversation analysis is now an independent section of the American Sociological Association. Ethnomethodological studies are increasingly honored by the wider profession as exemplary sociology, such as Michael Lynch's (1993) *Scientific Practice and Ordinary Action: Ethnomethodology and Social Studies of Science*, which received the 1995 Robert K. Merton Professional Award from the ASA Science, Knowledge and Technology section. News of ethnomethodology's practical relevance even to "applied" sociology and other professions is spreading, such as Maynard, Houtkoop-Steenstra, Schaeffer, and van der Zouwen (2002) on survey research, Maynard (2003) on diagnostic news in medicine (see Frederic W. Platt's 2003 review in the *Journal of the American Medical Association*), and Lucy Suchman (1987, 1994) on computer applications. Clearly, as Deirdre Boden knew as far back as 1990 (p. 185), "Ethnomethodology is here to stay."

ETHNOMETHODOLOGY'S ONTOLOGY

If "ethnomethodological theory" sets some ethnomethodologists back a few paces, "ethnomethodological ontology" should really set their teeth on edge, due to a marked reluctance to state, outright, "what is" – mostly eschewing misleading resemblances to philosophical statements about reality and what it contains. Ethnomethodology is clearly not a philosophy about "what is." But no more is Parsons's sociology a philosophy of "what is" other than derivative rephrasings of what Parsons, in his stated manner of discovery, asserts is empirically the case: *there are* social structures, *there are* norms and values, *there are* internalized common meanings and shared expectations. What might be appropriate "there are" statements concerning what ethnomethodologists find in their empirical studies?

One thing ethnomethodologists do not find in their studies is a macro-order as reported by macro-oriented sociologists – conceived as social structure, class relations, interest group competition, conflict, power struggles, cooperation, or products of structuration activities. But neither do they find micro-order as reported by micro-oriented sociologists – conceived as small group interaction, role-taking, role-making, subjective interpretation, conformity to status rules, rational decisionmaking, or structuration activities. Instead, ethnomethodologists assert that wherever in the society one looks, wherever one turns one's attention to the concrete activity empirically on display, one will find, right then and there, social practices productive of, by and for the members, all of the micro/macro matters of relevance for those members *in that specific setting* (Hilbert 1990). None of it is constructed as stable products exportable from the immediate setting as constraint at a later time except insofar as whatever it "is" for members can be reconstituted as something altogether different in terms of the contingencies at that "later time" (see Zimmerman and

Pollner 1970). In that sense, both micro and macro sociological matters, in whatever terms, are always embedded in the immediate here-and-now settings of their productions and are not recoverable at a later date as what-they-really-are either by members of other settings or by professional sociologists.

Ethnomethodologists' strong preference for empirical studies should remedy impressions that ethnomethodological assertions are made on the basis of logical necessity, such as a philosophy of radical context-embeddedness might dictate. Right there, *in that concrete setting*, is all any analyst needs to know about the micro/macro order that is of relevance to members of the setting. Setting members display the relevance in the immediacy of the here and now. There is no necessity, then, to account for local activity in terms of something not present – either internalized meaning or the culture at large. This is so whether we are witnessing a transient production of "immortal, ordinary society" (Garfinkel 2002) in common-sense situations in everyday life, or whether we are witnessing sociologists doing whatever they need to do to publish, for the world, the convincingness of their formal theories, their data-based claims about what kind of a thing society is "overall."

As Sharrock and Button put it, "ethnomethodology makes no attempt to construct a conception of the social whole" (1991: 143). They also note how easy it is to misread ethnomethodology as thereby "*denying* existence of any such whole." And indeed, this makes for endless mischief, for sociologists can easily and unceasingly display the convincingness of macro-sociological matters, matters which, for them, ethnomethodologists simply "refuse" to recognize. *Obviously*, they say, there are large-scale institutional phenomena that ethnomethodologists refuse to recognize, and they can produce the evidence, and the evidence is astonishingly convincing. But somebody is *doing* that, is the ethnomethodological reply, and that somebody is: professional sociologists themselves. That they are *doing* it does not discredit the activity, and that they are doing it so *well* is what attracts Garfinkel's great admiration. But *that* they are doing it is a phenomenon in its own right, the phenomenon to which ethnomethodology directs our attention.

If anything is axiomatic to ethnomethodology, then, it would be that "there are" social practices available for the seeing, and that wherever one finds them, social order will be *right there*. That these practices are not subjective or "interpretive" is indicated by their very empirical availability. That they are not individualistic is indicated by the fact that nobody is ever "free" to do just anything and have it count as competent membership. There is just as much constraint, on everyone, as Durkheim imagined (Hilbert 1992: 27–82), and trouble with the constraint leads to just as much anomie (Hilbert 1992: 83–103). But the constraint is observable in the very work being constrained. Members constrain one another, in that sense, though collectively they often experience the constraint as coming from outside the immediate setting – as policy, as tradition, as culturally mandated, as structural. This is a powerful impression, so powerful – and likewise so often cited in everyday discourse as "what society requires" – that it feeds directly into the very foundations and premises of most social research.

In teaching ethnomethodology I have had some success with an analogy to a jazz band jamming together, an improvisational session producing music known by none of the players in advance of playing. They "go along" with each other. None of them is free to play just any old thing. They are listening to one another as they play. They riff, they shift from key to key, they pass melody lines off to each other. What they play is not laid out in advance by composition, yet, if they are any good, the outcome will be something that deserves to have been written. They are satisfied in the end, but should they consult with one another and discover that every one of them was constrained during the playing, they might, in this ambitious analogy, be amazed by an impression that there was "something else" constraining all of them at the same time. Maybe the piece was actually composed by somebody after all, maybe they only recognized it as they played it but once recognizing it had no choice but to play it. Maybe God wrote it. Maybe they had heard it as small children. Maybe they had all dreamed it the night before. But they were certainly "going along" with something. Must be something big.

Naturally, jazz musicians would never be puzzled by the way I have described them, and they would not reach such conclusions about the origins of musical constraint. But this analogy suggests the kind of impressions people produce for one another all the time – something constrains all of us simultaneously. We experience it together. It must be reality. It must be society. It must be rules. It must be . . . something big. And when we want to, or if we need to – or if we are developing a social theory – we can find what it is and name it. As Durkheim cautioned in *The Elementary Forms of the Religious Life*, sociologists should not view this as superstition or deluded thinking. When people experience moral principles, religious truths, stable bureaucratic policy, or objective reality, they are experiencing something tangibly *real*: social constraint. That this constraint is concrete – real, not imagined; local, not "somewhere else"; empirical, not theoretical – is one of ethnomethodology's most distinctive offerings.

Probably the most counterintuitive ethnomethodological studies are those deriving from some early initiatives by Harvey Sacks in the 1960s and 1970s, then carried on by others in the tradition known as conversation analysis (see Sacks, Schegloff, and Jefferson 1974). Conversation analysis is taken up by John Heritage in CHAPTER 15, but I will comment on it briefly here. Conversation analysts have turned up empirical social practices whose detailed coordinations are measured in units of time down to tiny fractions of a second. These coordinated events are obviously not noticeable by conversationalists in cognitive ways, and in a certain sense they know nothing about them. But conversationalists nevertheless seem to "experience" them in embodied ways, at least to the extent that they are able to produce them collaboratively and respond to them in kind. More intriguingly, they appear to experience them as the same trans-contextual phenomena otherwise non-empirical but simply assumed as matters of common sense, that is as social structure – gender roles, for example, or status differences (West and Zimmerman 1977; Zimmerman and West 1975). Because of these embodied doings, Schegloff is able to speak of "doing being doctor" and "doing, and displaying doing, doctor" as opposed to conformity to exogenous demands of the doctor role – more generally "the doing of talk" or "doing the interaction" (Schegloff 1987: 219–20) – in explaining why sociologists do not have to resort to external structures beyond the here-and-now interaction to describe how it is that somebody is a doctor or somebody is a patient (cf. Wilson 1991). It is in that sense that the entire structural integrity of society, including whatever its members take to be factual reality (Hilbert 1992: 66–82), is ongoingly reproduced in ongoing behavior, not something external to the behavior which is causing it or making people experience it the way they do. That these sense-making practices are embodied but not cognitive – and in that sense social but not cultural – is fascinating. That they could be species-specific behavior is even more fascinating.

Conversation analysts have also expressed interest in the *distribution* of conversational events across myriad settings and interactions (Whalen, Zimmerman, and Whalen 1988). Wilson (1991) raises this question to address a "which is which" problem internal to the dynamics of conversational interaction: If "doing doctor" and "doing patient" are demonstrable productions of the here and now, what determines which participant does doctor and which does patient? Eschewing structural explanations, Wilson nevertheless argues that conversationalists bring to local settings certain foundational presuppositions of structure derived from previous exchanges. That these impressions are endogenously produced in every case does not prevent members from orienting to them subjectively as belief objects in the production of further here-and-now status differences. But as these structural impressions are not in themselves empirical, they ought not to be invoked by social science in accounting for here-and-now displays of doctor/patient identities.

I have commented at length about how ethnomethodology's focus on endogenous local practices has resulted in its being mistyped as one of several microsociologies (Hilbert 1990). But ethnomethodological interest in the distribution of these practices might just as easily cause it to be mistyped as a kind of macrosociology. This is instructive in itself in that it points, by contrast to common impressions, to a generic ethnomethodological indifference (Garfinkel and Sacks 1970) to structure at any level, favoring neither micro nor macro phenomena (Hilbert 1990). Whatever a distribution of local practices across space-time is, or however such a distribution might be conceived, it is not a "social whole" which Sharrock and Button (1991: 143) point out has no place in ethnomethodological studies. Local practices exhaust all possible sense of what "whole society" could possibly be. Nevertheless, social practices are themselves empirically distributed in space and time, somewhat as a quasi-ecology of events whose impacts on one another are biographical, temporal, and sequential. For example, a conversational exchange between an employer and an employee might have a bearing on conversations later that evening between a father and other family members, and it is little more than a mapping problem to show how someone moves from one conversational setting to another. Indeed an entire biography, from birth to death, could be conceived as a series of interactional exchanges linked in space-time by a body's motion from one local setting to another. A biography could be "drawn," in that sense, on a map (Hilbert 1990).

What might this overall distribution "look like" and how is it not macrosociological? To begin with, an ecology of sense-making activities is not indexed or referenced by investigations intended to describe society. It is uninteresting, as members' practices are themselves uninteresting. It occupies space-time in the manner of a population occupying territory, but it is not the society theorized via commonsense or professional methods of inquiry or description. It is not ordered, and it is neither acknowledged nor referred to in or through order-making practices, nor it is produced by those practices. It is the distribution of those practices. It is not social but exhibits social practices in concrete manifestations across space-time. While it is theoretically empirical, it is not stable and will not sit still for fly-over photography in the manner of macro-photographical maps. Its pieces and constantly shifting ecology are biographical, temporal, and sequential – and they are in principle empirical even if inaccessible for reasons quite different than why a "social whole," or "society in general," is inaccessible. A distribution of social practices is empirical, but not even the most dedicated of macro-sociologists will try to theorize it.

These considerations bear some momentary resonance with what Randall Collins calls "Interaction Ritual Chains" (1981, 1987), which he characterizes as empirical linkages between sites where myths of sacred objects are re-celebrated and sustained in the sense of Durkheim. Herein is the "ritual" of Interaction Ritual Chains, including their linkages across space-time as a distribution of Durkheimian ritual settings, places and moments where "the society" and everything equivalent to it are endlessly reproduced (Hilbert 1990). Collins allows that these ritual sites may be conversations. But the contrast between Collins's idea and ethnomethodology is just as illuminating. Collins uses his concept to forge a micro–macro link, wherein the details of local practices are conceived as micro-structure (thus connected to the misleading impression that ethnomethodology is microsociological) and their distribution is conceived as the "stuff" that gets reified by local practices (thus connected to the misleading impression that what gets theorized locally "exists" somewhere else in a pre-theoretical state). Ethnomethodology allows a more precise vision, distinguishing between what empirically (actually) and what theoretically (supposedly) is the case.

Thus ethnomethodologists can allow that "there are" social practices and "there are" distributions of these practices. Social practices happen simultaneously, all at once, no matter the cacophony of white noise one would pick up trying to record all of it. There is no order to be found there. Distributions of practical sense-making sites and the bodies that occupy them might be understood to be shifting and morphing in a never-ending state of flux, but there are no repetitions or naturally occurring categories – there are no natural patterns. Whatever relevance ritual chains have for sense production in an instance is no different than whatever conceptual resources local members bring from other instances, such concrete connections being empirical, embodied, temporal, and sequential. In any case, sense-making in an instance is a fully enacted accomplishment in that very instance – sometimes referred to as its "first time through" character – and whatever topics members orient to in an instance, those topics do not include the distribution of social practices any more than they include social practices themselves.

CONCLUDING REMARKS

I began by noting ambivalence among ethnomethodologists concerning social theory as it relates to ethnomethodology. Some boldly theorize ethnomethodology, others eschew all contact with theory; nearly all are cautiously nuanced in their renditions. I conclude with this same ambivalence, repeating that that ethnomethodology is not accessible as a program of research in fulfillment of a theoretical orientation, or a philosophy, no matter how compellingly the latter can be stated. Ethnomethodological studies are first and foremost empirical. Whatever can be said about ethnomethodology is no better than, and no different than, the quality of those studies. At the same time, though, ethnomethodologists are increasingly challenged to "say more" about what their studies offer the social sciences and to say it in ways that do not compromise the empirical integrity of the studies.

Bibliography

Atkinson, M. J., and Drew, P. (1979) *Order in Court: The Organisation of Verbal Interaction in Judicial Settings*. London: Macmillan.

Benson, D., and Hughes, J. (1991), "Evidence and Inference for Ethnomethodology," in G. Button (ed.), *Ethnomethodology and the Human Sciences*. Cambridge: Cambridge University Press.

Bittner, E. (1965) "The Concept of Organization." *Social Research* 32: 239–55.

Bittner, E. (1967) "The Police on Skid Row: A Study of Peace Keeping." *American Sociological Review* 32: 699–715.

Bjelic, D., and Lynch, M. (1992) "The Work of a (Scientific) Demonstration: Respecifying Newton's and Goethe's Theories of Prismatic Color," in G. Watson and R. M. Seiler (eds.), *Text in Context: Contributions to Ethnomethodology*. London: Sage.

Boden, D. (1990) "The World as it Happens: Ethnomethodology and Conversation Analysis," in G. Ritzer (ed.), *Frontiers of Social Theory*, New York: Columbia University Press.

Boden, D., and Zimmerman, D. H. (eds.) (1991) *Talk and Social Structure*. Cambridge: Polity.

Button, G. (ed.) (1991) *Ethnomethodology and the Human Sciences*. Cambridge: Cambridge University Press.

Clayman, Steve, and Heritage, John (2002) *The News Interview: Journalists and Public Figures on the Air*. Cambridge: Cambridge University Press.

Collins, R. (1981) "On the Microfoundations of Macrosociology." *American Journal of Sociology* 86: 984–1014.

Collins, R. (1987) "Interaction Ritual Chains, Power, and Property: The Micro–Macro Connection as an Empirically Based Theoretical Problem," in J. Alexander et al. (eds.), *The Micro–Macro Link*. Berkeley: University of California Press.

Coser, L. (1975) "Presidential Address: Two Methods in Search of a Substance." *American Sociological Review* 40: 691–9.

Coulter, J. (1991) "Cognition in an Ethnomethodological Mode," in G. Button (ed.), *Ethnomethodology and the Human Sciences*. Cambridge: Cambridge University Press.

Coulter, J. (1993) "Ethnomethodology and the Contemporary Condition of Inquiry," essay review of Richard A. Hilbert, *The Classical Roots of Ethnomethodology*. *Contemporary Sociology* 22: 261–3.

Cuff, E. C., Sharrock, W. W., and Francis, D. W. (1979) *Perspectives in Sociology*. London: Unwin Hyman.

Denzin, N. K. (1969) "Symbolic Interactionism and Ethnomethodology: A Proposed Synthesis." *American Sociological Review* 34: 922–34.

Denzin, N. K. (1970) "Symbolic Interactionism and Ethnomethodology," in J. Douglas (ed.), *Understanding Everyday Life*. Chicago: Aldine.

Drew, P., and Heritage, J. (eds.) (1992) *Talk at Work*. Cambridge: Cambridge University Press.

Fishman, M. (1980) *Manufacturing the News*. Austin: University of Texas Press.

Garfinkel, H. (1963) "A Conception of, and Experiments with, 'Trust' as a Condition of Stable Concerted Actions," in O. J. Henry (ed.), *Motivation and Social Interaction*. New York: Ronald Press.

Garfinkel, H. (1967) *Studies in Ethnomethodology*. Englewood Cliffs, NJ: Prentice Hall.

Garfinkel, H. (1988) "Evidence for the Locally Produced, Naturally Accountable Phenomena of Order*, Logic, Reason, Meaning, Method, Etc. in and as of the Essential Quiddity of Immortal Ordinary Society (I of IV): An Announcement of Studies," *Sociological Theory* 19: 103–9.

Garfinkel, H. (2002) *Ethnomethodology's Program: Working Out Durkheim's Aphorism*. Lanham, MD: Rowman & Littlefield.

Garfinkel, H. (2006) *Seeing Sociologically: The Routine Grounds of Social Action*. Boulder, CO: Paradigm.

Garfinkel, H., Lynch, M., and Livingston, E. (1981) "The Work of a Discovering Science Construed with Materials from the Optically Discovered Pulsar." *Philosophy of the Social Sciences* 11: 131–58.

Garfinkel, H., and Sacks, H. (1970) "On the Formal Structure of Practical Actions," in J. C. McKinney and E. A. Tiryakian (eds.), *Theoretical Sociology*. New York: Appleton-Century-Crofts.

Garfinkel, H., and Wieder, D. L. (1992) "Two Incommensurable, Asymmetrically Alternate Technologies of Social Analysis," in G. Watson and R. M. Seiler (eds.), *Text in Context*. Newbury Park, CA: Sage.

Heritage, J. (1984) *Garfinkel and Ethnomethodology*. Cambridge: Polity.

Heritage, J., and Maynard, D. W. (eds.) (2006) *Communication in Medical Care: Interactions between Primary Care Givers and Patients*. Cambridge: Cambridge University Press.

Hilbert, R. A. (1986) "Anomie and the Moral Regulation of Reality: The Durkheimian Tradition in Modern Relief." *Sociological Theory* 4: 1–19.

Hilbert, R. A. (1987) "Bureaucracy as Belief, Rationalization as Repair: Max Weber in a Post-Functionalist Age." *Sociological Theory* 5: 70–86.

Hilbert, R. A. (1989) "Durkheim and Merton on Anomie: An Unexplored Contrast and its Derivatives" *Social Problems* 36: 242–50.

Hilbert, R. A. (1990) "Ethnomethodology and the Micro–Macro Order" *American Sociological Review* 55: 794–808.

Hilbert, R. A. (1992) *The Classical Roots of Ethnomethodology: Durkheim, Weber, and Garfinkel*. Chapel Hill: University of North Carolina Press.

Hilbert, R. A. (1995) "Garfinkel's Recovery of Themes in Classical Sociology." *Human Studies* 18: 157–75.

Jalbert, P. L. (ed.) (1999), *Media Studies: Ethnomethodological Approaches*. Lanham, MD: University Press of America.

Lemert, C. (2006) "The Indexical Properties of Sociological Time," in H. Garfinkel, *Seeing Sociologically*. Boulder, CO: Paradigm.

Livingston, E. (1986) *The Ethnomethodological Foundations of Mathematics*. London: Routledge & Kegan Paul.

Livingston, E. (forthcoming) *Ethnographies of Reason*. Burlington, VT: Ashgate.

Lynch, M. (1985) *Art and Artifact in Laboratory Science: A Study of Shop Work and Shop Talk in a Research Laboratory*. London: Routledge & Kegan Paul.

Lynch, M. (1991) "Ordinary and Scientific Measurement as Ethnomethodological Phenomena," in G. Button (ed.), *Ethnomethodology and the Human Sciences*. Cambridge: Cambridge University Press.

Lynch, M. (1993) *Scientific Practice and Ordinary Action: Ethnomethodology and Social Studies of Science*. New York: Cambridge University Press.

Maynard, D. W. (1984) *Inside Plea Bargaining: The Language of Negotiation*. New York: Plenum Press.

Maynard, D. W. (1986) "New Treatment for an Old Itch," review of John Heritage, *Garfinkel and Ethnomethodology. Contemporary Sociology* 15: 346–9.

Maynard, D. W. (2003) *Bad News, Good News: Conversation Order in Everyday Talk and Clinical Settings.* Chicago: University of Chicago Press.

Maynard, D. W., and Clayman, S. B. (1991) "The Diversity of Ethnomethodology." *Annual Review of Sociology* 17: 385–418.

Maynard, D. W., Houtkoop-Steenstra, H., Schaeffer, N. C., and van der Zouwen, J. (eds.) (2002) *Standardization and Tacit Knowledge: Interaction and Practice in the Survey Interview.* New York: John Wiley.

Maynard, D. W., and Wilson, T. P. (1980) "On the Reification of Social Structure." *Current Perspectives in Social Theory* 1: 287–322.

Mehan, H., and Wood, H. (1975) *The Reality of Ethnomethodology.* New York: John Wiley.

Parsons, T. (1968 [1937]) *The Structure of Social Action.* New York: The Free Press.

Platt, F. W. (2003) "Review of Douglas W. Maynard, 'Bad News, Good News'," *Journal of the American Medical Association* 290: 3256–7.

Pollner, M. (1974) "Sociological and Common-Sense Models of the Labeling Process," in R. Turner (ed.) *Ethnomethodology.* Baltimore: Penguin.

Pollner, M. (1987) *Mundane Reason: Reality in Everyday and Sociological Discourse.* New York: Cambridge University Press.

Pollner, M. (1991) "Left of Ethnomethodology: The Rise and Decline of Radical Reflexivity." *American Sociological Review* 56: 370–80.

Rawls, A. (1996a) "Durkheim's Epistemology: The Initial Critique 1915–1924." *Sociological Quarterly* 38: 111–45.

Rawls, A. (1996b) "Durkheim's Epistemology: The Neglected Argument." *American Journal of Sociology* 102: 430–82.

Sacks, H., Schegloff, E., and Jefferson, G. (1974) "A Simplest Systematics for the Organization of Turn-Taking for Conversation." *Language* 50: 696–735.

Schegloff, E. (1987) "Between Micro and Macro: Contexts and Other Connections," in J. C. Alexander et al. (eds.), *The Micro–Macro Link.* Berkeley: University of California Press.

Sharrock, W., and Anderson, B. (1991) "Professional Scepticism," in G. Button (ed.) *Ethnomethdology and the Human Sciences.* Cambridge: Cambridge University Press.

Sharrock, W., and Button, G. (1991) "The Social Actor: Social Action in Real Time," in G. Button (ed.) *Ethnomethdology and the Human Sciences.* Cambridge: Cambridge University Press.

Suchman, L. (1987) *Plans and Situated Action: The Problem of Human–Machine Communication.* Cambridge: Cambridge University Press.

Suchman, L. (1994) "Working Relations of Technology Production and Use." *Computer Supported Cooperative Work* 2: 177–90.

Sudnow, D. (1965) "Normal Crimes: Sociological Features of the Penal Code in a Public Defender's Office." *Social Problems* 12: 255–72.

Sudnow, D. (1967) *Passing On: The Social Organization of Dying.* Englewood Cliffs: Prentice Hall.

Watson, G., and Seiler, R. M. (eds.) (1992) *Text in Context: Contributions to Ethnomethodology.* Newbury Park, CA: Sage.

West, C., and Zimmerman, D. H. (1977) "Women's Place in Everyday Talk: Reflections on Parent–Child Interaction" *Social Problems* 24: 521–9.

Whalen, J., Zimmerman, D. H., and Whalen, M. (1988) "When Words Fail: A Single Case Analysis." *Social Problems* 35: 335–62.

Whalen, M., and Zimmerman, D. H. (1987) "Sequential and Institutional Contexts in Calls for Help." *Social Psychology Quarterly* 50: 172–85.

Whalen, M., and Zimmerman, D. H. (1990) "Describing Trouble: Practical Epistemology in Citizen Calls to the Police." *Language in Society* 19: 465–92.

Wieder, D. L. (1970) "On Meaning by Rule," in J. D. Douglas (ed.), *Understanding Everyday Life*. Chicago: Aldine.

Wieder, D. L. (1974) *Language and Social Reality: The Case of Telling the Convict Code*. The Hague: Mouton.

Wilson, T. P. (1970) "Conceptions of Interaction and Forms of Sociological Explanation." *American Sociological Review* 35: 697–10.

Wilson, T. P. (1991) "Social Structure and the Sequential Organization of Interaction," in D. Boden and D. H. Zimmerman (eds.), *Talk and Social Structure: Studies in Ethnomethodology and Conversation Analysis*. Cambridge: Polity.

Wilson, T. P., and Zimmerman, D. H. (1979/80) "Ethnomethodology, Sociology, and Theory." *Humboldt Journal of Social Relations* 7: 52–88.

Zimmerman, D. H. (1970) "The Practicalities of Rule Use," in J. D. Douglas (ed.), *Understanding Everyday Life*, Chicago: Aldine.

Zimmerman, D. H. (1974) "Fact as a Practical Accomplishment," in J. D. Douglas (ed.), *Understanding Everyday Life*. Chicago: Aldine.

Zimmerman, D. H. (1976) "A Reply to Coser." *American Sociologist* 11: 4–13.

Zimmerman, D. H. (1992). "The Interactional Organization of Calls for Emergency Assistance," in P. Drew and J. Heritage (eds.), *Talk at Work: Social Interaction in Institutional Settings*. Cambridge: Cambridge University Press.

Zimmerman, D. H., and Pollner, M. (1970) "The Everyday World as a Phenomenon," in J. D. Douglas (ed.), *Understanding Everyday Life*. Chicago: Aldine.

Zimmerman, D. H., and West, C. (1975) "Sex Roles, Interruptions, and Silences in Conversation," in B. Thorne and N. Henley (eds.), *Language and Sex: Difference and Dominance*. Rowley, MA: Newbury House.

Zimmerman, D. H., and Wieder, D. L. (1970) "Ethnomethodology and the Problem of Order: Comment on Denzin," in J. D. Douglas (ed.), *Understanding Everyday Life*. Chicago: Aldine.

9

Rational Choice Theory

Raymond Boudon

Why Rational Choice Theory?

The basic principles underlying rational choice theory (RCT) can be summarized by three statements: (1) explaining a social phenomenon means making it the consequence of a set of statements which should all be easily acceptable; (2) a good sociological theory is a theory that interprets any social phenomenon as the outcome of individual actions; and (3) actions should be analyzed as "rational." M. Hollis (1977) puts it this way: "rational action is its own explanation." James Coleman (1986: 1) goes further, and states that an action can be held as "explained" if and only if it is treated as "rational": Thus "[r]ational actions of individuals have a unique attractiveness as the basis for social theory. If an institution or a social process can be accounted for in terms of the rational actions of individuals, then and only then can we say that it has been explained." As for Gary Becker, he introduces the crucial statement that the social sciences can analyze behavior along two basic dimensions, the rational and the irrational, the latter consisting in explaining behavior as the effect of impersonal forces: "The . . . utility-maximizing approach . . . is remarkably useful in unifying a wide class of behavior . . . I do not believe that any alternative approach – be it founded on 'cultural', 'biological', or 'psychological' forces – comes close to providing comparable insights and explanatory power" (Becker 1996: 4). Briefly, as soon as a social phenomenon can be explained as the outcome of rational individual actions, the explanation invites no further questions. In short, it contains no black boxes. By contrast, irrational explanations introduce necessarily various types of *forces* which raise further questions as to their nature or even reality. Becker makes the further point that the "utility-maximizing approach," another name for RCT, can be extended to include endogenous preferences. Thus, the pleasure drawn from playing or smoking can increase the need to play or smoke. One of the reasons why Becker's work is regarded as pathbreaking is that he has succeeded in answering, partially at least, a current objection against RCT, that is, while it can explain why individuals choose given means, it fails to explain why they follow their objectives or prefer one type of activity to another.

As Becker rightly maintains, a theory appears less convincing as soon as it evokes *psychological* forces, such as when cognitive psychologists explain that people tend to give a wrong answer to statistical problems under the effect of some "cognitive bias"; or when it evokes *biological* forces, as when sociobiologists such as Michael Ruse (1993) claim that moral feelings are an effect of biological evolution; or, finally, when it evokes *cultural* forces for example when sociologists claim that a given collective belief is the product of socialization. In contrast with rational explanations, such explanations raise further questions, that is, they include black boxes. Moreover, it is easy to find data incompatible with them. Thus, once we have explained that most Romans in the early years of the Roman empire believed in the old traditional Roman polytheistic religion *because* they had been *socialized* into it, we are confronted with the question as to why the Roman civil servants and the centurions, although they had been socialized into the old polytheistic religion, tended to be attracted by monotheistic religions such as the Mithra cult and subsequently Christianity (Weber 1988 [1922]). Moreover, the notion of socialization generates a black box that is apparently hard to open.

Nobody has yet been able to discover the mechanisms behind socialization in the way that the mechanisms behind digestion have been disentangled. I am not saying that *socialization* is a worthless notion, nor that there are no socialization effects, but merely that the notion is *descriptive* rather than *explanatory*. It identifies and christens various correlations between the way people have been raised and educated and their beliefs and behavior, but does not explain them.

THE POSTULATES OF RCT

The postulates of RCT are actually more numerous than the three already mentioned. As RCT is a family of theories with many versions, it is advisable to present the postulates in a general way in order to transcend the variants of the theory (Lindenberg and Fillieule 2005). The first postulate (P1) states that any social phenomenon is the effect of individual decisions, actions, attitudes and so forth. This is the classical principle of *methodological individualism*. A second postulate (P2) states that, in principle at least, an action can be understood. This is the principle of *Verstehen* (understanding) according to which any action should be treated as the effect of understandable motivations and/or reasons. Thus, it is understandable, as Émile Durkheim (1960 [1897]) suggests, that in a period of severe national or international crisis individuals are for a time distracted from their personal problems, thereby explaining a drop in the suicide rate in such situations. This example shows that some actions can be understood without being inspired by reasons. A third postulate (P3) states that any action is caused by reasons in the mind of individuals. Let us call P3 the postulate of *rationality*. A fourth postulate (P4) assumes that these reasons derive from the consideration by the actor of the consequences of his actions as he sees them. We will call P4 the postulate of *consequentialism* or *instrumentalism*. A fifth postulate (P5) states that actors are concerned mainly with the consequences for themselves of their action. This is the postulate of *egoism*. A sixth postulate (P6) maintains that actors are able to distinguish the costs and benefits of alternative lines of action and choose the line of action with the most favorable balance. P6 is the postulate of *maximization* or *optimization*.

THE ACHIEVEMENTS OF RCT

RCT has beyond any doubt inspired successful and convincing explanations of many puzzling social phenomena. Its scientific strength was even discovered before it was christened. Alexis de Tocqueville's work illustrates this point. Several of his analyses use what was later to be called RCT in his explanation of the relative stagnation of French agriculture at the end of the eighteenth century in comparison with British agriculture (Tocqueville 1986 [1856]). The "administrative centralization" characteristic of eighteenth-century France is the cause of the fact that there are many posts available to civil servants in France and that, given the importance of the central state, they are more prestigious than in England. These two factors provoke a rate of landlord absenteeism much larger than in England. Rich French landlords prefer to buy an appointment as a civil servant and leave their land. As the farmers who rent their land don't have the same capacity to innovate as the landowners, the rate of agricultural innovation is lower in France than in England. In England by contrast landowners have an interest in appearing to be innovators. If they want to be elected to Westminster, they see that they have to appear to the local voters to be able to improve their everyday lives, notably by introducing innovations which have positive effects for all. Finally, Tocqueville succeeds in explaining the macroscopic puzzling difference in the path of agricultural modernization between France and England at the end of the eighteenth century in terms of the effect of individual rational actions. The French context makes the landowner get a benefit in power, influence, prestige and eventually income by becoming a civil servant. The English context means that the landowner is rather incited to take care of his land and to appear as a dynamic innovator, even in the case where he has overriding political ambitions. Tocqueville's theory gives the impression of being self-sufficient, firstly because its empirical statements appear congruent with the observational data, and secondly because its statements explaining why the actors behaved the way they did are self-evident, not in the logical but in the psychological sense.

A second macroscopic puzzling question dealing with one of the most impressive events of the twentieth century provides a second illustration of the strength of RCT. Why did the Cold War last many decades and was then abruptly concluded? Why did the Soviet empire collapsed suddenly in the early 1990s and not 20 years before or after? General causes such as the low economic efficiency of the system and the violation of human rights can explain neither why it collapsed at that time nor why it collapsed so abruptly. The RCT can help in answering these questions. The Western world and the Soviet Union got involved in an arms race shortly after the end of World War II. Now the arms race has a "prisoner's dilemma" (PD) structure. If I (the US government) do not increase my military potential while the other (the USSR government) does, then I run a mortal risk. So, I have to increase it, although, as a government, I would prefer to spend less money on weapons and more on, say, schools, hospitals, or welfare since these would be more appreciated by the voters. In this situation, increasing one's arsenal is a dominant strategy, although its outcome is not optimal. The US and the USSR played this game for decades and accumulated so many nuclear weapons that each could destroy the planet several times. This "foolish" outcome was the product of "rational" strategies. The two super-actors, the two governments, played their dominant strategy and could not do better than marginally reducing their arsenal through negotiations. The game stopped when the PD structure which characterized the interaction between the US and USSR over decades was suddenly destroyed by the threat developed by the President Reagan of reaching a new threshold in the arms race by developing the SDI project, namely the star wars strategy. The project was so expensive that the Soviet Union saw that it could not follow without generating serious internal problems. So it did not follow, and in so doing lost its superpower status, which was uniquely grounded in its military strength. Of course, there are other causes of the collapse of the Soviet Union. But an essential one is that the PD game which had characterized the relations between the US and the USSR was suddenly broken by Reagan's move. In this case, an RCT approach helps in identifying one of the main causes of a major macroscopic historical phenomenon. It provides an explanation as to why Mikhail Gorbachev made a move which was going to be fatal to the USSR, and why the USSR collapsed at that point in time. In this case, we get an explanation without black boxes as to why the "stupid" arms race was conducted in the first place, and why it stopped suddenly at a given point in time, leaving one of the protagonists defeated. The explanation works because the RCT postulates, though reductionist, are not unrealistic: it is true that any government has to be "egoistical," that is it has to take care of the interests of its own nation.

Obviously, it would be easy to mention many modern works that owe their scientific value to the fact that they use the RCT model. One can think of the works of economists and sociologists, such as Mancur Olson (1965), Anthony Oberschall (1973), Samuel Popkin (1979), James Coleman (1990), Timur Kuran (1995), and Russell Hardin (1995), among many others, but also of historians, such as H. L. Root (1994), or political scientists such as B. Rothstein (2001). So, there is no doubt that RCT has produced many genuinely scientific contributions. This explains why, although it is widely criticized by many sociologists, it is also well established, as the audience of the journal created by Coleman, *Rationality and Society*, notably shows.

CAN RCT BE HELD AS A *GENERAL* THEORY?

So RCT is a powerful theory. But it also appears to be powerless when confronted with many social phenomena. We can build an impressive list of familiar phenomena it is unable to explain. This combination of success and failure is worth stressing since the social science community seems to be divided into two parties, those who hold the RCT as the new gospel and those who do not believe in this gospel. Also, this mixture of success and failure raises an important question as to its causes.

Two examples will illustrate the point that RCT appears powerless when confronted with important social phenomena. The effect of any single vote on any election turnout is infinitesimally small, so that according to RCT rational actors should refrain from voting, since the costs of voting are not zero. As one of these voters, I should prefer resting, walking, writing an article, or operating my vacuum cleaner to voting. Still, as many people do, I vote. So, RCT appears unable to explain why many people vote.

Many tentative "solutions" to this paradox have been proposed. People like to vote, contends one theory. People would have such strong regret if their ballot would have made a difference that they vote even though they know the probability of this event occurring is infinitesimally small, says another (Ferejohn and Fiorina 1974). If I do not vote, I run the risk of losing my reputation (Overbye 1995). Sometimes, the RCT is made more flexible thanks to the notion of "cognitive frames." Thus, G. A. Quattrone and Amos Tversky (1987) propose that the voter votes because he sees his motivation to vote as a sign that his party is going to win. Such a "frame" appears, however, not only ad hoc, but as introducing a black box. A. A. Schuessler (2000) introduces the conjecture that voters have an expressive rather than an instrumental interest in voting. None of these "solutions" has been widely accepted. Some of them, such as F. J. Ferejohn's and M. Fiorina's, display a high intellectual virtuosity. Still, they have not eliminated the "paradox."

Besides voting, other classical "paradoxes" can be mentioned. Maurice Allais's "paradoxes" show that, when confronted by lotteries, in many circumstances people do not make their choice in conformity with the principle of maximizing the expected utility (Allais and Hagen 1979; Hagen 1995). Bruno Frey (1997) has shown that people occasionally more easily accept some disagreement if no compensation is offered to them than when it is offered. Thus, in a study, people more easily accepted the presence of nuclear waste on their city's land when they were not offered compensation than when they were.

Sociology has produced many observations, which can be read as challenges to RCT. Thus, the negative reaction of social subjects against some given state of affairs has in many cases nothing to do with the costs they are exposed to by this state of affairs. On the other hand, actions can be frequently observed the benefit of which to the actor is zero or negative. In his *White Collar*, C. Wright Mills (1951) has identified what could be called the "overreaction paradox." He describes women clerks working in a firm where they all do the same tasks, sit in a great room, all have the same desks, the same working environment. Violent conflicts frequently occur over minor issues, as being seated closer to a source of heat or light. An outside observer would normally consider such conflicts irrational. As the behavior of the women would appear to him as strange in terms of the RCT model, he would turn to an irrational interpretation such as childish behavior. By so doing, he would confess that RCT cannot easily explain the observed overreaction paradox.

Psychologists have produced many experiments, including the classical "ultimatum game" (Hoffman and Spitzer 1985; Wilson 1993: 62–3), that resist RCT. In this game, player A can propose how a given amount of money should be shared between himself and B. B can only accept or refuse A's proposal. If he refuses, A and B get nothing. If B accepts, he gets the amount proposed by A. RCT predicts that A would propose, say, "80 percent of the sum for me, 20 percent for B." In most cases, however, A proposes rather a 50/50 sharing. Interestingly enough, researchers from Zurich have shown that a subject B would normally, in contradiction to RCT, refuse a sharing such as "80 percent for A, 20 percent for B," while when some specific part of his brain is inactivated by magnetic stimulation, he would accept it (Henderson 2006). These cases are painful news for RCT, since people behave according to its predictions in the ultimatum game when the normal operation of their brain is altered.

Many familiar observations cannot be interpreted satisfactorily in the RCT framework. In the conditions prevailing in most Western countries, political corruption has no tangible effects on the common man: he does not see or feel its effects. He considers corruption as unacceptable, though. Plagiarism can serve the interests of the plagiarized, since it draws public attention to the author. It is considered with severity, though. On some issues, as with the death penalty, I can have strong feelings, even though the probability that I am personally concerned is zero. In other words, in many circumstances, people are guided by considerations that have nothing to do with their own interests, nor with the consequences of their actions or reactions.

On the whole, psychologists, sociologists, and economists themselves have produced a huge number of observations which cannot easily be explained within the RCT frame. This raises two questions. Why does the RCT so often fail? Is there a model which would satisfy the scientific ambition behind RCT, namely trying to provide explanations without black boxes, and get rid of its defects?

REASONS FOR THE SHORTCOMINGS OF RCT

The social phenomena which RCT proves incapable of accounting for have many features in common. Three types of phenomena that evade RCT's jurisdiction can be identified.

Any behavior involves beliefs. To maximize my chances of survival, I look around before crossing the street. This behavior is dictated by my belief that, if I don't look around, I'm taking a serious risk. In such a case, the belief involved is commonplace. It is not worth the analyst's while to look at it more closely. To account for other items of behavior, however, it is crucial to explain the beliefs upon which they rest. Now, RCT has nothing to tell us about beliefs. So, a *first* type of phenomenon resistant to RCT includes things characterized by the fact that actors base their choices on non-commonplace beliefs.

We can postulate that an actor holds a given belief because he endorses a theory of which the belief is a consequence, and that endorsing a theory is a rational act. But, here, the rationality is *cognitive*, not *instrumental*: it consists in preferring the theory that enables the sociologist to account for given phenomena in the most satisfying possible way (in accordance with given criteria).

So, RCT runs into trouble because it reduces rationality to instrumental rationality. RCT followers have developed an interesting answer to this objection. Gerard Radnitzky (1987) maintains that endorsing a theory results from a cost-benefit analysis. Thus, a scientist stops believing in a theory, he contends, as soon as the objections raised against it make defending it too "costly". It is indeed difficult to explain why a boat hull disappears from the horizon before the mast, why the moon takes the shape of a crescent, why a navigator who maintains a constant direction returns to his starting point if we accept the theory that the earth is flat.

But what do we achieve in replacing the word "difficult" with the word "costly"? Defending a given theory is more "costly" *because* it is more difficult. We must then explain why this is so, and from instrumental rationality we come back to cognitive rationality. We prefer the Torricelli – Pascal theory of the barometer to the Aristotelian one because it is less costly to defend. But it is less costly because firstly it does not introduce the doubtful anthropomorphic idea that nature would dislike emptiness and secondly it predicts correctly why the quicksilver in a barometer rises higher at the bottom than at the top of a mountain. As long as we have not identified these differences, we cannot explain why it is more costly to defend the latter theory.

RCT is powerless with respect to a *second* category of phenomena: those characterized by the fact that actors are following *non-consequentialist prescriptive beliefs*. RCT is comfortable with prescriptive beliefs as long as they are consequential. RCT has no trouble explaining why most people believe that traffic lights are a good thing: despite the inconvenience they represent, I accept them because they have consequences that I judge beneficial. Here, RCT effectively accounts for both the belief and the reaction inspired by that belief. But RCT is mute when it comes to normative beliefs that cannot readily be explained in consequentialist terms (Boudon 2001, 2004). The subject in an "ultimatum game" acts against his own interest. The voter votes, even though his vote will have no effect on the election result. The citizen vehemently disapproves of corruption, though it doesn't affect him personally. The plagiarist gives rise to a feeling of repulsion, even when he hurts no one. We point an accusing finger at the imposter, though his machinations create problems for no one but himself.

RCT is powerless before a *third* category of phenomena, that involving behavior by individuals that we cannot assume to be dictated by self-interest. Regardless of where Sophocles' *Antigone* is being played, the viewer of the tragedy unhesitatingly condemns Creon and approves of Antigone. The reason RCT cannot explain this universal reaction is simple: the spectators' interests are in no way concerned by the matter before them. We therefore cannot explain their reaction by the possible consequences it would have for them, nor by any consequences at all because there are no such consequences. The spectator is not directly involved in Thebes' fate, because that fate belongs to the past and no one has any control over it any more. In this case the consequentialism and self-interest postulates are *ipso facto* disqualified.

Sociologists often find themselves confronted with this kind of phenomenon, since social actors are regularly called upon to evaluate situations in which they are not personally implicated. The death penalty threatens neither them nor their family or friends. Still, many have a strong opinion on the issue. How can a set of postulates that assumes them to be self-interested account for their reactions in situations where their interests are not at stake and there is no chance that they ever will be? These remarks lead to a crucial conclusion for the social sciences as a whole, namely, that RCT has little if anything to tell us about public opinion, a major subject for sociologists.

In sum, RCT is disarmed when it comes to phenomena involving non-commonplace beliefs, involving non-consequentialist prescriptive beliefs, and/or bringing into play reactions that do not, by the very nature of things, spring from any self-interest-based consideration.

BEYOND RCT: USING A BROADER THEORY OF RATIONALITY

The above considerations suggest that postulates P4, P5, P6 are welcome in some cases only. Reciprocally, the set of postulates P1, P2, P3 appears more general than the set P1 to P6. P1 defines what is usually called *methodological individualism*. The set of postulates P1, P2 defines *interpretive sociology* in Weber's sense (Weber 1922). The set P1, P2, P3 defines a version of interpretive sociology where actions are supposed to be rational in the sense where they are grounded on reasons in the actor's mind. I propose to identify the paradigm defined by this set as the *general theory of rationality* (GTR). It assumes that any collective phenomenon is the effect of human individual actions and that the action of an observed actor is always understandable, provided the observer has sufficient information, and finally that the causes of the actor's action are the reasons he has to undertake it.

Again RCT's failures result from its move to reduce rationality to its *instrumental* variety and neglect *cognitive rationality* and *axiological rationality*, the latter being, as we will see, an application of cognitive rationality to prescriptive problems. Conversely, it is essential for sociology to be aware that many classical and modern sociological studies owe their explanatory efficacy to the use of a *cognitive* version of rationality as opposed to the *instrumental* one.

Thanks to its broader notion of rationality, the GTR has all the advantages of RCT, above all offering explanations without black boxes, but not its disadvantages. This is the reason why it is commonly accepted, not only by philosophers, but by prominent classical and modern social scientists.

By creating his notion of "axiological rationality" or "evaluative rationality" (*Wertrationalität*) as complementary to, but essentially different from "instrumental rationality" (*Zweckrationalität*), Weber supported clearly the thesis that rationality can be noninstrumental, in other words that rationality should not be identified exclusively with instrumental rationality and *a fortiori* to the special form of instrumental rationality postulated by RCT (P1 to P6).

Many convincing classical and modern sociological analyses use implicitly, as in the case of Tocqueville, or explicitly, as in the case of Weber, the generalized conception of rationality which characterizes the GTR model. A few examples will illustrate this point.

COGNITIVE RATIONALITY

An example from Tocqueville (1986 [1856]) illustrates how the reasons for actors' beliefs and behavior are currently "cognitive. " He wondered why French intellectuals on the eve of the revolution firmly believed in the idea of Reason with a capital R, and why that notion had spread like wildfire among the public. It was an enigmatic phenomenon, not to be seen at the time in England, the United States, or Germany, and one with enormous macroscopic consequences.

Tocqueville's explanation consists in showing that Frenchmen at the end of the eighteenth century had strong reasons to believe in Reason. In France at that time, many traditional institutions seemed illegitimate. One such was the idea that the nobility was superior to the Third Estate. Nobles did not participate in either local political affairs or economic life; rather they spent their time at Versailles. Those who remained in the country held all the more tightly to their privileges, the poorer they were. This explains why they were designated with the name of a little bird of prey, the *hobereau*: a metaphor that spread immediately because it was perceived as fitting. The following equation was established in many minds: Tradition = Dysfunction = Illegitimacy, and, by opposition, Reason = Progress = Legitimacy. It was because this line of argument was latent in people's minds that the call of the *philosophes* to construct a society founded on Reason enjoyed immediate success.

The English, on the other hand, had good reason not to believe in those ideas. In England, the nobles played a crucial role: they ran local social, political, and economic life. The superiority attributed to them in people's customary thinking and by English institutions was perceived as functional and therefore legitimate. In general, traditional English institutions were not perceived as dysfunctional. Tocqueville proposes here, in other words, a brilliant GTR explanation of a puzzling macroscopic difference between France and England: people have reasons to react as they do, but these reasons are not instrumental (Boudon 2006).

An objection against GTR is that action is often grounded on false ideas and that in that case it cannot be held to be rational. Against this received idea, however, false beliefs can be grounded on strong reasons – on reasons perceived as valid by the subject – and in that sense be rational, as familiar examples show.

Vilfredo Pareto has rightly said that the history of science is the graveyard of all these false ideas which men have endorsed under the authority of scientists. In other words, science normally produces false ideas beside true ones. Now, nobody would accept the idea that these false ideas are endorsed by scientists under the effect of irrational causes, because their brains would have been wired in an inadequate fashion, or because their minds would have been obscured by inadequate "cognitive biases," "frames," "habitus," by class interests or by affective causes, in other words by the "biological," "psychological" or "cultural forces" evoked by Becker. Scientists believe in statements which often turn out to be false because they have strong reasons to believe them, given the cognitive context.

We do not believe any more in the idea that nature abhors a vacuum. Aristotle and most Greeks did, certainly not because they were irrational, but because they did not know how otherwise to explain many phenomena. The believers in the Aristotelian theory of the barometer, in the phlogiston, in ether or in the many other entities and mechanisms that appear now to us as imaginary had, in their time, given the cognitive context, strong reasons to believe in them. It was not immediately perceived as important that, when a piece of oxide of mercury is heated under an empty bell-glass, the drop of water that appears on the bell's wall should be taken into consideration. It was not immediately observed that it appears regularly, nor was it clearly perceived that it contradicts phlogiston theory. It was hard to predict that this drop of water would give Lavoisier the victory over Priestley.

Why should not the false beliefs produced by ordinary knowledge be explained in the same fashion as false scientific beliefs, namely as grounded in the mind of the social subject on reasons perceived by them as valid, given the cognitive context in which they move?

Needless to say, false beliefs should not *always* be explained in this fashion. Even scientists can hold false beliefs under the influence of passions and other genuinely irrational causes. But beliefs in false ideas *can* be caused by reasons in the minds of the actors. Even though these reasons appear to us as false, they can be perceived as right and strong by the actors themselves. To explain that they perceive as right what is wrong, we need not assume that their minds are obscured by conjectural

	Suicide attempted	Suicide not attempted	Total
Depression symptoms	a	b	$e = a + b$
No depression symptoms	c	d	$f = c + d$
Total	$g = a + c$	$h = b + d$	$i = a + b + c + d$

Figure 9.1

A causal presumption can be derived from the single piece of information a if a is much larger than e.g. i.

mechanisms of the kind Marxism ("false consciousness"), Sigmund Freud ("the unconscious"), Lucien Lévy-Bruhl (the *mentalité primitive*), and their many heirs imagined, nor by the "frames" evoked by RCT. In most cases, we get more acceptable explanations by assuming that, given the cognitive context in which they move, actors have strong reasons to believe in false ideas.

Elsewhere I have produced several examples showing that the rational explanation of beliefs we consider as normal in the case of false scientific beliefs can also be applied to ordinary knowledge. I have notably explored the cases of magical beliefs and of many false beliefs observed by cognitive psychologists (Boudon 2001).

I will limit myself to one example belonging to the second category. When psychiatrists are asked whether depression is a cause of suicide attempts, they would say it is. When asked why, they would answer that they have frequently observed patients exhibiting two features: many of their patients appear depressed and have attempted suicide. Of course, the answer reveals that the psychiatrists use *one* piece of information in the contingency table in figure 9.1: their argument is, namely, "a is high, hence depression is a cause of a suicide attempt."

Now, in order to conclude that there is a correlation between depression and suicide attempts, one has to consider, not one, but four pieces of information, not only a, but the difference $a/e - c/f$. So, the answer of the psychiatrists follows rules which are invalid. But this does not prove that we should assume, say, that the physician's brain is badly wired. More likely, they have subjectively strong and objectively valid reasons of believing what they believe. Suppose for instance that e in the figure would be equal to 20 percent, in other words that 20 percent of the physician's patients have depression symptoms, and that g would also be equal to 20 percent (20 percent of the patients have attempted suicide). Admittedly, higher figures would be unrealistic. With these assumptions, in the case where the percentage a of people presenting the two factors would be greater than 4, the two variables would be correlated, so that causality could plausibly be presumed. So, a physician who has seen, say, 10 people out of 100 presenting the two factors would have serious reason to believe in the existence of a causal relation between the two features.

In this example, the belief of the physician is not entirely false. In others, the beliefs produced by cognitive psychology appear unambiguously false. In most cases, I found, however, that these beliefs could be explained as grounded on reasons which the observer can easily understand.

Obviously, these reasons are not of the "benefit minus cost" type. They are of the cognitive type. The aim pursued by the actor is not to maximize something, but to determine whether something is likely or true. So, beside its instrumental dimension, rationality has a cognitive dimension. The GTR gives, on the whole, a more acceptable explanation of many phenomena than the eclectic widespread solution which tries to explain behavior by a mixture of instrumental rationality and irrational forces. The eclectic solution starts from the idea that *choice* can be considered *rational*, but *behavior* can be considered as including unavoidably *irrational* components, that is, being partially caused by sociocultural, anonymous forces beyond any control on the part of the individual (Elster 1989). By contrast, Weber, and before him Tocqueville among others, as well as the many modern sociologists defining themselves in terms of the Weberian version of interpretive sociology, start from the idea that the beliefs, preferences, and values of an individual can be analyzed as rationally selected by the individual. This latter theory implies, however, that we accept a theory of rationality including cognitive rationality, as well as the axiological declination of the latter, besides instrumental rationality.

The notion of cognitive rationality can be easily formalized: given a system of arguments {S} → P explaining a given phenomenon P, it is *cognitively rational* to accept {S} as a valid explanation of P if all the components of {S} are acceptable and mutually compatible and if no alternative explanation {S}′ is available and preferable to {S}.

The idea of explaining beliefs rationally can be illustrated by an example. The functionaries, military personnel, and politicians in ancient Rome were attracted by Mithraism and Christianity, and in modern Prussia by Freemasonry, because these cults were characterized by a vision of disembodied transcendence subjected to superior laws and a conception of the community of the faithful as a group to be organized hierarchically by means of initiation rituals. Now, the articles of faith in such religions were consistent with the social and political philosophy of these social categories. Their members believed that a social system could only function if under the control of a legitimate central authority and that that authority must be governed by impersonal rules. Their vision was of a functional, hierarchically organized society, and that hierarchy had to be founded on abilities and skills to be determined in accordance with formalized procedures, as was the case in the Roman and Prussian states. Taken together, these principles for the political organization of a "bureaucratic" state were, in their eyes, the reflection of a valid political philosophy. And they perceived the initiation rituals of Mithraism in the case of the Roman officers and civil servants or Freemasonry in the case of Prussian civil servants as expressing those same principles in a metaphysical-religious mode.

To cite another example, also from Weber: he explained why peasants had difficulty accepting monotheism because the uncertainty characteristic of natural phenomena did not seem to them at all compatible with the idea that the order of things could be subject to a single will. Monotheism was a notion which in and of itself implied a minimal degree of coherence and predictability.

AXIOLOGICAL RATIONALITY

Weber's "axiological rationality" is often understood as synonymous with "value conformity." I would propose rather to consider that the expression identifies the case where *prescriptive* beliefs are grounded in the mind of social actors on systems of reasons perceived by them as valid, exactly as *descriptive* beliefs (Boudon 2001).

Axiological rationality can be formally defined: given a system of arguments {Q} → N containing at least one axiological statement and concluding that the norm N is valid, all the components of {Q} being acceptable and mutually compatible, it is axiologically rational to accept N if no alternative system of arguments {Q}' preferable to {Q} and leading to prefer N' to N is available.

This intuition contained in Weber's notion was apparently already present in earlier thinkers, for example Adam Smith, which is itself an indirect proof of its relevance. While it is recognized that Smith's *Theory of Moral Sentiments* does not rest on RCT, it is sometimes believed that his better-known work *The Wealth of Nations* does. The following example shows, however, that even in this book, Smith uses also GTR.

Why, asks Adam Smith (1976 [1776]: bk. 1, ch. 10), do we consider it normal that the public executioner is paid a high salary? His qualifications are low. His job supposes a low level of training and competence. It takes a small part of his time. But, as the job is the most unpleasant of all, this should be compensated by a reasonably high salary. Other reasons justify the fact that physicians are well paid: their job is interesting and gratifying. They get satisfaction from practicing it. But as it implies a high level of responsibility, stress, and anxiety as well as exposure to criticism if a recommended cure fails, they should also be compensated for these negative aspects of the job by a reasonably high income. Other jobs require few qualifications, are not excessively unpleasant, and entail a low level of responsibility. In these cases a low salary is justified. In his discussion of salaries, Smith starts, in other words, from the idea that the salaries rewarding various types of activities are normally considered by people as more or less fair. Secondly these feelings of fairness are dictated by a more or less implicit system of reasons shared to a greater or lesser degree by all. Thirdly these reasons deal with a number of dimensions of a given job, and finally, given the characterization of a job on these dimensions, the public concludes that such and such job should be more or less highly paid. To use a concept from Smith's *Theory of Moral Sentiments*, the relative consensus emerging on the question as to whether a job should be more or less highly paid than another derives from the set of reasons developed by "impartial spectators," by individuals trying to figure out systems of reasons likely to be accepted by all.

First of all, Smith's analysis does not use RCT. People do not react as they do when they learn that some type of job is paid in the way it is because this would maximize some difference between benefits and costs. They have reasons to believe what they believe, but these reasons are not of the cost-benefit type, nor even of the consequential type. Smith's argument takes, rather, the form of a deduction from principles. People have the feeling that it is fair to pay a reasonably high salary to miners or to the public executioner on the basis reasons derived from principles, claims Smith. If miners were not paid more than, say, low-level clerks, this would perhaps generate consequences (such as a miners' strike, say), but these eventual consequences are not the causes of the fact that most people consider the miners should be paid more. People do not believe in this statement because they fear these eventual consequences.

Michael Walzer, a contemporary theorist of ethics, proposes analyses of some of our moral sentiments similar to Smith's (Walzer 1983). We consider conscription a legitimate recruitment method in the case of soldiers but not miners because the function of the former, but not of the latter, is vital in preserving the integrity of the nation. If conscription could be applied to miners, it could be applied to any and eventually to all kinds of activities, leading to a regime incompatible with the principles of democracy. In the same fashion, it is easily accepted that soldiers are used as garbage collectors in emergency situations. But it would be considered illegitimate to use them for such tasks in normal situations. In all these examples, collective moral feelings are grounded on reasons likely to be shared by many people, but not on reasons of the type considered in RCT.

A notion such as *fairness* can of course be affected by contextual parameters. Thus, in the ultimatum game, the 50/50 proposal is more frequent in societies where cooperation with one's neighbors is essential to the current economic activity than in societies where competition between neighbors prevails (Henrich et al. 2001). Such findings are not incompatible with a rational interpretation of moral beliefs, though. They show rather that a system of reasons is more easily evoked in some contexts than in others. In summary, while contextual variation in moral beliefs is generally interpreted as validating a cultural-irrational view of axiological feelings, the contextual-rational paradigm illustrated by the previous examples appears more satisfactory: as offering self-sufficient explanations, namely, explanations without black boxes.

THE VALIDITY OF REASONS

Why does an actor consider a system of reasons to be good? Immanuel Kant has written that looking for general criteria of truth amounts to trying to milk a male goat. We can only state that a theory is better or worse than another one. Priestley had strong reasons for believing the phlogiston theory was true. It became difficult to follow him only from the moment when Lavoisier had shown that all the phenomena Priestley had explained thanks to his phlogiston could be explained otherwise. In other words, we can be sure that a theory is better than another one, but *there are no general criteria of the strength of a system of reasons*. More generally, let us assume for a while that had we been able to identify the general criteria of truth or rationality, the next question would be: On which principles do you ground the criteria? And so on, ad infinitum.

Borrowing examples from the history of science has the advantage of clarifying the discussion about the criteria of rationality. But the conclusion to be drawn from the above example (that there are no general criteria of rationality) applies not only to scientific but to ordinary beliefs as well. And it applies not only to descriptive, but to prescriptive beliefs.

This latter point often meets some resistance as a consequence of a wrong interpretation of David Hume's uncontroversial theorem that "no conclusion of the prescriptive type can be drawn from a set of statements of the descriptive type." But it should be observed that a prescriptive or normative conclusion can be derived from a set of descriptive statements which are all descriptive, except one, so that the real formulation of Hume's theorem should be "no conclusion of the prescriptive type can be drawn from a set of statements *all* of the descriptive type." I have developed this point more fully in Boudon (2004). It is essential since it shows that the gap between prescriptive and descriptive beliefs is not as wide as many people think. It gives a clear meaning to Weber's assertion that axiological rationality and instrumental rationality are currently combined in social action, though they are entirely distinct from one another. As implied by the GTR model, cognitive reasons ground prescriptive as well as descriptive beliefs in the minds of individuals.

CONCLUSION

To summarize, we have defended three conclusions. Firstly, social action in the general case depends on beliefs. Secondly, beliefs, actions, attitudes should as far as possible be treated as rational, more precisely as the effect of reasons perceived by social actors as valid. Thirdly, reasons of the "cost-benefit" type should not be given more attention than they deserve. Rationality is one thing, expected utility another.

The rationality postulate should be introduced because social actors try to act in congruence with reasons they perceive as valid. This explains why their own behavior is normally meaningful to them. In some cases, the context makes these reasons of the "cost-benefit" type. In other cases, they are not, even if we accept that we should interpret the notions of cost and benefit in the broadest fashion: what are the costs and benefits to me of miners being better paid than low-level clerks, if I have no chance of ever becoming a clerk or a miner?

In the cases of interest to sociologists, people's actions are understandable because they are moved by reasons. But these reasons can belong to several types. Action can rest on beliefs or not; the beliefs can be commonplace or not; they can be descriptive or prescriptive. Prescriptive beliefs can be consequentially grounded or not. In all cases, the GTR model assumes that action has to be explained by its meaning to the actor; it supposes in other words that it is grounded in the actor's eyes on a system of reasons he perceives as valid.

One last point: the GTR is more promising than the eclectic version of RCT which supposes that actors are guided by "frames" and other "forces," for this eclecticism is balanced by the loss of the main advantage of RCT: providing self-sufficient explanations. It is also more promising than the "program-based behavior" model (PBBM) proposed by evolutionary epistemologists (Vanberg 2002), for the latter model unavoidably generates black boxes, in other words further questions of the type "Where does the program come from? Why do such actors endorse it while others do not?" As the GTR model has an answer to such questions, it is capable of generating self-sufficient explanations.

The GTR is more general than the RCT, but it cannot be applied to all phenomena. Irrationality should be given its rightful place. Traditional and affective actions also exist. Moreover, all actions rest on a ground of instincts. I look to my right and left when crossing a street because I wish to stay alive. Reason is the servant of passions, as Hume said. But passions need Reason: the rain dances and other magical rituals are motivated by the passion of the believers to survive, to see their crop grow; but nobody would consider that this passion in itself explains why they endorse the objectively invalid belief that the rituals are efficient.

The theory of rationality I have proposed raises finally some important questions which I will content myself with merely mentioning here. Does the fact that behavior and beliefs are normally inspired by strong reasons, though these reasons can be false, mean that any behavior or belief can be justified? The answer is no. Priestley believed in phlogiston, Lavoisier did not. The two had strong reasons for believing what they believed and they saw their reasons as valid. The latter was right, the former wrong, though. So, the strength of reasons is a function of the context.

Exactly like cognitive reasons, axiological reasons can become stronger or weaker, that is, be perceived as more or less valid over time, mainly because new reasons are invented. When it was shown that the abolition of capital punishment could not be held responsible for any significant increase in crime rates, the argument "capital punishment is good because it is an effective threat against crime" became weaker. This provoked a change in our moral sensibility toward capital punishment. There are no mechanically applicable general criteria of the strength of the reasons grounding prescriptive or descriptive beliefs. Still, irreversible changes in prescriptive as well as descriptive beliefs are currently observed because it happens currently that a system of reasons {S}' appears after a while to be better than the system {S}. This is exemplified in the *descriptive* case by Lavoisier and Priestley, in the *prescriptive* case by Montesquieu (who defended the idea that political power would be more efficient if it was divided) and Jean Bodin (who could not imagine that political power would be efficient without being concentrated). Montesquieu's and Bodin's beliefs as to what a *good* political organization *should be* were grounded on reasons the two perceived as valid. We know now that Montesquieu was right.

It can be readily shown that the above-mentioned "paradoxes" can be easily solved. They have no RCT solution but an easy GTR solution: plagiarism and corruption provoke a negative reaction not because of their consequences, but because they are incompatible with systems of reasons appearing to most people to be valid. The same is true of the other paradoxes: in the "ultimatum game" individuals pick up the 50/50 solution because they wonder which solution is *fair* and do their best to define fairness in this case. Against the RCT, they do not ask what is *good for them*. People reject corruption though it is neutral to them because they endorse a theory from which they conclude that it is unacceptable. In all theses cases, they display *teleological* behavior: they want to reach a goal. But the goal is to maximize one's interests or the satisfaction of one's preferences only in particular cases; it may be also to find the true or the fair answer to a question or to a situation. Given these various goals, they are rational in the sense that they look for the best or at least for a satisfactory system of reasons able to provide a ground to their answer.

Finally, a historical conjecture can be introduced. The success of RCT – of the utility-maximizing approach – in its genuine or eclectic versions is partly due to a sound reaction against the sociology which prevailed notably in the period 1960–80. Against the greatest classical sociologists, such as Tocqueville, Weber or Durkheim, the *homo sociologicus* was depicted by social scientists inspired by a Marxian or Nietzschean vulgate as the mere product of his social environment and as endorsing mere illusions on his own actions, objectives, and values as well as on the world generally. Unfortunately, against this model, RCT rediscovered the rationality of man only in its instrumental dimension.

Bibliography

Allais, M., and Hagen, O. (eds.) (1979) *Expected Utility Hypotheses and the Allais Paradox: Contemporary Discussions of Decisions under Uncertainty with Allais' Rejoinder.* Dordrecht: Reidel.

Becker, G. (1996) *Accounting for Tastes.* Cambridge, MA: Harvard University Press.

Boudon, R. (2001) *The Origin of Values.* London and New Brunswick: Transaction.

Boudon, R. (2004) *The Poverty of Relativism,* Oxford: Bardwell Press.

Boudon, R. (2006) *Tocqueville for Today,* Oxford: Bardwell Press.

Coleman, J. (1986) *Individual Interests and Collective Action: Selected Essays.* Cambridge: Cambridge University Press.

Coleman, J. (1990) *Foundations of Social Theory.* Cambridge, MA: Harvard University Press.

Durkheim, É. (1960 [1897]) *Le Suicide.* Paris: Presses Universitaires de France.

Elster, J. (1989) *The Cement of Society.* Cambridge: Cambridge University Press.

Ferejohn, F. J., and Fiorina, M. (1974) "The Paradox of Not Voting: A Decision Theoretic Analysis." *American Political. Science Review* 68(2): 525–36.

Frey, B. (1997) *Not Just for the Money: An Economic Theory of Personal Motivation.* Cheltenham: Edward Elgar.

Hagen, O. (1995) "Risk in Utility Theory, in Business and in the World of Fear and Hope," in J. Götschl (ed.), *Revolutionary Changes in Understanding Man and Society, Scopes and Limits.* Dordrecht: Kluwer.

Hardin, R. (1995) *One for All: The Logic of Group Conflict.* Princeton: Princeton University Press.

Henderson, M. (2006) "Why Say No to Free Money? Is Neuro-Economics Stupid?" *Times Online,* 7 October.

Henrich, J., Boyd, R., Bowles, S., Camerer, C., Fehr, E., et al. (2001) "In Search of Homo Economicus: Behavioral Experiments in 15 Small-Scale Societies." *American Economic Review* 91(2): 73–8.

Hoffman, E., and Spitzer, M. L. (1985) "Entitlements, Rights and Fairness. An Experimental Examination of Subjects' Concepts of Distributive Justice." *Journal of Legal Studies* 14: 259–97.

Hollis, M. (1977) *Models of Man: Philosophical Thoughts on Social Action.* Cambridge: Cambridge University Press.

Kuran, T. (1995) *Private Truths, Public Lies: The Social Consequences of Preference Falsification.* Cambridge, MA: Harvard University Press.

Lindenberg, S., and Fillieule, R. (2005) "Rationalité," in M. Borlandi et al., *Dictionnaire de la Pensée Sociologique.* Paris: Presses Universitaires de France.

Mills, C. W. (1951) *White Collar: The American Middle Classes.* New York: Oxford University Press.

Oberschall, A. (1973) *Social Conflict and Social Movements.* Englewood Cliffs: Prentice Hall.

Olson, M. (1965) *The Logic of Collective Action: Public Goods and the Theory of Groups.* Cambridge, MA: Harvard University Press.

Overbye, E. (1995) "Making a Case for the Rational, Self-Regarding, 'Ethical' Voter . . . and Solving the 'Paradox of Not Voting' in the Process." *European Journal of Political Research* 27: 369–96.

Popkin, S. (1979) *The Rational Peasant: The Political Economy of Rural Society in Vietnam.* Berkeley: University of California Press.

Quattrone, G. A., and Tversky A. (1987) "Self-Deception and the Voter's Illusion," in Elster J. (ed.), *The Multiple Self.* Cambridge: Cambridge University Press.

Radnitzky, G. (1987) "La Perspective économique sur le progrès scientifique: Application en philosophie de la science de l'analyse coût-bénéfice." *Archives de philosophie* 50: 177–98.

Root, H. L. (1994) *The Fountain of Privilege: Political Foundations of Economic Markets in Old Regime France and England.* Berkeley: University of California Press.

Rothstein, B. (2001) "The Universal Welfare State as a Social Dilemma." *Rationality and Society* 13(2): 213–33.

Ruse, M. (1993) "Une défense de l'éthique évolutionniste," in J. P. Changeux (ed.), *Fondements naturels de l'éthique.* Paris: Odile Jacob.

Schuessler, A. A. (2000) "Expressive Voting." *Rationality and Society* 12(1): 87–119.

Smith, A. (1976 [1776]). *An Inquiry into the Nature and Causes of the Wealth of Nations.* Oxford: Clarendon Press.

Tocqueville, A de (1986 [1856]). *L'Ancien Régime et la Révolution*, in *Tocqueville.* Paris: Laffont.

Vanberg, V. J. (2002) "Rational Choice vs. Program-Based Behavior: Alternative Theoretical Approaches and their Relevance for the Study of Institutions." *Rationality and Society* 14(1): 7–54.

Walzer, M. (1983) *Spheres of Justice: A Defence of Pluralism and Equality.* Oxford: Martin Robertson.

Weber, M. (1922) *Aufsätze zur Wissenschaftlehre.* Tübingen: Mohr.

Weber, M. (1988 [1922]). *Gesammelte Aufsätze zur Religionssoziologie.* Tübingen: Mohr.

Wilson, J. Q. (1993) *The Moral Sense.* New York: The Free Press.

Part III

Perspectives on Social and Cultural Analysis

10

Pragmatism and Symbolic Interactionism

JACK BARBALET

INTRODUCTION

Convention is not necessarily an adequate guide to understanding. As we shall see, the preceding statement implies a principle of pragmatism. It is also a necessary preface to any discussion of both pragmatism and symbolic interactionism as doctrines or bodies of thought on the one hand, and intellectual practices and their output, in the form of a literature and traditions of understandings, on the other.

The convention that is of concern here claims that symbolic interactionism is the expression of pragmatism in sociology. The term "symbolic interactionism" was first presented by Herbert Blumer (1937) and designed to articulate and advance the pragmatic social psychology of George Herbert Mead (1934). This latter Blumer summarized as three basic propositions: first, an actor's perception of and orientation to an object is a function of the meaning that actor imputes to the object; second, the meaning an actor ascribes to an object is a function of the processes of interaction in which the actor is implicated; third, the meaning ascribed to an object by an actor is likely to change over time as the actor's interactions change.

This convention, that symbolic interactionism is sociological pragmatism, requires serious qualification for the following reasons. Sociological pragmatism encompasses more than symbolic interactionism. Second, Mead's version of it is not an exclusive or unambiguous statement of pragmatism. Third, one implication of the previous claim is that symbolic interactionism may be subject to pragmatic challenge. Each of these issues will be discussed in this chapter. Additionally, the value of pragmatism – and especially the Jamesian version of it – will be demonstrated by applying it to a critique of rational choice theory. Both pragmatism and sociology are, importantly, reactions and alternatives to utilitarianism. The continuing relevance of pragmatism, therefore, can be demonstrated through its critique of a present manifestation of utilitarianism in the form of rational choice theory.

Pragmatism and Sociology

In summary, pragmatism is a method focused on the consequences of practical action. Charles Peirce regarded doubt, for instance, as a result of disjuncture between the requirements of human existence and its environment. Doubt stimulates inquiry and therefore science. In dispelling doubt these practices lead to a "fixation of belief" (Peirce 1966a). Thus knowledge does not represent reality, according to Peirce, but is an instrument for dealing with it (Peirce 1966b). Similarly, William James, in a paper first published in 1898, following Peirce's argument, held that to attain understanding of any object it is necessary to know what conceivable practical effects the object may produce and that it is the conception of these effects that constitutes the meaningful conception of the object (James 1920). The importance of the instrumentality of action rather than its environmental determination is also emphasized by John Dewey in another foundational statement of pragmatism (Dewey 1896).

The antecedents of action, especially external stimulation, while crucial to utilitarian accounts, are of secondary significance in pragmatism. Pragmatism, in understanding or forming a meaning of action, is concerned primarily with its consequences or outcomes. It follows that the distinction between thought and action is not accepted by pragmatism as implying that each is a different entity, as in Cartesian dualism, for instance, but refers only to distinct functions of engagement with the world. Finally, as each action necessarily changes the conditions for subsequent actions, pragmatism regards agency, for instance, and also interest, identity, and so on as things that are not given in persons prior to action but discovered, emergent, or constructed by them in the course of action. These principles, which are spelled out in different ways by the founders of philosophical pragmatism – Charles Peirce, William James, and John Dewey – and elaborated by pragmatic social psychologists – especially Charles Horton Cooley (1964) and George Herbert Mead (1934) – have resonance in much sociology.

Hans Joas, in a discussion of the work of the leading founders of the Chicago School, in particular William Isaac Thomas, Robert Park, Everett Hughes, and, of course, Herbert Blumer, demonstrates the primary influence of the pragmatism of Peirce and Dewey especially, but also Mead, on the theoretical outlook and research activities of this quintessential American sociological tradition (Joas 1987: 96–106). The influence of pragmatism on American sociology, however, cannot be confined to the Chicago School.

In terms of his focus, intellectual style and theoretical formation Thorstein Veblen, for instance, is not of the Chicago School. Yet his work is infused with pragmatism and relies on its assumptions. In his critique of economic science, for instance, Veblen complains against the idea that human organisms can be activated by external stimuli to follow a predetermined direction and that they would remain unchanged by the experience: "the hedonistic conception of man [as] a lightning calculator of pleasures and pains, who oscillates like a homogenous globule of desire of happiness under the impulse of stimuli that shift him about the area, but leave him intact" (Veblen 1919: 73). In place of such a conceptualization Veblen proposes that agents purposefully seek "realisation and expression in an unfolding activity" that "afford the point of departure for the next step in the process" and he proposes that within this process "both the agent and his [or her] environment" change (Veblen 1919: 74–5). What is true of the individual, Veblen immediately adds, is true of the group. This broad statement is not merely consistent with pragmatism but summarizes and paraphrases relevant passages of Peirce and James.

Veblen's account of human instinct is identical with James's (James 1890b: ch. 24). According to Veblen, human instinct alone "denotes the conscious pursuit of an objective end which the instinct in question makes worth while" (Veblen 1914: 5). Thus " 'instinct,' as contra-distinguished from tropismatic action [in humans], involves consciousness and adaptation to an end aimed at" (Veblen 1914: 4). As tropismatic action is action exhaustively described in terms of an external stimulus, it is invariant and fixed in its course. For Veblen, though, human instinct avoids such predetermination as it contains purposiveness – "adaptation to an end aimed at" – and coordinated object-awareness and self-awareness – "consciousness." Veblen's proximate source for this account is William James. James characteristically insists that the unique quality of human instinct is in the faculty of consciousness: because of "memory, power of reflection, and power of inference" the experience of instinctive impulses is always "in connection with a foresight of th[eir] results" (James 1890b: 390).

The influence of pragmatism has possibly been most forceful when least direct. Max Weber's seminal study, *The Protestant Ethic and the Spirit of Capitalism*, for instance, mentions pragmatism very briefly in a more or less dismissive footnote (Weber 1991: 232–3). It can be shown, however, that Weber's reading of James's *The Varieties of Religious Experience* (1902) made the writing of the *Protestant Ethic* possible, even though Weber rejects James's treatment of religion in terms of its underlying emotions as opposed to its doctrines, which Weber, on the other hand, sees as elemental.

The pragmatic method, as indicated above, accounts for a thing in terms of its consequences. This is also a key aspect of Weber's endeavors in *The Protestant Ethic*, in which the influence of a set of religious ideas on economic life is delineated (Weber 1991: 89–90). Nearly a decade prior to writing *The Protestant Ethic*, in 1895, Weber discussed religion in his inaugural lecture, "The Nation State and Economic Policy" (Weber 1994). In both works the social and cultural correlates of religion are identified and considered. But whereas in "The Nation State and Economic Policy" religion is a proxy for nation – Weber discusses German Protestants and Polish Catholics – in *The Protestant Ethic* religion is for the first time treated as an independent variable that is of interest because of the unintended consequences for which it is responsible, namely motivation for financial gain as an end in itself, which Weber summarizes as the "capitalist spirit" (Barbalet 2001). Many things occurred in the intervening period between the writing of these two works, but one of relevance for an understanding of the different treatment of religion in Weber's writing was his reading James's *Varieties*, in which is enunciated the principle that the significance of a religious experience is necessarily in its consequences (James 1902: 15–19). Weber extended consideration of the consequences of religious experience to economic relations and organization, and in doing so applied the pragmatic method to Reformation Protestantism. James's *Varieties* was the source of Weber's theoretical breakthrough (Barbalet 2007: 29–35).

From the examples above the relationship of continuity between distinct bodies of intellectual work can be seen as taking at least three forms. One is self-conscious indebtedness that constitutes a "tradition." In this case the nexus between pragmatism and the Chicago School, and also symbolic interactionism, is one in which later practitioners and theorists pay homage to earlier ones. Another possibility, exemplified in Veblen, is the application of pragmatic principles without drawing attention to their source. This is not the building of a tradition but the integration of earlier methods and findings (along with others) in the broad advancement of a science or research endeavor. Because this use of pragmatism does not draw attention to itself it is not typically seen as tradition-building, and therefore recognition of the links between the intellectual source and its later application is discovered and attributed by others. A similar and possibly more unlikely use of pragmatism – extensive, unacknowledged but significant – is in the work of Arthur Bentley, for example, founder of group theory in politics (Bentley 1949, 1954). A third relationship indicated in this discussion, through the example of Weber's *Protestant Ethic*, is that of denial or opposition, in which the importance of pragmatism is a signal though negative force or influence but nevertheless formative. Not only Weber's sociology of religion but also Durkheim's relies on Jamesian pragmatism in this third sense (Barbalet 2007: 35–9).

VARIETIES OF PRAGMATISM

In addition to the issue of multiple possibilities of inheritance, so that not only symbolic interactionism but other sociological formations may be expressions of pragmatism, there is the question of the constitution of pragmatism itself. It is, of course, important to acknowledge the unitary nature of pragmatism in order to distinguish it from other orientations and intellectual dispositions. But to do so is to operate at a highly general level of typological distinction or discrimination in which, say, idealism, rationalism, empiricism, and pragmatism are separated by distinctive features. When focus is directed to particular statements by exponents of a given theoretical orientation, on the other hand, divergence within the perspective and disagreements that constitute a large part of its intellectual vigor become salient and are in that sense more important than the umbrella of commonality that contains and encourages such differences.

At its inception the divergence alluded to in the previous paragraph was already manifest within pragmatism. Charles Peirce first introduced the term "pragmatism" as the name of a logical method for going beyond formalism and abstraction by indicating practical consequences that could be deduced from speculative and metaphysical claims, as indicated above (Peirce 1966a, 1966b). James drew on Peirce's method and developed it through consideration of relevant psychological mechanisms implicated in practical actions and their consequences (James 1920). In doing this James continued and expanded arguments he had presented a little earlier in related papers, "The Sentiment of Rationality" and "The Will to Believe," collected with others in 1897 as *The Will to Believe and Other Essays in Popular Philosophy* (1956). As the titles of these papers suggest, psychological rather logical elements of method were paramount for James, something to which Peirce took exception.

Indeed, because of these objections Peirce was moved to rename his method "pragmaticism" and reinforce his distance from James's approach, which James continued to call "pragmatism," by saying that the new name was "ugly enough to be safe from kidnappers" (Peirce 1966c, 1966d).

Of particular relevance in appreciating the singular thrust of Jamesian pragmatism is the way that certain data from his psychological theorizing are brought into his development of the pragmatic method. A general pragmatic notion, shared by all of its exponents, is that knowledge resides in concrete human acts. Among other things this means that knowledge, both of the external world and self-knowledge, cannot be merely given and therefore cannot be the passive outcome of past experience but must be based on ongoing experience projected into the future, for that is where the consequences of present action are found. James's appreciation of the significance of the consequences of action as future-located leads him to emphasize not merely psychological mechanisms as integral to pragmatism but more particularly emotions. It is only through emotions, James shows, that the future is apprehended; and, only an emotional basis of action can achieve or create one possible future against others. Before the details of this position are indicated, it is important to notice that not only does James bring emotional factors into the mechanisms of his pragmatic method, but also the insights of pragmatism infuse his psychology.

James's *The Principles of Psychology* (1890) is premised on an implicit Darwinism that leads him to write of the human organism as adapting to its environment through biological functions and processes. But James does not conceive the human organism as merely a product of external forces to which it is subjected. For James the human organism has interests that it is active in realizing, creating its own circumstances out of adaptive necessity. So it is with James's treatment of mind, as actively projecting from present experience into the future. James conceives the faculty of mind pragmatically: whereas empiricist approaches tend to treat human mind as subject to conditioning, as a passive imprint of past experiences, James regards mind as a selective and interested agent in the creation of its own future. "Only those items which I *notice* shape my mind," says James, and what is noticed is not accidentally achieved, which would lead experience to be "an utter chaos," but comes out of "selective interest" (James 1890a: 402; emphasis in original). James nominates emotions as the core basis or source of selective interest.

The discussion of James's theory of emotions in the relevant literature has focused almost exclusively on his treatment in chapter 25 of *Principles*, which proposes that in "coarse" emotions bodily or physical sensations are prior to emotional feelings. This is not James's theory of emotions, despite conventional assumptions, but part of his argument concerning the necessarily physical basis of emotions, which stands in contrast to the idea that emotions emanate from a source external to a person's experience of embodied self. James's more comprehensive account of emotions, which indicates their experiential nature and their role in self-identity and action, is developed in additional chapters of *Principles* and in the essays collected in the *Will to Believe*, which together provide a comprehensive theory of emotions (Barbalet 1999). Rather than outline the entirety of James's theory of emotions it will be sufficient to show how he demonstrates the necessity of emotions for understanding action on the basis of its future orientation.

All actions have consequences that cannot be contemporaneous with the action itself but are necessarily subsequent to it, so that at the present time the consequences of an action must occur in the future. This means that uncertainty is constant in social experience. James argues that the unease of futurity can only be settled by a feeling of expectancy, and that this feeling is the basis of rationality (James 1956: 77–8). In this affective or emotional displacement of uncertainty concerning the future the "emotional effect of expectation" is to enable actors to proceed in their practical affairs (James1956: 78–9). In this way rationality is characterized in terms of a particular emotional configuration that enables actors to effectively engage unknowable futures about which factual information – because it has not yet occurred – is simply not available. But the sentiment of rationality is not the only emotional apprehension of the unknowable future that James discusses.

In most social situations, James observes, action is taken in the absence of evidence concerning its most appropriate course (James 1956: 23–4). The general form of such a circumstance he calls a "forced option," a situation in which there is no possibility of not choosing (James 1956: 3). A paradigm case is trust. In order to achieve an outcome in a social context cooperation between persons is typically required. To effectively cooperate, one actor is frequently called upon to trust another. But whether trust is warranted can only be known after it is given. The decision to trust, therefore, cannot be based on relevant evidence. Under these circumstances the absence of evidence regarding a correct course of action means that deliberative calculation to aid decisionmaking is impossible, and an emotional rather than a logical choice or commitment is necessary if action is to occur at all.

James demonstrates the constructive significance of emotion through the case of the "Alpine climber" in which an actor's particular emotional commitment leads to a definitive concrete outcome (James 1956: 96–7). In order to avoid difficulty an Alpine climber must leap from a narrow and icy mountain ledge, a feat she has not previously performed. If she is engaged by the emotions of confidence and hope she is likely to accomplish what would otherwise be impossible. Fear and mistrust, on the other hand, are likely to lead to hesitation, which will increase the probability of missing her foothold, with the likely consequence of her falling to her death. Whichever emotion is engaged will be commensurate with a particular outcome, but with contrastingly different consequences. James's point is that the emotional component of action is significant in prefiguring its consequences. In that sense, an actor's emotional apprehension of her agency selects one possible future from the optional range.

The summary role of emotion in practical conduct or human agency, then, is to facilitate action even in the absence of information concerning its likely outcome, and emotion therefore displaces the need for action to rely on logic or calculation alone. The evidence on which deliberative calculation relies is simply not available for most social actions. The emotional contribution to agency is to overcome the uncertainty of an unknowable future by providing an emotional orientation to one possible future in the realization of a present action. Otherwise action could not occur.

The sociological relevance of the element of emotions in James's pragmatism is clear in the preceding remarks. Even in his philosophical discussion of the pragmatic theory of truth, for instance, there is discernible proto-sociological understanding.

In *Pragmatism* James describes the basis of truth as "a credit system" in which "You accept my verification of one thing, I yours of another" (James 1907: 207–8). He goes on to say:

> All human thinking gets discursified; we exchange ideas; we lend and borrow verifications, get them from one another by means of social intercourse. All truth thus gets verbally built out, stored up, and made available for everyone. (James 1907: 213–14)

Perhaps better known is his treatment of the self in *Principles*, comprising interactions between the "I" and the "Me," with a part of the Me, the social self, which forms and functions in terms of the recognition it receives from others (James 1890a: 292–300). The predominant discussion of the self in sociological social psychology, which focuses on trans-subjectivity as a means to the formation of self, and which occurs principally through a sense of the awareness and especially the evaluations of others, effectively summarizes this contribution of James to the thought of the later pragmatic social psychology of Cooley and Mead. Cooley, for instance, captures this notion by referring to the fact that persons "liv[e] in the minds of others without knowing it, just as we daily walk the solid ground without thinking how it bears us up" (Cooley 1964: 208). But in considering the formative content of pragmatic social psychology the differences between Cooley and Mead are as important as the overlapping elements of their theories.

Cooley's concept of the looking-glass self, for instance, in which an individual's self-evaluation and self-feeling derives from their apprehension of how others perceive and assess them (Cooley 1964: 184–5), develops James's notion of the social self. This idea of self-monitoring that is central to Cooley's looking-glass self is elaborated in Mead's notion of role-taking, in which the self has social agency through its capacity to anticipate the intentions of others (Mead 1934: 254). A difference between Cooley and Mead, though, is that whereas Cooley explicitly develops the emotional dimensions of this process, Mead neglects them – indeed rejects them – and emphasizes instead the cognitive dimensions of self (Mead 1934: 173). In all of this the social sources of self remain paramount and self's relation to the other is integral to self-formation. While Mead may underplay emotion in self-formation, he reiterates a crucial dimension of James's considerations in showing that the self which is interior to the individual person is also a social process. His argument is that the impulsive tendency, the "I," exchanges or communicates with the analytically distinct part or phases of the self, the "Me," in which socially sourced attitudes and understandings reside (Mead 1934: 173–8). Nevertheless, Mead's emphasis on cognition and symbol at the expense of emotion has had significant implications for the development of symbolic interactionism.

SYMBOLIC INTERACTIONISM

As its name suggests, symbolic interactionism is an approach that builds on the social formation of symbols, common or shared meanings, and their use in communication, both within the self and in self's orientation to others, in interactions between social agents. The term symbolic interactionism was coined by Herbert

Blumer in his elaboration of Mead's social psychology, but the sources of symbolic interactionism also include the work of early twentieth-century Chicago sociologists, including William Isaac Thomas, Robert Park and Everett Hughes. As with all intellectual traditions, the development of symbolic interactionism has led to different exponents emphasizing distinct elements of the approach, so that Blumer's original formulation has provided opportunity for modification, both theoretical and methodological, by what have become known as the Iowa School, the New Iowa School, and the dramaturgical approach, especially in the work of Erving Goffman (Hall 2007; Plummer 2000).

What unifies symbolic interactionism, however, is a set of assumptions shared by the different approaches that have developed within it. These include the notion that social processes necessarily contain an element of emergent contingency or unpredictability; that social agency is prior to structural determination, and therefore that institutions are conditional upon agency and interaction; and, finally, that self and society are terms for continuously connected processes and not distinct and separate entities. These assumptions are all pragmatic. They do not, however, complete pragmatic possibilities and especially those that are located in James's elaboration of the pragmatic method. The following discussion begins with Blumer's statement of symbolic interactionism.

Symbolic interaction functions through a process which Blumer calls "self-indication" (Blumer 1969: 83): the acting unit is "the self"; the self acts "in and with regard to the situation"; and action is "formed or constructed by interpreting the situation" (Blumer 1969: 85). Interpretation consists of three steps, according to Blumer: first, the acting self must "identify the things" the action is to deal with, such as tasks, opportunities, obstructions, distractions, and resources; second, it must "assess them in some fashion"; and third, it must "make decisions on the basis of the assessment" (Blumer 1969: 85). While it is required that action is necessarily constructed by the self through its interpretation of the situation, such interpretations are typically established through joint and reciprocal processes. Additionally, Blumer says, "previous interaction" generates "common understandings or definitions of how to act in this or that situation," which, he continues, "enable[s] people to act alike" (Blumer 1969: 86).

Two things stand out in this summary of Blumer's position. One is that the situation which the self acts with regard to is interpreted exclusively through cognitive processes. The other is the tension between, first, the requirements of "self-indication" that action be constructed by interpretations performed by the self, and second, the existence of a common stock of interpretations resulting from previous interactions which the self draws upon. This tension remains unresolved because of the commitment within symbolic interactionism to both the interpretive creativity of the self and at the same time an insistence that current understandings derive from previous interactions.

One difficulty which arises from the symbolic interactionist position, then, which has frequently been noted in the secondary literature, is that postulation of a creative and reflexive self serves to shade over the conservative and non-reflexive consequence of the stipulation that interaction produces interpretations subsequently drawn upon in the construction of action. In this latter instance the possibility of conflicting interpretations between actors is reduced by the implicit assumption that common understandings arise more or less spontaneously through joint and shared interactions. Jamesian pragmatism, on the other hand, simply cuts through this conundrum by indicating the limitations of a purely cognitive understanding of action that has become associated with symbolic interactionism.

Like Blumer, but for quite different reasons, James holds that action is creative and reflexive. From the perspective of Jamesian pragmatism, action is creative because in realizing a possible future it is generative of a transformative process, and in realizing one possible future – and therefore denying others – it reconstitutes the basis of subsequent action. The reflexivity inherent in Jamesian pragmatism is through the actor's emotional apprehension of intention and consequence. These are achieved not through construction and elaboration of cognitive interpretation, as with symbolic interactionism, but through emotional engagement.

The significant role of emotion in Jamesian pragmatism is incompatible with a further key element of Blumer's statement of symbolic interactionism. According to Blumer, actors might move from impressions of their situation to conceptual interpretations of it through a cognitive process of identification, assessment, and decisionmaking (Blumer 1969: 85). According to James, on the other hand, impression is transformed into conception through the mediation of emotion (James 1956: 117). Indeed, more recent research shows that social behavior cannot be guided by cognitions as they arise retrospective to events (Collins 1981: 990–4). Emotional forces, of which the subject may not necessarily be aware, are primarily responsible for social conduct and action. The capacity of cognitions to be implicated in agency is dependent upon their being affectively charged.

The observation that symbolic interactionism is overly cognitive and neglects emotions, which has been frequently made (Meltzer, Petras, and Reynolds 1975: 83–113; Stryker 2002: 144–52), requires careful consideration. With the development of the sociology of emotions from the mid-1970s, a number of publications have provided a symbolic interactionist account or theory of emotions (Denzin 1983, 1984; Finkelstein 1980; Lynch 1982; Shott 1979). The distinctive feature of all of them, however, is a continuing adherence to cognitivist principles in which emotion remains an object of cognitive interpretation. In these accounts emotion is denatured, its effective capacities undermined, and rather than being a factor in agency becomes an artifact of interpretation.

Susan Shott, for instance, refers to the "construction of emotion by the actor," a process that is "greatly influenced by situational definitions and social norms" (Shott 1979: 1318). She goes on to say that "within the limits set by social norms and internal stimuli, individuals construct their emotions; and their definitions and interpretations are critical to this often emergent process" (Shott 1979: 1323). Norman Denzin holds that emotions "are not mere cognitive responses to physiological, cultural or structural factors [but] interactive processes best studied as social acts involving self and other interactions" (Denzin 1983: 407–8). While they are not cognitive responses, according to Denzin, emotions are not efficacious in their own terms but exist as a result of cognitive apprehension through interpretation. Denzin says that emotions are "self-feelings" and that emotions terms, such as "anger," "hate," "guilt," and so on, refer only to these "mental states, interactional experiences and judgments of others . . . that persons feel and direct . . . towards themselves" (Denzin 1983: 404). These mental states and judgments are grist to the mill of symbolic interactionist interpretation.

These and similar accounts can be collectively described as the constructionist approach to emotions. Indeed, it is testament to the way in which symbolic inter-actionism accords with key threads of the intellectual culture of late modernity that the majority of sociologists and anthropologists, and large numbers of psychologists and philosophers, who have written on emotions over the last 25 years argue that emotions are constructed by interpretive processes on the part of the emoting subject. In the broadest terms the constructionist position holds that emotional experiences depend on situational or cultural cues and interpretations of them, and therefore that linguistic practices, values, norms, and currents of belief, all of which are influential in providing the content and framework of requisite interpretation, constitute the substance of experience of emotions. Biological and social structural factors have only the remotest relevance for this approach. A corollary of construc-tionism is that persons may voluntarily determine the emotions they experience, and therefore that the construction of emotions entails emotions management, a term associated with the work of Arlie Hochschild (1979, 1983), who, although not strictly a symbolic interactionist, draws upon and confirms leading element of sym-bolic interactionism as it relates to emotions.

The constructionist approach has enlivened discussion of emotions and drawn attention to the ways in which emotions are differentially experienced so that in different particular societies or the same society through historical time there are likely to be discernibly different types of emotions and emotional experiences. Indeed, the object of any emotion will be influenced by prevailing meanings and values, as will the way emotions are expressed; thus what is feared and how people show fear, for instance, indeed how they may experience fear, will necessarily vary between interpretive situations. But by treating emotions primarily as strategic evaluations derived from local meaning systems and individual interpretive prac-tices, the constructionist approach is arguably itself a captive of cultural preferences. It is important to accept that emotions that escape cultural tagging are not thereby without individual and social consequence. Indeed, there is much evidence that socially important emotions are experienced below the threshold of conscious awareness and cannot be fully accounted for in terms of an actor's interpretations of her situation, and are more likely to be determinative of the types of social inter-pretations agents draw upon (Scheff 1990).

Hochschild attempts to indicate the interpretive framework for the construction of emotions in terms of "feeling rules" (Hochschild 1979). It is particularly difficult in practice to locate such feeling rules and operationally describe them except at an essentially commonplace and possibly tautological level, such as: "At funerals the appropriate emotion is mourning." Indeed, what is meant by a funeral is a situation constructed by the emotion of mourning; what is meant by a party is a situation constructed by joyous feelings stimulated by shared food and drink. That feeling rules are subject to cultural and interpretive variation suggests that, rather than guide emotions, feeling rules are descriptions of particular emotional episodes. There are a number of reasons why this is so. First, as Pierre Bourdieu has shown, cultural regularization is a consequence of practice, not its cause (Bourdieu 1990); to the degree that there are feeling rules, they arise out of emotional experience and its preconditions, they do not determine emotional experience. Indeed, a close reading of her classic paper on emotion work and feeling rules reveals that Hochschild in fact demonstrates that feeling rules do not do what she claims for them.

While Hochschild shows that two respondents consciously engaged in emotion work, the evidence she provides indicates that their endeavors to effectively change their emotions failed to do so (Hochschild 1979: 561–2). Similarly, in her account of "rights" in the context of feeling rules, Hochschild confuses rejection of a right with refusal to lay claim to a right (Hochschild 1979: 565). Although Hochschild argues that emotions are induced in the subject or constructed through emotion work, it is more likely that when mixed emotions – or more properly, a mix of emotions – are experienced through complexity of situation or circumstance that provokes them, then, through a number of factors, particular emotions become backgrounded while others are foregrounded. A corrective reformulation of Hochschild's argument, then, would be to say that a respondent, through "emotion work," endeavors to resolve mixed feelings by consciously attempting to emphasize one and de-emphasize another. The success of such endeavors will be dependent upon the salience of context as much as the subject's efforts.

The approach to emotions that is found in symbolic interactionism and social or cultural constructionism is recent in the history of sociology. It is often stated that sociological interest in emotions began in the 1970s. In fact, however, sociological explanation through emotions is historically enduring. If sociology is thought of as beginning with the European Enlightenment, before it was legitimated with a name or organized as a discipline, through writers such as Giambattista Vico, Adam Ferguson, Adam Smith, and Jean-Jacques Rousseau, among others, human emotions were regarded as essential to accounts of the source and direction of social action and organization. With the professionalization of sociology in the late nineteenth and early twentieth centuries, through the work of Émile Durkheim, Vilfredo Pareto, Ferdinand Tönnies, Georg Simmel, and Edvard Westermarck, to mention only the most obvious, emotions continued to play a pivotal explanatory role. Indeed, even in Nietzsche's relevant work, which is frequently allied with constructionist thought, emotion is given a naturalistic as opposed to a constructionist form (Nietzsche 1992). Nietzsche emphasizes the significance of perspective not construction.

During the mid-twentieth century, emotions more or less ceased to be of interest to sociologists, who moved away from emotions and turned to values in accounting for social action and relationships. By the late twentieth century there was a return to sociological interest in emotions. What is new from this time is the concern not primarily to explain social processes in terms of emotions but to account for emotions in terms of social interactive and interpretive outcomes. The most obvious reason why this occurred is that sociology itself had changed. The scope of sociology had narrowed so that it engaged a much more constricted notion of the social than it had even in the late nineteenth and early twentieth centuries, and the concepts with which it worked were similarly truncated to focus on values and interactions, especially outside of political and economic organizations and pursuits. The expansive capacity of emotions to direct social relations and be foundation to institutions is replaced therefore with a concern for the individual's control of their emotions, emotions management, and the resulting cultural experience of what misleadingly appears as an interpretive construction of emotions.

Rational Choice Theory and the Pragmatic Critique

While symbolic interactionism accords with a number of leading cultural assumptions, especially concerning the constructive capacity of individuals through interpretive processes, another orientation, that is ostensibly the opposite of symbolic interactionism, in many ways shares similarities with it and is arguably also reflective of individuating aspects of advanced modernist culture. Rational choice theory, in the simplest terms, holds that social outcomes are determined by the choices individuals make in pursuit of their self-interest (see CHAPTER 9). The suggestion here is not that symbolic interactionism and rational choice theory are in any meaningful way equivalent but that there are elements in each that encourage comparison. Both function in terms of cognitive appraisals of opportunities for and imperatives in self-realization, one through the concept of rational self-interest, the other in terms of the notion of self-indication. Indeed, Blumer's understanding that action occurs through a decision made on the basis of appraising the tasks, opportunities, restraints, and resources available in a situation (Blumer 1969: 86), while not premised on a commitment to means – ends rationality, is closer to the agent-centered account of economistic rational choice theory than it is to mainstream sociology.

An "economic" explanation considers alternative possible choices taken by an actor, in order to achieve their purposes, in terms of a balance between the advantages, or "gains," and disadvantages, or "costs," that actor perceives. The "rational" choice is the one in which the gains are highest and the costs lowest. Sociological accounts, on the other hand, operate through quite different preconceptions, which are less concerned with the choice an individual makes between alternative possibilities and more concerned with the institutional arrangements that determine the set or types of choices that are available, the social allocation of means, the networks in which relations are embedded, the intermediaries who encourage or facilitate one choice over another, and so on.

Symbolic interactionism does not assume or imply that in seeking to achieve their purposes individuals will choose the highest gain over the lowest cost, and therefore that individuals are self-interested and rational in the economic sense. Indeed, symbolic interactionism "shadows" sociological accounts as characterized in the preceding paragraph by indicating the choices individuals make as a result of the operations of the social allocations, networks, and interactively formed meanings that predispose actors to a variety of "non-maximizing" options. The question to be raised here is the extent to which pragmatism and symbolic interactionism can develop a coherent and systematic critique of rational choice theory. If this may seem like an odd and perverse test it in fact simply reflects a standard form of relationship between sociology and economics and is therefore a reasonable expectation. Historically, sociology as a discipline developed through a critical engagement with economics. Marx's theory of state and society was forged through a critique of classical political economy; Durkheim similarly developed a theory of solidarity and normativity against the contractualist utilitarianism of nineteenth-century English economic theory; the core of Weber's sociology, similarly, has to be understood in terms of his antipathy to classical political economy and through his complicated relationship with the marginalist revolution. Parsons also developed his own char-

acteristic sociology in dialog with contemporary economic thought. What of pragmatic sociology?

Rational choice theory assumes that actors' preferences, which determine the
actions that realize their self-interest, will be consistent, stable, and exogenous, that
is, prior to the action or choice they take. The concept of the self developed by
James shows that these assumptions are inadequate for rational choice theory's own
purposes, namely explanation of self-interested action. An understanding of the self
requires consideration of three things, according to James: the constituent parts of
self, the emotions they arouse, and the actions they prompt, namely self-seeking and
self-preservation (James 1890a: 293). This third element clearly relates to self-interest, through which James's account directly links to the concerns of rational choice
theory. The significance of emotions, the second element, will be treated below. In
conceptualizing the self as comprising component parts, James begins with a principal distinction between the "I" and the "Me." The I, who knows, is the subject
of self, and the Me, which can be known, is the object or the empirical self. The
empirical self comprises three elements, which effectively constitute distinct selves.
These are the material self, comprising the body, its adornments and extensions;
the social self, which forms through the recognition it gets from others (which is
the only element of self conceptualized by symbolic interactionism); and the "spiritual" or subjective self, which is made of concrete manifestations of a person's
subjective faculties and disposition, including how a person regards herself, her
moral sensibility, conscience, and will (James 1890a: 292–7).

Each of the components of the Jamesian self is self-seeking, which satisfies the
behavioral foundation of rational choice theory. But the Jamesian self is a complex
not a simplex phenomenon, and self-interest becomes proportionately complex.
Maximization is not an imperative of the interest of each component of self. The
material or embodied self, including its adornments and extensions, accounts for
an interest in the body and its comforts or welfare, and the welfare of significant
others, who are extensions of the material self. The latter means that interests of a
material self will be subject to gender and age differentiation, depending on bodily
conditions and intimate associations. The social self, formed through the regard of
others, accounts for a quite different type of self-interest. Its needs are recognition
rather than maintenance. The interest of the subjective self is both more principled
and yet more susceptible to harm than the other two types of self-interest. This is
the self in which values predominate and may override utilities in satisfying self-
interest. But one may value risk as much as enlightenment. Subjective self-interest
is therefore responsible for ethical subordination of material self-interest as well as
moral lapses that threaten material welfare.

The Jamesian self offers solutions to certain perennial problems of utilitarian
egoism, such as the supposed contradiction between self-interest and altruism (James
1890a: 326). From the perspective of a complex Jamesian self, altruistic behavior
can be explained in terms of extensions of the material self. The material self's
extensions include not only immediate family members but under certain social
conditions may include total strangers. As an Australian tourist in Malaysia, for
example, the bad behavior I witness of a fellow Australian otherwise unknown to
me makes me blush with shame. This is not an instance of sympathy, but more
directly links another's self-interest to my own through a sense of common belong-

ing born of the contrast with the "strangeness" of the host society. Principled altruism through value-commitment, on the other hand, is sourced in the subjective self.

An important aspect of James's account of the empirical self is that its parts are linked to the actions they promote through the emotions they arouse (James 1890a: 293). In his discussion of the "rivalry and conflict of the different selves" James says that the particular self that one chooses is dominant and that through that choice the others are suppressed (1890a: 309–10). He also says that the self-feeling that achieves this simultaneous elevation and suppression of self is volitional: "our self-feeling is in our power" (1890a: 312). This summarizes experiences of a realization of self-interest or identity displacing a prior sense of having a number of possible choices reflecting different aspects of a person's engagements and evaluations. This much accords with rational choice theory. But by offering a complex rather than a simplex notion of self, the Jamesian approach provides a wider and more realistic account of what might constitute self-interest, including value aspirations and the regard of others as well as more straightforward utilities. These can each be classed as self-interest in the Jamesian schema because underlying all of them is an emotional engagement with distinct aspects of self. It is this part of the Jamesian self that has little resonance in rational choice theory, and is absent in non-Jamesian versions of pragmatism.

The efficacious emotional constitution of the Jamesian actor does not imply rational incapacity, impossibility of impartial abstraction and only labile self-interest (James 1890a: 328–9). Neither does the consolidation of the complex self through self-feeling deny the significance of social determination. Indeed, James indicates the pervasiveness of the social self in resolving the dynamics of self-formation (James 1890a: 315–17). But in actualizing self-interest, however conceived, choices are exercised and preferences acted upon. This engagement requires a conscious determination, but – as we shall see – both the engagement and its agent are best conceived as emergent rather than established and final.

A significant challenge to rationalistic accounts of behavior, and especially their consistency-of-preferences assumption, comes from discovery of a phenomenon known as preference reversals, first reported in an experimental study of gambling decisions (Lichtenstein and Slovic 1971), but which are found in a larger range of decisionmaking situations with general relevance for understanding preferences (Slovic and Lichtenstein 1983). The pattern of preference reversal identified by these studies emerges when subjects are given a choice between a pair of options (gambles, risks, policies) with nearly the same expected values: option A offers a high chance of a modest return; option B, a lower chance of a greater return. Most subjects choose option A. When subjects are then asked to price each option, option B is typically priced higher that option A, from which a preference for option B is inferred. These contrasting results contravene expectation of a consistent metric, irrespective of measurement procedure. Preference reversals have persisted in the face of determined efforts to minimize or eliminate them (see the studies reported by Slovic and Lichtenstein 1983: 598–9). Such reversals are not isolated phenomena, and therefore preferences and the choices they lead to cannot satisfy the consistency requirement of any theory of rational choice when information-processing considerations so strongly affect decisions (Slovic and Lichtenstein 1983: 597, 599, 603).

To describe the problem as one of information-processing or the "framing" of decisions (Tversky and Kahneman 1981) points in a general direction but does not identify the responsible mechanisms. More recently Tversky and Thaler have attempted to explain preference reversals in terms of stimulus-response compatibility:

> if the stimulus and the response do not match, additional mental operations are needed to map one into the other. This increases effort and error and may reduce the impact of the stimulus . . . Because the cash equivalence of a bet is expressed in dollars, compatibility implies that the payoffs, which are expressed in the same units, will be weighted more heavily in pricing bets than in choosing between bets . . . The compatibility hypothesis, therefore, explains the major source of preference reversal, namely the overpricing of low-probability high-payoff bets. (Tversky and Thaler 1990: 207)

Inventive as this explanation is, it cannot account for preference inconsistency in general.

Possible approaches to decisionmaking include: (1) the high reason approach, which holds that logical inference following more or less conscious induction of information provides the best available solution to any problem – on this basis choices are taken rationally; (2) the information process engineering approach holds that certain cognitive functions associated with the engineering of the human brain are responsible for the way problems are solved – on this basis choices are as rational as brain functions permit; (3) the affect inference approach holds that emotional appraisals both instantaneously limit the set of relevant choice options and at the same time set in motion dispositional responses to the chosen option – on this basis outcomes are likely to be substantively although not formally rational in terms of a person's complex (not simplex) self-interest. There is overwhelming evidence that affect or emotion not only plays a primary role in framing options for choice-taking but underlies rational thought. The high reason approach, however, explicitly denies the relevance of emotion, and the information process engineering approach is unconcerned with emotion, focusing exclusively on cognitive mechanisms.

The primacy of affect in information-processing and decisionmaking has been explained neurologically in terms of what Antonio Damasio has called somatic markers (Damasio 1994: 173–5). Somatic markers are emotionally borne physical sensations which indicate to those who experience them that an event, circumstance, or prospect is likely to be favorable or unfavorable, pleasurable or painful. In doing so they "dramatically reduce the number of options for consideration" (Damasio 1994: 175). The emotions that function in conjunction with somatic markers, which monitor and represent an actor's body images juxtaposed with their circumstances, are pre-conscious, more or less instantaneous, and drive the relevant cognitive processes. They are also readily seen as among the emotions to which James refers when indicating that the components of self are revealed to their subject through the emotions they provoke. The hypothesis accepted here, then, proposes that pref-

erence reversal results from the different emotional appraisals of the values represented in the alternate choices. The affective significance of risk-taking, for instance,
in which vulnerabilities and harms are salient, is very different from that of monetary worth, in which the payoff is only quantitatively meaningful.

This type of explanation allows us to make sense of another form of preference
reversal that cannot be explained by compatibility theory and relates to the issue
of the stability of preferences and their coherence. Practically all standard accounts
of rational choice assume strict morality insofar as they presume that a person's
actions will be consistent with their values. In practice, however, individuals frequently choose an action while recognizing that they would prefer not to exercise
that preference. This can be presented as a contradiction between self-interest and
conscience (March 1978: 603), but it could equally be regarded as a situation in
which two forms of self-interest, coexisting but incompatible, lead to preferences
that may or may not be acted upon. Discussion above regarding the complex self
prepares the ground for such a view.

If an individual's actions and their outcomes influence future preferences, then it
is likely that actions may be chosen not as a result of a preference but in order to
generate them. All competence attainment involves the selection of actions that the
individual expects or hopes will have effects on future abilities and associated preferences (March 1978: 596). More generally, individuals typically use present actions
to discover currently unknown or construct presently absent future preferences. All
curiosity-driven behavior is of this type. Learning about new situations and opportunities is exploration for new preferences. Indeed, it is rational to be strategic about
preferences, to specify goals different from the outcomes an individual would wish
to achieve. In March's words: "we consider the choice of preferences as part of an
infinite game with ourselves in which we attempt to deal with our propensities for
acting badly by anticipating them and outsmarting ourselves. We use deadlines and
make commitments" (March 1978: 597). On a more subjective level, individuals
typically are able to make sense of their actions only after they have been taken and
their consequences become apparent (March 1978: 601). It is the observation and
interpretation of the consequences of an action that allows individuals to find
meaning and merit in their actions and only then to be clear about what their preferences are. In this sense, then, preferences are the outcomes of actions rather than
their basis and only have clarity after the action has occurred and been subjectively
interpreted by the individual.

While the future consequences of a present action are necessarily uncertain, an
individual's preferences for those unknown consequences of present action will also
be uncertain. Thus, against the expectation of rational choice theory, the stability
of preferences and also their precision will necessarily be imperfectly achievable. In
terms of the experience of social actors this means that preferences cannot be pre-
given and unaffected by time but are achieved through engagement, discovered in
the meaning that actions acquire in terms of their consequences, and constructed
through curiosity and the acquisition of various competences. This account of preferences demonstrates pragmatic principles and is predicted by the Jamesian model
of the complex self discussed above. Preferences are unstable, inconsistent, endogenous, and imprecise. They are not necessarily prior to action. Through their interactions individuals discover and construct their preferences. This is where James and

symbolic interactionism entirely agree; as Blumer says, human behavior is emergent, continually constructed during its execution (Blumer 1969: 82).

CONCLUSION

We began with the problem of convention. Convention, like preference in utilitarian thought, is commonly taken to prefigure subsequent action. According to symbolic interactionism, however, convention derives from prior interaction. The understanding of events in terms of their consequences is characteristic of pragmatism in general. Within pragmatism, however, there is differential emphasis on emotional and cognitive mechanisms of consequence. Herein are alternative but compatible critiques of utilitarianism: emotional self-appraisal of needs of bodily maintenance, esteem satisfaction and value imperative, and also emergent meanings of an actor's interest, purpose, and preference.

Bibliography

Barbalet, J. M. (1999) "William James' Theory of Emotion: Filling in the Picture." *Journal for the Theory of Social Behavior* 29(3): 251–66.

Barbalet, J. M. (2001) "Weber's Inaugural Lecture and its Place in his Sociology." *Journal of Classical Sociology* 1(2): 147–70.

Barbalet, J. (2007) "Classical Pragmatism, Classical Sociology: William James, Religion and Emotions," in P. Baert and B. S. Turner (eds.), *Pragmatism and European Social Theory*. Oxford: Bardwell Press.

Bentley, A. F. (1949) *The Process of Government*. Evanston, IL: Principia Press.

Bentley, A. F. (1954) *Inquiry into Inquiries: Essays in Social Theory*, ed. S. Ratner. Boston: Beacon Press.

Blumer, H. (1937) "Social Psychology," in E. P. Schmidt (ed.), *Man and Society: A Substantive Introduction to the Social Sciences*. New York: Prentice Hall.

Blumer, H. (1969) *Symbolic Interactionism: Perspective and Method*. Engelwood Cliffs, NJ: Prentice Hall.

Bourdieu, P. (1990) *The Logic of Practice*. Cambridge: Polity.

Collins, R. (1981) "On the Microfoundations of Macrosociology." *American Journal of Sociology* 86(5): 984–1014.

Cooley, C. H. (1964) *Human Nature and the Social Order*. New York: Schocken Books.

Damasio, A. R. (1994) *Descartes' Error: Emotion, Reason and the Human Brain*. New York: Putnam.

Denzin, N. K. (1983) "A Note on Emotionality, Self, and Interaction." *American Journal of Sociology* 89(2): 402–9.

Denzin, N. K. (1984) *On Understanding Emotion*. San Francisco: Jossey-Bass.

Dewey, J. (1896) "The Reflex Arc Concept in Psychology." *Psychological Review* 3: 357–70.

Finkelstein, J. (1980) "Considerations for a Sociology of the Emotions." *Studies in Symbolic Interaction* 3: 111–21.

Hall, P. M. (2007) "Symbolic Interaction," in G. Ritzer (ed.), *Blackwell Encyclopedia of Sociology*. Oxford: Blackwell.

Hochschild, A. R. (1979) "Emotion Work, Feeling Rules, and Social Structure." *American Journal of Sociology* 85(3): 551–75.

Hochschild, A. R. (1983) *The Managed Heart: Commercialization of Human Feeling*. Berkeley: University of California Press.

James, W. (1890a) *Principles of Psychology*, vol. 1. New York: Henry Holt.

James, W. (1890b) *Principles of Psychology*, vol. 2. New York: Henry Holt.

James, W. (1902) *The Varieties of Religious Experience*. London: Longman, Green.

James, W. (1907) *Pragmatism: A New name for Some Old Ways of Thinking*. London: Longman, Green.

James, W. (1920) "Philosophical Conceptions and Practical Results," in W. James, *Collected Essays and Reviews*. New York: Longman, Green.

James, W. (1956) *The Will to Believe and Other Essays in Popular Philosophy*. New York: Dover.

Joas, H. (1987) "Symbolic Interactionism," in A. Giddens and J. Turner (eds.), *Social Theory Today*. Cambridge: Polity.

Lichtenstein, S., and Slovic, P. (1971) "Reversals of Preference between Bids and Choices in Gambling Decisions." *Journal of Experimental Psychology* 89(1): 46–55.

Lynch, R. (1982) "Play, Creativity and Emotion." *Studies in Symbolic Interaction* 4: 45–62.

March, J. G. (1978) "Bounder Rationality, Ambiguity, and the Engineering of Choice." *Bell Journal of Economics* 9(2): 587–608.

Mead, G. H. (1934) *Mind, Self and Society: From the Standpoint of a Social Behaviorist*, ed. C. W. Morris. Chicago: University of Chicago Press.

Meltzer, B. N., Petras, J. W., and Reynolds, L. T. (1975) *Symbolic Interactionism: Genesis, Varieties and Criticism*. London: Routledge & Kegan Paul.

Nietzsche, F. (1992) "On the Genealogy of Morals," in *Basic Writings of Nietzsche*. New York: Random House.

Peirce, C. S. (1966a) "The Fixation of Belief," in *Charles S. Peirce: Selected Writings*, ed. P. P. Wiener. New York: Dover.

Peirce, C. S. (1966b) "How to Make our Ideas Clear," in *Charles S. Peirce: Selected Writings*, ed. P. P. Wiener. New York: Dover.

Peirce, C. S. (1966c) "What Pragmatism Is," in *Charles S. Peirce: Selected Writings*, ed. P. P. Wiener. New York: Dover.

Peirce, C. S. (1966d) "Issues of Pragmaticism," in *Charles S. Peirce: Selected Writings*, ed. P. P. Wiener. New York: Dover.

Plummer, K. (2000) "Symbolic Interactionism in the Twentieth Century," in B. Turner (ed.), *A Companion to Social Theory*, 2nd edn. Oxford: Blackwell.

Scheff, T. J. (1990) *Microsociology: Discourse, Emotion and Social Structure*. Chicago: University of Chicago Press.

Shott, S. (1979) "Emotion and Social Life: A Symbolic Interactionism Analysis." *American Journal of Sociology* 84(6): 1317–34.

Slovic, P., and Lichtenstein, S.(1983) "Preference Reversals: A Broader Perspective." *American Economic Review* 73(4): 596–605.

Stryker, S. (2002) *Symbolic Interactionism: A Social Structural Version*. Caldwell, NJ: Blackburn Press.

Tversky, A., and Kahneman, D. (1981) "The Framing of Decisions and the Psychology of Choice." *Science* NS 211(4481): 453–8.

Tversky, A., and Thaler, R. H. (1990) "Anomalies: Preference Reversals." *Journal of Economic Perspectives* 4(2): 201–11.

Veblen, T. (1914) *The Instinct of Workmanship and the State of the Industrial Arts*. New York: Viking.

Veblen, T. (1919) "Why Economics Is Not an Evolutionary Science," in W. J. Samuels (ed.), *The Place of Science in Modern Civilization and Other Essays*. New York: Huebsch.

Weber, M. (1991) *The Protestant Ethic and the Spirit of Capitalism*. London: HarperCollins.

Weber, M. (1994) "The Nation State and Economic Policy," in P. Lassman and R. Speirs (eds.), *Weber: Political Writings*. Cambridge: Cambridge University Press.

11

Phenomenology

MICHAEL G. FLAHERTY

A quick search of *Sociological Abstracts* would bring the reader to hundreds of articles with variations on the word "phenomenology" in their titles. It is impossible, of course, to examine this large and disparate literature within the confines of a single chapter. Nonetheless, the sheer size of this literature is instructive, for it shows us that phenomenology has a seat at the sociological table. How did it get there, and what might the future hold? These are the questions I address in this chapter. I do so by reviewing the major contributions from Edmund Husserl, Alfred Schutz, Peter Berger, and Thomas Luckmann. In addition, I canvass some recent developments that presage continued growth.

ORIGINS AND AIMS

Joseph Kockelmans (1967: 24) describes phenomenology as "a sphere of ambiguity." He points out that the term has a long history in philosophy, with scholars defining it in divergent ways. Still, there is consensus that Edmund Husserl (1859–1938) was the first to use this term as the name for a systematic and distinctive philosophical position. Most of his writings were not translated into English until decades after his death (1960 [1931], 1965 [1910], 1970 [1936]).[1] And, in any event, his unadulterated thinking would not have been conducive to the further development of the social sciences. The upshot is that his influence on sociology has been almost entirely indirect. What we know about phenomenology is a (greatly modified) version of Husserl's doctrine that comes to us through the diligent efforts of his student, Alfred Schutz, and Schutz's students, Peter Berger and Thomas Luckmann.[2]

Husserl's agenda was nothing if not ambitious. Indeed, Kockelmans (1967: 25) characterizes it as "grandiose." According to Husserl, philosophy was in "crisis" – a word that appears repeatedly in his programmatic statements as well as the titles of his books (1965 [1910], 1970 [1936]). Philosophy was engrossed with trivialities rather than that which is essential. Husserl (1960 [1931]: 11) longed for a philosophy "grounded on an absolute foundation." What can we know with absolute certainty? Only the contents of our own consciousness, as Descartes concluded in his famous declaration, *Cogito ergo sum*. Husserl viewed Descartes as "the primally founding genius of all modern philosophy" (1970 [1936]: 73), and Kockelmans (1967: 25) argues that Husserl looked upon "his own work as a radicalization of Descartes' demand that all philosophical knowledge be founded in an absolutely certain insight."

Husserl (1965 [1910]: 96) hoped to redirect philosophy toward the "things themselves."[3] The uninitiated are likely to misinterpret this phrase as representative of an empirical or experiential stance, but that is not what he meant. In fact, from his perspective, there is no way for us to know the things of the world directly. We only have access to our own consciousness, avows Husserl. Consciousness mediates and colors our perceptions of the world as well as our thoughts, emotions, and physical sensations. Consciousness is what matters. The things themselves, then, are "essential forms of consciousness" through which we know the world (Husserl 1965 [1910]: 119); as such, they are antecedent to, and more fundamental than, experience. What we can study, what we must study, are the essential ways in which we are *conscious* of everything that constitutes our "life-world" (Husserl 1970 [1936]: 142).

Husserl (1960 [1931]: 4) was quite frustrated with what philosophy had become, and he saw the need for "*a radical new beginning.*" This would entail returning philosophical inquiry to its primordial mission: "Philosophy in its ancient origins wanted to be 'science,' universal knowledge of the universe" (Husserl 1970 [1936]: 65). To that end, he contended, philosophical inquiry must map the "invariant" structure and processes of human consciousness through systematic and meticulous description of its content (Husserl 1970 [1936]: 142). The essential forms of human consciousness are invariant because they are governed by universal laws, which can be discovered by means of phenomenological investigation. Hence, Husserl (1965 [1910]: 71) aspired to formulate something like a "rigorous science" of subjectivity – one that would, in his estimation, encompass everything.

It was not his intent, however, to mimic the sciences of his own era. He did not believe that empiricists were equipped to deal with the "*universe of subjective processes*" (1960 [1931]: 75). They would dismiss it, like the behaviorists, or reduce it to a materialistic substratum, in the manner of biologists. Husserl (1931 [1913]: 113) emphasized "*that Consciousness in itself has a being of its own*" which demands a unique epistemology. Consequently, he used the word "science" in an idiosyncratic way, and he asserted that phenomenological investigation "can in no way be an empirical analysis" (Husserl 1965 [1910]: 98). The examination of consciousness calls for an intuitive approach, not one rooted in experience (Husserl 1931 [1913]: 85). From Husserl's standpoint, those disciplines that refer to themselves as sciences are only engrossed in empirical ephemera. "All natural science is naive," according to Husserl (1965 [1910]: 85), because it assumes that our minds simply receive stimuli from the environment, thereby ignoring the a priori intervention of consciousness. Yet Husserl was equally critical of philosophical idealism. We inhabit a world of objects, but we only apprehend mental images of that world.

The essential forms of consciousness are not facets of the world itself, so they cannot be identified through observation in the traditional sense. How, then, does one *do* phenomenology? Husserl (1965 [1910]: 110, 1970 [1936]: 148) saw the path toward genuine scientific inquiry "blocked" by what he called the epoché of the "natural attitude." The word "epoché" is Greek for suspension or cessation. In everyday life, the natural attitude is to suspend doubt concerning the contents of consciousness. Put differently, the lifeworld is "taken for granted" (Husserl 1931 [1913]: 28). In order to escape from this cognitive cage, Husserl (1931 [1913]: 28) envisions a phenomenology with "absolute freedom from all presupposition." One must arrive at a presuppositionless frame of mind before one is ready to undertake systematic description of the objects of consciousness. Husserl used various terminology in reference to this special state of intuitive clarity. It is the "phenomenological epoché" (1931 [1913]: 110), or the "transcendental epoché" (1970 [1936]: 148), or the "transcendental-phenomenological epoché" (1960 [1931]: 26). Whatever its name, one suspends or transcends belief in all of one's presuppositions concerning the objects of consciousness. Synonymously, he referred to this method as "*bracketing*" because one must set aside or "place in brackets" all of one's assumptions (1931 [1913]: 110). Doing so enables the phenomenologist to describe or apprehend the contents of consciousness without recourse to preconceived notions about their ontological status.

Husserl had little to say about just how one is to set aside all of one's presuppositions. He offered examples of phenomenological analysis, but without specifying his technique. This has mystified his methods for succeeding generations of phenomenologists, some of whom have stepped into the breach by conceptualizing procedures of one kind or another. Maurice Natanson (1973: 6) contends that, if we seek unalloyed consciousness, phenomenology reverses the usual relationship between experience and skill: "The genuine beginner is an adept, not a novice. To begin, in this sense, is to start from the primordial grounds of evidence, from oneself as the center (not the sum) of philosophical experience." This observation is appealing but ultimately unsatisfying because, of course, it begs the question: How do we come to look upon the contents of our consciousness with a beginner's eyes?

Another intriguing answer can be found in an essay by Maurice Merleau-Ponty (1964 [1945]), "Cézanne's Doubt." In the title, he alludes to the phenomenological epoché, which the artist achieves through estrangement: "This is why Cézanne's people are strange, as if viewed by a creature of another species" (1964 [1945]: 16). Through this cultivated estrangement, "Cézanne returns to . . . primordial experience" (1964 [1945]: 16).[4] In contrast with Husserl's antipathy for empiricism, however, Cézanne's images are abstractions from recurrent observations: "He needed one hundred working sessions for a still life, one hundred and fifty sittings for a portrait" (1964 [1945]: 9). As we will see, this crucial adjustment opens the door to development of an empirically grounded version of phenomenology. Nevertheless, Merleau-Ponty (1964 [1945]: 17) maintains that, like Husserl, Cézanne attempts to drive past the particulars in an effort to arrive at the very essence of the things themselves: "Forgetting the viscous, equivocal appearances, we go through them straight to the things they present."

Most of Husserl's writings are programmatic in nature, but he did apply his perspective to the study of substantive topics. Indeed, he devoted an entire book to one of these subjects: *The Phenomenology of Internal Time-Consciousness* (Husserl 1964 [1928]). This subject appears thematically in several of his other books, as well. He (1931 [1913]: 234) distinguished between what he called cosmic or objective time and phenomenological time (i.e., the consciousness of one's own duration). In addition, his interest was piqued by the fact that the perceived passage of time is "a general peculiarity of all experiences" (1931 [1913]: 234). For Husserl (1960 [1931]: 43), "the all-embracing *consciousness of internal time*" serves as an essential foundation for "all other syntheses of consciousness." How is it, he asks, that we recognize the melody of a song, since we only ever hear one note at a time? We remember some notes and anticipate others while perceiving only one. As when we listen to a melody, self-consciousness is based upon our capacity to amalgamate successive events into a mental image of continuity through the integration of "memory and expectation" (Husserl 1964 [1928]: 79). He concludes that human beings have a "temporally constitutive consciousness" (Husserl 1964 [1928]: 47).

Husserl's legacy has enriched sociology. Both symbolic interactionism and ethnomethodology have been profoundly influenced by their inheritance. And, of course, there are scholars who espouse his namesake, phenomenological sociology. This, despite the fact that Husserl never intended any of them to be his heirs and would not have approved of the selective way they have scavenged from his bequest (Heap and Roth 1973). Unquestionably, he would have objected to the compromises they have made with the epistemology of the social sciences, but sociology is the beneficiary of their insistence that we cannot understand conduct without paying equal attention to consciousness.

SOCIOLOGY AND INTERSUBJECTIVITY

Husserl is the source and inspiration, but Alfred Schutz (1899–1959) is the pivotal figure in the emergence of phenomenological sociology. On its own terms, Husserl's work would have had little or no impact on sociology. Schutz is to Husserl what Blumer is to Mead: the student of a philosopher who devoted his life to bringing his mentor's outlook into sociology. In so doing, Schutz modified Husserl's doctrines by blending them with kindred, if sometimes foreign, streams of thought. Integrating the European sensibilities of Husserl, Max Weber, and Henri Bergson with the American insights of William James, John Dewey, and George Herbert Mead, he created a syncretic constructionism that served as a springboard for multiple strands of contemporary interactionist research.

Not surprisingly, Schutz (1967 [1932]: 3) was drawn to "the controversy over the scientific character of sociology." As with Husserl, he gave priority to fundamental issues of epistemology, and his predecessor's influence is apparent. "All facts," according to Schutz (1962: 5), "are from the outset facts selected from a universal context by the activities of our mind." It follows that there are no facts per se – only "interpreted facts" (1962: 5). Interpretation implicates consciousness which, in turn, implicates culture. Language intervenes, therefore, between one's observations and the environment: "All our knowledge of the world, in common-sense as well as in scientific thinking, involves constructs" (1962: 5). Yet, like Husserl, Schutz (1962: 5) rejected solipsism: "This does not mean that . . . we are unable to grasp the reality of the world. It just means that we grasp merely certain aspects of it."

In Europe, Schutz's scholarly activity had been an adjunct to his career in banking. Posted to New York in 1939 to prepare for transfer of the bank's head-quarters to the United States, he and his family were stranded there with the out-break of World War II (Wagner 1983: 70). He continued to work for the bank, but, wanting to establish an alternative career, Schutz joined the Department of Sociology at the New School for Social Research in 1943. Ever the doctrinaire thinker, Husserl (1931 [1913]: 147, 185) pursued the elusive possibilities of "pure" consciousness and "pure" phenomenology, but Schutz was never concerned with the purity of his own intellectual positions. Given his eclectic training (in law and social sciences at Vienna), he was a comparatively catholic theorist, and his sudden exile in America would only serve to magnify this inclination.

By the middle of the 1940s, a number of scholars had tried to read Husserl into sociology, but Schutz (1970 [1945]: 53) was openly critical of their efforts: "So far, social scientists have not found an adequate approach to the phenomenological movement." He recognized, however, that Husserl's emphasis on subjectivity would have to be tempered for a sociological audience by connecting it to the agenda of a canonical scholar. Further, Schutz (1967 [1932]: 5) realized that the most conge-nial candidate for this strategy was "Max Weber's 'interpretive sociology.'" As with all theorists, Weber's work lends itself to divergent perspectives. For Schutz (1967 [1932]: 6), he was a sociologist who had called upon his colleagues "to study social behavior by interpreting its subjective meaning as found in the intentions of indi-viduals." This mission statement dovetailed with the phenomenological focus on consciousness.

In Weber and Husserl, Schutz saw two scholars who put the onus on interpreta-tion. This made for methodological as well as conceptual parallels in their work. As Schutz (1967 [1932]: 6–7) put it, "the special aim of sociology demands a special method in order to select the materials relevant to the peculiar questions it raises." With his integrationist temperament, Schutz viewed Weber's formulation of ideal types as a procedure that was not antithetical to phenomenology. Indeed, Schutz's (1944, 1964) own use of ideal types is evident in essays such as "The Stranger" and "The Homecomer." Both ideal types and the intuition of essences produce an abstract distillation from innumerable specific instances – mindful for Husserl, empirical for Weber. Of course, while highlighting this family resemblance, Schutz had to downplay epistemological differences.

Despite his efforts to integrate them, Schutz (1967 [1945]) was critical of both Husserl's phenomenology and Weber's interpretive sociology. Weber had called upon his colleagues to seek interpretive understanding (*Verstehen*), thereby assum-ing in unexamined fashion one's capacity to transcend subjectivity. In contrast, Schutz confronted the issue that Weber sidestepped: How is intersubjectivity possi-ble? Simultaneously, Schutz's analysis of intersubjectivity challenged Husserl's reli-ance on intuition to explore his own mind. Husserl believed that it was possible to intuit transcendental (i.e., intersubjective) essences because they are a priori features of everyone's consciousness. Schutz rejects the notion that intersubjectivity is simply given in the nature of human consciousness. Instead, he argues that intersubjectivity is accomplished through socialization and social interaction.

Schutz wrought multiple dimensions of change in phenomenology. Through his efforts, the emphasis shifted from subjectivity to intersubjectivity, from consciousness to knowledge and meaning, from the intuition of essences to interpretation and typification. He sought to synthesize Husserl's philosophy with Weber's social science. And, subsequent to exile in the United States, he was eager to become acquainted with the foremost scholars in his new homeland. Characteristically, then, Schutz reached out to a leading American exponent of Weber's work: Talcott Parsons. Parsons had cited Schutz in his book, *The Structure of Social Action*, and Helmut Wagner (1983: 75) reports that Schutz "saw in him a thinker of related interests." In 1940, Schutz wrote a long exegesis of Parsons's book and mailed the draft to him with a complimentary letter inviting his assessment as well as face-to-face discussion. They exchanged several letters during 1941, but Parsons never agreed to meet with Schutz because he viewed Schutz's overture "as a demand for a 'far-reaching revision of my own work'" (Wagner 1983: 76).

Rebuffed by Parsons, Schutz continued to cultivate intellectual connections, but in a very different direction: that of American pragmatism (see CHAPTER 10). He was not unfamiliar with this school of thought before coming to the United States. Indeed, his earliest writings (1967 [1932]: 45, 66) intermingled ideas derived from the pragmatism of William James and the vitalism of Henri Bergson. Independently, but in parallel fashion, these men had explored the stream of consciousness and the experience of inner duration. Their separate lines of inquiry formed a confluence of inspiration for Schutz. Yet pragmatism would play a larger role in his later work – especially that aspect of it which proved to be most fertile for the further development of phenomenology. In his elaborate response to a provocative but deeply flawed essay by William James (1890), "The Perception of Reality," Schutz laid the foundation for what would come to be called the social construction of reality.

Here, in an American essay, Schutz found a perspective on reality that was quite compatible with Husserl's phenomenology. Both the title of James's essay and the gist of his argument suggested that it is our *perception* of reality that matters, not reality itself. He noted (1890: 291), moreover, that our perception of reality makes for many experiential "worlds" or "subuniverses" – an observation that would serve as a primitive model for Schutz. Frightened by the vertiginous implications of his own argument, however, James (1890: 299) backpedaled by claiming that the paramount reality was one of sensations.[5] Schutz (1962 [1945]: 229) was duly impressed by this trailblazing essay, but he objected to the way James reduced reality to "a psychology of belief and disbelief." For James, an early psychologist, reality was rooted within the individual: perceptions, sensations, and the like. Thus, Schutz (1962 [1945]: 229) set out "to free this important insight from its psychologistic setting."

Schutz began his essay, "On Multiple Realities," with a summary and critique of James. Crucially, Schutz (1962 [1945]: 208) rejected the reduction of reality to atomistic individualism because "the world is from the outset not the private world of the single individual but an intersubjective world, common to all of us." Schutz (1962 [1945]: 208, 213) countered James's psychology of belief with a sociology of "knowledge," or a "cognitive" sociology, but this sociology of knowledge was not the study of grand ideologies.[6] Rather, it was his intention (1962 [1945]: 208) to examine how people in everyday life collectively understand their shared world:

"All interpretation of this world is based upon a stock of previous experiences of it, our own experiences and those handed down to us by our parents and teachers, which in the form of 'knowledge at hand' function as a scheme of reference." With this statement, he repositioned the analysis of social reality under the rubric of the sociology of knowledge. This is the "common sense knowledge" which, two decades later, would be indispensable to Harold Garfinkel's (1967: 53) formulation of ethnomethodology.

Unlike James or Husserl, Schutz realized that the contents of one's consciousness can be neither universal nor utterly unique. In the book finished by his student, Thomas Luckmann, after Schutz's death (Schutz and Luckmann 1973: 243, 264), they stress that one's stock of knowledge is "socially conditioned" and a product of "socialization." It follows that each culture and subculture will have its own stock of knowledge. Yet Schutz also realized that if the contents of one's consciousness were utterly unique, each of us would be trapped in our own private world; it would be impossible to understand each other or coordinate our activities.

As was evident in his overture to Parsons, Schutz was intent on devising a theory of action. His theory was based upon the assumption that our interests are predominantly practical: "a pragmatic motive governs our natural attitude toward the world of daily life" (Schutz 1962 [1945]: 209). Drawing from both Weber and Husserl, Schutz (1962 [1945]: 210) established the scope of his theory as "the subjective meaning man bestows upon certain experiences of his own spontaneous life." In order to articulate this theory, he parsed our spontaneous life into an intricate vocabulary. Schutz (1962 [1945]: 211) defined conduct as "subjectively meaningful experiences of spontaneity, be they those of inner life or those gearing into the outer world." Thus, "conduct can be overt or covert" (1962 [1945]: 211), and he was careful to distinguish it from mere behavior. Schutz (1962 [1945]: 211) used the word "action" in reference to "[c]onduct which is based upon a preconceived project." One can plan or intend to think about something without this action affecting the world in a practical way, so Schutz's (1962 [1945]: 212) terminology culminated with "working," which he defined as "action in the outer world, based upon a project and characterized by the intention to bring about the projected state of affairs." As such, working is synonymous with social interaction – the requisite context for our construction of reality: "Among all the described forms of spontaneity that of working is the most important one for the constitution of the reality of the world of daily life" (1962 [1945]: 212).

Schutz (1962 [1945]: 228) avowed that the driving force behind working in the world (i.e., the social construction of reality) is our fear of death, which he labeled "the fundamental anxiety." Individually and collectively, human beings know that they are going to run out of time. Unique to human experience, then, is a self-conscious awareness of one's own mortality. According to Schutz (1962 [1945]: 228), we are driven to construct collective forms of meaning through social interaction in an anxious effort to transcend our own finitude: "From the fundamental anxiety spring the many interrelated systems of hopes and fears, of wants and satisfactions, of chances and risks which incite man within the natural attitude to attempt the mastery of the world, to overcome obstacles, to draft projects, and to realize them."

Time was a concept of unsurpassed importance for Husserl and Bergson as well as James, Dewey, and Mead. At the confluence of these lines of inquiry, Schutz made time a central issue in his own work. Like Husserl and Bergson, he differentiated *durée* (i.e., our inner experience of duration) from "objective or cosmic time" (Schutz 1962 [1945]: 215).[7] And, like the pragmatists, he used that distinction as a springboard for his analysis of "the time structure of the self" (1962 [1945]: 218). In the latter case, he is especially indebted to Mead, although not without explicit reservations. For example, Schutz adopted the pragmatist distinction between the I and the me as phases of the self in social interaction. The moment of action – the I – is a more or less uncertain step into the future, while the moment of reflection – the me – is the self's assessment of its own actions "only after it has carried out the act and thus appears . . . in memory" (Schutz 1962 [1945]: 216–17).

It was in his analysis of multiple realities and their constitutive features, however, that Schutz made his greatest contributions. James had posited the existence of subuniverses of reality, but Schutz (1962 [1945]: 230) rejected his terminology, opting instead to call them "finite provinces of meaning . . . because it is the meaning of our experiences and not the ontological structure of the objects which constitutes reality." The multiple realities do not represent what is out there in the world, as James would have it; rather, they are conventional (i.e., cultural) forms of experience structured by particular constellations of "relevance" and "selective" attention (Schutz 1962 [1945]: 227). Hence, we "bestow the accent of reality" on "a specific cognitive style" which is "consistent" across multiple instances of it (Schutz 1962 [1945]: 230).

If "the basic characteristics which constitute . . . [each] cognitive style" differ from each other, then, Schutz reasoned (1962 [1945]: 230), we should be able to specify realms of experience in terms of a particular combination of attributes. He identified six of these attributes. Each finite province of meaning has: (1) "a specific tension of consciousness"; (2) "a specific epoché"; (3) "a prevalent form of spontaneity"; (4) "a specific form of experiencing one's self"; (5) "a specific form of sociality"; and (6) "a specific time-perspective" (1962 [1945]: 230). In everyday life, for example, the characteristic tension of consciousness (i.e., degree of attentiveness) is "wide-awakeness"; the characteristic epoché is that of the natural attitude (i.e., "suspension of doubt"); working is the prevalent form of spontaneity; one experiences oneself as "the working self"; intersubjectivity is the typical form of sociality; and the dominant time-perspective is "standard time originating in an intersection between *dureé* and cosmic time" (1962 [1945]: 230–1). Different positions along these dimensions make for multiple realities: "All these worlds – the world of dreams, of imageries and phantasms, especially the world of art, the world of religious experience, the world of scientific contemplation, the play world of the child, and the world of the insane – are finite provinces of meaning" (1962 [1945]: 232). Like James, Schutz (1962 [1945]: 226) believed that there is a "paramount reality." It is not the private realm of sensations, however, but the intersubjective realm of everyday life.[8]

As a sociologist, Schutz had more to say about research methods than did Husserl, but his miscellaneous comments were more suggestive than definitive. There is, for instance, his observation (1962 [1945]: 220) that mutual communication is maximized during "face-to-face" interaction, or what he called a "We-relation." This would seem to represent endorsement of ethnography, but Schutz was never explicit on that issue. Instead, echoing Husserl, Schutz (1962 [1945]: 229) invoked the phenomenological epoché: "the suspension of our belief in the reality of the world as a device to overcome the natural attitude." This radical version of the Cartesian method was married to the Weberian use of ideal types in Schutz's (1944) paper, "The Stranger: An Essay in Social Psychology." With oblique wording, Schutz (1944: 506) hinted that the stranger is a prototype for sociological inquiry because "the cultural pattern of the approached group is to the stranger not a shelter but a field of adventure, not a matter of course but a questionable topic of investigation."[9] Despite this evocative statement, Schutz's contributions to sociology were decidedly analytical rather than empirical.

A POPULAR INGREDIENT

Notwithstanding his diligent efforts, phenomenology was still an exotic and unfamiliar school of thought when Schutz died in 1959. At that point, most of the writings by Husserl and Schutz were only available in German, which hampered dissemination of their ideas to an English-speaking audience. Moreover, even in the case of Schutz, phenomenology was characterized by an arcane and intimidating jargon. Peter Berger and Thomas Luckmann (1966) would change all of that with the publication of their enormously influential book, *The Social Construction of Reality*. Both of them studied with Schutz and earned their doctoral degrees at the New School for Social Research. In their hands, phenomenology would become far more popular, but only as one ingredient in a cosmopolitan cuisine.

Berger and Luckmann continued to do what Schutz had been doing, only more so because they amplified his efforts. Their primary agenda remained the application of phenomenology to the sociology of knowledge so as to change its focus from something like the history of ideas to a framework for the analysis of commonsense knowledge in everyday life. With Schutz, however, phenomenology was a prominent voice in a trio that included interpretive sociology and pragmatism. With Berger and Luckmann, phenomenology became one voice in a chorus that included Marx, Durkheim, Goffman, and just about everyone else who could be considered part of the sociological canon, as well as scholars from other disciplines – especially anthropology. In this way, Berger and Luckmann made phenomenology both accommodating and intelligible for English-speaking sociologists.

Prior to *The Social Construction of Reality*, Berger (1963) had written *Invitation to Sociology*, a very popular introduction to our discipline. In it, he had conceptualized a tripartite scheme that would structure his subsequent work with Luckmann: man in society, society in man, and society as drama. The individual is in society by virtue of his or her social location, which profoundly shapes the individual's behavior and life chances. By the same token, society is in the individual as a result of socialization, which involves learning the beliefs and commonsense knowledge at large in one's community. And society is akin to drama because it is enacted through the performance of social roles within face-to-face settings. In *The Social Construction of Reality*, Goffman's dramaturgical perspective would be subsumed within the dialectical tension between society as objective reality (i.e., man in society à la Marx and Durkheim) and society as subjective reality (i.e., society in man à la Cooley and Mead).

Berger and Luckmann adhered to the central tenets of Schutz's thinking, but they expressed certain principles with greater clarity, and they addressed problematic gaps in his work. They reasserted (1966: 25) that we experience multiple realities and that everyday life is the paramount reality, "to which consciousness always returns . . . as from an excursion." But, drawing further inspiration from George Herbert Mead, they placed much more emphasis on social interaction and language. Social interaction is where commonsense knowledge is created, sustained, and changed. "The reality of everyday life contains typificatory schemes," argued Berger and Luckmann (1966: 30–1), "in terms of which others are apprehended and 'dealt with' in face-to-face encounters." Moreover, socialization and the other effects of one's social location are realized through interaction.

Language is the principal vehicle for social interaction and, therefore, the social construction of reality. Berger and Luckmann (1966: 39) devoted much more attention to language than Schutz did, but this was in accord with his teachings on the inescapable relationship between meaning and intersubjectivity: "Language . . . typifies experiences, allowing me to subsume them under broad categories in terms of which they have meaning not only to myself but also to my fellow men." Itself a product of human creativity and consensus, language both inhibits and facilitates further invention. For Berger and Luckmann (1966: 37), "[e]veryday life is, above all, life with and by means of the language I share with my fellow men. An understanding of language is thus essential for any understanding of the reality of everyday life."

Unlike other organisms, contend Berger and Luckmann (1966: 47), "man's relationship to his environment is characterized by world-openness." Borrowing from Ruth Benedict (1934: 14), they invoked the "plasticity of the human organism" (1966: 49). With these phrases, they refer to the fact that a human infant arrives ready to learn whatever it needs to know, but, by the same token, is uncommitted to the particular cultural arrangements in its own community. On the one hand, this means that human groups are free to exercise enormous creativity in the social construction of reality, resulting in astonishing cultural diversity. On the other hand, it also means that human infants pose an unavoidable challenge to the intergenerational transmission of folkways. The community must restrict the behavioral repertoire of its infants to that which makes for cultural persistence. Benedict (1934: 23) summarized the issue most succinctly: "It is in cultural life as it is in speech; selection is the prime necessity." Her insight was echoed by Merleau-Ponty (1973 [1964]: 15): "About this time, children achieve vocal utterances of an extraordinary richness, emitting sounds that they will be incapable of reproducing later. There will be a selection, a kind of impoverishment." Their joint use of the word "selection" anticipated Berger and Luckmann's (1966: 51) similarly elegiac conclusion: the "world-openness of human existence is always, and indeed must be, transformed by social order into a relative world-closedness."

But how? Berger and Luckmann offer two answers. One, within the context of society as objective reality, is the process of institutionalization. The other, within the context of society as subjective reality, is the process of socialization. Lacking the instinctual programming that organizes the behavior of other organisms, human beings must construct social institutions that guide their behavior into culturally approved channels. Every human society confronts the same set of existential problems: making a living (economics), leadership and conflict resolution (politics), kinship (family), childrearing and other types of training (education), health and illness (medicine), and questions concerning the ultimate meaning of life (religion). All human societies must address these issues, but they do so in particular ways. In short, social institutions are culturally specific solutions to universal problems in human societies.

Social institutions have their origins in the habitualization of human interaction. Someone envisions a new way of doing things and expresses or externalizes these ideas, thereby making them available to others. Of course, it is not easy for the socialized person to even imagine truly innovative practices, and suggested changes are often rejected by one's community. Still, gradually or suddenly, others may embrace the suggested course of action and, over time, it may become the customary way of doing things among those people. Berger and Luckmann (1966: 54) assert that the essential criterion is intersubjectivity: "Institutionalization occurs whenever there is a reciprocal typification of habitualized actions by types of actors." The payoff is mutual predictability because the resulting social institution "provides the direction and the specialization of activity that is lacking in man's biological equipment" (Berger and Luckmann 1966: 53).

Social institutions have their origins in the *externalization* of human subjectivity (frustration with the status quo, innovative ideas, etc.), and they are "humanly produced" through social interaction (Berger and Luckmann 1966: 60), but, once they are ratified collectively, they evolve into objective features of society. Berger and Luckmann (1966: 60) define *objectivation* as "[t]he process by which the externalized products of human activity attain the character of objectivity." Put differently, social institutions have histories, although members of a society are rarely familiar with the actual details. Moreover, in accord with Durkheim (not Husserl or Schutz), Berger and Luckmann (1966: 58) point out that social institutions "are now experienced as possessing a reality of their own, a reality that confronts the individual as an external and coercive fact."

Those who initiate social institutions – the first generation if you will – typically have practical reasons for doing so. However, we must avoid the temptation of thinking that, for them at least, it is transparent that the new cultural practices are humanly produced. For themselves as well as their audience, the legitimation of novel cultural practices demands explanation and justification (Berger and Luckmann 1966: 93). These twin processes would be undermined by baldly confronting the ad hoc origins of all social institutions. Hence, even the first generation mystifies its own authorship by legitimating its actions on the basis of some suprahuman entity, such as nature or God. For example, the architects of the American Revolution did not legitimate their rebellion on the basis of naked self-interest, but because "they are endowed by their Creator with certain unalienable rights" (Shapiro 1966 [1776]: 78). Yet the most effective legitimation stems from a taken-for-granted (or natural) attitude toward all extant cultural practices on the part of succeeding generations, for whom things have always been this way. With intergenerational transmission, argue Berger and Luckmann (1966: 58), "institutionalization perfects itself" because the origins of social institutions become utterly opaque. Social

institutions originate within consciousness as innovative ideas, and ultimately return
to consciousness (albeit of succeeding generations) as taken-for-granted understandings of everyday life. Berger and Luckmann (1966: 61) refer to this process as
internalization, "by which the objectivated social world is retrojected into consciousness in the course of socialization."

Thus, Berger and Luckmann (1966: 61) conceptualize the social construction of
reality as three "moments in a continuing dialectical process": externalization,
objectivation, and internalization. Generally speaking, these processes are simultaneous, not sequential (1966: 129), and each of them has an essential implication
for sociological theory. With externalization, we see that society is a human product;
with objectivation, that society is an objective reality; and with internalization, that
human beings are social products (Berger and Luckmann 1966: 61). Together, these
processes make for the central paradox "that man is capable of producing a world
that he then experiences as something other than a human product" (Berger and
Luckmann 1966: 61). Indeed, the apotheosis of social reality occurs with its
reification.[10]

RECENT DEVELOPMENTS

Berger and Luckmann amplified the trend, begun by Schutz, of diluting phenomenology with mainstream sociological theory. This made for a popular and, arguably,
more powerful brew, but their writings were very abstract and no more empirically
oriented than those of Schutz. Commenting on the state of phenomenology during
the early 1970s, George Psathas (1973: 1) suggested that it was temporarily stalled
in a programmatic and exegetical phase: "As a function of the current stage of
development of a phenomenologically based social science, many of these authors
find it necessary to elaborate the theoretical and philosophical underpinnings of
their work before proceeding with their studies."

Beginning in the 1980s, however, phenomenology took a decidedly empirical
turn. Norman Denzin (1984) was a transitional figure. His work was empirically
grounded, not exegetical, but the title of his article, "Toward a Phenomenology of
Domestic Family Violence," implied monogamous devotion to a single theoretical
framework. The next generation of phenomenologically tinged sociologists would
be unabashedly empirical, but promiscuous with their conceptual inspirations.
Indeed, unlike Psathas and Denzin, they do not wear phenomenology on their
sleeves. They are inaugurating a pan-interactionism in which an empirically based
phenomenology is only one of several key components. The representative scholars
do not identify themselves as strictly phenomenological sociologists because this
new theoretical framework includes elements of symbolic interactionism, Goffman's
microstructuralism, and ethnomethodology.

One of the leading practitioners is Jack Katz (1988a), and his groundbreaking
book, *Seductions of Crime*, typifies this genre. Eschewing the traditional emphasis
on background factors such as race, class, and gender, Katz (1988a: 10) instead
concentrates on "the minutiae of experiential details in the phenomenal foreground"
– that is, the lived experience of one's own criminal behavior. There is, then, a
familiar emphasis on subjectivity, experiential creativity, and the social construction

of multiple realities: "What phenomenology uniquely has appreciated is not simply that a person's lived world is his artifact but that by experiencing himself as an object controlled by transcendent forces, an individual can genuinely experience a new or different world" (Katz 1988a: 8). This line of inquiry leads to a profound sense of irony concerning the dialectical and self-mystifying qualities of agentic conduct: "My overall objective in this book is to demonstrate that the causes of crime are constructed by the offenders themselves, but the causes they construct are lures and pressures that they experience as independently moving them toward crime" (Katz 1988a: 216).

Seductions of Crime is a data-driven treatise, and the empirical materials are quite diverse. Katz (1988a: 11) solicits "reports of shoplifting, burglary, and vandalism" from students in his classes; he assembles the findings of multiple ethnographic studies; he collects the published biographies and autobiographies of various criminals; and he makes extensive use of police records. In a further break with phenomenology's anti-empirical origins, Katz (1988b) advocates the use of analytic induction – an interpretive strategy first proposed by Florian Znaniecki (1934). Although rooted in an empirical epistemology, it bears more than a passing resemblance to Husserl's phenomenological procedures. One attempts to reduce particular instances of a phenomenon to its abstract essence. "The researcher is committed to form a perfect relation between data and explanation," as Katz (1988b: 130) puts it. "When encountering a 'negative case' – evidence contradicting the current explanation – the researcher must transform it into a confirming case by revising" the theory (1988b: 130). His refined and systematized version of analytic induction shares methodological kinship with Merleau-Ponty's (1964 [1945]: 17) insistence that "all the partial views one catches sight of must be welded together."

The twin themes of conceptual and methodological eclecticism are elaborated in a subsequent book, *How Emotions Work*. Here, Katz (1999: 7) formulates a "tripartite social-psychological theory" that incorporates elements of Freudian psychoanalysis with Mead and Goffman's interactionism and Merleau-Ponty's phenomenology of the body. Within this syncretic theoretical framework, Katz examines four of the common emotional experiences in everyday life: anger, laughter, shame, and crying. His approach is innovative, but his topic is in accord with the phenomenological focus on subjectivity. This book is thoroughly empirical, however. Katz assembles a sophisticated set of qualitative techniques for data collection, including extensive use of videotape. Once again, he makes sense of diverse data by means of analytic induction.

My own research offers another example of how phenomenological sociology has been subsumed by a pan-interactionism. Throughout the 1980s, there was considerable debate between scholars who espoused the constructionist and the positivist paradigms in the sociology of emotions. To support their respective positions, the constructionists pointed to cross-cultural variation in emotions whereas the positivists stressed cross-cultural uniformity. This debate rested on a fundamental misconception and its corollary: that the body is the only universal aspect of humanity and, therefore, that cross-cultural parallels in the emotions can only be predicated upon physiological processes. Rejecting this position, I demonstrated that the essential features of humor and amusement are derived from universal dynamics in the social construction of reality (Flaherty 1992). If, as Mehan and Wood (1975:

113) have argued, ordinary social interaction is "reality work," then we can understand the phenomenological essence of humor as "reality play" – intentional or
unintentional activity that involves a liberating and relatively harmless toying with
the tacitly assumed expectations apropos to a particular situation (Flaherty 1984:
75).

In my more recent work, I have turned to the study of variation in the perceived
passage of time (Flaherty 1999). Like the emotions, this topic represents a facet of
subjectivity (Ellis and Flaherty 1992), and, as we have seen, the investigation of
internal time consciousness has a long pedigree in the phenomenological literature.[11]
As with Katz, however, my research breaks with the past by virtue of being empirically grounded in narrative materials which are examined through a process of
analytic induction. The resulting theory aims at apprehending the phenomenological
essence of internal time consciousness, and that theory is constructed from the
conceptual building blocks we find in the writings of Mead, Schutz, Goffman, and
Garfinkel.

Relative to the objective or cosmic time of clocks and calendars, our subjective
experience of time can seem to pass slowly, quickly, or synchronously. This variation reflects the density of conscious information-processing occasioned by one's
immediate circumstances. Problematic circumstances provoke emotional concern
and cognitive involvement with self and situation, thereby increasing the density of
experience per standard temporal unit (e.g., minute). As a result, time seems to pass
slowly. Two different but related processes make for the impression that time has
passed quickly. First, some situations demand a great deal of challenging but
unproblematic activity (as in a "busy" interval). Given that one is familiar with,
and possibly trained for, the demands of this situation, one can act without much
self-consciousness or attention to time itself, thereby reducing the density of experience per standard temporal unit. When one looks back, time seems to have flown
by. Second, it is also the case that the erosion of episodic memory reduces the density
of experience in almost all remembered intervals, resulting in the nearly universal
feeling that "time flies." Finally, it is possible for one's experience to be roughly
synchronized with the time of clocks and calendars because familiarity with the
normal density of information-processing enables one to translate subjective experience into standard temporal units and vice versa.

Scott Harris is a third scholar whose work epitomizes recent developments in
phenomenological sociology. He takes "an interactionist approach" to the study of
equality in marital relationships (2006: 1), but, of course, it is not equality per se
which is at issue. Alluding to Berger and Luckmann's conceptual model, Harris
(2006: 1) contends that "equality is not an independent, objective, or self-evident
characteristic but is a socially constructed phenomenon." Likewise, his phenomenological roots are apparent when he "*attempts to bracket the 'truth' about the existence and meaning of inequality*" in order to open an analytical space for the
interpretive study of "claims-making" and the *perception* of equality and inequality
in marital relationships (Harris 2006: x).

In his writings, Harris shows us what has become of phenomenology. First, there
is a substantive focus on subjectivity – that is, how individuals define their relationships with others. Second, there is a syncretic theoretical framework that integrates
"symbolic interactionism, phenomenology, ethnomethodology," and Goffman's

microstructuralism (Harris 2006: 22). Although Harris (2006: 10) draws explicitly from the legacy of Alfred Schutz, he views it as "complementary to symbolic interactionism." Third, there is an unmistakably empirical orientation toward the analysis of narrative materials. Harris (2006: 72, 74) puts the word "data" in quotation marks to distance himself from mainstream positivism, but the fact that he invokes this term bespeaks a commitment to the evidentiary principles of intersubjectivity.

These traits are no less apparent in my own work as well as that of Katz. Ironically, then, phenomenology has earned a place at the sociological table, but only by evolving away from separatism and aligning itself with like-minded practitioners of the trade. It is, and will continue to be, a crucial component of the pan-interactionism that has emerged as a powerful paradigm in contemporary sociology.

Notes

1 One exception is Husserl's *Ideas* (1931 [1913]).
2 Harold Garfinkel, another of Schutz's students, will be dealt with elsewhere in this text.
3 Martin Heidegger (1962 [1927]: 50) famously echoes this slogan: "Thus the term 'phenomenology' expresses a maxim which can be formulated as 'To the things themselves!'"
4 Of course, the methodological utility of estrangement was anticipated by Georg Simmel (1971 [1908]).
5 As Erving Goffman (1974: 3) put it, "after taking this radical stand, James copped out; he allowed that the world of the senses has a special status, being the one we judge to be the realest reality." Goffman rejected the notion that any one of these worlds is more real than the others.
6 Subsequent contributions to the development of cognitive sociology include those of Cicourel (1974) and Zerubavel (1997).
7 Later, this distinction would be helpful in Garfinkel's (1967: 166) study of efforts by Agnes, the "intersexed" person, to manage her identity as a "normal female."
8 Goffman (1974: 5) would later mock the idea that the world of everyday life is "but one rule-produced plane of being."
9 Garfinkel (1967: 37) acknowledged his methodological debt to Schutz: "For these background expectancies to come into view one must either be a stranger to the 'life as usual' character of everyday scenes, or become estranged from them."
10 Berger (1967) elaborated on this model with a sociological theory of religion.
11 Further evidence of the importance of this topic can be found in the work of Eugene Minkowski (1970 [1933]).

Bibliography

Benedict, R. (1934) *Patterns of Culture*. Boston: Houghton Mifflin.
Berger, P. L. (1963) *Invitation to Sociology: A Humanistic Perspective*. Garden City, NY: Anchor.
Berger, P. L. (1967) *The Sacred Canopy: Elements of a Sociological Theory of Religion*. New York: Doubleday.

Berger, P. L., and Luckmann, T. (1966) *The Social Construction of Reality: A Treatise in the Sociology of Knowledge*. New York: Doubleday.

Cicourel, A. V. (1974) *Cognitive Sociology: Language and Meaning in Social Interaction*. New York: The Free Press.

Denzin, N. K. (1984) "Toward a Phenomenology of Domestic Family Violence." *American Journal of Sociology* 90: 483–513.

Ellis, C., and Flaherty, M. G. (eds.) (1992) *Investigating Subjectivity: Research on Lived Experience*. Newbury Park, CA: Sage.

Flaherty, M. G. (1984) "A Formal Approach to the Study of Amusement in Social Interaction." *Studies in Symbolic Interaction* 5: 71–82.

Flaherty, M. G. (1992) "The Derivation of Emotional Experience from the Social Construction of Reality." *Studies in Symbolic Interaction* 13: 167–82.

Flaherty, M. G. (1999) *A Watched Pot: How We Experience Time*. New York: New York University Press.

Garfinkel, H.(1967) *Studies in Ethnomethodology*. Englewood Cliffs, NJ: Prentice Hall.

Goffman, E. (1974) *Frame Analysis: An Essay on the Organization of Experience*. Cambridge, MA: Harvard University Press.

Harris, S. R. (2006) *The Meanings of Marital Equality*. Albany: State University of New York Press.

Heap, J. L., and Roth, P. A. (1973) "On Phenomenological Sociology." *American Sociological Review* 38: 354–67.

Heidegger, M. (1962 [1927]) *Being and Time*, trans. J. Macquarrie and E. Robinson. New York: Harper & Row.

Husserl, E. (1931 [1913]) *Ideas: General Introduction to Pure Phenomenology*, trans. W. R. Boyce Gibson. NY: Humanities Press.

Husserl, E. (1960 [1931]) *Cartesian Meditations: An Introduction to Phenomenology*, trans. D. Cairns. The Hague: Martinus Nijhoff.

Husserl, E. (1964 [1928]) *The Phenomenology of Internal Time-Consciousness*, ed. M. Heidegger, trans. J. S. Churchill. Bloomington: Indiana University Press.

Husserl, E. (1965 [1910]) *Phenomenology and the Crisis of Philosophy*, ed. and trans. Q. Lauer. New York: Harper & Row.

Husserl, E. (1970 [1936]) *The Crisis of European Sciences and Transcendental Phenomenology: An Introduction to Phenomenological Philosophy*, trans. D. Carr. Evanston, IL: Northwestern University Press.

James, W. (1890) "The Perception of Reality," in *The Principles of Psychology*, vol. 2. New York: Dover.

Katz, J. (1988a) *Seductions of Crime: Moral and Sensual Attractions in Doing Evil*. New York: Basic Books.

Katz, J. (1988b) "A Theory of Qualitative Methodology: The Social System of Analytic Fieldwork," in R. M. Emerson (ed.), *Contemporary Field Research: A Collection of Readings*. Prospect Heights, IL: Waveland.

Katz, J. (1999) *How Emotions Work*. Chicago: University of Chicago Press.

Kockelmans, J. J. (1967) "What Is Phenomenology?," in J. J. Kockelmans (ed.), *Phenomenology: The Philosophy of Edmund Husserl and its Interpretation*. Garden City, NY: Doubleday.

Mehan, H., and Wood, H. (1975) *The Reality of Ethnomethodology*. New York: John Wiley.

Merleau-Ponty, M. (1964 [1945]) "Cézanne's Doubt," in *Sense and Nonsense*, trans. H. L. Dreyfus and P. A. Dreyfus. Evanston, IL: Northwestern University Press.

Merleau-Ponty, M. (1973 [1964]) *Consciousness and the Acquisition of Language*, trans. H. J. Silverman. Evanston, IL: Northwestern University Press.

Minkowski, E. (1970 [1933]) *Lived Time: Phenomenological and Psychopathological Studies*, trans. N. Metzel. Evanston, IL: Northwestern University Press.

Natanson, M. (1973) "Phenomenology and the Social Sciences," in *Phenomenology and the Social Sciences*, vol. 1. Evanston, IL: Northwestern University Press.

Psathas, G. (1973) "Introduction," in G. Psathas (ed.), *Phenomenological Sociology: Issues and Applications*. New York: John Wiley.

Schutz, A. (1944) "The Stranger: An Essay in Social Psychology." *American Journal of Sociology* 49: 499–507.

Schutz, A. (1962 [1945]) "On Multiple Realities," in M. Natanson (ed.), *Collected Papers*, vol. 1, *The Problem of Social Reality*. The Hague: Martinus Nijhoff.

Schutz, A. (1964) *Collected Papers*, vol. 2, *Studies in Social Theory*, ed. A. Brodersen. The Hague: Martinus Nijhoff.

Schutz, A. (1967 [1932]) *The Phenomenology of the Social World*, trans. G. Walsh and F. Lehnert. Evanston, IL: Northwestern University Press.

Schutz, A. (1970 [1945]) *On Phenomenology and Social Relations*, ed. H. R. Wagner. Chicago: University of Chicago Press.

Schutz, A., and Luckmann, T. (1973) *The Structures of the Life-World*, trans. R. M. Zaner and H. T. Engelhardt, Jr. Evanston, IL: Northwestern University Press.

Shapiro, M. (ed.) (1966 [1776]) *The Constitution of the United States and Related Documents*. New York: Appleton, Century, Crofts.

Simmel, G. (1971 [1908]) "The Stranger," in D. N. Levine (ed.), *Georg Simmel: On Individuality and Social Forms*. Chicago: University of Chicago Press.

Wagner, H. R. (1983) *Alfred Schutz: An Intellectual Biography*. Chicago: University of Chicago Press.

Zerubavel, E. (1997) *Social Mindscapes: An Invitation to Cognitive Sociology*. Cambridge, MA: Harvard University Press.

Znaniecki, F. (1934) *The Method of Sociology*. New York: Farrar & Rinehart.

12

Feminist Theory

MARY EVANS

INTRODUCTION

Fifty years ago no volume on social theory would have included a chapter on feminist theory. That statement gives some indication of the extent to which feminist theory is a new area within social theory, but it does little to reflect the long history of theoretical engagement by women with the intellectual and the academic world. Feminist theory did not emerge out of a theoretical vacuum, and the "making" of feminist theory is both a subject in itself and one which has a great deal to say about both the content and the context of feminist theory. No account of feminist theory would therefore be complete without some recognition of the way in which feminists have engaged with social theory and offered contributions to it. At the same time it must also be acknowledged that the development of feminist theory in the academy owed a great deal to changes in both the curriculum and the recruitment to higher education in the West which took place from the 1960s onwards. In a very important sense, the history of feminist theory is also the history of liberal bourgeois society: society changed its understanding of the concept (and the gender) of the "citizen" in answer to the demands of feminism, but feminism also changed its demands in relation to the changing nature of the social world.

The history of feminist theory is as long as the Western tradition of written engagements with the social world. Wherever we locate the origins of the "modern" (the fourteenth century, 1492, 1789) we can identify women writers who have asked questions about their place in the social world and contested prevailing ideas about the role and the nature of women and the feminine. This challenge to the conventional has not always been conducted by women alone (for example, the most famous Western ally in the cause of the social emancipation of women must be John Stuart Mill), nor has it had a single focus, in the sense of a consistent challenge to the masculine or a demand for a full equalization of the social participation of women and men. In the eighteenth and nineteenth centuries, quite as much as in the twentieth and the twenty-first, there have been debates between women, and between women and men, about ideas of sexual equality and sexual difference. If we accept a liberal interpretation of the word "theory" then we can make a case for much that is part of the written tradition of the West making a contribution to the discussion of the social implications of the biological differences between the sexes. Literature and the visual arts in particular constitute a long testament to the different understandings of the social implications of male and female and the different ways in which those understandings have been challenged (Knott and Taylor 2005).

But that word "liberal" also has another importance in the history of feminism, for it has always been the case that questioning and examining the social meaning of biological difference has been a liberal preoccupation and supported by regimes or individuals who could be broadly described as liberal. As a general rule, in the West, the more authoritarian the regime the more unlikely it is to allow any intellectual or social space for the discussion of sexual difference. As sociologists we all know that the term "natural" has to be regarded with the largest degree of skepticism, but we might also note that this term has been widely used by "gender conservatives" to maintain (or enforce) conservatism about gender. Conservatism about gender, in the West, has taken the form of the assumption that women should occupy the private world of the household whilst men should direct and determine the public world. Gender conservatism has, in fact, rejoiced in the certainties of a binary vision about gender difference: men are men, made to hunt, fight, defend, and control the intellectual world, women are women, and as such are primarily responsible for all individual care that needs to be done in any society. (The majority of societies have been prepared to abandon all gender stereotypes at times of national emergency). Societies outside the West, however, and Mao's China is the best example, have been prepared to allow women an equal place with men in some aspects of the public world (notably the labor force), but have still maintained the pattern of the exclusion of women from public power. Marx is well known for his view that the entry of women into "public production" would also lead to their more general emancipation, and certain socialist societies organized the degree of child care which made this possible. Nevertheless – and notwithstanding everything which Foucault and the Foucauldians might have to say about the diffuse nature of power – women have been systematically excluded, within both capitalism and socialism, from those positions within power structures which have significant control over the lives of others.

This very general account of the social meaning of gender has included terms such as "nature," the "public," and the "private," which have now come to be a matter of considerable sociological debate. It is therefore perhaps useful at this point to review some of the history of the past 200 years of feminist theory and look at the ways in which feminist theory has developed and changed, and not least in terms of the ways in which these shifts and realignments have been a product of, quite as much as a confrontation with, more general ideological and material shifts in the social world. As sociologists we have to explain why ideas change – if they do – quite as much as the social impact and content of the ideas themselves. Thus the history of feminist theory should not just be a historical account of those ideas but also an account of the context in which those ideas changed, the relationship between changes in one part of the social world and others.

EARLY DEVELOPMENTS

The conventional starting point for accounts of the emergence of feminist theory in the West is the work of Mary Wollstonecraft, most particularly her *A Vindication of the Rights of Woman*, published in 1792 and dedicated to Talleyrand in a flowery note which includes the remark that "In France there is undoubtedly a more general diffusion of knowledge than in any part of the European world" (Wollstonecraft 1970). (Some 20 years later Wollstonecraft may have taken a somewhat less rosy view of French behavior, given Napoleon's less than egalitarian attitude to women.) What is important, however, about Wollstonecraft's work in the context of the twenty-first century is her conviction that the degree of the emancipation of women is related to the general progress and "enlightenment" of a society as a whole. In this she shares with Marx the view that the position of women in society has to be thought of in terms of the society as a whole. It is thus that Wollstonecraft – unlike, let us say, later writers on women such as John Stuart Mill – takes an organic view of society: improvement of one bit of the social world is not a matter of changing that one context but of an overall consideration and rearrangement of the various parts of the social world.

Wollstonecraft's *Vindication* was widely read at the time of its publication, and its views attracted, inevitably, both praise and censure. After her death, from puerperal fever, a number of female voices – not unlike that of the British newspaper the *Daily Mail* in the twenty-first century – commented that women, rather than reading Wollstonecraft, would do well to remember that "Girls must very soon perceive the impossibility of their rambling about the world in quest of adventures" (Tomalin 1974: 243). The debate about women, after Wollstonecraft and in response to Wollstonecraft, took the form that it was to take for the next 200 years: women (and occasionally male supporters of feminism) make claims for the equal treatment of women in both the social and domestic spheres; conservatives and anti-feminists resist the arguments in terms of the "natural" and unchangeable divisions between the sexes.

This dynamic in social theory about women can be identified throughout the nineteenth and much of the twentieth century, and within those years two major traditions in the discussion of the "woman question" can be observed. On the one hand were those, notably in Britain and the United States, who saw, and defended, the improvement in the education and civil status of women in terms of part of a general trajectory of social progress, whilst others saw the social position of women in society in terms of the structure of society itself. The first group, which in Britain included John Stuart Mill, the great women writers of nineteenth-century fiction such as the Brontës, George Eliot, and Elizabeth Gaskell, and the campaigners for women's higher and professional education, together with suffragists on both sides of the Atlantic, invoked changes in the social position of women in terms of the related improvements in society as a whole. A second group, which included Marx and Engels, saw the position of women as unchangeable within the context of bourgeois society. In *The Origins of the Family, Private Property and the State* Marx and Engels suggested a relationship between the social structure of society as a whole and the sexual division of labor: an analysis which called for an emancipation of women into public labor which was to inform the policies towards women of all state socialist societies (Marx and Engels 1984).

The divisions between these two groups on the question of the social status of women and men are, of course, part of the wider political and theoretical differences of the nineteenth and twentieth centuries between Marxism and liberal, and neo-liberal, accounts of the social world. Yet in some ways, and viewed from the perspective of the early twenty-first century, there are significant similarities, as much as differences, between these two groups on the question of women. The most marked similarity is the way in which protagonists of both groups use uncritically the terms male and female, masculinity and femininity. Marx, just as much as John Stuart Mill, takes the view that there are decidedly natural and fixed differences between women and men, differences which will be maintained regardless of other changes in social arrangements.

The theorist who did more than any other to shift this perception of the unalterable "nature" of male and female was Freud, whose ideas on the ways in which we learn and acquire our sexuality challenged centuries of ideas about masculinity and femininity. Freud famously remarked that he had little idea what women wanted, but even if he felt that he could not provide satisfactory answers on this point what he could, and did, do was to give women a crucial part in those relationships, both material and symbolic, through which we come to acquire our sexual identity. As feminist writers on Freud (Mitchell 1976; Sayers 1982) have pointed out, the father always occupies a somewhat more important role in Freud's account of the psychic world than the mother, but even given this, what he challenged is the view that individual human acquisition of "maleness" and "femaleness" is unproblematic. After Freud, and the integration of aspects of his work and that of other psychoanalysts into public institutions (the most obvious example of which is the work of John Bowlby on mother–child attachment: Bowlby 1973), there was no going back to the view that the terms man, woman, male, and female were anything other than deeply charged with meaning and the possibilities of diversity. Despite the hostility to Freud from both feminist and non-feminist critics, his work – and the particular reclamation of it by Juliet Mitchell – was to open up practices in the material world and the study of representation and the symbolic world.

It is therefore something of a paradox to find, as we do, in the middle of the twentieth century, that the second great icon of feminism, and feminist theory, Simone de Beauvoir, both refutes Freud's work and endorses an understanding of male and female which is organized around a rigid binary division. De Beauvoir, best known for *The Second Sex*, had initially little sympathy for organized feminism – that sympathy was to come later in her life – but what *The Second Sex* does do is to take issue with the social allocation of women to the household and to passivity. If there is a single theme which runs through de Beauvoir's work, her fiction just as much as *The Second Sex* and her other work of non-fiction, it is her revolt against the assignment of women to a social and emotional absence of agency. Whether it is in creating a heroine (in her novel *She Came to Stay*) who murders a female rival for a man's affections, or in *The Second Sex* and the four volumes of autobiography, where female activity and agency is endorsed, de Beauvoir exhorts women to step out of the socially defined strictures of being "the other" (de Beauvoir 1966). The "other" is, of course, the male, who possesses above all else the human capacity for transcendence and the ability to impress upon the world an individual will. In contrast to this, women are, in de Beauvoir's view, creatures who spend their lives following in the footsteps of men, ever willing to do their bidding and accept their definitions of reality. Women are, further, divided amongst themselves and endlessly in competition for access to those beings who might, in the twenty-first century, be described as the "alpha males."

In the last decade of her life de Beauvoir was to engage in many of the struggles of French and European feminism, most particularly for women's autonomous control over the technology of reproduction. But she never lost her commitment to the idea that both language and intelligence are gender-neutral; to her there was no such thing as a "female language," and the ways in which men and women think were to be viewed in the same way. The contribution of her fellow Frenchwomen (for example Cixous and Irigaray) to feminism was the enormously influential idea of the fundamental difference between the language and understanding of men and women; this, to de Beauvoir, was an untenable position (Marks and de Courtivron 1981). To de Beauvoir, the strength of feminism, indeed its appeal, was the possibilities it opened up for the transcendence of femininity; to Cixous et al. feminism was the celebration of the difference between men and women.

In their different ways, both de Beauvoir and the group identified with the "new" French feminism maintained a belief in the fixed nature of male and female. Even though difference was to be either transcended or celebrated it was still maintained, and there was little sense, for any of these writers, that the "nature" of gender was highly unstable and something that was, quite literally, "made up" in different social contexts. Notwithstanding de Beauvoir's famous remark that "women are made and not born," the actual argument of her work takes for granted less the fact of the fixed nature of femininity than that of the enduring nature of masculinity – and it is up to women, rather than men, to reposition the social meaning of their gender. For de Beauvoir, and generations of other Western feminists, the essential project of feminism is to gain for women the same rights as men, be they rights to paid employment or to autonomy of the person.

For over 200 years Western feminism has made a determined effort to acquire the same public and private civic status for women as that of men. In the nineteenth century Western feminism campaigned for various forms of institutional access (to the vote, to higher education, and to professional training for example) at the same time as feminists challenged the sexual double standards of their day. As writers on the history of sexuality have pointed out, for two centuries women have fought for the right to control of their bodies and for social recognition as autonomous sexual agents. From Wollstonecraft to de Beauvoir many of these demands were couched in a language of the betterment of the social world and an emancipatory model of human existence. Motherhood was long the stopping block to the discussion (and the practice) of the public emancipation of women, but two world wars, and the consumer revolution of the 1950s, very effectively put paid to the idea that mothers could remain, without paid employment, in the home and dependent on the support of a man. Certainly in the case of Britain in World War II, "history" moved rather faster than many social attitudes, and the acute and urgent need for labor power involved a rapid rewriting of the gendered script in relationship to both the home and the factory.

War, as historians have often pointed out, frequently drives social change. Between 1940 and 1945 this was certainly the case for Britain. Nevertheless, although women (most particularly unmarried women) took a larger share in production in World War II than had previously been the case, it was not in this period, but in the 1960s that the real challenges to the gender order became marked. De Beauvoir's *The Second Sex* was first published in 1949, and although the book was widely read at this time it was not explicitly allied to a social movement or a more generalized sense of discontent about the given arrangements of gender. This was, however, to be the case in the politically turbulent 1960s: the decade which (according to the poet Philip Larkin) invented sex also began the most radical rewriting of the sexual script in Western history: for the first time in that history feminist theory became a matter of general and popular discussion. Even if the complexities unleashed upon the world by feminist writers such as Judith Butler are seldom of concern outside the academy, feminism became a public part of Western culture, its major writers and theorists well known and widely discussed. "Women's lib," as second-wave feminism was popularly known, became a part of the popular culture of the West.

"Second-Wave" Feminism

The roots of this hugely influential feminism of the 1960s and 1970s lay less in scarcity than in plenty. The starting point for much that was to become commonplace in feminist theory was less the material deprivation which women shared (this discussion was to come later) than the personal and emotional thralldom in which women in the affluent West were kept. The book which made this point with a particularly dramatic rhetoric was Betty Friedan's *The Feminine Mystique*, first published in the United States in 1963 (Friedan 1963). The gist of Friedan's book was that in the affluent suburbs of the United States well-educated women were becoming depressed and miserable, confined to their homes and the domestic round. The cry of *The Feminine Mystique* was strikingly similar to that of Charlotte Brontë's most famous heroine Jane Eyre, who on reviewing the prospect of the calm and tranquil life before her asks, in a less material sense than Charles Dickens's *Oliver Twist*, for "more." Jane Eyre had cried out for change and diversity in 1847; now, over a hundred years later, another woman was voicing both her own dissatisfactions and those of her contemporaries at the same fate of domestic seclusion.

The Feminine Mystique was an immediate popular success, and Friedan became a globally known spokeswoman for the emancipation of women from the domestic hearth. She had identified what she called the "illness that has no name," and much of her book is about the waste (and in a sense the betrayal) of the education (particularly the higher education) that many women had received. With hindsight we can read the book as resistance to that home-centered consumer revolution which fueled Western economies in the 1950s and 1960s: the people who were to manage this newly equipped domestic space were assumed to be women, just as surely as it was taken for granted that no mother would wish to work outside the home.

Friedan's book stands at the very beginning of "second-wave" feminism and is in many ways far less radical than many of the later publications. It was in the early

1970s that a cluster of books was published, in both Britain and the United States, which argued that a revolution was needed in public attitudes about gender. This went much further than Friedan had ever envisaged: the books by Germaine Greer, Kate Millett, Sheila Rowbotham, Eva Figes, Shulamith Firestone, et al. were not about making certain changes to gendered social arrangements (more day care for example); they were about tearing up the existing social script about gender and rewriting it (Figes 1970; Firestone 1970; Greer 1971; Rowbotham 1973). Two main arguments emerged from the authors cited and the many others writing at this time: first, that misogyny was deeply entrenched in social practice, and, second, that the sexual division of labor was part and parcel of the structural order of neoliberal capitalism. In some authors these arguments overlapped; in others the emphasis was rather more on definitions and conditions of sexuality than conditions of labor.

By the end of the 1970s most Western societies had seen the emergence of a cluster of social demands which could be broadly defined as feminist: access for all women to contraception and abortion, much-enlarged state provision for child care, equal pay, and equal treatment in law. Britain passed, in 1967, a number of radical Acts of Parliament which drew on long campaigns about the reordering of sexuality and marriage, and throughout the 1970s other Western societies broadly followed the pattern of the British changes. By1980, the majority of Western societies had introduced legislation which 20 years previously might have been seen as impossible. The rate of social change about sexual life was widely described as the "sexual revolution," and it was clear, by this point, that a marked differentiation had appeared between liberal-democratic societies of the West and those of the rest of the world in terms of the personal liberties allowed to individual citizens. Inevitably, there was social resistance, a resistance which – in the context of debates about abortion and gay rights – has lost none of its vehemence with the passing of the years.

It might appear, from the above, that by the beginning of the 1980s Western feminism had achieved many of its early demands and there would be little recourse to further discussion of the "woman question." This proved to be entirely inaccurate, and the last two decades of the twentieth century saw an intellectual flowering of feminism which has been unparalleled at any other time or place. In part the emergence of a rich feminist intellectual tradition can be attributed to that increase in the number of women in higher education made possible through the reforms in higher education of the 1970s. The opening up of universities to large numbers of the age cohorts (a general Western phenomenon) included greater numbers of women, women who found that in the main the universities, and the wider intellectual and academic cultural world to which they now had access, was little changed by the wider advances in the social world. This situation was not to remain unchallenged.

The feminist theory that evolved in the last decades of the twentieth century was, in part, concerned with the politics of gender in the wider social world; feminist theory, through writers whose academic disciplines were often those involved in one way or another with social policy, has always had a developed sense of the social implications of ideas. But what also emerged – and was much more theoretically significant – was a tradition in feminist theory with two radical themes: first, the redefinition of those terms such as "nature," "gender," and "rights" which had long been a taken-for-granted part of academic debates, and, second, a challenge to nothing less than the gendered assumptions of various "classic" disciplinary traditions. In both cases writers took a highly skeptical view of post-Enlightenment accounts of the world and found that, rather than ushering in a more emancipatory view of gender, the 200 years since the end of the Enlightenment had seen an increasing rigidity in accounts of biological difference. In part, of course, this owed much to Foucauldian accounts of history; readings of history which did not endorse ideas about the long march of human progress opened up a space for feminists to take a less enthusiastic view of what was supposed to be women's "emancipation." Various writers began to suggest that the freedom to take part in the labor market on the same terms as men (terms which, by the end of the 1980s and given the impact of increasingly conservative economic policies, were often less secure than previously) was not, in itself, a mark of "emancipation."

If we take the first set of ideas we can identify within it writers from a number of academic disciplines, and the interdisciplinary nature of feminist theory has always been one of its distinguishing features. For example the historian Londa Schiebinger reiterated the question of eighteenth-century women when she asked "Does the mind have a sex?" (Schiebinger 1989). The philosopher Kate Soper questioned the extent to which "nature" was still used as an underlying assumption throughout the humanities and the social sciences and, in law, psychology, and political science respectively, Martha Nussbaum, Carol Gilligan, and Carole Pateman asked questions about the different meaning of rights and morality for men and women (Gilligan 1982; Nussbaum 1999; Pateman 1988; Soper 2005). What the work of these writers also opened up was the problem, within feminist theory, of essentialism – generally the assumption that there is a distinct and fixed difference between male and female which manifests itself in different ways of understanding, and acting within, the world. Essentialism had become an unacceptable theoretical position for many feminist writers by the end of the 1980s: the rhetorical strength and usefulness of the concept of the "essential" difference between men and women (most vehemently expressed in the 1970s slogan "All men are rapists") had now been replaced by a rejection of an idea which seemed to add nothing to the understanding of the ways in which gender and gender difference are socially created. Within feminism in the United States, in particular, there remained a sense of the political importance of maintaining the integrity of the word "woman," but for feminists in other contexts, and certainly in those countries where considerable traditions of the understanding of the social construction of the self were present, "woman" started to be a singularly problematic word.

DIFFERENCES AND CONTINUITIES

Yet the major challenge to gender essentialism came, in 1990, not from Europe but from the United States, in the first major book by the philosopher Judith Butler, *Gender Trouble* (Butler 1990). In essence, this book suggests that everyone – male and female, homosexual and heterosexual – is "performing" gender, and that this performance of gender is crucial for social stability and social cohesion. Butler gave gender a central building-block position in her account of the social world: without gender and gender differentiation, she suggests, the social world cannot function, and many of the ideas about social organization which we hold would prove to be meaningless. Butler's work (in *Gender Trouble* and in later books) has been hugely significant, not least because it offers a way of disconnecting ideologies about masculinity and femininity not just from people who are biologically male or female but also from any set of ideas which assumes the "natural" order of gender. In making gender a matter of both social construction and a degree of individual choice, Butler rejects any assumption that our gender identity is in any sense natural. The social acceptance and recognition of this argument would, she suggests, "have the effect of proliferating gender configurations, de-stabilizing substantive identity, and depriving the naturalizing narratives of compulsory heterosexuality of their central protagonists: 'man' and 'woman'" (Butler 1990). In effect, what Butler is doing here is arguing for both the theoretical instability of gender identity and the political and intellectual possibilities of that situation.

The theoretical implications of Butler's arguments have rightly been perceived as considerable, since what her work offers is a way of reinterpreting both the "real" world and the world of representation as contexts where individuals, rather than acting within their fixed gender identities, seek to establish them. Gender is thus not a given feature of the social world but one that is acquired, "made" in the sense that de Beauvoir suggested it but also less secure than she assumed. Women are "made" in de Beauvoir's view; they are always in the process of being made in that of Judith Butler. In the latter's writing we can see the possibilities of new forms of human engagement with biological sex difference, forms which in many ways are highly suitable for Western societies of the twenty-first century, where technology has shifted many of the boundaries of paid work and of reproduction. If we consider the practical implications of the disappearance of conventional gender behavior which Butler suggests, then we can see that many of the industries and much of the social behavior that actually depends on gender differentiation might disappear: a form of chosen androgyny does not involve sexual divisions of paid or unpaid labor or extensive consumerism organized around gender boundaries. Butler's less explicit emphasis is on the similarities between male and female; her most recent work has taken issue with the negative implications of masculinity rather than those of femininity, and she has also argued against all forms of campaigning (such as laws against pornography or legislation for equal pay) which seem to involve fixed definitions of male and female (Butler 1990). What Judith Butler is therefore not supporting is any form of feminism which champions a particular form of sexual identity, including that of lesbianism. In 1980 the poet Adrienne Rich wrote a widely influential paper entitled "Compulsory Heterosexuality," and Rich's argument in the paper underpinned many exercises, both theoretical and personal, which sought to remake sexual relations in terms which challenged what became known as "heteronormativity" (Rich 1980). Both gay men (and those later collectively known as "queer theorists") examined the ways in which history, theory, and social convention assumed heterosexuality but were also widely informed by what the literary critic Terry Castle was to describe as the "apparitional lesbian" (Castle 1993). As Castle included perceptions of Marie Antoinette in the ranks of those valuing the love of other women, it became clear that feminist theory had taken a challenging and imaginative leap into the understanding and definition of human sexuality.

Although Butler's work (and the equally radical work of writers such as Rich and Castle) has been highly influential, it has also, inevitably given Butler's views about political campaigns, had its critics, amongst whom Butler's fellow citizens Nancy Fraser and Martha Nussbaum have been perhaps the most vocal. The thrust of Fraser's arguments against Butler is that Butler ignores the material world: for Fraser shifts in gender identity within capitalism are perfectly acceptable and possible yet do nothing to challenge the underlying order of that world (Fraser 1998). Butler's reply is that – as we have seen above – the dilution of gender identity would threaten the patterns of consumption which depend upon them. Martha Nussbaum is similarly concerned with what she sees as Butler's refusal to recognize the validity of political and legislative campaigns that have long been associated with improvement in women's situation. Nussbaum writes:

> Butler's argument has implications well beyond the cases of hate speech and pornography. It would appear to support not just quietism in these areas, but a much more general legal quietism – or, indeed, a radical libertarianism. It goes like this: let us do away with everything from building codes to non-discriminisation laws to rape laws because they close the space within which the injured tenants, the victims of discrimination, the raped women, can perform their resistance. (Nussbaum 1999)

Resistance, Nussbaum goes on to point out, is crucial in Butler's work because it is only through resistance that individuals can challenge the very definitions that oppress them. To Butler a law which specifically bars discrimination against women is not a "good" law, but a very bad law, in that it maintains, indeed clearly supports, those same binary distinctions between men and women which inspire the discrimination in the first place.

Whatever view is taken of Butler's work there is no doubt that amongst the extensive feminist work of the late twentieth century she made the most radical contribution to thinking about gender, across all disciplines in the social sciences and the humanities. What is particularly useful about Butler's work, even to those with reservations about it, is that she provides a theoretical – and potentially cross-cultural – account of ways of destabilizing the subject and of discussing the ways in which identity is constructed. If we accept that we are all less than secure about our gender identity – and that our gender identity cannot be secure – then we can immediately see why human beings across all societies and all cultures should go to such (often extreme) lengths in order to stabilize what is otherwise fluid. In the contexts of gay studies, queer theory, literary criticism, social anthropology, the sociology of the body, and racial and ethnic identity, Butler's work has allowed us to see how we both pursue certainties about gender identity and construct both normative and essentialist assumptions around the terms "man" and "woman."

Whilst the value of Butler's work has been recognized as a major contribution to feminist theory there are others, contemporaries with Butler and from various disciplines and countries who take issue with the value of her work in the "real" world, in which, for example, women are routinely paid less than men and carry out the major part of caring responsibilities. The point that these writers stress is that biological difference – unlike gender difference – is for the most part not negotiable and that to ask women not to organize as "women" is to prolong significantly certain forms of social discrimination. For women outside the relatively affluent West, or for women in countries with strict religious rules about the behavior of male and female, to refuse to think about "women" could be regarded as collusion with male dominance. This criticism, however, could equally well be regarded as a question of political strategy rather than as a theoretical problem with Butler's work.

Amongst those many writers whose work has followed paths other than those set by Butler are women writing on the labor market, on education, on social policy, on literature, and on representation. Some of this work, although not all of it, has been untroubled by the ideas suggested by the possibilities of the fluidity of gender and has articulated much that has been of enormous value. Beverley Skeggs on gender and class, Sylvia Walby and Rosemary Crompton on gender and the labor market, Henrietta Moore on social anthropology, and Susan Bordo and Kathy Davis on the body are amongst those who have demonstrated the ways in which "gender free theory is no theory at all" (Bordo 1993; Crompton 2006; Davis 1997a, 1997b; Moore 1994; Skeggs 1997; Walby 1990). At the same time, many of these writers have drawn theoretical inspiration and direction from writers outside feminism: Beverley Skeggs's work, for example, whilst brilliantly illuminating the ways in which the acquisition of femininity is also a matter of the acquisition of a class-bound femininity, has acknowledged the relationship of her work to that of the French sociologist Pierre Bourdieu. In the same way, the other writers mentioned above (and many others) have both developed gendered theoretical perspectives within disparate disciplines whilst at the same time drawing on a canonical literature which in some cases may have had the most limited engagement with the question of gender.

ENLARGING FEMINISM

It is on the question of the part played by "classic" traditions in the making of feminist theory that we encounter a pattern of complexities within feminist theory. The decades which saw the emergence of second-wave Western feminism were also decades in which people of color and people from outside the West challenged many of the assumptions of what was taken to be "classic" theory. One of the first and best known of such challenges was the literary critic Edward Said's *Culture and Imperialism*, a book which took the West to task for refusing to recognize its colonial, and deeply exploitative, heritage (Said 1994). The central example used by Said to demonstrate his argument was a discussion of Jane Austen's *Mansfield Park*, a novel about a world economically supported by slave labor, in which that relationship has only the most minor of minor parts and is barely mentioned by the author.

Said's account of Jane Austen did not escape criticism. But apart from critical voices there were many who expressed sympathy with his view, and in the following decades other writers – for example Paul Gilroy and Gayatri Spivak – made the case for examining all forms of Western "theory" for its racial and ethnic assumptions (Gilroy 1996; Spivak 1999). The impact of this theoretical turn for feminist theory was considerable, for it opened up both a new set of political ideas about women (not least the relationship of white women to women of color) and suggested that many of the values which were a taken-for-granted part of feminism were themselves the very values which underpinned patterns of exploitation in the rest of the world. In this insistence on the inclusion of race, racial differences and social exploitation through race (and ethnic and religious differences) we can see two particular directions within feminist thought. The first is the challenge by black feminists to "white" assumptions, not the least of these challenges being to the long-term refusal of "white" feminism to see race and the social impact of racial difference. But, and very importantly for many black feminist writers (for example Patricia Hill Collins), the essential ingredient of black feminist thought should be its determination to deal with race and sex and class, rather than simply objectifying black women in terms only of their race (Collins 1989).

The second direction which feminist thought took when confronted by the social reality of the racial and class differences between women was to point out the global patterns of social and cultural privilege, patterns which, typically, allowed many Western women to profit by the poverty and deprivation of women outside relatively rich Western societies. For example, Arlie Hochschild and Barbara Ehrenreich wrote of the employment by white women in the United States of women from countries outside the West; this employment, almost always of women as domestic servants, made possible the paid employment of white women and, implicitly, the continuation of those social and political structures which ensured that the West was able to continue to profit from the material poverty of other parts of the world (Hochschild and Ehrenreich 2002).

The raising of this issue of racial divides between women brought with it a number of other questions which have remained complex and often divisive within feminism. Certain traditions within Western feminism had long recognized differences of class and race and the historical connections between the social emancipation of women, opposition to slavery, and postcolonial movements for the reclaiming of indigenous cultures (Carby 1984; Lorde 1984; Rowbotham 1973). But the post-Said arguments about race and ethnic difference took a rather different direction: here the questions became those of theoretical and political relativism. For example, to women in the West there was little doubt that practices such as the veiling of women or genital mutilation were unacceptable; but once these practices were put in the context of a colonized culture attempting to maintain its own religious and cultural patterns against those of the West they began to have rather different meanings. Women, particularly on the question of various dress codes, began to speak up for their own cultures and to argue that these were not enforced but freely chosen practices. By the beginning of the twenty-first century it had become apparent that feminism had to be a very broad church indeed to contain the various differences within it.

In this context, in which it has been made clear, by both argument and empirical demonstration, that there is as much that divides women as unites them, the appeal of arguments such as those of Judith Butler, which effectively aim to dissolve the cultural meaning of the term "man" and "woman," are very appealing. Butler's destabilization of identity as a political rather than an intellectual project has much to offer many feminists in the West who see the possibilities of a genderless citizen. However, this vision of the future (not, of course, unlike many of the futures envisaged by novelists, for example George Orwell in *Nineteen Eighty-Four*), has been widely attacked by those who see it as both a social agenda which abolishes all forms of protection for women (and by implication others with needs which differ from those of healthy males) and the theoretical nemesis of feminism. Without the category of woman, the argument goes, there can be no feminism.

At this point there is cause to reflect that in the 200 years since the publication of *A Vindication of the Rights of Woman* feminist theory has reached a point where it is both theoretically assured and influential and yet is seen in some quarters as a barrier to the human emancipation of women rather than as a means of liberation. In some contexts, notably outside the West, it is difficult to see how the abolition of the concept of "woman" would improve the lives of those actual women struggling to gain a measure of education, physical autonomy, and economic independence. At the same time, the example of communist China reminds us that gender differences can be at least formally dissolved and that what was done in Mao's China is being achieved in the capitalist West by the workings of the economy: the cost of basic subsistence together with the personal and material aspirational costs of a consumer society are such that women have become almost as fully integrated into the labor force, its values and those of consumption, as men. In this context the feminist theory which once, for example, decried the difficulties women faced in gaining paid employment or access to professional training have to a certain extent been overtaken, if not by events, then at least by the dynamics of capitalism.

To continue by considering the gendered differences in social experience which still exist in the West would inevitably involve a list which would include differences in male and female earnings and participation in the power structures of institutional life. The infamous "glass ceiling" has been broken in many contexts (in Britain, for example, by the first woman prime minister, and in mainland Europe by a number of very visible female politicians), but what remains – and remains most apparent in an area which is of the least interest to many in a secular society – is the barrier to women in senior positions in all religious faiths. The resistance, for example, to the idea of women bishops in the Church of England touches on a seam of such straightforward suspicion of the female and the feminine that is worthy of some of the religious leaders of the sixteenth century. Nevertheless the resistance is of considerable interest since it manifests a deep vein of the continuing strength of "natural" explanations of sexual difference.

The human experience which is inevitably associated with "natural" explanations of sexual difference is that of motherhood. Parenthood and fatherhood have little that can compete with the iconic status of motherhood is Western societies; the condition which killed Mary Wollstonecraft is also the situation in which women and femininity are most commonly celebrated. Technology and changes in social mores have now dissolved many of the traditional expectations of motherhood (not least the social protection and physical engagement of a male partner), but the impact on women of bearing children remains one of the great divides in the social world. Feminists have long campaigned for improvements in those social arrangements which most immediately have an impact on the condition of motherhood (more day care, better and more woman-friendly medical practices), and many of those demands have been achieved. Yet just as those demands are achieved so other questions arise, the issues, for example, of same-sex parenting and the responsibilities which women, rather than men, are supposed to have towards children. In all these debates, feminists have been actively involved in both critiques of the medical practices around reproduction (for example, the work of Ann Oakley and Sarah Franklin) and the various institutional practices (such as education) which seem to be most actively engaged in reproducing gender differences (Franklin 2007; Oakley 1981).

CONCLUSION

At the beginning of the twenty-first century it is therefore possible to define a considerable literature by feminists about the social condition of women throughout the world and to note the impact that some of this work has had on the actual practices of the social world. That last comment, however, has to be interpreted in two ways: first, in the sense that campaigns by feminists around certain issues have led to changes in the law or other institutional contexts, but second, that feminism has itself provoked, as is sometimes argued, a reordering of gendered behavior which has been socially disturbing, if not actually disruptive. This backlash against feminism has been associated with campaigns to reverse Western legal changes about, for example, access to abortion or active discrimination in favor of women in the workplace. So far there are few signs of coordinated campaigns to reverse the changes inspired by feminism, but we must note the statements by women writers of fiction (for example Doris Lessing and Fay Weldon) who have criticized significant aspects of feminist campaigns.

It is apparent that what has been achieved in the West is a considerable equalization in at least the civil status of women and men. What remains to be seen is the extent to which this equalization (in both debate and practice) actually challenges many of the assumptions of "classical" social theory. If we take the work of Marx, Weber, and Durkheim and examine it in the light of feminist theory we see, in large part, an absence of the discussion of gender per se, even if, as noted above, Marx (with Engels) did address the question of the relation of the sexual division of labor to other social divisions. But Weber and Durkheim (and later twentieth-century sociologists such as Parsons) attributed relatively little to gender divisions in terms of the overall structural organization of society. We can point out that Durkheim attributed the lower suicide rate of women to their greater engagement with others (an idea which, albeit often unattributed, supported a tradition within feminism which asserts the greater sense of emotional attachment to others on the part of women, rather than men) but discussion of gender as such is either absent or read in terms of "natural" binaries of male and female.

We can, therefore, read the classic tradition in sociology in the same way as others have read classic theoretical traditions in disciplines such as philosophy or political science: that these disciplines are therefore fatally flawed. However, whilst much of post-Enlightenment intellectual speculation accepts as given the "nature" of male and female (and it is not until well into the late twentieth century that there is any material basis or theoretical basis for a radical challenge to this view), what the classic tradition in sociology has to say about the social world stands, in many ways, the test of time and cannot be dismissed in terms of the "zombie concepts" which Beck has defined (Beck 2004). If we take just a view of the ideas first outlined in the nineteenth and early twentieth centuries by Marx, Weber, and Durkheim we can note that capitalism still flourishes and indeed has managed to acquire (after the fall of the Soviet Union) an added legitimacy as the "natural" form of human society; the "iron cage" suggested by Weber shows little sign of rotting away, and the question of the loss of social solidarity remains a potent source of social discussion. Studies of the United States and Britain suggest – as Marx predicted – that the gap between the rich and the poor would widen, and even if the West seems to be perplexed by what Offer has described as the problems of affluence, the nature of this affluence (largely a greater array of relatively low-cost consumer goods) does little to disturb long-term structural distinctions, most particularly in class (Offer 2005).

For all this, feminist theory has opened up new ways of studying the social world, not least in that context of the intersection of the social and the personal. Sociology has always encouraged us to recognize the social in ourselves (the driven creatures of the Protestant ethic or the authoritarian keepers of the institutional world), but the dimension which has been added is on that was once regarded as the preserve of psychology, that of intimate or personal relations. In this sense feminist theory could claim to have helped to increase vastly the scope of sociology and indeed the social. Anthony Giddens has suggested, in *The Transformation of Intimacy*, that feminism has contributed to the making of more "democratic" personal relations, and on this point there is some evidence that this has indeed been the case, although whether or not this new democracy is the result of ideological shifts rather than material ones has yet to be put to the test (Giddens 1992). The second part to his argument – that more democratic personal relations will underpin and inspire more democratic politics – has yet to be demonstrated; certain evidence (not least the disengagement of many Western citizens from the political system) suggests the contrary. Be that as it may, just as women came, in the twentieth century, to take a greater part in the world outside the household, so feminist theory has both charted and developed this shift and in doing so played its own part in the extension of the very idea of the "social."

Bibliography

Beck, U. (2004) "The Cosmopolitan Turn," in N. Gane (ed.), *The Future of Social Theory*. London: Continuum.

Bordo, S. (1993) *Unbearable Weight*. Berkeley: University of California Press.

Bowlby, J. (1973) *Separation*. London: Hogarth Press.

Butler, J. (1990) *Gender Trouble*. London: Routledge.

Carby, H. (1984) "White Women Listen," in Centre for Contemporary Cultural Studies, *The Empire Strikes Back: Race and Racism in Seventies Britain*. London: Hutchinson.

Castle, T. (1993) *The Apparitional Lesbian*. New York: Columbia University Press.

Collins, P. H. (1989 "Black Feminist Thought." *Signs* 14(4): 745–73.

Crompton, R. (1990) *Gendered Jobs and Social Change*. London: Unwin Hyman.

Crompton, R. (2006) *Employment and the Family*. Cambridge: Cambridge University Press.

Davis, K. (1997a) *Reshaping the Female Body*. London: Routledge.

Davis, K. (1997b) *Feminist Perspectives on the Body*. London: Sage.

De Beauvoir, S. (1966) *The Second Sex*. New York: Bantam.

Figes, E. (1970) *Patriarchal Attitudes*. London: Faber & Faber.

Firestone, S. (1970) *The Dialectic of Sex*. London: The Women's Press.

Franklin, S. (2007) *Dolly Mixtures: The Remaking of Genealogy*. Durham, NC: Duke University Press.

Fraser, N. (1998) "Heterosexist Capitalism?" *New Left Review* March/April: 140–9.

Friedan, B. (1963) *The Feminine Mystique*. London: Penguin.

Giddens, A. (1992) *The Transformation of Intimacy*. Cambridge: Polity.

Gilligan, C. (1982) *In a Different Voice*. Cambridge, MA: Harvard University Press.

Gilroy, P. (1996) *The Black Atlantic: Modernity and Double Consciousness*. London: Verso.

Greer, G. (1971) *The Female Eunuch*. London: Mackibbon & Kee.

Hochschild, A., with Ehrenreich, B. (eds.) (2002) *Global Woman: Nannies, Maids and Sex Workers*. New York: Metropolitan Books.

Knott, S., and Taylor, B. (2005) *Women, Gender and Enlightenment*. London: Palgrave.

Lorde, A. (1984) "The Master's Tools," in *Sister Outsider*. Trumansburg: Crossing Press.

Marks, E., and Courtivron, I. (eds.) (1981) *The New French Feminisms*. Brighton: Harvester.

Marx, K., and Engels, F. (1984). *Origin of the Family, Private Property and the State*. London: Penguin.

Millett, K. (1977) *Sexual Politics*. London: Virago.

Moore, H. (1994) *A Passion for Difference*. Cambridge: Polity.

Nussbaum, M. (1999) "The Professor of Parody." *New Republic* February.

Oakley, A. (1981) *From Here to Maternity*. Harmondsworth: Penguin.

Offer, A. (2005) *The Challenge of Affluence*. Oxford: Oxford University Press.

Pateman, C. (1988) *The Sexual Contract*. Cambridge, Polity.

Rich, A. (1980, "Compulsory Heterosexuality." *Signs* 5(4): 631–60.

Rowbotham, S. (1973) *Hidden from History*. London: Pluto.

Said, E. (1994) *Culture and Imperialism*. London: Vintage.

Sayers, J. (1982) *Biological Politics*. London: Tavistock.

Schiebinger, L. (1989) *The Mind Has No Sex*. Cambridge, MA: Harvard University Press.

Skeggs, B. (1997) *Formations of Class and Gender*. London: Sage.

Soper, K. (2005) "Feminism and Enlightenment Legacies," in S. Knott and B. Taylor (eds.), *Women, Gender and Enlightenment*. London: Palgrave.

Spivak, G. (1999) *A Critique of Post-Colonial Reason*. Cambridge, MA: Harvard University Press.

Tomalin, C. (1974) *The Life and Death of Mary Wollstonecraft*. London: Harcourt Brace.

Walby, S. (1990) *Theorising Patriarchy*. Oxford: Blackwell.

Wollstonecraft, M. (1970) *A Vindication of the Rights of Woman*. London: Dent.

13

Postmodern Social Theory

Jan Pakulski

Consideration of postmodern social theory (PST) brings us into a highly contested territory. Both the notion of social theory – a coherent body of knowledge that highlights the key aspects of "the social," conceptualizes its key dimensions, and organizes causalities in an explanatory fashion – and the adjective "postmodern" are subject to intense debates and critical scrutiny (e.g. Delanty 1999; Ritzer 1997; Turner 2000, 2007). The position adopted here is that the adjective "postmodern" has a substance and distinctive – a but also multiple – meanings, and therefore requires elucidation, and that social theory is possible and desirable in its traditional role as a guide to social change. Below I overview those multiple meanings of the terms "postmodern," "postmodernity," and "postmodernization," cast a glance on the key early exponents of postmodern social theory (PST), and reflect on the complex origins of postmodern theorizing as a prolegomena to a more extensive presentation of one version of PST: a sociological argument on "postmoderniza-tion" as intensification and extension of modern trends. On the way, I note some disagreements with the more radical "postmodern" formulations, especially of an epistemological nature.

Social theory in its classical sociological form is not only possible but, in fact, urgently needed to assist in "making sense" of rapidly changing social configura-tions. This is because these configurations – the ways in which individuals "band together" and act – have been changing particularly fast and wide thus generating widespread theoretical confusions and public anxieties. The confusions concern mainly the adequacy of classical theoretical heritage, the conceptualizations and explanations of social change inherited mainly from the canonical texts of nine-teenth- and early twentieth-century thinkers. The anxieties reflect uncertainties that social change inevitably amplifies, as well as maladies that accompany alterations in familiar institutions and patterns of everyday life. Good theoretical accounts, those that combine comprehensiveness with empirical fit, minimize both the confu-sions and the anxieties. They also respond to public expectations that social theory both enlightens and anticipates, that it domesticates the unknown, especially its most traumatic aspects, by naming, identifying causal connections, and charting the trends. This is why changes in patterns of social relations, especially those organized into institutions, have always constituted the main domain and the central referent of social theory.

While focusing on the social realm, the patterned social relations (configurations), social theory also encompasses the non-social factors: natural-ecological, biological, economic, etc., but only to the extent they affect the social realm. New developments in biology (especially genetics), environmental ecology, informatics, etc. make it necessary to consider these non-social factors in a more explicit manner (mainly as conditions of social action), but they do not warrant the change in what we consider the nature of "the social," and therefore do not alter the analytical borderlines of the social sciences, especially sociology. However, they do prompt a rapid differentiation within the sociological domain. This differentiation, apparent in all disciplinary domains, is, in fact, one aspect of social change that a good social theory is expected to account for in the first place.

PST has as its main object "postmodern" social change or "postmodernization," as well as the products of this change, postmodern social configurations. The latter are sometimes referred to as "postmodernity" or the "postmodern condition." As signaled by the quote marks, all these terms, while popular, need further elucidation. The prefix "post" indicates both the historical transcendence (passing of a threshold, transcending modernity) and the tentative nature of theoretical formulations, uncertainty as to the direction of change beyond the fact that we are no longer living in modern society. It implies a sociohistorical discontinuity, a redirection of change, an ending of a distinctive (modern) period with its specific social forms and cultural outlooks. This distinctive period of modernity is typically dated as starting in the south-western part of Europe around the fifteenth to sixteenth centuries, and culminating in the nineteenth to twentieth centuries. Some historians, like Arnold Toynbee (1954 [1934]) date the postmodern redirection in Europe as early as the 1870s; art historians typically locate the origins of "postmodern style" and sensitivities to the interwar decades of the twentieth century; social scientists see "postmodernization," a continuous social and cultural reconfiguration, as a much later development, typically following World War II and accelerating during the turbulent 1960s and 1970s. One symptom of discontinuity is the very popularity of the prefix "post" applied frequently (one is tempted to say indiscriminately) in social analyses and popular discourses; another is a pervasive sense of "disorganization" and "disorder"; still another is a consensus as to what "modernity" means. If Minerva's owl spreads its wings at dusk, if such a consensus can be achieved only retrospectively, it clearly indicates that we are leaving behind modern social and cultural forms.

The origins of the term, and its connotations, have strong connections with aesthetic criticism, especially in visual arts and architecture. These connections shaped the trajectory of the postmodern intellectual movement and the deployment of the terms in social analysis. They facilitated the initial spread of the terms in the domains of humanities, especially cultural/literary studies. Perry Anderson (1998) suggests that the postmodern intellectual movement originated in the historical, philosophical, and aesthetic domains but promptly expanded into the social sciences (especially sociology and social geography) more or less at the same time as it started to dominate cultural studies, especially at new universities that benefited from a rapid expansion of tertiary education. Its early supporters were thus outside the influence and control of traditional academic and disciplinary establishments – a factor that contributed to radicalism, diversity, and eclecticism. As Hobsbawm (1994: 517) observed, "By the 1990s there were 'postmodern' philosophers, social scientists, anthropologists, historians and other practitioners . . . Literary criticism, of course, adopted it with enthusiasm. In fact, 'postmodern' fashions, pioneered under various names ('deconstruction', 'post-structuralism', etc.) among the French-speaking intelligentsia, made their way into US departments of literature and thence into the rest of the humanities and social sciences."

THE POSTMODERN APPROACH

One of the distinctive features of the postmodern movement was a combination of epistemological radicalism, including the critical questioning of the "Enlightenment legacy," with substantive liberalism, programmatic openness to all themes, disciplinary domains, and traditions. The radical epistemological position – arguably the least clearly articulated by movement intellectuals – deserves some critical scrutiny, partly because it generated the most provocative (and most critically received) postmodern pronouncements.

According to such key postmodern intellectuals as Jean-François Lyotard, the intellectual response to accelerated social change warrants a radical revision in some key metatheoretical assumptions, including the meaning of "the social realm," as well as ideological underpinnings, such as the faith in social progress, emancipation, the effectiveness of formal organization, and the possibility of securing objective and reliable social knowledge. There is a danger that these assumptions, labeled by Lyotard (1984 [1979]) the "metanarratives" of modernity, will obscure the view of change. This is a central point made by the early advocates of postmodern approach, most of them philosophers. They have promoted not only new "postmodern theories" (in the plural, to stress the fragmentation of disciplinary domains) that capture the key features of "postmodern condition," but also a new style of theorizing, a "postmodern approach." Such an approach has been derived from the works of (mostly German) critical thinkers: Friedrich Nietzsche, Max Weber, Georg Simmel, and Martin Heidegger, and subsequently developed by predominantly French intellectuals, such as Michel Foucault, François Lyotard, and Jacques Derrida. At the heart of the new approach one can find a mixture of critical skepticism, irony, and ambivalence, as well as the tendency to focus on the discursive/narrative foundations of knowledge and language–power relations. Such a mixture, according to the movement intellectuals, opens the way for a more reliable and less ideologically distorted knowledge.

In line with this programmatic critical-skeptical intention, the early postmodern thinkers focused mainly on "deconstruction," the questioning of "old certainties," critical re-evaluation of discourses and the accompanying knowledge–power nexus.

They also advocated a "paradigmatic switch" that engenders ironic self-orientation by encompassing, as an object of critical reflection, the social scientific analysis itself. That helped, in turn, in revealing the blind spots and unexamined assumptions of modern theorizing – the latter no longer adequate in the postmodern condition. Such a form of critical reflection, aware of its own epistemological foundations, prospects, and limitations, was welcomed as promising a more socially adequate knowledge.

Initially, this promise was looking good. The insights of postmodern philosophers have been promptly developed in a sociological realm by such thinkers as Jean Baudrillard (1994, 1998, 2006), Zygmunt Bauman (1992, 1997, 2006), Ulrich Beck (1992, 2002, 2006) and his collaborators (Beck et al. 1994), Stephen Crook and his colleagues (1992; Pakulski and Waters 1996), Anthony Giddens (1987, 1991), Mike Featherstone (1995, 2007), Fredric Jameson (1992, 1998), Scott Lash (1990) and his collaborators (Lash and Urry 1987, 1994), David Harvey (1989, 2001, 2005), and Barry Smart (1993, 1998, 2000). What are the key features of postmodern *social* theory, as suggested by these key proponents, and what are the core postmodern social trends they identify?

Perhaps the best way of answering these questions is by starting with negative references, that is, what the postmodern social thinkers oppose and object to. This is in line with seeing "postmodernism" as an intellectual movement that is unified more by what it is against than what it is for. The key critical references in all movement intellectual products, including the postmodern social analyses, seem to be theoretical structuralism, especially Marxist structuralism, especially in its politicized versions that embrace scientism, economic determinism, a focus on class conflict, and anticipation of socialist revolution. Equally widespread are critical references to ("the mainstream") modernization theory, especially its liberal Parsonian form that anticipates the progressive value-shift towards universalism, secularism, achievement, affective neutrality, instrumentalism, and self-orientation. Both are charged with four faults: ideological bias towards apology (assuming progress, emancipation, etc.); misplaced abstraction that severs the link between social theory and everyday experience of/in society; simplification (under the guise of abstraction and universalism) that ignores diversity; and predictive pretension that results in false anticipations (and proliferation of unanticipated "anomalies"). In contrast to both, the advocates of postmodernization are critical of the social (dis) order, embrace diversity, acknowledge limited capacities to predict (but a possibility of accurate anticipation), and promote a type of critical reflection that engages popular feelings, anxieties, and concerns. They are also skeptical as to the possibility of effective "social engineering" through discovering universal law-like regularities, especially the primary determinants and movers of social forms, and applying them as policy guides. Moreover, the key feature of the postmodern approach is also shared skepticism about progress, especially the evolutionary liberal schemes predicting widening rationality, value-universalism, freedom, and affluence-generated happiness. Their assessments of postmodern condition tend to be skeptical and critical, but not in terms of identifying terminal "crises," but rather revealing certain social maladies as perennial and chronic. This skeptical criticism is well summarized in a series of dichotomies derived from Bauman's (1992) seminal work:

modern features	versus	postmodern features
determinism (natural laws)		contingency, chance, probability
universalism, similarity in time/space		particularism and localism
confidence, transparency, sense of reality		uncertainty, skepticism, ambiguity
sense of order, clarity, and certainty		sense of disorder, provisionality
institutional monism and universalism		institutional pluralism, diversity
sense of constraint, limitation		freedom of choice and stylization

It is not hard to identify in these dichotomies the "core" critical edge of post-modern social analysis. In many ways, it is similar to the critical edge of the previous anti-positivist intellectual movement that reoriented European social thought from 1890 to 1930 (Hughes 1974). Like their early twentieth-century predecessors (who included Dilthey, Weber, Simmel, and Pareto), the proponents of the "postmodern turn" question the underlying assumptions about the persistence of stable and deterministic social structures (versus actors), are skeptical about universal causalities (versus particular patterns, contingencies), and doubt the possibility of predictions (versus probabilities). Postmodern analysis seems to avoid this criticized form of systematic-cum-systemic theorizing, avoids generalizations and "blanket" predictions, and its proponents seldom aim at producing cumulative knowledge. Rather, in a Simmelian fashion, they offer loose reflections that capture both new social developments and the accompanying popular sensitivities and tastes. Also, in a Weberian fashion, they stress the importance of actors, complex contingencies, and probabilistic regularities. The dominant mood is critical: the postmodern thinkers are debunking, deconstructing, demystifying, questioning, and criticizing. It is backed by generalized skepticism: we are better off aware of uncertainties and contingencies than guided by dubious explanatory constructs combined with "meta-narratives" of progress and emancipation. Closely related to this critical orientation is a tendency for critically monitoring and reflecting upon (rather than systematically analyzing) social change, focusing on specific and particular (rather than general and typical) developments, producing "rich descriptions" (rather than formulating hypotheses), all combined with terminological innovations, often beyond obvious need. That attracts the accusations of atheoretical bias, descriptivism, esotericism, imprecision, and jargon-infestation (e.g. Sokal and Bricmont 1999).

POSTMODERN SOCIAL THEORY

It is important to note that PST emerged largely as a by-product of the postmodern approach, as a result of a critical and skeptical reflection on the state of social knowledge. And it emerged relatively late – the main texts were published in the 1980s and 1990s – thus carrying a strong imprint of the critical spirit engendered in the postmodern movement. This affected both its content, especially the strong philosophical references, and its form: typically critical essays, reflections, and observations.

Though the key critical referents of PST – modernity and modern conditions – have seldom been defined in a systematic way, there seems to be a consensus that they include the key features identified by the "classical" theorists: Marx, Tocqueville, Durkheim, Weber, and Simmel, elaborated later by such "modernization theorists" as Parsons and Inkeles. In these renditions, modernization implies progressive rationalization – especially through formal legalism and market transactions – that displaces traditional conduct; hierarchical organization adopted in all domains of life, especially state administration; democratization as reflected in equalization of statuses, relations, and lifestyles; the ubiquitous "division of labor" that transpires in occupational and scientific-disciplinary specialization; the separation between "high" and "low" culture, the latter subject to "massification"; and gradual individualization engendered in the expansion of liberal norms, laws, rights, and popular outlooks. The outcomes of these processes have been variously described as "modern Western," "modern capitalist," "class," "mass," "democratic," "organized," and "industrial" forms of society.

Postmodernization implies a move away from these modern social configurations. While some theorists suggest that postmodernization also implies a break with the very central "modern" values engendered in the Enlightenment movement (rationalism, secularism, liberalism), these suggestions remain largely rhetorical, and most postmodern theorists adhere to these values, at least in practice (as opposed to declarations). One can summarize the contrast between the modern and postmodern features in another series of dichotomies:

modern society (condition)	versus	postmodern society (condition)
focus on production and productive roles		focus on consumption
industrial production and organization		postindustrial production and organization
embedded institutions		disembedded (floating) institutions
class structures and allied lifestyles		complex hierarchies and niche lifestyles
stable employment and sequential careers		episodic employment and lateral moves
stable core identities (class, ethnic, etc.)		fluid, multiple, situational identifications
hierarchical national cultures (mass)		diverse multicultural and subcultural mosaic
"cleavage" and organized national politics		issue- and leader-oriented global politics
national focus and policymaking		global-local focus, opportunistic policies

Another way of characterizing postmodern social theory is by identifying some critical changes in focus and emphasis. Thus the advocates of postmodern social analysis suggest five substantive shifts in focus:

- from structural to cultural: more attention given to culture, especially popular culture, with its vicissitudes and uncertain value-bases. This attention typically combines with interest in consumption (especially mass symbolic) and identity (re)formation;

- from mass production to mass consumption and lifestyle, communication, and mass media: focus on mass consumption, especially of symbols/ information, on mass-mediated communication, and on popular (versus elite) culture;
- from interaction to discourse: a "linguistic/symbolic shift" reflected in more attention paid to representations, especially in popular media and discourses;
- from institutions to actors and networks: focus on flexible social networking based on temporary consensus rather than norms/rules and on the role of influential actors/agents of change. This is often combined with interest in changing identifications and the propagation of "model" images, especially in the domains of popular culture and politics;
- from typical to diverse and marginal: increased interest in non-typical (often specific and marginalized) social-cultural configurations, such as sexual, ethnic, religious, lifestyle, etc. minorities and their cultures.

As one may also expect, there is some disagreement among the theorists as to the scope of postmodernization, a degree of departure from modern social configurations. Some, like Bauman and Harvey, see contemporary societies, especially their cultures, as already "postmodern" (though Bauman has recently abandoned this term and opts for a more specific and continuity-implying label of "liquid modernity"). Others, like Baudrillard and Crook et al., refer more cautiously to ongoing processes of "postmodernization" understood as a directional trend, and are either skeptical or agnostic about the possibility of mature "postmodern" society. Still others, like Beck and Giddens, adhere to a view of epochal discontinuity, but distance themselves from the postmodern movement by adopting alternative labels of "second" or "late" modernity (analogous to "liquid" or "reflexive" modernity à la Bauman and Scott) and by embracing a new "globalization perspective." This signals a double split within the movement: between more radical "postmodernists," who share the perception of radical change (beyond the modern) and follow the postmodern approach, and the less radical postmodernists, who just explore social discontinuities and new "postmodern trends" without committing themselves to epistemological innovations. The second divide is between the faithful adherents committed to embracing the postmodern idiom, and the "defectors" who, while initially supporting the movement, now explore alternative theoretical frameworks (such as "globalization theory").

THE KEY FIGURES

Postmodern social thinkers stress discontinuities in social development and have less confidence than their predecessors in our capacity to identify the general regularities and causal complexes. For most of them, contingency rules OK. Thus in his *Postmodern Condition* (1984), Jean-François Lyotard reflects critically on the state of knowledge in contemporary society. His analysis contains not only a radical criticism of the epistemological foundations of scientific knowledge in general, but also more specific comments about sociological knowledge, the latter as a sociological account of commodified knowledge under the impact of information and communication technologies. Knowledge, according to Lyotard, consists of narratives, that is, a mixture of norms, stories, popular wisdoms, fables, and myths. The "postmodern condition" is characterized by increasing public realization that scientific knowledge is not different from other forms of popular knowledge: like all social knowledge, it is a type of discourse, a "metanarrative" or a grand story of a totalizing type. Claims of those who see scientific knowledge as uniquely objective, true, and universally valid are greeted with incredulity or skepticism. This incredulity extends to all "metanarratives," including Marxism (a story of human emancipation) and mainstream social theory (a story of progress, secularization, rationalization, etc.), and constitutes a distinctive mark of the postmodern approach (1993). The accuracy and legitimacy of metanarratives are questioned, and so is their claim to privileged epistemological status; instead, the postmodern critics like Lyotard claim, their true nature as "language games" opens the way for critical revaluation of their substance and social function.

Lyotard's countryman Jean Baudrillard (e.g. 1988, 1994, 1998, 2006) focuses attention on popular culture and the mass media. He sees postmodernity as a trend – a correlate of expanding mass media and mass consumption – and as the beginning of a new era brought by the proliferation of mediated communication, symbolic consumption, and the compression of time and space. This results in self-referentiality of signs, intensified consumption of signs (e.g. brands), and the emergence of social order based on symbolic consumption. Our everyday experience is now so pervaded by images and representations, most of them electronically mediated, that the old distinction between "reality" and "representation" is obsolete. "Representations" are now a (the?) major part of our experience of "reality." In fact, the difference between them blurs, as indicated by the often used inverted commas. Thus people respond to media images of the Iraq war, rather than the actual events, the latter either hidden from scrutiny and public gaze and/or formatted by journalistic/media practices. This opens the way for radical differences in perceptions and accounts, as proven by moon landing conspiracy theories. We no longer live in "reality," he claims, but in a highly mediated "hyper-reality," an important part of which is a "world of self-referential signs" (1988, 1994). Our response to the loss of reality is to engage in "panic productions" of what we try to convince ourselves is real, but can only be "hyper-real," simulated. Baudrillard traces the "phases of the image" (or loss of "reality") through four steps, from mere representation to hyper-real "simulation." This may explain why our contemporary culture is so absorbed by creative nostalgia (retro fashions and musical tastes, the "heritage-ization" of history, "traditional" family values) and pastiche (mock-federation domestic architecture, theme parks, skansen-type replicas). It might even shed some light on the proliferation of quasi-religious beliefs, such as scientology and creationism, and widespread environmental anxieties, the latter fed by reports of environmental risks and ecological disasters, as well as sci-fi fantasies and widely propagated urban mythologies (e.g. native wisdoms, spiritual paths, "law and order solutions"). Baudrillard also writes of the "disappearance" of the masses and classes through self-dissolution into mass-mediated simulations. Under the postmodern condition of progressive commodification and mediation, the social realm – the webs of patterned social relations – is a by-product of second-order simulacra, that is, interpretations of media-propagated images.

Baudrillard's (1994) emphasis on the representing ("simulating") power of the media has led him to highly controversial questioning the existence of the social realm. Society, or "the social," does not escape the fate of increasingly mediated and simulated reality: it becomes "invisible" and can only be "hyper-simulated." It therefore loses its capacity to explain. Subsequently (e.g. 2006) he adopted a more moderate view, that the new electronic and digitalized media just undermine the reality and autonomy of social relations ("the social"). His British counterparts, Mike Featherstone (1988, 1995, 2007) and Zygmunt Bauman (1992), locate the notion of "postmodern" more firmly in the realm of social relations, and give it a more clear historical locus. Both see contemporary society as evolving beyond modernity, and they define "postmodern" as an emergent global social configuration with its own distinctive organization, cultures, and popular mentalities. "[T]o speak about postmodernity," according to Featherstone (1988: 198), "is to suggest an epochal shift or break from modernity involving the emergence of a new social totality with its own distinctive organizing principles." These principles derive mainly from intensified consumption, especially of images and signs that accompany the gradual "decoupling" of highly commodified popular culture from the social realm. In a similar tone, Bauman (1992, 1997) charts the changing culture, social relations, and popular sensitivities. He stresses the discontinuity between modern concerns with regulation, supervision, and other forms of imposing order, and the new postmodern celebration of individual freedom, spontaneity, and choice, the latter reflected particularly in stylized consumption. More recently, Bauman (2003, 2005, 2006) has stressed the fluid and "disembedded" nature of social relations that proliferate together with postmodern culture – a configuration of "liquid modernity." Perhaps more importantly, he also provides a model of postmodern analysis in a form of a loose sociological reflection that pays attention to both new social formations and the accompanying mentalities, sensibilities, and popular concerns.

On the other side of the Atlantic, Richard Rorty (1989, 1993, 1998, 2007), a philosopher, David Harvey (1989, 2001, 2005), a social geographer, and Fredric Jameson (1992, 1998, 2007), a cultural critic, offer a version of postmodern social theory highly Marxist in its theoretical inspiration, in which the postmodern condition is closely identified with "late" or "consumer" capitalism. All three analyze postmodern trends as a continuation of modern developments: a more rapid and global circulation of capital, spacial reorganization of investment, intensification of consumption, gradual commodification of culture, collapse of styles and high/low cultural tastes, increasing populism of standards, and fragmentation of classes and political realignments as reflected in the proliferation of ephemeral movements. Postmodernism, according to Jameson, represents a new mode of representation, life experience, and aesthetic sensitivity, all of which reflect the latest stage of capitalist development. The key features of this stage (that evolved out of the market capitalism of the nineteenth century and the monopoly capitalism of the early twentieth century) is the global division of labor, intense consumption, especially of images, a proliferation of the mass media, and an increasing saturation of society with information technology. Above all, late capitalism integrates aesthetic production into general commodity production, thus intensifying mass consumption of ever more novel goods. Jameson identifies the features of postmodern cultural configuration, a new "mode of production" in late capitalism, as including: the blurring of distinctions between popular/commercial and high-brow/classic culture; the weakening of the historical dimension with the emphasis on current experience and the organization of space (most conspicuous in contemporary architecture); the spread of electronically reproduced images; a wide use of pastiche; and a decline in affectivity that reduces the need for emotional engagement in cultural consumption. In his quest for "cognitive mapping" of contemporary culture in relation to the late capitalist economy and society, Jameson links the postmodern configuration with the popular ethos, lifestyles, and mentalities of "the yuppies," the young segments of a professional-managerial class, and with a new wave of American economic, cultural, and military domination.

Across the Pacific in Australia, Stephen Crook and his colleagues (1992; Pakulski and Waters 1996) developed a less radical theoretical vision focusing on "postmodernization" – a continuous process of "reversals (hence the prefix 'post') through acceleration" of the core processes of modernization (hence the references to classical theory). This allows them to relate clearly the processes of postmodernization to modernization, and explain the former as a continuation of modern trends, rather than a radical sociohistorical breach. This also means that their theoretical formulation maintains a strong nexus with classical social theory. Thus the "reversal through acceleration" transforms commodification into hyper-commodification, social differentiation into hyper-differentiation, and rationalization into hyper-rationalization. Postmodernization involves not only acceleration-cum-rerouting of social change, but also the blurring of boundaries between social, cultural, and political domains. For Crook and his colleagues, this means that flows of social action are no longer contained in social institutions. In fact, many forms of action take the form of more fluid "social arrangements" that lack clear normative founding and the accompanying solidity and durability. It also means that postmodernization generates widespread uncertainty, "fear of the future," and poses (again) the problem of social order.

So, what are the connotations and denotations of postmodern social theory, and who are "postmodern social theorists"? As suggested above, PST can be defined as a sub-category of social theory. It encompasses those explanatory accounts of social reconfigurations that maintain a critical orientation and embrace the notion of discontinuity. Another, and much broader (and therefore often favored), way of circumscribing PST is by treating it as a body of social knowledge, that is, knowledge concerning social relations ("the social"), produced by key movement intellectuals. Considering the fact that postmodernism constitutes a very broad and amorphous intellectual movement – a reticulate network of intellectuals linked mainly by shared oppositions and dislikes, some common positive emphases (e.g. on discontinuity and social fluidity), terminological preferences, frequent cross-references, and shared debates – such a definition would be blurred.

This brings us to a difficult question of identity and composition: who is in and who is out of the movement. Like all intellectual movements (e.g. contemporary feminism, environmentalism, and neo-Marxism), the postmodern movement is rather amorphous. Moreover, the recent (what looks like) defections from the movement – or at least a reluctance to embrace the key identifying terms (such as "postmodern" or "postmodernity") by some prominent pioneers of the movement, such as Bauman, raises further problems of identification. Not only do the boundaries of the movement look more blurred, but also its identifications seem to be weaker and more transient. Today it is less clear than at the beginning of the new century who are the key movement intellectuals and how strong is their identification with, and commitment to, the postmodern movement. Thus at least four important figures, Zygmunt Bauman, Scott Lash, Ulrich Beck, and Anthony Giddens, have recently questioned their self-identification with the "postmodern theoretical camp." Bauman (1997: 17–20) sees postmodern theory as a preliminary statement superseded by ideas spun around "liquid modernization." Lash (1994), seems to be abandoning the commitment to "postmodern" and "reflexing modernization" for what he prefers to call "vitalism." Giddens (1991, 2000) opts for labeling the new social forms as "late modern," "radicalized modernity," and "high modernity" characterized by "post-traditional social order" in which individual identities are constantly reshaped as a part of an ongoing reflective accomplishment. To Giddens, the adjective "postmodern" describes the most extreme features of late modern society. Similarly, Beck (2006), an initial sympathizer (if not a supporter of the movement), today prefers to use the concept of "reflexive modernity" as a descriptor of choice for current social and cultural configurations. The latter places more emphasis on continuous individualization and re-creation of identities than on social discontinuities. This may indicate a decline of the movement. Such historical declines of intellectual movements are typically harbingered by weakening identifications, defection of supporters, weathering networks, shrinking intellectual production (especially publications), and declining popularity of the key concepts. It is too early to offer a verdict about the vitality of the postmodern movement.

THE SOCIAL FRAMEWORK

This brings us to the *social* origins and development of the movement (its *intellectual* origins have been traced admirably by Perry Anderson [1998]). The critical clues as to these origins are: shared references that allow for identification of the key pioneers and seminal texts, a strong concentration of postmodern social analyses (publications) in the late 1980s and 1990s that helps in mapping the developmental trajectory, and the shared "critical" orientation of postmodern analyses combined with a shared sense of discontinuity and fluidity (as reflected in the prefixes "post" or qualifying terms "late," "reflexive," "fluid," etc.) that betray the formative concerns and preoccupations.

There is no doubt that the postmodern movement is a response to accelerating social change, especially those aspects of change that affect "everyday life" in the most advanced Western societies: daily experiences, popular concerns and feelings, mass orientations, consumption, lifestyles, and popular culture – and through them the ways in which we relate to others. Over the last decades of the twentieth century the change seemed to be particularly rapid and pervasive, partly due to the impact of the new electronic media and the rapid spread of commodified popular culture, increasingly global in scope. These processes, and the accompanying sense of historical-biographical discontinuity-cum-uncertainty, was articulated well by the pioneers of the postmodern movement, especially in the wave of publications in the 1980s and 1990s at the peak of the popularity of the postmodern idiom.

While all advocates of the postmodern approach subscribe to the notion of discontinuity, a break with modernity, they seldom clearly mark the watershed. Most, however, would agree that the social developments in advanced societies in the mid-twentieth century, particularly after World War II, especially the proliferation of popular consumer culture and the global informational-media revolution (especially the spread of TV) that accompanies a global spread of ideas and market relations (e.g. Crook et al. 1992) . This consensus offers some pointers as to the social roots of the movement, especially its distinctive critical-skeptical orientation engendered in the attempts at a critical revision of the classical theoretical heritage. The classical social theories, one might argue (as well as their twentieth-century "updates"), especially in their dominant Marxist and "mainstream" (modernization) renditions, have lost their plausibility and relevance, and this loss became most apparent – especially to observers in advanced societies – in the last decades of the twentieth century. This was a gradual process. The classical heritage looked quite plausible in guiding our understanding and anticipation of social change (notwithstanding the differences in predictions among the "classics" themselves) until roughly the mid-twentieth century. Then, to use the language of Kuhn, the "anomalies" started to pile up in the form of increasingly "unexpected," "puzzling," and "chaotic" social developments. It is these cumulative anomalies – the developments that "do not fit" the anticipated developmental paths, do not sit well with the accompanying world-views and popular creeds, and therefore require ad hoc adjustments – that triggered the postmodern intellectual movement, especially its social-theoretical part. Since the strength and popularity of this movement seem to be proportionate to the scope of anomalies (and the sense of puzzlement they generated), it is useful to list these anomalous developments as the supporting argued link:

- The despotic evolution of Soviet Russia and the rise of fascism, especially German Nazism, followed by its spread throughout Europe, South America, and the Middle East was a surprising "anomaly" to both Marxists and modernization theorists. Both developments proved difficult to accommodate with the "class conflict," "modern trends" and progressive-emancipatory expectations. Stalinism evolved in a nationalistic and despotic direction. The fascist ascendancy also looked contradictory (irrational, socially "regressive," etc.). Perhaps most puzzling was the effective political and ideological uniformization of fascist and communist societies and the systematic violence embraced by both regimes, most evident in the horrors of Gulag and the Holocaust. They have badly shaken the evolutionary and universalistic assumptions of modern theory in all its versions.
- The post-World War II developments, especially the proliferation of the electronic media and rapidly diversifying popular culture, were less shocking; nonetheless they seemed at odds with the predictions of structural functionalists and Marxists alike. Again, the global spread of culture industries combined with a "postindustrial" shift from manufacturing to service production proved challenging to the key theoretical predictions. The proposed theoretical modifications (including the Frankfurt School analyses, industrial society, mass society, and "postindustrial" accounts) helped to defuse a sense of

theoretical inadequacy. It is characteristic, however, that some of these accounts (especially by Ralf Dahrendorf and Daniel Bell) resorted to the prefix "post" in order to signal the need for a radical reworking of the modern theoretical heritage.

• The turbulent last decades of the twentieth century proved particularly "anomalous" and therefore provoking. They witnessed not only the massive expansion of the electronic media – seen by McLuhan (2001 [1964]) as revolutionary in their impact on mental processes and popular perceptions – but also a rapid expansion of market relations (investment and trade) combined with a new international "division of labor" that brought with it Western "deindustrialization" and "flexible" forms of employment. They also witnessed "refolutions" (revolutions through peaceful reforms), elite-led "national autonomy" movements resulting in the dissolution of the Soviet bloc and the Soviet Union itself.

• The developments starting the new millennium have further reinforced the sense of puzzlement and anxiety by highlighting the fragility and vulnerability of the social order to disruptive influences. The spread of religious fundamentalism (Islamic, Christian, Jewish, Hindu) was a surprise – incompatible with modern trajectories. Their cross-national political mobilization was a shock to all observers, particularly those embracing Marxism or the "mainstream" modernization theory – both dominant in educational curricula and policy debates. The terrorist attacks by shadowy "non-state agents," the confused response of the American government, and the outbursts of ethno-racial xenophobia around the issues of migration and cultural rights have added to puzzlement and frustration. In a similar way, environmental anxieties entered the mainstream of social concerns in a largely unpredicted way. With the massive publicity given to climate change, this time attributed to routine human activities, the mass anxieties about future and the awareness of "risks" have intensified.

This list may be skewed towards unexpected and anomalous developments, and the accompanying failure of the social sciences to explain and anticipate. However, as noted by William Saroyan, we get very little wisdom from success. The anticipation of failure proved creative by provoking intellectual ferment among social thinkers, especially the World War II and post-war generations educated in the modern canon. The disparities between this canon, dominant in the educational curricula and policy debates, on the one hand, and the increasingly "anomalous" developments, on the other, have proved fertile grounds for critical revisions of the modern theoretical heritage.

As usual, the most radical critical revisions originated outside the established centers of learning (the Ivy League and Oxbridge universities), involved academics and public intellectuals who operated at the periphery of "normal" social science, latched on to formerly marginalized philosophical traditions (Nietzsche, Weber, Heidegger), and encouraged provocative formulations that travel fast-n-easy through the mass media networks. To the readers of Coser and Kuhn, this form of intellectual ferment-cum-innovation triggered on the peripheries, outside the "core" institutions, is hardly surprising.

The critical factor was undoubtedly the ease of communication. The audience for these critical reflections promptly expanded beyond the traditional academic-intellectual circles. Postmodern critics could address the mass educated audience in a similar way as postmodern artists and philosophers entered the arena of popular culture with their reflections and commentaries, typically in the form of critical essays. The electronic mediation of academic and popular cultures (increasingly merging into one), the proliferation of tertiary education, and the swelling ranks of the "chattering classes" all facilitated movement mobilization and growth. The focus on popular experiences, sensitivities, anxieties, and the highly accessible form of cultural commentary and intellectual reflection that the critics favored, added to the easy accommodation of postmodern analyses within the diversifying popular culture. Its essays, especially social commentaries accessible to non-experts, became an integral part of this culture.

Perhaps the most important fertilizer for postmodern critical revisions came from what was widely perceived as a failure of Marxism, especially in its critical-explanatory and social-emancipatory functions. The intellectual debris of post-Soviet Marxism provided ready-made models for postmodern reflection. Criticism of Soviet–Chinese socialism was one convenient starting point; another was a series of Frankfurt School "updates" that provided theoretical pointers to postmodern analyses of contemporary "culture industries." This accompanied, one should stress, a brief revival of structural Marxism, a key initial competitor to postmodern interpretations. However, this Marxist revival, which could stifle the postmodern movement, proved short-lived. Neither the initially fashionable structural analyses of Althusser and Poulantzas, nor the highly abstract "analytical Marxism," nor, finally, the "dependency/world system" accounts have dealt satisfactorily with the new developments, including the rise of corporate elites, the "death of class," the Soviet collapse, the messy postcommunist developments, the ascendancy of "Asian tigers" and the industrial growth of China. Moreover, the Marxist "updates" shared another weakness: they ignored the "everyday life" aspect, the experience of living in a heavily mediated and rapidly changing society. This gap between the abstract structural accounts and the "everyday" experience contributed to the demise of structural Marxism – and the initial popularity of its postmodern competitor. The less abstract, less doctrinal, more modest and more sociologically informed post-modern accounts, especially by Harvey and Jameson, have helped to fill a gap left by withering Marxism in the sense of providing more relevant and convincing theoretical "updates," critical of contemporary consumer capitalism but free from the dubious eschatologies of class exploitation, social polarization, revolution, and the ultimate socialist emancipation.

To some extent, these accounts are updates on updates – a reinterpretation of many themes initiated by Max Weber, and the critical theorists of the Frankfurt School (especially Theodor Adorno and Walter Benjamin). Like their early twenti-eth-century predecessors, the postmodern thinkers prefer to debunk illusions rather than prophesy crises, highlight new developments and complex contingencies rather than formulate general regularities. Postmodern theorizing, in other words, has provided a fresh idiom for social criticism previously monopolized by Marxism. However, as argued below, it has also encountered a formidable competitor in the form of growing "globalization theory." The latter is partly competitive and partly complementary, focusing on the spacial aspects of social change, and on sociopolitical actors and arenas.

CRITICISMS

Critics of PST, recently more numerous than supporters of the movement, point to some problems. First, PST tends to contain too much radical critical epistemology and not enough positive sociology, especially macrosociology. Postmodern analyses tend to be both too abstract in embracing high-level generalizations and too specific in focusing on particular, often marginal, social and cultural developments. If PST is to perform its sensitizing-explanatory role by rendering meaningful and intelligible past and current social-historical developments, critics point out, it should have a more robust substantive core, a more specific historical focus, and a more solid empirical base. Second, PST is criticized for being too fragmented, unsystematic in its focus. While pursuing a noble aim of bringing social theorizing closer to "everyday life," and while focusing on everyday experiences and identifying popular anxieties, the postmodern reflection, critics charge, fails to discriminate between the central and marginal, universal and particular, typical and specific. It tends to highlight cultural currents, popular moods and sensibilities, while ignoring their "social substratum." Therefore it risks marginalization, especially when facing the competitor in the form of burgeoning "globalization theory." Third, PST focuses on cultural trends and popular mentalities but tends to ignore the sociopolitical trends and key "crucial episodes," such as the peaceful collapse of Soviet communism, the postcommunist liberalization of the social and economic order, the diffusion of democratic governments, the spread of environmental concerns, etc. Fourth, PST is criticized for its relentless analytic innovation. While the emphasis on discontinuities and the tendency to veer into the domains of philosophy, social geography, or cultural anthropology are understandable (they reflect the origins of the movement and its key critical concerns), the tendency to multiply concepts and coin new terms for almost any observed regularity is an obvious weakness. It exposes PST to accusations of analytical promiscuity, imprecision, and jargon-peddling.

This necessarily potted summary of criticisms may give a biased impression. The critics are often excessively harsh: they seldom do justice to the historical innovativeness of Foucault's analyses, the provocative brilliance of Baudrillard's commentaries, the synthetic sophistication of Bauman's essays, the sociological anchoring of Ritzer's interpretations, and the comprehensiveness of Harvey's and Jameson's studies. The "mainstream" version of PST produced by these thinkers deserves more recognition than granted by the critics. While this "mainstream" postmodern account allies itself with the new postmodern intellectual movement, it also maintains strong links with classical sociological theory. This is most apparent in the postmodern analyses of modernization and its maladies, to which we now turn. The major advantage of postmodern social theory over its closest competitors, especially globalization theory, rests in its capacity to articulate and account for the new social maladies and the accompanying popular concerns, especially about social (dis)order. This point, essential in shaping the future of PST, deserves special attention.

MODERNIZATION AND ITS DISCONTENTS

As noted by Fukuyama (1999), social order is back on the agenda of social analysis. This is due to disruptions in the "international" and internal "societal" order. The former takes the form of the post-Cold War reshuffles and repositioning, and, perhaps more importantly, the failure of states and international organizations to stabilize peaceful relations. The latter seems to be weakening in advanced societies, as reflected in the erosion of established models of (bureaucratic) organization, (nuclear) family, (class) politics, and (national) identity, economy, and culture. These disruptions are non-revolutionary, and they take a form of cumulative erosion, rather than "crises." Taken together, they mark the end of the certainties that permeated the "golden age" of post-war liberal-democratic capitalism. These certainties reflected the established modalities of life, and they encompassed the widespread belief in the effectiveness of modern strategies of building social order through the strengthening of the state – both its external sovereignty and its internal administrative capacities – through bureaucratic organization based on the principle of hierarchical authority and rule-compliance; through gradual extension of legal regulation, including the governmental control of (national) economies, cultures, and societies; through legally safeguarded individual rights in civil, political welfare, and cultural domains; through organized national, ethno-religious-regional, and class identities and the accompanying ("social cleavage") party politics; through hierarchical (high-brow-lowbrow, vanguard-popular) national cultures; through stable occupational divisions reflected in careers, status expectations, as well as established lifestyles and outlooks; and finally through systematic socialization in nuclear families based on hierarchical and gender-specific norms.

These modalities, and the accompanying certainties, started to crumble in advanced societies in the post-World War II decades. Since these developments have been widely recognized and commented upon, a cursory listing will suffice: The weakening of "corporate deals" and the collapse of the Cold War superpower arrangements, combined with the proliferation of supranational blocs (EU, NAFTA, ASEAN) and non-state actors, from TNCs and NGOs through drug cartels and terrorist networks to global movements, and the assertions of formerly peripheral states and regions (China, Asian Tigers, India), have undermined the global sense of order and predictability. The position and status of the USA as a "sole super-power" and the world safeguard of the liberal order has been undermined, especially in the wake of Chinese ascendancy, the "war on terror" and the Iraq debacle. Similarly, the organizing capacities of nation-states and their core institutions have weakened, with large corporations operating internationally, and national elites embracing non-interventionist, deregulatory, low-tax strategies of growth. These deregulatory strategies have been almost universally embraced: by neoliberals, neo-conservatives, and in Great Britain by "New Labour." Internally, class identities, cultures, and politics have been decomposing, together with their institutional articulations (unions, class parties), thus undermining corporatist "deals," and the role of the state as a social "broker-cum-manager" of social order. A rapid shift from industrial organization (factory system, autonomous industrial enterprise, national economy) to "postindustrial" service provision by large but often amorphous corporate networks that operate internationally, in an increasingly deregulated environment, has been shaking the foundations of occupational divisions, identities, and lifestyles. The "de-industrialization" of advanced societies – a shift of manufacturing and simple services to the areas of cheap labor – has accompanied "flexible" reorganization that undermines the stability of employment, predictable careers, and the accompanying occupational status hierarchies. This is exacerbated by the declining willingness of governments to intervene (especially through restrictive regulation and redistribution) into labor market processes and corporate governance. The latter has undergone a significant change, with managerial decisions increasingly shifting into the hands of central financial controllers, resulting in increased employment mobility, uncertainty and, in many low- and medium-skill areas, deteriorating working conditions. While employment remains high, fueled by rapidly rising credit-consumption, especially of information and communication technologies and entertainment, it tends to favor the young, skilled, and flexible, those ready to and capable of adjusting to changing expectations. Increasingly, career trajectories are replaced by lateral "shifts" and episodic "flexible" contract employment. The discontent among the lower ranks (rather than classes), many of them "flexibly" deployed, is defused by widening access to credit and consumption opportunities, absorbed into deviant subcultures (often associated with drug use), and suppressed by widening surveillance-cum-control, including privatized security and prison industries (the latter mainly in the USA). When it surfaces, it is through outbursts of violence and low-level urban deviance associated with social marginalization. As noted by Garland (2001: 194), the social reactions to deviance and crime have changed more than the deviance and crime themselves, in line with increasing security consciousness. "This desire of security, orderliness, and control, for the management of risk and the taming of chance is, to be sure, an underlying theme in any culture. But in Britain and America in recent decades that theme has become a more dominant one."

The change affects social hierarchies by increasing their fragmentation and complexity. The winners are few and dispersed, their legitimacy based on educational credentials (cultural capital) and economic "achievement," the latter often associated with predatory business and financial ventures. They are socially amorphous – do not cluster into conscious and culturally cohesive collectivities of classes, status groups, or establishments. Moreover, they lack the sense of confidence and status trappings of the old ruling classes – a fact that weakens their social legitimacy and identity. Instead of social groupings, they form fickle top "layers" of corporate executives, property owners, and finance and investment experts, located predominantly in the vicinity of metropolitan corporate headquarters, with increasingly diverse, often bohemian, lifestyles. Complex, multidimensional, and local social "maps," especially those recognizing the role of cultural and social capitals, capture the character of complex social hierarchies better than ladder-like socio-economic or status-occupational gradations (e.g. Bourdieu 1984; Brooks 2000; Pakulski 2004).

The socially stabilizing role of the family has been weakened by progressive individualization. This is reflected in the rapidly increasing divorce rates, declining birth rates, and a rapid shift from a complementary to a partnership model. While divorce lowers the burden associated with failed relations, it also undermines the stable environment for the socialization of children. Families have fewer children, which is a result of liberation and social autonomization of women, and a reflection of abandonment of pro-natal state policies. Similarly, the partnership model, while promoted by the highly educated, the liberally minded, and feminists, is less a matter of preference and choice, and more a necessity: fewer and fewer families can maintain their lifestyles on single income. Two-income families have to reshape and renegotiate their tasks and duties – or face serious strain in their relations.

The common trend in governance is away from "social regulation" and towards the marketization and privatization of services, mixing nationalized and private delivery, and dismantling centralistic administration, typically accused of rigidity, inefficiency, and high cost. The aspiration is for "effective governance" in which cost-efficiency combines with flexibility, thus allowing for periodic tax cuts and adjustments to diversifying demand ("flexible services"). This is increasingly difficult because national governments have a reduced capacity to shape "their" economies, as financial markets expand internationally and transnational corporations move production around the world. The collapse of Soviet communism and the liberalization of eastern Europe, the rapid entry of China into the world market, the expansion and liberalization of the European Union, and the widening of free trade agreements marked the end to state-regulated national economies and to the socialist experiment with central economic planning-cum-management. One intended effect has been de-étatization marked by states shedding their social responsibilities. Since this is often portrayed as a "global trend," one unintended consequence has been a spread of anti-globalist sentiment, often fusing nationalism with a sense of insecurity. This is most clearly articulated in attitudes towards mass migrations, especially a "forced" circulation of people that occurs mainly from the peripheries to the core (refugees, illegal migrants, and "undocumented" job-seekers) (e.g. Casteles 2003). The migrations are as large (estimated by the UN Population Division in 2005 at 185–192 million, up from about 175 million in 2000 and circa 120 million in the 1990s) as they are traumatic – both for migrants and the "receiving" populations. For the former, migration is typically an escape from deprivation and persecution into "3D" (dangerous, difficult, and dirty) work; for the latter it is often seen as an invasion of foreigners who "steal jobs" from the locals, dilute national cultures, and spread criminality (e.g. Garland 2001; *World Migration 2005*).

The end of the "golden age" presented a major challenge for the "Fordist" industrial enterprises and bureaucratic organization, especially in the USA and Europe, with intense product diversification, constant innovation, intensification of production technologies, and internationalization of production, all requiring high employment flexibility, complex management, and constant monitoring of demand. The more radical responses have been termed "post-Fordist." They are consistent with the trends noted above, especially with the "flexible" labor organization. "Flexible" technologies (computers in design/production, international "component manufacturing") coincide with "flexible" organization (financial and strategic management, JIT, quality, teamwork, task-monitoring) and proliferating "flexible labor," highly mobile, often sub-contracted or employed on a part-time basis. The onset of "post-Fordism," and especially the new "enterprise system" in service provision, have coincided with a rapid rise in productivity (estimated by Sennett [2006] at exceeding wages by over 300 percent in 1995–2006). The digital revolution has been affecting not only "flexible" manufacturing ("Toyotism"), retail ("WalMartization"), and simple services ("McDonaldization"), but also white-collar tasks in complex service provision. (Head 2005). The super-rational "enter-prise system" adopted in large retail/distribution, health services, telecommunication, IT, and educational firms, combines task standardization with electronic tagging that allow for monitoring and rationalization of complex processes. The growing number of "managed care organizations" (such as AmTech and TeleTech in the USA) adopt the elements of this system, thus increasing their efficiency and effective-ness. While in many cases this increases top-down supervision, lowers staff com-mitment, and marginalizes older workers, the typical victims of rationalization and downsizing (e.g. Head 2005), in leading high-tech (IT, biotech) firms, the new system opens up the bottom-up channels of communication and initiative that empower the staff and feeds into flexible innovation (e.g. Brown and Deguid 2006).

By the mid-twentieth century the focus of mass culture had shifted from mechani-cal print to new electronic media: radio, film, gramophone records, and (after World War II) television. The powers of "extension" of these media were much greater and more immediate than those of print. The Frankfurt School thinkers, especially Walter Benjamin, welcomed new technologies (especially film) in the 1930s as a challenge to the elitist "aura" of high culture and a path to democratization. Some 30 years later, Marshall McLuhan was preaching the revolution that would come in the wake of television overcoming what he saw as alienating, hierarchical, and individualizing aspects of print-based mass cultures. The electronic "cool" media required active participation of the viewer in the construction of meaning, they are kaleidoscopic rather than linear, and encourage the sense of involvement that under-lies the integrative "global village" effect. It is the form, the medium itself, rather than the content, that generates this effect – a clear contrast to Baudrillard's subse-quent conclusions about the social impact of mass consumption of signs.

There has also been a broad consensus among the observers of contemporary culture. Modern culture is not only highly commodified (accessed mainly as con-sumer product), but also intensely (doubly) rationalized, popularized, diversified and globalized. The different value-spheres require the work of distinctive cultural "experts," while the production and distribution of cultural goods is subject to technical rationalization (as in the technologies of video-making and music record-ing). The commodification of culture facilitates its mass expansion as popular con-sumer culture, heavily dominated by American production. While the commodification and mass expansion of culture has often been portrayed as degradation, it also marks – as noted earlier – a significant democratization of cultural consumption, weakening of cultural exclusions, and erosion of hierarchy. Cultural consumption also diversifies into "vertical" sub-cultural segments and lifestyle-related niches – increasingly cross-cutting and weakening the old national and ethno-regional divi-sions. Popular forms, proliferating with the mass media, appeal across class and national boundaries thus resulting in proliferation of age-generational, regional, and lifestyle segments .This differs from the anticipations of Frankfurt School thinkers predicting the "massification" and "standardization" of mass (popular) culture. In contrast, the followers of French sociologist Pierre Bourdieu see culture and knowl-edge (especially cultural competency legitimized through high education) as a form of capital. Here, the question of a "mass" culture is set aside in favor of a return to the culture-class/elite nexus (e.g. 1984). The "distinction" of elite culture, according to Bourdieu, is linked to formal features that mirror social distinction. Elite tastes (like chamber music) are formalized and abstract, reflecting the elite claim to "abstraction" from the demands of work and ordinary life. The (anti-)taste of lower classes and strata, by contrast, is for the useful and immediately gratifying in a reduction of "art" to "life." Culture is thus part of the changing system of class-ification: tastes and preferences locate one in a complex field that is social as well as cultural. Within this field, the capacity to produce (and be seen to produce) pure aesthetic judgments is a form of capital that can be invested and deployed to secure favorable social positions.

Perhaps it is the interface of the liberal trends in the economy and high consumption with popular culture that generates most "disorganization" and provokes uncertainty and anxiety. Both are propelled by new information and communication technologies, especially computerization, that revolutionize the delivery of images and sound – increasingly cheaply, individually, and on demand (podcasting, the internet). The problem is that it produces both a long mass-consumption-driven economic boom, accompanied by widening consumer choices and almost full employment, as well as social dislocations and pathologies. On the positive side, it is associated with affluence, increasing consumption, and economic growth in the core; with widening availability of goods and services, including widening access to information; with increasing cosmopolitanism and postmaterial orientations; and with declining social distances (gender, ethno-racial), prejudices, and discrimination. On the negative side, intensifying popular cultural consumption undermines intellectual elites, widens the opportunities for manipulation, "hollows the middle" (especially in the US and UK), facilitates the erosion of citizenship rights (especially following security scares), and spreads a "risk society" syndrome focused mainly on environmental concerns. Many of these trends look familiar to the observers of the first (1790–1840) and second (1890–1920) "industrial revolutions" – both of which were associated with rapid cultural reconfigurations. However, the current trends look distinctive, mainly because they are so strongly driven by (political, corporate, and cultural/media) elites, so firmly anchored in the domain of popular culture, mass consumption, and easy communication, all in the contest of weakening associations and identities. They generate widespread concerns mainly because of the changing role of the state – its gradual withdrawal from the role of the key social organizer of national culture, underwriter of social pacts, and guarantor of (widening) citizenship rights, including social/welfare rights. State interventions, while powerful, are increasingly restricted to enforcement of law and order (especially national security) and strengthening the "business infrastructure." Citizens are increasingly seen and treated as consumers. Managing society and culture is seen as incompatible with freedom and consumer choice. Therefore the fashionable developmental strategies pursued by national elites focus on the reduction and minimization of state intervention in social life.

While the followers of "globalization theory," the key competitor to PST, see these trends as a part of general "weakening of national boundaries," the "hyper-extension" interpretation depicts globalization as a side effect of intense differentiation combined with hyper- commodification and rationalization, the former associated with an international division of labor, the latter transpiring with the widening scope of market relations. Both are responsible for the specific "market-liberal" nature of globalization that diminishes some regulatory powers of nation-states. It affects social configurations as both a cultural current – a popular outlook incorporated into all the products of popular culture – as well as influential and popular elite outlooks that affect politics and policy. The ruling elites, as well as big sections of compliant publics, are increasingly skeptical of social intervention-ism, partly in response to the intellectual climate generated by the media and popular culture, and partly in response to elite persuasion that point to dysfunctions of interventionist policies ("governability crisis," "fiscal crisis," "welfare depen-dency crisis," "legitimation crisis") and publicize the collapse of socialism as the evidence of failed state interventionism.

Changes in work, politics, and popular culture are accompanied by a fracturing and weakening of identities, especially those associated with "master collectivities" and established roles. Modern society used to provide a set of shields against change-generated uncertainties and anxieties in the form of these strong "master" identities that underlay the social anchoring in nations, classes, local communities, and fami-lies, the latter accompanied by gender-specific norms. This anchoring, and the accompanying identities, as noted by Kellner (1995), Warde (1996), and Bradley (1996), have been weakening and fracturing due to the combined effects of differ-entiation, consumption, and proliferating mass-mediation. For Crook at al. (1992) "master identities" are victims of social differentiation, internal fracturing, and the accompanying cultural decomposition. Kellner (1995, 2003) attributes this mainly to media spectacles. Warde (1996, 1997) and Bauman (1997) see the process as a correlate of consumption practices. It is proliferating consumer roles – rather than productive roles – that are the main site for the accomplishment of the "lifestyle" choices, the latter increasingly reflected in identifications. The nexus between con-sumption and identity makes each a matter of anxiety. Consumption- and lifestyle-generated identifications (one is hesitant to call them identities, because of their fleeting and situational nature) are superficial, requiring constant reinforcement. Consumption is hazardous because each choice has consequences for identity: a wrong choice marks the carefully presented surface of self. Warde argues that there are mechanisms in place to prevent consumption from causing identity anxieties; they range from advertising and consumer guides to delegation, convention, and complacency.

The process of decomposition of old "master identities" – especially class, gender, and ethno-national – has been exacerbated by communications technologies McLu-han's radical claims that electronic media not only make available previously inac-cessible cultural objects but change the way in which we experience the world seems to be widely accepted. Cultures shaped by television (and now the internet) process "reality" in different ways to print cultures. They generate consumption/lifestyle identifications that are more fleeting and situationally evoked than the old "master identities." The waning of class identities (together with class organizations, cul-tures, politics) represents a transformation of social into cultural relations. It is also the reflection of unwillingness to mobilize class idiom by political elites. Class identi-ties weaken together with class organizations and the whole social constellation of "class politics" (e.g. Pakulski and Waters 1996).

The process of fracturing and decomposition is aided by trends in popular culture. Commodified popular cultures seldom promote just "products"; typically they promote (life)styles, totalizing images in which looks, outlooks, and actions form recognizable models that can be chosen and easily emulated, typically through stylized consumption. They invariably contain the elements of packaged identification that aims at adding stability to the promoted consumption. If consumption is salient to identity, so too must be cultural globalization: wherever we live in the advanced world, we watch American TV programs on Chinese or Korean sets, drive Japanese cars and wear clothes made in China, Indonesia, or India, but fashioned in the international design centers of New York, London, or Milan. This also means that identifications based on these models are manipulable and fickle; they band adherents together into weak "imagined communities," often with generational referents – yuppies, boomers, greens, X-ers, sophisticatos, bobos, etc. – that are easily dissolved and fail to give a sense of belonging, let alone a consistent normative guidance. They are easily adopted and shed, like the lifestyles (and consumption patterns) they promote. National and familial identities seem to be exceptions; they prove more stable and are often mobilized as "fall-backs" – a fact that is seldom appreciated as a source of political pathologies. However, they seem to be under pressure from above and below: from above comes media- and consumption-based global culture, from below come alternative projections of "imagined communities" from religious groups, indigenes, migrants, and sub-nationalists. These processes can meet each other in a "hybridization" or "creolization" of culture that multiplies the bases of collective identification and establishes complex relations with national cultures. Current debates about multiculturalism (salient not only in settler and high-migration societies, such as the UK, US, Canada, and Australia, but also in migration-affected France, Germany, and Italy) echo these themes.

This has some serious implications for social solidarities that weaken, become less culturally embedded, more vulnerable to manipulations. Beck (2002) points to the long-lasting trends in the weakening of community and familial solidarities. Industrial society, according to him, was really quasi-traditional, generating social classes and the modern family surrogates for community and household that could provide secure roots for stable identities. Only recently has the full impact of modernization been felt. The eclipse of class and family throws the individual on her own resources. Selves must be constructed "reflexively" from resources to hand (e.g. media) in an increasingly risky world. For Giddens (1991), too, the "radicalization" of modernity accelerates change, including the "dis-embedding" of individuals from traditional identity supports. In modern societies, individuals achieve a measure of ontological security by reposing trust in expert systems that range from banks to health-care organizations. Expert systems institutionalize reflexivity and provide stable, seemingly risk-free, environments. They also sequester experience, removing pain and death from public view. In a radicalized ("late") modernity we are more aware of the high-consequence (but low-probability) risks of failure in systems, while the agenda of "life politics" problematizes sequestration. The tasks of constructing specific identities and sustaining them through appropriate lifestyles and consumption thus fall more heavily on increasingly socially dis-embedded individuals. So, a radicalized late modernity brings a radicalized individualism that puts more pressure on us to make choices about selfhood while removing (quasi-)traditional identity supports. Both Beck and Giddens seem to imply that social "solidarity," in either of Durkheim's senses (mechanical or organic), is a thing of the past. But intensely solidaristic groups and communities – from charismatic churches to lifestyle groups and youth gangs – are a prominent feature of contemporary culture. The contradiction is only apparent: when the task of individualized, reflexive selfhood becomes too hard to bear, we take flight to an all-embracing community, or media-provided model, or a doctrine that provides for all our social-psychological needs. But this leaves unanswered questions about the origins and status of contemporary solidary groups. One solution is to argue that somehow traditional or premodern "sociality" (in Maffesoli's term) has been revitalized in contemporary circumstances. On Maffesoli's (1995) view, an intense solidarism that is not mediated by (modern) institutions is a kind of biological given, a manifestation of the life-force. The erosion of institutions and old identities simply allows forces of association to reassert themselves in a new form.

THEORETICAL SYNTHESIS: POSTMODERNIZATION

Alternatively – as already implied in the overview above – these developments can be interpreted in a more dramatic way as symptoms of a movement away from "modern" forms of social organization as such. On this view, the crises of organized society marks the radical reorganization of modern society, away from the modern configurations. There is some evidence to warrant this view. Regularities and institutional patterns that have defined modern societies – from class to work to family structure and cultural tastes – have fragmented or radically changed shape. Accepted and modern hierarchies of determination, in which economic factors determine the shape of political and cultural processes, for example, have been eroded or reversed. Contemporary consumer cultures, spread through the accessible media, dissolve master identities and the accompanying social solidarities into fleeting identifications backed by fickle commitments subject to easy manipulation. If we grant for the moment that it is plausible to argue that contemporary societies are moving beyond recognizably modern configurations, two questions arise. Can the idea of "postmodernity" be given any sociological content? Can we give a satisfying account of the processes that drive "postmodernization"?

As suggested above, there are three types of affirmative answers to the first question. The first suggests that the postmodern condition is the scandalous mirror-image or inversion of the modern. Some French theorists, such as Michel de Certeau, Gilles Deleuze, and Michel Maffesoli, seem to suggest such an inversion. Ideas of "progress" and "emancipation" are abandoned in favor of a valorization of the play of desire and the celebration of difference. Universal and objective standards (as of truth, goodness, and beauty) are rejected in favor of relative and variable local standards ("my" or "our" truths). Organization and functional differentiation of social relations are seen as oppressive. Disorganization and de-differentiation are celebrated as a basis of "neo-tribalism."

The second positive answer suggests that postmodern configurations should be understood as new forms of advanced social order, where "social" and "order" retain most of their modern connotations but take different forms. For some analysts, such as Harvey and Jameson, developments in postmodern culture embody the logic of the recent development of (consumer-oriented) capitalism. For sociologists such as Bauman or Featherstone, a decentered and globalized postmodern order is built around consumption and pluralized lifestyles.

The third answer is arguably the most radical. On this view, the postmodern is post-societal or even post-social. For Baudrillard, the world is saturated by sounds and images from mass media, eroding the distinction between "representation" and "(social) reality" producing the "end of the social." Needless to add, such a view denies the possibility of postmodern social theory as a comprehensive explanatory construct; at the very best, what is possible is a "sensitizing" critical social commentary.

None of these answers is satisfactory. The postmodern intellectual movement needs a more comprehensive social theory that can fulfill its key cognitive and social functions: facilitate the understanding of change, absorb (explain) the anomalies, reduce anxieties by squaring social developments with expectations, generate a sense of familiarity. Therefore a fourth answer is suggested – one more embedded in classical theory, general and comprehensive. It can be summarized in four points:

- Since the pace of social change has intensified, and the outcomes – the social configurations, patterned social relations – are *in statu nascendi*, the processual focus – on the process of postmodernization – offers the best option for theoretical advancement. It is necessary to identify and focus on the key processes of postmodernization that operate across the social spectrum, across the field of social relations.
- These processes are not new. In fact, the sources of postmodern social dynamics are firmly anchored in processes constitutive of modern society. What is new is the intensity of those processes ("hyper-") combined with their specific interaction across the time-space and sectoral boundaries.
- The processes of postmodernization, like their predecessors (processes of modernization), are open-ended in the sense of being capable of generating a broad diversity of social configurations. However, in the initial stage of their operation they appear as "destabilizing" and "corrosive" of the old social forms, thus generating a widespread sense of social fluidity ("liquid society") and uncertainty, triggering popular anxieties and posing the "problem of order."
- The responses to the problem of order are also partly old and partly novel; they take the form of a variety of "social ordering" – attempts at stabilizing the patterns of social relations through institutionalization. What is novel is some of the (reflexive) strategies of ordering, and a high degree of flexibility, readiness for negotiated adjustment.

On the most abstract level, modern society, a type of society that emerged in Europe and North America in the late nineteenth century, was a product of four constitutive processes. First and foremost it was a result of long-lasting *rationalization*, that is, changes in intellectual technology, the dominant mode of thinking, from emulative (traditional) to deliberate and calculative (rational). It was Max

Weber who identified the sources of (uniquely and peculiarly Western) rationalism, mainly in the exemplary action of Protestant divines, analyzed its forms (especially the instrumental and substantive) and, above all, charted its spread. Rationalization transpired in widening market relations, scientific outlooks, legal formalism, bureaucratic organization, professional ethos, national power-politics, technical art, etc. Modernization has been closely identified with this Western (in origin) progressive rationalization of various domains of life. At the heart of these processes lay a tendency, indeed a compulsion, for systematic and deliberate calculation in terms effectiveness/efficiency and according to chosen standards. Rationalization, especially in its instrumental form, increased both the effectiveness and predictability of action, though it also widened the scope of unintended consequences. Progressive rationalization, transplanted from the West to other regions and cultures, generated bureaucratically organized societies, promoted formal legalism, science, and marketization, and shaped complex webs of class, status, and command relations. It also generated disenchanted and reflexive cultures, including formalized and technique-based art. The dynamics of modernity, seen by Weber as "fate," an "iron cage," were complex, because rationalization progressed by leaps and spread slowly to non-Western societies, depending on historical circumstances (the "trucks"), and the actions of powerful elites (the "switchmen"), the latter identified with charismatic leaders.

The second and parallel constitutive process of modernization has been identified by Marx as progressive *commodification*, that is, involvement of objects, ideas, qualities – and importantly for Marx also human labor – in the process of (market) exchange, thus increasing alienation. Commodity production-cum-exchange contrasts with, and replaces, traditional forms of obligation-based exchange, thus resulting in a social expansion of "markets." When commodified, goods, services, and qualities acquire exchange value that widens their circulation but also shapes social relations of reciprocity and exchange. While the core elements of Marxist historical materialism have proven dubious, the proposition of progressive commodification (especially of intellectual processes and knowledge) as a "master process" shaping contemporary society seems to have withstood the test of time. While Marx focused his attention on the consequences of the commodification of labor, his twentieth-century followers, especially Adorno, Horkheimer, and Benjamin, commented on the commodification of culture, especially in the context of the proliferation of popular consumer culture. This aspect of "cultural commodification" marks the developmental path of modern capitalism in its "core" advanced form.

The third process is social *differentiation* (cum integration), most famously identified by Durkheim as a constitutive process of the modern "division of labor." While its origins are hazy – Durkheim suggested some critical increases in social interaction ("moral density") accompanying demographic concentration (in proto-cities?), as the main propellant of differentiation – the consequences have been analyzed with clarity. Particularly important for Durkheim is that differentiation encourages further differentiation (as "resolution" of competition) and a new form of social integration. Thus progressive differentiation implies increasing social complexity combined with the formation of "organic" social bonds that are based on the recognition of complementarity. This form of social integration is stronger than the older "mechanical" bonds based on similarity (shared beliefs and outlooks). It supersedes the older forms in large social settings, and it paves the way for the spread of individualism – a typically modern outlook (and social norm) appreciating and promoting the distinctiveness and uniqueness of each human being. Modernization is thus identified primarily with growing social complexity (specialization-cum-hierarchy), organic integration, and a spreading "cult of the individual." Anomic pressures minimized by integrative-regulative activities were famously linked by Parsons with the evolving value systems and the coordinating role of state governments.

Finally, one should add to the list of the constitutive processes of modern society *individualization*, the term recently popularized by Beck (2002) and seen as the emergence of the socially produced autonomous self. We owe the classical sociological formulations of this process to Georg Simmel and G. H. Mead and, to a lesser extent, Sigmund Freud. Simmel provided a compelling argument about the sources of individualization, identified with a growing focus of perception and judgment on the individual human subject. He saw it as a correlate and by-product of urban-metropolitan life marked by dense and complex social interactions. Pre-modern life, according to him, was characterized by ascribed and "concentric" group membership (family, clan, village), and the resulting strong all-enveloping collective identities. Modern urban life results in complex cross-cutting, voluntary and partial membership in complex social networks. Each group and association in these networks generates specific but partial identifications (reflected in complex obligations). This results in unique "portfolios" of identification – individual identities. Such identities, according to Simmel, require constant reflexive reconciliation. Mead charted the developmental dynamics of the individual self in those complex webs, especially the process of internalization of the "generalized other." While the major contributions of Freud were in the psychological (rather than sociological) domain, his late account of tensions between widening cultural constraints and the instinctual desires adds to the central account of modern individual identity and "expressive-repressive" culture.

The destabilizing and paradoxical effects of postmodernization arise from the "hyper-extensions" of the core processes of modernization: commodification, rationalization, differentiation, and individualization. They not only interact, but also increase in pace, scope, and intensity, and operate on social forms that are already modernized. This hyper-extension can give the appearance of reversals. Thus hyper-commodification results in the extension of commodity relations well beyond what traditionally constituted market transactions, thus drawing into the orbit of market relations once non-commodified regions (e.g. knowledge/intellectual property, images and styles, family relations, worship/televangelism). Hyper-rationalization appears as splits in "expert cultures," and it transpires in a wide diversity of "value-rational" responses (often confused with irrationality) and pluralizes modes of rationalization (e.g. enterprise systems, the "new politics" of social movements, fundamentalisms, and new age cults). In the cultural sphere, hyper-rationalization appears as the proliferation of recipes for desirable effects: from marital happiness and spiritual satisfaction, through a successful career and progressive social involvement, to an attractive personality, social attractiveness, and effective dating. In contrast to the modernizing versions, however, the techniques start to proliferate and mix beyond the separated areas of expertise. Thus serious political and corporate decisions are made with the assistance of "personal" and "spiritual" advisors; lifestyle choices are harmonized with deep and hidden desires. Religious doctrines and practices are subject to interpretive hyper-rationalization no less than more mundane pursuits. Hyper-differentiation appears as the proliferation of specializations, lifestyles, and outlooks into fragments that are subsequently recombined in an unpredictable and hybrid fashion (e.g. cross- and multi-disciplinary areas, Bund-like groupings, syncretic lifestyles, multi-media, transdisciplinary science). The proliferation of interdisciplinarity in science, for example, leads to paradoxical proximities, whereby a geneticist, a mathematician, and a chemist working on a similar problem may communicate more easily among themselves than among their disciplinary colleagues. Hence a proliferation of problem-teams, task-forces, and brain trusts that utilizes the advantages of this de-differentiation resulting from hyper-differentiation. Finally, the process of hyper-individualization results in a cultural (value-normative) shift whereby everyone is expected to demonstrate a capacity for judgment and choice, and to shape their life in a conscious, intentional manner, as a self-centered project. What in the past constituted an option, often welcomed as modern liberation, now becomes a (burdensome) compulsion (e.g. consumer choices, lifestyle choices, political preferences). One articulation of hyper-individualism is in the erosion of collective identities mentioned above; another is in the changing form of family and gender relations.

Is postmodern social theory in this "hyper-extension" version capable of responding to the popular expectation of explaining social change – and perhaps even assisting in strengthening social order? Only to some extent. While providing an explanatory framework, it points to the sources of (chronic) social disorder. In that sense, it suggests that social order is a fragile accomplishment, increasingly difficult to attain at the time of accelerated (hyper-)change. What is viable is a pursuit of order in the form of ongoing "social ordering" that takes multiple forms: "modern ordering" through social organization and institutionalization; neo-traditional ordering through reinforcement of old social norms, values, and underlying solidarities; and the new "reflexive ordering" that aims at imposing regularity and predictability in conduct through negotiations between the key actors. This negotiated ordering takes the forms of "local understandings," "social pacts," and agreements that have a non-institutional character, and therefore more flexibility.

CONCLUSION

The future of PST is uncertain. This is not only because it is still underdeveloped, and because the movement within which it evolved is showing signs of decomposition, but also because it has a serious new competitor in the novelty stakes in the form of "globalization theory" (e.g. Berger and Huntington 2003; Robertson 1992; Waters 1999). The origins of globalization theory and the "globalization camp" are similar to the origins of PST – both were triggered by dissatisfaction with the old theoretical frameworks and multiplying anomalies. The accounts in terms of globalization deal well with the key "anomalies" and have an alluring simplicity, mainly due to their reliance on a single master concept. While attempts to develop a comprehensive postmodern social theory persist, the "mainstream" postmodern analysis continues its critical, somewhat anarchic and wildly diverse growth, mainly on the boundaries of traditional social science disciplines (cultural studies, media studies, minority studies, etc.). The apex of its popularity, as marked by a proliferation of publications, university courses, conferences, and symposia, was reached in the late 1990s. Since then, there has been a notable decline, perhaps a symptom of the withering away of an intellectual movement that engenders theoretical production.

Bibliography

Anderson, P. (1998) *The Origins of Postmodernity*. London: Verso.

Baudrillard, J. (1988) *Jean Baudrillard: Selected Writings*. Stanford: Stanford University Press.

Baudrillard, J. (1994) *Simulacra and Simulations*. Ann Arbor: University of Michigan Press.

Baudrillard, J. (1998) *The Consumer Society*. London: Sage.

Baudrillard, J. (2006) *The System of Objects*. London: Verso.

Bauman, Z. (1992) *Intimations of Postmodernity*. London: Routledge.

Bauman, Z. (1997) *Postmodernity and its Discontents*. Cambridge: Polity.

Bauman, Z. (2003) *Liquid Love*. Cambridge: Polity.

Bauman, Z. (2005) *Liquid Life*. Cambridge: Polity.

Bauman, Z. (2006) *Liquid Times: Living in an Age of Uncertainty*. Cambridge: Polity.

Beck, U. (1992) *Risk Society*. London: Sage.

Beck, U. (2002) *Individualization*. London: Sage.

Beck, U. (2006) *Power in the Global Age*. Cambridge: Polity.

Beck, U., Giddens, A., and Lash, S. (1994) *Reflexive Modernization*. Cambridge: Polity.

Berger, P. L., and Huntington, S. (2003) *Many Globalizations*. New York: Oxford University Press.

Best, S., and Kellner, D. (1991) *Postmodern Theory: Critical Interrogations*. New York: Guilford.

Best, S., and Kellner, D. (1997) *The Postmodern Turn*. New York: Guilford.

Bourdieu, P. (1984) *Distinction*. London: Routledge.

Bradley, H. (1996) *Fractured Identities*. Cambridge: Polity.

Brooks, D. (2000) *Bobos in the Paradise*. New York: Simon & Schuster.

Brown, J. S., and Dequit, P. (2006) *The Social Life of Information*. Cambridge, MA: Harvard Business School.

Casteles, S. (2003) "Towards a Sociology of Forced Migration and Social Transformation." *Sociology* 37(1): 13–34.

Castells, M. (1997) *The Power of Identity*. Oxford: Blackwell.

Crook, S., Pakulski, J., and Waters, M. (1992) *Postmodernization*. London: Sage.

Delanty, G. (1999) *Social Theory in a Changing World*. Cambridge: Polity.

Featherstone, M. (1988) *Postmodernism*. London: Sage.

Featherstone, M. (1995) *Undoing Culture*. London: Sage.

Featherstone, M. (2007) *Consumer Culture and Postmodernism*, 2nd edn. London: Sage.

Fukuyama, F. (1999) *The Great Disruption*. New York: The Free Press.

Garland, D. (2001) *The Culture of Control*. Chicago: University of Chicago Press.

Giddens, A. (1987) "Structuralism, Post-structuralism and the Production of Culture," in A. Giddens and J. H. Turner (eds.), *Social Theory Today*. Stanford: Stanford University Press.

Giddens, A. (1991) *Modernity and Self-Identity*. Cambridge: Polity.

Giddens, A. (2000) *Runaway World*. London: Routledge.

Harvey, D. (1989) *The Condition of Postmodernity: An Enquiry into the Origins of Cultural Change*. Oxford: Blackwell.

Harvey, D. (1989) *The Condition of Postmodernity*, pt. II. Oxford: Blackwell.

Harvey, D. (2001) *Spaces of Capital*. London: Routledge.

Harvey, D. (2005) *Paris, Capital of Modernity*. London: Routledge.

Head, S. (2005) *The New Ruthless Economy*. Oxford: Oxford University Press.

Hobsbawm, E. J. (1994) *Age of Extremes*. New York: Abacus.

Hollinger, R. (1994) *Postmodernism and the Social Sciences: A Thematic Approach*. Thousand Oaks, CA: Sage.

Hughes, H. S. (1974) *Consciousness and Society*. New York: Paladin Press.

Huntington, S. (1993) *The Third Wave*. Norman: University of Oklahoma Press.

Jameson, F. (1992) *Postmodernism, or, The Cultural Logic of Late Capitalism*. Durham, NC: Duke University Press.

Jameson, F. (1998) *The Cultural Turn*. New York: W. W. Norton.

Jameson, F. (2007) *Archeologies of the Future*. New York: W. W. Norton.

Kellner, D. (1995) *Media Culture*. London: Routledge.

Kellner, D. (2003) *Media Spectacle*. London: Routledge.

Lash, S. (1990) *Sociology of Postmodernism*. London: Routledge.

Lash, S., Giddens, A., and Beck, U. (1994) *Reflexive Modernisation*. Cambridge: Polity.

Lash, S., and Urry, J. (1987) *The End of Organized Capitalism*. Cambridge: Polity.

Lash, S., and Urry, J. (1994) *Economies of Signs and Spaces*. London: Sage.

Lyotard, J.-F. (1984 [1979]) *The Postmodern Condition: A Report on Knowledge*. Minneapolis: University of Minnesota Press.

Lyotard, J.-F. (1993) "Answering the Question: What Is Postmodernism?" and "Note on the Meaning of 'Post-,'" in T. Docherty (ed.), *Postmodernism: A Reader*. New York: Columbia University Press.

Maffesoli, M. (1995) *The Time of the Tribes*. London: Sage.

McLuhan, M. (2001 [1964]) *Understanding Media*. London: Routledge.

Pakulski, J. (2004) *Globalising Inequalities*. Sydney: Allen & Unwin.

Pakulski, J., and Waters, M. (1996) *The Death of Class*. London: Sage.

Ritzer, G. (1997) *Postmodern Social Theory*. New York: McGraw-Hill.

Ritzer, G. (1998) *The McDonaldization Thesis*. London: Sage.

Robertson, R. (1992) *Globalization: Social Theory and Global Culture*. London: Sage.

Rorty, R. (1989) *Contingency, Irony and Solidarity*. Cambridge: Cambridge University Press.

Rorty, R. (1993) "Postmodernist Bourgeois Liberalism," in T. Docherty (ed.), *Postmodernism: A Reader*. New York: Columbia University Press.

Rorty, R. (1998) *Truth and Progress*. Cambridge: Cambridge University Press.

Rorty, R. (2007) *Philosophy as Cultural Politics*. Cambridge: Cambridge University Press.

Sennett, R. (2006) *The Culture of the New Capitalism*. New Haven: Yale University Press.

Smart, B. (1993) *Postmodernity*. London: Routledge.

Smart, B. (1998) "Modern Reason, Postmodern Imagination," in V. E. Taylor and C. E. Winquist (eds.), *Postmodernism: Critical Concepts*. London: Routledge.

Smart, B. (1999) *Facing Modernity*. London: Sage.

Smart, B. (2000) "Postmodern Social Theory," in B. Turner (ed.), *The Blackwell Companion to Social Theory*, 2nd edn. Oxford: Blackwell.

Sokal, A. D., and Bricmont, J. (1999) *Fashionable Nonsense*. New York: Picador.

Toynbee, A. (1954 [1934]) *A Study of History*. Oxford: Oxford University Press.

Turner, B. (ed.) (2000) *The Blackwell Companion to Social Theory*, 2nd edn. Oxford: Blackwell.

Warde, A. (1996) *Consumption Matters*. Oxford: Blackwell.

Warde, A. (1997) *Consumption, Food and Taste*. London: Sage.

Waters, M. (1999) *Globalization: The Key Concepts*. London: Routledge.

World Migration 2005. International Organization for Migration. UN publication 882.

14

Social Constructionism

Darin Weinberg

Few terms in social theory ignite controversy like the term social constructionism.[1] While embraced as a creed by scholars working throughout the human sciences, it is also the focus of some of the most passionate criticism one is likely to find in the academy. Some of this criticism is levied from outside the social sciences and is based largely on caricature and misunderstanding (cf. Gross and Levitt 1994; Sokal and Bricmont 1998). But much of it also comes from social scientists themselves, who fear that social constructionism threatens the very foundations of their craft (cf. Boudon 2004). I do not share this fear, and in this chapter seek to put it to rest. Indeed, I argue not only that it poses no threat to the social sciences but that a commitment to some form of social constructionism is an indispensable feature of all social scientific research. It is only if they are socially constructed that things might be amenable to sociological analysis. Hence the question we should be asking is not the categorical: Are we or are we not constructionists? It is one of degree: Are there any aspects of our lives that must inevitably fall beyond the reach of social scientific understanding? I argue that social constructionists are best understood as those least willing to forsake the promise of the social sciences and, therefore, most dedicated to extending their reach into knowledge domains wherein they have hitherto been discounted. Social constructionism thus entails a thoroughly sociological regard for *all* knowledge forms (including, of course, those produced by social scientists).

Quite obviously, this is a partisan definition in a contested theoretical field. While few would dispute the claim that social constructionism is in some sense concerned with the sociology of knowledge, there is a wide range of opinion as to what "knowledge" ought to mean in this context. Peter Berger and Thomas Luckmann, for example, clearly intended their classic text *The Social Construction of Reality* (1967) as a contribution to the sociology of knowledge, but the knowledge they sought to analyze was, following Alfred Schutz, the commonsense knowledge of lay members of society rather than philosophically or scientifically validated knowledge. They specifically avoided problematizing the epistemological standards by which

competing claims to knowledge are judged. Likewise, many constructionist researchers focus on news programming and other products of the mass media but very
rarely explicitly attend to their epistemic merits, except to sometimes summarily
discount them by way of uncritical contrasts with received scientific wisdom
(Woolgar and Pawluch 1985). This research certainly yields important insights but,
because it neglects epistemological questions, contributes little to our understanding
of knowledge as such. To my mind, social constructionism's most original and
important contributions to social theory per se stem from its unyielding *empirical*
investigations of what counts as genuine knowledge and why. Therefore the themes
I emphasize in this chapter highlight how social constructionism has contributed to
our understanding of what knowledge is, and the comparative value of the social
sciences for illuminating knowledge as an empirically observable and researchable
phenomenon rather than a merely imagined normative ideal.

The chapter is divided into five parts. I first trace the multiple origins of social
constructionist thought, paying particular attention to Marxian ideology critique
and, more broadly, to what is often called the sociology of error. I note the more
prominent debates and challenges that emerged among early social constructionists
who sought to show the social forces governing the ideas of others without thereby
undermining their own claim to intellectual authority. In part two I consider the
contributions of the "strong program" in the sociology of scientific knowledge.
Emphasis is given to the consequences of adopting the "principle of symmetry,"
or the principle that both true and false beliefs must be explained in the same
way. Part three addresses the so-called "practice turn." Here I consider the main
sources and key ideas of those who advocate an understanding of knowledge as
competent performance rather than as beliefs or propositions that mirror things-
in-themselves. In part four I discuss the concept of reflexivity. Here I consider the
value of explaining our own research practices sociologically. I conclude with a
brief statement of what I take to be the distinctive virtues of the social constructionist approach.

THE ROOTS OF SOCIAL CONSTRUCTIONISM

It is all too common in writings on the origins of social constructionism to rest
content with a tracing of the phrase itself back to certain landmark texts like Berger
and Luckmann's (1967) *The Social Construction of Reality* or Spector and Kitsuse's
(1987) *Constructing Social Problems*. Without discounting the importance of these
texts, I would contend that it is deeply misleading to conflate the term "social construction" (or any other term) with the concept(s) it is meant to capture (Skinner
1989). As Lynch (1998: 29) notes, since its introduction into the social scientific
lexicon, the term "social construction" has been adopted by "diverse constituencies . . . for different reasons." These constituencies have put the term to a wide
variety of uses, many of which are plainly incompatible. Most of these constituencies also have intellectual roots that go considerably deeper than the trendy terms
in which they sometimes express their views. Much more important than tracing
the roots of the term social construction itself, then, is to trace the roots of the
various intellectual movements within which this term has found a home.

Nowadays using the term "social construction" is usually meant to convey that something that has been widely considered beyond the scope of social influence is actually the product of specific sociohistorical or social interactional processes. Hence, social constructionism thrives particularly vigorously among social scientists interested in the study of such matters as beauty, gender, morality, pathology, race, science, and sexuality. Whereas it was once widely believed that these phenomena were determined by fixed natural and/or metaphysical laws and were therefore sociohistorically invariant, social constructionists have repeatedly demonstrated the extent to which their characteristics are, in fact, culturally relative or historically specific. The conceptual resources with which such demonstrations are achieved hail from a wide variety of theoretical traditions both within and beyond the social sciences (Holstein and Gubrium 2008). But for present purposes it will be useful to begin with the three most prominent founders of modern social theory: Émile Durkheim, Max Weber, and Karl Marx. Each of these writers set major precedents for social constructionist social theory.

Despite his common association with positivism, Durkheim has exercised a considerable influence on social constructionist research through his later thought as exhibited, for example, in *Primitive Classification* (1963) and *The Elementary Forms of the Religious Life* (1954). In these writings, Durkheim argued that systems of classification reflect the social organization of the societies in which they occur. Though it may be debated whether he was referring to "knowledge" in the conventional sense, his influence can be seen in the work of various important twentieth-century anthropologists like E. E. Evans-Pritchard who articulated and effectively promoted a culturally relativist sociology of knowledge (Douglas 1980). This turn toward classification and the sociology of knowledge in anthropology provided important precedent for a diverse assortment of writers including Pierre Bourdieu, Mary Douglas, Peter Winch, and Michel Foucault who, in their turn, have also become important figures in the constructionist canon. A more direct Durkheimian influence can also be seen in the work of David Bloor and other contributors to the "strong program" in the sociology of knowledge (cf. Bloor 1982), of whom I will have more to say below.

Because social constructionists tend to stress the diverse meanings social actors confer upon their experiences, Weber's role in legitimating and popularizing *Verstehen* sociology must be acknowledged as an important precedent. Weber's thoughts on *Verstehen* reflect the influences of a variety of earlier writers associated with German idealism, including such patriarchs of the constructionist tradition as Immanuel Kant, Wilhelm Dilthey, and Friedrich Nietzsche. Though the specifics of Weber's often obscure reflections on social action, rationality, and knowledge are rarely given explicit coverage in constructionist texts, he must nonetheless be credited with helping to create a space wherein subjective meaning could be considered a legitimate topic for social scientific study. Were it not for Weber's influence, the social sciences may well have provided far less fertile soil for social constructionist cultivation than has in fact been the case. More concretely, Weber's writings on ideal types, meaning, values, and rationalization also exercised a variety of specific influences on other seminal contributors to the constructionist canon, including Alfred Schutz, Karl Mannheim, members of the Frankfurt School, and Jürgen Habermas.

Among the classical theorists, it is Marx who has had the greatest impact on social constructionism by way of his writings on ideology. Marx developed this concept to suggest how people can suffer from a *false consciousness* that renders them complicit in their own oppression. This idea was developed by later Marxists like Georg Lukács and Antonio Gramsci, whose elaborations on concepts like *class consciousness*, *reification*, and *hegemony* have exercised immense influences on social constructionist research by linking the putative legitimacy of ideas to the interests of actors sufficiently powerful to influence the standards by which their legitimacy is measured. This linkage of what societies regard as valid knowledge to the power structures comprising those societies has remained a lively and fruitful enterprise. Beyond its Marxian roots, the linkage of power and knowledge can be seen in the social constructionist traditions stemming from the postcolonial writings of people like Edward Said, Stuart Hall, and the Birmingham School of cultural studies, Michel Foucault's studies of power/knowledge, Pierre Bourdieu's studies of symbolic violence, the feminist standpoint theories of people like Dorothy Smith, and, of course, Howard Becker's, Edwin Lemert's, and Erving Goffman's studies of labeling.

Transforming the Marxian critical concept of ideology into a general and non-critical concept of knowledge as such, Karl Mannheim (1936) called for the sociological analysis of all knowledge (except natural science) as socially embedded and constructed. This was, of course, a monumental precedent for social constructionism, but it tended to undermine the possibility of critiquing knowledge claims by leveling the epistemological ground between critic and the object of critique. Mannheim's sociology of knowledge was therefore looked upon by his Marxist contemporaries with considerable suspicion. Indeed, it has been precisely this difficulty of reconciling the sociology of knowledge (which seeks to explain ideas with reference to their social contexts) with epistemology (which seeks to establish procedures for validating ideas), that has, since Mannheim, continued to provoke the most passionate debate amongst social constructionists and their critics (cf. Hacking 1999; Hollis and Lukes 1982; Wilson 1970). Mannheim (1936) sought to achieve this reconciliation by both exempting the natural sciences from his purview and by arguing that a "socially unattached intelligentsia" (p. 155) might succeed in overcoming the biases inherent to their original class positions. However, he gave no real account of how they could do so and has been taken to task by critics for ducking the problem more than truly resolving it (cf. Merton 1937; von Schelting 1936).

Berger and Luckmann (1967) also exempted the natural sciences from their analysis and, rather than seeking to resolve the tension with epistemology, simply declared it beyond the scope of the sociology of knowledge:

> To include epistemological questions concerning the validity of sociological knowledge in the sociology of knowledge is somewhat like trying to push a bus in which one is riding . . . Far be it from us to brush aside such questions. All we would contend here is that these questions are not themselves part of the empirical discipline of sociology. They properly belong to the methodology of the social sciences, an enterprise that belongs to philosophy and is by definition other than sociology. (Berger and Luckmann 1967: 13)

Like Berger and Luckmann, most social constructionists have sought to avoid direct confrontations with either the natural sciences or epistemology. Hence, it has been common to distinguish between the natural and social dimensions of studied phenomena and confine attention to the social construction of the latter (as when feminist scholars distinguished between biologically determined *sex* and socially constructed *gender*, or when medical sociologists distinguished between biologically determined *disease* and socially constructed *illness experience* or *disability*). Likewise, most constructionists have passed the buck when it comes to dealing with the difficult question of distinguishing truth and falsity, or, for that matter, establishing any technique for arbitrating the intellectual value of competing claims once the presumption to possess universal epistemological criteria has been abandoned. They instead rely implicitly on the epistemological standards of their own respective disciplines, or sub-disciplines, to assert the legitimate authority of their ideas and sociologically reductionist accounts of the ideas of those they study. The result is that most social constructionists have been forced to choose between an unsustainably parochial relativism and what Bloor (1991: 12) called the sociology of error. More precisely, they have had either to advocate a permanent suspension of questions concerning the comparative value of their own ideas and those they study, or dogmatically insist that their own ideas are epistemologically sound and those they study amount to mere myths and illusions. In any case, most social constructionists have remained studiously silent on the question of how we might more reasonably, justly, compassionately, or systematically arbitrate the intellectual value of competing claims. It is this silence that has most consistently infuriated critics.

Social constructionist theory has also drawn a great deal from the legacy of what is often called microsociology. For the most part this tradition stems from the American pragmatist tradition inaugurated by people like Charles Pierce, William James, John Dewey, and George Herbert Mead. In contrast to many of their European predecessors, the pragmatists tended to emphasize creative agency over structurally deterministic explanations of social events and to highlight how social order can be a product of egalitarian negotiation rather than exploitation and domination. Central to this theoretical program was the tenet that human experience of the world is always mediated by the socially inherited meanings actors actively confer upon it. The Chicago School of sociology enthusiastically embraced this tenet, as may be seen in W. I. Thomas's famous theorem, "If men define situations as real, they are real in their consequences" (Thomas and Thomas 1928: 572). The turn away from structural determinism toward a focus on the situated negotiation of meaning was codified by Herbert Blumer (1969) into what he christened symbolic interactionism. Long before Berger and Luckmann published *The Social Construction of Reality*, symbolic interactionists took it as axiomatic that whatever grasp people have of the world is inevitably mediated by socially constructed symbolic devices. Through labeling theory and, later, the "social worlds" perspective first outlined by Anselm Strauss, Tomatsu Shibutani, and Howard Becker, symbolic interactionists have made major contributions to the constructionist canon (cf. Clarke 1990; Star 1989; Wiener 1981).

However, it was not until the advent of ethnomethodology in the 1960s that critical attention was given to questions of epistemology as such. Harold Garfinkel and Harvey Sacks (1970) notoriously recommended a policy of indifference to received sociological wisdom in studies of the routine production of social order. Sociology was thus placed on an epistemological par with all other forms of practical reasoning (including water witching!). The presumption that epistemology might somehow facilitate the transcendence of our ordinary practical reasoning skills was abandoned in favor of a radically empirical approach to the study of what Mel Pollner (1987) has called mundane reason – not the normative ideal of Reason valorized in the academy, but the actual, empirically observable, ways in which people organize judgments of rationality and competence as they go about their everyday lives. Beginning in the late 1970s this approach was trained directly on the research practices of natural scientists and mathematicians, thus making even more explicit the anti-epistemological ambitions implicit in Garfinkel's program.[2] Though its relation to social constructionism has sometimes been contested (Button and Sharrock 1993; Lynch 2008), there can be no questioning the fact that ethnomethodology has exerted a profound influence on the development of social constructionist studies throughout a very wide range of research domains (see CHAPTER 8).

By explicitly forsaking a priori justifications of epistemological privilege in favor of a thoroughly empirical regard for rationality *in action*, ethnomethodologists have given powerful impetus to the social constructionist agenda. However, they also invited some rather thorny questions that have haunted not only their own work but that of others who have followed the radically anti-foundationalist path. Perhaps most significantly: if they endorse neither the positivist presumption of direct observational access to the world nor any rationalist presumption to possess a universally valid epistemology, then exactly what grounds can ethnomethodologists, or any other anti-foundationalists, provide to support the intellectual legitimacy of their claims? By far the most prominent answer to this question has been to reference the real-time contingencies of academic dialog (cf. Lynch 1993: 144–7). In other words, rather than staking claim to any *principled* entitlement to intellectual respectability, ethnomethodologists offer both a retrospective claim (and a prospective pledge) to have been (and to continue to be) competently responsive to the contingent demands of academic dialog as they emerge *in situ* – that is, in any actual case. This is a pretty good answer that is well supported by the manifest fact that ethnomethodology has been taken quite seriously indeed throughout the social sciences. However, it also begs some important questions.

Given the historically enduring fact that academic dialog tends to be a deeply fragmented, contentious, and polysemous set of activities, what exactly could it mean to be adequately responsive to its contingencies? Aren't we inevitably compelled to make hard choices about whom and what to take seriously amongst a din of ongoing, cross-cutting academic disputes and discussions? Armed with foundationalist, or unquestioned, standards of epistemic authority, we are a good deal better equipped to make and defend these choices than we are if, following the ethnomethodological lead, we seek to improvisationally negotiate whatever epistemic landscapes in which we may find ourselves. The improvisational solution to the problem of epistemic legitimacy can also seem rather anemic and parasitic insofar as it conspicuously fails to provide guidance as to how one might legitimately devise and defend epistemic standards of one's own. So it is that we find the bulk of contemporary constructionist research situated between the horns of an apparent dilemma. Either (1) refuse to problematize one's epistemic standards and slip into a parochial relativism or mere sociology of error, or (2) actively problematize those standards thereby confining oneself to the ephemeral posture of what Theodor Adorno (1990) called a negative dialectic with the orthodoxies of others. Adopting the first option one remains vulnerable to the charge of blind dogmatism, while adopting the second option relegates one to the posture of gadfly or perpetual critic and systematically undermines one's capacity to defend any manner of constructive and/or cumulative research program. To my mind, the most important developments in contemporary constructionist theory stem from efforts to resolve this dilemma.

THE SOCIOLOGY OF SCIENTIFIC KNOWLEDGE

Proponents of the strong program in the sociology of scientific knowledge (SSK) have exercised a profound influence on social constructionism (see CHAPTER 23). Scientific knowledge is the archetypal empirical example of valid knowledge in Western societies. It therefore provides the indispensable critical case for social constructionists who would hope to move beyond the sociology of error. Barry Barnes, David Bloor, Simon Schaffer, Steve Shapin, and others associated with the Science Studies Unit at the University of Edinburgh, are widely credited as the first to consistently treat the theoretical contents of the natural sciences and mathematics as amenable to sociological explanation (but see also Bourdieu 1975, 1990a; Fleck 1979). Building on Thomas Kuhn's (1970) groundbreaking book *The Structure of Scientific Revolutions*, Barnes, Bloor, and company articulated cogent critiques of the claim that sound science and epistemology are beyond the scope of sociological explanation. In Shapin's (1995: 297) words:

> SSK set out to construct an "anti-epistemology," to break down the legitimacy of the distinction between "contexts of discovery and justification," and to develop an anti-individualist and anti-empiricist framework for the sociology of knowledge in which "social factors" counted not as contaminants but as constitutive of the very idea of scientific knowledge ... SSK developed in opposition to philosophical rationalism, foundationalism, essentialism, and, to a lesser extent, realism.

However, despite their fierce opposition to philosophically foundationalist construals of science and mathematics, SSK remained equally fiercely committed to defending the sociology of science as itself a thoroughly scientific rather than anti-scientific research program (cf. Barnes 1974; Bloor 1991). Just like any other scientific enterprise, the sociology of science, they argued, must be a wholly naturalistic form of empirical inquiry dedicated to the production of maximally general theoretical laws that provide causal explanations of the phenomena under consideration. Far from being antithetical to the scientific ethos, they insisted their sociologically relativist understanding of scientific knowledge was required by it (Barnes and Bloor 1982: 21–2). The indisputable fact that beliefs regarding what is and is not credible knowledge vary both culturally and by historical period requires the sociologist of knowledge to adopt a value-free naturalism that neither consecrates nor denigrates particular beliefs but seeks only to explain why people have adopted them. The

Edinburgh School succeeded in articulating a theoretically powerful and radically sociological alternative to philosophically foundationalist arguments regarding the nature of valid knowledge. In doing so, they decisively established their studies as both the most important precedents and most important critical foils for all sociologists of knowledge who have since sought to follow in their wake.

The Edinburgh School offered macro-sociological explanations of scientific knowledge. The fact that controversy has been endemic to the scientific enterprise provided Edinburgh scholars excellent opportunities to use fine-grained descriptions of the arguments asserted by scientific disputants to empirically demonstrate the manifest variance in their willingness to be persuaded by one another's reasoning. These episodes provided stark evidence that neither scientific reason nor the experimental findings brought to bear in these debates provided unequivocal grounds for their resolution. Hence, they inferred, the causes of both the disputes and their resolutions must be found beyond the manifest conduct of the debates themselves – that is, in the social structurally determined interests and intellectual dispositions scientific disputants brought to those debates (Barnes 1977; Shapin and Schaffer 1985). With relatively minor modifications this approach was applied at a more microsociological level of analysis by Harry Collins and his colleagues at the University of Bath (cf. Collins 1985). The sociological study of scientific controversies and their closures became a prime device for demonstrating both the disunity of scientific rationality and the insinuation of broader social interests, dispositions, and processes into the very heart of scientific theory development. Because scientific knowledge production, it appeared, is inevitably socially interested, scientific knowledge must therefore be recognized as inevitably socially constructed.

Echoing broader Durkheimian tendencies in anthropology and sociology toward the study of "belief systems," the Edinburgh and Bath schools cast the beliefs of scientists as relatively coherent conceptual schemes comprising general propositions woven together by a diverse set of Wittgensteinian family resemblances. Scientific practice was seen to consist primarily in efforts to expand the scope of particular conceptual schemes by applying them to new cases in ways that could be justified among one's peers. Hence, the benchmarks of scientific validity were identified as the locally agreed upon epistemic standards of particular scientific movements rather than somehow transcendental epistemologies or ontologies. In opposition to foundationalist philosophy of science, SSK appealed to empirical cases of science in action to show that the progressive articulation of what Kuhn (1970) called scientific paradigms is demonstrably not governed by any discernibly uniform methodology nor the intrinsic nature of things studied but by the creative inclinations of scientists themselves. However, because these inclinations are governed by the shared and relatively enduring interests of those involved, the continuous propagation of a paradigm does not result in its disintegration. Rather, epistemic standards remain as stable and enduring as are the shared social interests of those who honor them. Intellectual consensus follows shared interests. The empirical confirmation of scientific theories is thus cast as analogous to the empirical confirmation of witchcraft documented by Evans-Pritchard among the Azande (Bloor 1991: 138–46).

Bloor's impartial and symmetrical characterization of the reasons scientists and the Azande hold to their respective belief systems exhibits the SSK axiom requiring a totally value-neutral and naturalistic regard for the causes of people's beliefs. This so-called "principle of symmetry" has proven a valuable rhetorical tool in SSK's struggle to emancipate the sociology of knowledge from the sociology of error imposed upon it by foundationalist philosophers of science. It has allowed SSK to align itself with the value-neutrality espoused by scientists since the Enlightenment and to mount the serious, and credible, charge that philosophical foundationalism amounts to little more than a vestige of the theological dogmatism against which the likes of Galileo had to struggle. However, the principle of symmetry also has costs. Though a thorough account of these costs is beyond the scope of this chapter (see Freedman 2005; Pels 1996), it will suffice to note here that the posture of value-neutrality implies a level of detachment from the world under study and an apparent commitment to what John Dewey called the "spectator theory" of knowledge that is difficult to reconcile with the interest-governed theory of scientific knowledge with which SSK explains the scientific work of others. If, as Bloor (1991: 7) has argued, SSK style explanations must be reflexively applicable to SSK itself, this tension seems to present a rather considerable problem. To date, there are conspicuously no SSK case studies of the social interests governing SSK. Insofar as reflexivity is a fundamental tenet of SSK, this seems a rather puzzling omission. One particularly plausible explanation for it is that the presumption to value-neutrality very seriously hobbles the prospects of reflexively identifying the interests governing SSK analysis.

Despite this gap in its literature, SSK has done much to lead the way toward a viable solution to the social constructionist dilemma of reconciling the production of tenable epistemic standards with a thoroughly naturalistic, or empirical, regard for the processes through which that production takes place. SSK may have so far downplayed the extent to which sociology too is socially constructed, but this need not require others to do so (cf. Bourdieu 1988; Calhoun 2007; Turner and Turner 1990). However, if this is to be made a viable enterprise we must refine SSK's principle of symmetry. While all "good reasons" for holding a belief are inevitably socially constructed, or provisionally institutionalized normative conventions, it does not follow that they are equivalent to other kinds of social causes of belief (Freedman 2005; Kusch 1999). A viable approach to reconciling the assertion of tenable epistemic standards with a thoroughly sociological understanding of their production will require a more careful, and less reductionist, regard for the relation between our commitments to particular epistemic standards and our other social interests.

THE PRACTICE TURN

At least since Marx penned his famous "Theses on Feuerbach," social scientists have found much to value in the notion of practice. Its appeal has been various. Marx himself saw the concept of practice, or "human sensuous activity," as a resource with which to avoid the antinomy of idealism and materialism. This would, in turn, free us from "the chief defect of all previous materialisms" which was to understand "the object, reality, what we apprehend through our senses . . . only in the form of *object* or *contemplation*" (Marx 1983: 155). The erroneous cleavage of reality from human sensuous activity resulted in a false Cartesian dichotomy between mind and body – subject and object – that prevents our properly grasping either the nature of knowledge or the worldly causes and consequences of our various intellectual habits. Marx insisted that contemplation does much more than ethereally reflect upon the nature of reality. It is, for better or worse, a product, feature, and consequential producer, of reality. Hence, for Marx, the idea that knowledge could ever be "detached" or "disinterested" is at best a mistake and at worst a ruse designed to mask the complicity of intellectual authority with political and economic power.

The ideas that reason and knowledge are not detached and disinterested, but historically conditioned and materially embodied forms of practical engagement with the world are also central to American pragmatist thought. The pragmatists argued that knowledge production, scientific or otherwise, should be freed from the misconceived dream of transcending the human condition. Epistemic standards should instead reflect our much more realistic concerns to merely improve the human condition. By pragmatist lights, the acquisition of knowledge thus consists not in developing what Richard Rorty (1980) called a mirror of nature but in developing habits and practical skills that promote the good of the individual and society. Moreover, grounded as they are in the pursuits of actual communities, epistemic standards are best understood with reference to the interests and activities of those for whom they hold rather than as abstract, universally valid principles. Pragmatists advise us to expect our epistemic terms of reference to be multiple and to change along with the changing conditions under which they are applied. The comparative evaluation of knowledge claims is not forsaken but is nested deeply within the specific practical contexts within which it must inevitably be accomplished.

While these Marxist and pragmatist ideas never completely disappeared, their influence declined dramatically during the mid-twentieth century as structuralist, positivist, and otherwise scientistic sensibilities overtook the social sciences. Due primarily to felt social pressures to emulate the natural sciences, mid-century social scientists embraced the principles of value-neutrality, detachment, and disinterested inquiry, and thereby installed Cartesian fallacies into the heart of mainstream social science. The contemporary resurgence of interest in the idiom of practices reflects the widespread rejection of structuralism, positivism, and scientism by many of the most important social theorists of the last 40 years (cf. Alexander 1982; Bourdieu 1990b; Calhoun 1995; Collins 1991; Foucault 1980; Garfinkel 1984; Giddens 1984; Habermas 1984; Smith 1989; Turner 1996). It also reflects a broader set of social scientific interests and challenges, including the antinomy between structure and agency, that between macro and micro levels of analysis, the ramifications of the fact that social action is embodied, and an increasingly meticulous regard for the phenomenology, temporality, and spatiality of "lived experience" and social interaction (cf. Schatzki, Knorr-Cetina, and von Savigny 2001). These are, of course, a mutually implicative set of themes, but it is important to note that the practice turn in contemporary theory consists only in a partial confluence of relatively distinct research programs. The practice turn has also been influenced by many of the major philosophical developments of the twentieth century, including the phenomenology of Martin Heidegger, Maurice Merleau-Ponty, and Michael Polanyi; Ludwig Wittgenstein's insights regarding language use and rule-following; Michel Foucault's genealogical investigations; Richard Rorty's anti-representationalism, and post-structuralism more generally.

Proponents of the practice turn take seriously what SSK, following the philosopher Mary Hesse, calls the thesis of finitism (cf. Barnes, Bloor, and Henry 1996). This is the idea that all our criteria for adequate understandings of the world, including our scientific understandings, are inevitably learned. That is, they are the products of our particular, *finite*, experiences and the specific, *finite*, techniques we have acquired practically to cope with our lives. To the extent that we share epistemic standards at all they have been forged in, and enforced through, specific collaborative efforts to more effectively manage the myriad practical challenges we encounter. These standards, like any other tools, are things we devise and learn to use in the accomplishment of particular tasks. It follows, then, that epistemic standards well suited to one domain of practical activity may or may not be well suited to another. For example, the criteria we have devised to judge epistemic excellence in Western university settings may or may not be suitable outside those settings. The criteria we use to judge excellence in the study of demographic trends may or may not be adequate to the study of conversation, and so on. By these lights, it is only under the specific conditions of their practical use that we may judge either the adequacy of our epistemic standards themselves or the adequacy with which they have been applied in any given case. Hence we may note that various types of scientist may hold various levels of commitment to different epistemic standards depending upon the types of research in which they participate.

Relatedly, insofar as they are devised, learned, and applied in the course of specific practical activities, it follows that in the first instance epistemic standards are tied to those activities rather than the particular people who participate in them. Whereas philosophically foundationalist epistemologies have tended to cast knowing as a relationship between an isolated rational mind (or linguistic proposition) and an enduring and self-consistent natural world, proponents of the practice turn tend to cast knowing as a matter of observably competent performance within a particular domain of practical activity (cf. Chaiklin and Lave 1993; Hutchins 1995; Lynch 1993; Weinberg 2002). Epistemic standards are thus seen to pertain to more than just the use of descriptive, explanatory, or logical propositions. They extend to the whole range of discursive and non-discursive competences required to adequately participate in a given practical domain. By these lights, epistemic standards cease to exist as fixed universal rules for validly linking "the mind" or "language" with a preformed natural world and come instead to be seen as provisional and socially situated rules for defining and identifying adequate performance.

And because their valid definition, identification, and practical engagement is inevitably predicated on these provisional and socially situated rules, the ontological characteristics of both knowing subjects and known objects lose their fixity and universality. Whatever characteristics subjects and objects are observed to possess are held to exist only in and through the embodied activities comprising the particular practical domains wherein they are observed to occur (cf. Bourdieu 1990b; Coulter 1989; Goodwin 1994; Knorr-Cetina 1999; Pickering 1995). Hence, for example, I have shown in my own work how the mental illnesses and addictions held to afflict patients in two recovery programs were given empirical form and causal force only in and through the distinctive patterns of therapeutic practice found in these programs (Weinberg 2005). Not only were patients' disorders identified and engaged in ways bearing no evident relationship to formally codified nosologies like the *DSM IV*, but assessments of both their presence and absence in patients' behavior were dictated only by the moral economy of program practice. Genetic, neurological, and other kinds of biological evidence that might be used to great advantage in other settings for the treatment of mental disorder had absolutely no part in it. This is not to argue, as some social constructionists have in the past, that ontology ought to be reduced to epistemology. Rather, it is to argue that neither our various ontologies nor our various epistemologies should be divorced from the historically and culturally situated social practices in which they arise, develop, and are given meaning and value.

The idiom of practice calls our attention to the fact that theorizing, language use, social action, and worldly events more generally, derive both their intelligibility and their value only from the socially constructed contexts within which they are observed. These social contexts may be those within which events actually occur, as when people observe and track the practical upshot of one another's actions in the course of interacting with each other. But they may also be the social contexts of more distant observers, like social scientists, who track the practical upshot of people's behavior for their own social scientific activities (Bourdieu 1984, 1987). Because different people know and value different things about these social contexts they often interpret events differently.[3] This is as true of social scientists as it is of the people they study. Neither segments of human behavior nor any other worldly events have intrinsic or unequivocal meaning. Their meanings are instead multiple and projected upon them by actors with any number of different practical interests in them. However, this by no means forecloses on the possibility of evaluating different accounts of events as more or less helpful or astute given the practical purposes for which these accounts are made. But such evaluations, and a critical consideration in the social construction of our epistemic standards, must involve identifying just what those practical purposes happen to be.

REFLEXIVITY

The expression reflexivity has a wide variety of definitions (cf. Ashmore 1989; Lynch 2000; Woolgar 1988), only some of which are pertinent here. One early definition was given by Garfinkel (1984: 4), who wrote of the "essential reflexivity of accounts of practical action." By this he meant to note the inevitable fact that, in order to make sense of one another, interactants formulate the meaning of each other's actions in light of more inclusive formulations of their relationships and their ongoing interactions. In keeping with the idiom of practice, the meaning of social action is thus seen to derive solely from its perceived practical relevance to the ongoing accomplishment of some shared activity. Pollner (1991) has called this endogenous reflexivity, reflexivity as an inevitable feature of the ordinary forms of collective action that social scientists study, and distinguished it from what he called referential reflexivity, or reflexivity as not only a topic of social scientific inquiry but a resource for it. Just as ordinary activities are seen to be reflexively organized and to reflexively constitute their realities, so too are scientific activities seen to do so (cf. Drew, Raymond, and Weinberg 2006; Holstein and Gubrium 1995). By these lights, reflexivity is conceived as a locally achieved phenomenon largely of interest to those who study dyadic or small group interactions.

Another prominent understanding of reflexivity takes a more macrosociological view. Ulrich Beck, Anthony Giddens, and Scott Lash (1994) have noted a global trend among late modern societies wherein the epistemological privilege historically accorded technical and scientific expertise itself becomes problematized, a process they have dubbed "reflexive modernization." In a related trend, factions in different political, cultural, and economic struggles have grown increasingly savvy in their ability to use experts as mercenaries – as is evident, for example, in debates concerning global warming, intelligent design, and the linkage of cigarette smoking and cancer. Scientific and technological projects are thus seen to be deeply embedded in and bound up with wider social, economic, and political activities that not only influence the direction of their development but contribute to the stability or instability of their perceived epistemic legitimacy and, indeed, the perceived legitimacy of science and technology in general. This insight has led prominent intellectuals as otherwise dissimilar as Michel Foucault and Jürgen Habermas to cast aspersions on the very possibility of dissociating technical or scientific expertise from the regimes of power within which they operate and to question the compatibility of scientific expertise and liberal democracy (see also Jasanoff 2005; Turner 2003).

We see, then, that both (1) the micro-interactional practices that engage particular researchers with their research subjects and professional colleagues, and (2) the macro-interactional practices that engage scientific (including social scientific) projects, movements, and disciplines with their wider social contexts have become the foci of empirical sociological investigation. This research decisively demonstrates, at both micro and macro levels of analysis, that the social sciences cannot be dissociated from the social worlds they seek to understand. They are, inevitably, constituent features of those worlds. Hence, beyond the litany of powerful theoretical arguments against philosophical foundationalism (Weinberg 2008), we may also point to any number of empirical demonstrations of the fact that a detached, disinterested, or value-free social science is now, and has always been, an ill-conceived illusion. Social scientific knowledge is itself socially constructed. However, it by no means follows that the interests that govern social scientific work are reducible to mere economic greed, political ambition, tribalism, or any other such generically specified interests. Following Bourdieu (1975), we may instead find that, depending on the level of institutional autonomy achieved among members of a scientific community, the interests governing their research are more or less uniquely adapted to their positions in that scientific community. Moreover, we may also find that people's interests change along with changes in their practical understanding of their research and/or their position in the social world (Pickering 1995). Therefore, the critical question is not whether or not knowledge production is governed by social interests – of course it is – but, rather, which specific interests, to what extent, how stable are these interests, and why?

A growing contingent of social scientists now takes seriously the idea that by reflexively interrogating the interests served by social scientific work we may succeed in making it a subtler and more valuable craft (cf. Bourdieu and Wacquant 1992; Camic 1996). To the extent that we have lost faith in Berger and Luckmann's (1967:

13) foundationalist claim that devising "the methodology of the social sciences . . . belongs to philosophy and is by definition other than sociology," we increasingly appreciate the need to naturalize our regard for own epistemic bearings, locating them empirically in the historical legacy of our craft and in our worldly aspirations for that craft, rather than the otherworldly realm of a putatively transcendental analytic logic. Forsaking the false dream of achieving what Rorty (1991: 13) has called a "God's eye point of view" of the world, means that we must assume responsibility for the mortality of our epistemic projects and the techniques by which we seek to see them through. This entails acquainting ourselves *empirically* with the worldly circumstances of our research, their attendant possibilities for learning and progress, and then devising the specific role(s) we would hope for our research to play in realizing those possibilities. If we no longer countenance the claim that knowledge consists in articulating the sentences in which nature would, if she could, describe herself, then we must provide more justifiable statements of what it is we think our research is, and ought to be, doing.

Some of the best-known efforts in this regard have construed the work of social scientists predominantly as a form of writing, calling attention to many of the textual techniques by which epistemic authority is conveyed (cf. Atkinson 1990; Clifford and Marcus 1986; Van Maanan 1988; Woolgar 1988). However, as often as not, these exercises have been undertaken not to epistemically ground the social sciences but to deconstruct and destabilize them. While critical interrogations of the pretenses of academic writing are by no means without value, they do little to overcome what I have been calling the constructionist dilemma of reconciling the production of tenable epistemic standards with a thoroughly empirical regard for the processes through which that production takes place. Moreover, they overlook the fact that writing is itself only one component of a much more richly organized round of *collective* activity that both influences and is influenced by what we write. Epistemic authority, and the legitimacy of the various epistemic standards upon which it rests, is not achieved unilaterally through textual tricks, but *collectively*, as all of us engaged in a given domain of knowledge production proffer mutually critical assessments of the value of our own and each other's contributions to the work and worlds we share (Pels 2000; Wacquant 1992: 36–46; Weinberg 2002, 2006). Empirically informed reflexive dialog hones our research skills by facilitating a more explicit regard for the specific nature of our collective work in all its myriad forms and the distinctive resources and constraints that attend the specific conditions under which it is accomplished. Indeed, this point can be generalized. Far from being threatened, all knowledge production stands to benefit considerably from a detailed regard for the myriad macro and micro social conditions that shape, facilitate, and constrain it.

CONCLUSION

Because social constructionism is far too diverse, both theoretically and substantively, to yield to a chapter-length synopsis, I have been content to provide only a more focused discussion of the aspects of social constructionism most interesting and important from the standpoint of contemporary social theory. To my mind, these are those aspects that pertain to the nature of knowledge as such and its relation to the worlds it concerns. Too often both boosters and critics of social constructionism alike have assumed that to argue something is socially constructed is to argue it is mythical or unreal. This assumption, of course, requires that it be possible to distinguish between the mythic and the real in ways that avoid implicating culturally and/or historically specific epistemic standards. This is precisely what I have argued here is impossible.

Neither nature, nor logic, nor the words of those we study provide guarantees that our descriptions correspond, in the positivist sense, with the things they are about. Instead, our interpretations, descriptions, analyses, and theories are socially constructed to do particular kinds of work. Their forms are thoroughly mediated by the interests and practical involvements for which they are devised. But, *contra* Descartes, these interests and practical involvements do not necessarily distort our understanding. Because no understanding of the world is disinterested or divorced from practical action, it is senseless to speak of distortion without also speaking to the specific, socially constructed, standards by which distortion is measured. These standards are inevitably contestable, in science and philosophy no less than anywhere else (Habermas 1987: 408–9). Hence, if and when epistemic disputes arise they are not, and could never be, resolved by recourse to fixed natural or logical standards. They can be resolved only by recourse to the provisional standards we ourselves create in light of the specific practical projects we hope to fulfill. These standards embody our claims to power/knowledge and we must expect to be held accountable for them. But while our claims are certainly fallible and may be flawed, they are by no means always arbitrary. Their legitimacy resides in the practices they make possible and in our willingness to defend them in open and inclusive dialog.

Notes

1   For present purposes I am treating the term "social constructionism" as synonymous with terms like "constructionism," "social constructivism," etc. Though I am aware that these terms are sometimes used to draw more refined lines of theoretical distinction, more often they are used interchangeably.

2   One might also call this research anti-ontological insofar as Garfinkel and his colleagues wished to demonstrate how both ideas *and their worldly referents* are constructed through socially situated practice. In other words, they sought to demonstrate how ideas and the things those ideas concern are socially constructed in tandem. Hence, for example, Garfinkel, Lynch, and Livingston (1981: 137) insist their analysis is not of ideas as such but the optically discovered pulsar itself as a "cultural object." The notion that ideas and their worldly referents are co-constructed has since become a major concern of so-called posthumanist or post-social investigators like Michel Callon, Donna Haraway, Bruno Latour, John Law, Karen Knorr-Cetina, and Andrew Pickering. I have more to say on this below.

3   Stephen Turner (1994) notes an unfortunate tendency among some practice theorists to neglect this fact and treat practices as if they implicate identical contents in the minds of their participants. While it may be sensible to speak of the enforcement of normative standards as causes of people's capacities to share in social practices, we should not assume these capacities take identical forms.

Bibliography

Adorno, T. W. (1990) *Negative Dialectics*. London: Routledge.

Alexander, J. C. (1982) *Theoretical Logic in Sociology*, vol. 1. Berkeley: University of California Press.

Ashmore, M. (1989) *The Reflexive Thesis*. Chicago: University of Chicago Press.

Atkinson, P. (1990) *The Ethnographic Imagination*. London: Routledge.

Barnes, B. (1974) *Scientific Knowledge and Sociological Theory*. London: Routledge.

Barnes, B. (1977) *Interests and the Growth of Knowledge*. London: Routledge & Kegan Paul.

Barnes, B., and Bloor, D. (1982) "Relativism, Rationalism and the Sociology of Knowledge," in M. Hollis and S. Lukes (eds.), *Rationality and Relativism*. Oxford: Blackwell.

Barnes, B., Bloor, D., and Henry, J. (1996) *Scientific Knowledge*. Chicago: University of Chicago Press.

Beck, U., Giddens, A., and Lash, S. (1994) *Reflexive Modernization*. Cambridge: Polity.

Berger, P. L., and Luckmann, T. (1967) *The Social Construction of Reality*. New York: Anchor.

Bloor, D. (1982) "Durkheim and Mauss Revisited: Classification and the Sociology of Knowledge." *Studies in the History and Philosophy of Science* 1(4): 267–97.

Bloor, D. (1991) *Knowledge and Social Imagery*, 2nd edn. Chicago: University of Chicago Press.

Blumer, H. (1969) *Symbolic Interactionism*. Englewood Cliffs, NJ: Prentice Hall.

Boudon, R. (2004) *The Poverty of Relativism*. Cambridge: Bardwell.

Bourdieu, P. (1975) "The Specificity of the Scientific Field and the Social Conditions for the Progress of Reason." *Social Science Information* 14(5): 19–47.

Bourdieu, P. (1984) "Social Space and the Genesis of Groups." *Theory and Society* 14(6): 723–44.

Bourdieu, P. (1987) "What Makes a Social Class? On the Theoretical and Practical Existence of Groups." *Berkeley Journal of Sociology* 32: 1–18.

Bourdieu, P. (1988) *Homo Academicus*. Stanford: Stanford University Press.

Bourdieu, P. (1990a) "Animadversiones in Mertonem," in J. Clarke, C. Modgil, and S. Modgil (eds.), *Robert K. Merton*. London: Falmer.

Bourdieu, P. (1990b) *The Logic of Practice*. Stanford: Stanford University Press.

Bourdieu, P., and Wacquant, L. J. D. (1992) *An Invitation to Reflexive Sociology*. Chicago: University of Chicago Press.

Button, G., and Sharrock, W. (1993) "A Disagreement over Agreement and Consensus in Constructionist Sociology." *Journal for the Theory of Social Behaviour* 23(1): 1–25.

Calhoun, C. (1995) *Critical Social Theory*. Oxford: Blackwell.

Calhoun, C. (ed.) (2007) *Sociology in America*. Chicago: University of Chicago Press.

Camic, C. (1996) "Alexander's Antisociology." *Sociological Theory* 14(2): 172–86.

Chaiklen, S., and Lave, J. (eds.) (1993) *Understanding Practice*. Cambridge: Cambridge University Press.

Clarke, A. (1990) "A Social Worlds Research Adventure: The Case of Reproductive Science," in S. Cozzens and T. Gieryn (eds.), *Theories of Science in Society*. Bloomington: Indiana University Press.

Clifford, J., and Marcus, G. E. (eds.) (1986) *Writing Culture*. Berkeley: University of California Press.

Collins, H. M. (1985) *Changing Order*. London: Sage.

Collins, P. H. (1991) *Black Feminist Thought*. New York: Routledge.

Coulter, J. (1989) *Mind in Action*. Atlantic Highlands, NJ: Humanities Press International.

Douglas, M. (1980) *Evans-Pritchard*. Sussex: Harvester.

Drew, P., Geoffrey R., and Weinberg, D. (eds.) (2006) *Talk and Interaction in Social Research Methods*. London: Sage.

Durkheim, É. (1954) *The Elementary Forms of the Religious Life*. New York: The Free Press.

Durkheim, É., and Mauss, M. (1963) *Primitive Classification*. Chicago: University of Chicago Press.

Fleck, L. (1979) *Genesis and Development of a Scientific Fact*. Chicago: University of Chicago Press.

Foucault, M. (1980) *Power/Knowledge*. New York: Pantheon.

Freedman, K. L. (2005) "Naturalized Epistemology, or What the Strong Programme Can't Explain." *Studies in the History and Philosophy of Science* 36: 135–48.

Garfinkel, H. (1984) *Studies in Ethnomethodology*. Cambridge: Polity.

Garfinkel, H., Lynch, M., and Livingston, E. (1981) "The Work of a Discovering Science Construed with Materials from the Optically Discovered Pulsar." *Philosophy of the Social Sciences* 11: 131–58.

Garfinkel, H., and Sacks, H. (1970) "On Formal Structures of Practical Actions," in J. C. McKinney and E. A. Tiryakian (eds.), *Theoretical Sociology*. New York: Appleton Century Crofts.

Giddens, A. (1984) *The Constitution of Society*. Berkeley: University of California Press.

Goodwin, C. (1994) "Professional Vision." *American Anthropologist* 96(3): 606–33.

Gross, P. R., and Levitt, N. (1994) *Higher Superstition*. Baltimore: Johns Hopkins University Press.

Habermas, J. (1984) *Theory of Communicative Action*, vol. 1. Boston: Beacon Press.

Habermas, J. (1987) *The Philosophical Discourse of Modernity*. Cambridge, MA: MIT Press.

Hacking, I. (1999) *The Social Construction of What?* Cambridge, MA: Harvard University Press.

Hollis, M., and Lukes, S. (eds.) (1982) *Rationality and Relativism*. Oxford: Blackwell.

Holstein, J. A., and Gubrium, J. F. (1995) *The Active Interview*. London: Sage.

Holstein, J. A., and Gubrium, J. F. (eds.) (2008) *The Handbook of Constructionist Research*. New York: Guilford.

Hutchins, E. (1995) *Cognition in the Wild*. Cambridge, MA: MIT Press.

Jasanoff, S. (2005) *Designs on Nature*. Princeton: Princeton University Press.

Knorr-Cetina, K. (1999) *Epistemic Cultures*. Cambridge, MA: Harvard University Press.

Kuhn, T. S. (1970) *The Structure of Scientific Revolutions*, 2nd edn. Chicago: University of Chicago Press.

Kusch, M. (1999) *Psychological Knowledge*. London: Routledge.

Lynch, M. (1993) *Scientific Practice and Ordinary Action*. Cambridge: Cambridge University Press.

Lynch, M. (1998) "Towards a Constructivist Genealogy of Social Constructivism," in I. Velody and R. Williams (eds.), *The Politics of Constructionism*. London: Sage.

Lynch, M. (2000) "Against Reflexivity as an Academic Virtue and Source of Privileged Knowledge." *Theory, Culture, and Society* 17(3): 27–56.

Lynch, M. (2008) "Ethnomethodology as a Provocation to Constructionism," in J. A. Holstein and J. F. Gubrium (eds.), *The Handbook of Constructionist Research*. New York: Guilford.

Mannheim, K. (1936) *Ideology and Utopia*. New York: Harvest.

Marx, K. (1983) "Theses on Feuerbach," in *The Portable Karl Marx*. London: Penguin.

Merton, R. K. (1937) "The Sociology of Knowledge." *Isis* 27(3): 493–503.

Pels, D. (1996) "The Politics of Symmetry." *Social Studies of Science* 26: 277–304.

Pels, D. (2000) "Reflexivity: One Step Up." *Theory, Culture and Society* 17(3): 1–25.

Pickering, A. (1995) *The Mangle of Practice*. Chicago: University of Chicago Press.

Pollner, M. (1987) *Mundane Reason*. Cambridge: Cambridge University Press.

Pollner, M. (1991) "Left of Ethnomethodology: The Rise and Decline of Radical Reflexivity." *American Sociological Review* 56(3): 370–80.

Rorty, R. (1980) *Philosophy and the Mirror of Nature*. Oxford: Blackwell.

Rorty, R. (1991) *Objectivity, Relativism, and Truth*. Cambridge: Cambridge University Press.

Schatzki, T. R., Knorr-Cetina, K., and von Savigny, E. (eds.) (2001) *The Practice Turn in Contemporary Theory*. London: Routledge.

Shapin, S. (1995) "Here and Everywhere: Sociology of Scientific Knowledge." *Annual Review of Sociology* 21: 289–321.

Shapin, S., and Schaffer, S. (1985) *Leviathan and the Air Pump*. Princeton: Princeton University Press.

Skinner, Q. (1989) "Language and Political Change," in T. Ball, J. Farr, and R. L. Hanson (eds.), *Political Innovation and Conceptual Change*. Cambridge: Cambridge University Press.

Smith, D. E. (1989) *The Everyday World as Problematic*. Boston: Northeastern University Press.

Sokal, A. D., and Bricmont, J. (1998) *Fashionable Nonsense*. New York: Picador.

Spector, M., and Kitsuse, J. I. (1987) *Constructing Social Problems* New York: Aldine/de Gruyter.

Star, S. L. (1989) *Regions of the Mind*. Stanford: Stanford University Press.

Thomas, W. I., and Thomas, D. S. (1928) *The Child in America*. New York: Knopf.

Turner, B. S. (1996) *The Body and Society*, 2nd edn. London: Sage.

Turner, S. (1994) *The Social Theory of Practices*. Chicago: University of Chicago Press.

Turner, S. (2003) *Liberal Democracy 3.0*. London: Sage.

Turner, S., and Turner, J. (1990) *The Impossible Science*. Newbury Park: Sage.

Van Mannan, J. (ed.) (1988) *Representation in Ethnography*. Thousand Oaks, CA: Sage.

von Schelting, A. (1936) Review of *Ideologie und Utopie* by Karl Mannheim. *American Sociological Review* 1(4): 664–74.

Wacquant, L. J. D. (1992) "Toward a Social Praxeology: The Structure and Logic of Bourdieu's Sociology," in P. Bourdieu and L. J. D. Wacquant, *An Invitation to Reflexive Sociology*. Chicago: University of Chicago Press.

Weinberg, D. (2002) "Qualitative Research Methods: An Overview," in D. Weinberg (ed.), *Qualitative Research Methods*. Oxford: Blackwell.

Weinberg, D. (2005) *Of Others Inside: Insanity, Addiction and Belonging in America*. Philadelphia: Temple University Press.

Weinberg, D. (2006) "Language, Dialogue, and Ethnographic Objectivity," in P. Drew, G. Raymond, and D. Weinberg (eds.), *Talk and Interaction in Social Research Methods*. London: Sage.

Weinberg, D. (2008) "The Philosophical Foundations of Constructionist Research," in J. A. Holstein and J. F. Gubrium (eds.), *The Handbook of Constructionist Research*. New York: Guilford.

Wiener, C. (1981) *The Politics of Alcoholism*. New Brunswick: Transaction.

Wilson, B. R. (ed.) (1970) *Rationality*. Oxford: Basil Blackwell.

Woolgar, S. (ed.) (1988) *Knowledge and Reflexivity*. London: Sage.

Woolgar, S., and Pawluch, D. (1985) "Ontological Gerrymandering: The Anatomy of Social Problems Explanations." *Social Problems* 32: 214–27.

15

Conversation Analysis as Social Theory

JOHN HERITAGE

Conversation analysis (CA) emerged as a recognizably distinct approach to the analysis of social life in the privately circulated lectures of Harvey Sacks (1992 [1964–72]). Its earliest publications, initially placed in non-sociological journals such as *American Anthropologist* (Schegloff 1968), *Semiotica* (Schegloff and Sacks 1973), and *Language* (Sacks, Schegloff, and Jefferson 1974), became visible to sociologists as an outgrowth of Harold Garfinkel's ethnomethodology (Douglas 1970; Sudnow 1972; Turner 1974). In 1975, Harvey Sacks was killed in an automobile accident, and the hiring freeze in American universities consequent on the oil shock and "stagflation" of the 1970s (Wiley 1985) forced almost all the first generation of CA graduate students into other walks of life. Dominant sociological figures of the 1970s lined up to dismiss CA as dustbowl empiricism (Coser 1975), or "do it yourself linguistics" (Goldthorpe 1973), or a "re-enchantment industry" fit only for the counter-cultural hippies of southern California (Gellner 1975). Under these circumstances CA was all but extinguished as a field of sociological analysis.

The early 1980s witnessed a resurgence of the field. The resistance of sociological journals to publish CA research resulted in the creation of several significant anthologies. Regenerated during the subsequent years of the decade, the field has now grown to become the dominant method for the sociological study of interaction, and reaches into anthropology, linguistics, communication, cognitive science, and electrical engineering. Published papers run into the thousands, and the method is practiced in many dozens of countries on all the continents of the world. Citation rates for classic CA papers have roughly doubled during each of the past two decades, and Sacks, Schegloff, and Jefferson's (1974) effort at "do it yourself linguistics" is now, according to the editor of *Language*, "by far the most cited" and downloaded paper in the journal's 80-year history (Joseph 2003).

In this essay, I suggest some ways in which CA represents a contribution to social theory. These suggestions may be thought to be tendentious, not least because Coser's calumny stuck and CA is sometimes thought of as a kind of atheoretical empiricism – a method without a substance, as he so unfortunately phrased it. This latter point of view strikes me as self-evidently false, and in what follows I sketch the CA contribution to a view of social interaction as a social institution, I give a brief account of how its institutional order articulates with other elements of social systems, and conclude with a view of CA as a contribution to a theory of self–other relations.

BACKGROUND

The proximate origins of CA are to be found in the work of Erving Goffman and Harold Garfinkel. These two giants of American social theory essentially inaugurated the study of everyday life as a research focus in its own right. They did so by dissenting from the dominant view of post-World War II sociology that the specifics of the everyday world are too random and disorderly to support systematic analysis. However they arrived at their forms of dissent from very different perspectives.

Emerging from a specifically Durkheimian tradition (Goffman 1955, 1956; Goffman and Verhoeven 1993), Goffman started from the perspective that what he came to call the interaction order (Goffman 1983) is an institutional order in its own right. The interaction order, he argued, comprises a complex set of interactional rights and obligations which are linked both to "face" (a person's immediate claims about "who s/he is" in an interaction), more enduring features of personal identity, and also to large-scale macro social institutions. Goffman also observed that the institution of interaction underlies the operation of other social institutions, mediating the business they transact, and he repeatedly rejected the idea that it is a kind of colorless, odorless substrate through which sociological and psychological processes exert their influence on human affairs (Goffman 1964; Kendon 1987). The interaction order that Goffman depicts is structural and driven by a logic which is external to the individual and which supports an objective hermeneutics of individual accountability. As Goffman wrote in the introduction to *Interaction Ritual*: "I assume that the proper study of interaction is not the individual and his psychology, but rather the syntactical relations among the acts of different persons mutually present to one another" (Goffman 1967:2).

It is this external normative order of "syntactical relations" that provides for the sequential ordering of action (Goffman 1971) and which also provides for action's public accountability. In turn, this enmeshes the individual in a web of lines and associated face claims (Goffman 1955), thereby permitting persons to analyze one another's conduct and arrive at judgments about personal motives and identities. It is a core feature of social order.

Harold Garfinkel arrived at convergent conclusions from a very different starting point: phenomenologically inspired theoretical investigations of the subjectively meaningful character of human social action. Having studied with Parsons at Harvard, Garfinkel apprehended clear deficiencies in the treatment of action, reasoning, mutual understanding, and social representations in *The Social System* (Parsons 1951) and other studies emanating from Harvard during that period (Garfinkel 1960, 1967; Heritage 1984a, 1987). Drawing on the researches of Alfred Schutz (Schutz 1962), his objections centered on the lack of process in Parsons's treatment of action, its failure to conceptualize the dynamic and methodical basis in terms of which actions are produced and recognized, weaknesses in the treatment of processes of mutual understanding in the context of action, and failures to grasp the dynamic reproduction of collective knowledge and representations accompanying this process.

Drawing on experiments with games and other "breaching experiments" which engineered departures from everyday expectations (Garfinkel 1963), Garfinkel concluded that shared methods of practical reasoning inform both the *production* of action, and the *recognition* of action and its meanings. In fact, he argued, we produce action methodically to be recognized for what it is, and we recognize action because it is produced methodically in this way. As Garfinkel made the point in his own inimitable prose: "the activities whereby members produce and manage the settings of organized everyday affairs are identical with members' procedures for making these settings accountable" (Garfinkel 1967). His experiments clearly indicated that social actions, shared understandings, and, ultimately, social institutions are underpinned by a complex body of presuppositions, tacit assumptions, and methods of inference – in short, a body of methods or methodology – that informs the production and recognition of culturally meaningful objects and actions (see CHAPTER 8).

Methods of commonsense reasoning are fundamentally adapted to the recognition and understanding of events-in-context. In Garfinkel's analysis, ordinary understandings are the product of a circular process in which an event and its background are dynamically adjusted to one another to form a coherent "gestalt." Garfinkel described this process, following Mannheim, as "the documentary method of interpretation," and he argued that it is a ubiquitous feature of the recognition of all objects and events, from the most mundane features of everyday existence to the most recondite of scientific or artistic achievements. In this process, linkages are assembled between an event and its physical and social background using a variegated array of presuppositions and inferential procedures. The documentary method embodies the property of reflexivity: changes in an understanding of an event's context will evoke some shift or elaboration of a person's grasp of the focal event and vice versa. When it is employed in a temporally dynamic context, which is a characteristic of all situations of social action and interaction, the documentary method forms the basis for temporally updated shared understandings of actions and events among the participants.

CONVERSATION ANALYSIS

Conversation analysis, developed by Harvey Sacks in association with Emanuel Schegloff and Gail Jefferson, emerged at the intersection of the perspectives developed by Goffman and Garfinkel. The two men most centrally involved in its foundation, Harvey Sacks and Emanuel Schegloff, were both students of Erving Goffman at the University of California at Berkeley during the 1960s, and also had frequent and extensive contact with Harold Garfinkel at UCLA during the same period (Schegloff 1992a). From Goffman, CA took the notion that talk-in-interaction is a fundamental social domain that can be studied as an institutional entity in its own right. From Garfinkel came the notion that the practices and procedures with which parties produce and recognize talk are talk's "ethnomethods." They form the resources which the parties unavoidably must use and rely on to produce and recognize contributions to interaction which are mutually intelligible in specific ways, and which inform the participants' grasp of the context of their interaction in a continuously updated, step-by-step fashion. This fusion is directly expressed in one of the earliest published papers in CA:

> We have proceeded under the assumption . . . that in so far as the materials we worked with exhibited orderliness, they did so not only for us, indeed not in the first place for us, but for the co-participants who had produced them. If the materials (records of natural conversation) were orderly, they were so because they had been methodically produced by members of the society for one another. (Schegloff and Sacks 1973)

From these early papers and Sacks's lectures (Sacks 1992 [1964–72]), CA emerged as a study of the institution of conversation that focuses on the procedural basis of its production. This basis was conceived as a site of massive order and regularity, whose normative organization and empirical regularities could be addressed using the sorts of basic observational techniques that a naturalist might use in studying animals or plants (Sacks 1984a). As it has emerged, the field has consolidated around two basic theoretical and methodological assumptions.

The structural analysis of action in ordinary conversation

Fundamental to the inception of CA is the notion that social interaction is informed by institutionalized structural organizations of practices to which participants are normatively oriented. It is this structural assumption, which is fundamentally associated with Goffman, that differentiates CA as an approach to the *study of social action* from sociolinguistics, which focuses on variations in language (such as accent and dialect) and their sociological determinants, and the sociology of language, which fundamentally considers languages in relation to the nation-state and other macro-level social processes.

Within this view structure underlies variations in its implementation. Associated with this view is the notion that these organizations of practices – as the conditions on which the achievement of mutually intelligible and concerted interaction depends – are fundamentally independent of the motivational, psychological, or sociological characteristics of the participants. Rather than being dependent on these characteristics, conversational practices are the medium through which these sociological and psychological characteristics manifest themselves.

It is this structural assumption which informs, in fact mandates, the basic CA imperative to isolate organizations of practices in talk without reference to the sociological or psychological characteristics of the participants. For example, a structured set of turn-taking procedures is presupposed in the recognition of an "interruption." Moreover, both the turn-taking procedures and the associated recognizability of interruptive departures from them are anterior to, and independent of, empirical distributions of interruptions as between males and females or between powerful and powerless individuals. It is thus only after the structural features of, for example, turn-taking and interruption have been determined that it is meaningful to search for the ways in which sociological factors such as gender, class, ethnicity, etc., or psychological dispositions such as extroversion, may be manifested – whether causally or expressively – in interactional conduct.

From its inception, CA has placed a primary focus on the sequential organization of interaction. Underlying this notion are a number of fundamental ideas. First, in doing some current action, speakers normally project (empirically) and require (normatively) the relevance of a "next" or range of possible "next" actions to be done by a subsequent speaker (Schegloff 1972). Second, in constructing a turn at talk, speakers normally address themselves to preceding talk and, most commonly, the immediately preceding talk (Sacks 1987, 1992; Schegloff and Sacks 1973). Speakers design their talk in ways that exploit this basic positioning (Schegloff 1984), thereby exposing the fundamental role of this sequential contextuality in their utterances. Third, by the production of next actions, speakers show an understanding of a prior action and do so at a multiplicity of levels – for example, by an "acceptance," an actor can show an understanding that the prior turn was possibly complete, that it was addressed to them, that it was an action of a particular type (e.g. an invitation) and so on. These understandings are (tacitly) confirmed or can become the objects of repair at any third turn in an ongoing sequence (Schegloff 1992b).

CA starts from the presumption that all three of these features – the grasp of a "next" action that a current projects, the production of that next action, and its interpretation by the previous speaker – are the products of a common set of socially shared and structured procedures. CA analyses are thus simultaneously analyses of action, context management, and intersubjectivity because all three of these features are simultaneously, if tacitly, the objects of the actors' actions. Finally, the procedures that inform these activities are normative in that actors can be held morally accountable both for departures from their use and for the inferences which their use, or departures from their use, may engender. This analytic perspective represents a crystallization into a clear set of empirical working practices of the accumulated assumptions embodied in a wide range of ethno-scientific approaches described elsewhere (Heritage 2002a).

The primacy of ordinary conversation

The second assumption can be stated more briefly. It is that "ordinary conversation" between peers represents a fundamental domain for analysis and that the analysis of ordinary conversation represents a basic resource for the extension of CA into other "non-conversational" domains. This conception was first expressed in work on turn-taking (Sacks, Schegloff, and Jefferson 1974), by which point it had become apparent that ordinary conversation differs in systematic ways from, for example, interaction in the law courts or news interviews. The conceptualization of these differences has developed substantially in recent years (Drew and Heritage 1992; Heritage 2005; Heritage and Clayman, forthcoming).

There is every reason to view ordinary conversation as the fundamental domain of interaction, and indeed as a primordial form of human sociality (Schegloff 1996a). It is the predominant form of human interaction in the social world and the primary medium of communication to which the child is exposed and through which socialization proceeds. It thus antedates the development of other, more specialized, forms of "institutional" interaction both phylogenetically in the life of society and ontogenetically in the life of the individual. Moreover, the practices of ordinary conversation appear to have a "bedrock" or default status. When they are subject to processes of historical change these tend to be slow and unrecognized, nor are they generally subject to discursive justification (by reference, for example, to logic, equity, or efficiency) in ways that practices of interaction in legal, medical, pedagogical, and other institutions manifestly are. Research is increasingly showing that communicative conduct in more specialized social institutions embodies task- or role-oriented specializations and particularizations that generally involve a narrowing of the range of conduct that is generically found in ordinary conversation (see below). The latter thus embodies a diversity and range of combinations of interactional practices that is unmatched elsewhere in the social world. Interactional conduct in institutional environments, by contrast, embodies socially imposed and often irksome departures from that range (Atkinson 1982).

ORDERS OF ANALYSIS

Acceptance of the notion that conversation embodies a specific institutional order invites investigation of its constituent practices in terms of their contribution to fundamental aspects of conversational and social organization. A number of domains of organization are the objects of continuing investigation (Schegloff 2006).

Turn-taking

The first is what Schegloff (2006) calls the "turn-taking" problem, which concerns "who should talk or move or act next and when should they do so." Turns at talk are valued in their own right and they represent a scarce resource because, ordinarily, only one person can talk at a time. Even in two-party conversation the coordination problem is considerable: granted that one party has the floor, how is it to be managed that the speaker's turn has ended and the recipient should begin talking? The problem is significantly greater in multi-party interactions. A solution to this problem is necessary for coordinated social action to occur at all.

In the well-known analysis developed by Sacks, Schegloff, and Jefferson (1974), the turn-taking problem is solved via a normative system in which single units of talk are allocated to speakers, at the end of which a next speaker (which includes a current one) is allocated a next unit via an ordered set of rules. The significance of this solution is that it is stated in terms of units of talk and rules for their allocation, rather than persons and their social attributes. An institutional problem is resolved in a completely institutionalized way.

An important facet of this solution is that, through the turn-taking system, the parties administer rights both to claim occupancy of a turn-space and to "own" the talk which is implemented within it – the latter being particularly apparent in the management of turns in which a second speaker completes a first speaker's sentence (Lerner 1989, 2004). Though the implementation of these rights is most often semi-automated and outside the sphere of what Giddens (1984) calls discursive consciousness, violations of these rights (for example in interruptions [Jefferson 2004a; Schegloff 2000]) become visible as complainable departures from the norms of turn occupancy (Schegloff 2002). The turn-taking system is not merely "technical," it is also "moral" – a dimension which it shares with other systems through which the interaction order is managed.

Sequence organization

A second problem is the "sequence organizational" problem and concerns "how successive turns or actions are formed up to be 'coherent'" (Schegloff 2006). The central insight that drives the CA approach to this problem is that contributions to interaction anticipate, invite, and in some cases require responses. This is largely because these contributions are situated in an action space within which social rights and obligations are mobilized. Turns at talk offer or request goods and services (including information), position their producers relative to others in social relations and epistemic space, and undertake courses of action embracing narrative, play, humor, and. beyond these, the whole kaleidoscope of conjoint human conduct from shaking hands to making love.

The starting point for work on sequential organization was the observation that some first actions make certain kinds of next actions unavoidably relevant, to the point that if the relevant next action is not done it will be "noticeably absent," and may be the object of sanctions or other remedial measures (Sacks 1992 [1968]; Schegloff 1968). A central property of these sequences of actions, termed adjacency pairs, is that of "conditional relevance." Conditional relevance is readily apparent as a feature of greetings (which require return greetings), questions (which require answers, or at least responses), and related actions.

This analysis opened up two crucial features of the "sequence organizational problem". First and prospectively in time, it provided a mechanism through which an agent can get another to do something (Heritage 1984a; Schegloff and Sacks 1973). At the same time it provides an institutionalized motivation for the other to respond – to avoid sanctions, or the inferences which might otherwise be drawn from failure to respond. Second, and retrospectively in time, it provided a mechanism through which mutual understandings might be managed in interaction. For the second action, in being designed as a response to the first, must perforce display an analysis of what kind of "first" it is. And the doer of the first can inspect the second action to determine whether the second embodied an appropriate or correct understanding of the first. Embedded in sequence structure therefore is an apparatus through which intersubjective understandings of social actions can be displayed, checked, and, where necessary, corrected (Schegloff 1992b, 2007).

Adjacency pairs provide an armature around which secondary organizations can form. These organizations can be schematically represented as expansions that are organized in relation to a "base" adjacency pair (figure 15.1). Most of these expansions address the appropriateness of first actions, management of the prospects that desirable second actions will come to pass, and management of situations in which those second actions depart from the expectations (or desires) of the producers of first actions. Detailed description of these organizations is beyond the scope of this chapter, but they are extensively described in Schegloff (2007).

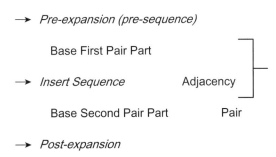

Figure 15.1 Adjacency pairs and their expansions

Of course social interaction is not exclusively built up from actions embodying this level of normative constraint. A majority of actions invite response without requiring it and are less constraining of its content. A conceptualization recently developed by Stivers and Rossano (2007) suggests that pressure to respond is mobilized through a variety of dimensions of action, including gaze, intonation, epistemic imbalance between actors, and aspects of interrogative syntax (or morphology). In this viewpoint, more "relaxed" sequences of interaction are mobilized and realized in a step-by-step process through these locally implemented response-mobilizing resources, while the more canonically constraining adjacency pair formats involve the simultaneous deployment of many if not all of them.

Intersubjectivity and repair

Little can be achieved in interaction if the parties cannot grasp what is being said to them or grasp it incorrectly. Indeed as Schegloff (2006: 77) has noted, "if the organization of talk in interaction supplies the basic infrastructure through which the institutions and social organization of quotidian life are implemented, it had better be pretty reliable, and have ways of getting righted if beset by trouble." The organization of repair consists of a coordinated set of practices designed to address problems of speaking, hearing, or understanding talk (Schegloff, Jefferson, and Sacks 1977). These practices are implemented within a narrowly defined temporal space that begins in the speaker's current turn, extends through the responsive turn, and ends at the initial speaker's next turn. Correspondingly, the organization of repair is distinctively formed and implemented as between speaker-initiated and executed repairs, and repair that is initiated and/or executed by a recipient. Repair must necessarily involve practices for identifying what is being (or to be) fixed and which is the replacement, and these differ between speakers and recipients.

Similar to turn-taking, the organization of repair is generally designed to respect the rights of speakers to "say what they wish to say" and to own it. By definition, a current speaker has the first opportunity to fix problems encountered in an ongoing turn at talk, and if unfixed problems are encountered by recipients the latter will tend to *initiate* repair on the prior speaker's talk rather than attempting to fix it unilaterally (Schegloff, Jefferson, and Sacks 1977) or, in contexts where the speaker's turn is in trouble, wait for the speaker to solicit assistance (Goodwin and

Goodwin 1986). Moreover unilateral fixes, when they occur, tend to be disguised or off-record (Jefferson 1987), or indeed "abdicated" (Jefferson 2007). However the rights of speakers in the context of repair do not extend indefinitely. In a remarkably apt, but imaginary, illustration of a Wittgensteinian language game, Stanley Cavell (1968: 159) observes that:

> "It is always conceivable" that, for example, the language game(s) we now play with the question "What did you say?" should not have been played. What are we conceiving if we conceive this? Perhaps that when we ask this of A, only A's father is allowed to answer, or that it is answered always by repeating the next to last remark you made, or that it is answered by saying what you wished you had said, or perhaps that we can never remember what we just said, or perhaps simply we have no way of asking that question . . .

And he asks:

> What would our lives look like, what very general facts would be different, if these conceivable alternatives were in fact operative? (There would, for example, be different ways and purposes for lying; a different social structure; different ways of attending to what is said; different weight put on our words; and so forth.)

The organization of repair is implicated in another great principle of conversational organization: the principle of progressivity (Schegloff 1979). In a brilliant passage, Schegloff (2007: 14–15) frames the issue in this way:

> Among the most pervasively relevant features in the organization of talk-and-other-conduct-in-interaction is the relationship of adjacency or "nextness." . . . Moving from some element to a hearably-next-one with nothing intervening is the embodiment of, and the measure of, progressivity. Should something intervene between some element and what is hearable as a/the next one due – should something violate or interfere with their contiguity, whether next sound, next word or next turn – it will be heard as qualifying the progressivity of the talk, and will be examined for its import, for what understanding should be accorded it. Each next element of such a progression can be inspected to find how it reaffirms the understanding-so-far of what has preceded, or favors one or more of the several such understandings that are being entertained, or how it requires reconfiguration of that understanding.

Schegloff notes that the organization of repair is sensitive to this fundamental principle of progressivity at the within-turn level where the progression of an action is at issue (Schegloff 1979), and at the level of sequence where progression involves a jointly constructed course of action (Schegloff 2007). Within the matrix of repair practices, progressivity is pitted against intersubjectivity (Heritage 2007a) and, as Schegloff (2006: 79) also notes, these practices "make intersubjectivity always a matter of immediate and local determination, not one of abstract and general shared facts, views or stances." As Garfinkel (1967: 30) repeatedly noted, shared understanding is constructed from a multiplicity of methods of talking. The organization of repair permits humans to exploit these multiplex connections between language and the world, while providing a safety net when our high-wire act with language goes awry.

The epistemic order

A large proportion of interaction involves the conveying of information. In this process persons continually position themselves with respect to the epistemic order: what they know relative to others, what they are entitled to know, and what they are entitled to describe or communicate. This activity is the object of highly elaborated management practices (Pomerantz 1980). Epistemic positioning is, first and foremost, conducted with reference to co-interactants in the here and now, but may also involve non-present others, commonsense knowledge, and more abstract and socially patterned rights and obligations to knowledge.

Epistemic positioning is conducted through the entire resources of language and sequence organization (Goodwin 1979; Goodwin 1996; Heritage 2007b). For example, declarative sentences ordinarily establish a positive epistemic gradient between speaker and hearer. Declaratives encode the speaker's right to know and to assert what is being declared, rights which are commonly predicated on the assumption that the speaker knows something that the recipient does not. Correspondingly, interrogative sentences ordinarily establish a negative epistemic gradient between speaker and hearer. They encode the speaker's desire to obtain information, a desire which is commonly predicated on the assumption that the question recipient knows something that the questioner does not.

These gradients can be adjusted through practices of turn design (Pomerantz 1988). The assertion that "John's coming" can be epistemically downgraded in certainty ("John may be coming"), or presented as a matter of belief ("I think John's coming"), or hearsay ("Bill says that John's coming" [Pomerantz 1984a]). Correspondingly, the question "Is John coming?" can be adjusted to reduce the negative gradient between speaker and recipient: "John's coming isn't he?" or "Surely John's coming?". Numbers of interactional practices are available to subvert or resist the positionings that these designs instantiate (Heritage 1998, 2007b; Raymond 2003; Schegloff and Lerner 2006).

Over and above turn design, considerable sequential resources are devoted to establishing and securing relative epistemic positioning. For example, pre-announcement sequences ("Did you hear about X?") are commonly implemented prior to informings as a means of establishing that what is purportedly and projectedly new information is indeed new (Terasaki 2004). Similar issues attend the delivery of stories (Goodwin 1984, 1986; Sacks 1974). Responses to information recurrently contain elements that allow tellers to infer that the epistemic gradient on which their action was based was indeed the case, and that what was said was informative to the recipient. For example, the word "oh" is virtually dedicated to this task (Heritage 1984b, 1998, 2002b).

Other practices addressed to the epistemic order between interactants include sequential positioning: a first describer has implied epistemic authority in relation to some described state of affairs relative to a second speaker even when the parties are in full agreement. Thus a range of additional practices is required when the epistemic claims related to going first and going second require modification (Heritage and

Raymond 2005; Raymond and Heritage 2006; Schegloff 1996b; Stivers 2005). In another dimension of interaction, the selection of referring expressions embodies very precise recognition of who and what an interlocutor knows, while also encoding nuanced information about the purposes of utterance (Sacks and Schegloff 1979; Schegloff 1972, 1996c; Stivers 2007). Finally speakers may show exceptional caution in describing states of affairs that fly in the face of mundane expectations and commonsense knowledge (Jefferson 2004b; Sacks 1984b).

The intensity with which epistemic positions, rights, and obligations are indexed and policed in practices of turn design and sequence organization is vivid testimony to their fundamental status within social relations. This is not simply a matter, important though it is, of the construction of epistemic communities and cultures. It is also intertwined with the ownership of experience and of rights to its expression. Very fundamental rights to knowledge and opinion accrue to persons who have them by virtue of personal experience (Sacks 1984b), and the interactional policing of epistemic claims is arguably central to the management and maintenance of personal identity (Raymond and Heritage 2006). Correspondingly, reconciliation of personally owned knowledge and experience with the "better knowledge" of distinctively expert and empowered epistemic communities is a central dilemma for modern societies in which expert knowledge (for example, of "risk") cannot be directly translated into the coin of personal experience.

Social solidarity

A common theme from the social contract theory of the seventeenth century through to contemporary game theory and ethology is that social relations in groups involve a tradeoff between competition and cooperation (Byrne and Whiten 1988; Dunbar 1996; Goffman 1971). To conceptualize this tradeoff in social interaction it is useful to draw on Brown and Levinson's (1987) extension of Goffman's analysis of face. In Brown and Levinson's analysis, each person is conceived as having two kinds of face wants: (1) positive face wants involving the desire for affirmation and acceptance, and (2) negative face wants involving the desire to remain unimpeded. This extension itself echoes the social contract tradition of political theory, in particular the concepts of liberty advocated by Hobbes and Rousseau respectively (Berlin 1969). In the spirit of Goffman's treatment of Durkheim's concept of ritual, social interaction can be viewed as driven by social contract considerations writ small, and as an arena within which individuals pursue personal objectives while maximizing and, where necessary, trading off, both of these classes of face wants.

Almost, if not all, social actions position both the actor and the recipient in social space, thereby defining (or at least proposing) a social relationship between them. Greetings, for example, invoke recognition of another and invite reciprocation and ratification of that recognition. Requests assert the legitimacy of the requested thing, the requester's right to request it of the recipient, and invoke the requestee's obligation to supply it and so on. As Goffman (1971: 95) noted, even the act of speaking expresses a right to speech and a corresponding obligation to listen. The sequence organizational conventions of the interaction order provide important resources that tilt social action in favor of cooperation.

A primary resource is preference organization. This term describes the formats of turns in which, broadly speaking, affiliative and disaffiliative actions are performed. Granted a first action that requires response, affirming and affiliative actions are done briefly and with no delay, while disaffiliative and rejecting actions are signaled by delay and other pre-indications that there is trouble ahead. The import of this patterning, which is highly regular and clearly insitutionalized, is that the probability of affiliative actions actually occurring is maximized, while the probability of disaffiliative actions actually occurring is minimized (Davidson 1984; Pomerantz 1984b; Sacks 1987).

Just as significant in this regard is conduct when face-threatening rejections are produced. As Goffman (1971) was among the first to note, rejections are overwhelmingly associated with accounts. In a context in which a first action embodies a range of ways in which speakers presuppositionally position themselves relative to recipients in terms of needs, desires, rights, and obligations, accounts address which one of these presuppositions is defective. In this context, inability and other kinds of "no fault" accounts predominate (Heritage 1984a) for the simple reason that they manage contexts of rejection so that contingent grounds are invoked rather than those that threaten the presumptive relationship between the parties. In this connection, accounts function as "secondary elaborations of belief" that preserve not only the status quo of the relationship, thereby permitting its future use, but also, and ultimately, the normative underpinnings of social action itself (Heritage 1987, 1988).

While the discussion has so far focused on second (responsive) actions, it is of course the case that large numbers of first actions are also (potentially) face-threatening. Requests intrude on recipients' negative face (Brown and Levinson 1987), as does troubles-telling (Jefferson 1980, 1988), while the delivery of bad news may damage both the positive and negative face of its recipients. Complex sequential negotiations surround these activities (Maynard 2003; Schegloff 1988), and turn design is routinely the object of efforts to maintain a balance between the assertion of entitlement to a good and a recognition of the contingencies that may surround its provision (Curl, Drew, and Ogden forthcoming). More generally, persons in interaction must continually position themselves relative to one another in terms of rights and obligations, the imposition of burdens on others, hierarchy and social distance, and of course the formulation of positions of relatedness, friendship, and love (Brown and Levinson 1987). Goffman (1955) recognized these concerns as lying at the core of social order:

> An unguarded glance, a momentary change in tone of voice, an ecological position taken or not taken, can drench a talk with judgmental significance. Therefore, just as there is no occasion of talk in which improper impressions could not intentionally or unintentionally arise, so there is no occasion of talk so trivial as not to require each participant to show serious concern for the way he handles himself and the others present.

After decades of research on language and social interaction, the relevance of these concerns is beyond question.

THE INTERACTION ORDER AS AN INSTITUTION

What kind of institution is the interaction order as sketched in these few paragraphs? At its most basic it is an institutional order that regulates the relationships within the simplest social system there can be. This social system comprises just two persons: self and other. In a famous discussion, John Rawls (1971) suggests that human cooperation might be maximized if the principles underpinning a just and fair society were conceived and agreed by persons who could not know in advance what their actual position in such a society was to be. Such a state of affairs is of course wholly counterfactual. Yet, with regard to the rights and obligations of the interaction order, the Rawlsian conception may be less far-fetched. All human interaction involves continuous interchange between the roles of speaker and hearer. Rights and obligations to speak and listen fluctuate accordingly and are accommodated within a turn-taking system that administers opportunities to act without much reference to the particular actors involved. In sequence organization, rights to mobilize response are available to all competent users of the language on every occasion of its use. In acts of speaking, a person may at any point be the producer, or the recipient, of talk that is in need of repair. The rights and obligations associated with those roles are distributed in accordance with the primary rights of the speaker – as agent – to be understood in the way that he or she wishes to be understood, and the secondary rights of recipients to demand that speakers make themselves clear. In regard to knowledge, epistemic gradients can fluctuate from moment to moment between participants depending on the topic, or its details, under discussion. The management of solidary face relationships is an obligation of speakers just as it is of recipients, and at all points in interaction.

It is perhaps for just these reasons that a powerful sense of injustice can be mobilized by departures from the conventions of the interaction order – the interruptions, snubs, and impositions of persons who could have, and should have, known better and acted differently. By the same token, it may not be unrealistic to find in the pragmatics of communication a universal foundation for a theory of freedom and justice (Habermas 1970, 1979). At the same time, as Parsons (1951) was pre-eminent in recognizing, a normative order is not to be confused with an empirical one. Symmetrical rights in a fluctuating interactional order do not translate into symmetrical rights in a social one. An "equal opportunity" interaction order self-evidently does not translate into "equal opportunity" social relations, nor is the interaction order any prophylactic against inequality. The manipulation of expectations is almost certainly a fundamental feature of hominid evolution (Byrne and Whiten 1988), and the manipulation of normative expectations is a mechanism of social advantage. Indeed departures from symmetrical rights, whether enforced through the medium of interaction or by other means, may be a central means by which the "oil" of power is gleaned from the "shale" of interaction.

THE INTERACTION ORDER AND SOCIETAL INSTITUTIONS

It is clear that, as Goffman (1983) observed in his presidential address to the American Sociological Association, the interaction order is an institution that mediates the operation of other institutions in society. Without the interaction order, the institutions which are the primary subject matter of sociology – the economy, polity, law religion, war-making, the reproductive (family, socialization, education), and the reparative (medicine) – cannot function. All of them rest on the institution of talk. Moreover, as Schegloff (2006) notes, the institution of talk can survive the collapse of these other institutions more or less unscathed. And indeed it survives across historical time and changing social structures: with some adjustments for culture and diction, we can "follow" the interactions portrayed in Shakespeare and Euripides, Chaucer and Aeschylus.

At the same time, it is clear that the interaction order undergoes significant modification when it is pressed into institutional purposes. No one could mistake questioning in a school classroom, for the give and take of question and answer in ordinary conversation (Heritage 1984a; Levinson 1992). Nor could either of these be confused with questioning in a courtroom (Atkinson and Drew 1979; Drew 1992), a news interview (Clayman and Heritage 2002), or a medical consultation (Boyd and Heritage 2006). Within the interactional matrix of these institutions, every resource that can be deployed to make conversation "ordinary" can be deployed to make these interactions expressive of institutional purpose and asymmetry (Drew and Heritage 1992).

In his address, Goffman wrestled with the interaction order's intrication within normative systems which, whether based on the fundamentals of class, race, and ethnicity or lodged in institutional roles or both, lead to social outcomes that are distant from the Rawlsian ideal. He was right to do so. In many languages, interactants are grammatically obligated to encode markers of relative status between speaker and hearer. In such languages orientations to relative social status, because they are grammaticalized, are built into the structure of every act of communication (Agha 1994; Brown and Gilman 1960; Enfield 2007). In the absence of sanctions and regulation, the interaction order offers no defense against the dynamics of exclusion, or of in-group formations (Goodwin 2006), nor against unconscious institutional racism in the interactional treatment of persons, nor the outcomes of that treatment (Stivers and Majid 2007; van Ryn and Fu 2003), nor, again, against the confluences of interactional and social power which it mediates (Kollock, Blumstein, and Schwartz 1985; West 1984a, 1984b). Investigation into how interaction is embedded in the reproduction of race, class, and gender inequalities, though overdue, is a clear prospect for contemporary CA research (Kitzinger 2005a, 2005b; Land and Kitzinger 2005; Speer 2005).

CONCLUSION

In his war diary of 1918, Georg Simmel (1923) distinguished between sociological legacies that are in cash and in real estate. Viewed in these terms, both the method and the substance of CA have a distinctly landed appearance. They are paradigmatic in Kuhn's (1962) sense of the term. An existing, but evolving, body of methods and findings ranging across data collection, representation, and analysis have become broadly standard in the field. The method and its substance are contiguous with, and capable of interfacing with, other styles of sociological analysis, including both qualitative and quantitative methods. The relevance of the method and its substance across a range of disciplines from electrical engineering, robotics, and cognitive

science, through linguistics, psychology, and anthropology are widely acknowledged. Applications of the method to the study of social institutions are so extensive
as to be beyond the descriptive scope of this chapter. In short, a large amount of
highly fertile sociological territory has been recovered from the chaotic riparian
swamps to which the analysis of interaction was consigned by an earlier generation
of scholars from Parsons (1951) to Chomsky (1957).

All but invisible to most sociologists, CA has also evolved into a large-scale,
cross-cultural, cross-linguistic field. It is a major contributor to an emerging cross-
disciplinary domain of study that asks what it is to be distinctively human, and that
responds in terms of converging trends in neurobiology, zoology, evolutionary
theory, anthropology, and psychology (Enfield and Levinson 2006). The questions
to which this field is addressed are strikingly similar to those that animated Mead's
(1934) analysis of mind, self, and society nearly a century ago – the distinctive
nature of mind (and mind-reading) and human intentionality (Astington 2006), its
embeddedness in stable sequences of interaction, its involvement in self and identity,
and its cultural, social, and anthropological variability.

The distinctively sociological contribution of CA to this enterprise is to establish
the existence of stable organizations of human interaction, and to situate them
firmly within an understanding of social relations. It is a very considerable elaboration of the theoretical inheritance accrued from Goffman and Garfinkel and, more
distally, from Durkheim and Mead. It has involved a paradigm shift in the conceptualization of human action from the notion of a (or even "the") structure of
social action (Parsons 1937) to a pluralized conception of variegated structures
(Atkinson and Heritage 1984) designed to meet the fundamental exigencies of
human life described here, together with others described elsewhere (Schegloff
2006).

At the end of "On Face Work," Goffman (1955) observed that "universal human
nature is not a very human thing." However the same claim may not so easily be
made about the interaction order. Sacks, Schegloff, and Jefferson's (1974) model of
turn-taking has held up across numerous languages, as have the Schegloff-originated
models of repair and person reference (Enfield and Stivers 2007). Even minutiae of
interaction, such as systematic practices for showing that a question was inappro-
priately asked, have been found across languages as diverse and distant as English
and Mandarin (Heritage 1998; Wu 2004). In the preface to *Presumptive Meanings*,
Levinson (2000: xiv) observes that:

> Current perspectives on the relation between universal human nature and cultural
> factors often seem to me to be inverted: for example, language is held to be essentially
> universal, whereas language use is thought to be more open to cultural influences. But
> the reverse may in fact be far more plausible: there is obvious cultural codification of
> many aspects of language from phoneme to syntactic construction, whereas the uncodi-
> fied, unnoticed, low-level background of usage principles or strategies may be funda-
> mentally culture-independent . . . Underlying presumptions, heuristics and principles of
> usage may be more immune to cultural influence simply because they are prerequisites
> for the system to work at all, preconditions even for learning language.

Perhaps there is, after all, an interaction order for all of humankind.

Acknowledgment

I would like to thank Steve Clayman and Paul Drew for their comments on an earlier draft of this chapter.

Bibliography

Agha, A. (1994). "Honorification." *Annual Review of Anthropology* 23: 277–302.

Astington, J. W. (2006). "The Developmental Interdependence of Theory of Mind and Language," in N. C. Enfield and S. C. Levinson (eds.), *Roots of Human Sociality*. London: Berg.

Atkinson, J. M. (1982). "Understanding Formality: Notes on the Categorisation and Production of 'Formal' Interaction." *British Journal of Sociology* 33: 86–117.

Atkinson, J. M., and Drew, P. (1979). *Order in Court: The Organisation of Verbal Interaction in Judicial Settings*. London: Macmillan.

Atkinson, J. M., and Heritage, J. (eds.) (1984). *Structures of Social Action: Studies in Conversation Analysis*. Cambridge: Cambridge University Press.

Berlin, I. (1969). "Two Concepts of Liberty," in I. Berlin, *Four Essays on Liberty*. London: Oxford University Press.

Boyd, E., and Heritage, J. (2006). "Taking the History: Questioning During Comprehensive History Taking," in J. Heritage and D. Maynard (eds.), *Communication in Medical Care: Interactions between Primary Care Physicians and Patients*. Cambridge: Cambridge University Press.

Brown, P., and Levinson, S. C. (1987). *Politeness: Some Universals in Language Usage*. Cambridge: Cambridge University Press.

Brown, R., and Gilman, A. (1960). "The Pronouns of Power and Solidarity," in T. A. Sebeok (ed.), *Style in Language*. Cambridge, MA: MIT Press.

Byrne, R., and Whiten, A. (eds.) (1988). *Machiavellian Intelligence: Social Expertise and the Evolution of Intellect in Monkeys, Apes and Humans*. Oxford: Oxford University Press.

Cavell, S. (1968). "The Availability of Wittgenstein's Later Philosophy," in G. Pitcher (ed.), *Wittgenstein: The Philosophical Investigations*. London: Macmillan.

Chomsky, N. (1957). *Syntactic Structures*. The Hague: Mouton.

Clayman, S., and Heritage, J. (2002). *The News Interview: Journalists and Public Figures on the Air*. Cambridge: Cambridge University Press.

Coser, L. (1975). "Two Methods in Search of a Substance." *American Sociological Review* 40: 691–700.

Curl, T., Drew, P., and Ogden, R. (forthcoming). *Linguistic Resources for Social Action*. Cambridge: Cambridge University Press.

Davidson, J. (1984). "Subsequent Versions of Invitations, Offers, Requests, and Proposals Dealing with Potential or Actual Rejection," in J. M. Atkinson and J. Heritage (eds.), *Structures of Social Action*. Cambridge: Cambridge University Press.

Douglas, J. (ed.) (1970). *Understanding Everyday Life*. Chicago: Aldine.

Drew, P. (1992). "Contested Evidence in a Courtroom Cross-Examination: The Case of a Trial for Rape," in P. Drew and J. Heritage (eds.), *Talk at Work: Social Interaction in Institutional Settings*. Cambridge: Cambridge University Press.

Drew, P., and Heritage, J. (eds.) (1992). *Talk at Work*. Cambridge: Cambridge University Press.

Dunbar, R. (1996). *Grooming, Gossip and the Evolution of Language*. London: Faber & Faber.

Enfield, N. J. (2007). "Meanings of the Unmarked: How 'Default' Person Reference Does More Than Just Refer," in N. J. Enfield and T. Stivers (eds.), *Person Reference in Interaction: Linguistic, Cultural and Social Perspectives*. Cambridge: Cambridge University Press.

Enfield, N. J., and Levinson, S. C. (eds.) (2006). *Roots of Human Sociality: Culture, Cognition, and Interaction*. London: Berg.

Enfield, N. J., and Stivers, T. (2007). *Person Reference in Interaction: Linguistic, Cultural and Social Perspectives*. Cambridge: Cambridge University Press.

Garfinkel, H. (1960). "A Comparison of Decisions Made on Four 'Pre-Theoretical' Problems by Talcott Parsons and Alfred Schuetz." Unpublished mimeo, UCLA.

Garfinkel, H. (1963). "A Conception of, and Experiments with, 'Trust' as a Condition of Stable Concerted Actions," in O. J. Harvey (ed.), *Motivation and Social Interaction*. New York: Ronald Press.

Garfinkel, H. (1967). *Studies in Ethnomethodology*. Englewood Cliffs, NJ: Prentice Hall.

Gellner, E. (1975). "Ethnomethodology: Re-enchantment Industry or Californian Way of Subjectivity." *Philosophy of the Social Sciences* 5: 431–50.

Giddens, A. (1984). *The Constitution of Society: Outline of the Theory of Structuration*. Berkeley: University of California Press.

Goffman, E. (1955). "On Face Work." *Psychiatry* 18: 213–31.

Goffman, E. (1956). "The Nature of Deference and Demeanor." *American Anthropologist* 58: 473–502.

Goffman, E. (1964). "The Neglected Situation," in J. J. Gumperz and D. Hymes (eds.), "The Ethnography of Communication." *American Anthropologist* 66(6, II): 133–6.

Goffman, E. (1967). *Interaction Ritual: Essays in Face to Face Behavior*. Garden City, NY: Doubleday.

Goffman, E. (1971). *Relations in Public: Microstudies of the Public Order*. New York: Harper & Row.

Goffman, E. (1983). "The Interaction Order." *American Sociological Review* 48: 1–17.

Goffman, E., and Verhoeven, J. (1993). "An Interview with Erving Goffman, 1980." *Research on Language and Social Interaction* 26(3): 317–48.

Goldthorpe, J. H. (1973). "Revolution in Sociology." *Sociology* 7: 449–62.

Goodwin, C. (1979). "The Interactive Construction of a Sentence in Natural Conversation," in G. Psathas (ed.), *Everyday Language: Studies in Ethnomethodology*. New York: Irvington.

Goodwin, C. (1984). "Notes on Story Structure and the Organization of Participation," in M. Atkinson and J. Heritage (eds.), *Structures of Social Action*. Cambridge: Cambridge University Press.

Goodwin, C. (1986). "Audience Diversity, Participation and Interpretation." *Text* 6(3): 283–316.

Goodwin, M. H. (1996). "Informings and Announcements in their Environment: Prosody within a Multi-Activity Work Setting," in E. Couper-Kuhlen and M. Selting (eds.), *Prosody in Conversation*. Cambridge: Cambridge University Press.

Goodwin, M. H. (2006). *The Hidden Life of Girls*. Oxford: Blackwell.

Goodwin, M. H., and Goodwin, C. (1986). "Gesture and Coparticipation in the Activity of Searching for a Word." *Semiotica* 62(1/2): 51–75.

Habermas, J. (1970). "Toward a Theory of Communicative Competence," in H. P. Dreitzel (ed.), *Recent Sociology No. 2*. New York: Macmillan.

Habermas, J. (1979). *Communication and the Evolution of Society*. London: Heinemann.

Heritage, J. (1984a). *Garfinkel and Ethnomethodology*. Cambridge: Polity.

Heritage, J. (1984b). "A Change-of-State Token and Aspects of its Sequential Placement," in J. M. Atkinson and J. Heritage (eds.), *Structures of Social Action*. Cambridge: Cambridge University Press.

Heritage, J. (1987). "Ethnomethodology," in A. Giddens and J. Turner (eds.), *Social Theory Today*. Cambridge: Polity.

Heritage, J. (1988). "Explanations as Accounts: A Conversation Analytic Perspective," in C. Antaki (ed.), *Understanding Everyday Explanation: A Casebook of Methods*. Beverly Hills: Sage.

Heritage, J. (1998). "'Oh'-Prefaced Responses to Inquiry." *Language in Society* 27(3): 291–334.

Heritage, J. (2002a). "Ethno-Sciences and their Significance for Conversation Linguistics," in G. Antos, K. Brinker, W. Heinemann, and S. Sager (eds.), *Linguistics of Text and Conversation: An International Handbook of Contemporary Research*. Berlin: De Gruyter.

Heritage, J. (2002b). "'Oh'-Prefaced Responses to Assessments: A Method of Modifying Agreement/Disagreement," in C. Ford, B. Fox, and S. Thompson (eds.), *The Language of Turn and Sequence*. Oxford: Oxford University Press.

Heritage, J. (2005). "Conversation Analysis and Institutional Talk," in R. Sanders and K. Fitch (eds.), *Handbook of Language and Social Interaction*. Mahwah, NJ: Erlbaum.

Heritage, J. (2007a). "Intersubjectivity and Progressivity in References to Persons (and Places)," in N. J. Enfield and T. Stivers (eds.), *Person Reference in Interaction: Linguistic, Cultural and Social Perspectives*. Cambridge: Cambridge University Press.

Heritage, J. (2007b). "Constructing and Navigating Epistemic Landscapes: Progressivity, Agency and Resistance in Initial Elements of Responses to Yes/No Questions." Paper presented at the annual meeting of the American Sociological Association.

Heritage, J., and Clayman, S. E. (forthcoming). *Talk and Social Institutions*. Oxford: Blackwell.

Heritage, J., and Raymond, G. (2005). "The Terms of Agreement: Indexing Epistemic Authority and Subordination in Assessment Sequences." *Social Psychology Quarterly* 68(1): 15–38.

Jefferson, G. (1980). "On 'Trouble-Premonitory' Response to Inquiry." *Sociological Inquiry* 50: 153–85.

Jefferson, G. (1987). "On Exposed and Embedded Correction in Conversation," in G. Button and J. R. E. Lee (eds.), *Talk and Social Organisation*. Clevedon, UK: Multilingual Matters.

Jefferson, G. (1988). "On the Sequential Organization of Troubles-Talk in Ordinary Conversation." *Social Problems* 35(4): 418–41.

Jefferson, G. (2004a). "A Sketch of Some Orderly Aspects of Overlap in Natural Conversation," in G. Lerner (ed.), *Conversation Analysis: Studies from the First Generation*. Amsterdam: John Benjamins.

Jefferson, G. (2004b). "'At first I thought': A Normalizing Device for Extraordinary Events," in G. Lerner (ed.), *Conversation Analysis: Studies from the First Generation*. Amsterdam: John Benjamins.

Jefferson, G. (2007). "Preliminary Notes on Abdicated Other Correction." *Journal of Pragmatics* 39: 225–61.

Joseph, B. D. (2003). "Reviewing our Contents." *Language* 79(3): 461–3.

Kendon, A. (1987). "Erving Goffman's Contributions to the Study of Face-to-Face Interaction," in P. Drew and A. Wootton (eds.), *Erving Goffman: Explorations in the Interaction Order*. Cambridge: Polity.

Kitzinger, C. (2005a). "Heteronormativity in Action: Reproducing Normative Heterosexuality in 'After Hours' Calls to the Doctor." *Social Problems* 52: 477–98.

Kitzinger, C. (2005b). "Speaking as a Heterosexual: (How) Does Sexuality Matter for Talk-in-Interaction?" *Research on Language and Social Interaction* 38: 221–65.

Kollock, P., Blumstein, P., and Schwartz, P. (1985). "Sex and Power in Interaction: Conversational Privileges and Duties." *American Sociological Review* 50: 24–46.

Kuhn, T. (1962). *The Structure of Scientific Revolutions*. Chicago: University of Chicago Press.

Land, V., and Kitzinger, C. (2005). "Speaking as a Lesbian: Correcting the Heterosexist Presumption." *Research on Language and Social Interaction* 38: 371–416.

Lerner, G. (1989). "Notes on Overlap Management in Conversation: The Case of Delayed Completion." *Western Journal of Speech Communication* 53: 167–77.

Lerner, G. (2004). "Collaborative Turn Sequences," in G. Lerner (ed.), *Conversation Analysis: Studies from the First Generation*. Amsterdam: John Benjamins.

Levinson, S. C. (1992). "Activity Types and Language," in P. Drew and J. Heritage (ed.), *Talk at Work*. Cambridge: Cambridge University Press.

Levinson, S. C. (2000). *Presumptive Meanings: The Theory of Generalized Conversational Implicature*. Cambridge MA: MIT Press.

Maynard, D. (2003). *Bad News, Good News: Conversational Order in Everyday Talk and Clinical Settings*. Chicago: University of Chicago Press.

Mead, G. H. (1934). *Mind, Self, and Society*. Chicago: University of Chicago Press.

Parsons, T. (1937). *The Structure of Social Action*. New York: McGraw-Hill.

Parsons, T. (1951). *The Social System*. New York: The Free Press.

Pomerantz, A. M. (1980). "Telling My Side: 'Limited Access' as a 'Fishing' Device." *Sociological Inquiry* 50: 186–98.

Pomerantz, A. M. (1984a). "Giving a Source or Basis: The Practice in Conversation of Telling 'What I Know'." *Journal of Pragmatics* 8(4): 607–25.

Pomerantz, A. M. (1984b). "Agreeing and Disagreeing with Assessments: Some Features of Preferred/ Dispreferred Turn Shapes," in J. M. Atkinson and J. Heritage (eds.), *Structures of Social Action: Studies in Conversation Analysis*. Cambridge: Cambridge University Press.

Pomerantz, A. M. (1988). "Offering a Candidate Answer: An Information Seeking Strategy." *Communication Monographs* 55: 360–73.

Rawls, J. (1971). *A Theory of Justice*. Cambridge, MA: Harvard University Press.

Raymond, G. (2003). "Grammar and Social Organization: Yes/No Interrogatives and the Structure of Responding." *American Sociological Review* 68: 939–67.

Raymond, G., and Heritage, J. (2006). "The Epistemics of Social Relations: Owning Grandchildren." *Language in Society* 35: 677–705.

Sacks, H. (1974). "An Analysis of the Course of a Joke's Telling in Conversation," in R. Bauman and J. Sherzer (eds.), *Explorations in the Ethnography of Speaking*. Cambridge: Cambridge University Press.

Sacks, H. (1984a). "Notes on Methodology," ed. G. Jefferson from various lectures, in J. M. Atkinson and J. Heritage (eds.), *Structures of Social Action*. Cambridge: Cambridge University Press.

Sacks, H. (1984b). "On Doing 'Being Ordinary'," in J. M. Atkinson and J. Heritage (eds.), *Structures of Social Action*. Cambridge: Cambridge University Press.

Sacks, H. (1987). "On the Preferences for Agreement and Contiguity in Sequences in Conversation," in G. Button and J. R. E. Lee (eds.), *Talk and Social Organisation*. Clevedon, UK: Multilingual Matters.

Sacks, H. (1992 [1964–72]). *Lectures on Conversation*, 2 vols. Oxford: Blackwell.

Sacks, H., and Schegloff, E. A. (1979). "Two Preferences in the Organization of Reference to Persons and their Interaction," in G. Psathas (ed.), *Everyday Language: Studies in Ethnomethodology*. New York: Irvington.

Sacks, H., Schegloff, E. A., and Jefferson, G. (1974). "A Simplest Systematics for the Organization of Turn-Taking for Conversation." *Language* 50: 696–735.

Schegloff, E. A. (1968). "Sequencing in Conversational Openings." *American Anthropologist* 70: 1075–95.

Schegloff, E. A. (1972). "Notes on a Conversational Practice: Formulating Place," in D. Sudnow (ed.), *Studies in Social Interaction*. New York: The Free Press.

Schegloff, E. A. (1979). "The Relevance of Repair for Syntax-for-Conversation," in T. Givon (ed.), *Syntax and Semantics 12: Discourse and Syntax*. New York: Academic Press.

Schegloff, E. A. (1984). "On Some Questions and Ambiguities in Conversation," in J. M. Atkinson and J. Heritage (eds.), *Structures of Social Action*. Cambridge: Cambridge University Press.

Schegloff, E. A. (1988). "On an Actual Virtual Servo-Mechanism for Guessing Bad News: A Single Case Conjecture." *Social Problems* 35(4): 442–57.

Schegloff, E. A. (1992a). "Introduction," in G. Jefferson (ed.), *Harvey Sacks, Lectures on Conversation*, vol. 1, *Fall 1964-Spring 1968*. Oxford: Blackwell.

Schegloff, E. A. (1992b). "Repair after Next Turn: The Last Structurally Provided for Place for the Defense of Intersubjectivity in Conversation." *American Journal of Sociology* 95(5): 1295–1345.

Schegloff, E. A. (1996a). "Turn Organization: One Intersection of Grammar and Interaction," in E. Ochs, S. Thompson, and E. Schegloff (eds.), *Interaction and Grammar*. Cambridge: Cambridge University Press.

Schegloff, E. A. (1996b). "Confirming Allusions: Toward an Empirical Account of Action." *American Journal of Sociology* 104(1): 161–216.

Schegloff, E. A. (1996c). "Some Practices for Referring to Persons in Talk-in Interaction: A Partial Sketch of a Systematics," in B. Fox (ed.), *Studies in Anaphora*. Amsterdam: John Benjamins.

Schegloff, E. A. (2000). "Overlapping Talk and the Organization of Turn-Taking for Conversation." *Language in Society* 29(1): 1–63.

Schegloff, E. A. (2002). "Accounts of Conduct in Interaction: Interruption, Overlap and Turn-Taking," in J. H. Turner (ed.), *Handbook of Sociological Theory*. New York: Plenum.

Schegloff, E. A. (2006). "Interaction: The Infrastructure for Social Institutions, the Natural Ecological Niche for Language and the Arena in which Culture is Enacted," in N. J. Enfield and S. C. Levinson (eds.), *The Roots of Human Sociality: Culture, Cognition and Interaction*. New York: Berg.

Schegloff, E. A. (2007). *Sequence Organization in Interaction: A Primer in Conversation Analysis*, vol. 1. Cambridge: Cambridge University Press.

Schegloff, E. A., Jefferson, G. and Sacks, H. (1977). "The Preference for Self-Correction in the Organization of Repair in Conversation." *Language* 53: 361–82.

Schegloff, E. A., and Lerner, G. H. (2006). "Beginning to Respond." Unpublished manuscript, UCLA.

Schegloff, E. A., and Sacks, H. (1973). "Opening Up Closings." *Semiotica* 8: 289–327.

Schutz, A. (1962). *Collected Papers*, vol. 1, *The Problem of Social Reality*. The Hague: Martinus Nijhoff.

Simmel, G. (1923). "Aus dem nachlassenen Tagebuch," in *Fragmente und Aufsatze*. Munich: Drei Masken.

Speer, S. (2005). *Gender Talk: Feminism, Discourse and Conversation Analysis*. London: Routledge.

Stivers, T. (2005). "Modified Repeats: One Method for Asserting Primary Rights from Second Position." *Research on Language and Social Interaction* 38(2): 131–58.

Stivers, T. (2007). "Alternative Recognitionals in Initial References to Persons," in N. J. Enfield and T. Stivers (eds.), *Person Reference in Interaction: Linguistic, Cultural, and Social Perspectives*. Cambridge: Cambridge University Press.

Stivers, T., and Majid, A. (2007). "Questioning Children: Interactional Evidence of Implicit Bias in Medical Interviews." *Social Psychology Quarterly* 70(4): 424–41.

Stivers, T., and Rossano, F. (2007). "Mobilizing Response." Unpublished mimeo, Max Planck Institute for Psycholinguistics, Nijmegen, Netherlands.

Sudnow, D. (ed.) (1972). *Studies in Social Interaction*. New York: The Free Press.

Terasaki, A. K. (2004). "Pre-Announcement Sequences in Conversation," in G. Lerner (ed.), *Conversation Analysis: Studies from the First Generation*. Amsterdam: John Benjamins.

Turner, R. (ed.) (1974). *Ethnomethodology*. Harmondsworth: Penguin.

van Ryn, M., and Fu, S. S. (2003) "Paved with Good Intentions: Do Public Health and Human Service Providers Contribute to Racial/Ethnic Disparities in Health?" *American Journal of Public Health* 93: 248–55.

West, C. (1984a). *Routine Complications: Troubles with Talk between Doctors and Patients*. Bloomington: Indiana University Press.

West, C. (1984b). "When the Doctor Is a 'Lady': Power, Status and Gender in Physician–Patient Encounters." *Symbolic Interaction* 7: 87–106.

Wiley, N. (1985). "The Current Interregnum in American Sociology." *Social Research* 52: 179–207.

Wu, R.-J. R. (2004). *Stance in Talk: A Conversation Analysis of Mandarin Final Particles*. Amsterdam: Benjamins.

16

Globalization Theory

JOHN BOLI AND FRANK J. LECHNER

Sociological theories of globalization vary significantly in terms of their underlying epistemologies, focal points, and empirical import. The three theoretical perspectives of primary concern here – world-system theory, world polity theory, and globalization theory – derive from different theoretical traditions, conceive globalization in dissimilar ways, and emphasize different aspects of globalization. We provide some insight into these variations but concentrate on the substance of the theories. For each, we ask: What is the theoretical core of the perspective? What does it posit as the primary driving forces in globalization? What consequences of globalization are its primary concern? To what empirical phenomena does it draw attention? What empirical phenomena does it neglect? We comment only briefly on how well each holds up under empirical scrutiny. Apart from discussing the three main lines of argument, we also touch on related globalization perspectives but must omit many relevant complexities and controversies.

We refrain from conceptual analysis of the term globalization, mainly because consensus about it is practically unthinkable. The literature is replete with definitions and explications: globalization is flows of goods, capital, people, and information (Held et al. 1999), or it is the decrease in geographic constraints on interaction (Waters 2001), or it is the rise of a global, information-based network society (Castells 1996), or, from a more critical and politically engaged standpoint, it is economic liberalization, neoliberalism, and the expansion of corporate capitalism (McMichael 2005). Scholte (2005), who prefers to view globalization as "deterritorialization," provides a useful critical analysis showing that many such definitions are inadequate or redundant. We limit ourselves here to explaining what globalization means from different theoretical perspectives, recognizing that different theories deal with different aspects of a broad and elastic concept.

CULTURAL THEORY: GLOBALIZATION AS
RECONCEPTUALIZATION AND HYBRIDITY

Roland Robertson ushered the concept of globalization into the social sciences in a series of essays written in the 1980s and collected in a single volume in 1992.[1] Robertson had found his way to the analysis of globalization through work in the sociology of religion and critical analysis of modernization theory. In an early book, Nettl and Robertson (1968) argued against prevailing views of modernization as a single path leading to a largely standard modern society. Rather, they emphasized the global field of societies and states that acts as a point of reference for any given society. Comparisons are endemic, both past and present. States and societies compare themselves with other states and societies, not just with their own histories or lines of development. The goals they purse depend heavily on what they learn from such comparisons; reflexivity, emulation, and borrowing are central. States' ability to pursue these goals depends heavily on the nature of their interdependence with the larger world. Modernization was thus not a sequence of evolutionary stages but a "global culture of modernization," as Robertson (1991: 211) later would describe it.

Robertson's studies in religion yielded further insight into globalization as a cultural process. Fundamentalism was on the rise in the 1970s and 1980s, and most interpretations of this religious resurgence viewed it as regressive or reactionary withdrawal from modernity. Robertson (1992: ch. 11) saw it instead as part and parcel of the globalization process (see also Lechner 2005). In his view, fundamentalism is one way for societies to come to grips with the globalizing world with which they are so ineluctably interdependent. Globalization challenges established identities and meaning systems by confronting them with many apparently viable alternatives, thereby relativizing national and local identities. As the chief cultural predicament of societies in a globalized world, relativization implies that fundamentalist impulses are universal, not peculiar to Islam or the Christian right. Fundamentalism is inherent in a key axis of global cultural tension, the universalism-particularism dialectic (more on this below). Global culture universalizes problems of meaning and identity, of value and belief, but it also legitimates distinct, particular identities and meaning systems. Fundamentalists respond to the global condition by constructing particular visions of world order and distinct systems of value and belief, but these responses are not parochial. They are proclaimed as universalistic truths, as candidates for globalization with greater or lesser resonance in global society. Fundamentalism is thus globalization at work, and it resonates widely because it offers simplified and comprehensive visions of the world that travel well because they are easily digested.

In analyzing the global condition, then, Robertson has taken a neo-Parsonian "cultural turn" (Robertson 1992: ch. 2) grounded in concrete elements of global change. Globalization "refers both to the compression of the world and intensification of consciousness of the world as a whole" (Robertson 1992: 8). Compression of the world (or "space-time compression," the phrase made famous by Harvey 1989), reflects the development of technologies of rapid travel and communication since the eighteenth century. A journey that once required months now requires less than a day; a message that once must travel for weeks now arrives in milliseconds. The shrinking world impels expanding consciousness of ever larger geographical and social spaces, above all consciousness of the world as a single interconnected society, an all-encompassing yet distinct arena of culture and action. As indicated above, the globe has become a frame of reference for social actors, just as the "nation" became a frame of reference in the early modern period of European nation-building and the "Roman world" was a frame of reference during the centuries of Roman imperial hegemony. "Consciousness of the world as a whole," coupled with Robertson's emphasis on increasing interdependence among peoples and places, impels states, national societies, individuals, and religio-ethnic groups to take into account actors, identities, movements, and so on, that reach far beyond local and national frames of reference. Processes of identity, meaning-making, and action reflect global shrinking and global awareness.[2]

This is the global condition that makes relativization so prominent. Relativization characterizes the relationships among all of the key elements of what Robertson (1992: 27) calls the "global field" or "global-human condition." These elements are selves (individuals), national societies, the world system of societies, and humankind (humanity as a whole). As seen above, national societies are relativized with respect to the world system of societies. They are also relativized with respect to humankind, which complicates identity and action considerably. National citizenship, so central to modern identity, is an exclusive status, while humankind entails a Kantian universalistic (world) citizenship that adheres in all people. This relationship produces the familiar dynamic of conflict and inconsistency between universal human rights and citizen rights, impelling not only much meaning-making on the part of states and societies but also much social mobilization on behalf of or against migrant world citizens who do not hold national citizenship where they live. Similarly, the construct of humankind relativizes the system of societies: if humankind as a whole is foremost, the *Realpolitik* of interstate competition and self-interested action loses its legitimacy. All of these globalization-induced cultural tensions generate great dynamism in world society.

The universalism-particularism dialectic operates in two directions. One is the universalism of the particular, i.e., the legitimacy enjoyed by peoples and cultures insofar as they maintain their integrity and authenticity. In the global ideology of cultural relativism, societies have a right to their own cultures and traditions (cultural imperialism is illegitimate) and they should not be judged by standards outside their own cultures (ethnocentrism is pernicious). What is more, societies have an obligation to establish a unique and distinctive identity. Failure to do so projects an image of weakness, passivity, or a too eager acceptance of outside influences. But this distinctive identity is not for local consumption alone; in the global condition, it is to be trumpeted to the larger world. Thus, global culture constantly expands as new forms of particularism (including various fundamentalisms) strive to make themselves known.

The other direction of the dialectic is the particularism of the universal, for which Robertson (1995) coined the term "glocalization." When universalistic cultural elements, ideologies, and institutions encounter local contexts, they change. Local actors adapt the universal to local conditions and interests, often in surprising ways. McDonald's in East Asia is much more than just a fast food joint (Watson 2006); Coca-Cola is so indigenized that many Indians think it is an Indian company. Local meaning systems foster varied interpretations of global cultural influences – fans of *Dallas* (Liebes and Katz 1990) or of George Lamming's novels (Griswold 1987) experience even highly packaged popular culture in strikingly different terms depending on the local context. The global context thus is less homogenizing than many have claimed (or feared).

Largely compatible with Robertson's analysis, an independent strain of cultural globalization theory has emerged in anthropological studies of national and local cultures. Exemplified most prominently by the work of Ulf Hannerz (1987, 1990, 1996), and in part prompted by world-system theory's concern about cultural imperialism (below), this perspective raises fundamental questions about the nature of local culture and identity. Hannerz conducted extensive field research in the central Nigerian town of Kafanchan, noting the legacy of the British colonial period but also learning about a multitude of influences in this polyglot crossroads that engender a vibrant, rich, and innovative local culture. He realized that "local" culture is never "pristine" or "tradition-true." Traditions are borrowed, they may be short-lived, they derive from many forms of exchange with outside cultures both near and far. Local culture mixes and stirs the many influences to which it is subject, creating a complex stew containing many different tastes.

Hannerz describes the mixing and stirring of local culture as "hybridization" and "creolization," processes not peculiar to colonialism or imperialism but routinely in operation for local cultures in most locales and for much of human cultural history. Globalization intensifies hybridization and increases the distance that cultural influences can travel, making it possible for particular influences to reach all parts of the world. Much hybridization occurs at a less than global level, however, often involving geographical or cultural neighbors. For this reason, Hannerz prefers to speak of the "transnationalization" of culture in a way analogous to Scholte's (2005) concept of supraterritoriality. When he assesses the amount of space occupied by various cultural influences in local cultures, he finds only a modest share deriving from globalized cultural elements.

Turned the other way around, a creolized culture has certain advantages in reaching out to the globe. Taylor (1997) shows, for example, how West African singer and percussionist Youssou N'Dour has mixed French, Cuban, jazz, hip hop, and soul elements with traditional Senegalese griot (praise singer) musical forms to create distinctive songs that appeal to many disparate audiences. This is glocalization in reverse: the globalized forms are reinterpreted at the local level and then globalized anew. Tomlinson (1991) pushes this analysis further in an illuminating critique of the cultural imperialism thesis. To continue with Hannerz's terminology, if all cultures are hybrid cultures and creolization is the normal state of affairs, how are we to decide what is "truly" local or indigenous? Why is the cultural adaptation entailed by modern forms of interchange more pernicious than that of earlier forms? What does it mean to say that local cultures are being undermined by irresistible globalization forces? Tomlinson recognizes that cultures sometimes die, but the culprit in such cases is not cultural "contamination" but military conquest and annihilation.

WORLD-SYSTEM AND RELATED THEORIES: GLOBALIZATION AS THE HISTORY OF CAPITALISM

Rooted in the French historical tradition associated with the *Annales d'histoire économique et sociale*, the influential journal founded in 1929 by Marc Bloch and Lucien Febvre, world-system theory crystallized in the work of Immanuel Wallerstein (1974–89). Brought to full prominence by Fernand Braudel, the Annales School rejected prevailing emphases on politics, signal events, and elite individuals in favor of "total histories" dealing with economic, technical, social, and cultural processes affecting the everyday lives of entire populations. It also insisted on the importance of the *longue durée*, seeking to understand social change over extended historical periods. Another important element in world-system theory's genesis was dependency theory, a mostly Latin American theoretical tradition which itself was stimulated by the structuralist (*desarrollista*) school initiated by Raúl Prebisch, an Argentinian economist who argued that colonialism had locked Latin American economies into a subordinate position on the "periphery" of the world economy, producing mainly primary export products at disadvantageous terms of trade while falling ever further behind developed "center" countries in terms of high value-added production. The periphery was therefore in a state of dependency vis-à-vis the center, not "undeveloped" but "badly developed" and thus unable to make the shift from primary production to manufacture. These ideas formed the baseline for dependency theory, which coalesced in the 1970s.

In its radical form, as in the work of Frank and Amin, dependency theory relied on Marxian epistemology, insisting on the primacy of relations of production and the centrality of political economy, that is, the interplay between economic forces (means and relations of production, property relations, the structure and distribution of capital) and political arrangements. It was thus a materialist theory, and its Marxian underpinnings led to the conclusion that political arrangements are subordinate to economic forces. They also pointed to a revolutionary political stance: only the overthrow of capitalism on a worldwide scale could free the periphery from its enslavement to the core. World-system theory agrees, and its proponents often see themselves as engaged in a global class struggle on behalf of workers and peasants seeking to break the iron grip of global capitalism.

Core of the theory

World-system theory is a theory of history, and the history it theorizes is that of global capitalism. Wallerstein's three-volume magnum opus, *The Modern World-System*, begins with the "long sixteenth century" (Braudel's term, roughly 1480–1640), the take-off period of the capitalist world economy. Western European powers colonized coastal areas in many parts of the world, using their superior weapons and naval technology to extract resources (gold and silver, slaves, exotic foods) and open up markets for manufactured goods. Merchants developed trading systems in eastern and northern Europe to obtain grain, timber, furs, and other basic goods. Plantation economies emerged in colonized areas, especially in the Americas, worked in large part by slave and indentured labor to supply sugar, coffee, rum, and cotton. A world division of labor emerged. The core of the world system (northern France and the Low Countries, England, northern Italian cities) shifted toward manufactures while relying on peripheral areas for agricultural and other primary products. Backed by the power of increasingly capable states, capitalist classes in the core fashioned a self-reinforcing cycle of economic and military superiority. Core industrialization in the eighteenth and nineteenth centuries increased the core's relative advantages, yielding a phase of intense colonization that brought virtually the entire globe into the capitalist world economy under the tutelage of globe-spanning empires centered around competing core powers.

Contrary to conventional economic arguments, for world-system theory (as for Prebisch) large portions of the world are poor and poorly developed not because they are excluded from the capitalist world economy but because they have long been incorporated into it in a structurally subordinate position. Frank (1966) famously called this feature of the world economy the "development of underdevelopment," as capitalist incorporation undercut local industries and trading systems and reversed prior economic progress (see e.g. Rodney 1972 on Africa).

Crucial to the world-system approach is the fact that, while the capitalist world system comprises a single interconnected world economy, the political system is composed of multiple independent (sovereign) states. Interstate competition reinforces capitalist competition and impels core states to promote and protect the interests of their respective capitalist classes. Given the high mobility of capital relative to other factors of production (labor and land), interstate competition also allows capitalists to play states off against one another. The contrasting case is a world empire, in which a single state (Rome being the classic example) exerts political control over the associated world economy. World empires are characterized by tributary relations (payments in return for autonomy) on the periphery and political control at the core to prevent the emergence of a powerful merchant/capitalist class that could threaten the political, military, and religious elites atop the empire. The multi-centered character of late medieval Europe militated against the establishment of a new trans-European empire and facilitated the heavy dependence of monarchs on major capitalist houses (e.g. the Fuggers in the sixteenth century, the Rothschilds in the nineteenth). Capital thus could act with far greater freedom than in a world empire.

The dynamics of the world system derive from inherent properties of capitalism, which are captured in the up-and-down cycles of the world economy known as Kondratieff waves or K-waves. Named for the Russian economist who first posited their existence in the 1920s, K-waves last 40 to 60 years and consist of an expansionary A-phase followed by stagnation or contraction in the B-phase.[3] Most theories of the K-wave cycle attribute A-phase expansion to a burst of innovation and technical development producing new "leading industries" (e.g. cotton and textile manufacturing in the eighteenth century, steel and railroads in the nineteenth century) that facilitate rising profits and rapid capital accumulation. Contraction ensues when the leading industries can no longer keep up the pace of innovation and the new markets they have created become saturated. The A-phase expansion of resources and capital eases tensions in the core, both among capitalists and between capital and labor, as some of the economic growth benefits the workers (proletariat) in the core and thereby lowers class-based tensions. It also facilitates military build-ups (Goldstein 1988), however, and spurs the search for new markets in areas not yet incorporated into the world economy. Contraction in the B-phase, in the form of falling rates of profit, excess production, rising unemployment, social unrest, and so on, intensifies core competition and the struggle for hegemony over the world system as a whole. Wars of ever larger scale ensue; examples often adduced include the "first world war" between Britain and France in the eighteenth century, partially waged in North America, and the world wars of the twentieth century.

Contractions in the world economy and increased competition in the core can work to the benefit of the semi-periphery, those political units that have achieved a moderate level of economic development and serve as a buffer zone between the core and the periphery. Challengers to the dominant core powers normally arise in the semi-periphery, often by means of a repressive state that limits the penetration of foreign (core) capital and mobilizes extraordinary military power while pushing state-led industrialization. The prototypical case is Prussia, which united Germany and mobilized for militarized development to reach core status in the late nineteenth century. The USA similarly rose from peripheral to core status in the nineteenth century, under a relatively limited state that was nonetheless strong enough to crush resistance in its own periphery (the South) and reorient its primary production to the North rather than Britain.

While K-wave cycles represent the principal economic dynamic of the world system, hegemonic competition is the principal political dynamic. Three powers have gained hegemonic status in modern capitalism's history: the United Provinces of the Netherlands in the seventeenth century, Britain in the nineteenth century, and the USA in the twentieth century. Periods of large-scale or protracted warfare are crucial in hegemonic shifts. The Netherlands briefly achieved hegemony following the Thirty Years War that exhausted continental land powers, using its advanced naval technology and commercial acumen to dominate world trade. Britain built the world's largest naval and commercial fleets in the eighteenth century and gained hegemony in the nineteenth century in the wake of the Napoleonic Wars. Its hegemony was reinforced by its leading position in nineteenth-century industrialization – textile manufacturing, coal and steel production, railroads, and so on. The breakthrough for the USA came with World Wars I and II, often seen as two phases of a single systemic crisis. Hegemonic rise and fall, for world-system theorists, is as inevitable as economic cycles. The advantages that powered the new hegemon's rise eventually are superseded by competing powers, the costs of world-systemic control and maintenance become excessive, rising costs of production lead to capital flight. The current hegemon, the USA, is struggling with just these problems (Wallerstein 2003), threatened by China's rapid rise from peripheral to near-core status on a rocket that has been fueled in considerable part by investment capital from the core.

In more abstract terms, then, world-system theory conceives of the world economy as comprised of three zones: core, periphery, and semi-periphery. The core is the leading zone, characterized by relatively free markets for labor, land, and capital; advanced technology, skilled labor, and, therefore, high labor productivity; large amounts of capital and ongoing capital accumulation; and consequent advantages in terms of resources and coercive power that enable it to dominate the world economy. The periphery, heavily subjugated to and exploited by the core, was initially characterized by coercive forms of labor (serfdom, slavery, indentured status, and the like), limited markets in land and capital, low levels of technology and labor skill, low productivity, and limited capital accumulation. The semi-periphery occupies an "in-between" zone of mid-level development, exploited by the core but exploiting parts of the periphery. It thereby mediates tensions between core and periphery, contributing to the overall stability of the world system but also posing a threat to the core.

Over time, of course, the general level of development of the world economy has risen. The leading sectors in the core are no longer manufacturing industries but a growing array of sectors engaged in the production and application of knowledge, along with "pure" capitalist sectors like financial services. Technology-intensive manufacturing has shifted to the semi-periphery, labor-intensive manufacturing to the periphery. Correspondingly, marketization of the factors of production in the semi-periphery and periphery has been extensive, and coercive means of labor control have declined. Uneven development remains the rule in the periphery because core powers exercise "neocolonial" (economic rather than political) control. However, export-led development in the semi-periphery, organized by states working in close cooperation with (and imposing few regulations on) private capital to take advantage of low labor costs ensured by weak or non-existent labor organizations, has produced more dynamic development in numerous countries and increased the pressure on core countries that are burdened by much higher labor and social costs of production.

Given its Marxian foundation and economic emphasis, world-system theory brings two interrelated issues to the fore: exploitation and inequality. The core exploits the non-core, capital exploits labor. Exploitation increases capital accumulation in the core but inhibits it in the periphery, thus maintaining the basic world-system structure. Severe inequality results, heavily favoring the core over the non-core, capital over labor, global and national elites over the middle and lower classes. Inequality is tempered in core countries where labor is well organized (the welfare states of western and northern Europe) but is all the worse elsewhere. Individual countries may rise and fall but the stratification structure is largely undisturbed, and the inherent tendency of the capitalist world economy is to increase inequality.

While world-system theory is essentially materialist, it projects a vital role for cultural ideology in system dynamics (Lechner and Boli 2005). Capitalists bombard the public realm with ideologies of free markets and trade, strong individualism, and limited states – classic liberal ideas repackaged as global neoliberalism and embedded in economic governance bodies like the IMF (International Monetary Fund) and WTO (World Trade Organization). Uninhibited capitalism is the surest means of producing the greatest good for the greatest number; the greatest good is maximum consumer choice and consumption. Capitalism stokes the fires of racism and sexism to justify systemic exploitation and stratification. "Counter-systemic" resistance movements, which gather annually at the World Social Forum, see through the ideological smokescreens laid down by global capitalism, returning fire with analyses and images blaming capitalism for poverty, war, environmental degradation, state repression, and much more. Culture is, thus, the "ideological battleground of the modern world-system" (Wallerstein 1990). But the battle is fought largely on capitalism's terrain and on highly unequal terms, given the far greater resources at the command of capitalist classes.

The unequal material and ideological contest between capital and its opponents does not entail the permanent victory of capitalism, however. Ever faithful to Marx, world-system theorists remain convinced of the ultimate collapse of global capitalism due to its internal contradictions (Wallerstein 2004). Capitalism must expand to new markets and new sites of production to survive its periodic crises of overproduction and falling accumulation, but sows the seeds of its own destruction because of the environmental devastation and counter-systemic movements that it evokes.

Globalization in world-system terms is thus the formation, differentiation, and elaboration of the capitalist world economy. What globalizes are the techniques, goals, structures, and values of capitalism in a global division of labor marked by steep stratification. The driving force is economic competition buttressed by interstate political and military competition for regional and global domination. Core capitalist enterprises drive globalization; core states construct and control global governance mechanisms to protect and promote capitalist interests. Resistance to capitalism also globalizes in the form of counter-systemic social movements and ideologies, but the consequences of globalization are mostly negative: inequality, poor working conditions, environmental degradation, cultural imperialism, and so on.

World-system theory has moved in new directions in the past two decades, leading to changes in the nomenclature but not in the basic thrust of the theory. On the one hand, scholars likes Chase-Dunn and Hall (1997) have generalized the theory, studying small- and medium-scale systems such as the stateless tribal systems of indigenous peoples in pre-Columbian North America and the Mesopotamian region conquered by the Akkadians after 2400 BC. On the other hand, scholars such as Abu-Lughod (1989) and Frank and Gills (1993) have extended the analysis much further back in time, arguing that a single world system has prevailed since AD 1300 or even 5000 BC. These two new directions, described by the moniker "world systems research," complement one another insofar as studies of "minisystems" show how they contributed to lines of development leading to the modern world system.

Related theories

A prominent relative of world-systems theory is study of the transnational capitalist class (TCC), exemplified in the work of Sklair (2001, 2002) and Robinson (2004). TCC theorizing posits the emergence in recent decades of a global ruling class, interacting through dense networks that exclude all but the most powerful, and dominating the global system in its own interests. Robinson's conceptualization follows Marx's classic model of class formation: "the TCC is the capitalist group that owns or controls transnational capital" (2004: 36 n.1). This group mobilizes as a class "for itself" to shape the policies and programs of individual states and, especially, major global economic governance bodies like the IMF and WTO. The emerging result, for Robinson, is a transnational capitalist state analogous to national capitalist states, "captured" (indeed, largely created) by the TCC and managing to ensure that capitalist interests and ideologies dominate global development. Sklair promotes a broader concept of the TCC that has four components: a "corporate fraction" (Robinson's focus) that owns and controls transnational corporations (TNCs), a "state fraction" of globalizing bureaucrats and politicians, a "technical fraction" of globalizing professionals, and a "consumerist fraction" of merchants and media. Sklair insists on the high degree of interaction and circulation of individuals among these four fractions and the general coincidence of interests among them, which is embodied most centrally, in his view, by the "culture-ideology of consumerism." Consumerism implies that "the meaning of life is to be found in the things that we possess. To consume, therefore, is to be fully alive, and to remain fully alive we must continuously consume" (Sklair 2002: 62). The TCC, particularly the corporate and merchants/media fractions, push consumerist ideology deep into every society. The ideology facilitates the commodification of ever more aspects of daily life and aligns individual values and attitudes with the interests of the TCC. Globalization driven by the TCC thus induces far-reaching homogenization of consumption patterns, individual aspirations and world-views, political structures, symbolic culture, and so on.

One of the more interesting theoretical approaches to globalization, building on but also departing from world-system ideas, is the analysis of global commodity and value chains (Gereffi and Korzeniewicz 1994; Gereffi, Humphrey, and Sturgeon 2005; Schmitz 2004). Detailed study of specific industries, production systems, and networks takes pride of place in this work. Key theoretical issues revolve around the accumulation of capital (rents) in value chains – which segments of the chain benefit most and which benefit least? – and chain governance mechanisms. Most of the theoretical and empirical work in this tradition points to disproportionate benefits for companies in developed countries that control, initiate, or manage value chains. Value chain analysis thus accords well with world-system theory's assertions about peripheral subordination to the core. Regarding governance, Gereffi, Humphrey, and Sturgeon (2005) use three chain characteristics (transaction complexity, transaction codification, and supplier capabilities) to explain the degree of formal coordination and power asymmetries in value chains. They point to a gradual shift toward chain governance structures that are less controlled by developed country companies and better integrated into local economies, a trend counter to world-system theory. Virtually all of the policy proposals emerging from this tradition seek to improve the benefits to the less developed countries, in part through state policies and in part through company and entrepreneurial strategies to occupy higher value-added nodes on the chains (Schmitz 2004).

Another related perspective, stimulated by the collapse of communism and the resurgence of the USA as the "world's only superpower," is theory of empire, sometimes presented as an alternative to "neoliberal" accounts of globalization. Works in this vein have flourished since the USA's invasions of Afghanistan and Iraq in 2002–3. Some, such as Foster (2006), Harvey (2003), and Smith (2004), view American domination as rather ordinary imperialism like that of Britain in the nineteenth century, though of greater power and scope. As the leading capitalist power, the USA bears the burden of making the world safe for capital by providing the global public goods (order, stability, governance institutions) that only the dominant state can provide. American imperialism is for these authors entirely consistent with American history, which they see as imperialist from very early on but never avowedly so. In Ferguson's (2004) variant, US imperialism is both necessary and beneficent; he argues that peace and prosperity have thrived only where the US presence has been clear and vigorous. Wood (2005) analyzes imperialism historically (Roman, Chinese, and Spanish "empires of property," Arab Muslim, Venetian, and Dutch "empires of commerce," British settler-colony imperialism) to argue that US imperialism is both more sweepingly global and less directly political than earlier forms. The key for the contemporary "empire of capital" is maintaining the free flow of capital throughout the globe, not controlling territory.

Wallerstein (2003) himself goes against the grain of most imperialism analyses, emphasizing the decline of American hegemony since the Vietnam War and viewing the latest burst of American militarism as a further hastening of that decline (see also Johnson 2007). For Wallerstein, the US empire is coming to an end as a new round of struggle among core powers takes shape. The obvious challenger, China, has rapidly risen from peripheral to semi-peripheral status and seems destined to become a major core power in the near future.

For most theories of empire, globalization as such is not a central topic. Some analysts (Petras and Veltmeyer 2001) explicitly reject the globalization perspective, arguing that it is an ideological device masking the pernicious inequality and exploitation of capitalist imperialism. On the whole, imperialism arguments recognize only a one-sided globalization that amounts to little more than Americanization.

Such is not the case for a much-discussed and rather elusive treatment by Hardt and Negri (2000). They reject the view that US-led capitalist domination is essentially a new round of classic imperialism. The USA may be the world's only superpower but Empire is not American hegemony superseding older European powers: *"no nation-state can today form the center of an imperialist project.* Imperialism is over" (2000: xiv; italics in original here and below). Rather, Empire is a *"decentered and deterritorialising* apparatus of rule that progressively incorporates the entire global realm within its open, expanding frontiers" (2000: xii). Empire is global networks of production, exchange, technique, media management, and so on, that are assuming global sovereignty and thereby displacing or subordinating nation-states. Empire is global capitalism, as in world-system theory, but it is a new form of postmodern capitalism in which global agencies exercise extensive regulation in the interests of capital. It is also, Hardt and Negri claim, a vulnerable form of capitalism in that it empowers (and gains its strength from) "the multitude," i.e. all those who work or are in need of work. The multitude's potential to disrupt Empire and fashion a "spontaneous and elementary communism" (2000: 294) derives from its increasing concentration in forms of "immaterial labor," by which they mean information, symbolic production, and the manipulation of affect. Immaterial labor fosters cooperative relations among the multitude because it is homogenous (unlike the highly differentiated character of industrial occupations), it operates largely autonomously, and it engenders democratic impulses in the form of demands for global citizenship that would return control of social space to the multitude. Hardt and Negri thus share the long-term optimism of world-system theorists regarding a bottom-up restructuring of global capitalism conditioned by problems inherent in global capitalism itself.[4] In their various ways, authors writing in this vein bolster popular and political critiques that inspire the "anti-" or "other-" globalization movement, a broad range of groups and organizations that challenge the injustices of capitalist world society and advocate egalitarian alternatives (Notes from Nowhere 2003).

WORLD POLITY THEORY: GLOBALIZATION AS THE ENACTMENT OF WORLD CULTURE

Arising almost contemporaneously with world-system theory, world polity theory rejects the materialist, actor-centric epistemology of Marxian analysis in favor of a "deep-culture" or institutional approach. It combines Durkheimian attention to the role of symbolic rituals in defining and affirming social reality with Weberian emphasis on the sources and dynamics of societal rationalization. Its chief architect, John W. Meyer, initially developed this deep-culture approach, commonly described (for historical reasons we must omit) as neoinstitutional theory, in studying educational systems and credentialing. Deliberately setting aside education's avowed purposes – transmitting knowledge and values, i.e. socializing individuals – Meyer (1977) brought to light the institutional effects of schooling. For example, at the individual level, education defines broad social status: the high school dropout has a much lower social status than a college graduate, and this status difference in and of itself strongly affects individual life chances regarding employment, occupation, leisure activities, and so on. At the societal level, education creates child and youth age-grade categories (and, hence, distinct "markets" for clothing companies or toy designers), legitimates particular bodies of knowledge (which companies and states learn to incorporate into their operations, e.g. psychological testing), and so on. More generally, Meyer insisted on education's mutual interpenetration with the broader cultural environment in which it is embedded, arguing that schools and schooling both reflect and help shape fundamental conceptions of social reality, actors, knowledge, and much more.

Meanwhile, Meyer and his colleague Michael Hannan were directing a large cross-national quantitative project studying education, economic development, and political structures around the world in the post-war period (Meyer and Hannan 1979). One of the central topics of the project was the post-war expansion of schooling. Multivariate analyses demonstrated that schooling expansion was essentially a self-generating process, i.e. it was rampant in all regions of the world and was largely independent of national characteristics such as level of economic development, type of political regime, and ethnic heterogeneity (Meyer et al. 1977). Formal education thus appeared to have become a global process, even a global imperative – an obligation that states would ignore only to their peril and shame. Assuming responsibility for a standardized national educational system, free and obligatory at the lower levels, appeared to have become a standard feature of a global cultural model of the state. The suspicion arose that many other features of modern world society might also have "gone global" in this way, becoming embedded in an overarching world culture and spreading through a set of differentiated authority structures constituting a globe-spanning world polity.

Core of the theory

World polity theory begins with the ontological core of world culture – a diffuse, inchoate, but broadly institutionalized set of definitions of the nature of reality. Cultural ontology defines nature, the universe, gods, society, groups, organizations, individuals, and so on. It defines the characteristics, capacities, and pathologies of social entities – the individual, the state, the organization, the ethnic group – and imbues these entities with varying forms of sacrality, purpose, and meaning (Meyer, Boli, and Thomas 1987). Most central are the individual, highly sacralized (Elliott, forthcoming) and anointed as the ultimate source of sovereign authority, and the state, which organizes the sacred nation on behalf of the citizenry and assumes primary responsibility for the two great purposes of the human project, progress and justice. Also significant are the family and the religio-ethnic group, though the individualist bias of world culture gnaws at the collectivist bonds defining these entities.

Modern world culture insists on the rational capability of entities: they can identify alternative courses of action, compare costs and benefits, and choose optimal actions accordingly. The ends toward which action is to be oriented (Weber's value rationality) are defined within deep culture as a set of "interests" that entities are to pursue. Rational action is strongly legitimated as the superior mode of behavior, and the rationalized cultural environment offers an enormous array of rationalized means by which actors can pursue their interests. They include scientific and technical knowledge, systematic accounting, principles of organization, jurisprudence, interaction skills, educational curricula, and on and on. The paradox of rationalized world culture is that purportedly rational actors engage much more in cultural "enactment" than in rational action. Actors enact the cultural models of actors and actorhood that the cultural environment supplies, seeking to actualize the models in themselves and in the organizations through which they act. Here world polity theory adopts a decidedly Durkheimian mode: enactment is a ritualized process of affirming the identity, meaning, and sacrality of actors through purportedly rational action. The catch is that the demonstrable rationality of most action is unknown or, at best, dubious. Actors, whether individuals, organizations, or states, generally lack the resources, information, and expertise required to behave optimally. Rationality is not simply "bounded"; it is beyond the reach of most actors most of the time. In consequence, rationality usually is *ex post facto* wishful thinking. To maintain the fiction of their rationality, actors in hindsight construct rationalized explanations of their behavior, selectively editing the past and present to put the right foot forward for the future.

This analysis leads world polity theory to predict considerable structural and rhetorical isomorphism among actors (a prominent theme that Meyer was instrumental in bringing into organizations research [Powell and DiMaggio 1991]). States are primary candidates for isomorphic structuration because they face precisely those conditions that make ritualized rationality most compelling: complex and uncertain environments, rapid change, insufficient or over-abundant information, internal organizational incoherence, ever-increasing demands from the external environment and internal forces, and so on. In addition, states are culturally depicted (not least by much academic theorizing) as aggressive competitors struggling for resources and status in an anarchic interstate system, a world-view which compels states both to embrace change and to drink deeply from every available source of legitimacy. New states are thus likely to adopt prevailing global cultural models of the state more or less wholesale (Meyer et al. 1997). For example, they adopt formal constitutions, build school and health care systems, organize military and police forces, pass labor laws, and so on. Older states are likely to be receptive to changes driven by global cultural trends as long as the changes are accompanied by reasonably authoritative claims regarding their necessity, legitimacy, and effectiveness. When, for example, the international women's movement made women's empowerment a global principle grounded in considerations of justice and women's personhood, established states realized that they had a responsibility to extend political rights to women in the 1920s (Berkovitch 1999). When protecting the natural environment became a global cultural principle backed by scientific claims of the intimate co-dependency of the human and natural worlds, established states rapidly created environmental protection agencies in the 1970s (Frank 1997).

For world polity theorists, these examples show that world cultural change readily produces changes in actor identity and interests and, thus, changes in the structure and behavior of actors. The efficacious, responsible, well-constituted state could ignore schooling in the eighteenth century, women's rights in the nineteenth century, or the environment through most of the twentieth century. In earlier times, states did not know that their interests extended to such matters. Authoritative theories of the instrumental advantages and moral necessity of these interests had yet to be constructed and institutionalized in world culture. Once in place, however, these theories embed new interests in global models of the state, and both new and old states eventually (and, often, suddenly) find implementation of these new interests obvious, natural, and reasonable. The same logic applies to other actor entities: the more deeply they are embedded in world culture, the greater the global isomorphism they display. Thus, TNCs are especially likely to rely on standard technical means (for example advanced accounting principles, complex financial instruments), turn to common sources of expert advice (organizational, engineering, design, and environmental management consultants), adopt similar measures of corporate social responsibility, and so on.

World polity theory recognizes the power capabilities of states and TNCs, the influence of capitalist groups on states and intergovernmental organizations, and other key features of world-system theory. With its emphasis on world culture, however, it also recognizes a major globalizing role for international nongovernmental organizations (INGOs). INGOs are especially important in forming, debating, crystallizing, and propagating world culture (Boli and Thomas 1997, 1999). Other global actors (states, TNCs, IGOs) also do much world cultural work, but INGOs range over a much broader array of social sectors and they are much less constrained than power actors by the rigors of competition and interest-oriented constituencies. Hence, for many INGOs world cultural work is their primary activity. They make rules for globalized sports, codify best practices for globalized professions, set technical standards for product functionality and safety, and so on. INGOs are also especially highly engaged in promoting global actor models and the means of actualizing them. They push theories of the efficacy or efficiency of scientific, technical, legal, and other forms of knowledge that define actor properties, strengths, and weaknesses. They push innumerable specific instrumental means deemed suitable for the attainment of actor interests. They also push normative claims derived from the global moral order to urge actors to behave responsibly with respect to broad conceptions of virtue and justice (Boli 2006). Often such normative pursuits take the form of global social movements that promote equality and respect for those whom globalization excludes or victimizes: the poor, the marginalized, the oppressed, the exploited.

INGOs are important for another, related, reason: they provide the best window through which to examine the content of world culture. In this claim world polity theory is self-consciously tautological: it reads the content of world culture from the structures, operations, and purposes of INGOs while arguing that INGO structures, operations, and purposes are enactments of world culture. Thus, for example, Boli and Thomas (1997) infer that world culture defines and legitimates the individual as the central social entity because INGOs are constructed primarily around individuals – as members, voters, officers, intended beneficiaries of INGO activities, and so on. Collective entities such as the family, religio-ethnic group, village, or social class are much less central to world culture because they are rarely embedded in INGOs, even as beneficiaries. Similarly, they infer that world culture is highly rationalized because most INGOs operate in highly rationalized sectors – science, technique, production, professions, information, standardization, accounting, and the like – and most INGOs are formally organized structures employing rationalized means of action. INGOs thus reflect or embody world culture while they also propagate it and help shape it through their everyday work. This thrust in world polity analysis reinforces and overlaps with other work describing the rise of a "global civil society" (Keane 2003), "activists beyond borders" (Keck and Sikkink 1998), or a "third force" (Florini 2000) mostly distinct from states and the world market that increasingly crystallizes new global problems, influences the global policy agenda, and negotiates the link between global and local settings.

As we have seen, world-system theory depicts a world of divergent development, with great differentiation between core, semi-periphery, and periphery. World polity theory implies considerable convergent global development due to isomorphism processes that homogenize actor interests, structure, and action. Homogenization is slowed, however, by two factors. One is the considerable gap between actor models, however passionately embraced, and practical action. The deep and broad legitimation of world culture impels actors to adopt global models and purposes. Rhetorical adoption is easy; practical implementation is not. Actualization of the models requires material resources, expertise, organizational acumen, political will, and much more. Many actors – states, individuals, corporations, IGOs – are ill equipped to meet these requirements. Expressed commitments to effective national health care, improved personal leadership skills, or full compliance with international accounting standards remain pipe dreams far beyond practical actor capabilities. Organizational inertia, interest groups, and local cultures inhibit or distort the implementation of world cultural models and methods. Actors may embrace world cultural models and purposes only rhetorically, masking their true intentions in acts of bad faith undertaken solely to gain legitimacy. These and other factors ensure that loose coupling between world culture and local situations is widespread and routine. Isomorphism is on the rise but world culture is not a steamroller flattening all cultural variation in one sweep (Lechner and Boli 2005).

A second brake on world culture's homogenization effects derives from legitimations of diversity and difference that inhere in world culture itself (Lechner and Boli 2005). Here world polity theory resembles Robertson's analysis of the universalism of particularism. World culture defines social entities and their identities in diffuse terms, but it is not diffuse about identity as such: actors have identities; actors should ponder and explore their identities; actors should develop unique and distinctive identities. Modern actors should "break the mold," strike off in new directions, "make something of the self." Above all, modern actors should be "true to the self." Difference and diversity are thus deeply legitimated. Authenticity is prized.[5] Particularism is championed universally. This cultural logic impels individuals, organizations, religio-ethnic groups, etc. to emphasize or invent anew distinct features, habits, traditions, and mores. Particularly highly empowered in this respect are peoples who are oppressed or exploited by mammoth global forces – "indigenous peoples," who constitute a reservoir of authentic (primordial) diversity of great value to humanity, and migrant peoples, strangers in a strange land, whose right to their own languages and cultures is well ensconced in world culture (and therefore much debated). The right to be different is also an obligation, though the distinctiveness that results often has an air of superficiality about it.

World polity theory is evidently compatible with globalization theory à la Robertson and Hannerz. Both perspectives begin with culture and conceive globalization as the construction of transcendent (supraterritorial or deterritorialized) cultural constructs, though world polity theory adds the neoinstitutional argument. World polity theory is less compatible with world-system theory, though not entirely so. Both world-system and world polity theory discuss global social movements, albeit not in common terms. World-system theory treats counter-systemic movements as seemingly automatic, natural responses to globalizing capitalism's exploitation and inequality – from this point of view, environmental movements typically challenge the logic of capitalist accumulation in response to actual environmental harm caused by capitalist actors. World polity theory offers a deep-culture explanation for many social movements – they represent the ritual affirmation and reconstruction of the sacred individual, nation, nature, etc. – that extends to many types of movements not treated by world-system theory. From this point of view, environmental movements serve as carriers of world-cultural scripts and may mobilize transnationally even in settings not directly affected by environmental devastation (Frank, Longhofer, and Schofer 2007).

An important limitation of world polity scholarship is its modest historical range, concentrating on the post-war period and reaching back only to the mid-nineteenth century. It has rather little to say about the preceding three or four centuries, which are so integral to world-system theory's understanding of global capitalism. Meyer, Boli, and Thomas (1987) refer to Christendom's role in the emergence of the world polity and world culture but a comprehensive genealogy corresponding to Wallerstein's three-volume opus is lacking. Garrett's (2001) enlightening analysis of Christendom's vital role in the emergence of natural law and human rights ideologies could serve as a model for such an endeavor.

CONCLUSION

Theories of globalization, exemplified by the perspectives we have summarized, are a vital part of sociological theory more generally. Inspired to varying degrees by Marx, Weber, and Durkheim, students of globalization are creatively rethinking both the analytical approaches and substantive issues that marked the now classical traditions. In particular, they are trying to capture the distinctive features of the contemporary "global age." Relative to early efforts, such as Marshall McLuhan's notion that "[a]s electrically contracted, the globe is no more than a village" (1994: 4), the recent advances in scholarship jointly offer a more systematic analysis that has also generated more fruitful research. According to one argument about the nature of global transformations, the current age is wholly different from the preceding "modern" age since much of social life occurs beyond the constraints of the nation-state (Albrow 1996). The authors we have reviewed here take different positions on this point, with Wallerstein emphasizing long-term continuities, Meyer treating nation-state institutions as enactments of world culture, and Robertson agreeing that globalization entails the reorganization of human experience. They also vary in the extent to which they view theory as a form of critique: in contrast with Robertson and Meyer's mainly academic scholarship on "generic" globalization, which interprets resistance to current globalization in the context of an emerging world culture (Lechner and Boli 2005: ch. 7), Wallerstein aligns more closely with the anti-capitalist rhetoric and "critical" analysis of globalization inherent in "global justice" movements (Evans 2005). While Robertson and Meyer take a more "cultural" approach to globalization by comparison with Wallerstein's "materialist" analysis, at their most ambitious they also aim to overcome the old dichotomies in social theory. In spite of the differences among them and the limitations of each individual research direction we have reviewed, globalization theorists collectively help to shape the agenda of sociological theory for the twenty-first century. The key scholarly task, their work implies, is to understand the nature and organization of world society.

Notes

1 The term "globalization" was not new; Waters (2001) reports instances of its use from around 1960, and Scholte (2005: 50) traces its cognates "globalize" and "globalism" back to Reiser and Davies (1944).

2 Scholte's (2005) critical analysis arrives at a similar conceptualization: the essence of globalization is "supraterritoriality" or "deterritorialization." The supraterritorial is that which transcends territorial boundaries and identities. It is not limited by considerations of geography or spatial location. It is "transworld simultaneity and instantaneity" (p. 61).

3 Kondratieff posited four phases in each cycle: inflationary growth, recession, deflationary growth, and depression. Most world-system work simplifies the cycle into two phases.

4 Due to its high-flown rhetoric, sweeping generalizations, and paucity of empirical referents, Hardt and Negri's analysis has evoked extensive criticism. Dean and Passavant (2003) offer a thoughtful collection of critical essays.

5 Ritzer (2004) devotes an entire book to a critique of globalization's transformation of cultures into inauthentic (commodified, standardized, meaningless) shadows of themselves. Globalization creates what he calls non-places, non-things, non-people, and non-services (2004: ch. 3), replacing everything that is authentic with woefully McDonaldized substitutes.

Bibliography

Abu Lughod, J. (1989) *Before European Hegemony: The World System A.D. 1250–1350*. New York: Oxford University Press.

Albrow, M. (1996) *The Global Age: State and Society Beyond Modernity*. Stanford: Stanford University Press.

Berkovitch, N. (1999) *From Motherhood to Citizenship: Women's Rights and International Organizations*. Baltimore: Johns Hopkins University Press.

Boli, J. (2006) "The Rationalization of Virtue and Virtuosity in World Society," in M.-L. Djelic and K. Sahlin-Andersson (eds.), *Transnational Governance: Institutional Dynamics of Regulation*. Cambridge: Cambridge University Press.

Boli, J., and Thomas, G. M. (1997) "World Culture in the World Polity: A Century of International Non-Governmental Organization." *American Sociological Review* 62(2): 171–90.

Boli, J., and Thomas, G. M. (eds.) (1999) *Constructing World Culture: International Non-governmental Organizations Since 1875*. Stanford: Stanford University Press.

Castells, M. (1996) *The Information Age*, vol. 1, *The Rise of the Network Society*. Oxford: Blackwell.

Chase-Dunn, C. (1998) *Global Formation: Structures of the Global Economy*, updated edn. Boulder, CO: Rowman & Littlefield.

Chase-Dunn, C., and Hall, T. D. (1997) *Rise and Demise: Comparing World-Systems*. Boulder, CO: Westview.

Dean, J., and Passavant, P. (eds.) (2003) *Empire's New Clothes: Reading Hardt and Negri*. New York: Routledge.

Elliott, M. A. (forthcoming) "Human Rights and the Triumph of the Individual in World Culture." *Cultural Sociology*.

Evans, P. (2005) "Counterhegemonic Globalization," in T. Janoski, et al. (eds.), *The Handbook of Political Sociology*, Cambridge: Cambridge University Press.

Ferguson, N. (2004) *Colossus: The Price of America's Empire*. New York: Penguin.

Florini, A. M. (ed.) (2000) *The Third Force: The Rise of Transnational Civil Society*. Washington, DC: Carnegie Endowment for International Peace.

Foster, J. B. (2006) *Naked Imperialism: The US Pursuit of Global Dominance*. New York: Monthly Review Press.

Frank, A. G. (1966) "The Development of Underdevelopment." *Monthly Review* 18: 4–17.

Frank, A. G., and Gills, B. K. (eds.) (1993) *The World System: Five Hundred Years or Five Thousand?* London: Routledge.

Frank, D. J. (1997) "Science, Nature, and the Globalization of the Environment, 1870–1990." *Social Forces* 75: 411–37.

Frank, D. J., Longhofer, W., and Schofer, E. (2007) "World Society, NGOs, and Environmental Policy Reform in Asia." *International Journal of Comparative Sociology* 48(4): 275–95.

Garrett, W. R. (2001) "Religion, Law, and the Human Condition," in P. Beyer (ed.), *Religion in the Process of Globalization*. Wurzburg: Ergon.

Gereffi, G., Humphrey, J., and Sturgeon, T. J. (2005) "The Governance of Global Value Chains." *Review of International Political Economy* 12(1): 78–104.

Gereffi, G., and Korzeniewicz, M. (1994) *Commodity Chains and Global Capitalism*. Westport, CT: Greenwood Press.

Goldstein, J. (1988) *Long Cycles: Prosperity and War in the Modern Age*. New Haven: Yale University Press.

Griswold, W. (1987) "The Fabrication of Meaning: Literary Interpretation in the United States, Great Britain, and the West Indies." *American Journal of Sociology* 92: 1077–1117.

Hannerz, U. (1987) "The World in Creolisation." *Africa* 57(4): 546–59.

Hannerz, U. (1990) *Cultural Complexity: Studies in the Social Organization of Meaning*. New York: Columbia University Press.

Hannerz, U. (1996) *Transnational Connections: Culture, People, Places*. London: Routledge.

Hardt, M., and Negri, A. (2000) *Empire*. Cambridge, MA: Harvard University Press.

Harvey, D. (1989) *The Condition of Postmodernity: An Enquiry into the Origins of Cultural Change*. Oxford: Blackwell.

Harvey, D. (2003) *The New Imperialism*. Oxford: Oxford University Press.

Held, D., McGrew, A., Goldblatt, D., and Perraton, J. (1999) *Global Transformations: Politics, Economics and Culture*. Cambridge: Polity.

Johnson, C. (2007) *Nemesis: The Last Days of the American Republic*. New York: Holt.

Keane, J. (2003) *Global Civil Society?* Cambridge: Cambridge University Press.

Keck, M. E., and Sikkink, K. (1998) *Activists Beyond Borders: Advocacy Networks in International Politics*. Ithaca, NY: Cornell University Press.

Lechner, F. J. (2005) "Religious Rejections of Globalization," in M. Juergensmeyer (ed.), *Religion and Global Civil Society*. Oxford: Oxford University Press.

Lechner, F. J., and Boli, J. (2005) *World Culture: Origins and Consequences*. Oxford: Blackwell.

Liebes, T., and Katz, E. (1990) *The Export of Meaning: Cross-Cultural Readings of "Dallas."* New York: Oxford University Press.

McLuhan, M. (1994 [1964]) *Understanding Media: The Extensions of Man*. Cambridge, MA: MIT Press.

McMichael, P. (2005) "Globalization," in T. Janoski et al. (eds.), *The Handbook of Political Sociology*, Cambridge: Cambridge University Press.

Meyer, J. W. (1977) "The Effects of Education as an Institution." *American Journal of Sociology* 83(1): 55–77.

Meyer, J. W., Boli, J., and Thomas, G. M. (1987) "Ontology and Rationalization in the Western Cultural Account," in G. M. Thomas, J. W. Meyer, F. O. Ramirez, and J. Boli (eds.), *Institutional Structure: Constituting State, Society, and the Individual*. Newbury Park, CA: Sage.

Meyer, J. W., Boli, J., Thomas, G. M., and Ramirez, F. O. (1997) "World Society and the Nation-State." *American Journal of Sociology* 103(1): 144–81.

Meyer, J. W., and Hannan, M. T. (eds.) (1979) *National Development and the World System*. Chicago: University of Chicago Press.

Meyer, J. W., Ramirez, F. O., Rubinson, R., and Boli-Bennett, J. (1977) "The World Educational Revolution, 1950–1970." *Sociology of Education* 50: 242–58.

Nettl, J. P., and Robertson, R. (1968) *International Systems and the Modernization of Societies: The Formation of National Goals and Attitudes*. New York: Basic Books.

Notes from Nowhere (eds.) (2003) *We Are Everywhere: The Irresistible Rise of Global Anti-Capitalism*. London: Verso.

Petras, J., and Veltmeyer, H. (2001) *Globalization Unmasked: Imperialism in the 21st Century*. New York: Zed Books.

Powell, W. W., and DiMaggio, P. J. (eds.) (1991) *The New Institutionalism in Organizational Analysis*. Chicago: University of Chicago Press.

Reiser, O. L., and Davies, B. (1944) *Planetary Democracy: An Introduction to Scientific Humanism and Applied Semantics*. New York: Creative Age Press.

Ritzer, G. (2004) *The Globalization of Nothing*. Thousand Oaks, CA: Pine Forge.

Robertson, R. (1991) "The Globalization Paradigm: Thinking Globally," in D. Bromley (ed.), *Religion and the Social Order*, vol. 1, *New Developments in Theory and Research*. Greenwich, CN: JAI Press.

Robertson, R. (1992) *Globalization: Social Theory and Global Culture*. London: Sage.

Robertson, R. (1995) "Glocalization: Time-Space and Homogeneity-Heterogeneity," in M. Featherstone, S. Lash, and R. Robertson (eds.), *Global Modernities*. London: Sage.

Robinson, W. I. (2004) *A Theory of Global Capitalism: Production, Class, and State in a Transnational World*. Baltimore: Johns Hopkins University Press.

Rodney, W. (1972) *How Europe Underdeveloped Africa*. London: Bogle-L'Ouverture Publications; Dar es Salaam: Tanzanian Publishing House.

Schmitz, H. (ed.) (2004) *Local Enterprises in the Global Economy: Issues of Governance and Upgrading*. Cheltenham: Edward Elgar.

Scholte, J. A. (2005) *Globalization: A Critical Introduction*, 2nd edn. New York: Palgrave/St. Martin's Press.

Sklair, L. (2001) *The Transnational Capitalist Class*. Oxford: Blackwell.

Sklair, L. (2002) *Globalization: Capitalism and its Alternatives*. Oxford: Oxford University Press.

Smith, N. (2004) *The Endgame of Globalization*. New York: Routledge.

Taylor, T. (1997) *Global Pop: World Music, World Markets*. New York: Routledge.

Thomas, G. M., Meyer, J. W., Ramirez, F. O., and Boli, J. (1987) *Institutional Structure: Constituting State, Society, and the Individual*. Newbury Park, CA: Sage.

Tomlinson, J. (1991) *Cultural Imperialism: A Critical Introduction*. London: Pinter.

Wallerstein, I. (1974–89) *The Modern World System*, vol. 1, *Capitalist Agriculture and the Origins of the European World-Economy in the Sixteenth Century*; vol. 2, *Mercantilism and the Consolidation of the European World-Economy, 1600–1750*; vol. 3, *The Second Era of Great Expansion of the Capitalist World-Economy, 1730–1840s*. New York: Academic Press.

Wallerstein, I. (1990) "Culture as the Ideological Battleground of the Modern World-System." *Theory, Culture and Society* 7: 31–55.

Wallerstein, I. (2003) *The Decline of American Power*. New York: New Press.

Wallerstein, I. (2004) *World-Systems Analysis: An Introduction*. Durham, NC: Duke University Press.

Waters, M. (2001) *Globalization*, 2nd edn. London: Routledge.

Watson, J. L. (ed.) (2006) *Golden Arches East: McDonald's in East Asia*, 2nd edn. Stanford: Stanford University Press.

Wood, E. M. (2005) *Empire of Capital*. London: Verso.

Part IV

Sociology and the Social Sciences

17

Genetics and Social Theory

Oonagh Corrigan

Introduction

The term "revolution" has been used to describe developments in the fields of genetic science and molecular biology during the past 20 years. The fast pace of technological change, the huge financial investment in genetics and biotechnology, the emergence of an ever-increasing array of genetic tests in the clinic and the increasing blurring of boundaries between biology and culture have prompted an explosion of sociological contemplation and empirical work. Social scientists are not alone in these endeavors, and other disciplines such as moral philosophy, law, medicine, and public policy have been drawn into deliberation on the so-called ELSI (ethical, legal, and social issues) aspects of the "new genetics." However, despite this ardent focus of attention on genetics the cup of social theory is far from running over.

Sociology has a long and at times hostile relationship with the biological sciences. While founding figures of the discipline such as Auguste Comte and Émile Durkheim respected the rigors of the natural scientific method, they were keen to distinguish sociology from the other natural sciences, highlighting sociology's unique position in demonstrating the role of social institutions and in determining social behavior, interaction, and identity formation. The nature versus nurture debate raged for much of the twentieth century. Lombroso's theories on criminal behavior in the late nineteenth century, based on an evolutionary model of human development that could identify the propensity of such behavior by scientific and statistical methods such as measuring human skulls, have been rightly vilified by sociologists. In the 1970s too, Edward O. Wilson's sociobiology, a theory of human behavior and society premised largely on a convergence of Charles Darwin's theory of evolution and a crude hypothesis about the function of human genes, has been severely criticized by most sociologists. Such theories have drawn on the biological sciences to explain human behavior and social interaction. The popularity too of social constructionism in recent decades has tended not only to undermine scientific authority in general but has contributed towards a polar opposition between biological and sociological explanations for human behavior. Human behavior and social interaction are viewed primarily as determined by social conditions, and explanations based on biology are seen as reductionist and false. Although in recent years the "sociology of the body" has come to be regarded as making a valued contribution to the neglected issue of the body by sociologists, here too the literature tends to position biological accounts as false, highlighting instead its social construction.

What sense, then, are we to make of the new genetics? Is this simply a scientific enterprise that falsely explains human behavior, interaction, and identity, one which should be exposed and opposed by sociologists for its false assumptions? I suggest that we need to approach the field more openly, and in particular that theories should be aligned closely to empirical work in this regard. Yes, we need to assess whether, like Lombroso's theories which once provided legitimacy for the stigmatization of certain races and groups within society, the new genetics too is a dangerous ideology. But we should also question the extent to which social theories locked into a view that the biological sciences lead inexorably to biological reductionism can contribute to an understanding of the complexities of the role played by molecular biology and genetics in contemporary society. As this chapter will demonstrate, theoretical contributions depicting a largely gloomy landscape where the specter of eugenics and notions of genetic determinism loom large, fail to capture the complexities of the new genetics era. One confounding factor for social theorists is that failure is as much a feature of the new genetics as is success. Much of the initial theorizing is premised on an expectation that genetics has the power to reshape our biology and social relations, yet science's failure in human genetic engineering to deliver promised cures anticipated from the much-publicized Human Genome Project, as well as the failure of the biotech financial sector to secure longer-term financial success and the refusal of the public to accept GM foods in Europe, all stand in contrast to the anticipation, hype, and publicity that surround genetics. However, DNA has become a successful "cultural icon," and while the biotech sector has yet to be regarded as a financial success, endeavors have attracted multibillion-dollar investments by governments and funding bodies in Western and newly emerging Eastern market economies. Furthermore, the number of genetic tests now available in the clinic is rising, and patient groups have increasingly become involved not simply as passive recipients of genetic knowledge, tests, research, and treatments but as active "genetic citizens" involved in securing the hoped-for benefits in terms of treatments and cures for disease. Hype, hope, and fear have characterized scientific endeavors and challenge social theorists to make sense of the new milieu of science and society.

"OLD" GENETICS AND EUGENIC IDEOLOGY

As already indicated, the recent focus of attention has been on the so-called "genetics revolution" associated with large financial investments, and the unprecedented scientific activity in molecular biology and genetics that has been taking place since the late 1980s. Nevertheless, as sociologists and other scholars are keen to demonstrate, the so-called "new genetics" cannot be divorced from its history despite the desire by scientists to draw clear lines of demarcation between present practices and much of the disreputable and ideologically driven quasi science that fueled past eugenic practices. Furthermore, as historian Evelyn Fox Keller (2000) argues, much of the twentieth century can be understood both scientifically and culturally as "the century of the gene." This chapter begins, then, with an account of the history of the "old" genetics and its relationship with eugenics, as it is important to understand the legacy this has created for contemporary understandings, practices, and concerns.

Gregor Mendel's explanations of heredity in the latter half of the nineteenth century created the foundation for modern genetics. Based largely on experiments in peas and the fruit fly, he established that traits were passed intact, with each member of the parental generation transmitting half of his and her hereditary factors to each offspring, with traits such as brown eyes "dominant" over others.

Genetic theories coalesced with Darwin's (1994 [1859]) ideas of natural selection, and spawned the social movement of eugenics which prevailed during the early twentieth century. Furthermore, the rise of medicine, and in particular public health and welfare policy, as well as a more general approach of seeing biology as a solution to social problems such as crime, drunkenness, and poverty was the broader societal context within which eugenics took hold.

While genetics provided explanations for the transmission of physical characteristics such as hair color, finger length, and certain diseases such as Huntington's Chorea, eugenics was formulated on the theory that behavioral characteristics were also inherited. The idea of eugenics, a process for selectively breeding humans in order to preserve and promote "desirable" characteristics, was first formulated by the scientist and cousin of Darwin, Francis Galton. A major motivation underpinning many eugenicists was the idea of human progress. The idea of progress was not based solely on the advancement of scientific knowledge but also on genetic improvement. Interestingly, it was at a meeting held by the Sociological Society in England in 1904 that Galton described eugenics as "the science which deals with all influences that improve the inborn qualities of a race; also with those that develop them to the utmost advantage" (Johnson 1914: 99). The ultimate goal of eugenics was the improvement of the human race, or, more specifically, to preserve the "purity" of certain ethnic groups or "races" (Stephan 1996). Galton intended eugenics to extend to any technique that might serve to increase the representation of those with "good genes," in this way accelerating evolution.

Eugenics was as much a social movement as a scientific one, and while eugenics has become most closely associated with the Nazi regime, in the early twentieth century Fabian socialists and leftist intellectuals were also enthusiastic supporters (Paul 1995). Appearing to offer technocratic solutions to social problems and the prevalent anxieties of the time about the perceived social and biological degeneration of modern societies, eugenic programs were as popular in liberal social democratic spheres as they were in totalitarian regimes. Many endeavors focused on promoting the improvement in human stock through so-called "positive eugenics," including such practices as the encouragement of "good breeding" (Richards 2004) and improvements in the health and fitness of "human stock." However, eugenics programs also had darker, more sinister aspects. Galton proposed that the human race might also be improved by eliminating society's so-called "undesirables."

Encompassing both "positive" and "negative" aspects, these ideas increased in popularity during the early decades of the twentieth century. Programs emerged in various Western countries manifesting themselves in multiple forms, ranging from "better baby" competitions, to contraception and abortion facilities, through to compulsory sterilization.

A human genetics program emerged, focusing on the analysis of various conditions, particularly those seen to be creating a burden for society. The so-called "feebleminded" were a particular focus. Psychologist and eugenicist Henry Goddard was of the opinion that "feeblemindedness" was a hereditary condition of the brain that made those who had inherited it more prone to becoming criminals, paupers, and prostitutes. Societal problems such as poverty, vagrancy, prostitution, and alcoholism were understood by eugenicists as primarily the outcome of a person's genetic inheritance rather than emanating from social, political, and economic factors. Research in human heredity was carried out in laboratories to develop eugenically useful knowledge. Much of this research was based on case studies of particular families. Histories and family pedigrees of the Jukes family, for example, a US family of paupers, criminals, harlots, epileptics, and mental defectives, were recorded and used for decades as a textbook example of how heredity shaped human behavior. The pedigree chart was used to track the presence or absence of a given trait (phenotype) through two or more generations of a family. By using the pedigree charts, eugenicists gave the impression that vague behaviors are well-established genetic traits, whereas most pedigrees made by the eugenicists showed nothing about biological heredity and were anecdotal in nature. A visiting scientific committee to the Eugenics Record Office in 1935 found that the collection of data was haphazard, that many questionnaires were improperly completed by the family members themselves, and that second- or third-hand reports were trusted. The committee concluded that virtually all pedigree information collected over the preceding quarter-century was worthless for genetic purposes. Nevertheless, such was the ideology surrounding eugenics that the belief in heredity of behavioral characteristics prevailed.

The mental and behavioral characteristics of different "races" was also a focus of the eugenics movement, and in northern Europe and the United States eugenics was frequently used to support ideas of the existence of a superior white, middle-class Protestant elite, such as the so-called Aryan race. Beginning in 1907, compulsory sterilization laws were passed in many states in the US, with Denmark and Germany passing such measures in the 1930s. While these countries adopted compulsory sterilization programs designed to prevent the continued breeding of those deemed to be undesirable, the eugenic movement in Nazi Germany led not only to the sterilization of hundreds of thousands of individuals but ultimately to Hitler's final solution, the Holocaust, where millions of "undesirables" were murdered. In Nazi Germany the so-called "undesirables" included Jews, Gypsies, the mentally defective, and those with genetic diseases such as Huntington's Chorea. Nevertheless, while Nazi Germany is popularly seen as the extreme point of eugenics, many eugenicists of all political persuasions opposed the Nazi excesses and, of course, eugenics was well developed long before the Nazis came to power. Interestingly, state negative eugenics was most developed in the social/liberal countries of northern Europe and North America, with the Catholic Church being the only really effective opposition in the rest of the world. Therefore, while historians and social and political scientists have documented the horrors of Nazi eugenics, their work also suggests the need to be attentive to the complexities and broad spectrum of eugenic practices.

BIG SCIENCE: ETHICS, AND THE NEW GENETICS

Driven by political ideology and associated with the dangers of nationalism, eugenics, at least how it had been practiced, fell into disrepute following the end of the Nazi period. Scientists were keen to distinguish the many shoddy scientific studies associated with eugenic programs from the scientific theories of Mendel and Darwin, and the science of genetics was not accorded the same degree of importance during the immediate post-war period. Although the process for discovering the chromosomal location of genes and their relation to each other continued, this task was a laborious, difficult, and slow one. Despite the discovery by James Watson and Francis Crick in 1953 of the physical structure of DNA (the molecular structure that holds genetic information), which was considered to be a landmark scientific breakthrough, scientists still faced a daunting task in identifying all the genes of the human body. By the 1980s, however, genetic maps were good enough to allow scientists to go "hunting" for genes among families of people with inherited diseases such as Huntington's disease and cystic fibrosis. Nevertheless, it was the invention of PCR (polymerase chain reaction) technology that accelerated the pace of gene discovery (Rabinow 1997) by enabling DNA to be replicated and amplified. This technique, along with the availability of new high-speed computer sequencing technology, helped facilitate the global endeavor to map and sequence the entire human genome.

The Human Genome Project marks the entry of genetics into what scholars of science and technology studies have termed "big science" (Galison and Hevly 1993; Weinberg 1961), and officially began in 1990 with the aim of completing the genetic sequencing of certain forms of bacteria, yeast, plants, animals, and ultimately human beings. As with previous big science projects this was a large-scale collaborative project, coordinated by the US Department of Energy and the National Institutes of Health; the UK's Wellcome Trust was also a major partner, and additional contributions came from Japan, France, Germany, China, and others. In all, 20 research groups from six countries were involved. One-third of the human genome was sequenced in the UK at the Sanger Institute. The scale and cost of the project were huge. It is estimated that work carried out in sequencing the single gene responsible for cystic fibrosis alone cost between US$50 million and US$150 million. Headed by James Watson in the USA, who played a key role as both scientist and political lobbyist, the project was as much a political and economic endeavor as a scientific one. The project's aims were to identify all genes, determining the sequences of the 3 billion chemical base pairs that make up human DNA, and to store this information in databases.

The ethos underpinning the project was based on the notion of a "public commons" (Olson 2002) – that information should be for the common good of all society and should be made freely available via the internet to scientists worldwide.

For many of those involved in developing the project, such as John Sulston, former director of the UK's Sanger Centre, this was a crucial moral and democratic justification and motivating factor (Sulston and Ferry 2002). Nevertheless, as Nowotny, Scott, and Gibbons (2001) argue, in contemporary society the boundaries between the private and public spheres of science have merged, and the two strands are now co-produced. The twin goals of the new biotech era are the generation of health and wealth. Alongside the public effort there was an understanding that the private biotech sector was crucial to capitalize on the knowledge generated, and to transform it into useful technologies and products such as new drugs and treatments. A further muddying of the waters between private and public involves the patenting of genes and genetic testing kits, including activities by a rival private venture company, Celera Genomics. Such activity threatened to undermine the exercise as one based on a public commons ethos (Olson 2002). Nevertheless, public good and ensuring public interests have been key (albeit merely rhetorical) themes of the project's organizers. Alongside scientific research, the establishment of programs of research into the social, ethical, and policy implications of genomics have been seen as crucial to promotion, education, and guidance regarding the conduct of genetic research and the development of related medical and public policies. This has prompted a proliferation of deliberation of these issues and given sociology a role in seeking both to conduct research and contribute to policy formation. Unsurprisingly, one of the first concerns to be discussed by scholars was the extent to which the new genetics could be separated from the eugenic practices of the past.

A NEW EUGENICS?

There are now well over one thousand genetic tests available in UK clinics alone, and while acknowledging some fundamental differences between the past and present, the increasing prevalence of genetic testing has led a number of social scientists to view contemporary genetic practices as a continuation or resurrection of eugenic programs, albeit in a modified form. Troy Duster for example, suggests that the introduction of genetic testing and screening programs has created a "back door" to eugenics (1990). Duster clearly warns against the dangers in the development of prenatal testing for genetic defects, gene therapies, and genetic solutions to problems associated with various racial minority groups. He documents an increasing propensity to see crime, mental illness, and intelligence as expressions of genetic dispositions, and sees current genetic practices as perpetuating the dual myths that race is a genetic trait and that problems stemming from racial inequality can be fixed biologically. Feminists and disability scholars, too, have expressed concern about the social implications of genetic testing, especially as it frequently results in aborting those fetuses identified as having a defective gene. While acknowledging that the recent implementations of practices and policies related to genetic technologies are very different from the past, Ann Kerr and Tom Shakespeare (2002), warn that there is a fine line between contemporary policies and practices on abortion and diseases and the past practice of compulsory sterilization and deviancy. They argue that genetics reinforces medical-genetic definitions of disability, encourages judgments about the social worth of disabled persons, and ultimately involves decisions about what kinds of persons ought to be born. The eugenics of the past was based on state-organized social programs, whereas today interventions based on genetic knowledge are largely a matter of individual choice. However, as a number of sociologists have noted, what is presented as an individual "choice" about reproductive decisionmaking masks the extent to which such choices are governed by social norms which are reinforced by public health screening and "education" programs (Jallinoja 2001; Kerr and Cunningham-Burley 2000; Petersen and Bunton 2002).

The most pessimistic theories on eugenics have been put forward by Giorgio Agamben (1998) and Zygmunt Bauman (1989), who share the view that genocide and other forms of eugenic practice are the inevitable outcomes of modernity. Agamben's ideas are a development of Michel Foucault's concept of biopolitics (Foucault 1981), which claim that modern power is characterized by a fundamentally different rationality than that of sovereign, pre-modern power. Whereas sovereign power was characterized by the right of the sovereign to decide over life and death, modern power is characterized by a productive relation to life. From the late nineteenth century the life, health, and wellbeing of the population all became a central concern for the management of society. For Foucault, the transition from sovereign power to biopower centers on the new political subject becoming a target of a regime of power that operates through governance of the variabilities of biological life itself (Rabinow and Rose 2006). Here the management of health at the level of both the individual and the population is a key concern for modern forms of rationality and governmentality. Agamben (1998) argues that the political management of life and death involves the moral judgment of whose life is worth preserving. While this expresses itself in contemporary modern biomedicine and various health and social welfare practices, it also inevitably involves the elimination of certain sub-populations by the state as part of the goal for the health and welfare of the population at large. For Agamben, the Holocaust is the ultimate exemplar of biopower. As Nikolas Rose notes, for Agamben the concentration camp is "the biopolitical paradigm of the modern," where the collective body of the people becomes a resource for politics and the purging of defective individuals becomes an essential part of the care for life (Rose 2001: 3). However, Rabinow and Rose (2006) disagree that the elimination of populations stems from the inherent rationality of modernity. Rather, they suggest that, while Agamben's ideas have their merits, they are based on a highly general philosophical deployment of the term biopolitics that is "totalizing and misleading" and that the Holocaust was an extraordinary exception emerging only as a result of particular set of historical and technical conditions (2006: 3). Identifying a new configuration of race, health, genealogy, reproduction, and knowledge that are intertwined, Rabinow and Rose develop the concept of biopower to reflect the genetics and new biomedical knowledges and practices in the twenty-first century.

Anxieties about the dangers of a new kind of eugenics have also been expressed by Jürgen Habermas (2003). However, Habermas follows a slightly different tack to other commentators in that what concerns him is not so much the problematic ways in which choices and identities are being socially engineered or the shaping of the social, but rather that individuals and subsequent generations are being biologically engineered and manipulated. Whereas in the past eugenic practices were aimed at future populations based on the encouragement of natural traits through selective breeding, new practices such as human genetic engineering and stem cell technologies are predicated on the irrevocable alteration of an individual's genetic makeup. Given that such alterations could subsequently be passed on through biological inheritance to future generations, Habermas sees the new genetics as having the potential to fundamentally and irrevocably alter human nature. Like Habermas, Fukuyama (2002) understands human nature to be rooted in our biological being, in particular in our genes. For him the important issues at stake are the capacities of biotechnology, in particular through the development of genetic engineering, cloning, and stem cell technologies, to alter human nature and transform our values, and thus move us into a "posthuman" stage of history. His concern about the power of biotechnology to alter not only human behavior but also social institutions leads him to argue for strong international regulations to obstruct any technological advance that he sees as having the potential to disrupt the unity or the continuity of human nature, and thereby the human rights that are based upon it. These theories have generated much debate, sitting awkwardly as they do with other social theories insofar as they are premised largely on a biological view of human nature that presuppose a biological essence to human identity, and as such they contravene many contemporary concepts based on the "social construction" of the body (see CHAPTER 26).

GENES ARE US?

By contrast a number of other theorists are more concerned with the social and cultural power of genetics to construct a false account of what it is to be human. Genetics, they argue, promotes an essentialist ideology reducing the qualities of human identity to mere biology. Echoing more widespread nature versus culture debates and social theoretical opposition to sociobiology, Abby Lippman (1991, 1992) and others since have coined the term "geneticization" to refer to the growing tendency to describe health and disease, the causes and the cures of illness, in genetic terms to the detriment of social and other environmental explanations involved in shaping the manifestation and meaning of bodily characteristics and behavior. Building upon the concept of medicalization, whereby individuals come to perceive their bodies in conformity with biomedical categories, geneticization is conceptualized as a problematic process based on false biological reductionist and deterministic assumptions which generate a sense of fatalism, whereby individuals see themselves as predominantly determined by their genes. Dorothy Nelkin and Susan Lindee (1995), for example, argue that the gene has become a very powerful cultural icon, and that a process of genetic essentialism is occurring whereby what it is to be human is increasingly understood in genetic terms. Such geneticization, these critics argue, stems from highly exaggerated claims made by scientists and the ways in which powerful metaphors, such as "genetic blueprint" and "book of life," are used to describe the human genome. The media in particular are seen to play a vital role in conveying and promoting the iconic status of the gene. Indeed, the gene, as Nelkin and Lindee argue, has become "much more than a biological structure, a unit of heredity, or a sequence of DNA; it has also become a powerful cultural icon. It is ... both a scientific concept and a powerful social symbol, the gene has many

powers" (Nelkin and Lindee 1995: 2). Suggesting that contemporary understandings of genetics represents a "mirage" (Conrad 1999) based on "biofantasies"
(Petersen 2001), sociologists have attempted to challenge its iconic status by revealing the failure of genetics to live up to the promises made, and point to lack of evidence about the extent to which genes cause common diseases, as has been suggested
in exaggerated claims made by scientists and the media.

Nevertheless, concerns about geneticization are not shared by all scholars in this
area. Other theorists suggest that the concept of genetic determinism and the extent
to which the wider public have come to understand themselves as biological beings
determined by their genes have been overstated. Carlos Novas and Nikolas Rose
(2000), for example, maintain that such approaches over-simplify shifts in the forms
of personal identity that arise as a result of the growing awareness of genetic risk.
They claim that knowledge of the new genetics does not so much result in individuals seeing themselves and their lives along predetermined genetic lines, but rather
transforms their identities and relations with medical experts in novel and unexpected ways. The growth in various forms of patient activism, such as those coalesc-
ing around web-based forums and patient organizations (Novas 2006), that not
only raise funds to find cures for genetically based diseases but also help direct scientific agendas, are evidence, they argue, of a more active, self-actualizing form of
personhood. At the same time, a number of commentators have noted that culture
is becoming increasingly biologized. Paul Rabinow, for example, has coined the
term "biosociality" (Rabinow 1992) to refer to the new forms subjecthood and
social and political practices that are emerging. He sees these as providing a possible
basis for overcoming the nature/culture split.

RECONCEPTUALIZING NATURE AND CULTURE

Fox Keller (1992) also sees the new genetic era as one in which the forces of nature
and nurture are radically reconceived. While the genetics associated with early
twentieth-century eugenics was based on the immutability of nature (save for the
elimination of genetic traits through systems of breeding control), the success of
molecular biology has led to the reconceptualization of nature as an increasingly
malleable entity. This blurring of the distinction between nature and culture has of
course been argued by other cultural theorists. In her writings about human and
animal reproduction, and in particular in her account of the making of Dolly the
cloned sheep, anthropologist Sarah Franklin (2003, 2007) speaks of the culturing
of biology and the biologizing of culture. Also, cultural theorist and feminist Donna
Haraway (1991), in her celebratory accounts of the breaking down of distinctions
between nature and culture, sees human genetic engineering and manipulation as
playing a key role in women's emancipation from their bodily limitations. Such
developments, she argues, can provide life-enhancing reconfigurations and the means
to overcome our biological, neurological, and psychological limitations. However,
for Fox Keller (1992), the blurring boundaries between nature and culture have
some unintended negative consequences. Fifty years ago, fears about the specter of
eugenics had been quelled as the aims of genetics operated under a clear demarcation between biology and culture where molecular biology seemed to have little if

any bearing on human behavior. However, the power of the new genetics to prevent the birth of those with genetic defects and its promise to alter behaviors and conditions associated with genetic defects now makes the distinction between biology and culture more difficult to sustain. What was harmful about early twentieth-century eugenics was not the biological manipulation of the gene pool but its social engineering. According to Fox Keller, this does not mean we are returning to another form of explicit social engineering, or a new eugenics period. However, she urges caution about the presentation of the various preventative and treatment options, as "individual choices." Rather, we must recognize such choices are increasingly influenced by a new reinforced distinction that is being drawn between the normal and the abnormal:

> I suggest that the distinction that had earlier been made by the demarcation between culture and biology (or between nature and nurture) is now made by a demarcation between the normal and the abnormal; the force of destiny is no longer attached to culture, or even to biology in general, but rather to the biology or the genetics of disease. . . . The freedom molecular biology promises to bring is the freedom to rout out the domain of destiny inhering in "disease causing genes" in the name of an unspecified standard of normality – a standard that remains unexamined not simply by oversight but by the internal logic of the endeavor. (Fox Keller 1992: 298)

THE RECONFIGURATION OF RACE

Excited by the possibilities of the new genetics to overcome binary divisions between nature and culture, Paul Gilroy (2000) has a utopian vision for the reconceptualization of race. Alongside developments in molecular medicine, the neurosciences, and reproductive technologies, the new genetics is now seen as having a major impact on conceptions of race and difference. As David Skinner (2006) notes, following World War II, and in response to the horrors of eugenics, science was put to the service of anti-racism, with notions of race as a biological category being marginalized. However, the biological sciences, and genetics in particular, are attaching a renewed significance to concepts such as race. Responses to this have prompted opposing visions of what this means for racism. As previously stated, Duster (1990) is wary of a "back door to eugenics", while Gilroy (2000) welcomes opportunities for the new genetics to ultimately make redundant false notions of biological difference based on racial distinctions. While Duster and Gilroy are in agreement that race takes on a renewed emphasis with the rise of the new genetics, they dispute the effects. For Duster the association of certain genetic conditions and racial groups, such as sickle cell disease with black ethnic populations, leads to prejudicial stereotyping of such populations, furthering existing health inequalities. By contrast, Gilroy suggests that the scientific accuracy of genetics testing will refute prejudices based on previously held false beliefs about racial difference based on mere skin color, and thus lead to a better understanding of race and difference. Skinner, however, sees both these utopian and dystopian scenarios as problematic and overly simplistic. Rather than envisioning a wholly utopian or dystopian view, he sees the consequence of a new genetic understanding of race as generating public discourses which "are likely to be complex and varied – at some points destabilizing and at others reinforcing notions of absolute differences between peoples and populations" (Skinner 2006). Here too, though, Skinner points to the dissolving distinction between nature and culture as indicative of a reassessment of kinship and ancestry that at times reinforces biological relatedness and at others reconfigures them. While genetic testing for disease and paternity testing focus on the primacy of biological relatedness, developments in reproductive technology such as surrogacy and egg and sperm donation challenge the importance of biological ties in family life. Furthermore, as Skinner argues, while the contemporary popularity of ancestry and genealogical tracing would appear to reinforce the importance of biological ties, studies indicate that they do not supersede other ways of making sense of identity. In line with Novas and Rose (2000), who claim that, far from generating resignation to fate and passivity, new genetic technologies oblige individuals to formulate life and risk management strategies, Skinner argues genetics would appear to provide a means for individuals to establish new forms of human agency and subjecthood.

THE VALUE OF GENES

The new genetics has been accompanied by an interest in the special properties of the genes of certain nations and indigenous communities. In this context genes are a resource for scientists and pharmaceutical companies to generate increased knowledge about the function and properties of particular genes with the potential to capitalize on this knowledge by generating new drugs. The rise of private and public tissue collection has created enormous storehouses of biological matter (and bioinformation) with great potential for generating commercial value. At the same time, liberal interpretations of novelty and innovation that have prevailed since the 1980s have made the patenting of genes and gene sequences by companies and researchers a routine phenomenon (Hayden 2007). Drawing on Marx's theory of "surplus value," Catherine Waldby (2000, 2002) has coined the term "biovalue" to convey the notion of a surplus value of vitality and instrumental knowledge for human biological material. Value here refers not simply to the economic surplus generated by the procurement of genes and other human biological materials that generate income for biotech and pharmaceutical companies, but also to their moral value. Such endeavors rely on the collection of DNA and frequently other forms of data, including health-related data from individuals within the population under study. While various discourses, including the concept of "the gift" (Tutton 2002), have been invoked to present this moral element as one based on altruism, the dominant moral concept deployed is that of informed consent. Informed consent gives ethical legitimacy to the collection of DNA insofar as it is understood to promote human agency and respect the rights of individuals to determine the uses to which their body parts can be put (Corrigan 2003, 2004). Informed consent is premised on notions of individual autonomy (Corrigan 2003; Wolpe 1998) and as such has provided little moral legitimacy for research to collect genetic samples from populations that value collective decisionmaking. In the South Pacific island of Tonga, for example, the islanders opposed individual informed consent procedures for the collection by scientists of their population's DNA as they argued this ignored the traditional Tongan role of the extended family in decisionmaking (Burton 2002). In the case of the Human Genome Diversity Project, a project involving the collection of human DNA from populations around the globe in order to study the diversity and unity of the entire human species, researchers attempted to avoid opposition to the research by using group consent. However, this too has been rejected by many indigenous populations, who criticized this approach for failing to address critical social issues of group identity and community rights (Reardon 2001). Many indigenous peoples and environmental NGOs oppose the granting of patents on biological materials such as genes, plants, animals, and humans invoking the concepts of biocolonialism and biopiracy to highlight the exploitation of indigenous communities and developing countries whose genetic materials have been used with the intent of developing the health and wealth of Western economies. In response to this critique, policymakers and scientists have produced models of benefit-sharing (Hayden, forthcoming) where profits generated and/or health-related benefits are offered to those populations providing DNA samples.

GENETIC CITIZENS

Concerns about the commercial interests and the adequacy of informed consent alone to provide ethical legitimacy have also been raised about the new breed of biobanks and human genetic databases in Western countries. Following the controversy and eventual collapse of the deCODE Iceland Project in the late 1990s, an Icelandic-sector genetic database that had departed from the normal practice in research of gaining specific informed consent from participants and had formed a coalition with the industrial sector, issues surrounding the ethics and governance of such projects have been brought to the fore. The controversy that soon followed the Icelandic case is indicative of the kinds of issues that have been raised in relation to subsequent biobank proposals. In particular, the involvement of a commercial company with monopoly rights over scientific discoveries emerging from the project generated concerns about the commercialization of these materials and the fact that sensitive personal health-related information was being collected without the explicit, informed consent of individuals. However, in ensuing ethical debate and policy discussions, full informed consent was seen as difficult to achieve given the inability to know in advance the eventual uses to which the collection of samples would be put. Furthermore, following the rejection by the public of genetically modified foods in Europe, policymakers were concerned about what they conceived to be public mistrust or misunderstanding of genetics. Public opposition to genetically modified foods has furthered debate on the public understanding of science, the role of democracy and the necessity for governance and regulation. While policymakers and scientists frequently suggest such opposition is based on a public deficit of scientific knowledge, social scientists reject this. For example, Bryan Wynne (Wynne 1993) claims that the public understands only too well the provisional nature of scientific knowledge and is aware that problems can emerge in the future that are in the present unknown. More recently, in response to a perceived breakdown of the public's trust in science, attempts have been made by science funding agencies, policymakers, and governmental bodies to adopt public engagement strategies and to develop means of exploiting the opportunities offered by new genetics without undermining public trust. As Corrigan and Petersen (2008) note in relation to genetic databases, this has produced various strategies aimed at the "engendering of trust – or rather the management of mistrust which has become a central issue for contemporary risk governance." These strategies are often presented as part of a more inclusive democratic process of government and entail such activities as the setting up of citizen's juries and carrying out surveys and public consultation exercises. Such work is often undertaken by sociologists and other social scientists. Some such research draws upon Rawls's theory of deliberative democracy (Rawls 1971), and here social scientists often work alongside moral philosophers (Burgess 2005) as part of the multidisciplinary bioethics field. However, others sociologists remain skeptical about these endeavors, claiming that such exercises are designed to stave off the kind of public opposition that has thwarted the deployment of genetically modified foods rather than being a genuine attempt to make the practice of science a more democratic one. Certainly, as Marli Huijer argues, "from the perspective of democracy rather than science, the challenge is how to conceptualize democratic negotiation and decisionmaking processes on global science projects" (Huijer 2003: 480).

HOPE AND FUTURE PROMISES

There are a growing number of patient initiatives in pursuit of genetics research and in the hope for finding genetic cures. In the US, PXE International, a non-profit-making organization established by patients and their families, is one such example (Novas 2006). It has been successful in lobbying the government and encouraging researchers to undertake clinical studies to help find cures for the disease PXE, and has established a blood and tissue registry with rights on how such material is used, and a share in the intellectual property that arises from it. Furthermore, patient groups can challenge the commercialization of genetics, as in the case of disease advocacy organization the Canavan Foundation, which sued the Miami Children's Hospital (the owner of the patent on the gene linked to the disease) for restricting research and access to genetic testing. However, as Petersen and Bunton claim:

> In a "free market" economy not everyone is able to "participate" equally in decision-making about the introduction of new genetic technologies, and not everyone has access to the conditions, products and services that are seen as necessary to maintaining or advancing health and well-being. (2002: 205)

Furthermore, the engagement of patients in the investments of the new genetics is premised on hopes for new treatments and cures that have yet to be realized. The promissory nature of the new genetics and associated stem cell technologies is, for Fox Keller (1992), the key to understanding its scientific, political, and economic impetus. It is not simply the force of science that drives developments but, just as important, the cultural success in capturing the imagination of scientists and public alike about the possibility of controlling nature and our biological destinies. Techniques involving the genetic modification of plants and animals that began to emerge in the late 1970s were accompanied by an ideological expansion of molecular biology – institutionally, culturally, and economically. In particular, anticipation about the kinds of possibilities that genetics opens up in relation to the control of nature helped mobilize scientific endeavors and raise expectations and visions of the future. Notions of a biotechnology revolution underpinned by scientific, governmental, and regional policy initiatives designed to bring about the twin objectives of wealth and health creation have generated widespread expectations about the rapid impact of biotechnology. Sociologists highlight the ways in which promoters of new technologies build expectations through the creation and citation of technological visions. Nevertheless, the process of development is far from smooth. As sociologists of science and technology studies have shown, "genetic advances are incremental, haphazard, contested and complex. Science is partial, unreliable, incomplete and sometimes inaccurate, despite the hyperbole of researchers" (Shakespeare 1999: 681). Paul Nightingale and Paul Martin (2004) argue that, counter to expectations of a revolutionary model of innovation, biotechnology innovation is instead following a historically well established process of slow and incremental change. These commentators note that most research fields can be seen to move through various cycles of hype and disappointment, expressing tensions between generative visions on the one hand and the material "messiness" of innovation on the other.

CONCLUSION

This chapter has drawn on some of the key theoretical perspectives on contemporary genetic practices but is by no means an all-encompassing account of work in this area. Undoubtedly social theorists are in agreement that genetics and associated technologies have had, for good or ill, an impact upon social relations and human identities, and in redefining social norms. However, whereas some theorists such as Habermas (2003) and Fukuyama (2002) attribute to genetics powerful capabilities to radically alter human cells and transform "human nature," others, such as Nightingale and Martin (2004), suggest that the process whereby genetic knowledge can be transformed into useful applications is a messy, slow, and contingent one. Gene therapy and stem cell technologies have so far been largely unsuccessful, and there are very few cures yet for diseases caused solely by a genetic mutation, much less conditions that involve multi-factorial disease where genes are thought to play a role alongside other biological and environmental factors. Nevertheless, a myriad of genetic tests are now commonly in place, and while these are generally used to confirm the existence of a known genetic mutation where the potential for such disease is already suspected through its pre-existence in the family, knowledge about such mutations can have a profound effect on individuals and their families. Here sociology, largely through empirical research based on ethnographic approaches, has made a useful contribution in understanding their effect. Such studies reveal the dilemmas and experiences faced by those confronted with knowledge of having, or having the ability to pass on, genetic mutations. To regard this as a new, emerging form of eugenics would be rather misleading, but as Kerr and Shakespeare (2002), Fox Keller (1992), and others have argued, we need to be aware of the norms governing "freedom," reproductive "choice," and the "normal and pathological."

Paternity testing too is a subject that is starting to be addressed by sociologists. Given that paternity testing is a tool that can be used to identify the biological father, questions about the implications of this and other associated reproductive technologies for gender and family relations are extremely important and require sociological analysis. The growing popularity of genetic tests for genealogy searching (Nash 2004) illustrates further reconfigurations of kin relations and notions of race and geographical identities. Here companies promote genetic tests that purport to establish information regarding an individual's biological lineage and the geographical location of his or her ancestors. The ways in which these tests are being deployed by individuals, as well as by institutions regulating populations and their entitlements, as in the case of government immigration and indigenous land rights, is an important issue for social theory to address.

The use of DNA in forensics has huge implications for criminal justice systems and human rights. The UK now has the largest DNA crime database in the world, with over 5 percent of UK population samples included on the database and with predictions that one in four UK males will soon have their DNA samples stored on it. This, and the use of genetic information by other institutions, are likely to be issues for further deliberation. Furthermore, while Nowotny, Scott, and Gibbons (2001) and others explain some of the contemporary shifts between science and society as features of the collapse of polar oppositions such as "science and society," "nature and nurture," and "private and public," more work is required to examine and make sense of the messiness of this milieu. In particular, issues concerning the political economy demand considerable attention.

Finally, sociology needs to be reflective regarding its potential in contributing towards ethical and policy-related processes. Francis Fukuyama is a former member of the USA's President's Council on Bioethics, and other social theorists mentioned in this chapter have taken part in various bioethics commissions and studies into issues surrounding genetics. Social theory, as always, needs to remain useful in explaining social phenomena and should be tethered closely to the empirical world it seeks to explain. In the area of genetics, social theory can be deployed as a tool for policy and governance, and it is incumbent upon social theorists to reflect upon this process too.

Bibliography

Agamben, G. (1998) *Homo Sacer: Sovereign Power and Bare Life*. Stanford: Stanford University Press.

Bauman, Z. (1989) *Modernity and the Holocaust*. Cambridge: Polity.

Burgess, M. (2005) "Ethical Analysis of Representation in the Governance of Biotechnology," in E. F. Einsiedel and F. Timmermans (eds.), *Crossing Over: Genomics in the Public Arena*. Calgary: University of Calgary Press.

Burton, B. (2002) "Proposed Genetic Database on Tongans Opposed." *BMJ* 324(7335): 443a.

Conrad, P. (1999) "A Mirage of Genes." *Sociology of Health & Illness* 21: 228–41.

Corrigan, O. P. (2003) "Empty Ethics: The Problem with Informed Consent." *Sociology of Health and Illness* 25: 768–92.

Corrigan, O. P. (2004) "Informed Consent: The Contradictory Ethical Safeguards in Pharmacogenetics," in R. Tutton and O. P. Corrigan (eds.), *Genetic Databases: Socio-ethical Issues in the Collection and Use of DNA*. London: Routledge.

Corrigan, O. P., and Peterson, A. (2008). "UK Biobank: Bioethics as a Technology of Governance." in H. Gottweis and A. Petersen (eds.), *Biobanks: Governance in Comparative Perspective*. London: Routledge.

Darwin, C. (1994 [1859]) *The Origin of Species*. London: Senate.

Duster, T. (1990) *Backdoor of Eugenics*. London: Routledge.

Foucault, M. (1981) *History of Sexuality*, vol. 1, *An Introduction*, trans. R. Hurley. London: Penguin.

Fox Keller, E. (1992) "Nature, Nurture and the Human Genome Project," in D. J. Kelves and L. Hood (eds.), *The Code of Codes*. Cambridge, MA: Harvard University Press.

Fox Keller, E. (2000) *The Century of the Gene*. Cambridge, MA: Harvard University Press.

Franklin, S. (2003) "Re-Thinking Nature-Culture: Anthropology and the New Genetics." *Anthropological Theory* 3: 65–85.

Franklin, S. (2007) *Dolly Mixtures: The Remaking of Genealogy*. Durham, NC: Duke University Press.

Fukuyama, F. (2002) *Our Posthuman Future: Consequences of the Biotechnology Revolution*. London: Profile Books.

Galison, P., and Hevly, B. (1993) *Big Science: The Growth of Large-Scale Research*. Chicago: University of Chicago Press.

Gilroy, P. (2000) *Between Camps: Nation, Culture and the Allure of Race*. Harmondsworth: Penguin.

Habermas, J. (2003) *The Future of Human Nature*. Cambridge: Polity.

Haraway, D. (1991) *Simians, Cyborgs and Women: the Reinvention of Nature*. New York: Routledge.

Hayden, C. (2007) "Taking as Giving: Bioscience, Exchange and the Politics of Benefit Sharing." *Social Studies of Science* 37: 729–58.

Huijer, M. (2003) "Reconsidering Democracy: History of the Human Genome Project." *Science Communications* 24: 479–502.

Jallinoja, P. (2001) "Genetic Screening in Maternity Care: Preventive Aims and Voluntary Choices." *Sociology of Health & Illness* 23: 286–307.

Johnson, R. H. (1914) "Eugenics and So-called Eugenics." *The American Journal of Sociology* 20: 98–103.

Kerr, A., and Cunningham-Burley, S. (2000) "On Ambivalence and Risk: Reflexive Modernity and the New Human Genetics." *Sociology* 34: 283–304.

Kerr, A., and Shakespeare, T. (2002) *Genetic Politics: From Eugenics to Genome*. Cheltenham: New Clarion Press.

Lippman, A. (1991) "Prenatal Genetic Testing and Screening: Constructing Needs and Reinforcing Inequities." *American Journal of Law and Medicine* 17: 17–50.

Lippman, A. (1992) "Led Astray by Genetic Maps: The Cartography for the Human Genome and Health Care." *Social Science & Medicine* 35: 1469–76.

Nash, C. (2004) "Genetic Kinship." *Cultural Studies* 18: 1–33.

Nelkin, D., and Lindee, S. (1995) *The Gene as a Cultural Icon*. New York: W. H. Freeman.

Nightingale, P., and Martin, P. (2004) "The Myth of the Biotech Revolution." *Trends in Biotechnology* 22: 564–9.

Novas, C. (2006) "The Political Economy of Hope: Patients' Organizations, Science and Biovalue." *Bioethics* 1: 289–345.

Novas, C., and Rose, N. (2000) "Genetic Risk and the Birth of the Somatic Individual." *Economy and Society* 29: 485–513.

Nowotny, H., Scott, P., and Gibbons, M. (2001) *Re-thinking Science: Knowledge and the Public in an Age of Uncertainty*. Cambridge: Polity.

Olson, M. V. (2002) "The Human Genome Project: A Player's Perspective." *Journal of Molecular Biology* 319: 931–42.

Paul, D. (1995) *Controlling Human Heredity: 1865 to the Present* Atlantic Highlands, NJ: Humanities Press.

Petersen, A. (2001) "Biofantasies: Genetics and Medicine in the Print News Media." *Social Science & Medicine* 52: 1255–68.

Petersen, A., and Bunton, R. (2002) *The New Genetics and the Public's Health*. London: Routledge.

Rabinow, P. (1992) "Artificiality and Enlightenment: From Sociobiology to Biosociality." *Essays on the Anthropology of Reason*. Princeton: Princeton University Press.

Rabinow, P. (1997) *Making PCR: A Story of Biotechnology*. Chicago: University of Chicago Press.

Rabinow, P., and Rose, N. (2006) "Biopower Today." *Biosocieties* 1: 195–218.

Rawls, J. (1971) *A Theory of Justice*. Cambridge, MA: Harvard University Press.

Reardon, J. (2001) "The Human Genome Diversity Project: A Case Study in Coproduction." *Social Studies of Science* 31: 357–88.

Richards, M. (2004) "Perfecting People: Selective Breeding at the Oneida Community (1869–1879) and the Eugenics Movement." *New Genetics & Society* 23: 47–71.

Rose, N. (2001). "The Politics of Life Itself." *Theory Culture Society* 18: 1–30.

Shakespeare, T. (1999) " 'Losing the Plot?' Medical and Activist Discourse of Contemporary Genetics and Disability." *Sociology of Health & Illness* 21: 668–88.

Skinner, D. (2006) "Racialized Futures: Biologism and the Changing Politics of Identity." *Social Studies of Science* 36: 459–88.

Stephan, N. L. (1996) *The Hour of Eugenics: Race Gender and Nation in Latin America*. New York: Cornell University Press.

Sulston, J., and Ferry, G. (2002) *The Common Thread: A Story of Science, Politics, Ethics and the Human Genome*. London: Bantam.

Tutton, R. (2002) "Gift Relationships in Genetic Research." *Science as Culture* 11: 523–42.

Waldby, C. (2000) *The Visible Human Project: Informatic Bodies and Posthuman Medicine*. New York: Routledge.

Waldby, C. (2002) "Stem Cells, Tissue Cultures and the Production of Biovalue." *Health* 6: 305–23.

Weinberg, A. M. (1961) "Impact of Large-Scale Science on the United States." *Science* 161–4.

Wolpe, P. (1998) "The Triumph of Autonomy in American Bioethics: A Sociological View," in R. DeVries and J. Subedi (eds.) *Bioethics and Society*. Englewood Cliffs, NJ: Prentice Hall.

Wynne, B. (1993) "Public Uptake of Science: A Case for Institutional Reflexivity." *Public Understanding of Science* 2: 321–37.

18

Economic Sociology

RICHARD SWEDBERG

There exists no single and generally accepted definition of economic sociology, and one reason for this is that the term is used by economists as well as sociologists. Gary Becker, for example, views economic sociology as the study of non-economic phenomena with the help of microeconomics. The definition that will inform this chapter, however, is the one that is most often used by sociologists and that is also much more common. This is that economic sociology is that part of sociology that deals with economic phenomena, and that analyzes these with the help of sociological concepts and methods.

As a sub-discipline of sociology, economic sociology traces its historical roots primarily to Max Weber and Karl Marx, but also to Émile Durkheim and Georg Simmel. Among Marx's works *Capital* is obviously central, but many of his other writings are of great interest to modern economic sociology (e.g. Marx 1906, 1970, 1973). Max Weber's contributions include in particular *The Protestant Ethic and the Spirit of Capitalism, General Economic History*, and *Economy and Society*. The last of these three important works contains a chapter in which Weber attempts to outline a theoretical program for what he termed *Wirtschaftssoziologie* (Weber 1958 [1904–5], 1978 [1922], 1981 [1923]).

While Durkheim was more interested in such topics as morality and religion than in the economy, he is also the author of *The Division of Labor*, which argues that the social effects of the modern exchange economy may be as important as its purely economic effects (Durkheim 1984). Simmel similarly argues, in *The Philosophy of Money*, that the cultural effects of money equal its economic effects (Simmel 1990).

After around 1920, the area of economic sociology fell more or less into oblivion, even if a few outstanding economists and sociologists turned to the topic with much creativity. This small number includes, first and foremost, Joseph Schumpeter (1883–1950), Karl Polanyi (1886–1964), and Talcott Parsons (1902–79). While they all created high-quality works, they nonetheless did not succeed in making economic sociology itself generally accepted.

Joseph Schumpeter viewed "economic sociology" as an integral part of what he called "social economics"; he also published a few essays in economic sociology as well as the sociologically inspired *Capitalism, Socialism and Democracy* (Schumpeter 1991, 1994 [1942]). Karl Polanyi made a frontal attack on the market economy in *The Great Transformation*; he also formulated a new and important conceptual apparatus for a socio-economic or sociological approach in other writings (Polanyi 1957 [1944]; Polanyi, Arensberg, and Pearson 1971 [1957]). Talcott Parsons, finally, applied his general systems approach to the economy in a study co-authored with Neil Smelser (Parsons and Smelser 1956).

In the mid-1980s, and more or less independent of all earlier work in the field, economic sociology suddenly began to come alive again on a broad scale, and it has continued to do so ever since. Since this time important changes have taken place in the theoretical approach of economic sociology. New topics have been added to its agenda, and a number of advances have been made in analyzing various areas of the economy.

THE PRESENT STATE OF ECONOMIC SOCIOLOGY

When economic sociology was revived in the 1980s, this primarily took place in the United States; and this is also where modern economic sociology is most developed. Economic sociology, however, has during the last decade or so also developed strongly in Europe. While it seems to be catching on also in Latin America and Asia, it is by no means as accepted and institutionalized as economic sociology is in the United States and Europe.

Modern American economic sociology often refers to economic activities as being *embedded* in social structures, a term from Polanyi that Mark Granovetter has popularized (Granovetter 1985). The idea that economic activities are *socially constructed*, as opposed to given by nature in one unchangeable form, represents another fundamental idea. US sociologists have also often drawn heavily on the following three traditions in their work: cultural sociology, organizational sociology, and network analysis.

Economic sociology is today represented at several of the major universities in the United States, such as Stanford, Cornell, and so on. In numerical terms, one can speak of a steady increase in the number of economic sociologists since the 1980s, even if exact figures are not available.

For the reader who is interested in knowing exactly what is being taught in courses in economic sociology in the United States, there exists a collection of syllabi and other teaching resources, made available through the American Sociological Association (ASA). The fact that the ASA recently published a third edition of these course descriptions is itself a sign that the field is growing and becoming more institutionalized (Anderson et al. 2006). Pointing in the same direction of increased institutionalization is also the fact that there now exist three readers in economic sociology, namely *The New Economic Sociology: A Reader* (edited by Frank Dobbin), *The Sociology of Economic Life* (edited by Mark Granovetter and Richard Swedberg), and *Readings in Economic Sociology* (edited by Nicole Woolsey-Biggart). The second is the most popular reader in the field and was recently reissued in a second and expanded edition (Granovetter and Swedberg 1992, 2001; cf. Biggart 2002; Dobbin 2004).

In the United States a sure sign that a sub-field in sociology is being taken seriously is that it gets its own section at the ASA, and this is also what has happened with economic sociology. After some lobbying by Wayne Baker and other people, the section for economic sociology came into being in 2001, and today it has various prizes, a newsletter (*Accounts*), a webpage, and so on. At one of the ASA's recent meetings it was reported that the economic sociology section currently has the largest number of student members (in percentage terms). This fact indicates that the field is very popular among graduate students.

Many of those who helped to introduce economic sociology in the mid- to late 1980s are still active in the field and keep making contributions. This is true, for example, of Mark Granovetter, who is seen by many as *the* quintessential economic sociologist because of his extremely influential article "Economic Action and Social Structure" (Granovetter 1985; see also e.g. Granovetter 1995a, 1995b, 2002). Through this article Granovetter launched the term "embeddedness" and forcefully advocated the use of networks analysis in economic sociology, an agenda he has continued to work on. Similarly Harrison C. White, Granovetter's thesis adviser at Harvard University and a very influential figure in economic sociology, has continued to deepen his analysis of markets, which goes back to the early 1980s (White 1981). White's *Markets from Networks* represents his most important contribution in this respect (White 2001).

Some other pioneers from the 1980s who have continued to contribute to the field are Viviana Zelizer and Bruce Carruthers. Viviana Zelizer has continued to do work on different types of monies and currencies, and her studies have become increasingly influential. But she has also branched out in new directions, such as consumption and the way that economic factors and intimacy are often interrelated (e.g. Zelizer 1994, 2002). Bruce Carruthers, who began his career with a study of the financial market in eighteenth-century London (Carruthers 1996), has not only co-authored the first undergraduate textbook in economic sociology but also done important work on a number of topics, including credit and credit-rating systems (Carruthers 2005; Carruthers and Babb 2000).

While the average age of the key people is probably somewhere in the fifties, a younger generation is also emerging. The people who are part of this new generation have already shown what they can do. Important work has, for example, been carried out by Sarah Babb and Marion Fourcade-Gourinchas. The former has studied the role of economists in twentieth-century Mexico (Babb 2001), and the latter has produced a comparative study of the emergence of modern economics (Fourcade-Gourinchas 2001, forthcoming). Together the two have carried out a study of the way that neoliberalism has been received in France, England, Chile, and Mexico (Fourcade-Gourinchas and Babb 2003).

Other young scholars who belong in this category of new and coming people include Nina Bandelj (2007), Brook Harrington (2007), Rakesh Khurana (2002, 2007), Greta Krippner (2001), Valery Yakubovich (2002), Milan Zafirovski (2001), and Ezra Zuckerman (1999). The topics they cover run from investments to embeddedness to labor markets in Russia.

Before turning to the topic of major themes in modern economic sociology, the situation outside of the United States needs to be discussed. This means, first of all, Europe, and in Europe, first of all France. It has gradually been realized outside of France that several of the country's major sociologists have been very interested in economic topics. This is especially true of Pierre Bourdieu and Luc Boltanski but also, to some extent, of Raymond Boudon and Bruno Latour.

Bourdieu's early work on Algeria contains a very suggestive analysis of various economic phenomena that differs on many points from mainstream American economic sociology (see especially Bourdieu 1979, but also see his last contribution to economic sociology in Bourdieu 2000). While mainstream economic sociology focuses on embeddedness, networks, and the social construction of the economy, Bourdieu has a much more structural approach to economic phenomena. Drawing on the concepts of habitus, field, interest, and capital (social, cultural, and so on), Bourdieu is less interested in how the official economy works than in how people live their lives as part of the economy, struggling with – and against – the existing economic power structure. One reason why Bourdieu's analysis is considerably more realistic than that of mainstream economic sociology, has to do with its emphasis on the concept of *interest*. Much of mainstream economic sociology, in contrast, primarily traces the impact of social relations, and leaves interest (including the search for profit) to the economists.

Luc Boltanski draws less on a structuralist approach than Bourdieu, emphasizing instead the ways in which economic actors view reality and justify their actions (Boltanski and Thévenot 2006). His basic idea is that economic actors develop so-called conventions, as part of their efforts to coordinate economic actions, and that these conventions constitute a few standard ways of thinking about reality and justify why certain actions should be taken. What is novel in Boltanski's approach is primarily the emphasis on justification; the idea of the importance of conventions is something that he shares with the so-called school of conventions which consists mainly of economists (see e.g. Storper and Salais 1997).

Together with Eve Chiapello, Boltanski has also published a major study entitled *The New Spirit of Capitalism*, in which it is argued that we are currently witnessing the emergence of a new type of capitalism, *network capitalism* (Boltanski and Chiapello 2005). Social scientists, the two authors argue, have added to the ideology of this project through their naive advocacy of networks, decentralization, and flexible production – all of which according to Boltanski and Chiapello are part of "the new spirit of capitalism."

While the works of Bourdieu (who died in 2002) and Boltanski currently dominate economic sociology in France, it would be incorrect to leave the reader with the impression that little else has been produced in this country than the studies by these two authors. Important work on the role of economists in French life has, for example, been produced by Frédéric Lebaron, who is a student of Bourdieu (e.g. Lebaron 2000). Philippe Steiner, trained as a historian of economic thought, has helped to develop a sociology-of-knowledge approach to economic thought in France, made a splendid study of the approach of the Durkheimians to economic sociology, and has also written on economic sociology in general (Steiner 2001, 2005).

There is also Michel Callon, who has spearheaded the application of actor network theory (ANT) to the economy, questioning in particular the theory of markets (see

CHAPTER 7). One of Callon's interesting ideas is close to the notion of externality, namely that the market "overflows" in a number of ways, and in this manner affects society. He is best known, however, for his thesis that economic theory creates the reality that it studies – the so-called performativity thesis (Callon 1998; *Economy and Society* 2002; for a critical appreciation, see especially MacKenzie, Muniesa, and Siu, 2007). Finally, Emanuelle Lazega is currently working on an important study of a commercial court in Paris (for a sample, see Lazega 2003; see also the work by Yves Dezalay on international economic arbitration, e.g. Dezalay and Garth 1996).

In the days of Max Weber and Werner Sombart, German scholars dominated the field of economic sociology, something that is not the case today, even if such major figures in social theory as Jürgen Habermas and Niklas Luhmann have done some interesting work in the field (e.g. Luhmann 1982 [1970]; for Habermas, see Sitton 1998). Nonetheless, there is one area where German economic sociologists have been in the forefront, and that is in the sociology of finance.

Led by Karin Knorr-Cetina, a number of interesting and imaginative studies of finance have been carried out, typically with an ethnographic dimension (e.g. Knorr-Cetina and Bruggers 2002; Knorr-Cetina and Preda 2005). Modern electronic markets, it has for example been shown, are far more social than one might think. It should also be noted that Knorr-Cetina draws heavily on sociology of science and phenomenology in her research. By doing so, she has helped to broaden the repertoire of contemporary economic sociology.

Before leaving Germany, the work of Jens Beckert and Christoph Deutschmann must be mentioned. The former has produced some interesting theoretical work in economic sociology, including a study of the role of uncertainty in economic life (Beckert 1996). He has also recently published a pioneering comparative study of inheritance in the nineteenth century (Beckert 2007). Christoph Deutschmann, in contrast, looks more at macro phenomena, especially how capitalism has turned into a kind of religion in modern times (Deutschmann 2001).

While work in economic sociology in the other European countries is not as highly developed as in France or Germany, some interesting individual contributions have nonetheless been produced. Geoffrey Ingham, Nigel Dodd, and some other people in England have, for example, looked at money from a sociological perspective (e.g. Dodd 1994; Ingham 1998, 2004). Patrik Aspers has carried out a study of the market for fashion photography in Sweden, and Olav Velthuis has studied the art market in the Netherlands (Aspers 2001; Olav Velthuis 2005).

What is happening in economic sociology outside of Europe and North America is little known. It seems clear, however, that the interest for economic sociology is on the rise in for Russia (see especially the work of Vadim Radaev, e.g. Radaev 1997). From various sources it also appears that occasional courses on economic sociology are being taught in Latin America and Asia – but details are missing, and there is little knowledge in the United States and Europe about what type of research is being carried out.

NEW DEVELOPMENTS

The last 10 to 15 years in economic sociology have been characterized by dynamic growth, and many new developments have taken place. Some new topics have been broached, such as wealth, entrepreneurship, and the role of law in the economy. Earlier insights have also been elaborated upon and developed in new directions. The latter is, for example, true of Mark Granovetter's ideas about embeddedness and Harrison White's theory of production markets. There is also the ongoing attempt to consolidate economic sociology by going back to the classics and learn from these (for Weber, see e.g. Swedberg 1998).

Theory and theory-related advances

When economic sociology was revived in the mid-1980s sociologists were basically at a loss when it came to theory. There was a strong sense that sociologists should develop their own approach, and that this approach should differ from that of mainstream economics – but that was about all. The heritage of economic sociology, especially the ideas of Max Weber on *Wirtschaftssoziologie*, was not an option since they were little known. To draw on Marx's work did not seem as much of an option either, since the days of radical sociology were over.

It was in this situation that Mark Granovetter came up with the suggestion that one might be able to unite the ideas of Karl Polanyi on embeddedness with the new and evolving approach of networks analysis (Granovetter 1985). Following this suggestion, the task of economic sociology would be to trace the way that economic actions are structured in networks. Economic actions, in brief, do not follow the short and direct paths of maximization, as the economists claim; they rather follow the considerably more complex paths of networks.

This embeddedness project has been quite successful, and during the recent decade it has been tested and added to by Granovetter himself as well as by his students and some other followers. Attempts have, for example, been made to establish theoretically (and empirically) what balance is needed between embedded relationships and pure market relationships (e.g. Uzzi 1996, 1997).

During the last 10 years this perspective has also been challenged, and one may speak of a general attempt to go beyond embeddedness and replace it with some totally different approach. One of these challenges came from Pierre Bourdieu, who several times criticized the embeddedness approach for its failure to deal with structural factors. In Bourdieu's own theory there is especially the concept of field that takes care of the structural dimension and which allowed him to handle macro issues, something that Granovetter is less interested in doing.

Other critics argue that the embeddedness leaves too much of economic thought intact, since it takes as its point of departure that there exist economic actions that need to be embedded in the social structure. This criticism is somewhat misguided since Granovetter has been a consistent and sharp critic of mainstream economic theory and the tendency to treat economic action as something separate from the social (for a general discussion of the problems of embeddedness, see especially Krippner et al. 2004; see also Krippner 2001).

Some economic sociologists have been considerably less critical of economics than Granovetter, and they often draw on the work of various members of so-called new institutional economics. They also argue that Granovetter has difficulty in dealing with the role of institutions in economic life (as opposed to networks), and that sociologists have much to learn on this score from economists, such as Douglass (e.g. Nee and Ingram 1998).

Whether economic sociologists should draw on game theory or not represents another issue that has recently been raised, and for which the embeddedness approach provides little guidance. Since a few years back the major American journals in sociology often contained analyses that make use of game theory; this is also an approach that has become part of mainstream economics.

So far economic sociologists have remained suspicious of game theory, and have at the most shown sympathy for the attempt to mix empirical analysis with game theory of the type that can be found in the work of Avner Greif (Greif 1998, 2005; see e.g. Swedberg 2001). All in all, we may conclude that economic sociology is currently characterized by several theoretical approaches, and that a firm theoretical core of the type that can be found in mainstream economics is definitely missing.

Various theoretical alternatives to the embeddedness approach have also been explored during the last decade, including the works that make up the early or classical tradition in economic sociology. Another reason for paying attention to these early works may be academic legitimation; there is also a sense that economic sociology does have a past, and that this past deserves to be better known.

Most of this interest in the past has gone into exploring the work of Karl Polanyi and Max Weber. The latter produced several studies that are relevant for economic sociology, including one on the stock market that has recently been translated (Weber 2000). The scholarship on Karl Polanyi's work has also accelerated during the last decade, and includes an important study by economic sociologist Fred Block (2003) on the coming into being of *The Great Transformation*. This last work, it may be added, was also recently reissued by Block, with a preface by Joseph Stiglitz.

Joseph Schumpeter and Georg Simmel are two other classics in economic sociology whose works continue to fascinate. This is particularly true for Simmel's work on money and Schumpeter's theory of the entrepreneur. The beginnings of a secondary literature on *The Philosophy of Money* have slowly started to emerge even if much work remains to be done before Simmel's work on the economy is exhausted (e.g. Poggi 1993). Schumpeter's stature as an economic sociologist is, by contrast, well established; one of his lesser-known essays on the entrepreneur has also recently been translated into English (Schumpeter 2003; Swedberg 1991).

While it was common in the 1980s for economic sociologists to be quite hostile to economics, it has gradually come to be better understood that modern economics is a multifaceted science and that it contains many ideas and works that are of much relevance to economic sociology. Some economists have also come to think that they can improve their own analyses by opening these up to sociological concepts and ways of thinking. The work of Herbert Simon has, for example, continued to be close in spirit to that of economic sociology, and so has that of George Akerlof (e.g. Akerlof and Kranton 2000; Schelling 2006). By now there also exist full-scale attempts by economists to theorize social interactions (e.g. Gui and Sugden 2005; Manski 2000).

What economists write on development has also continued to be of theoretical relevance, and many economic sociologists follow the works of such people as Jeffrey Sachs, Amartya Sen, and Joseph Stiglitz with much interest (Sachs 2000, 2005; Sen 1999; Stiglitz 2003). Some economic sociologists have also been attracted to Douglass North's attempt to recast the concept of institution and introduce it into economic analysis (e.g. North 1990, 2005). There also exists a certain fascination with behavioral economics, especially its attempt to introduce emotions and the notion of fairness into economics (e.g. Berezin 2004; Camerer 2004).

New developments in analyzing old topics (networks, markets; and firms)

In Granovetter's article from 1985 it was argued, to repeat, that economic activities were not simply embedded in social relations but in *networks*. Many of Granovetter's early students at New York University at Stony Brook in the 1980s also used network analysis in their studies of the economy. Some of them focused on the kind of networks that can be found around firms, while others analyzed the networks that are formed by directors sitting on several boards, so-called interlocks. While big hopes were initially attached to the latter type of study, it was eventually realized that research on interlocks had a limited – but still important – function to fulfill (e.g. Mizruchi 1996).

One of the many strengths of networks analysis is that it represents a flexible tool with which a number of social phenomena can be approached, and recent developments in economic sociology tend to confirm this (e.g. Zuckerman 2003). Networks analysis has, for example, been used to explore various types of economic interactions that cannot be categorized either as some form of custom or some type of organization. These intermediary social forms – which are sometimes referred to as "network forms of organization" – have also been studied.

A special mention should also be made of the work of Ronald Burt (1992, 1993, 2005). In a very influential and much-cited work from the early 1990s he suggested that entrepreneurship can be understood with the help of networks analysis. His basic idea is that the entrepreneur connects two groups of people (say, sellers and buyers), who otherwise would be socially disconnected. The entrepreneur, in his capacity as a middleman, straddles according to this argument a so-called "structural hole."

That networks analysis is very flexible can be illustrated by mentioning a few more articles that draw on this approach. In one of these – co-authored by Paul DiMaggio and Hugh Louch (1998) – a specific kind of consumer purchase is analyzed, namely purchases for which people use their networks of friends and acquaintances. These are then contrasted to purchases, where the buyer does not need a referral or network, and it is shown that people prefer to use acquaintances and the like when, for example, they buy second-hand cars and houses.

Another example of a suggestive network analysis can be found in the work of John Padgett, who has become something of an expert on the early history of Florence (Padgett and Ansell 1993). The famous Medici family, he shows, held its power partly because of its skill in building and at crucial moments activating various types of economic and political networks. Padgett's work also illustrates the technical skills that are needed to work with networks theory today.

Next to networks, *markets* have been one of the most popular topics in economic sociology from the very beginning of its revival in the mid-1980s. One of the very first articles that helped to launch economic sociology in the early 1980s was, for example, devoted to precisely this topic. Its author was Harrison C. White, a physicist turned sociologist and a major figure more generally in twentieth-century sociology. After a break in working on markets in the early 1990s, White came back to this topic, adding several new features to his earlier model (White 2001). One of White's followers has also added to his ideas on how the identity of market actors is related to their place in the market (Aspers 2001).

White argues that the typical (industrial) market has a small number of actors who, by signaling to one another through price and volume, may turn into a group with a stable social structure – in brief, into a market. An alternative theory to that of White, however, has been suggested by Neil Fligstein, according to which the characteristic feature of modern markets is their emphasis on *stability* (1996; for an elaboration see Fligstein 2001). Market actors do not want volatility in price or cutthroat competition, according to this argument; they want stable markets and as few surprises as possible.

A special mention must also be made of the elegant study by Joel Podolny on the role of status in markets (Podolny 1992; for later elaborations and additions, see Podolny 2005). Podolny's argument is that buyers are willing to pay a premium for status, something which is obviously profitable for the seller. Having status, however, also restricts the seller to a small market since he or she would otherwise lose status (and the earlier market).

Not only networks and markets have been on the agenda of economic sociology for two decades by now, but also *firms*. One major reason for this is that sociologists since a long time back have done work in organization theory and, as part of this, studied firms. Many sociologists are also employed in business schools, where organization theory is often taught.

One important contribution that sociologists have made to the analysis of firms, and which has grown considerably in importance during the last decade, is population ecology (e.g. Hannan and Carroll 1995). Instead of just analyzing one or a few firms, the focus of this type of approach is on whole populations of firms in some area of the economy (say railroads, newspapers, or breweries). The task then becomes to study how these populations of firms come into being, expand, and gradually decline.

Another type of analysis which has become popular during the last decade looks at *the diffusion* in a population of firms of ideas, ways of doing things, and the like. The way that the social relations between the firms are structured will clearly influence the speed and range of the diffusion. One of the best-known studies of this type has been authored by Gerald Davis and looks at the way that knowledge about ways to block hostile takeovers spread among US firms in the 1980s (Davis 1991).

An important novelty, when it comes to recent sociological research on firms, has to do with entrepreneurship. While this topic was occasionally touched on in the 1980s, one could not speak of a full sociology of entrepreneurship – something which, however, is possible today (e.g. Swedberg 2000; Thornton 1999). Mark Granovetter, for example, has helped to theorize why people who are not particularly entrepreneurial in their home countries become successful entrepreneurs once they are in a foreign environment. The secret, Granovetter suggests, is that extended family ties may prevent entrepreneurship in the home country, but will be absent in the new country – with successful entrepreneurship as a result (Granovetter 1995a).

Additions have also been made to Alfred Marshall's well-known ideas about industrial districts, especially by Annalee Saxenian through her study of Silicon Valley (Saxenian 1996). By contrasting the decentralized and informal social structure of Silicon Valley to the centralized and formal social structure of Route 128, Saxenian has tried to pinpoint the factors that are conducive to entrepreneurship and those that are not. Her study also contains information about Frederick Terman, the fascinating Dean of Engineering at Stanford, who more or less invented the formula of Silicon Valley (business–state–university cooperation).

New topics: finance, law, stratification, comparative and historical studies

While there exists a distinct continuity to the study by economic sociologists of such topics as networks, markets, and firms, even if new and interesting contributions have also been made during the last decade, this is less the case with the topics that now will be discussed. These are finance, law, stratification, and comparative-historical studies.

In finance, for example, a series of important developments has taken place during the last decade, set off by the decision to deregulate the banking sector in the early 1980s. Sophisticated analyses of the social mechanisms that operate in this type of market have begun to appear, as exemplified by the work of such people as Donald MacKenzie, Yuval Millo, and Ezra Zuckerman. The former argues in a major monograph that the development of the option market in the United States shows that economic theory to some extent creates the reality that it analyzes. In making this argument, MacKenzie draws heavily on Callon's theory of "performativity" (MacKenzie 2006; see also MacKenzie and Millo 2003). Another example of a recent and important study of the social mechanisms that operate in modern financial markets is that of Ezra Zuckerman. The main focus of his work is to show that firms that are not tracked by security analysts are systematically undervalued in the market (Zuckerman 1999).

Economic sociology has also brought ethnography and culture to the study of money and finance, and thereby altered the kind of questions that can be asked and also what kind of material to look for (e.g. Abolafia 1996). In this way, for example, Viviana Zelizer has been able to show that people in their everyday lives do not see money as some unitary substance, but rather divide it up into different monies or currencies (Zelizer 1994). Karin Knorr-Cetina and Urs Brugger have used phenomenology to analyze what it means for people such as brokers to interact with one another with the help of computers (Knorr-Cetina and Brugger 2002; see also Aspers 2001).

Economists started to analyze law, together with legal scholars interested in an economic approach, many years before economic sociology came alive. While the field of law and economics quickly became very strong, legal topics initially attracted little attention among economic sociologists. Slowly, however, it has been realized that law constitutes a central part of the modern economy, and a broad program for how to analyze its role from a sociological perspective has recently been formulated (Swedberg 2003b). This program outlines the task that an "economic sociology of law" may want to undertake; it also points to a small number of already existing studies which are highly relevant in this context.

Lauren Edelman is one of the pioneers in introducing a sociological approach to law and economics. She has especially suggested that one should bring together the study of organizations with that of law; and one of her earliest studies that does this deals with due process in the workplace (Edelman 1990). The same approach is also used in another study that analyzes a related subject, namely the legalization of the workplace (Sutton et al. 1994).

But other topics than the workplace have also been studied in the nascent economic sociology of law. One study, for example, attempts to show how networks analysis may be of help in analyzing the social structure of illegal cartels (Baker and Faulkner 1993). Another looks at the new types of property that have evolved in eastern Europe as part of the privatization process (Stark 2001).

The claim that the study of stratification and wealth represents a new development for economic sociology may sound strange to anybody, except for sociologists. Has not economic sociology always studied these topics, from Marx to C. Wright Mills and beyond? Questions of inequality, however, are generally handled in sociology in a special sub-field called stratification, and not in economic sociology. And wealth, as it turns out, is rarely studied at all in contemporary sociology. Recently, however, stratification experts and economic sociologists have begun to study wealth and how it is related to the workings of the economy (e.g. Keister and Moller 2000; Spilerman 2000).

Another illustration of the attempt to bring together the study of stratification with the workings of the economy can be found in the work of Victor Nee (1989). Using recent changes in China as his empirical example, Nee argues that, when a society goes from having an economic system based on redistribution to one of exchange via the market, this also tends to be reflected in its stratification. This so-called market transition theory has led to a lively debate among sociologists (for a discussion of the literature, see e.g. Cao and Nee. 2000).

Before concluding this overview of recent developments in economic sociology, something needs to be said about the recent attempt by practitioners in this field of study to develop a historical as well as a comparative economic sociology. Sociologists have a long and successful tradition of analyzing historical and comparative topics, and it can be argued that they have a comparative advantage in this area in relation to economists.

One of these historical studies tries to follow the social construction of a whole industry, and another the evolution of accounting (Carruthers and Espeland 1991; Granovetter and McGuire 1998). Other studies focus on different countries and periods, basically making the argument that economic activities can be organized in many different ways. Marion Fourcade-Gourinchas makes, for example, this point for economic theory itself, by showing how economic theory reflects the social environment of the countries in which it happens to have emerged (Fourcade-Gourinchas 2001, forthcoming). Frank Dobbin has made the interesting and ambitious argument that not only do the industrial policies of various countries differ, but they also reflect the way that political power is organized (Dobbin 1994).

CONCLUDING REMARKS

It is clear that economic sociology has developed very strongly since its revival in the mid-1980s. Not only its first decade of existence, but also its second, have been very dynamic. Signs indicate that more growth is to be expected, because of the huge number of graduate students who are interested in economic sociology and also because of the growing tendency for sociology departments around the world to offer courses in this topic.

While it seems obvious that economic sociology is here to stay as a distinct sub-field of sociology, it is less clear what its impact on economics ultimately will be or its importance more generally for the understanding of economics in social science. At the moment, the impact of economic sociology on economics is negligible in the sense that only a very small number of economists read sociology or are interested in what sociologists are doing. A few exceptions exist, but they remain exactly that, exceptions.

On the other hand, there is also the fact that economists themselves as well as many other social scientists are today starting to pay attention to the role that institutions, norms, and social interactions are playing in economic life. Whether one wants to label this latter trend "economic sociology" or not is perhaps not so important – as long as a genuinely social perspective is introduced into the analysis of economic phenomena. With this caveat in mind, one may argue that economic sociology is here to stay not only as a sub-field of sociology but also as a general approach to economic analysis.

Bibliography

Abolafia, M. (1996) *Making Markets: Opportunism and Restraint on Wall Street*. Cambridge, MA: Harvard University Press.

Akerlof, G., and Kranton, R. (2000) "Economics of Identity." *Quarterly Journal of Economics* 15: 715–53.

Anderson, E., et al. (2006) *Economic Sociology: Syllabi & Instructional Materials*, 3rd edn. New York: American Sociological Association.

Aspers, P. (2001) *Markets in Fashion: A Phenomenological Approach*. Stockholm: City University Press.

Babb, S. (2001) *Managing Mexico: Economists from Nationalism to Neoliberalism*. Princeton: Princeton University Press.

Baker, W., and Faulkner, R. (1993) "The Social Organization of Conspiracy: Illegal Networks in the Heavy Electrical Industry." *American Sociological Review* 58: 837–60.

Bandelj, N. (2007) *From Communists to Foreign Capitalists: The Social Foundations of Foreign Direct Investment in Post-Socialist Europe*. Princeton: Princeton University Press.

Beckert, J. (1996) "What Is Sociological about Economic Sociology? Uncertainty and the Embeddedness of Economic Action." *Theory and Society* 25(6): 803–40.

Beckert, J. (2007) *Inherited Wealth: Inheritance in France, Germany, and the United States since 1800*. Princeton: Princeton University Press.

Berezin, M. (2004) "Emotions and the Economy," in N. Smelser and R. Swedberg (eds.), *The Handbook of Economic Sociology*, 2nd edn. New York and Princeton: Russell Sage Foundation and Princeton University Press.

Biggart, N. W. (1989) *Charismatic Capitalism: Direct Selling Organizations in America.* Chicago: University of Chicago Press.

Biggart, N. W. (ed.) (2002) *Readings in Economic Sociology*. Oxford: Blackwell.

Block, F. (2003) "Karl Polanyi and the Writing of *The Great Transformation*." *Theory and Society* 32(3): 275–306.

Boltanski, L., and Chiapello, E. (2005) *The New Spirit of Capitalism*. London: Verso.

Boltanski, L., and Thévenot, L. (2006) *On Justification: Economies of Worth*. Princeton: Princeton University Press.

Bourdieu, P. (1979) "The Disenchantment of the World," in *Algeria 1960*. Cambridge: Cambridge University Press.

Bourdieu, P. (2000) *Les Structures sociales de l'économie*. Paris: Seuil.

Burt, R. (1992) *Structural Holes: The Social Structure of Competition*. Cambridge, MA: Harvard University Press.

Burt, R. (1993) "The Social Structure of Competition," in R. Swedberg (ed.), *Explorations in Economic Sociology*. New York: Russell Sage Foundation.

Burt, R. (2005) *Brokerage and Closure: An Introduction to Social Capital*. Oxford: Oxford University Press.

Callon, M. (ed.) (1998) *The Laws of the Market*. Oxford: Blackwell.

Cao, Y., and Nee, V. (2000) "Comment: Controversies and Evidence in the Market Transition Debate." *American Journal of Sociology* 105: 1175–89.

Camerer, C., et al. (eds.) (2004) *Advances in Behavioral Economics*. Princeton: Princeton University Press.

Carruthers, B. (1996) *City of Capital: Politics and Markets in the English Financial Revolution*. Princeton: Princeton University Press.

Carruthers, B. (2005) "The Sociology of Money and Credit," in N. Smelser and R. Swedberg (eds.), *The Handbook of Economic Sociology*, 2nd edn. New York and Princeton: Russell Sage Foundation and Princeton University Press.

Carruthers, B., and Babb, S. (2000) *Economy/Society: Markets, Meanings, and Social Structure*. Thousand Oaks: Pine Forge Press.

Carruthers, B., and Nelson Espeland, W. (1991) "Accounting for Rationality: Double-Entry Bookkeeping and the Rhetoric of Economic Rationality." *American Journal of Sociology* 97: 31–69.

Davis, G. (1991) "Agents without Principles? The Spread of the Poison Pill through the Intercorporate Network." *Administrative Science Quarterly* 36: 583–613.

Deutschmann, C. (2001) "Capitalism as a Religion? An Unorthodox Analysis of Entrepreneurship." *European Journal of Social Theory* 4(4): 379–86.

Dezalay, Y., and Garth, B. (1996) *Dealing in Virtue: International Commercial Arbitration and the Construction of A Transnational Legal Order*. Chicago: University of Chicago Press.

DiMaggio, P., and Louch, H. (1998) "Socially Embedded Consumer Transactions: For What Kind of Purchases Do People Most Often Use Networks?" *American Sociological Review* 63: 619–37.

Dobbin, F. (1994) *Forging Industrial Policy: The United States, Britain and France in the Railroad Age*. Cambridge: Cambridge University Press.

Dobbin, F. (2001) "Why the Economy Reflects the Polity: Early Rail Policy in Britain, France, and the United States," in M. Granovetter and R. Swedberg (eds.), *The Sociology of Economic Life*, 2nd edn. Boulder, CO: Westview.

Dobbin, F. (ed.) (2004) *The New Economic Sociology: A Reader*. Princeton: Princeton University Press.

Dodd, N. (1994) *The Sociology of Money: Economics, Reason and Contemporary Society*. Cambridge: Polity.

Durkheim, É. (1984) *The Division of Labor in Society*. New York: The Free Press.

Economy and Society (2002) Theme issue: *The Technological Economy* [The Theories of Michel Callon]. 31(2): 175–306.

Edelman, L. (1990) "Legal Environments and Organizational Governance: The Expansion of Due Process in the American Workplace." *American Journal of Sociology* 95: 1401–40.

Fligstein, N. (1990) *The Transformation of Corporate Control*. Cambridge, MA: Harvard University Press.

Fligstein, N. (1996) "Markets as Politics: A Political-Cultural Approach to Markets." *American Sociological Review* 61: 656–73.

Fligstein, N. (2001) *The Architecture of Markets: An Economic Sociology of Twenty-First-Century Societies*. Princeton: Princeton University Press.

Fourcade-Gourinchas, M. (2001) "Politics, Institutional Structures, and the Rise of Economics: A Comparative Study." *Theory and Society* 30: 397–447.

Fourcade-Gourinchas, M., and Babb, S. (2003) "The Rebirth of the Liberal Creed: Paths to Neoliberalism in Four Countries." *American Journal of Sociology* 108: 533–79.

Fourcade-Gourinchas, M. (forthcoming) *Economists and Societies: Discipline and Profession in the United States, Great Britain and France*. Princeton: Princeton University Press.

Granovetter, M. (1985) "Economic Action and Social Structure: The Problem of Embeddedness." *American Journal of Sociology* 91: 481–510.

Granovetter, M. (1994) "The Problem of Explanation in Economic Sociology," in N. Nohria and R. Eccles (eds.), *Networks and Organizations*. Cambridge, MA: Harvard Business School Press.

Granovetter, M. (1995a) "The Economic Sociology of Firms and Entrepreneurs," in A. Portes (ed.), *The Economic Sociology of Immigration*. New York: Russell Sage Foundation.

Granovetter, M. (1995b) *Getting A Job: A Study of Contacts and Careers*, 2nd edn. Chicago: University of Chicago Press.

Granovetter, M. (2002) "A Theoretical Agenda for Economic Sociology," in M. Guillen et al. (eds.), *The New Economic Sociology*. New York: Russell Sage Foundation.

Granovetter, M., and McGuire, P. (1998) "The Making of an Industry: Electricity in the United States," in M. Callon (ed.), *The Laws of the Market*. Oxford: Blackwell.

Granovetter, M., and Swedberg, R. (eds.) (1992, 2001) *The Sociology of Economic Life*, 1st and 2nd, rev., edns. Boulder, CO: Westview Press.

Greif, A. (1998) "Self-Enforcing Political Systems and Economic Growth: Late Medieval Genoa," in R. Bates et al. (eds.), *Analytical Narratives*. Princeton: Princeton University Press.

Greif, A. (2005) *Institutions and the Path to the Modern Economy: Lessons from Medieval Trade*. Cambridge: Cambridge University Press.

Gui, B., and Sugden, R. (2005) *Economics and Social Interaction: Accounting for Interpersonal Relations*. Cambridge: Cambridge University Press.

Hannan, M., and Carroll, G. (1995) "An Introduction to Organizational Ecology," in G. Carroll and M. Hannan (eds.), *Organizations in Industry*. New York: Oxford University Press.

Harrington, B. (2007) *Pop Finance: Investment Groups in the United States*. Princeton: Princeton University Press.

Ingham, G. (1998) "On the Underdevelopment of 'The Sociology of Money'." *Acta Sociologica* 41: 3–18.

Ingham, G. (2004) *The Nature of Money*. Cambridge: Polity.

Keister, L. and Moller, S. (2000) "Wealth Inequality in the United States." *Annual Review of Sociology* 26: 63–81.

Khurana, R. (2002) *Searching for a Corporate Savior: The Irrational Quest for Charismatic CEOs*. Princeton: Princeton University Press.

Khurana, R. (2007) *From Higher Aims to Hired Hands: On the Professionalization in Business Schools*. Princeton: Princeton University Press.

Knorr-Cetina, K., and Brugger, U. (2002) "Global Macrostructures: The Virtual Societies of Financial Markets." *American Journal of Sociology* 107: 905–50.

Knorr-Cetina, K., and Preda, A. (eds.) (2005) *The Sociology of Financial Markets*. New York: Oxford University Press.

Krippner, G. (2001) "The Elusive Market: Embeddedness and the Paradigm of Economic Sociology." *Theory and Society* 30: 775–810.

Krippner, G., et al. (2004) "Polanyi Symposium: A Conversation on Embeddedness." *Socio-Economic Review* 2: 109–35.

Lazega, E. (2003) *Networks in Legal Organizations: On the Protection of Public Interest in Joint Regulation of Markets*. Inaugural Lecture of the Wiarda Chair, December. Faculty of Law, Utrecht University.

Lebaron, F. (2000) *La Croyance économique: Les Économistes entre science et politique*. Paris: Seuil.

Luhmann, N. (1982 [1970]) "The Economy as a Social System," in *The Differentiation of Society*. New York: Columbia University Press.

MacKenzie, D. (2006) *An Engine, Not a Camera: How Financial Models Shape Markets*. Cambridge, MA: MIT Press.

MacKenzie, D., and Millo, Y. (2003) "Constructing a Market, Performing Theory: The Historical Sociology of a Financial Derivatives Exchange." *American Journal of Sociology* 109: 107–45.

MacKenzie, D., Muniesa, F., and Siu, L. (eds.) (2007) *Do Economists Make Markets? On the Performativity of Economics*. Princeton: Princeton University Press.

Manski, C. (2000) "Economic Analysis of Social Interactions." *Journal of Economic Perspectives*, 14(3): 115–36.

Marx, K. (1906) *Capital: A Critique of Political Economy*. New York: The Modern Library.

Marx, K. (1970) *A Contribution to the Critique of Political Economy*. New York: International Publishers.

Marx, K. (1973) *Grundrisse: Foundations of the Critique of Political Economy*. New York: Vintage Books.

Mizruchi, M. (1996) "What Do Interlocks Do? An Analysis, Critique and Assessment of Research on Interlocking Directorates." *Annual Review of Sociology* 22(1996): 271–98.

Morris, M., and Western, B. (1999) "Inequality in Earnings at the Close of the Twentieth Century." *Annual Review of Sociology* 25: 623–57.

Nee, V. (1989) "A Theory of Market Transition: From Redistribution to Markets in State Socialism." *American Sociological Review* 54: 663–81.

Nee, V., and Ingram, P. (1998) "Embeddedness and Beyond: Institutions, Exchange, and Social Structure," in M. Brinton and V. Nee (eds.), *The New Institutionalism in Sociology*. New York: Russell Sage Foundation.

Nee, V., and Swedberg, R. (eds.) (forthcoming) *The Economic Sociology of Capitalism*. Princeton: Princeton University Press.

North, D. (1990) "Institutions." *Journal of Economic Perspectives.* 5(12): 97–112.

North, D. (2005) *Understanding the Process of Economic Change*. Princeton: Princeton University Press.

Padgett, J., and Ansell, C. (1993) "Robust Action and the Rise of the Medici, 1400–1434." *American Journal of Sociology* 98: 1259–1319.

Parsons, T., and Smelser, N. (1956) *Economy and Society: A Study in the Integration of Economic and Social Theory*. New York: The Free Press.

Podolny, J. (1992) "A Status-Based Model of Market Competition." *American Journal of Sociology* 98: 829–72.

Podolny, J. (2005) *Status Signals: A Sociological Study of Market Competition*. Princeton: Princeton University Press.

Poggi, G. (1993) *Money and the Modern Mind: Georg Simmel's Philosophy of Money*. Berkeley: University of California Press.

Polanyi, K. (1957 [1944]) *The Great Transformation*. Boston: Beacon Hill.

Polanyi, K., Arensberg, C., and Pearson, H. (eds.) (1971 [1957]) *Trade and Market in the Early Empires*. Chicago: Henry Regnery.

Radaev, V. (1997) "Practising and Potential Entrepreneurs in Russia." *International Journal of Sociology* 27(3): 15–50.

Sachs, J. (2000) "Notes on a New Sociology of Economic Development," in L. Harrison and S. Huntington (eds.), *Culture Matters*. New York: Basic Books,.

Sachs, J. (2005) *The End of Poverty: Economic Possibilities for Our Time*. New York: Penguin.

Saxenian, A. (1996) *Regional Competition: Culture and Competition in Silicon Valley and Route 128*. Cambridge, MA: Harvard University Press.

Schelling, T. (2006) *Strategies of Commitment and Other Essays*. Cambridge, MA: Harvard University Press.

Schumpeter, J. (1991) *The Economics and Sociology of Capitalism*, ed. R. Swedberg. Princeton: Princeton University Press.

Schumpeter, J. (1994 [1942]) *Capitalism, Socialism and Democracy*. London: Routledge.

Schumpeter, J. (2003) "Entrepreneur," in R. Koppl (ed.), *Austrian Economics and Entrepreneurial Studies*. Amsterdam: Elsevier.

Sen, A. (1999) *Development as Freedom*. Oxford: Oxford University Press.

Simmel, G. (1990) *The Philosophy of Money*, 2nd edn. London: Routledge.

Simon, H. (1997) "The Role of Organizations in an Economy," in H. Simon, *An Empirically Based Microeconomics*. Cambridge: Cambridge University Press.

Sitton, J. (1998) "Disembodied Capitalism: Habermas' Conception of the Economy." *Sociological Forum* 13(1): 61–83.

Spilerman, S. (2000) "Wealth and Stratification Processes." *Annual Review of Sociology* 26: 497–524.

Stark, D. (2001) "Recombinant Property in East European Capitalism." *American Journal of Sociology* 106: 993–1027.

Steiner, P. (2001) "The Sociology of Economic Knowledge." *European Journal of Social Theory* 4(4): 443–58.

Steiner, P. (2005) *L'École durkheimienne et l'économie*. Geneva: Droz.

Stiglitz, J. (2003) *Globalization and its Discontents*. New York: W. W. Norton.

Storper, M., and Salais, R. (1997). *Worlds of Production: The Action Frameworks of the Economy*. Cambridge, MA: Harvard University Press.

Sutton, J., Dobbin, F., Meyer, J., and Scott, R. (1994) "The Legalization of the Workplace." *American Journal of Sociology* 99: 944–71.

Swedberg, R. (1991) *Schumpeter: A Biography*. Princeton: Princeton University Press.

Swedberg, R. (1998) *Max Weber and the Idea of Economic Sociology*. Princeton: Princeton University Press.

Swedberg, R. (ed.) (2000) *Entrepreneurship: The Social Science View*. Oxford: Oxford University Press.

Swedberg, R. (2001) "Sociology and Game Theory: Contemporary and Historical Perspectives." *Theory and Society* 30(3): 301–35.

Swedberg, R. (2003a) *Principles of Economic Sociology*. Princeton: Princeton University Press.

Swedberg, R. (2003b) "The Case for an Economic Sociology of Law." *Theory and Society* 32(1): 1–37.

Thornton, P. (1999) "The Sociology of Entrepreneurship." *Annual Review of Sociology* 25: 19–46.

Uzzi, B. (1996) "The Sources and Consequences of Embeddednes for the Economic Performance of Organizations: The Network Effect." *American Sociological Review* 61: 674–98.

Uzzi, B. (1997) "Social Structure and Competition in Interfirm Networks: The Paradox of Embeddedness." *Administrative Science Quarterly* 42: 35–67.

Velthuis, O. (2005) *Talking Prices: Symbolic Meanings of Prices on the Market for Contemporary Art*. Princeton: Princeton University Press.

Weber, M. (1958 [1904–5]) *The Protestant Ethic and the Spirit of Capitalism*. New York: Charles Scribner's Sons.

Weber, M. (1978 [1922]) *Economy and Society: An Outline of Interpretive Sociology*, 2 vols. Berkeley: University of California Press.

Weber, M. (1981 [1923]) *General Economic History.* New Brunswick, NJ: Transaction Books.

Weber, M. (2000) "Stock and Commodity Exchanges: Commerce on the Stock and Commodity Exchanges." *Theory and Society* 29: 305–84.

White, H. (1981) "Where Do Markets Come From?." *American Journal of Sociology* 87: 517–47.

White, H. (2001) *Markets from Networks*. Princeton: Princeton University Press.

Yakubovich, V. (2002) "Between Exchange and Reciprocity: Matching Workers with Jobs in a Local Russian Labor Market." PhD thesis, Stanford University, Department of Sociology.

Zafirovski, M. (2001) *Exchange, Action and Social Structure: Elements of Economic Sociology*. Westport, CT: Greenwood.

Zelizer, V. (1994) *The Social Meaning of Money*. New York: Basic Books.

Zelizer, V. (2002) "Intimate Transactions." in M. Guillen et al. (eds.), *The New Economic Sociology*. New York: Russell Sage Foundation.

Zelizer, V. (2004) "Culture and Consumption," in N. Smelser and R. Swedberg (eds.), *The Handbook of Economic Sociology*, 2nd edn. New York and Princeton: Russell Sage Foundation and Princeton University Press.

Zuckerman, E. (1999) "The Categorical Imperative: Securities Analysts and the Illegitimacy Discount." *American Journal of Sociology* 104: 1398–1438.

Zuckerman, E. (2003) "On Networks and Markets." *Journal of Economic Literature* 41(2): 545–65.

19

Cultural Sociology

ISAAC REED AND JEFFREY C. ALEXANDER

A foundational principle of cultural sociology is that meaning is relational – that the meanings of symbols, words, tropes, metaphors, ideologies, and so on emerge in concert and contrast to other meanings of social import. This is as true of the terms "culture" and "cultural sociology" as it is of anything else. In particular, cultural sociology in its current use and meaning emerges both diachronically in contrast to the humanities, anthropology and the sociology of culture, and synchronically in relation to the core sociological terms of structure, action, and critique.

FROM THE HUMANITIES TO CULTURAL SOCIOLOGY, VIA THE SOCIOLOGY OF CULTURE

The old-fashioned definition of culture, which had as its institutional locus the humanities departments of elite Western universities in the early and mid-twentieth century, referred to what Matthew Arnold called "the best that has been thought and said." Culture was, according to this definition, intellectual and artistic activity and the artifacts produced by this activity, and to have culture was to possess the ability to interpret these artifacts, and the taste to distinguish the good ones from the bad ones. Simultaneously, Western anthropology developed a totalizing concept of culture that was expected to do the comparative work of differentiating the peoples of the world. Culture was thus the counterpoint to the concept of "human nature" which formed the subject of physical anthropology.

Over and against these definitions, the sociology of culture has developed a more nuanced, and more critical, account of the role of the symbolic and the artistic in society. The pretensions of the humanities' definition of culture, and the construction of the literary, dramatic, and musical canon that went along with it, were revealed as the tools of social exclusion and the maintenance of hierarchy. Furthermore, by carefully examining the aesthetics of both popular cultural artifacts, and the creative cultural activities of classes, races, and genders traditionally excluded from the realm of high arts production and appreciation, the sociology of culture has been essential to the deconstruction of the high/middle/lowbrow culture typology. Meanwhile, historical sociology has shown the connections between the anthropological imagination and various nationalist and colonialist projects of nineteenth-century Europe, whereby the totalizing concept of culture was complicit in the exoticization and simultaneous subordination and colonization (and sometimes extermination) of native populations. Extensive debates about the political valences and historical guilt of the concept of culture have ensued. But perhaps more importantly for ongoing empirical research, sociologists have found the anthropological concept of culture to be underspecified; for sociology, differentiating culture from nature is not enough. Rather, culture must be defined in relation to society, history, and individual psychology, and, furthermore, the differentiation between culture and nature must be itself be examined historically with an eye towards its varying social effects (many anthropologists have also come to this conclusion). Thus while sociology has drawn extensively on symbolic, structuralist, and linguistic anthropology for its own studies of culture, it has resisted the temptation to directly conflate culture with the social as such, and the culture/society distinction has been a productively unstable one.

In approaching culture as a social object of study, then, the sociology of culture forms a sub-field alongside the sociology of religion and the sociology of science, and takes within its purview both high literature and pulp fiction, Fellini films and Hollywood schlock, art music and rock "n" roll. With the advent of the production of culture perspective in the 1970s, centered around the work of Richard Peterson, and the concepts of field and cultural capital, drawn from the work of Pierre Bourdieu, this sub-field has gained both empirical purchase and theoretical sophistication. In taking culture as its object of study, however, the sociology of culture tends to bring to bear both methods and theories which were designed for the study of other sociological phenomena, and tends, still, towards the inclination that social structure and the actions of individuals can be used explain culture, as opposed to the other way around. This is the basic meaning of "reduction" which, by tracing culture's "reflection," "mediation," "expression," "determination by," "isomorphism with," or "homologous relation to" deeper and more real social networks, class tensions, or material realities, explains culture and gives the sociology *of* culture its name.

Yet the sociology of culture so constituted begs certain questions, and remains theoretically incomplete, and it is in the encounter with this incompleteness that one finds the origins of cultural sociology. Why are social actors so interested in cultural artifacts in the first place, as opposed to other, functional equivalent, status markers? Does the role of culture in modern and late capitalistic societies exceed its use as a tool for buying and selling, and status differentiation? Despite their suspicions about how modern rationality emptied the world of meaning, both Durkheim and Weber had moments where they viewed the construction and use of social meaning as the most basic social process in all societies, and Marx made clear in his passage on commodity fetishism that the supposed difference between a "civilized" Englishman and an African "savage" was an illusion – both worshiped at the altar of something that, for them, gave life meaning.

It is thus that cultural sociology emerges from the opposition between the humanities and the sociology of culture to offer both a concrete and an analytic definition of culture. Concretely, culture refers to those social objects and activities which are primarily or exclusively symbolic in their intent or social function, such as art, music, and sports. Analytically, culture refers to the symbolic and ideational element of any social action, social relationship, or historical pattern. Culture is signifiers and their signifieds, gestures and their interpretation, intended and unintended meanings, written discourse and effective speech, situational framing and scientific paradigms, moral and political ideals, and so on. The methodologies for studying culture so conceived range widely, and include surveys of attitudes and beliefs, participant observation, ethnography, structured and unstructured interviews, textual analysis of written and visual media, and conversation analysis. Ultimately, however, all of these methods involve the interpretation of meaning, and thus cannot be mapped directly from the methods of the natural sciences, though the extent to which scientific methods can be adapted to the study of culture is a matter of significant dispute.

What must be remembered, however, is that non-reductionist cultural sociology remains interested, ultimately, in the explanation of social action – it is not a return to the full, un-ironic engagement of aesthetics, and it is not a version of *de gustibus non est disputandum* (on this, see Born, forthcoming). The point is not to give up on the explanation of taste – or on the explanation of any other social phenomenon – but rather to approach this task of explanation from a perspective that makes meaning central, and refuses to set the relationship of meaning to society *in advance* as one in which real interests, structures, and opportunities drive the ephemeral imaginations of those who interpret culture.

This brings us the central terms of sociological theory in relation to which cultural sociology defines itself, and which, in its more ambitious theoretical moments, it attempts to reform: structure, action, and critique.

CULTURE AS STRUCTURE

Repeatedly in sociological theory and research, culture is distinguished from social structure. Talcott Parsons distinguished the cultural from the social system in a strictly analytic fashion (his student Niklas Luhmann would later claim that this should in fact be a concrete distinction). And Parsons suggested that the study of culture in all its symbolic elaborations could be left to anthropology, and that sociology could focus on the place where culture and social structure met, namely, on the institutionalization of values and norms. Structural functionalism suggested that culture, through normative interpenetration, could perform an integrative function in the service of social equilibrium, and thus that social change came with a breakdown in value consensus (as in Chalmers Johnson's theory of social revolution).

These assertions were subjected to relentless attack for suppressing the role of strife and domination in society (and in the use of culture). However, it is perhaps more instructive, now, to notice a deeper problem with structural functionalism, namely its interpretive deafness. By approaching culture as "norms and values," structural functionalism not only projected certain liberal ideals onto its model of society, but, more significantly, evacuated meaning from culture, robbing its analysis of nuance and empirical specificity. For, an engagement with the multiple layers of the symbolic immediately reveals that culture in modern societies is neither homogenous nor consensual. Rather, the size and makeup of collectivities that share certain symbolic articulations vary significantly (from small religious cults to large voting populations), and these symbolic articulations are contested both within and without collectivities.

Mid-century Marxism and post-1960s conflict theory insisted that culture was more of a guarantor of hierarchy, exploitation, and inequality, and thus saw culture as ideology. And though the political commitments and theoretical presuppositions of conflict theory were fundamentally at odds with those of Parsonian functionalism, one can discern in the studies of the objective basis of systematically distorted communication, and in references the political and economic functions of ideology, very similar problems to those that plagued the structural-functional approach. Here too, culture is assumed to be relatively uniform, at least in its social effects, and its study is guided by theoretical intuitions about the workings of the social system, and in particular the exploitation of labor. Thus Marxist repudiations of culture as ideology also suffered from a lack of musicality, and inattention to the empirical details of culture's varied production, performance, and reception.

In both cases, these problems were exacerbated by imagining social structures as hard, real, and external to the actor, in opposition to culture as a more pliable and less efficacious possession of individual minds. Furthermore, both structural functionalism and Marxism were embedded in teleological philosophies of history and social evolution that enabled them to locate the appropriate relations between social structure and culture in an *a priori* theoretical manner. As these teleologies came to be seen as more the meaningful, ideational constructions of sociologists' own cultures than ontological certainties about actual societies, the strict scientific distinction between social structure and culture began to break down, as did the various conceptions of their relationship. This breakdown created an opening for sociology to develop the tools necessary for a more sensitive and empirically sophisticated approach to culture in its collective forms. This has been accomplished by studying culture as a structure in its own right, a theoretical development that has taken three central forms.

The study of symbolic boundaries, associated with the work of Michele Lamont (*Money, Morals and Manners*, 1994), has shown how actors construct and maintain meanings as a mode of ordering, including, and excluding their fellow humans, over and against the exigencies of social structure. Thus, the economic basis for class is overwritten by an attribution of certain moral qualities to certain humans, based on criteria (including religion, race, and so forth) that may cross-cut the expectations of more reductively minded sociologists who would map class consciousness directly onto economic position, and so on.

The study of discourse and its relationship to power, based on the pioneering work of Michel Foucault, has enabled sociologists to examine not only articulated boundaries, but also unstated exclusions, and more generally the cultural construction of certain taken-for-granted "positivities" of modern life. Thus one can examine from a reflexive historical perspective how certain kinds human subjects (for example, insane people and medical patients) and social problems (for example, homosexuality) came to be of such great concern, and how their meaningful construction affected the way they were dealt with, inside and outside of mainstream society. Though Foucault's work has been largely appropriated in the humanities as a set of theorems concerning power and knowledge more appropriate to critical theory than to empirical sociology, his early studies of madness, medicine, and the episteme of the classical and modern ages are in fact rich historical reconstructions of landscapes' meaning, and their essential role in the social processes of treatment, exclusion, and philosophical understanding. These issues are developed in Foucault's *Madness and Civilization* (1988 [1964]) and in Mukerji (1990).

Finally, the conception of culture as a structure in its own right has enabled the sociological transformation of a set of tools from literary theory and semiotics. Culture can be studied as a social text, replete with codes, narratives, genres, and metaphors. Then, culture can be examined in both its concrete and analytic auton- omy from social structure, which enables us to isolate and make clear its effects (and its varying political valences) from a sociological point of view. So, for example, the long struggle for women's rights in the United States can be seen as a discursive battle for civil inclusion, according to which a new set of actors came to be coded in a democratic and morally positive way (see Alexander 2006). This conception of culture suggests, moreover, that social structures themselves are interpreted variably by social actors, and thus must be attended to hermeneutically by cultural sociolo- gists, with an eye to their meaningful aspects, their locality, and their historical specificity (see Alexander 2003; Geertz 1973).

Culture in action

Since culture is often contrasted to social structure, and furthermore associated with subjectivity, then it should not be surprising that it has often been erroneously con- flated with action and its related terms: agency, reflexivity, and consciousness. However, as culture has become recognized as a structure in its own right, the rela- tionship of culture to action has become a key component of sociological theory and research. The ongoing debate about culture and action has its roots in two dif- ferent sociological traditions, both of which contribute to contemporary cultural sociology. On the one hand, the analytic tradition, descending from Parsons's for- malization of Max Weber's means–ends approach to action, approached culture in terms of the ways culture sets the ends of action. Action is thus structured not only by interests, but by norms as well. Originally opposed to economistic accounts of social action, the strictly analytic approach to purposive action has been revived in contemporary sociological debates about agency and rationality. But a deeper under- standing of the role of culture for action has been developed from within this tradi- tion by recognizing culture as an internal environment for action, arguing thus that culture orients action by structuring subjectivity. Social actors respond to sets of internal typifications of the social world and thus are dependent upon meaningful symbolization in setting their goals, and in imagining how they can go about meeting them. By reintroducing the symbolic as an environment of action full of rich narratives and morally and emotionally loaded oppositions, this approach integrates the expanded approach to culture-as-structure elaborated above.

On the other hand, the pragmatic tradition, descending from George Herbert Mead and Herbert Blumer, rejects the means–ends characterization of action outright, and suggests instead that actors constantly negotiate situations in an improvisatory way, attempting to make sense of and solve both social and physical problems as they arise. Originally, because of its distance from the analytic abstractions of the Parsonian tradition, and its tendency towards methodological individualism, this tradition was not really oriented towards culture per se, though it had a conception of the use of symbols and framing on the micro level. Increasingly, however, the descendants of this tradition have developed a conception of culture-as-use that conceives of the knowledgeable agent as the link between culture and society. It is actors, in social situations, that draw on culture when institutional consistency breaks down.

Thus the contemporary debate is structured by two positions, that of culture-in-action (illustrated in Swidler 1986), and that of culture as thick environment for action (see Alexander 1988). Both approaches have significant insights to offer. The first emphasizes that actors continually work to render coherent and solvable discursive and institutional problems that arise in the flow of social life. The second emphasizes the way in which the social world is constructed for the actor by previous interpretations and collective languages. In either case, these approaches suggest the importance of culture for the study of social life. For example, we should perhaps discuss the discursive repertoires of politicians, and the resonance of these repertoires with the shared codes of their audience-electorates, as opposed to the "revealed preferences" of either. The contrasts between the two approaches have, however, produced significantly different forms of theory and research.

One important manifestation of the symbolic interactionist tradition has been Gary Fine's development of the concept of idiocultures, whereby small groups develop an idiosyncratic set of meanings (beliefs, knowledge, and customs) that forms the basis for mutual understanding and further interaction and action. Thus cooks in various classes of restaurants develop an aesthetic language that enables them to communicate with each other concerning the manifestly practical problems of smell and taste.

Alternately, Robin Wagner-Pacifici has developed the concept of social drama within the more analytic tradition of action and its environments, so as to enable the study of social situations where symbolic and physical violence interact. In studying terrorist kidnappings, standoffs between government and its discontents, and surrenders, she develops a deep understanding of morally loaded environments for action. When the social fabric is breached, actors must work within certain dramatic frameworks, and with certain obtainable identities. Thus, in a standoff between the Freemen of Montana and the US government, it was a mediator who had fought in Vietnam and, like some of the leaders of the Freemen, had formed his core identity in the crucible of that experience and its subsequent narration who was able bridge the symbolic gap between the antagonists. Action was deeply structured by the symbolic environments of traumatic memory and the enactment of masculinity.

The specificity of the kinds of meanings that are enacted, however, points to both the possible misinterpretations of the relationship between action and culture, and to the way forward in the theoretical debate. For the exclusive emphasis on culture as it is used by actors can support the naturalistic approach to social structure and thus an understanding of culture as unstructured and primarily the possession of individuals. In this conception, it is meaning-less institutions that set the parameters of the action problem, and culture is merely the way actors make sense of things as they are solving it, perhaps important for filling out an explanation, but not essential to it. The environments to action approach is faced with a similar danger, for insofar as it retains vestiges of Parsons's action frame of reference, it can be taken to indicate that sociology can produce, in theory alone, a mechanistic explanation of the interaction of norms and interests that will apply everywhere, regardless of cultural differences.

Perhaps most significantly, it is important that action theory be prevented from becoming a sort of existential meditation on the capacities (or incapacities) of human freedom, rather than a way to examine the social contingencies of actually existing meaning. If the knowledgeable agent becomes a sort of philosophical and methodological hero, whose reflexivity about her location in structure ultimately makes her the master of the cultural formations in her head, then the sociological purpose of examining cultural structures is vitiated, as collective meaning formations melt away in the face of agency and knowledge as developed by Anthony Giddens in *The Constitution of Society* (1984).

Thus the way forward in the action-culture debates lies in the development of a meaning-full account of action through a theorization of social performance, by linking action theory to Erving Goffman's dramaturgical sociology and Kenneth Burke's literary theory, but also Judith Butler's reconception of the poststructuralist tradition of social thought. By thinking of social situations of varying scope (from small group interactions to media events watched by millions) as dramas being played out on a public stage, with certain actors and audiences, props and social powers, emergent scripts and cultural backgrounds, we can conceive of the exigencies of social action in a thoroughly cultural way that does not reduce meaning to social structure. Action, then, is the putting into scene of certain intended and unintended meanings. This is to say that the theorization of action not only has to take into account cultural structures, but must further focus on how actions are themselves interpretations of these structures, and thus responds to logics of meaning and identity underneath the interests and norms that were once supposed to do the work of explaining them; this argument is developed in Alexander, Giesen, and Mast 2006.

CULTURE AND CRITIQUE

The sociologically inspired critique of culture used to be based almost entirely on references to the social as existing outside of culture itself. It was thus diametrically opposed to the sense of criticism associated with the detailed reading of the literary canon, and with humanistic studies more generally. The obvious exception was Marxist literary criticism, in particular that of Georg Lukács and Raymond Williams, which entered into literary texts themselves to find the logics of ideology. While their work foreshadowed the development of cultural studies, it remained nonetheless within the discourse of suspicion about culture, usually understood as bourgeois culture (and its discontents). This, in the course of twentieth-century criticism and the invention of cultural studies, was expanded into the study of the many varieties of hegemonic culture, to the point where Gramsci's term was no longer associated with a specifically Marxist perspective, but rather used as the touchstone of cultural criticism from the perspective of almost any dominated or oppressed social group.

There is, in this form of cultural study, a deep and ongoing tension between the process of debunking ideology, and the more diffuse and obscure process of "deconstruction." The latter term – taken from Derrida but usually combined with a Foucauldian analysis of power/knowledge – has, at times, produced an overarching suspicion of all norms and normalcy, and indeed the very process of making normative claims about how society should be ordered. This has had a strange effect on the academic left, introducing a strand of extreme skepticism which would be entirely incomprehensible to Marxists with a strong sense of the utopian promise of revolution. In reforming the project of critique, cultural sociology attempts to avoid this aspect of the postmodern turn.

Instead, cultural sociology aims to connect the normative orientation towards democracy, social inclusion, and the critique of power with the interpretation of cultures, asking what the basis is, in extant social meaning, for the improvement of the conditions under which humans live together. The project of hermeneutics, once associated with the conservative aesthetic hierarchies of the German philosophical tradition, can now be seen as a rich source of critique in a post-positivist and post-orthodox-Marxist age, as exemplified by the work of Michael Walzer. The epistemological implication of his work is that sociological critique must abandon its pseudo-scientific assumption of an exterior stance or view from nowhere, and develop critical distance through extensive engagement, dialog, and interpretation. Thereby, critical perspectives on contemporary societies will share some of the empirical purchase of cultural sociology, and will attend to the communicability of new normative understandings of justice and equality. More generally, insofar as sociological critique is no longer beholden to scientific certainty, revolutionary upheaval, and the genre of debunking, its normative repertoire of critical tropes, subtle ironies, and imagined ideals can be expanded (for a fuller version of this argument, see Reed 2007).

THE CULTURAL TURN IN SOCIOLOGY: EMPIRICAL MANIFESTATIONS

Ultimately, then, the theoretical reorientation implied by cultural sociology has enabled sociologists to approach a variety of sub-fields of empirical research from a different perspective. This is what is known as "the cultural turn." Though the end goal is often the same – the explanations of sets of patterned social actions – the means to that end now involve ferreting out the varied meanings of a dominant discourse, examining the signification systems embodied in rituals, and asking how social life is lived according to symbolic frameworks.

Sociology's ongoing preoccupation with modernity, and the history of state formation, has led to a focus on the constitution of nations as collective identities. In explaining economic takeoff in western Europe, the consolidation of the power of states, and the emergence and importance of democratic publics and the free press, sociologists have increasingly focused on the construction of nations as "imagined communities" and "discursive fields," and nationalism as "a unique form of social consciousness" (for example in Anderson 1991; Greenfeld 2007 [1992]; Spillman 1997).

The sociology of sex and gender has likewise experienced a cultural overhaul. While feminist and queer theory have questioned the naturalness of the sex/gender distinction, sociological research has examined the effects of actually existing cultural schemas of gender and sex for social outcomes, including family structure, women's tendency to join or opt out of the workforce, and the ongoing existence of sexism in wage levels and status attainment. These studies examine gender as both a highly rigid structure of meaning, but also its varying enactment by women and men who attempt to negotiate the political and economic contradictions of modern society (for instance in Blair-Loy 2003; Hays 1996; Stacy 1990).

Finally, sociology's longstanding normative concern with democracy and its incipient populism has also taken a cultural turn. For example, analyses of American political participation and activism have investigated how certain meanings either enable or discourage civic participation. The results have often been counterintuitive: doctrines of individual empowerment encourage activity and public responsibility, while norms of civility and politeness discourage political conversation and involvement which is developed in Eliasoph (1998) and Lichterman (1996).

REINTERPRETING THE CLASSICS

Culture has thus moved towards the center of sociological discourse, as both a topic of study and a perspective from which to view the social. As reinterpretation is a primary form of theoretical advance, the perhaps predictable result of this has been that, simultaneously, the classics of social theory have come to be seen in a new light. New readings of Karl Marx, Max Weber, and Émile Durkheim have emerged.

While all twentieth-century Marxisms have given more importance to culture and ideology than did the crude economic Marxist orthodoxy that followed Marx's death, the turn to culture in the 1960s and 1970s is evident in the increasing attention given to Marx's analysis of commodity fetishism in *Capital*, as well as to the importance of the early, humanist, and perhaps even idealist-Hegelian, Marx. Either way, Marx is read as attentive to the capacity of meaning as a social force. One important result of this has been the way structuralist and poststructuralist theories of language have merged with Marxist historiography to produce a central thesis concerning postmodernism, namely that the postmodern age is one in which the workings of capitalism are increasingly dependent on signifiers as well as signifieds, that is, on the relational field of social symbolism. These approaches are illustrated in Jameson (1992) and Baudrillard (1981 [1972]).

Likewise, the last 40 years have seen a recovery of Weber's sociology of art, as well as continuing debate over *The Protestant Ethic and the Spirit of Capitalism*. However, most significantly, the concern with culture has also entered in to Weberian debates about the consolidation of state power and the institutionalization of rational bureaucracy. Here, sociologists have increasingly read Weber as a hermeneutic student of rationality as cultural form specific to Western history. In doing so, Weber's concerns are read as not so different from Foucault's, and bureaucracy is less a mechanism to be uncovered than a form of symbolic action to be interpreted. This interpretation is developed in Gorski (2003).

Finally, the cultural turn in sociology has seen a renaissance and reconsideration of Durkheim later works, and in particular, *The Elementary Forms of Religious Life* (1912). This work has come to be seen as a key prolegomenon to the symbolic study of society as general project, including to the study of the role of culture in modern, industrial societies. Durkheim is thus read as uncomfortable with the materialist interpretations given to *The Division of Labor in Society* and as having made a key epistemic break in the years between the publication of *Suicide* and *Elementary Forms* (see Alexander 1986). As a result, Durkheim can be seen as a precursor to cultural structuralism in his emphasis on the autonomy of symbolic forms, and the importance of belief and ritual for the organization of society.

CULTURAL SOCIOLOGY: "NEW CLASSICS"

Another aspect of this process of reinterpretation has been the emergence of new classic texts, required reading for any cultural sociologist. Though the cultural sociological canon, if there is one, is a dynamic and expanding group of texts, here we mention three.

Wilhelm Dilthey's essay, "The Construction of the Historical World in the Human Sciences" (1976) marked the author's departure from psychologism and entry into the study of meaning as itself a structure. It thus sets the stage for twentieth-century hermeneutics, and, eventually, for cultural sociology itself. Dilthey begins from German Romanticism's emphasis on the internal self and the complexities of subjective experience, and thus rejects any equation of the social and natural sciences. But he also rejects the notion that the human sciences and the interpretation of history are thus doomed to be unsystematic and arbitrary in their conclusions. Rather, he suggests that the interpretation of society and history must look towards the shared, background meanings which make individual subjectivity and experience possible, and that these meanings will contain the key to producing explanations of historical events and social phenomena.

Ferdinand de Saussure's *Course in General Linguistics* (1998) provided the essential tools for the task Dilthey had set. In his structural theory of language, linguistic signs are divisible into signifier and signified, and meaning is determined relationally and is thus "arbitrary and conventional." Saussure's ideas on language – already intended, in his writings, to describe processes of symbolization more broadly – became the basis for structural anthropology, and more generally, the theoretical movements of structuralism and poststructuralism. Saussure's theory of meaning provides cultural sociology with the ability to study chains of signification empirically, and thus map in detail the collective representations to which Durkheim attributed so much force.

The essays collected in Clifford Geertz's *Interpretation of Cultures* (1973) brought Saussure's and Dilthey's insights together, and helped launch the contemporary cultural turn. Geertz's controversial concept of "thick description" articulated the methodological inclination of cultural sociology to get inside actors' meanings. But it was what Geertz brought to his own efforts at thick description which expanded indefinitely the scope of cultural sociology. Geertz was able to use the concepts of humanistic and aesthetic criticism – such as genre, trope, metaphor, etc. – to describe social phenomena such as sporting events, the performance of state power, and religion. In his later work, Geertz suggested that this effort represented a "blurring" of genres of academic writing – between literary criticism and anthropology, for example. This may be so. But what Geertz's work also suggested was a new, self-sustaining, and coherent genre of sociological writing, in which the tools of criticism were put to a different, and distinctly sociological use, namely, the development of understanding for the purpose of social explanation.

FURTHER THEORETICAL QUESTIONS FOR CULTURAL SOCIOLOGY: REFRAMING "INTERPRETATION"

As a burgeoning paradigm for empirical research, cultural sociology – which began as an argument against the reductionisms of the sociology of culture and the cynicism of Marxist literary criticism – must confront its own positive knowledge claims, rather than rest content as a counterpoint or "alternative" to the mainstream sociological instinct to be suspicious of culture. This is to say that, in the future, cultural sociology must come to a fuller self-understanding, through an examination of the epistemologically and methodologically fraught term *interpretation*.

First, cultural sociology must provide a self-consistent account of the role of the investigator in social analysis. Though most cultural sociologists accept neither scientific norms nor postmodern normlessness as the parameters for their truth claims, what norms they do accept is an important issue to discuss in the abstract. In particular, it seems clear that sociologists want the meanings they reconstruct to be translatable, so that cultural comparison is possible, so as to perceive more clearly the varied relationships of meaning in action. Thus even single case studies or ethnographies implicitly contain a comparison, at least to the investigator's own meaningful social contexts, and this comparative consciousness forms an important basis for the development of theory and research in cultural sociology. Thinking along these lines intersects with advances in the sociology of knowledge, and in particular with the sociology of science in the form of the "strong program" associated with David Bloor.

The second question concerns how forms of interpretation common to cultural sociology may apply outside the domain of what is either analytically or concretely called culture. A lot of work within poststructuralist theory has examined the symbolic and discursive basis for what sociologists are more likely to call social structure, namely, institutional formations, social sanction and exclusion, and even violence, as argued in Butler (1989). The extent to which these aspects of social life can actually be explored empirically, however, remains to be explored in terms of the philosophy of social science. Thus, for example, we need to ask how even the reconstruction of political strategies and economic exigencies involves the interpretation of highly reified and strictly executed meaning.

Finally, cultural sociology – which frequently claims the importance of local knowledge, the contingency of interpretation, and the constructedness of social reality over and against the more standard forms of social structural analysis – must come to terms with the historical dimension of sociological analysis. Both "culture" and "history" are terms which, in academic discourse, tend to be used to defy the universalist claims of sociological theories that aspire to scientific status. Thus it is not surprising that many of their theoretical concerns and epistemological quandaries overlap. History, as a profession, has taken on board – to a certain degree – the claims of culture. Cultural sociology, likewise, should take on the great problems of comparative-historical sociology – the transition to modernity, the origins and maintenance of capitalism, the nature of the colonial encounter, the causes of social revolutions – which have for so long been comprehended under the aegis of political economy.

Bibliography

Alexander, J. (1986) "Rethinking Durkheim's Intellectual Development II: Working out a Religious Sociology." *International Sociology.* 1(2): 189–201.

Alexander, J. (1988) *Action and its Environments: Toward a New Synthesis.* New York: Columbia University Press.

Alexander, J. (2003) *The Meanings of Social Life: A Cultural Sociology.* New York: Oxford University Press.

Alexander, J. (2006) *The Civil Sphere.* New York: Oxford University Press.

Alexander, J., Giesen, B., and Mast, J. (eds.) (2006) *Social Performance: Symbolic Action, Cultural Pragmatics, and Ritual.* New York: Cambridge University Press.

Anderson, B. (1991) *Imagined Communities.* New York: Verso.

Baudrillard, J. (1981 [1972]) *For a Critique of the Political Economy of the Sign.* St. Louis: Telos.

Baudrillard, J. (2006) *The System of Objects.* New York: Verso.

Blair-Loy, M. (2003) *Competing Devotions: Career and Family among Women Executives.* Cambridge, MA: Harvard University Press.

Born, G. (forthcoming) "The Social and the Aesthetic: Methodological Principles in the Study of Cultural Production," in I. Reed and J. Alexander (eds.), *Meaning and Method: The Cultural Approach to Sociology.* Boulder, CO: Paradigm.

Butler, J. (1989) *Gender Trouble: Feminism and the Subversion of Identity.* New York: Routledge.

Dilthey, W. (1976) "The Construction of the Historical World in the Human Studies," in H. P. Rickman (ed.), *Wilhelm Dilthey: Selected Writings.* New York: Cambridge University Press.

Eliasoph, N. (1998) *Avoiding Politics: How Americans Produce Apathy in Everyday Life.* New York: Cambridge University Press.

Foucault, M. (1988 [1964]) *Madness and Civilization: A History of Insanity in the Age of Reason.* New York: Vintage.

Geertz, C. (1973) *The Interpretation of Cultures.* New York: HarperCollins.

Giddens, A. (1984) *The Constitution of Society: Outline of the Theory of Structuration.* Cambridge: Polity.

Gorski, P. (2003) The *Disciplinary Revolution: Calvinism and the Rise of the State in Early Modern Europe.* Chicago: University of Chicago Press.

Greenfeld, L. (2007 [1992]) *Nationalism: Five Roads to Modernity.* Cambridge, MA: Harvard University Press.

Hays, S. (1996) *The Cultural Contradictions of Motherhood*. New Haven: Yale University Press.

Jameson, F. (1992) *Postmodernism, or, the Cultural Logic of Late Capitalism*. Durham, NC: Duke University Press.

Lamont, M. (1994) *Money, Morals, and Manners: The Culture of the French and American Upper-Middle Class*. Chicago: University of Chicago Press.

Lichterman, P. (1996) *The Search for Political Community: American Activists Reinventing Commitment*. New York: Cambridge University Press.

Mukerji, C. (1990) *A Fragile Power: Scientists and the State*. Princeton, NJ: Princeton University Press.

Reed, I. (2007) "Cultural Sociology and the Democratic Imperative," in I. Reed and J. Alexander, *Culture, Society, and Democracy: The Interpretive Approach*. Boulder, CO: Paradigm.

Reed, I., and Alexander, J. (eds.) (2007) *Culture, Society, and Democracy: The Interpretive Approach*. Boulder, CO: Paradigm.

Reed, I., and Alexander, J. (eds.) (forthcoming) *Meaning and Method: The Cultural Approach to Sociology*. Boulder, CO: Paradigm.

Saussure, F. de (1998) *Course in General Linguistics*. New York: Open Court.

Spillman, L. (1997) *Nation and Commemoration*. New York: Cambridge University Press.

Stacy, J. (1990) *Brave New Families: Stories of Domestic Upheaval in Late Twentieth-Century America*. Berkeley: University of California Press.

Swidler, A. (1986) "Culture in Action: Symbols and Strategies." *American Sociological Review*. 51(2): 273–86.

Wagner-Pacifici, R. (2000) *Theorizing the Standoff: Contingency in Action*. New York: Cambridge University Press.

20

Historical Sociology

KRISHAN KUMAR

WHY "HISTORICAL SOCIOLOGY"?

In one sense, an entry on "historical sociology" in a *Companion* of this kind might seem redundant, if not actually counter-productive. If one believes, with C. Wright Mills, that "all sociology worthy of the name is 'historical sociology'" (Mills 1959: 146), then history should inform all branches of sociology. There should not be a separate, potentially ghettoizable, sub-field called "historical sociology," comparable to "family sociology" or the "sociology of education." Those areas have their subject – the family, the educational system. What is the "subject" of historical sociology? Is it not rather simply an approach, a way of doing sociology? What if we were to turn it around, and say "sociological history"? The meaningless of specifying an object of study becomes immediately apparent. No historian would think of teaching a course in "sociological history," yet it is quite common now to find sociologists teaching courses in historical sociology, or "comparative-historical sociology."

The peculiarity of this is even more evident if we recall the establishment of the discipline of sociology in the nineteenth century. Nearly all the important practitioners – Karl Marx, Alexis de Tocqueville, Max Weber, Georg Simmel – were historical in their approach (see e.g. Abrams 1982). Even Émile Durkheim, usually accounted the least historically minded of the "founding fathers," declared that "it is only by carefully studying the past that we can come to anticipate the future and to understand the present" (Durkheim 1977: 9). Anyone attempting to describe and explain large-scale social changes – as all the major early sociologists conceived their task – was forced to consider history, even if they were sometimes tempted to abridge and schematize it by their use of general categories ("from militant to industrial society," "from mechanical to organic solidarity," "from *Gemeinschaft* to *Gesellschaft*," etc). For what is "social change" but history? The idea that sociology could do without history would have seemed incomprehensible to them, as it would have done to any student of the human sciences at the time (only economics perhaps then began its long and disastrous turn away from history).

It is clear that, in this respect at least, the legacy of the founding fathers has not been lasting. Sociology has had to rediscover, slowly and painfully, its kinship with history. It is as if the famous injunction of E. H. Carr's – "the more sociological history becomes, and the more historical sociology becomes, the better for both" (Carr 1964: 66) – has failed to have its desired effect. Whatever the case with history – and the retreat there, from the social sciences, is evident too (Thomas 2006) – sociology has manifestly not taken upon itself to become historical, not at least as a mainstream assumption. It has indeed accepted history, but on its own terms. "Historical sociology" has become an accepted and even respected branch of the discipline – there is a flourishing section, for instance, within the American Sociological Association – but it has, like most areas of sociology, had to resign itself to being a sub-field, an enclave within the discipline, with its own methods and even to a good extent its own characteristic concerns. Hence the need to specify it as a specialized area, alongside "economic sociology," or "cultural sociology," or "the sociology of religion."

THE RECOVERY OF HISTORICAL SOCIOLOGY

Why did sociology, despite its earlier embrace, part company with history? Why has the relationship had to be re-established? The usual explanation still seems the correct one. At the end of the nineteenth and in the early twentieth centuries, especially in the developing discipline of anthropology, social scientists reacted against the dominant evolutionism of the previous epoch. Though evolutionism and the use of history were not and are not the same thing (see e.g. Nisbet 1970), their common reference to time and to long-term social change made them joint targets of the new functionalism, which insisted on the need to understand social order before – and perhaps, as the more urgent task, instead of – social change. Social scientists were directed to examining the institutions and structures of "social systems" – conceived in an essentially universalist, ahistorical way – as a way of understanding how they contributed to the maintenance of social order and social integration. This led away from a "diachronic" to a more "synchronic" approach to the study of society. The teachings of Bronislaw Malinowski in anthropology and of Talcott Parsons in sociology were especially influential in this reorientation of social science in the 1920s and 1930s. Consequently for much of the period from the 1930s to the 1960s history was more or less banished from mainstream sociology, at least in the West (in the Soviet Union Marxism substituted for sociology, which at least had the effect of keeping historical approaches alive).

There was a marked revival of historical sociology in the 1960s – a revival that can be seen as marking the beginning of the second "long wave" of historical sociology (the first can be seen as lasting from the mid-eighteenth-century Enlightenment to the 1920s) (Smith 1991). What seems to have driven it was – in the face of the challenge of the Soviet Union and the communist model – an attempt to understand the basis of Western capitalist societies, and in particular their robust ability to withstand the challenges of communism and working-class revolution. Ironically this marked a continuation of the functionalist project, but now with a historical twist that sought to uncover the historical origins of the long-term stability of Western societies. Despite the differences of subject matter, this concern is what linked such major works of historical sociology as Neil Smelser's *Social Change in the Industrial Revolution* (1959), Reinhard Bendix's *Work and Authority in Industry* (1956) and *Nation-Building and Citizenship* (1964), Clark Kerr and others' *Industrialism and Industrial Man* (1960), and S. M. Lipset's *First New Nation* (1963). A particular aspect of this inquiry – the conflict between democracy and dictatorship in modern states, and the social requisites of democracy – was a central feature of two other influential works of historical sociology of this period, S. M. Lipset's *Political Man* (1960) and S. N. Eisenstadt's *The Political Systems of Empires* (1963). One might also mention, as part of the general concern with the problems of "modernization" shared by all these works, Robert Bellah's pioneering study, *Tokugawa Religion: The Cultural Roots of Modern Japan* (1957), and Ronald Dore's *Education in Tokugawa Japan* (1965).

It was partly in response to this school – dominated by Parsonian concerns of consensus and integration – that a reaction set in in the later 1960s, leading to a second phase of the second long wave of historical sociology. Once more purely intellectual influences were matched by significant political and social changes. The 1960s saw the rebirth of conflict in the West, in the form of student protests, worker militancy, and the black movement in the United States. An important stimulus to this revival were the massive "national liberation" struggles throughout the Third World, as former colonies threw off European imperial rule. One consequence of the turmoil was the return of conflict theories of society, especially of its major representative, Marxism. Marxism, critically interrogated and fruitfully applied, was the guiding spirit of Barrington Moore Jr.'s *Social Origins of Dictatorship and Democracy* (1969), the work usually taken as marking the opening of the new wave in historical sociology.

Moore sought to understand the different "routes to modernity" taken by countries such as Britain, the United States, France, Russia, China, and India. Some had ended up as democracies, some as dictatorships. Moore found the key in the different resolutions of the "peasant problem," and in the managing of the transition to capitalist relations in the countryside. Much of the study was taken up with the analysis of various forms of revolution, the "capitalist revolutions" of the English and French particularly, but also the American Civil War seen in similar terms. Against these examples, which largely produced democracies, were seen the communist revolutions of Russia and China and their dictatorial outcomes (in India the future still was uncertain, Moore thought).

Moore's powerful and wide-ranging work set the agenda for much of the historical sociology of the 1970s and 1980s (see. e.g. Adams, Clemens, and Orloff 2005b). It was the self-confessed inspiration of the influential study by his Harvard student Theda Skocpol, *States and Social Revolutions* (1979). This comparative study of revolutions in France, Russia, and China once more engaged with Marx, but the "state-centered" perspective that Skocpol brought to bear on her cases evidently derived from Tocqueville and Weber. The fiscal crisis of the state, rivalry between state elites, international competition, and the pressures of the international system: these were the factors that Skocpol showed were the principal causes of the revolutions (though, as if it were necessary to pay due respect to both Marx and Moore, Skocpol also tried, less successfully, to integrate this analysis with class struggles in the countryside).

Revolutions and radical social movements indeed were the focus of some of the best work in historical sociology in the 1970s and 1980s. Here insights from Tocqueville and Weber, with their stress on the state, politics, and culture, increasingly challenged the economically based interpretations of the Marxists. Charles Tilly was a leading spirit in this, with a cascade of works beginning with *The Vendée* (1964) and continuing with *From Mobilization to Revolution* (1978) and later *European Revolutions, 1492–1992* (1993). But Marx remained important, especially as shown in the work of the British Marxist historians Eric Hobsbawm, Lawrence Stone, and E. P. Thompson, who had considerable influence on the historical sociology of these decades. Thompson's magisterial *The Making of the English Working Class* (1963) held pride of place, but Hobsbawm's studies in the history of labor and labor movements – e.g. *Primitive Rebels* (1959) and *Labouring Men* (1964) – were also important, as was Stone's *Causes of the English Revolution* (1972). Sociologists and historians engaged in a highly productive debate about the political potential of working-class movements, much of it concerning the fate of working-class movements in the nineteenth century and beyond (see e.g. Kumar 1988). William Sewell's *Work and Revolution in France* (1980), which showed how the culture of work can decisively influence working-class politics, was an influential study, as was Craig Calhoun's *The Question of Class Struggle* (1983), a skillful interrogation of E. P. Thompson's model of English working-class development.

Marx was also evidently the inspiration for one of the most powerful and enduring stands of historical sociology, the "world-system" model of Immanuel Wallerstein as expounded in his three-volume study, *The Modern World System* (1974–89). The significance of this work lay not simply in its analytical power but in its stimulus to the investigation of non-Western societies, something largely neglected in the earlier period. By treating the capitalist world as a single global system, Wallerstein – originally himself an Africanist – was able to suggest an ongoing interaction of all the cultures and societies of the world, at least since the sixteenth century. Not only did Wallerstein himself, in a continuing stream of publications over three decades, actively develop and propagate this model, but at his base, the Fernand Braudel Center at the State University of New York at Binghampton, he gathered around him an immensely fertile and productive group of scholars – Giovanni Arrighi, Terence Hopkins, Christopher Chase-Dunn, Caglar Keyder – who also explored and elaborated the model in a series of wide-ranging investigations of the historical development of different societies across the globe (see e.g. Arrighi 1994; Chase-Dunn 1989; Keyder 1987).

It might have been thought that sociologists, with their interest in Marx and Weber, would have been active contributors to debates on "the transition from feudalism to capitalism." But with the exception of the world-system school – which in any case avoided any detailed investigation of the feudal past – sociologists seemed reluctant to tackle this important area of historical sociology. There was R. J. Holton's *The Transition from Feudalism to Capitalism* (1985), largely a critical review of the ideas of Adam Smith, Marx, and Weber on the transition; later Richard Lachmann's *Capitalists in Spite of Themselves* (2000) more creatively synthesized Marx and Weber to provide an original account of the different routes out of feudalism taken by different European nations in the early modern period. Beyond that, there was some reference to the great work of Marc Bloch, *Feudal Society*

(English translation, 1961), and a general awareness that the Annales School of French historians, with their emphasis on structure and *la longue durée*, would be particularly congenial to sociologists. Fernand Braudel's trilogy *Civilization and Capitalism 15th–18th Century* (1981–4) occasionally got respectful mention, but its strongly materialist approach may have put off sociologists increasingly influenced by "the cultural turn" in sociology. At any rate it scarcely figures in the work of historical sociologists. Nor was there any general recognition in the sociological literature of the importance of the work of the American historian Robert Brenner on the agrarian origins of capitalism (see Aston and Philpin 1985). This neglect of significant contributions by historians is a recurrent feature of contemporary historical sociology, to which I shall return.

One might make one further general point here. Some of the best work in historical sociology in these decades was done under the influence of Marxism, even when, perhaps especially when, in disagreement with Marx. Whatever the fate of Marxism as a general social theory, it remains the case that of all the theoretical traditions Marxism is the one that most insistently demands an engagement with history. "Historical materialism," as the name implies, is historical through and through; for Marx human beings are constituted by history, they are historical beings ("the cultivation of the five senses is the work of all previous history"). Even before the fall of the Soviet Union, social theorists had begun to turn away from Marxism. Culture and politics came to occupy center-stage. This necessary reassertion of the importance of meaning and values, and of the state and political power, nevertheless seemed to mean a turning away from an approach that, for all its emphasis on the economic, offered the most wide-ranging and comprehensive interrogation of the historical record as a necessary means of understanding our present condition. For historical sociology, nothing could be more suggestive or stimulating. One has to hope that the current disfavor into which Marxism has fallen will prove to be temporary, more a reaction to recent political events than a permanent shift. To abandon it – especially in a period in which global capitalism seems to be flexing its muscles as never before, and in which Marx therefore seems as relevant as at any previous time – would be to deprive historical sociology of one of its most important sources of inspiration, and a continuing resource for large-scale and imaginative engagement with the past.

A THIRD WAVE?

By the late 1980s it was generally felt that historical sociology had come of age – or, at least, that it had achieved a reasonable degree of respectability in the profession. This had perhaps always been truer of Europe, where journals such as the *British Journal of Sociology*, the *Sociological Review* and the *Archives Européennes de Sociologie* had for long carried historical articles, and sociologists such as Philip Abrams, Anthony Giddens, Bryan Turner, and W. G. Runciman had produced an impressive body of work marked by a strong concern with history. But it had taken longer in America, despite the prominence of scholars such as Barrington Moore, Theda Skocpol, Charles Tilly, and Immanuel Wallerstein. A suspicion of history had been a marked feature of American sociology for most of its development, and it took time to overcome this. Given the global prominence of American sociology, it was therefore symbolically important that historical sociology now received recognition in the discipline there. By the mid-1980s there was a sufficient body of high-quality work for Randall Collins to announce that this was "the golden age of historical sociology" (Collins 1985: 107).

A good marker of this was the appearance of an important exercise in scholarly stocktaking, a volume edited by Theda Skocpol with the title *Vision and Method in Historical Sociology* (1984). Here a largely younger generation critically assessed the work of their teachers in historical sociology – Bendix, Moore, Tilly, and others. Equally telling was the publication of a number of other works of stocktaking by some of the senior practitioners in the field, such as Charles Tilly's *As Sociology Meets History* (1981) and *Big Structures, Large Processes, Huge Comparisons* (1984), and Philip Abrams's *Historical Sociology* (1982). By 1991 Dennis Smith could publish a full-length survey under the title *The Rise of Historical Sociology*. All this meant that there was now a sufficient body of scholarly work that could be the material for critical reflection. These reviews and assessments have continued throughout the subsequent decades, testifying to the current health and vitality of the field (see Adams, Clemens, and Orloff 2005a; Delanty and Isin 2003; Mahoney and Rueschmeyer 2003; McDonald 1996).

There were other signs as well. Historical sociologists were now well represented at the annual meetings of the American Sociological Association, and the ASA's section on "Comparative and Historical Sociology" had a healthy membership and a lively newsletter. Historical articles no longer featured only in "outlier" journals such as *Comparative Studies in Society and History*, the *Journal of Historical Sociology*, *Social Science History*, and – an early leader in the field among sociological journals – *Theory and Society*, but in the central journals of the profession, the *American Sociological Review*, the *American Journal of Sociology*, and *Sociological Theory*. It was also particularly important that historical sociology was well represented at the elite American research universities – not just the "Ivies," Harvard, Princeton, Columbia, and – latterly – Yale, but at some of the major public universities, such as the University of California at Berkeley and Los Angeles and the University of Michigan. These gave undoubted luster to the subject – but also, because of their greater resources, the sense that historical sociology was "something of a luxury good – the sociological equivalent of a Paneria watch or a Prada bag" (Adams, Clemens, and Orloff 2005b: 30). Graduates doing work in historical sociology were assured that there would be jobs, but that the number of institutions open to them would be relatively small, though highly prestigious.

Nevertheless there was no doubting the burgeoning of research in historical sociology in the 1980s and 1990s, with the younger generation particularly well represented. This has led some scholars to talk of a "third wave" of historical sociology, with the break-up of the Marxist paradigm that set the agenda of questions for the "second wave" sociologists of the 1970s and early 1980s (Adams, Clemens, and Orloff 2005b: 32–63.). This is a moot point. What we see rather is a mixture of old and new, with some strong continuities but also some new emphases and new directions.

Thus there has been continued historical work on states and state-formation. This very much builds on the 1970s, with the appearance then of such important works as Perry Anderson's *Lineages of the Absolutist State* (1974), Charles Tilly's edited volume, *The Formation of National States in Western Europe* (1975), and Gianfranco Poggi's *The Development of the Modern State* (1978). There was also the rediscovery of the historical essays of Otto Hintze (1975), with its Weberian emphasis on the primacy of politics and of conflicts between states. Since then there have been Michael Mann's imposing multi-volume study, *The Sources of Social Power* (1986–93), John A. Hall's *Power and Liberties* (1986), Charles Tilly's *Coercion, Capital and European States, AD 990–1992* (1992), Thomas Ertman's *Birth of the Leviathan* (1997), and George Steinmetz's edited volume, *State/Culture* (1999). Paul Corrigan and Derek Sayer, in *The Great Arch: English State Formation as Cultural Revolution* (1985) took up a challenge from E. P. Thompson (and Antonio Gramsci) in attempting a comprehensive sociological history of the English/British state. The have been some important recent studies in particular of the fascist state, such as Mabel Berezin's *Making the Fascist Self* (1997) and Michael Mann's *Fascists* (2004). The influences in all these are mixed, but there is no mistaking the imprint of Weber and Hintze alongside newer approaches from cultural sociology, law, and international relations. It is here perhaps that the departure from Marx is at its clearest, given Marxism's notoriously negligent treatment of the modern state and the nature of political power (though the Gramscian modification of this tradition has been highly influential).

Revolution too represents a continuity, at least in the sense of its systematic and comparative study. In 1991 Jack Goldstone produced his long-awaited *Revolution and Rebellion in the Early Modern World*, something of an anomaly in the spirit of the times in its insistence on the strongly material – in this case demographic – basis of revolutions. But in the meantime two things had happened to reshape thinking about revolutions. There was the Iranian revolution of 1979, which with its strongly religious character threw many theories into the melting pot; and there were the anti-communist revolutions of 1989 in central and eastern Europe, which also upset many views that revolution no longer applied to Europe and was largely a phenomenon of the "Third World." Taken with the general revival of fundamentalist religion across the world and the decline of secular Marxist movements, theorists were forced to re-examine the revolutionary tradition and to propose new ways of thinking about the past and future of revolution. The result has been an explosion of studies in the area, in which older thinkers such as Fanon have joined newer thinkers such as Foucault in supplying some of the analytical tools, though both Marx and Tocqueville remain highly resilient (see e.g. Foran 2005; Goodwin 2001; Kumar 2001; Skocpol 1994).

A newer entrant into the field of historical sociology has been nations and nationalism – another area neglected by the Marxists, and indeed most of the early sociologists, with the partial exception of Weber. Here too there have been precursors in the more immediate past: Ernest Gellner briefly elaborated a theory of nationalism in his *Thought and Change* (1964), and his student Anthony Smith had already in the 1970s begun his extensive array of publications on the subject. There was also the pioneering study of Michael Hechter, *Internal Colonialism* (1974), with its examination of the different nations of the United Kingdom. But it was not until Gellner put his thoughts on nationalism into a full-scale book, *Nations and Nationalism* (1983), that the subject really took off among sociologists. A key work was

Anthony Smith's *The Ethnic Origins of Nations* (1986), which linked modern nations to their distant ethnic pasts. More "modernist" in conception, seeing with Gellner nations as essentially new inventions, was Benedict Anderson's stimulating *Imagined Communities* (1983) and the historian Eric Hobsbawm's *Nations and Nationalism since 1780* (1990). Nationalism was indeed an area where many disciplines were fruitfully engaged, with historians, anthropologists, sociologists, and political scientists in constant interaction.

But all agreed on the crucial importance of history for elucidating the main problems in the field. Political scientist John Armstrong, in his *Nations before Nationalism* (1982), tended to side with the "primordialists," such as Anthony Smith; historian John Breuilly, in *Nationalism and the State* (1982), with the modernists. Also modernist in orientation was sociologist Rogers Brubaker's *Citizenship and Nationhood in France and Germany* (1992), which identified two ideal types of nationhood, "civic" and "ethnic," through a careful historical comparison of the main representatives of the two types. Another powerful contribution of a sociologist was Liah Greenfeld's *Nationalism: Five Roads to Modernity* (1992), which argued for the early invention of nationalism in sixteenth-century England. This was challenged by Krishan Kumar, *The Making of English National Identity* (2003), but a lively debate on the antiquity or otherwise of nations and nationalism has remained one of the most notable features of contemporary work in the field (see e.g. Ichijo and Uzelac 2005). Currently one might say, given the extent of the interest among younger sociologists, that this area bids fair to remain one of the strongest concerns of historical sociology. What is particularly striking is the rise in interest among American sociologists, in what had been until the 1990s a field largely tilled by British and other European sociologists (even though several worked in America). A notable example is Miguel Centeno's examination of a neglected field, the sense of nationhood – or the absence of it – in Latin America, in his *Blood and Debt: War and the Nation State in Latin America* (2002); also good, for the same region, is Jonathan Eastwood's *The Rise of Nationalism in Venezuela* (2006).

State, revolution, nation: these are topics that belong fairly squarely to the main tradition of historical-sociological analysis so that, whatever the shifts of emphasis between the 1960s and 1990s, they represent fundamental continuities. The same can be said of historical studies of working-class movements, a staple of the 1960s and 1970s but now – as part of the movement away from Marxism – somewhat rarer. But there have been some penetrating studies of the nineteenth-century French working class in Mark Traugott's *Armies of the Poor* (1985), Ronald Aminzade's *Ballots and Barricades* (1993), and Roger Gould's *Insurgent Identities* (1995). These studies show the still continuing influence of some of Charles Tilly's earlier work, especially (with Louise and Richard Tilly) *The Rebellious Century, 1830–1930* (1975), as well as that of William Sewell. Noticeably lacking, as in the past, is any similar attention to the historical development of the middle and upper classes – though Julia Adams's *The Familial State: Ruling Families and Merchant Capitalism in Early Modern Europe* (2005) is a good step in that direction. But we badly need studies to complement such work by historians as Arno Mayer's *The Persistence of the Old Regime* (1981), which indicates the social and political importance of the upper classes of European societies well into the twentieth century, despite general processes of "bourgeoisification." Historical sociology, moreover, has too often followed the old pattern of considering classes as worlds unto themselves, insulated from each other, without seeing that their dynamic interaction is the key to their development. Since Marx's writings such as the *Eighteenth Brumaire of Louis Bonaparte* give us as good a model as need be of how to do this, it is ironic that it is largely left-wing history and sociology that has developed the model of the compartmentalized class – Thompson's *The Making of the English Working Class* being in this respect an unfortunate influence.

NEW DEPARTURES, WIDER HORIZONS

What of the newer developments in historical sociology? A major event was the first complete English translation of Norbert Elias's *The Civilizing Process* (1978–82), a work actually first published in German in 1939 but which had virtually disappeared in the intervening period. Elias traced the process by which, starting from the "court society" of the higher nobility and the absolutist monarchs, European societies gradually rid themselves of internal violence and the coarser forms of social interaction, leading to a general pacification of society and a gentling of manners. Part of the appeal of Elias's approach was his extensive use of manuals of manners and etiquette, introducing a welcome element of everyday life into his analysis and indicating a set of cultural tools that might be profitably employed by other historical sociologists. Gradually filtering into the consciousness of sociologists – a process energetically aided by disciples such as Eric Dunning, Stephen Mennell, and Johan Goudsblom – Elias's work received widespread acclaim, although his influence has been diffuse and hard to pin down with any precision. A number of studies of the history of food and eating habits – e.g. Stephen Mennell's *All Manners of Food* (1985) – acknowledge his inspiration, as do some studies of sport, but it is hard to think of any major work of historical sociology that could be firmly called "Eliasan." Certainly he has so far had greater impact on European – and more on Continental than British – sociology than American, and that might be part of the story, given the global dominance of English-language sociology (it was the translation of Elias's work into English that boosted his reputation even on the Continent). But one can expect an increasing amount of work in historical sociology to reflect Elias's original and wide-ranging approach.

This is all the more likely given the popularity among sociologists of the work of Michel Foucault, whose interests and approaches in many respects parallels Elias's. The more immediate impact of Foucault's work, most of which appeared in the 1960s and 1970s, was in social theory. But his studies of prisons and penitentiaries (*Discipline and Punish*, 1975), of insanity and its institutional treatment (*Madness and Civilization*, 1961), and of sexuality and its discontents (*History of Sexuality*, 1976), are also deeply historical and have found echoes in several major studies, as in Andrew Scull's *Museums of Madness* (1979) and *The Most Solitary of Afflictions: Madness and Society in Britain 1700–1900* (1993). A particular focus has been the Foucauldian concept of "governmentality" and his concern with moral regulation, as in Alan Hunt's *Governing Morals* (1999) and David Wagner's *The New Temperance* (1997). Not surprisingly this has also been a theme central to the work of some feminist sociologist, such as Nicola Beisel's *Imperiled Innocents*

(1997), a study of the notorious anti-obscenity campaign of Anthony Comstock in nineteenth-century America.

It is noticeable, nevertheless, that the contribution of feminist sociologists – or of other sociologists working on women – has in general not matched that of others scholars in the field of historical sociology. This is particularly surprising in view of the enormous amount of excellent work done by feminist *historians* in recent decades – outstanding among whom have been Louise Tilly, Joan Scott, Catherine Hall, Leonore Davidoff, Lynn Hunt, Lyndal Roper, and many others. Davidoff and Hall's *Family Fortunes: Men and Women of the English Middle Class 1780–1850* (1987) could indeed stand as an exemplary model for historical sociologists of gender and the family. Once more the striking thing is the lack of attention on the part of sociologists to relevant historical work. The field is certainly not entirely barren – Pavla Miller's *Transformations of Patriarchy in the West, 1500–1900* (1998) is a notable study, as is Karen Hansen's *A Very Social Time: Crafting Community in Antebellum New England* (1994), an account of the significant role of women in the public life of mid-nineteenth-century New England; and sociologists of sexuality such as Jeffrey Weeks (e.g. *Making Sexual History*, 2000) have made important contributions. Moreover sociologists such as Sylvia Walby and Mary McIntosh have frequently incorporated history into their analyses of family and gender relations. But compared to anthropologists, historians, political theorists, philosophers, and literary theorists, sociologists have been conspicuously marginal in the historical debates concerning the family, marriage, sex, and gender. Perhaps it is the very abundance and quality of the work of feminist historians – and historically minded feminist political theorists and philosophers, such as Carole Pateman and Jean Elshtain – that discourage sociologists from attempting to emulate them. But this is too important a field for sociologists to abandon to historians and political theorists.

More promising among the newer developments is the field of "collective memory." This too takes off from some earlier work – the work in particular of Durkheim's disciple, Maurice Halbwachs, stretching from his early *The Social Frameworks of Memory* (1925) to his posthumously published *The Collective Memory* (1950). Halbwachs insisted that even the most individual of memories were the product of collective or social experiences; time itself was socially conceived, dependent on the way different groups organize it for their own purposes. Memory could also be spatially ordered: one of Halbwachs's most original works – *La Topographie légendaire des évangiles en terre sainte* (1941) – was a study of the shifting locations of the revered pilgrimage sites in the Holy Land, and of their varying place in the collective memory of various Christian groups over time.

Sociology has been slow to follow in Halbwachs's footsteps. Anthropologists, in the work of Evans-Pritchard and his followers, were quick to enter the field. So too were social psychologists, as shown in David Middleton and Derek Edwards's edited collection, *Collective Remembering* (1990). Literary historians made a strong showing, with such outstanding and influential works as Paul Fussell's *The Great War and Modern Memory* (1975). Even geographers weighed in, as in David Lowenthal's stimulating *The Past Is a Foreign Country* (1985). Most active, perhaps not surprisingly, have been the historians, in such innovative studies as Eric Hobsbawm and Terence Ranger's edited collection, *The Invention of Tradition*

(1983), Raphael Samuel's *Theatres of Memory* (1994), on British popular memory, John Gillis's excellent collection, *Commemorations* (1994), on national identity, and Pierre Nora's multi-volume *The Realms of Memory* (1984–92), a panoramic survey of the collective memories of the French. And of course there has been a wave of Holocaust studies, attempting to assess its impact on the collective memory of Jews and others (see e.g. Novick 2000). All these works by scholars from varying disciplines have had an influence far outweighing anything yet done by sociologists.

An early sociological work in the field, Edward Shils's *Tradition* (1981), fell on stony ground, perhaps because there was so little to fertilize it in the discipline at the time. But sociology is belatedly catching up. The doyen in this field is Barry Schwartz, with numerous studies including *George Washington: The Making of An American Symbol* (1987) and *Abraham Lincoln and the Forge of National Memory* (2000). A thoughtful and wide-ranging general account, *How Societies Remember* (1989), was provided by Paul Connerton. Lynn Spillman considered commemorative practices in Australia and the United States in her *Nation and Commemoration* (1997). Jeffrey Olick gathered a number of scholars together to provide a useful conspectus of the field in *States of Memory* (2003), and went on to make his own effective contribution in *In the House of the Hangman* (2005), a study of German collective memory in the immediate post-World War II period. Eviatar Zerubavel has made a number of valuable studies of the social uses of history, as in *Time Maps: Collective Memory and the Social Shape of the Past* (2003); and another consistent contributor in the field of historical sociology, Robin Wagner-Pacifici, has recently offered *The Art of Surrender* (2005), an illuminating comparative account of how the rituals surrounding military surrender in three different historical periods reveal both current postures and future fault lines between the contending parties. Finally sociology has also taken on the Holocaust, most powerfully in Zygmunt Bauman's *Modernity and the Holocaust* (1989), but also as the outstanding example of historical "trauma," as in Bernard Giesen's *Triumph and Trauma* (2002). Currently one might say that collective memory is becoming one of the most promising areas of historical sociology – perhaps because it is one of the few that seems to have been genuinely open to the contributions by scholars in other disciplines.

Lastly, in this account of newer developments, one might consider the return to religion. This indeed is going back to the roots, since religion was the subject of the best-known work of historical sociology of the classical period, Weber's *The Protestant Ethic and the Spirit of Capitalism* (1920) – not to mention Weber's other historical studies of the world religions of Islam, Hinduism, and Judaism. Bryan Turner, in such works as *Weber and Islam* (1974), was an early interrogator of some of Weber's key findings, and has continued to produce wide-ranging works of comparative-historical analysis, such as *Orientalism, Postmodernism and Globalism* (1994). David Martin too questioned some of the traditional assumptions about religion in the modern world, in such historically informed works as A *General Theory of Secularization* (1978). Others were slower to realize the continued importance of religion, and to move beyond debates about "secularization" to re-examine some of the traditional ideas about religion's historic role and destiny. But things began to shift in the 1980s and 1990s, stimulated no doubt by the renewed challenge of Islam and by "fundamentalist" revivals in many other parts of the world, among Jews, Christians, Hindus, and Buddhists.

The result has been some exciting new work among sociologists. Rodney Stark essayed an interpretation of *The Rise of Christianity* (1996), making skillful use of data on contemporary religious movements, such as the Moonies and the Mormons. Robert Wuthnow produced an ambitious historical account, *Communities of Discourse* (1989), which compared religious and secular ideologies from the Reformation to the nineteenth century. Philip Gorski, one of the most assiduous promoters of the return to religion, argued in *The Disciplinary Revolution* (2003) for the importance of religion – specifically Calvinism – in state-formation in a number of leading northern European countries in the early modern period. Geneviève Zubrzycki, in *The Crosses of Auschwitz* (2006), presented a fascinating analysis of the centuries-old relation between religion and nationalism in Poland, using as her starting point a contemporary dispute between Poles and Jews about the meaning of Auschwitz. Also with a focus on nationalism was Khaldoun Samman's *Cities of God and Nationalism* (2007), a bold foray into the two-millennia history of the "world cities" of Mecca, Jerusalem and Rome, and the threat posed to their traditional cosmopolitanism by the nationalism of the modern period. All these works – the latter by younger scholars – indicate what is a veritable renaissance in the historical sociology of religion, and suggest that this will be a central area of future work in the field.

PROMISE AND PERFORMANCE

There is no doubting the renewed energy and enterprise of historical sociology. After a hiatus of more than half a century, the field has re-emerged to engage some of the best minds in the discipline. Particularly important is the involvement of a large number of younger scholars. The case for understanding societies in time, the conviction that a sociology without history is thin and superficial, have entered the consciousness and practice of a sufficient number of sociologists for us to feel that a critical threshold has been passed. Historical sociology is here to stay.

But inevitably there are caveats. There are challenges that still need to be met, gaps that ought to be filled, criticisms that must be addressed. The mission of historical sociology is far from accomplished.

The easiest to deal with are the gaps. There are a number of areas of contemporary concern that historical sociologists have been very slow to engage with, once more leaving the field to others. Globalization is one such (see CHAPTER 16). This cries out for historical analysis, and it has begun to get some from historians, as in A. G. Hopkins's edited collection, *Globalization in World History* (2002), Bruce Mazlish and Ralph Buultjens's edited volume, *Conceptualizing Global History* (2004), and Jürgen Osterhamel and Niels Petersson's *Globalization* (2005). There is also Christopher Bayly's masterful *The Birth of the Modern World 1780–1914: Global Connections and Comparisons* (2004). Given the increasing interest in globalization among sociologists, this seems an obvious field in which scholars could and should undertake historical work. How "new" is globalization? How are we to understand the current phase of globalization by comparison with other phases in the past? Are we indeed in a radically new situation, demanding new ways of thinking about the contemporary world? These questions seem to need urgent attention, but they are not on the whole currently getting this from sociologists. Paul Hirst and Grahame Thompson's pioneering *Globalization in Question* (1996) stands out as something of a lone contribution, and even there the historical analysis is rather perfunctory. The same is true of what is generally considered the leading text in the field, *Global Transformations* (1999), by David Held and others, as well as more recent accounts such as Robert Holton's *Making Globalization* (2005). The influential work on globalization by Anthony Giddens and Ulrich Beck makes historical assumptions but is remarkably lacking in historical analysis and investigation.

Sociologists of globalization acknowledge the need for history but do not seem to wish to undertake the task. This is all the more puzzling since, in the world-systems approach of Wallerstein and others, sociologists can claim to have marked out a position on globalization well before others – with a few exceptions such as the "world historian" William McNeil – entered the field. Since the world-systems approach turned on macro-historical analysis, one might have assumed that in the newer guise of globalization theory the same would have been true. It has not been so and, without history, globalization theory runs the risk of becoming schematic and mechanical.

A linked area is the whole question of "the rise of the West," and the need to address the Eurocentric quality of much thinking in history and sociology. This is the question classically posed by Weber in *The Protestant Ethic* and more generally in his studies of non-Western religions. Did the West really invent modernity, or even capitalism? A whole generation of historians from both East and West has recently been examining the received accounts in classical sociology and Western thought more generally. Works by R. Bin Wong (1997), Sanjay Subrahmanyam (1990), and Kenneth Pomeranz (2000) have been transforming our understanding of the relations between the West and the rest of the world, and in particular our assumptions of Western superiority in economic and technological developments in the crucial early modern period. Historical anthropology too has made an invaluable contribution (see e.g. Abu-Lughod 1989; Goody 1996, 2004). Here again is an area one would have thought crucial to sociology, in view of the working assumptions of so many of the classical sociologists and the inheritance that they have passed on to us. But it is so far a thinly worked field of historical sociology. There are some good edited collections, such as Shmuel Eisenstadt's *Multiple Modernities* (2002), and his own impressive *Japanese Civilization: A Comparative View* (1996). Jack Goldstone too has valiantly entered the fray, in some wide-ranging articles (e.g. 2002) that are a prelude to a full-scale work. But sociologists generally have seemed unwilling to take on the challenge – perhaps understandably daunted by the range and quantity of historical work that they would have to absorb, much of it dealing with non-Western societies.

A third area is empire and imperialism. This has experienced a major resurgence recently, fueled partly by debates about the "American empire," but also by the sense that empires may have much to teach us about an increasingly multicultural and perhaps post-national world. Sociologists such as Karen Barkey and von Hagen (1997), Michael Mann (2003), and George Steinmetz (2005) have made some valuable contributions in this area. But little in sociology yet matches the contribution of political scientists and political theorists such as Michael Doyle (1986), Sankhar Muthu (2003), and Jennifer Pitts (2005), still less the work of historians such as

Anthony Pagden (1995), David Armitage (2000), or John Eliott (2006). It is true that empire figured only marginally in the writings of the early sociologists (though Marx gives a considerable lead). But given its persistence and even revival in the modern world it is surprising that it is only now that some sociologists are turning to it. This is particularly regrettable given the enormous amount of excellent historical work done on empires, and the instructive range of cases that are available for consideration (as Eisenstadt showed in his early but somewhat cumbersome sociological work, *The Political Systems of Empires* (1963) – a work that had virtually no successors).

This brings us to the problem that has been mentioned a number of times in this survey. Historical sociologists have shown a marked degree of reluctance to engage with the work of historians or even to make much use of it in their own studies. This has not always been the case – both Barrington Moore and Theda Skocpol, for instance, drew profusely on historical studies in their work on revolutions and social change, as did the earlier generation of Smelser, Bendix, and Bellah. But the very success of historical sociology since that time has meant that current historical sociologists have felt that they should, or at least can, engage mainly with the work of other historical sociologists rather than that of historians (see Abbott 1994). So works on revolution, for instance, by historical sociologists will contain ample references to Skocpol, Goodwin, Goldstone, and Foran, but hardly any to notable work by, say, John Dunn or Fred Halliday or Perez Zagorin. In studies of class and class conflict, one looks in vain for more than passing references to the work of Patrick Joyce or Ross McKibbin; work on capitalism and modernity will use Wallerstein and Anderson but not Carlo Cipolla or Jonathan Clark. In many areas of growing interest to sociologists – war, the military, fascism, empire – historians such as Eric Hobsbawm, Victor Kiernan, Michael Howard, John Eliott, Geoffrey Parker, Mark Mazower, Geoffrey Hosking, and Dominic Lieven remain severely underused.

Partly, as these names imply, the problem is one of the general ignorance by American scholars of work done across the Atlantic (the opposite problem is not so acute). But a more serious issue might be the rigid insistence that work in historical sociology must be "theoretical" and "comparative" – and historians are often neither, at least not to the satisfaction of many sociologists. The fact that many individual studies contain important theoretical insights, with clear implications for comparative analysis, is often ignored. And yet what could have been more suggestive for the theoretical and comparative study of revolution than Tocqueville's account of the coming of the French Revolution, *The Ancien Régime and the Revolution* (1856)? What more illuminating about nations and nationalism than Eugen Weber's *The Modernization of Rural France, 1870–1914* (1976)? Again and again studies by historians of individual cases have lit up whole areas of general concern to the sociologist. Historical sociology ignores the work of historians at its peril, and is certainly the poorer for the neglect. The excessive striving towards "theory," here as elsewhere in sociology, can have pernicious effects.

Much of this reflects what remains the most serious weakness of historical sociology: its insulation and "ghettoization." Historical sociology has been given its head by the profession, but at the price of becoming yet another specialization, another area or "sub-field" of the discipline, with its own section, its own networks, its own professional activities, its own favored journals. At least in the United States, and to a lesser extent elsewhere, historical sociology has failed so far to transform the discipline, to make it feel that history should inform every important sociological study, not merely those with an obvious historical subject such as the Reformation or the French Revolution. Charles Tilly, a long-standing and leading practitioner in the field, some time ago protested at the "institutionalization" of historical sociology – the "fixing of a labeled specialty in sections of learned societies, journals, courses, a share of the job market." This would, he feared, have a stultifying effect, because "institutionalization may well impede the spread of historical thinking to other parts of sociology. The other parts need that thinking badly" (quoted in Smith 1991: 3). Tilly's fears have to a good extent been realized. Sociologists in general have been quite prepared to let historical sociology flourish in its own enclosure, so long as its practitioners did not disturb others or attempt to convert them to the ways of historical sociology.

To some extent historical sociologists have only themselves to blame. Historical sociologists have too often assumed that their task is to apply social theory to the past rather than to show the relevance of history to the present. They have wished to do history better than historians, to demonstrate that as against the "unreflecting," "untheoretical" historians, they can bring social theory to bear on the great questions of state formation, revolution, and religious change. That way they will explain the things that historians ignore or sweep under the carpet – large questions of causality, for instance. That has been the message of some of the best-regarded exercises in historical sociology, from Skocpol's studies of revolution to Ertman's account of the divergent development of modern states and Gorski's emphasis on religion in the creation of new states. The most admired works of historical sociology have barely anything to say about the present – so that, for instance, when the Iranian revolution of 1979 occurred sociologists of revolution had to scramble to find ways of dealing with what seemed an unexpected novelty. Similarly Richard Lachmann's *Capitalists in Spite of Themselves* is an elegant exercise in historical explanation. But having shown why England, France, and Italy found different solutions to the transition to capitalism in early modern Europe, we are left wondering as to the long-term consequences of these differences, and what additional factors will have to be found to account for subsequent developments, especially where these diverge substantially from the situation of the sixteenth and seventeenth centuries (Ertman's *Birth of the Leviathan* leaves us with a similar question).

There is of course nothing to be said against history per se, whether written by historians or sociologists. Sociologists have shown that they can do as good or even better history than historians, including the use of archival material. But their colleagues in sociology have understandably felt that perhaps this is of little concern to them, where there seem no implications for the study of present-day society. If there is a division of labor between historians and sociologists, one form of this is that historians concentrate on the past and sociologists on the present. This does not mean that history is irrelevant to the present – far from it, that is, or should be, the whole point of a sociology informed by history. What it does mean is that historical sociologists have a greater obligation than historians to show the relevance of their studies to the present, otherwise they risk being sidelined and shunted off into the ghetto reserved especially for them.

It is worth noting that this is a point that has been forcefully made in the case of historians themselves. "The function of the historian," said E. H. Carr (1964: 26), "is neither to love the past nor to emancipate himself from the past, but to master and understand it as the key to the present." Others have expressed a similar thought differently. All history is "contemporary history," said Benedetto Croce, "because, however remote in time events thus recounted may seem to be, the history in reality refers to present needs and present situations wherein those events vibrate" (quoted in Carr 1964: 21). Then, though with a different emphasis, there is C. Wright Mills's pithy remark, echoing a sentiment of George Santayana's, that "we study history in order to get rid of it" (Mills 1959: 154). All these comments stress the relevance of history to the present, whether as a means of understanding it or of freeing ourselves from it. Not only can we not study the past except through the prism of present concerns (whether or not we acknowledge that); we cannot get a true sense of our situation in the present except by the light that the past casts on it.

This is something that, ironically, sociologists seem to need to grasp even more than historians. One might have thought that sociologists, whose main concern has always been contemporary society, would when they turn to history have been most aware of it (after all, it was to understand the different attitudes towards business of Protestants and Catholics in his own time that led Weber to investigate the origins of "the Protestant ethic"). Instead they seem to want to show that they can be as good as or better than the historians. There is a kind of antiquarianism here that is quite remarkable. The best history, whether it is Edward Gibbon on the rise and fall of the Roman empire or Jacob Burckhardt on the civilization of the Renaissance, has a pointed message for its contemporary readers. Others have been equally convinced of the value of using the past to cast light on the present. Historical novelists, such as Walter Scott, have always seen this as their purpose, as have the great history painters, such as David. Following the great examples of Handel and Verdi, the Russian composer Modest Mussorgsky chose historical subjects for his operas, most famously *Boris Godunov*, when he wished to comment on the contemporary condition of Russia. When, towards the end of his life, he attempted another such exercise, he chose, in *Khovanshchina*, to portray the violent political conflicts that attended the birth of the state created by Peter the Great – conflicts between the old ("Moscow") and the new ("St. Petersburg") that he thought had marked Russian history ever since. "The past in the present," he wrote to his friend Vladimir Stasov in explaining his design, "that's my task!" It is a view of their enterprise that many historical sociologists still need to learn.

Bibliography

Abbott, A. (1994) "History and Sociology: The Lost Synthesis," in E. H. Monkkonen (ed.), *Engaging the Past: The Use of History Across the Social Sciences*. Durham, NC: Duke University Press.

Abrams, P. (1982) *Historical Sociology*. Shepton Mallet, Somerset: Open Books.

Abu-Lughod, J. L. (1989) *Before European Hegemony: The World System A.D. 1250–1350*. New York: Oxford University Press.

Adams, J., Clemens, E. S., and Orloff, A. S. (eds.) (2005a) *Remaking Modernity: Politics, History, and Sociology*. Durham, NC: Duke University Press.

Adams, J., Clemens, E. S., and Orloff, A. S. (2005b.) "Introduction: Social Theory, Modernity, and the Three Waves of Historical Sociology," in *Remaking Modernity: Politics History, and Sociology*. Durham, NC: Duke University Press.

Armitage, D. (2000) *The Ideological Origins of the British Empire*. Cambridge: Cambridge University Press.

Arrighi, G. (1994) *The Long Twentieth Century: Money, Power and the Origins of Our Times*. London: Verso.

Aston, T. H., and Philpin, C. H. E. (eds.) (1985) *The Brenner Debate: Agrarian Class Structure and Economic Development in Pre-Industrial Europe*. Cambridge: Cambridge University Press.

Barkey, K., and von Hagen, M. (eds.) (1997) *After Empire: Multiethnic Societies and Nation-Building*. Boulder, CO: Westview Press.

Carr, E. H. (1964) *What Is History?* Harmondsworth: Penguin.

Chase-Dunn, C. (1989) *Global Formation: Structures of the World Economy*. Oxford: Blackwell.

Collins, R. (1985) *Three Sociological Traditions*. Oxford: Oxford University Press.

Delanty, G., and Isin, E. F. (eds.) (2003) *The Handbook of Historical Sociology*. London: Sage.

Durkheim, É. (1977 [1938]) *The Evolution of Educational Thought: Lectures on the Formation and Development of Secondary Education in France*, trans. P. Collins. London: Routledge & Kegan Paul.

Eliott, J. H. (2006) *Empires of the Atlantic World: Britain and Spain in America 1492–1830*. New Haven: Yale University Press.

Foran, J. (2005) *Taking Power: On the Origins of Third World Revolutions*. Cambridge: Cambridge University Press.

Goldstone, J. A. (2002) "Efflorescences and Economic Growth in World History: Rethinking the 'Rise of the West' and the Industrial Revolution." *Journal of World History* 13(2): 323–89.

Goodwin, J. (2001) *No Other Way Out: States and Revolutionary Movements, 1945–1991*. Cambridge: Cambridge University Press.

Goody, J. (1996) *The East in the West*. Cambridge: Cambridge University Press.

Goody, J. (2004) *Capitalism and Modernity*. Cambridge: Polity.

Hintze, O. (1975) *The Historical Essays of Otto Hintze*, ed. F. Gilbert. New York: Oxford University Press.

Ichijo, A., and Uzelac, G. (eds.), (2005) *When Is the Nation? Towards an Understanding of Theories of Nationalism*. London: Routledge.

Keyder, C. (1987) *State and Class in Turkey: A Study in Capitalist Development*. London: Verso.

Kumar, K. (1988) *The Rise of Modern Society: Aspects of the Social and Political Development of the West*. Oxford: Blackwell.

Kumar, K. (2001) *1989: Revolutionary Ideas and Ideals*. Minneapolis: University of Minnesota Press.

Mahoney, J., and Rueschmeyer, D. (eds.) (2003) *Comparative Historical Analysis in the Social Sciences*. New York: Cambridge University Press.

Mann, M. (2003) *Incoherent Empire*. London: Verso.

McDonald, T. J. (ed.) (1996) *The Historic Turn in the Human Sciences*. Ann Arbor: University of Michigan Press.

Mills, C. W. (1959) *The Sociological Imagination*. New York: Oxford University Press.

Muthu, S. (2003) *Enlightenment Against Empire*. Princeton: Princeton University Press.

Nisbet, R. (1970) *Social Change and History: Aspects of the Western Theory of Development*. New York: Oxford University Press.

Novick, P. (2000) *The Holocaust and Collective Memory: The American Experience*. London: Bloomsbury.

Pagden, A. (1995) *Lords of All the World: Ideologies of Empire in Spain, Britain and France c.1500–c.1800*. New Haven: Yale University Press.

Pitts, J. (2005) *A Turn to Empire: The Rise of Imperial Liberalism in Britain and France*. Princeton: Princeton University Press.

Pomeranz, K. (2000) *The Great Divergence: China, Europe, and the Making of the Modern World Economy*. Princeton: Princeton University Press.

Skocpol, T. (1994) *Social Revolutions in the Modern World*. Cambridge: Cambridge University Press.

Smith, D. (1991) *The Rise of Historical Sociology*. Cambridge: Polity.

Steinmetz, G. (2005) "Return to Empire: The New U.S. Imperialism in Comparative Historical Perspective." *Sociological Theory* 23(4): 339–67.

Subrahmanyam, S. (1990) *The Political Economy of Commerce: Southern India 1500–1650*. Cambridge: Cambridge University Press.

Thomas, K. (2006) "New Ways Revisited." *Times Literary Supplement*, October 13: 3–4.

Turner, B. S. (1974) *Weber and Islam: A Critical Study*. London: Routledge & Kegan Paul.

Wong, R. B. (1997) *China Transformed: Historical Change and the Limits of European Experience*. Ithaca, NY: Cornell University Press.

21

The Sociology of Religion

MICHELE DILLON

Before Max Weber and Émile Durkheim made religion a central analytical focus for sociology, anthropologists had made the crucial intellectual move wrestling the study of religion away from theology and abstract scholastic debates about faith and divinity. The classical comparative studies of religion in "primitive" or pre-industrial societies produced by the British anthropologists James Frazer (e.g. 1935 [1890]), William Robertson Smith (e.g. 1997 [1894]), Edward Tylor (e.g. 1950 [1891]), and Andrew Lang (e.g. 1899) established the fact that religion was a cultural phenomenon and as such, open to cultural and sociohistorical analysis. And an additional boost came from psychology, specifically from the American pragmatist William James (1898) and his thesis that religion could be studied objectively and scientifically, i.e. by its visible practical consequences.

But while these various studies contributed to setting the groundwork for the sociology of religion, the historical context of their publication was also significant and continues to shadow the sociology of religion. These books were published in the late nineteenth century, an era when, not unlike the present moment in history, intellectuals, poets, and politicians struggled with questions over the very structures of the modern social order and the character of human society. Expanding rationality, technological and scientific triumphs, Darwinism, Freud's discovery of the unconscious, industrial strife, and fledgling nationalist movements all converged to suggest that religion belonged to the primitives and would have little practical consequence in modern society other than perhaps for culturally defensive purposes.

This is the Janus-faced inheritance of the sociology of religion. On one side, confidence that religion can be studied scientifically as an exciting social, cultural, and historical phenomenon. On the other side, the lurking suspicion that what we study is really something else disguised as religion and even if we are sure it is religion, that it really is not as relevant as we claim, or only has relevance in explaining deviations from modernity as apparent allegedly in the world-views of fundamentalists, those who are different from us moderns. This inheritance in large part accounts for the long preoccupation in the field with the puzzle of secularization and the (somewhat

ironic) emergence in recent years of intellectual talk of the post-secular. In this chapter,
I review the central theoretical strands that have shaped and comprise the sociology
of religion, a narrative that inevitably begins with Weber and Durkheim.

MAX WEBER'S SOCIOLOGY OF RELIGION: DEFINITION AND METHODOLOGY

Max Weber's writings on religion demonstrated both the significance of different
historical and cultural contexts on the evolution, development, and societal implications of different religions as well as drawing attention to the intricate cultural
intertwining of religion and societal structures. Although Weber never offered a
formal definition of religion, it is clear from his writings that what he saw as sociologically significant was the substantive content of beliefs: how do particular beliefs
about salvation orient social actors to the world and motivate social action? Different world religions produce different world-orientations with different practical
consequences for the sorts of institutions and authority structures that emerge. If
the early Calvinists' concerns about salvation could indirectly work to produce the
expansion of capitalism through the rationalization of the idea of the calling, what
other non-religious processes and outcomes might be understood by recognizing the
tracks of underlying religious ideas and interests?

   It is these empirically demonstrable Weberian insights – though perhaps indirectly
influenced by William James's pragmatism (see CHAPTER 10) – on the practical
societal consequences of religious world-views that gave sociologists the charge to
consider religion in terms of particular social-historical contexts. Although Weber
himself modeled the comparative study of religion on a macro historical-cultural
plane, the practical challenges encountered in conducting large-scale comparative
studies, coupled with the sociological exceptionalism of particular national contexts,
has made the comparative study of religion (and of other social processes) less normative than we might expect given Weber's dominance in the discipline. Yet, as I
note in a later section, the changing global currents portend a shift in this tide.
Nonetheless, sociologists of religion have produced many comparative local-based
studies showing precisely that, as Weber underscored, different beliefs and different
contexts impact the religion-social action nexus. Further, Weber's definition of sociology as the interpretive study of subjectively meaningful social action (1978: 4–5)
has been influential in accounting for the pervasiveness of ethnographic studies of
religion as various researchers seek to understand how specifically located individuals and groups make sense of their world despite the apparent anomalies between
their beliefs and the social contexts of their everyday interaction.

ÉMILE DURKHEIM'S SOCIOLOGY OF RELIGION: DEFINITION AND METHODOLOGY

Unlike Weber, Durkheim was very deliberate in setting about elaborating a specifically scientific methodology for the sociological study of religion. He was committed
to offering precise definitions of religion, church, and the sacred/profane such that

sociologists would be able to both recognize and differentiate between religion and non-religion. While Durkheim acknowledged that the "science of comparative religions is greatly indebted" to Frazer (2001 [1912]: 25), and while he drew on the writings of Frazer, Lang, Tylor, and Robertson Smith, among others, Durkheim was also at pains to carve a social science of religion that went beyond the "old methods of the anthropological school" (2001 [1912]: 79). Their objective, he argued, was "to reach beyond national and historical differences to the universal and truly human bases of religious life" independent of their social setting (2001 [1912]). While sharing the anthropologists' scientific objectives of seeking understanding of "the religious nature of man," Durkheim was emphatic that since religion was not inherent in the individual, but "a product of social causes, there can be no question of determining it apart from a social setting" (2001 [1912]).

Durkheim's incessant emphasis that sociology should explain social facts, social phenomena, in terms of their social rather than their individual manifestations pervades his discussion of religion. This emphasis on the social setting and social consequences of religion, and persuaded by Tylor's argument that a narrow definition of religion as belief in a supreme being would exclude tribal beliefs in spiritual beings (2001 [1912]: 31), led Durkheim to offer an expansive definition of the sacred. Durkheim argued that all religions make a classificatory distinction between the sacred – all those things set apart and forbidden – and the profane (2001 [1912]: 36), and what is deemed sacred does not inhere in the thing itself but is so defined by the particular society: "What makes a thing holy is . . . the collective feeling attached to it" (2001 [1912]: 308). "Since neither man nor nature is inherently sacred, this quality of sacredness must come from another source" (2001 [1912]: 76), and that source is society. Hence, "it is the unity and the diversity of social life that creates both the unity and the diversity of sacred beings and things" (2001 [1912]: 309).

Durkheim also explicated a clear definition of what constitutes religion as a social practice, stating, "Religious phenomena fall quite naturally into two basic categories: beliefs and rites. The first are states of opinion and consist of representations [symbols]; the second are fixed modes of actions [specific practices]" (2001 [1912]: 36). What we believe, or what we worship, and how we worship comprises the domain of religion. And not surprisingly, following Durkheim's emphasis on the collective nature of social life, religious beliefs and rites or rituals are not unique to the individual but are, and must necessarily be, shared collectively:

> Religious beliefs proper are always held by a defined collectivity that professes them and practices the rites that go with them. These beliefs are not only embraced by all the members of this collectivity as individuals, they belong to the group and unite it. The individuals who make up this group is bound to one another by their common beliefs. A society whose members are united because they share a common conception of the sacred world and its relation to the profane world, and who translate this common conception into identical practices, is what we call a church. Now historically, we find no religion without a church. (2001 [1912]: 42–3)

Despite Durkheim's own historical-anthropological foray into the study of Australian totemism which formed the basis for his sociology of religion (and for his sociology of knowledge more generally; see Turner 2005: 287–8), he did not see the historical antecedents of a phenomenon as necessary to sociological analysis. This is, of course, a major difference between Durkheim and Weber. And though Durkheim emphasized the centrality of beliefs to religion, he was not interested in the content of belief per se but in how those beliefs tied the believers into the larger collectivity. Durkheim was thus interested in the functions of collectively shared beliefs and practices and specifically, as also elaborated in *Suicide*, how these related to social integration. This perspective on religion is well represented in the plethora of empirical studies today documenting the many varied ways that religion appears to have a socially integrating function.

WEBER, DURKHEIM, AND SECULARIZATION

The secularization thesis has its origins in both Weber's and Durkheim's analyses of religion. Weber's infamous words in the closing pages of *The Protestant Ethic and the Spirit of Capitalism* were simultaneously prophetic and misleading. Weber concluded:

> The Puritan wanted to work in a calling; we are forced to do so. For when asceticism was carried out of monastic cells into everyday life, and began to dominate worldly morality, it did its part in building the tremendous cosmos of the modern economic order. This order is now bound to the technical and economic conditions of machine production which to-day determine the lives of all individuals who are born into this mechanism, not only those directly concerned with economic acquisition, with irresistible force. . . . In [Richard] Baxter's view the care for external good should lie on the shoulders of the "saint like a light cloak, which can be thrown aside at any moment." But fate decreed that the cloak should become an iron cage. . . . In the field of its highest development, in the United States, the pursuit of wealth, stripped of its religious and ethical meaning, tends to become associated with purely mundane passions, which often actually give it the character of sport. . . . The modern man is in general, even with the best will, unable to give religious ideas a significance for culture and national character which they deserve. (1904–5: 181–3)

Weber rightly predicted that the rationality of modern society would extend well beyond the economic sphere into all the crevices of everyday life. And he rightly recognized what has come to be known as US exceptionalism – that developments in American society take on a different, more accentuated hue than found in other Western capitalist societies. It was America's exceptionalism in regard to religion, however, that Weber did not fully appreciate. And although there is some slight ambiguity in Weber in regard to secularization – he was emphatic that scientific knowledge, for example, cannot answer the values questions that modern society must necessarily confront – nevertheless, his presumption that religion would lose its significance in rationally advanced societies contributed to reigniting the cinders of secularization theory throughout much of the twentieth century.

Durkheim's conceptualization of the evolving place of religion in modern society was far more ambiguous. On the one hand, Durkheim recognized that, with the rise of modern society, and especially the increase in individualism (required by the specialized division of labor) and the progressive expansion in science as the basis of knowledge, the dogmatic hold of traditional religious systems would wane (cf. 2001 [1912]: 325). He argued that

> the realities to which religious speculation is applied are the same realities that will later serve as the objects of scientific reflection: nature, man, and society. The mystery that seems to surround them is entirely superficial and dissipates upon closer observation: lift the veil with which the mythological imagination has cloaked them, and they appear as they are. Religion endeavors to translate these realities into an intelligible language that is no different in kind from the language employed by science; both involve connecting things to one another, establishing internal relations between them, classifying them, and systematizing them. . . . Both, in this respect, pursue the same goal; scientific thought is merely a more perfect form of religious thought. It seems natural, then, that religion should progressively fade as science becomes more adept at completing its task. . . . What science disputes in religion is not its right to exist but its right to be dogmatic about the nature of things, the kind of special competence it claimed for its knowledge of man and the world. In fact, religion does not know itself. It knows neither what it is made of nor what needs it satisfies. Far from handing down the law to science, it is itself an object of scientific study! . . . [And since] religious speculation has no proper object, religion clearly cannot play the same role in the future that it has in the past. (2001 [1912]: 324–5)

At the same time however, Durkheim also recognized that scientific knowledge alone is not sufficient to affirm the bonds necessary to social integration. Thus, he did not see science and religion in conflict with one another but as having interdependent functions. Science provides knowledge, but religion and its functional equivalents provide action – the "moral remaking" that exists around sacred rituals and beliefs. Hence, he argued, "science could not possibly take religion's place. For if science expresses life, it does not create it" (2001 [1912]: 323). It does not revitalize social ties. Durkheim argued, moreover, that religion would maintain itself as a social fact, a social reality that science could not deny; in short, religion would adapt and transform itself rather than disappear (2001 [1912]: 324–6). Precisely because Durkheim saw religion or the sacred as that which compels individuals to assemble, to act in unison (and therein to bend their individual impulses to the moral or social force of the collectivity), and as a consequence to be strengthened in their individual and collective ability to cope with the joys and sorrows of everyday life (2001 [1912]: 311, 313, 309), he regarded religion as eternally necessary.

> There is something eternal in religion, then, that is destined to survive all the particular symbols in which religious thought has successfully cloaked itself. No society can exist that does not feel the need at regular intervals to sustain and reaffirm the collective feelings and ideas that constitute its unity. . . . Now, this moral remaking can be achieved only by means of meetings, assemblies, or congregations in which individuals, brought into close contact, reaffirm in common their common feelings: hence those ceremonies whose goals, results, and methods do not differ in kind from properly religious ceremonies. (2001 [1912]: 322)

Notwithstanding Durkheim's claims regarding the enduring facticity of religion and its socially integrative power, subsequent cohorts of sociologists were generally more embracing of Weber's prediction (and Durkheim's partial acknowledgment too) that religion would be undermined by the progressive forces of rationality and science. Secularization theory has undergone a variety of emphases (see e.g. Tschannen 1991), but its core assumption is that social change is invariably accompanied by a progressive pattern of decline in the authority and significance of religion in society, both in public culture and in individual lives.

The appeal of evolutionary theories that propose a relatively uncomplicated, linear, and progressive model of social change helps to account for the embrace of the secularization thesis. After all, the march of history – as evaluated by Weber, Durkheim, and Marx too – was a history demonstrating the ever-expanding division of labor and its related increase in the production capacity and resources of modern capitalist societies. Rationality, notwithstanding its excesses – variously denoted by Weber's iron cage, Durkheim's pathologies, and Marx's alienated labor – was widely recognized as the *modus operandi* of modern capitalist society. And within this evolutionary framing, the presumption that religion would be driven further and further to the margins by the dominance of reason and science in everyday life made intellectual sense. Moreover, if modern individuals were to be disenchanted, why would they (re)turn to religion in a society where the allure of mass consumption seemed far more powerful and comforting?

This view of advancing secularization was further bolstered as a result of the towering presence of Talcott Parsons in sociology for much of the twentieth century. Parsons completed his doctorate in sociology at the University of Heidelberg, the same university where Max Weber had been a professor until his death in 1920, and he subsequently played a critical role in making Weber's work accessible to American students. In 1930, Parsons's translation of Weber's *Protestant Ethic and the Spirit of Capitalism* was published, and Weber's *Theory of Social and Economic Organization* was published in 1947 – translated, edited, and with an introduction by Parsons. And although Parsons's general theorizing in *The Structure of Social Action* (1937) owes much to both Weber and Durkheim (and to Pareto), his subsequent essays on religion and culture (e.g. 1963) were strongly Weberian.

MODERNIZATION AND THE DIFFERENTIATION OF INSTITUTIONAL SPHERES

Following Weber, Parsons (1963) argued that the significance of religion was critical to understanding the historical development and culture of modern society. And, importantly, following Weber's discussion of the rational differentiation of societal spheres, Parsons also argued that, just as society evolves and becomes more complex in its structure and institutions, so too does religion. Just as the economy, the family, and the legal system, for example, become more differentiated and specialized in the societal functions they perform, religion too becomes differentiated from these specialized institutional functions and creates its own system of differentiation (Christianity differentiated itself from Judaism, Protestantism differentiated itself from Catholicism, and so on with the differentiation of discrete Protestant denominations; Parsons 1963: 392–3).

The process of structural differentiation and autonomous specialization was a central strand in Parsons's modernization theory. Although modernization theory acknowledged the structural differentiation within religion, it was also implicit (following Weber) that religious values – as sources of ultimate justification – would necessarily lose their public relevance, and in Luckmann's (1967) terms become invisible. In fact, even if relegated to the private sphere, modernization theorists saw traditional religious attachments as a hindrance to modernization and consequently argued that it was necessary to pry individuals from such attachments (Smelser 1968: 134).

Structural differentiation, as explained by Neil Smelser, means that the economy, politics, science, and other institutional spheres no longer relied on the justification provided by religious beliefs and sanctions but developed their own autonomous rationality: "Insofar as [autonomous rationality] replaces religious sanctions, secularization occurs in these spheres" (1968: 135). Similarly, religious and other value systems necessarily "undergo a process of secularization as differentiation proceeds" and lose their all-encompassing legitimacy within the religious sphere (as in other spheres) and adopt mechanisms that are not directly sanctioned by religious values. "Hence there is a paradoxical element in the role of religious or nationalistic belief systems. Insofar as they encourage the breakup of old patterns, they may stimulate economic modernization. Insofar as they resist their own subsequent secularization, however, these same value systems may become impediments to economic advance and structural change" (Smelser 1968).

AMERICAN RELIGIOUS EXCEPTIONALISM: FREEDOM AND DENOMINATIONALISM

Modernization theorists held American society as the apogee of modernization. And where else could one find such clear-cut evidence of institutional differentiation than right within the specific context of the US? Most notably, functional differentiation was vividly seen in the legal-rational, institutional separation of church and state (Parsons 1963). This historical differentiation affirmed that the church has its specific functions and sphere of authority and the state has its discrete institutional functions and authority, and each sphere does not (in principle) impede or tread on the specialized functions of the other. This highly rational arrangement contrasted with the European situation, where church and state since the time of Constantine had long been inexorably tied to one another, and which in the Reformation era did not lead to the splitting of church and state but to a realignment of church and state, whether of Protestantism and the state in England during the reign of Henry VIII, or of Catholicism and the state in France, Ireland, etc. The remnants of these alignments still play out locally in various guises today in Europe.

In the US, however, the institutional differentiation between church and state cannot be seen simply as the result of modernization's inexorable force in requiring increased rationalization and secularization per se. It was emergent, rather, from a more complicated convergence of historical circumstances: America's interlinked history of immigration and religious freedom which gave rise to denominationalism. Both religious freedom and denominationalism are core, interrelated strands in the narrative of American religious exceptionalism, the view that religion in America is substantively different, more vibrant, than in other Western democratic countries.

Religious freedom

The coupling of religion and freedom in American everyday life and its attendant impact on the vitality of church activity was especially striking to Alexis de Tocqueville during his travels in the eastern part of America in the 1830s. Coming from France, with its very different, European experience of a hierarchical, state-established, dominant religion, de Tocqueville observed that, in America, "the spirit of religion and the spirit of freedom . . . are intimately united and . . . reign in common" (1946 [1835]: 308). And, importantly, de Tocqueville reported that this spirit generated rather than diminished religious activity. Thus he wrote:

> In the United States on the seventh day of every week the tradition and working life of the nation seems suspended; all noises cease; a deep tranquility, say rather the solemn calm of meditation, succeeds the turmoil of the week, and the soul resumes possession and contemplation of itself. On this day, the marts of traffic are deserted; every member of the community, accompanied by his children, goes to church, where he listens to strange language which would seem unsuited to his ear. . . . On his return home he does not turn to the ledgers of business, but he opens the book of Holy Scripture; there he meets with sublime and affecting descriptions of the greatness and goodness of the Creator, of the infinite magnificence of the handiwork of God, and of the lofty destinies of man, his duties, and his immortal privileges. (1946 [1840]: 143)

Although de Tocqueville's observations come from a snapshot of the 1830s, and although they would not in any case meet the canon of scientific sociology that was soon to be established by his compatriot, Auguste Comte, the significance of de Tocqueville in the American cultural imagination is such that his historical portrait of religion in American life is the received view. Few empirical studies of religion in the US were conducted in the hundred years between de Tocqueville's visit and the establishment of national opinion polls in the 1940s. The few existing historical studies of particular communities document the strong cultural presence of the church in the early decades of the twentieth century, but they also present a picture of differentiation in individuals' religious activity (e.g. Dillon and Wink 2007; Lynd and Lynd 1929). Nonetheless, while religious activity in America has always been less uniform than might be inferred from de Tocqueville, the fact remains that the practical ethos of religious freedom that is uniquely American has complicated the secularization trajectory of American society and has made the contrast between it and Europe even more striking today than in past centuries.

Denominationalism

Denominationalism, the second, related strand in the narrative of American exceptionalism, refers both to the institutional reality reflected in the diversity of Christian churches and sects present in America from the early seventeenth century onwards and to the cultural acceptance of the idea of religious freedom, an ethos given accentuated emphasis during the revolutionary period. As the American religious historian Sydney Ahlstrom (1972: 381–2) has pointed out, denominationalism as an idea implicitly rejects the notion that there is one true church, and by extension, the view that any single church should enjoy the privileges of state protection. Denominationalism, therefore, can be seen as part of the secularizing process, demonstrating that the differentiation between spheres (e.g. church and state) is also accompanied by a differentiation within any given sphere (the splitting of the church, following the Reformation, into multiple, different churches or denominations).

Institutional differentiation (of church and state, and among denominations) contributed to making religious activity part and parcel of the cultural fabric of what it means to be an American – giving religion its legitimate place among other culturally sanctioned activities (work, recreation). Since the revolutionary era, American freedom has invariably meant a populist belief in freedom of choice (cf. Hatch 1989), and, in regard to religion, successive generations have interpreted this freedom as the freedom to choose not an anti-religious stance (as seen in French anti-clericalism, for example) but to actively choose and switch among denominational options. Therefore, as modernization scholars have argued, "To be modern means to be see life as alternatives, preferences and choices – self-conscious choice implies rationality" (Apter 1965: 10). The quirk in American society is that this rationality is exercised by many in favor of religion rather than its eschewal.

Thus the structure of denominational choices available to Americans appears to have enhanced rather than attenuated the plausibility of religion. This scenario was unexpected not only by modernization scholars but also by those coming from a more micro-analytical and phenomenological perspective. Most notably, Peter Berger (1967) argued that societal contexts characterized by denominationalism rather than by a dominant monopoly (one true) church, would experience the decline of religion; in this view, religious pluralism would inevitably breed uncertainty in regard to religion and threaten the plausibility of any and all religious belief systems. If there are so many religious options, as evidenced by diverse denominations, how can individuals sustain belief in the truth of their chosen option? Berger stated:

> when different religious systems, and their respective institutional "carriers" are in pluralistic competition with each other. . . . The problem [becomes] . . . one of constructing and maintaining subsocieties that may serve as plausibility structures for the demonopolized religious systems. . . . For the individual, existing in a particular religious world implies existing in the particular social context within which that world can retain its plausibility. (1967: 49–50)

When the everyday life in a given community revolves around one (true) church, individuals in that here and now would not be prompted to imagine that there may be an alternative church (or truth). This was the experience for most people growing up in Europe; you went to the Catholic church (in Italy, Ireland, France) or to the Anglican church (in England) or to the Lutheran church (in Sweden), and this act

was not a decision as such – it was habit and it was the habit over many generations, and was not given a second thought. By contrast, growing up in America
presented an array of local choices, especially pronounced from the mid-nineteenth
century onwards. If for whatever reason one was prompted to leave one's own
particular (inherited) church, the alternative was not no church (as was practically
the case in Europe), but, to the contrary, a plurality of alternatives from which to
choose. California, unlike Puritan New England, is not renowned for its religious
fervor. Yet in the 1930s, while it had only two movie theaters, it had many different
churches, including Lutheran, Presbyterian, Episcopal, Congregational, Unitarian,
Free Methodist, Mormon, Plymouth Brethren, Evangelical, Christian Science, Apos-
tolic Church, Seventh Day Adventist, Catholic, Russian Orthodox, as well as a Unity
Center, and Hebrew Orthodox, Reihaisho Hershinto, and Buddhist temples (Dillon
and Wink 2007: 24). This is American religious pluralism. With all of these options
available, one can readily appreciate that Berger's predictions concerning the implau-
sibility of religious truth might well have been borne out.

The empirical reality, of course, is that the increased differentiation within the
religious sphere in the US, and the ethos of religious freedom that denominationalism both reflected and encouraged as a practical matter, did not render religion
implausible, it rendered it all the more plausible – providing a niche for (almost)
everyone. As underscored by Will Herberg (1955), denominational identity was a
culturally necessary marker of patriotism, decency, and civic commitment in post-
war America. The situation in Britain and Europe, however, was quite different;
and not surprisingly, given their trends indicating a slide away from traditional or
church-based institutional religion, British and European sociologists were among
those who most readily embraced the secularization thesis (e.g. Dobbelaere 1981;
Wilson 1966). This move, however, opened up other avenues of sociological inquiry
into religion, most notably conceptual and empirical work on sects (e.g. Wilson
1959), a preoccupation with its origins in Weber.

RATIONAL CHOICE THEORY AND SUPPLY-SIDE LOGIC

Although there were early critics of secularization theory on both sides of the Atlantic (e.g. Greeley 1982; Martin 1978), it was the persisting contrast in religious
vibrancy between the US and western Europe that prompted a major turn in sociological theorizing in the US away from the secularization thesis. Rational choice
scholars of religion adopted a framework drawing out the implications for religious
vitality derived from the competitive religious environment that denominationalism
fostered. Already in the 1960s, Peter Berger had pointed out the contrasting distinction between the monopolistic control of the church in western Europe and the
pluralistic situation created by American denominationalism. He argued:

> The key characteristic of all pluralistic situations, whatever the details of their historical
> background, is that the religious ex-monopolies can no longer take for granted the
> allegiance of their client populations. Allegiance is voluntary and thus, by definition,
> less than certain. As a result, the religious tradition, which previously could be authori-
> tatively imposed, now has to be marketed. It must be "sold" to a clientele that is no

longer constrained to "buy." The pluralistic situation is, above all, a market situation. In it, the religious institutions become marketing agencies and the religious traditions become consumer commodities. And at any rate a good deal of religious activity in this situation comes to be dominated by the logic of market economics. (1967: 137)

The metaphor of the religious market was given further elaboration by a group of social scientists who have come to be identified with a rational choice approach to religion. This perspective conceptualizes the individual religious adherent as a rational actor, and conceptualizes the societal context in terms of a religious marketplace in which different firms (denominations) compete for the loyalty of consumers by actively selling distinct religious products whose rewards are perceived as being more compensatory and satisfying than their costs (e.g. Finke and Stark 1992; Iannaccone 1990, 1995).

In 1980 Rodney Stark and William Bainbridge published a paper which they stated was "the pivotal work in a series of papers, published and forthcoming, which present a new exchange paradigm for analyzing and explaining religious phenomena" (1980: 114). Among the several deductive propositions outlined, they argued that "humans seek what they perceive to be rewards and avoid what they perceive to be costs" (1980: 115); thus "they will tend to act rationally to maximize rewards and minimize costs" (1980: 118). Stark and Bainbridge defined "compensators" – faith that empirically unsubstantiated rewards *will be* obtained – as key to their theory of religion; faith in intangible promises, in the likely rewards of a given belief system is what motivates individuals to persist in religious behavior (exchanging compensators for rewards; thus believers avoid sinful behavior now in order to triumph in heaven [1980: 123]). Stark and Bainbridge deduced that "religion must emerge in human society" because supernatural belief acts as a general compensator system for individuals as they confront existential questions (1980: 124).

Having outlined a framework for seeing the individual as a rational religious actor, Stark and his collaborators then turned their gaze to the religious marketplace. Finke and Stark (1992) elaborated a "new approach to American religious history," one that argued that "religious organizations can thrive only to the extent that they have a theology that can comfort souls and motivate sacrifice" (1992: 5). Their statistical analysis of detailed historical data in America from 1776 to 1980 led them to conclude that the churching of America was driven by the entrepreneurial activities of church preachers who actively sought to make adherents out of unbelievers. Importantly, they found that the winners in the American religious economy, those who increased their market share, were those upstart sects like the Methodists and the Baptists whose "emotion-packed messages centered on experience with the sacred and warned of the evils of the secular" (Finke and Stark 1992: 85). The losers, by contrast, were the established denominations – especially Congregationalists and Episcopalians – whose complacency and theological elitism did not appeal to the masses (1992: 85–6).

Finke and Stark thus elaborated a supply-side theory of religion; they argued that, while there will always be a latent demand for religion – people invariably need compensators as they wrestle with existential questions about the meaning of life (Stark and Bainbridge 1980) – this demand needs to be stoked by entrepreneurial churches (supplier firms) that are able to provide a religious product that will be seen as a good investment. Notably, in the rational choice perspective, a good religious investment is not one that comes easily and allows for free riders (e.g. Iannaccone 1995); to the contrary, as the fortunes of the American denominations attest, it is the churches that are strict in their religious demands and in the costs they impose (and hence offer the promise of greater rewards) that are the more successful (Finke and Stark 1992).

For rational choice scholars, a pluralistic religious economy produces religious vitality: the more clearly demarcated choices are available (because there are more specific firms/denominations competing), the more religious exchange behavior is fostered. This approach thus rejects the assumptions of secularization theory, seeing it as being applicable to the monopolized religious context in Europe but unsuited to American denominationalism and its twin, religious freedom; monopolies breed laziness, whereas competition breeds vitality (Finke and Stark 1992: 19). Therefore, notwithstanding Berger's (1967) observation that market economics would characterize a pluralistic religious context, Finke and Stark argue that Berger's core understanding that the sacred canopy of one, true religion covering the whole society is shattered by religious pluralism is a Eurocentric perspective, and one that is contravened by the religious vitality produced by American religious pluralism (1992: 18–19).

The explanatory power of the rational choice framework in making sense of the historical and contemporary vibrancy of religion in the US was seen as such a significant development in the sociology of religion that it (taken along with other American-based studies of the diversity and vitality of American institutional religion) prompted Stephen Warner (1993) to announce an "emerging new paradigm" in the early 1990s. In the years since, the early advocates of rational choice and other scholars have tested the paradigm's claims using diverse data sources from both the US and elsewhere, and several researchers have taken issue with the varying assumptions and claims promulgated by its proponents (see Chaves and Gorski 2001 for a critical review). On the other hand, several researchers have found it analytically useful to think about changes in religious beliefs and in macro-institutional practices in terms of the monopoly/competitive influences in the religious environment.

CHANGES IN THE RELIGIOUS-SPIRITUAL MARKETPLACE

US/European exceptionalism continues unabated today. Americans are far more likely than their European and Canadian peers to express belief in God and in the afterlife, to affiliate with a religious tradition, and to attend religious services. And while religiously framed moral debates on abortion, gay rights, and end-of-life issues are not uncommon in other Western societies, they are an ongoing feature of American local and national politics. In Europe, cultural secularization is such that Europe's Christian past has become politically controversial and is seen as an inappropriate collective memory for the European Parliament to acknowledge in the new Constitution for a unified Europe. By contrast, in America, the irony is not the attempt to diminish the church in everyday life (a ritual played out locally every Christmas season contesting/advocating the display of religious symbols in the public square), but the great expectations that are invested in the church. American churches have so many non-religious functions – providing an array of social welfare, education, counseling, and therapeutic services – it is easy to forget that their primary purpose is worship. American policymakers, civic leaders, and citizens alike look to the church to solve the ills of modern society. These problems are the byproduct of social arrangements in which instrumental rationality, as Weber predicted, appears triumphant over values rationality, and the moral, socially responsible individualism envisaged by Durkheim has been sidelined by the dominance of contractual relations. Hence, the religious sphere by default becomes the system of integration; it is burdened with picking up the pieces from the fragmentation of the self and of social ties, and with redeeming the malfunctioning of the state, the economy, and the family.

The continuing viability of the church as a bridge between the self and society has come into question, however, with the proliferation of non-church-based spiritual seeking. Since the mid-1960s, a vastly expanded spiritual marketplace with a diverse mix of Eastern philosophies and practices, alternative ways of thinking about the sacred, and a variety of self-help therapeutic groups and manuals addressed at satisfying the individual's inner needs (e.g. Glock and Bellah 1976; Roof 1993, 1999; Wuthnow 1998), has produced a growing trend toward the uncoupling of religion and spirituality in the US (e.g. Roof 1993, 1999; Wuthnow 1998). This uncoupling, however, is far from straightforward. The ambiguity of the sacred that was problematic for Durkheim as for the early anthropologists has come full circle, evident in the multiplicity of ways in which scholars and ordinary individuals construe what spirituality denotes. The emphasis on the varieties of religious experience first elaborated by William James (1902) receives support today from the diverse ways in which individuals are negotiating religious and spiritual involvement (e.g. Roof 1999).

And, once again, what spirituality means to Europeans is different in important ways from what it means in America; the differing significance of religion in both settings matters to how spirituality is construed. For Europeans, as Stifoss-Hanssen argues, "Spirituality is expressed by atheists and agnostics, by people deeply engaged in ecology and other idealistic endeavors, and by people inspired by religious impulses not easily understood by classic religious concepts (e.g. sacredness). My point is that a big area of study is at risk of being left out if sacredness is used as the central defining concept. . . . I recommend putting existentiality in the place of sacredness" (1999: 28).

In the US, by contrast, spirituality includes existential spirituality but it also includes a large proportion of individuals who specifically and intentionally seek the sacred, and indeed many who do so in varying ways through institutionalized religion. Americans who describe themselves as spiritual but not religious include those who are born-again Christians but who bypass churches and organized religion in order to prioritize a personal relationship with Jesus (e.g. Roof 1999). These individuals clearly are culturally different from seekers who engage in Eastern spiritual practices only, and from those who negotiate a spirituality that is derived from a diverse mix of religious and spiritual traditions (e.g. Dillon and Wink 2007; Roof 1999; Wuthnow 1998).

The expansion of the spiritual marketplace has resulted in considerable controversy about the social and personal implications of unchurched spirituality. In particular, a number of American cultural critics (e.g. Bellah et al. 1985) have argued for a connection between Americans' increased interest in spiritual seeking and the increased narcissism of contemporary society, a trend that is perceived as being detrimental to civic engagement. Coming from a Durkheimian–Parsonian values-consensus/societal integration perspective, Robert Bellah, for example, argues that a therapeutic, self-centered, and narcissistic individualism underlies spiritual seeking and that these self-oriented interests are displacing the socially responsible individualism that has historically characterized American society. In this view, the "triumph of the therapeutic" (Rieff 1966) in post-1960s America and the growth of interest in both psychotherapy and spirituality is portrayed as reflecting a desire for immediate gratification among individuals for whom feeling good has become the prime goal in life.

In essence, the elevation of personal experience as the arbiter of moral authority and its lack of grounding in the external authority imposed by an institutionalized religious tradition is seen as detrimental to the practices of spiritual and social commitment associated with church participation (Bellah et al. 1985). Whereas churches play a critical role in the creation of a responsible community, spiritual seeking appears less suited to providing the same resources (cf. Bellah et al. 1985). Typically, it does not entail the same degree of exposure to the parables of service to others repeated in scriptural readings and sermons, the church-based friendship connections that encourage collaboration in volunteer activities, and the organized service and care opportunities that many churches provide their members. In short, skepticism toward an individualized spiritual seeking fits well with the sociological view that social institutions are essential to the maintenance of community and society.

Research (e.g. Dillon and Wink 2007) comparing church-centered religious participation and a more individualized sacred-spiritual seeking shows, however, that as long as individuals are *disciplined* in their spiritual practices – that they actually engage in spiritual practices (e.g. meditation) and do so on a regular basis, rather than simply describe themselves as spiritual – then the consequences of spiritual seeking are not as detrimental for civic engagement and concern for others as some critics have suggested. Like church participation, disciplined spiritual seeking too can function to bridge the self and society. It is true that individuals who are attracted to spiritual seeking are different in many respects from those who are church-goers. But common to both, is the recognition that the sacred matters, though how they define and integrate the sacred in daily life varies (Dillon and Wink 2007).

In any case, the increased interest in spirituality in America again complicates what sociologists can say about secularization. On the one hand, there have been notable declines in recent decades in church attendance and in the proportion of those who express a denominational affiliation (Hout and Fischer 2002). Further, among those who are committed to church, and especially so among Catholics, there is a remarkable autonomy shown in regard to the authority of church officials on a variety of moral and social issues. These varying empirical realities can be taken as evidence of the march of secularization. On the other hand, the stability of belief in God and the afterlife, the vitality of local congregations, the continuing evidence of religious institutional loyalty, and the evidence of commitment to new forms of spiritual engagement make the counter-point. Moreover, this evidence of the continuing relevance of religion/spirituality cannot be dismissed as being confined to the private sphere alone. To the contrary, the popularity of Christian-themed movies and rock music, the persistence of civil religious rituals and discourse in American public life, and the salience of religious values in shaping voting and public policy debates suggest that religious attachments and influences cannot so easily be pried from the public sphere.

RELIGION AND GLOBALIZATION

One consequence of the paradigmatic shift from classical secularization theory to rational choice supply-side models is the tendency to de-emphasize the comparative study of religion. If the US is so different from Europe, and it is – historically, culturally, and institutionally – why should sociologists embark on comparative studies of religion and society? Any emphasis on exceptionalism, whether American or indeed European exceptionalism (see Davie 2001) can have the effect of making the study of religion particularistic as researchers concentrate on understanding religion in its specific local guises; thus in the US, for example, there has been a lot of emphasis on studying local congregations.

This trend is counterbalanced, however, by the increased scholarly attention to globalization (see CHAPTER 16). As sociologists pay attention not just to the economic but to the cultural, social, and political dimensions of globalization (e.g. Robertson 1992), the study of issues and themes related to religion and globalization will most likely gain momentum. Among other transformations, globalization challenges our traditional understanding and conceptualization of territorial and cultural-intellectual boundaries (e.g. Sassen 2007), and this expansion necessarily challenges the conceptual definitions of religion and of religious borders that have characterized sociology. Thus, as Peter Beyer argues, "a more important question to pose of contemporary religion than what religion is or what religion does (the substantive versus functional debate) is the question of what religion and the religions are becoming" (2003: 58).

Apprehending these emergent processes can take many forms. We already see an increase in sociological attention to globalized religious movements and the changing global religious landscape. David Martin's (2002) study of Pentecostalism in Latin America and Southeast Asia is a case in point, while in Europe the changing religious, political, and cultural dynamics resulting from the steady increase in Europe's Muslim population are beginning to receive careful scholarly attention (e.g. Al Sayyad and Castells 2007). Some of this interest is driven, of course, by the re-emergence of fundamentalist religion (e.g. Giddens 2003), and its heightened association with the globalization of terror and the religious framing of violence both by its perpetrators and cultural commentators (e.g. Huntington 1996); these linkages were first addressed by Weber in his analysis of the different world-orientations of world religions including Islam (e.g. Weber1978: 623–8). Though controversial, Weber's elaborations of different world-religious types (e.g. the Protestant capitalist, the Islamic warrior) can be retrieved to re-energize the global comparative study of religion and politics. Apart from the study of global religious movements and transnational religious identities, sociologists of religion also have a timely opportunity to investigate how the trend toward decentralization and non-hierarchical authority made possible (if not required) in the globalizing, network society changes the contours of religious organizations, inter-institutional relationships, and collective identity (cf. Castells 2000).

Although the study of religion should be a fruitful cross-disciplinary endeavor, and while talk of intra- and inter-disciplinary boundaries may sound old-fashioned given today's intellectual zeitgeist of a post-disciplinary world, one specific challenge for sociologists of religion is not to cede the study of religion and globalization to globalization scholars, but to make the study of globalizing processes a core area within the sociology of religion. Otherwise, the explanations offered of how religion and globalization impact each other may be only partial, especially if they are not grounded in the accumulated knowledge produced by sociologists of religion in regard to the multiple and multilayered ways in which religious beliefs and practices intertwine in expected and unexpected directions with the institutional, cultural, and sociohistorical contexts in which they are embedded.

Post-secular society

The need for comparative study is further prompted by the recent murmurings in intellectual circles. Most notably, the idea that we are now living in a post-secular society has gained considerable currency following the implicit theoretical shift indicated by Jürgen Habermas (2002) in his continuing appraisal of the economic, political, and intellectual pathologies of modernity. Rethinking his analysis of the relation between religion and rationality, Habermas concedes "the continuity of religion in secularized environments" and the preservation of "sacred scriptures and religious traditions," such that he now recognizes that a reflexively understood religion, rather than a rationality devoid of religion, can help human society to deal with "a miscarried life, social pathologies, the failures of individual life projects, and the deformation of misarranged existential relationships" (quoted in Nemoianu 2006: 26). Thus Habermas states: "It is in the best interest of the constitutional state to act considerately toward all those cultural sources out of which civil solidarity and norm consciousness are nourished" (Nemoianu 2006: 27). Habermas's new openness to the cultural relevance of religion contrasts with the view articulated in his theory of communicative action which required that "the authority of the holy is gradually replaced by the authority of an achieved consensus. This means a freeing of communicative action from sacrally protected normative contexts . . . the spellbinding power of the holy, is sublimated into the binding/bonding force of criticizable validity claims and at the same time turned into an everyday occurrence" (Habermas 1987: 77; cf. Dillon 1999).

The notion of a post-secular society has intellectual appeal. It simultaneously references the secularization of society while also affirming that something may have changed such that we are in a post-phase. It affirms the Enlightenment while recognizing that Enlightenment thought did not get everything right. Sociologically, however, it is uncertain how accurate, and ultimately how useful, this term is. If post-secular society refers to "the continuity of religion in secularized environments," we must wonder whether those environments were ever truly secularized or whether secularization was only partial (and thus not really meeting the

Weber–Parsons definition of secularization); or whether it means that religion has re-emerged in what was for a time a secularized society (though this notion would be at odds with the evolutionary march of secularization as the end point of history). We must also probe whether and in what ways the post-secular society is substantively different from the "Christianizing" of secular society – the leveraging of the church (i.e., religious values) on the state – observed by Parsons (1963)?

Further, if we embrace the notion of post-secular society, are we implying that we once knew the secular society (or that we could legitimately call certain societal contexts secular)? If so, where was that secular society? And when was it secular? And if a given society was secular (until whenever), what evidence do we see today that it is now post-secular? These are not simply rhetorical questions, but can be answered by much-needed empirically sound comparative-historical research.

In the meantime, in evaluating the analytical usefulness of embracing the idea of the post-secular society, we should heed the lessons of sociology's past misperceptions. One thing we have learned in late modernity is to be suspicious of grand, generalizing claims. We have come to know that modern society is a complex mosaic of institutional and cultural unevenness, that sees the rational and the non-rational mixed up in all kinds of unanticipated ways, and in the most unexpected of places. Because religion, ultimately, has to be carried either tacitly or explicitly by individuals and collectivities, we need to be attentive to how the specific social and cultural contexts in which individual lives are lived shape how religion is construed and practiced, and how those contexts temper the generalized inferences we make about religion. Thus while it may well be empirically true to talk about specific post-secular enclaves, locales, or even societies, (and to talk about specific secular communities, societies, etc.) it would be a distortion of the complexity of societal processes and of everyday life to sweepingly shroud the current era in the West, not to mention the global face of religion, in a post-secular veil.

We can and should unveil the religious, the secular, and the post-secular – but it needs to be accomplished with empirical attentiveness to the differentiated processes that can then help to illuminate what is really going on. And, if we find that indeed all three terms – or even any two of the three – are necessary to explaining the nature of our current societal experience, then perhaps we should reconsider why it is apparently the case that, despite the evident gains for rationality and progress, there is nonetheless a need for some kind of "transcendental grounding" (Habermas 1987: 397) that human society cannot avoid. This question undoubtedly would give sociologists much to ponder and contest for many years to come.

Bibliography

Ahlstrom, S. (1972) *A Religious History of the American People*. New Haven: Yale University Press.
Al Sayyad, N., and Castells, M. (eds.) (2007) *Muslim Europe or Euro-Islam? Politics, Culture, and Citizenship in the Age of Globalization*. Lanham, MD: Lexington Books.
Apter, D. (1965) *The Politics of Modernization*. Chicago: University of Chicago Press.
Barbalet, J. (forthcoming) "Pragmatism and Symbolic Interactionism," in Bryan Turner (ed.), *Social Theory*. Oxford: Blackwell.

Bellah, R., Madsen, R., Sullivan, W., Swidler, A., and Tipton, S. (1985) *Habits of the Heart: Individualism and Commitment in American Life.* Berkeley: University of California Press.

Berger, P. (1967) *The Sacred Canopy.* Garden City, NY: Doubleday.

Beyer, P. (2003) "Social Forms of Religion in Contemporary Society," in Michele Dillon (ed.), *Handbook of the Sociology of Religion.* New York: Cambridge University Press.

Castells, M. (2000) "Toward a Sociology of the Network Society." *Contemporary Sociology* 29: 693–9.

Chaves, M., and Gorski, P. (2001) "Religious Pluralism and Religious Participation. *Annual Review of Sociology* 27: 261–81.

Davie, G. (2001) "Patterns of Religion in Western Europe: An Exceptional Case," in R. Fenn (ed.), *The Blackwell Companion to Sociology of Religion.* Oxford: Blackwell.

Dillon, M. (1999) "The Authority of the Holy Revisited: Habermas, Religion, and Emancipatory Possibilities." *Sociological Theory* 17: 290–306.

Dillon, M., and Wink, P. (2007) *In the Course of a Lifetime: Tracing Religious Belief, Practice, and Change.* Berkeley: University of California Press.

Dobbelaere, K. (1981) *Secularization: A Multi-Dimensional Concept.* London: Sage.

Durkheim, É. (2001 [1912]) *The Elementary Forms of Religious Life,* trans. C. Cosman. New York: Oxford University Press.

Finke, R., and Stark, R. (1992) *The Churching of America: Winners and Losers in the Religious Economy.* New Brunswick, NJ: Rutgers University Press.

Frazer, W. (1935 [1890]) *The Golden Bough: A Study in Magic and Religion.* New York: Macmillan.

Giddens, A. (2003) *Runaway World: How Globalization is Reshaping our Lives.* New York: Routledge.

Glock, C., and Bellah, R. N. (eds.) (1976) *The New Religious Consciousness.* Berkeley: University of California Press.

Greeley, A. (1982) *Unsecular Man: The Persistence of Religion.* New York: Schocken.

Habermas, J. (1987) *The Theory of Communicative Action,* vol. 2. Boston: Beacon Press.

Habermas, J. (2002) *Religion and Rationality: Essays on Reason, God, and Modernity.* Cambridge, MA: MIT Press.

Hatch, N. (1989) *The Democratization of American Christianity.* New Haven: Yale University Press.

Herberg, W. (1955) *Protestant–Catholic–Jew: An Essay in American Religious Sociology.* New York: Doubleday.

Hout, M., and Fischer, C. (2002) "Explaining the Rise of Americans with No Religious Preferences: Politics and Generations." *American Sociological Review* 67: 165–90.

Huntington, S. (1996) *The Clash of Civilizations and the Remaking of World Order.* New York: Simon & Schuster.

Iannaccone, L. (1990) "Religious Participation: A Human Capital Approach." *Journal for the Scientific Study of Religion* 29: 297–314.

Iannaccone, L. (1995) "Voodoo Economics: Reviewing the Rational Choice Approach to Religion." *Journal for the Scientific Study of Religion* 34: 76–89.

James, W. (1898) *Collected Essay and Reviews.* New York: Longman, Green.

James, W. (1902) *The Varieties of Religious Experience.* New York: Longman, Green.

Lang, A. (1899) *Myth, Ritual and Religion.* New York: Longman, Green.

Luckmann, T. (1967) *The Invisible Religion: The Problem of Religion in Modern Society.* New York: Macmillan.

Lynd, R., and Lynd, H. (1929) *Middletown: A Study in Contemporary American Culture*. New York: Harcourt, Brace.

Martin, D. (1978) *A General Theory of Secularization*. New York: Harper & Row.

Martin, D. P. (2002) *Pentecostalism: The World their Parish*. Oxford: Blackwell.

Nemoianu, V. (2006) "The Church and the Secular Establishment." *Logos* 9: 17–42.

Parsons, T. (1937) *The Structure of Social Action*. New York: The Free Press.

Parsons, T. (1963) "Christianity and Modern Industrial Society," in E. Tiryakian (ed.), *Talcott Parsons: Sociological Theory and Modern Society*. New York: The Free Press.

Rieff, P. (1966) *The Triumph of the Therapeutic*. Harmondsworth: Penguin.

Robertson, R. (1992) *"Globalization": Social Theory and Global Culture*. London: Sage.

Roof, W. C. (1993) *A Generation of Seekers: The Spiritual Journeys of the Baby Boom Generation*. San Francisco: Harper & Row.

Roof, W. C. (1999) *Spiritual Marketplace: Baby Boomers and the Remaking of American Religion*. Princeton: Princeton University Press.

Sassen, S. (2007) *A Sociology of Globalization*. New York: Norton.

Smelser, N. (1968) *Essays in Sociological Explanation*. Englewood Cliffs, NJ: Prentice Hall.

Smith, W. R. (1997 [1894]) *Lectures on the Religion of the Semites*. London: Routledge/Thoemmes.

Stark, R., and Bainbridge, W. S. (1980) "Towards a Theory of Religion: Religious Commitment." *Journal for the Scientific Study of Religion* 19: 114–28.

Stifoss-Hanssen, H. (1999) "Religion and Spirituality: What a European Ear Hears." *International Journal for the Psychology of Religion* 9: 25–33.

Tocqueville, A. de (1946 [1835]) *Democracy in America*, vol. 1, introd. Phillips Bradley. Repr. New York: Knopf.

Tocqueville, A. de. (1946 [1840]) *Democracy in America*, vol. 2. introd. Phillips Bradley. Repr. New York: Knopf.

Tschannen, O. (1991) "The Secularization Paradigm: A Systematization." *Journal for the Scientific Study of Religion* 30: 396–415.

Turner, B. (2005) "The Sociology of Religion," in C. Calhoun, C. Rojek, and B. Turner (eds.), *The Sage Handbook of Sociology*. Thousand Oaks, CA: Sage.

Tylor, E. (1950 [1891]) *Primitive Culture*. New York: Harper & Row.

Warner, R. S. (1993) "Work in Progress Toward a New Paradigm for the Sociological Study of Religion in the United States." *American Journal of Sociology* 98: 1044–93.

Weber, M. (1976 [1904–5]) *The Protestant Ethic and the Spirit of Capitalism*, trans. T. Parsons, introd. A. Giddens. New York: Scribner's/Allen & Unwin.

Weber, M. (1978) *Economy and Society*, vol. 1, ed. G. Roth and C.Wittich. Berkeley, CA: University of California Press.

Wilson, B. (1959) "An Analysis of Sect Development." *American Sociological Review* 24: 3–15.

Wilson, B. (1966) *Religion and Secular Society*. London: Watts.

Wuthnow, R. (1998) *After Heaven: Spirituality in America Since the 1950s*. Berkeley: University of California Press.

22

Demography

John MacInnes and Julio Pérez Díaz

There shall be no more thence an infant of days, nor an old man that hath not filled his days: for the child shall die an hundred years old . . . (Isaiah 65: 20)

Consider men as if even now sprung up out of the earth, and suddenly, like mushrooms, come to full maturity, without all kind of engagement to each other. (Hobbes 1984 [1651])

Mankind is like the sea, ever ebbing or flowing, every minute one is born another dies. Those that are the people this minute, are not the people the next minute. In every instant and point of time there is a variation. No one time can be indifferent for all mankind to assemble. (Filmer 1991 [1680])

INTRODUCTION

As a discipline, demography must appear to be one of the least suitable candidates for inclusion in a volume on social theory. It is the intellectual and institutional child of the modern European bureaucratic state. For military, economic, and administrative reasons, the state came to be interested not only in the size of its component population, its evolution and reproduction, but in all kinds of data relevant to the management of its resources, both domestically and in its overseas colonies. Here lies the institutional genesis of demography and its close associates, the census, map and science of statistics (Anderson 1991; Mackenzie 1981; Marsh 1982). To this day most demographers work directly for the state, while its more autonomous academic practitioners are almost invariably tied closely to state and supra-state organizations, such as the United Nations or European Union. It is thus hardly surprising that much of the "theory" that demographers use, and especially its core concept of the "demographic transition," has been driven at times by the interests of states in general and that of the United States in particular (Hodgson 1983, 1988, 1991; Szreter 1993).

The content and subject matter of demography also appear relentlessly technical, descriptive, and atheoretical: more a question of arithmetic than social theory. Moreover, this is a vision many demographers themselves embrace. Mills's (2005) survey of recent articles in the journal *Demography* found that they employed exclusively theories from other disciplines, most notably those of the household economics of Becker (1960, 1991). To the extent that contemporary demography has its "own" theory it is that of the "demographic transition," but the latter has been plagued by both its political distortion and the failure of the most extensive attempts to reconcile the theory with the empirical evidence available (Coale 1986; Hodgson 1988; Robinson 1997) such that one of its most prominent theorists, Paul Demeny (1972) could summarize it thus: "in traditional societies, fertility and mortality are high. In modern societies, fertility and mortality are low. In between there is the demographic transition."

SOCIOLOGY AND DEMOGRAPHY

This perhaps explains why it is unusual to find many references to demography in contemporary sociology. Sociological texts (e.g. Giddens 2006) rarely include any reference to demographic analysis. Yet this absence is rather paradoxical, since sociology deals with themes that are directly related to population: the family and its evolution, population "aging," migration, gender relations, and so on. In institutional terms, in many countries it is not possible to study demography to degree level: its teaching is subsumed under sociology, economics, or related subjects. Moreover sociology makes much use of the output of demography as a discipline in the form of "population studies." It is, after all, rather difficult to study social change without paying some attention to the changing demographics of different societies. Finally this absence is fairly recent. In the interwar period many sociologists, such as Kingsley Davis in the USA or David Glass in Britain, took a keen interest in demography. Indeed Davis's sociological theory of modernization and fertility decline (1937) was almost certainly a key source of Parsons', later sociology of the family. However the focus of this interest – low fertility and the prospect of population stagnation or decline – also helps explains its rapid waning in the "baby boom" years of the 1950s and 1960s.

It is demography's technical and methodological aspects that sociology especially tends to ignore, as if these were indeed a question of arithmetic. An unintended but largely uncontested intellectual division of labor has grown up between the two disciplines such that demography studies and predicts the volume of population and its components in different societies (total population, fertility rates, dependency ratios, mortality rates, population pyramids, and so on) while sociology studies what these people think and do, the structure of social relations between them, social change, and so on. This can be seen, for example, in the development of the "sociology of the body" (see CHAPTER 26). The latter hardly studies what only bodies can do – give birth, have sex, reproduce, die – for that can safely be left to demography. Sociology of the body rather focuses on the interpretation of the changing symbolic meanings attached to bodies or represented by them in different social contexts.

This intellectual division of labor is not, of course, innocent. We think it has its roots in two related but distinct phenomena. One is the way it suited Enlightenment liberalism to deny the carnal origins of human beings, as can be vividly seen in the exchange between Hobbes and Filmer that opens this chapter. For the anti-patriarchalists, like Hobbes, it seemed as if the only way to assert both the rights of the citizen against the divine right of kings and assert the triumph of politics over nature was to split off the civic and social mind from the natural or supernatural body. To this day most social scientists are predisposed both to prefer "nurture" to "nature" accounts of human behavior, and to see a fairly clear dividing line between them.

However, we think that the struggle against patriarchalism has advanced sufficiently over the last four centuries to allow us to contest the law of the father without ceasing to see children as the offspring of their biological parents. But we are interested here only in one legacy of this split: the relative indifference of sociology as a discipline to the sexual reproduction of people and the effort, time, energy, and resources it requires, as opposed to sociology's focus on the social reproduction of the roles, structures, institutions, or discourses they might come to occupy. To make a perhaps crude generalization, for most sociology, most of the time, reproduction has meant *socialization* (MacInnes 1998).

The other root may lie in the institutional genesis of demography, and its intimately related twin, statistics, as the emerging bourgeois state's chief quantity surveyor. Its business was indeed technical and applied: to count rather than to understand. This technocratic character, together with its over-intimate connections as a discipline in its early years with the eugenics movement (Hodgson 1991; Soloway 1990; Szreter 1996), perhaps explains the relative disinterest of sociology in contemporary demography: especially compared to the much closer relationship between the disciplines in the first half of the twentieth century. In the 1920s and 1930s the first versions of what was later to become demographic transition theory appeared in sociology journals.

DEMOGRAPHY AND ECONOMICS

At first, the development of what might commonly be thought of as "theory" in demography is to be found in works of classical political economy, where population enters as an economic variable alongside others such as the size of the workforce, growth of economic activity, the level of prices or supply of fertile land. However, this has led to a situation where any work containing the term "population," regardless of how it is understood, can be considered as part of a the evolution of demography, as far back as Plato's *Republic*. For example, Malthus is often thought of as a founding father of the discipline, when it is far from clear that he was a demographer at all. He paid little or no attention to the dynamics of population as such. Indeed his specifically political objective was to demonstrate that the relationship between population volume and the supply of land must make any fundamental social change impossible, in contrast to the claims of the French

Revolution. When, later, Marx, for example, critically analyzed Malthus's approach, that did not turn him into a "demographer." What Marx, Malthus, and others such as Ricardo in his "Law of Diminishing Returns" studied, was not population as such but rather the relation between size of population, considered as a stock, and other economic variables. The central question of population was simply quantitative: its size.

This relationship has been turned somewhat on its head by Gary Becker's "Household Economics" which seeks to analyze the family as a reproductive institution by treating its "product" – children – as analogous to a consumer durable and the family as an economic enterprise much like any other. While such an approach may have the merit of integrating the analysis of production and reproduction (a theme we return to below) it has attracted criticism, bordering on derision, from sociologists and other economists alarmed at the kind of assumptions Becker's model requires (Blake 1968; Robinson 1997). At the same time it has inspired rather lurid flights of fancy by those determined to perceive any and every aspect of social life in exclusively market terms, such as the apparently serious claim by Posner and Landes (1978) that low fertility might be addressed by auctioning babies.

DEMOGRAPHY AND THE CONCEPT OF POPULATION

Here, on the contrary, we present an alternative vision of demography and its place in social theory by suggesting that it is precisely in its methodology, usually regarded as merely technical, that demography has a decisive and distinctive theoretical contribution to make. In turn the essence of this methodology is precisely to leave behind the idea of population as a quantitative economic variable, a stock of people, and instead focus on that aspect of population that only demography can properly consider: a population's capacity to reproduce itself or population as a reproductive *system*. From our point of view the early origins of demography as the study of population reproduction are rather to be found in the works of early statisticians such as William Petty, John Gaunt, or Edmund Halley, who developed various tools for analyzing population trends which over time have culminated in the what we see as the essential *theoretical* component of modern demography: *the life table*.

Demography is the study of population. This apparent statement of the obvious conceals an essential ambiguity in the term "population" that is fundamental to understanding demography and its relation to other social sciences and to biology. The term population can be taken to refer to any group of human beings considered as a "stock," as a defined group of persons at a point in time: the number of inhabitants of a territory, a social class, or any group sharing a common characteristic. It is in this sense, for example, that we find the term used in statistics to refer to a wider group from which a sample to be studied has been drawn.

However the term population also has another meaning, rooted in biology, which for us is paramount: a population is something that reproduces itself over time. For human beings reproduction is sexual, and, like other living organisms, humans are mortal. This dependence of human beings as a species upon their sexual genesis has a number of important consequences. First they exist as two sexes, which creates the possibility of both sexual and gender relations. Second the maintenance of the human species over time requires sufficient reproductive sexual activity to produce successive generations of human beings, such that there are enough births to at least partially replace those members of the population who die. In this sense population is not a stock but a flow, so that the composition of the currently living is continually changing as people die and others are born, and the volume at any point in time of the population, considered as a stock, is determined by the rates of mortality and fertility. In this sense there is also only one, global, human population, insofar as its reproduction is not in any way dependent upon any particular segment of that population located in a particular state or territorial unit successfully reproducing itself. When demography, and other social sciences use the term in the plural, this can refer only to administratively defined stocks: typically the inhabitants or sometimes the legal residents or again citizens of states.

This confusion between two discrete meanings of the term population is well illustrated by the attempt of the distinguished demographer Livi Bacci (1990) to define the term. On the one hand he distinguishes a population from "transitory or occasional collectivities" such as might be found in a "sports stadium a factory or an army." A population needs continuity over time, he argues. This requires reproduction and therefore implies relations of reproduction that "unite parents and children and guarantee the succession of generations." However, he adds, a population is also characterized by its specific character and limits, usually, but not exclusively, territorial, but also sometimes ethnic or religious. Populations, however, are not eternal. They rise and fall, he argues, especially as a consequence of migration. They can die out, as a result of chronic low fertility, or by the fusion of previously separate populations. We see here the analytical contradiction resulting from demography's intimate relation with (territorially based) states. States like to regard their inhabitants as populations both for purely instrumental reasons and because it reinforces their banally nationalist "natural" character (Billig 1995). This is true no matter how "transitory or occasional" they may prove to be (and in the *longue durée* of history no state endures for ever).

However, even the most "applied" demography has to recognize that such states are neither hermetically sealed nor historically immutable. One need only look at the map of Europe since 1989 to see a remarkable procession of discursive "populations" appear and disappear in a fashion absolutely analogous to the emptying and filling of a sports stadium. The problem is twofold. Having legs, people move. Reproduction relations spill over state boundaries as migration locates successive generations in supposedly distinct populations. Being social and historical rather than biological entities, states expand and contract territorially, sometimes to nothing at all. Thus to treat a population as a system of reproduction we have to exercise extreme caution in reducing population systems to specific territorial areas, or treating fertility and immigration on the one hand, or mortality and emigration on the other, as distinct phenomena: they may be bound together by the nature of territorial boundaries that may have little direct effect on population dynamics. As we shall see, if we are insufficiently cautious, we can easily fall into essentially racist forms of argument about the natural characteristics of distinct *populations*.

LIFE EXPECTANCY AND THE REPRODUCTIVE REVOLUTION

How can we best distinguish how population(s) reproduce themselves? What is fundamental is not the size of population that a given technological, economic, and social order might sustain. The size of a population, as a stock, tells us nothing about how that population reproduces itself over time, and crucially, the volume of births and associated reproductive effort that goes into maintaining it: what might be called the balance between life and death. We take life expectancy to be perhaps the most important demographic indicator, as it is at the core of reproduction. Over the last two centuries, life expectancy, and thus the manner in which populations reproduce themselves, has undergone a fundamental and unrepeatable change. If life expectancy is short, a population can reproduce itself only by means of sustaining a high rate of births. Conversely, if the means can be found to increase life expectancy, the volume of population at any point in time can be maintained or even increased with a much lower, and even declining, rate of births.

What distinguishes pre-"demographic transition" populations from our contemporary demographic reality almost everywhere beyond sub-Saharan Africa is that in the former the balance between life and death was a thoroughly wretched one: low life expectancy and high mortality rates at early ages meant a constant struggle to keep the birth rate, and thus the supply of generally miserably short lives, sufficiently high to maintain the population. This struggle was periodically aggravated by a variety of demographic crises: epidemics, poor harvests, warfare. The Black Death, which probably killed off about one-third of the population of Europe in the fourteenth century, is well known. However, it is often forgotten that as recently as 1918–19 "Spanish flu" killed anywhere between 30 and 100 million people worldwide. Troop movements associated with World War I accelerated and globalized its reach. It probably had its origin in the US, but killed between 7 and 17 million in India, and wiped out one-quarter of the populations of Alaska and Samoa (Patterson and Kyle 1991; Potter 2001).[1] The historical breakthrough to demographic security is very recent. In the most fortunate states it stretches back two centuries. In most it occurred only in the course of the twentieth century: for many only in the last few decades. An indication of this progress is given by figure 22.1, which traces female life expectancy at birth for different regions of the world over the last half-century.

The demographic transition in Spain reveals the nature of this breakthrough with particular clarity, as it occurred relatively late and rapidly, and with good enough statistical records to allow us to chart its course precisely. Between the 1880s and 1940s, life expectancy at birth doubled from 37 to 76 years. Life expectancies at birth deal in averages which can never reveal the full story. A better measure is to take the age by which half of an original birth cohort have met their deaths. Until the generations born towards the end of the 1880s (and therefore reaching this age in first two decades of the last century) this age was less than 25. Just over half a century later those born just after the end of the civil war could wait until their eighties before they had witnessed the death of half their peers (Cabré i Pla 1999).

Much valuable effort has gone into exploring the causes of this dramatic, and increasingly global, change and the relative importance of the contributions of

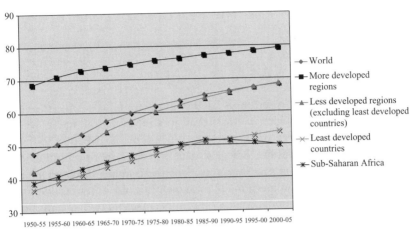

Figure 22.1 Female life expectancy in years at birth, world and regions 1950–2005
Source: United Nations Population Division. Population Database 2006 revision.

technological and economic change, improvements in public health, medical knowledge, and so on (Boserup 1996; McKeown 1979). However, this has had, as a less welcome side effect, the tendency to see this demographic change as exclusively a "result" caused by other social and economic factors. This has been facilitated by the willingness of demography to eschew theory and keep "explanations" where they belong: in other disciplines, especially economics. Much less effort has gone into exploring the consequences of the other side of this two-way relationship: the impact on economic and social development of an unprecedented fall in the volume of social effort devoted to population reproduction (Peréz Diaz 2004). As we argue below, we think that demography, and in particular the changing dynamics of population reproduction, holds the key to explaining the unprecedented pace and volume of change in gender relations in post-transition societies. This does not mean, of course, substituting one determinist explanation with another, such that demographic change becomes the "cause" of modernity. It does, however, mean taking account of the vital demographic component of social and economic change without which it is almost impossible to understand key aspects of modern society.

Again the case of Spain makes our point particularly clearly, but the story for the rest of Europe is basically similar. By 1990 the crude birth rate in Spain was less than one-third of what it had been one hundred years earlier: about 10 births per 1,000 women each year, compared to over 35. Yet throughout this period, except for the crises caused by flu epidemic and the civil war, there never ceased to be more births than deaths in the population, such that population doubled over this time (Blanes, Gil, and Pérez 1996).

Such a spectacular result was achieved because the efficiency of the reproductive system underwent a fundamental transformation, rather like the shift from a steam engine to an internal combustion engine, rooted above all in the reduction of infant and child mortality. This had two results, direct and indirect. Directly, less early mortality meant longer lives. We might compare the situation to that of a hotel where the average length of stay of its guests increased. When the guests stay longer

Table 22.1 Expectation of life at birth, Vietnam, 1950–2005

	Males	Females
1950–1955	39.1	41.8
1955–1960	41.3	44.6
1960–1965	43.5	47.4
1965–1970	45.7	50.2
1970–1975	47.7	53.1
1975–1980	53.7	58.1
1980–1985	56.8	61.2
1985–1990	61.1	64.9
1990–1995	66.1	69.6
1995–2000	69.0	72.4
2000–2005	71.2	74.9

Source: United Nations Population Division, Population Database 2006 revision.

the hotel manager has fewer vacated beds to fill with new arrivals. Indeed, unless the flow of new guests slows down dramatically, the hotel would soon be overflowing. The demographic transition thus quadrupled global population across the twentieth century. Indirectly, fewer female deaths in the years before reaching their fertile years meant that fewer potentially life-producing lives were "wasted" from the perspective of the reproductive system. This means that fertility rates and mortality rates themselves do not capture the full impact of the change. The key indicator was in fact identified in 1960s by the French demographer Louis Henry (1965) as the rate of reproduction of *years of life*.

A shown in figure 22.1, this fundamental change has spread the world over, with the exception of sub-Saharan Africa, where the AIDS pandemic has reversed what had always been a halting growth in life expectancy. An illuminating example is Vietnam. Between 1965 and 1973 the USA dropped more bombs on this small country than were used in World War II. An estimated 1.4 million Vietnamese combatants and between 1 million and 4 million civilians were killed, and up to 4 million suffered dioxin poising resulting from the use of chemical defoliants such as agent orange. Despite this onslaught, life expectancy continued to *rise*, to levels approaching those of Europe, as table 22.1 shows.

Overall, some of this increased efficiency resulted in the unprecedented expansion of world population (shown in figure 22.2), but, as in the case of Spain, improvements in efficiency have usually been translated fairly quickly into declining fertility. For example, the fertility rate for the world as a whole is now approaching the level of the United States in the 1950s. This revolution, which demographers usually call the "demographic transition" but which we prefer to call the "reproductive revolution" (MacInnes and Pérez Díaz 2005), has had three main consequences, crucial to modernity, which have also tended to be obscured by the concentration on the exploration of its non-demographic "causes." These are a fall in the strategic political importance of fertility, or sustaining a high birth rate; the decline of patriarchy and direct state control of women; and a transformation in the age structure of populations (population aging). We will look at each of these in turn, attempting

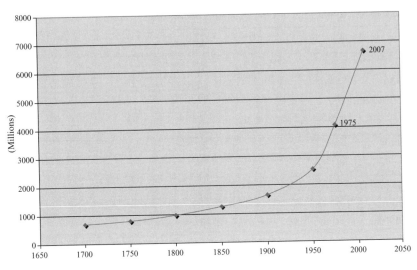

Figure 22.2 World population, 1700–2007
Source: UN Population Fund.

to show how what we see as critical demographic theory can correct the frequently alarmist and usually incorrect analyses of these topics that issue not least from demographers themselves. However before we do so, let us return briefly to what we see as the theoretical core of demography: the "currency" of reproduction: years of life.

YEARS OF LIFE: AGE GROUPS, GENERATIONS AND LIFE TABLES

In the social sciences we make use of the concept of age groups so regularly that they end up becoming an object of investigation in themselves. But although we often talk of the characteristics, behavior, and changes in "age groups," such groups have no more material an existence than Hobbes's mushrooms. Today's 14-year-olds will be 15 next year, and 50 in another thirty-six. Such use of the word "age" is a perversion of language, because it ends up converting it into some kind of fixed, unchanging, reality through which individuals pass, when it is the individuals who are real, and it is the ages that pass through them. The distinction between ages and the individuals who have them is fundamental. We can, of course, equate age group and life course, imagining that a cross-sectional division of age groups also gives us a picture of a succession of life stages, from infant to senior citizen, but the cost of doing so is to rule out that which we are usually concerned to investigate in the first place: *social change*.

Considered as a birth cohort or generation in the demographic sense, individuals' ages become closer to their authentic meaning: sequential, temporary, stages of a life course. An early appreciation of the sociological significance of the life table approach is that of Ryder (1965), who saw the *cohort* – a group of people *born* at the same calendar time – as the key concept of demography:

the passage of time is identified for the individual constituent elements as well as for the population as a whole. . . . Individual entries and exits are dated, and the difference between date of entry and date of observation, for the individual, is his age at that time. Age is the central variable in the demographic model. It identifies birth cohort membership . . . It is a measure of the interval of time spent within the population, and thus of exposure to the risk of occurrence of the event of leaving the population, and more generally is a surrogate for the experience which causes changing probabilities of behavior of various kinds. Age as the passage of personal time is, in short, the link between the history of the individual and the history of the population

The problem of course, is that given the hegemony of the one-off cross-sectional survey (and not without reason: it is quick and cheap) we often do not have data by birth cohort. This is slowly changing as information technology innovation has rendered both longitudinal and repeated cross-sectional survey data easier and cheaper to collect, but for the moment at least, the transversal view of society dominates, and not only for technical or methodological reasons. Politically, the transversal survey yields fast, affordable, policy-relevant results. When a week is a long time in politics, a genuine understanding of the roots of social change lies further down the agenda than immediate policy-relevant period indicators. Ideologically, the kind of dataset produced by the survey is a perfect analog of the "nation" reproduced in the minds of its members via their perception of the way transverse simultaneity links their diverse individual experiences as they march onward together down calendrical, homogeneous, empty time (Anderson 1991: 25–34). Homogeneous empty time of the kind in which men might indeed spring up "like mushrooms" and in which not only the popular but also the scientific imagination could find it not only possible but obvious to imagine the "people" as a constant, measured *inter alia* by its volume, contained by the borders of "its" territory and quite unaffected by the continual sea-like change in its composition.

It is here that demography furnishes us with a key analytical tool: the life table, and the Lexis diagram, named after its nineteenth-century "inventor" although Vandeschrick (2001) suggests that this is a misnomer (figure 22.3). Lexis diagrams effectively present three variables in one plane, by plotting both calendrical time (on the horizontal axis) and "personal time" or generational age (on the vertical axis). The experience of each generation thus appears as a 45-degree line in the chart, and various characteristics can be computed for different coordinates rather than the vertical slice presented by the results of a cross-sectional survey at a particular point in time. It is an extremely useful tool since if we have sufficient data (and one of the merits of demography's association with the state is often the availability of a great range of high-quality data) it allows us to separate out the effects of age and historical time, and thus look at the experience of successive generations across the life course, thus dispensing with static "age groups."

This is especially useful when we consider the impact of the reproductive revolution, for one if its effects, as a direct result of the democratization of longer life expectancy, is not only to change the distribution of "age groups" in a society, but also, by altering the life courses of successive generations, substantially to change the characteristics of those who comprise these age groups across calendrical time. As a result, what has often been a useful method in sociology –

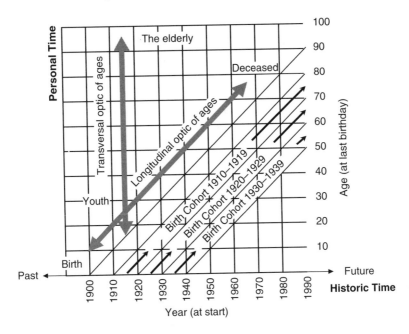

Figure 22.3 A lexis diagram

using the results of cross-sectional survey broken down by age to construct a model of what a generational life course might look like – becomes increasingly unreliable because of the pace of both demographic and social change. Just as the experience of today's youth does not reflect the past life course of older people, neither does the experience of today's older people tell us much about the future of today's youth. This might appear to carry stating the obvious to new heights, but on the contrary, it is an "insight" that constantly gets forgotten. Let us look at some examples.

POPULATION PYRAMIDS

Perhaps the best-known image of demography is that of diagrams depicting the age structure of a population as a pyramid with a distinctive shape. The rapid changes experienced by these pyramids in recent years highlights the demographic transformations we have referred to. Everywhere the weight of the old and so-called "oldest old" in the population is growing, and that of the young decreasing, resulting in a change in the shape of these pyramids from a triangle to rectangle, as shown in figure 22.4. This is referred to by demographers and others as "population aging," usually summoning up fears of whether the "dependency" of the old must pose an unsustainable burden on the welfare state, where it exists. The imminent retiral of the "baby boom" cohorts adds to this pessimism (Demeny 2003; Lutz, O'Neill, and Sherbov 2003).

However, precisely because they are based on *age groups*, this is a rather distorted way to portray what might be thought of as modernity's greatest achievement: the generalization of longer life expectancy. The pyramids tell us about social change

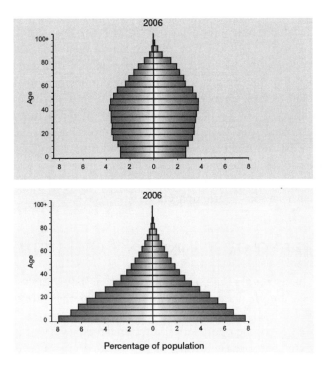

Figure 22.4 Population pyramid diagrams from the UN Population Division's Population Ageing 2006 Wallchart (UN publication ST/ESA/SER.V251). Reproduced by permission

only so long as we assume that the characteristics of the component layers of the pyramid do not change over time. Only if we confuse age and historical time can we even imagine the phenomenon of population "aging" in the first place. Age is not and *cannot* be a characteristic of a population. It is a characteristic of those individuals who comprise it. A population might come to have relatively more older people within it, but that is a very different thing, especially if, as we have already suggested, social change means that the characteristics of age groups are far from static. The power of this dubious metaphor lies rather in what it manages to imply: that a population with a higher average age is not a great achievement, but rather some kind of problem. That aging populations, like aging individuals, are slow, less "flexible" or dynamic, in decline or about to die out. This perhaps reflects a rather older propensity in demography to regard at least some early deaths as desirable, from Malthus through to its flirtation with eugenics in the first half of the last century. It is politically far easier to summon up fear of "population aging" in abstract terms than to suggest that it would be better if grannie or grandad died sooner.

There are two simple points to make about population aging, that have been largely overlooked in the contemporary debate. Much of the concern focuses on the calculation of "dependency ratios" based on the ratio of those of "working age" (16 to 64) to those aged 65 or over. However, age structure has an increasingly weak relationship to real dependency ratios because economic activity patterns have altered much faster. The feminization of employment has almost doubled women's employment in Europe over the last half-century. Meanwhile the vast increase in higher education and training has meant that youngsters enter the labor market much later than before (Mason and Jensen 1995; Peréz Diaz 2004). Conversely a rapidly falling proportion of older workers stay on till the formal age of retirement. Increased living standards, the more rapid accumulation of assets across the life course, and expanding opportunities for leisure encourage them to swap income for time. The net result of these changes has been that the ratio of those in employment to the rest of the population has been positive or neutral across the last half-century in most European countries. The second is that this ghostly army of the "dependent" old is actually a vast supplier of income, assets, and time, both to younger generations and to each other (MacInnes 2006). The caring needs of elderly people are substantially met by their peers. The biggest single source of childcare in Europe after parents themselves is . . . grandparents.

The Strategic Importance of Fertility

Modern states have always had a keen interest in population questions both because they need an adequate quantity of recruits for their armies or labor for their offices and factories and also because they fear the prospect of any relative decline in the "quality" of their population compared to other states. In the nineteenth and early twentieth centuries such fears were expressed in straightforwardly racial and eugenic language, across the political spectrum (MacInnes and Pérez Díaz 2007; Solway 1990; Szreter 1984; Teitelbaum and Winter 1985). They now tend to be expressed in debates about the quality of the education and training systems.

In the 1920s and 1930s the impact of the fertility decline released by the reproductive revolution brought forth alarmist claims from both progressive and conservative analysts about the impending "death" of the nation, either through demographic weakness or military defeat (Spengler 1926). The intellectual architect of the UK welfare state, William Beveridge, could assert that the "revolutionary fall of fertility among the European races within the past fifty years, while it had some mysterious features, was due in the main to practices as deliberate as infanticide" (1925: 10). Keynes (1937) speculated about the "Economic effects of a declining population" in *The Eugenics Review*. Alva Myrdal virtually invented the Scandinavian welfare state model by arguing cogently in her 1939 work *Nation and Family* that, while moral campaigns denouncing "family limitation" simply spread knowledge about contraception, the thorough collectivization of childrearing costs might deliver a different result (Myrdal 1968).

Differential fertility (the phenomenon whereby those with higher levels of education or higher incomes tended to be among the first to have smaller families) awakened the specter of national or racial degeneration and brought forth a eugenic response that took a long time to finally wither away. The rise of Nazism and the experience of the Holocaust made directly eugenic language less easy to use; however, in Britain its swansong came as late as Sir Keith Joseph's notorious 1974 Egbaston speech:

> The balance of our population, our human stock is threatened. . . . a high and rising proportion of children are being born to mothers least fitted to bring children into the

world and bring them up. They are born to mothers who were first pregnant in ado-
lescence in social classes 4 and 5. Many of these girls are unmarried, many are deserted
or divorced or soon will be. Some are of low intelligence, most of low educational att
ainment.... They are producing problem children, the future unmarried mothers,
delinquents, denizens of our borstals, sub-normal educational establishments, prisons,
hostels for drifters. Yet these mothers, the under-twenties in many cases, single parents,
from classes 4 and 5, are now producing a third of all births.

Nowadays this discourse tends to be presented in terms of the preservation
of national culture, the provision of adequate education, the problems of integration, and so on. Either way the conclusion reached is broadly similar. Fertility
is falling below replacement level in almost every affluent society, with the possible
exception of the United States (Bongaarts 2002; Caldwell and Schindlmeyer
2003; Frejka and Calot 2001; Frejka and Ross 2001; Goldstein, Lutz, and Testa
2003; Lesthaeghe and Willems 1999). Too low a rate of (the right sort of) fertility
must aggravate population aging and, in the longer term, threaten national eviscera-
tion via population decline (Chesnais 1998; Grant et al. 2004). Yet such an
argument merely threatens to reproduce the interwar debate about differential class
fertility and racial degeneration in international and explicitly racist terms. There
is no global fertility shortage. The fear, although it is rarely presented directly as
such, is rather that "they" are having too many children, while "we" are not having
enough.

There are two issues to consider here. One, as we have indicated, is the tendency
to confuse population as a reproductive system with the stock of people in a state,
such that both demographers and politicians can speak about a state's "population
replacement level" of fertility as though immigration did not exist. The other is a
struggle between employers and states, conducted within a discourse of "work–life
balance" over how much each should bear the costs of the further socialization of
childcare costs.

After the interlude of the baby boom of the 1950s and 1960s, fertility fell to new
lows throughout Europe, especially in the Mediterranean and former Soviet countries. This led to renewed interest in natalist policies and a rash of ad hoc measures
by state and regional governments to encourage more or earlier babies, either
through fiscal transfers or measures to facilitate "work–life balance" (McDonald
2005; MacInnes 2006; MacInnes and Pérez Díaz 2007; Neyer 2003; OECD 2001).
Many of these unwittingly repeat the essentials of Myrdal's early study. Fertility
change has been closely tied up with other social changes, such as a drift of most
major early life transitions (termination of education, entry to the labor market,
emancipation from the parental home, formation of a stable partnership, parenthood) to later ages, a compression in the length of men's working lives (fewer hours
per year for fewer years) and, of course, a rapid and substantial expansion in
women's education and employment. As notable as the feminization of employment
and the collapse of the male breadwinner system has been the collapse of marriage
as an institution. Not only has the proportion of children born outside of marriage
exploded (so that in many European countries only a minority of children are born
to married parents), "legitimacy" has, for the first time, become almost irrelevant,
divorce rates have risen steadily, and many states, by recognizing gay marriage, have

explicitly broken the link between the marriage contract and sexual reproduction. This led many conservative analysts to lament the decline of the family (Davis 1937; Fukuyama 1999; Lasch 1977), and more radical analysts to discern a "transformation of intimacy" (Beck and Beck-Gernsheim 1995; Giddens 1992) and states to puzzle over how women might best be encouraged to be both mothers and workers (Brewster and Rindfuss 2000; Castles 2003).

However, the longitudinal perspective afforded by a critical demography suggests quite a different conclusion. It is hardly surprising if the leap in the efficiency in reproduction has freed labor up to go elsewhere, in much the same way as technological innovation and economic progress has done in agriculture and industry. Societies with high fertility and mortality had been universally characterized by systematic restrictions to any alternative use of what was in some ways their most important means of production: women's bodies. This ranged from the direct regulation of reproductive sexuality through such institutions as marriage, proscriptions against adultery or other sexual activity outside marriage, restriction of divorce and the prohibition of abortion and other forms of contraception through to the prevention of women entering the public sphere on anything like equal terms to men. However, as the progress of liberal thought found it harder to resist feminist argument (Mann 1994) it also gradually found it less *necessary* to do so. Indeed, states faced with labor shortages and over-full employment in the long boom of 1945 to 1970 played an active role in the feminization of employment. Over the course of the twentieth century, and especially in its final third, states gradually decided that they had "no business in the bedroom" (a phrase coined by future Canadian prime minister Pierre Trudeau in a 1967 television interview) and controls over sexuality, both plastic and reproductive, were relaxed or abolished.

Nor is it surprising that the much looser social control of sexual reproduction made possible by the fruits of the reproductive revolution has started to rob the family (and especially its patriarchal head) of the power it previously enjoyed, as well as rendering its internal affairs increasingly public. But de-industrialization and what might be called "de-familization" have one fundamental difference. Much longer lives means the survival at the same point in time of more generations. This further changes the distribution of reproductive work as parents and grandparents and other family members increasingly share the burden. Orthodox demography has tended to understand this development in terms of the second demographic transition, whereby changes in values drove renewed changes in demographic behavior (Inglehart 1975; Van de Kaa 1987). However, in our view the relationship might better be seen the other way around: an utterly changed system of population reproduction made materially possible what had previously been only a utopia: the destruction of the foundations of patriarchy and the generalization, for the first time, of the idea of the fundamental equality of the sexes.

It is often forgotten just how recent has been both the withdrawal of the state from the bedroom and the dismantling of the systematic restriction of alternatives to motherhood for women via "equal rights" policies. Both have been made possible by the demographic transformations that the reproductive revolution has ushered in. If we wish to understand why patriarchy has weakened so dramatically in many states in a few decades after reigning supreme for millennia, demography is a good place to start.

THE REGULATION OF FERTILITY AT "HOME" AND ABROAD

In the course of the twentieth century governments gradually discovered that rapidly decreasing fertility was compatible not only with population stability but also population growth, while the upward turn in fertility rates in the "baby boom" after World War II drew their attention away from domestic demographic issues to that of differential fertility within a global perspective. In the climate of the Cold War it was feared that too rapid population growth in the "Third World" might choke off economic growth and open the door to the spread of communism. This was accompanied by alarmist predictions of what "population explosion" might happen if mortality there continued to fall but fertility remained unchecked (e.g. Ehrlich 1968). As a result attention within demography switched to the search for a model of the demographic transition that might provide policy recipes for the achievement of the swiftest possible fertility falls in "developing" countries (Hodgson 1988; Szreter 1993). One of the largest ever social science projects was launched at the University of Princeton to mine the history of Europe for what insights could be gleaned from the fall of fertility there (Coale 1986).

Old ideas often die hard, however. Demographers, politicians, and others struggle to free themselves from the idea that low or "below replacement" fertility is a problem, and search for "blockages" to higher fertility, chiefly in the form of arguments that the relative economic cost of children has increased, or that employment has become less compatible with parenting. There is no doubt that even in a socially protected and regulated labor market children impose restrictions and burdens on parents, particularly working ones. However, the question is not whether these exist, but whether any change in their relative weight might account for falling fertility. The answer is controversial, but our view is a resounding "no." There is a simpler explanation for falling fertility. Fewer people choose to become parents, and parents in turn have fewer children because, for almost the first time in history, they have the freedom to make this choice.

Part of the problem here is rooted in demography's continued reliance on other disciplines for its theoretical ideas, rather than paying sufficient attention to the explanatory power of its own contribution. It is all too easy for sociology, economics, or political science to take a "variable" such as fertility, from demography and seek explanations for it – whether in the form of accounting for the decline of fertility thorough changes in economic behavior or values and attitudes, or searching for policy remedies for what is wrongly assumed to be a social problem. But such efforts tend to overlook the way the laws of operation of the reproductive system have been transformed by the reproductive revolution and the withering of patriarchy.

THE CONTEMPORARY SITUATION OF DEMOGRAPHY

Paradoxically, the "atheoretical" and empirical character of demography has reinforced its scientific character and saved it from disciplinary disintegration. Because of its applied character and intimate relation with the state, and the way in which the latter, both at central and local level, has developed ever more rigorous systems for the collection and recording of reliable data, demography has been able to base itself on data which is carefully defined, exists in very long time series, and lends itself to comparative analysis. It is the only field of social science in which we can draw upon regular census data: that is, data on (almost) all individuals, rather than on samples. The fact that states are interested in having accurate and timely data on the number, whereabouts, and other basic characteristics of their inhabitants has led to the development not only of national but also international databases with a steadily increasing range of valuable information. To this can be added other information from more specific official surveys on such issues as the labor market, health, crime, household composition, and so on, including surveys with an invaluable longitudinal or panel component, such as the European Community Household Panel Study or its successor, European Union Statistics on Income and Living Conditions. Statistical methods for analyzing this data have been revolutionized by the development of information technology that facilitates calculations and analysis that simply could not be undertaken only a few years ago, as well as making such analysis ever more accessible to the social scientist with only a minimum of quantitative expertise. It has also led to new techniques such as Event History Analysis, which has its roots in biology and epidemiology, but is now being applied to great effect in demography and sociology.

However, this tremendous advance at the level of the availability and coverage of data and techniques for its analysis has not been accompanied by a corresponding development of demographic theory. Instead it has been left to the economists, from Malthus to Boserup, Easterlin, and, above all, Becker, to explore and develop theories of demographic change, while a somewhat lesser role has been taken by sociologists, such as Dumont and later Kingsley Davis, Alva Myrdal, and, above all, Talcott Parsons (1956). This helps to explain why, although there is universal recognition that demographic change has been a fundamental aspect of the rise of modernity, particularly the explosion of world population that started in the eighteenth century and now appears to be reaching its conclusion, this demographic revolution has always been seen as an effect of other, more basic, social and economic changes, rather than some kind of revolutionary change in its own right. Our argument here, however, is that the reproductive revolution has been one equal in status and importance to the already well-known and discussed political and economic revolutions (Hobsbawm 1962).

DEMOGRAPHY IN THE ERA OF POPULATION MATURITY

The end of the explosive growth of global population is now in sight. As a result the demographic map of the world, in terms of the distribution and demographic behavior of population, has been in constant evolution, and the themes of interest and discussion in demography has undergone almost constant change. Let us focus on what seem to us to be the two further key areas of development, beyond the issue of population aging and fertility decline that we have already discussed.

Life expectancy

Current attention has come to be focused on what, if any, are the limits to the growth of life expectancy. Recent statistical studies of mortality in what might be called the "oldest old," those surviving to 100 years and more, have questioned the classical assumption of Gompertz that the probability of dying increased exponentially with age. What has been more recently discovered it that at very advanced ages the probability of dying changes from exponential to linear. This apparently trivial finding in fact has tremendous theoretical implications, for if the survival curve is not logistic, neither does it have an upper limit. Any final limit to longevity ceases to be predictable (Horiuchi and Wilmoth 1998). However, the rectangularization of survival curves, together with quite unexpected advances in the survival rates of the very old, have given rise to new unknowns that it has become urgent to address, not least for practical purposes, especially making any reliable population projections. This question has theoretical relevance too, insofar as it has led to discussion between evolutionary biologists and sociologists (Gavrilov and Gavrilova 2001). With the rise of longevity, increased interest has focused on morbidity and what has come to be called "healthy life expectancy" or the number of years people can expect to live in good health. Changing ages of death have also changed the pattern of pathologies that bring it about, together with patterns of ill health in general. This has come to be known as the epidemiological transition, with obvious implications for the demand for health care, and other public services.

Migration

For the first time in history, more people in the world now live in cities than in the country, while the nature of urban spatial mobility has changed substantially even over the last two decades. The global spread of the reproductive revolution first experienced in Europe has altered geostrategic global politics: the Chinese and Indian states are no longer potential but actual world power players Added to this, the technology of mobility has revolutionized international migration, revealing the vast distance between states' desire to control population movements and their empirical ability to do so. At the same time new empirical data sources have opened up, following states' needs to monitor this process, and try to understand and predict future population movements.

This process of migration raises hitherto underexplored theoretical questions for demography as a discipline as soon as it treats population at anything less than a global level, for it raises the question of the logical basis of the frontier used to define any movement as migration. Here states' capacity to marry the nationalist imagination to state regulation and the technical tools of analysis of demography comes up against the reality of people's increasing mobility (Adams and Kasakoff 2004) as economic development and technical innovation have brought down transport costs, while the internet and innovation in information technology has revolutionized communications and transformed what has been variously called time-space convergence, compression or distanciation (Giddens 1990; Harvey 1989; Janelle 1969). Urry's (2000) suggestion that such mobility renders classical sociology virtually irrelevant has been dismissed as what Michael Mann has referred to as "Globaloney" by Favell (2001). Held et al. (1999) and Torpey (2000) have shown how the world of the late nineteenth century, before more affluent states started to police and seal their borders, may have been still more mobile than that of the early twenty-first. Zelinsky (1971), in a work that deserves more attention than it has received, has made the useful suggestion that demography might think in terms of a migration transition.

CONCLUSION

We have argued that there are two main reasons why social theory ought to pay more attention to demography than it has perhaps done in the past. The first is empirical. We are living through a period of very rapid demographic change bound up with the processes of modernization that has seen an upward leap in life expectancy whose upper limits still remain far from clear. This revolution has ushered in other demographic changes such as declining fertility and nuptiality, the redistribution of world population, and vast changes in migration patterns both within and between states. These demographic changes have manifold and profound social consequences, such as alterations in the structure and power of the family, the decline of patriarchy, intergenerational relations, and the future shape of globalization. The second is theoretical. By focusing on longitudinal processes, the analytical tools of a critical demography, which we have argued can be seen as rooted in the development of the life table and its analogs, have much to offer social theory trying to understand processes of social change. It can do this through its capacity to distinguish different dimensions of time and thus bring biography and history together in a way that does not "flatten" individuals' experiences into the kind of structural snapshot of society offered by the one-off transversal survey. By remembering, like Filmer, that society comprises mortals with a sexual genesis, and not just social roles or positions in structure or discourse that need filling, we have a better chance of understanding contemporary social change.

Note

1   Ironically it was called "Spanish" flu because the non-belligerent status of that country freed its press from the censorship that restricted reporting of the epidemic in combatant states.

Bibliography

Adams, J. W., and Kasakoff, A. B. (2004) "Spillovers, Subdivisions, and Flows: Questioning the Usefulness of 'Bounded Container' as the Dominant Spatial Metaphor in Demography," in S. Szreter, H. Sholkamy, and A. Dharmalingmam (eds.), *Categories and Contexts: Anthropological and Historical Studies in Critical Demography*. New York: Oxford University Press.
Anderson, B. (1991) *Imagined Communities*, 2nd edn. London: Verso.

Beck, U., and Beck-Gernsheim, E. (1995) *The Normal Chaos of Love*. Cambridge: Polity.

Becker, G. S. (1960) "An Economic Analysis of Fertility," in *Demographic Change in Developed Countries*. Princeton: National Bulletin of Economic Research.

Becker, G. S. (1991) *A Treatise on the Family*. Cambridge, MA: Harvard University Press.

Beveridge, W. H. (1925) "The Fall of Fertility among the European Races." *Economica* 5: 10–27.

Billig, M. (1995) *Banal Nationalism*. London: Sage.

Blake, J. (1968) "Are Babies Consumer Durables? A Critique of the Economic Theory of Reproductive Motivation." *Population Studies* 22(1): 5–25.

Blanes, A, Gil, F. and Pérez, J. (1996) *Población y actividad en España: evolución y perspectivas*. Colección Estudios e Informes, 5. Barcelona: Servicio de Estudios de "la Caixa."

Bongaarts, J. (2002) "The End of the Fertility Transition in the Developed World." *Population and Development Review* 28(3): 419–43.

Boserup, E. (1996) "Development Theory: An Analytical Framework and Selected Application." *Population and Development Review* 22(3): 505–15.

Brewster, K. L., and Rindfuss, R. R. (2000) "Fertility and Women's Employment in Industrialized Nations." *Annual Review of Sociology* 26: 271–96.

Cabré i Pla (1999) *El sistema català de reproducció*. Barcelona: Proa.

Caldwell, J. C., and Shindlmayr, T. (2003) "Explanations of Fertility Crisis in Modern Societies: A Search for Commonalities." *Population Studies* 57: 241–63.

Castles, F. (2003) "The World Turned Upside Down: Below Replacement Fertility, Changing Preferences and Family-Friendly Public Policy in 21 OECD Countries." *Journal of European Social Policy* 13(3): 209–27.

Chesnais, J. C. (1998) "Below Replacement Fertility in the European Union (EU-15): Facts and Policies 1960–1997." *Review of Population and Social Policy* 7.

Coale, A. J. (1986) "The Decline of Fertility in Europe since the Eighteenth Century as a Chapter in Demographic History," in A. J. Coale and S. Cotts-Watkins (eds.), *The Decline of Fertility in Europe: The Revised Proceedings of a Conference on the Princeton European Fertility Project*. Princeton: Princeton University Press.

Davis, K. (1937) Reproductive Institutions and the Pressure for Population." *Sociological Review* 29: 284–306.

Demeny, P. (1972) "Early Fertility Decline in Austria-Hungary: A Lesson in Demographic Transition," in D. Glass and R. Revelle (eds.), *Population and Social Change*. London: Edward Arnold.

Demeny, P. (2003) "Population Policy Dilemmas in Europe at the Dawn of the Twenty-First Century." *Population and Development Review* 29(1): 1–28.

Ehrlich, P. R. (1968) *The Population Bomb*. New York: Ballantine Books.

Favell, A. (2001) "Migration, Mobility and Globaloney: Metaphors and Rhetoric in the Sociology of Globalisation." *Global Networks* 1(4): 389–98.

Filmer, R (1991 [1680]) *Patriarcha and Other Writings*, ed. J. P. Sommerville. Cambridge: Cambridge University Press.

Frejka, T., and Calot, G. (2001) "Cohort Reproductive Patterns in Low-Fertility Countries." *Population and Development Review* 27(1): 103–32.

Frejka, T., and Ross, J. (2001) "Paths to Sub-Replacement Fertility: The Empirical Evidence." *Population and Development Review* 27(supplement): 213–54.

Fukuyama, F. (1999) *The Great Disruption*. Profile Books: London.

Gavrilov, L. A, and Gavrilova, N. S. (2001) "Biodemographic Perspectives on Human Longevity." *Population: An English Selection*, 13(1): 197–221.

Giddens, A. (1990) *The Consequences of Modernity*. Cambridge: Polity.

Giddens, A. (1992) *The Transformation of Intimacy: Love Sexuality and Eroticism in Modern Societies*. Cambridge: Polity.

Giddens, A. (2006) *Sociology*. Cambridge: Polity.

Goldstein, J., Lutz, W., and Testa, M. (2003) "The Emergence of Sub-Replacement Family Size Ideals in Europe." *Population Research and Policy Review* 22(5–6): 479–96.

Grant, J., Hoorens, S., Sivadasan, S., van het Loo, M., DeVanzo, J., Hale, L., Gibson, S., and Butz, W. (2004) *Low Fertility and Population Ageing: Causes, Consequences, and Policy Options*. Santa Monica: RAND.

Harvey, D. (1989) *The Condition of Postmodernity*. Oxford: Blackwell.

Held, D., McGrew, A., Goldblatt, D., and Perraton, J. (1999) *Global Transformations: Politics, Economics and Culture*. Cambridge: Polity.

Henry, L. (1965) "Réfléxions sur les taux de réproduction." *Population* 1: 53–76.

Hobbes, T. (1984 [1651]) *De Cive*. Oxford: Clarendon Press.

Hobsbawm, E. J. (1962) *The Age of Revolution 1789–1848*. London: Weidenfeld & Nicolson.

Hodgson, D. (1983) "Demography as Social Science and Policy Science." *Population and Development Review* 9: 1–34.

Hodgson, D. (1988) "Orthodoxy and Revisionism in American Demography." *Population and Development Review* 14: 541–69.

Hodgson, D. (1991) "The Ideological Origins of the Population Association of America." *Population and Development Review* 17: 1–34.

Horiuchi, S. and Wilmoth, J. R. (1998) "Deceleration in the Age Pattern of Mortality at Older Ages." *Demography* 35(4): 391–412.

Inglehart, R. (1975) *The Silent Revolution: Changing Values and Political Styles among Western Publics*. Princeton: Princeton University Press.

Janelle, D. (1969) "Spatial Reorganization: A Model and Concept." *Annals of the Association of American Geographers* 59: 348–64.

Keynes, J. M. (1937) "Some Economic Consequences of a Declining Population." *The Eugenics Review* 29(1): 13–17.

Lasch, C. (1977) *Haven in a Heartless World: The Family Besieged*. New York: W. W. Norton.

Laslett, P. (1991) *A Fresh Map of Life: The Emergence of the Third Age*. Cambridge, MA: Harvard University Press.

Lesthaeghe, R. (2001) *Postponement and Recuperation: Recent Fertility Trends and Forecasts in Six Western European Countries*. Interuniversity Papers in Demography. Brussels: Interface Demography (Soco) Vrije Universiteit Brussel.

Lesthaeghe, R., and Willems, P. (1999) "Is Low Fertility a Temporary Phenomenon in the European Union?" *Population and Development Review* 25(2): 211–28.

Livi Bacci, M. (1990) *Introduzione all demografia*. Turin: Loescher.

Lutz, W., O'Neill, B., and Scherbov, S. (2003) "Europe's Population at a Turning Point." *Science* 299(28): 1991–2.

McDonald, P. (2001) *Theory Pertaining to Low Fertility*. International Union for the Scientific Study of Population Working Group on Low Fertility Conference "International Perspectives on Low Fertility: Trends, Theories and Policies," Tokyo.

McDonald, P. (2005) "Fertility and the State: The Efficacy of Policy." IUSSP XXV International Population Conference, Tours, France.

MacInnes, J. (1998) *The End of Masculinity* Milton Keynes: Open University Press.

MacInnes, J. (2006) "Work–Life Balance in Europe: A Response to the Baby Bust or Reward for the Baby Boomers?" *European Societies* 8(2): 223–49.

MacInnes, J., and Pérez Díaz, J. (2005) "The Reproductive Revolution." IUSSP XXV International Population Conference, Tours, France.

MacInnes, J., and Pérez Díaz, J. (2007) " 'Low' Fertility and Population Replacement in Scotland." *Population Space and Place* 13(1): 2–21.

Mackenzie, D. (1981) *Statistics in Britain, 1865–1930: The Social Construction of Scientific Knowledge*. Edinburgh: Edinburgh University Press.

McKeown, T. (1979) *The Role of Medicine: Dream, Mirage or Nemesis*. Princeton: Princeton University Press.

Mann, M. (1994) "Persons, Households, Families, Lineages, Genders, Classes and Nations," in *The Polity Reader in Gender Studies*. Cambridge: Polity.

Marsh, C. (1982) *The Survey Method*. London: Allen & Unwin.

Mason, K. O. (1997) "Explaining Fertility Transitions. *Demography* 34(4): 443–54.

Mason, K. O., and Jensen, A.-M. (eds.) (1995) *Gender and Family Change in Industrialized Countries*. Oxford: Clarendon Press.

Mills, M. (2005) " 'Theory and 'Demography': A Longitudinal Empirical Analysis from 1964 to 2004." IUSSP XXV International Population Conference, Tours, France.

Myrdal, A. (1968) *Nation and Family*. Cambridge, MA: MIT Press.

Neyer, G. (2003) *Family Policies and Low Fertility in Western Europe*. MPIDR Working Paper. Rostock: Max Planck Institute for Demographic Research.

OECD (2001) "Balancing Work and Family Life: Helping Parents into Employment." *Employment Outlook 2001*: 129–66.

Parsons, T. (1956) "The American Family: Its Relations to Personality and to the Social Structure," in T. Parsons and R. F. Bales (eds.), *Family Socialization and Interaction Processes*. London: Routledge & Kegan Paul.

Patterson, K. D., and Pyle, G. F. (1991) "The Geography and Mortality of the 1918 Influenza Pandemic." *Bulletin of the History of Medicine* 65(1): 4–21.

Pérez Díaz, J. (2004) *Madurez de Masas*. Madrid: IMSERSO.

Posner, R., and Landes, E. (1978) "The Economics of the Baby Shortage." *Journal of Legal Studies* 7: 323–48.

Potter, C. W. (2001) "A History of Influenza." *Journal of Applied Microbiology* 91(4): 572–9.

Robinson, W. C. (1997) "The Economic Theory of Fertility Decline over Three Decades." *Population Studies* 51: 63–74.

Ryder, N. B. (1965) "The Cohort as a Concept in the Study of Social Change." *American Sociological Review* 30: 843–61.

Soloway, R. A. (1990) *Demography and Degeneration: Eugenics and the Declining Birthrate in Twentieth-Century Britain*. Chapel Hill: University of North Carolina Press.

Spengler, O. (1926) *The Decline of the West*. London: Allen & Unwin.

Szreter, S. (1984) "The Genesis of the Registrar General's Social Classification of Occupations." *British Journal of Sociology* 35: 522–46.

Szreter, S. (1993) "The Idea of Demographic Transition and the Study of Fertility Change." *Population and Development Review* 19: 659–702.

Szreter, S. (1996) *Fertility, Class and Gender in Britain, 1860–1940*. Cambridge: Cambridge University Press.

Teitelbaum, M. S., and Winter, J. M. (1985) *The Fear of Population Decline*. Orlando, FL: Academic Press.

Torpey, J. (2000) *The Invention of the Passport: Surveillance, Citizenship and the State*. Cambridge: Cambridge University Press.

Urry, J. (2000) *Sociology Beyond Societies: Mobilities for the Twenty-First Century*. London: Routledge.

Van de Kaa, D. J. (1987) "Europe's Second Demographic Transition." *Population Bulletin* 42(1). Washington DC: Population Reference Bureau.

Vandeschrick, C. (2001) "The Lexis Diagram: A Misnomer." *Demographic Research* 4(3): 97–124.

Zelinsky, W. (1971) "The Hypothesis of the Mobility Transition." *The Geographical Review* 61(2): 219–49.

23

Science and Technology Studies: From Controversies to Posthumanist Social Theory

SOPHIA ROOSTH AND SUSAN SILBEY

Science and Technology Studies (STS) names a heterogeneous body of research, scholars, journals, professional associations, and academic programs that focus on the history, social organization and culture of science and technology. Begun in the 1960s in response to the recognizable growth in science in the contemporary world and to the educational and economic policy implications of this explosion of scientific research and development, STS also responded to issues of public responsibility that seemed to be engendered by technological innovation. In the 1960s, the Vietnam War encouraged scientists to become politically active; in 1975, the Asilomar Conference on Recombinant DNA set a precedent in which scientists regulated their own community, established formal norms, and supported legally enforceable guidelines for research; and in the early 1980s, public recognition of the AIDS epidemic sparked rumors of the virus's origin in laboratory mishaps. The burgeoning synergy of attention and concern in the late twentieth century produced, by the twenty-first century, a continuous concatenation between science and public policy concerns. By the time STS first emerged as an interdisciplinary conversation, significant accounts of the work of scientists, the production of scientific knowledge, and the impact of technological innovation had been produced in each of the social sciences from their distinctive disciplinary perspectives. Across the diverse research traditions, however, there seemed to be a shared or received view of science as the work of great minds, usually male, discovering nature's hidden patterns and mechanisms. If the "focused confluence" of research begged for integration (Edge 1995: 3–24), STS scholarship not only integrated the existing scholarship but revised these conventional accounts of science.

EARLY SOURCES

The earliest roots of STS can be traced to the sociology of knowledge and the philosophy of science, representing opposing positions on the possibilities of transcendent, universal knowledge of nature. The theoretical materials of STS developed from debates between those seeking to establish secure empirical methods for understanding nature and the sociologists who insisted that our access to nature, as well as other minds, was inevitably filtered through our collectively created forms of cognition and communication. If Comte (1896: vol. 1, p. 2) taught that we must discover "invariable relations of succession and resemblance" in human society using the same scientific methods as we study the world of nature, Durkheim challenged the reductionism of science for understanding human society, insisting that we consider social phenomena *sui generis*, as things in the themselves. Although "social facts" are the consequences of human interaction, they are nonetheless "endowed with coercive power," constraining the possibilities of human action and agency (Durkheim 1950).

In the early decades of the twentieth century, Mannheim, building on Kant and Durkheim and enamored of Dilthey, sought a sociology that would provide objective knowledge while also capturing "authentic experience," empathetic, lived experience of persons that was more than could be represented by simple calculable and external facts and statistics (Kaiser 1998). In his major work, *Ideology and Utopia* (1936 [1929]), Mannheim developed the concept of ideology into a full-blown theory of knowledge that became the impetus for both the American and European sociology of science. Mannheim extended the notion of ideology from mere interests, psychological, material, or otherwise, to a more comprehensive world-view, with embedded assumptions, perspectives, and lenses through which experience and information are inevitably apprehended and interpreted. Mannheim argued that all knowledge develops from particular, concrete situations which provide the constitutive presuppositions that ground all knowledge-making and knowledge claims. Thus, sociology of knowledge must, according to Mannheim, analyze all knowledge claims to expose their ultimate presuppositions, as well as the social and historical situation from which they emerged. Mannheim was adamant, however, that he was not describing moral or epistemological relativism, which he believed was as ethically dangerous as the moral poverty of the natural sciences. Rather, Mannheim argued that by identifying the particular social bases of perspectives we can place knowledges in relation to each other, what he described as relationism, producing a new kind of objectivity. In America, Merton (1937, 1968 [1941], 1973 [1942]) critiqued Mannheim's account of the sociology of knowledge for its failure to differentiate among different types of knowledge and for failing to recognize the uniqueness of science as a way of making knowledge. If Mannheim had devoted less attention to the natural sciences, it was because modes of understanding nature, he thought, had produced unprecedented danger: science had led to disproportionate development of human capacities without developing a parallel capacity for understanding human action and the governance of people rather than things. If the project of analyzing the production of knowledge was incomplete, it would be taken up in the 1970s by the Edinburgh school of STS, known as the sociology of scientific knowledge, by subjecting science to Mannheim's sociological critique, which Merton had failed to do.[1] But we get ahead of ourselves.

Before the sociology of science and knowledge was taken up in the STS of the 1970s, it was resisted at home, in Europe, by scientists and by philosophers. The logical positivists of the 1920s Vienna circle were part of a continuing effort to secure for empirical science epistemological foundations challenged by the constructivism of sociology. Whereas nineteenth-century Comtean and twentieth-century logical positivism were initially defined by their embrace of the verifiability principle, which posits that statements bear meaning only if they can be confirmed by sense data (Ayer 1936), positivism has since become a label used polemically to refer to naive empiricism. Positivists assigned discussions about "what is real" to metaphysics, as irrelevant and beyond the purview of science. Positivists were concerned with specifying what could science legitimately reveal, and how far beyond immediate sense data we could make empirical claims. Thus, one of the central philosophical questions of logical positivism concerned processes of scientific induction, especially generalizations (across observations) that are themselves incapable of direct empirical verification. Rudolf Carnap of the Vienna circle of logical positivists attempted to resolve the problem of induction by defining simplicity as an ideal of explanatory parsimony that could be applied to validate unverifiable generalizations.

Karl Popper, writing in Vienna at a time when the dominant intellectual movements were Marxism and psychoanalysis as well as logical positivism, produced a theory of scientific fact-making that inverted the positivists' problem of verifiability by focusing on processes of falsifiability. By his forceful development of a positivist program of research, Popper may have provided an opening toward the constructivism (that would emerge prominently in STS). Although Popper was not an admirer, in any way, of constructivism, by describing how scientists use powers of both deduction and falsification to make predictions, disproving hypotheses rather than verifying statements, Popper provided an opening for others. Popper took issue with conventionalists' claim that theoretical systems are neither verifiable nor falsifiable, arguing that the entire effort of science was to falsify claims and hypotheses. He specifically argued that the distinction between falsifiable and non-falsifiable systems could be made on the basis of experimental methodology, and much of his work identified and developed the techniques for positivist scientific methods.

Ludwik Fleck, working in Poland at about the same time as Popper and Mannheim, was writing against the Vienna circle and logical positivism. Building on Durkheim's injunction to sociologists to treat "social facts as things," Fleck theorized not social facts but the production of *scientific* facts, naming the community of persons who mutually exchange ideas and maintain intellectual interaction a "thought collective." The "thought collective," a carrier for the historical development of a field of thought, parallels Durkheim's "social group" whose continuous interactions generate inescapable, normative practices and constraints, i.e. social facts. In this way, Fleck defines a scientific fact as a thought-stylized conceptual relation that can be investigated from the perspective of history and psychology (both individual and collective), but argues that it cannot be constructed exclusively from these perspectives alone. Fleck argues that a thought collective and its thought style leads perception, trains it, and produces a stock of knowledge. Thought style sets the preconditions for any cognition, determines what can be counted as a reasonable question and a true or false answer, provides context, and sets limits to judgment about the nature of "objective reality." In this way, Fleck emphasized the theory-ladenness of observations, directly challenging the naive empiricism of the logical positivists for whom sense data came first and inductive theorizing followed.

By the 1930s, Fleck and Mannheim aside, science was understood to be a bounded activity in which science impacts society, and technology – as applied science – develops linearly from (basic) science. The entire process was regarded as a value-free, amoral enterprise that is legitimated by the claims both that its truths exist independent of, and prior to, any social authority and that it has provided the grounds of human progress. This "internalist" account described an essentially autonomous and asocial process consistent with positivistic philosophies of science as a self-regulated search for timeless, universal, irrefutable facts. Facts are themselves understood, in this received or traditional conception of science, to exist independent of the procedures for making or discovering them. "Scientific facts were considered to exist in a realm outside of the blood, sweat and tears of our everyday sensual and material world, outside of history, outside of society and culture" (Restivo 2005: xi). This understanding of science is best illustrated by the work of Robert K. Merton (1973 [1942]). Writing during and immediately after World War II, Merton believed that Mannheim had mistakenly treated all knowledge and knowledge production as the same, failing to understand how the practices and norms of science were distinct. He first identified four norms that supposedly governed the activities of scientists: universalism, communalism, disinterestedness, and organized skepticism (Merton 1973 [1942]; cf. Hollinger 1983). In later work, he identified norms of originality, reward, and humility (1968 [1941]). Ironically, by taking up Mannheim's project, Merton seem to come to a very different conclusion, describing science in terms more consistent with the historically conventional internalist account than with the sociology of knowledge: autonomous scientific practices characterized by a unique and timeless ethos. Fine work by Merton and his students on the social organization and institutionalization of science was soon swamped by the criticism for its failure to emphasize ways in which these norms failed to provide an accurate picture of scientific behavior or to recognize shared practices across different forms of knowledge production. Gieryn, a student of Merton, would later break with Merton's theory by describing how the very distinction between science and non-science must be kept up, maintained, and sustained. In his model of "boundary work" – the expulsion of that which is defined as non-science, the expansion of science to maintain explanatory authority over previously non-scientific realms, and the maintenance of scientific autonomy – Gieryn (1999) eschewed the structural functionalism that constrained Merton's work but built from it and promoted a thoroughly constructivist account of science.

By the 1960s, however, few realms of human action were immune from acknowledgment of their historicity, including science. Within each of the traditional social science disciplines (history, philosophy, sociology, economics, anthropology, and political science), germs of a more complex understanding of science and technology were developing. Even within the sciences, critical thinking about basic assumptions and paradigms was developing, for example, work by biologists Stephen Jay Gould and Richard Lewontin about the sciences of race (cf. Chorover 1979; Gould 1981, 1996; Hammonds, forthcoming; Harding 1993; Lewontin 1991; Lewontin, Rose, and Kamin 1984). Despite diverse theoretical, pragmatic, and disciplinary sources, science and technology studies seemed to force an orienting consensus that science is a social institution. Thomas Kuhn, deeply influenced by the work of Ludwik Fleck, argued in his groundbreaking *The Structure of Scientific Revolutions* (1996 [1962]) that science does not progress by accumulating ever more accurate descriptions of nature. Rather, new scientific paradigms are produced in opposition to previous paradigms, but the shape of the new paradigm cannot be predicted in advance. Kuhn defined paradigms as a coherent body of knowledge, as "an accepted model or pattern" (1996 [1962]: 23) with a series of questions defined and refined by scientists that constitute a scientific tradition that shapes the way questions are asked and information is gathered. Paradigms become dominant because they are more able than their competitors to answer questions that are deemed relevant at a particular historical moment while accounting for anomalies that have accumulated under the previous paradigm. By rejecting the belief that science followed a logical progress towards truth and placing Popperian theory within a historical context, Kuhn set the groundwork for later analyses of scientific knowledge production, namely the Sociology of Scientific Institutions (SSI) and the Sociology of Scientific Knowledge (SSK).

As in any field of cultural production, STS is constituted more by its oppositions and debates than by a single theoretical paradigm, set of research questions, or canon of readings. Although engaged discourse may generate scholarly production, STS may be more fractious than other scholarly fields or interdisciplinary engagements. Because STS scholarship takes the creation of knowledge as its object of study, it has been hyper-reflexive about its own knowledge-production practices, leading to extended yet insightful debate. Sometimes referred to as the science wars, these scholarly disputes suffused much of academia in the 1990s, where they went by a more generic label as "culture" wars. One line of cleavage developed about the strength and depth of a constructivist account and the sufficiency of internalist histories of science. Another derives from the conjunction of science and technology within the same intellectual rubric, and yet other lines of cleavage developed from epistemological debates and professional competitions among the constituent disciplines. This self-reflexive critique in a heterogeneous joining of topics and disciplines has produced an abundance of shorthand expressions and acronyms to describe the distinctive camps and orientations. For example, some observers distinguish the scholarship of STS from the subject of study, the latter (science, technology, and society) a subject that can be studied via STS or through any traditional discipline such as history, sociology, or philosophy without adopting any particular epistemological position with regard to the social construction of science. Those who focus on the sociology of scientific knowledge (SSK) distinguish themselves from those who do the social construction of technology (SCOT) or the social history of technology (SHOT) or the sociology of scientific institutions (SSI). The STS coalition probably speaks more to the marginality of science and technology to the central concerns of the constituent disciplines than to any necessary or comfortable marriage between the study of science and of technology or across the disciplinary perspectives. Because the history, social organization, and logic of science has been a topic of minor interest for each of the disciplines (in comparison, for example, to concerns about state development, inequality, or freedom), scholarly communities addressing science and/or technology in each discipline were relatively small and perhaps particularly guarded. Nonetheless, the divergent perspectives and heated debates have energized the field, producing an abundant literature in books and academic journals, a substantial network of professional associations, and dozens of departments offering undergraduate and advanced degrees in STS.[2]

Covering an enormous array of topics, STS scholarship has proliferated beyond easy categorization. Several recent publications have nonetheless built synthetic, yet varying, accounts of STS from its various disciplinary streams (e.g. from history, Golinski 1998; Proctor 1991; from sociology, Barnes, Bloor, and Henry 1996; Shapin 1993; from political theory, Rouse 1987; from philosophy of science, Hacking 1999. In addition, see Biagoli 1999; Fischer 2007; Hackett et al. 2007; Haraway 1994; Hess 1997; Rouse 1992; Sismondo 2004; Traweek 1993). For purposes of textual organization, we will describe STS scholarship within two very general rubrics: first, work that looks at the institutionalization, reception, and appropriation of science and technology, and second, research that looks more centrally at the production of science and technology than at their appropriation, distribution, regulation, and use. Across this diverse collection of research, one finds an array of theoretical positions and resources. If there was a structural functional orientation in Merton's early work, those who took up the topic of the institutionalization of science pursued diverse theoretical paths, none of which was unique to STS. If one can find a common thread, and it is tendentious at best, there was a consistent muckraking materialism that revels in exposing the play of interest, power, and privilege where Merton had observed norms of disinterest, humility, communalism, and universality. Where Merton had identified a basic norm of skepticism, the STS critics describe convention and credulity. If SSI was a project devoted to discovering how scientific facts were produced through institutional hierarchies of interest and power as well as debate and consensus, SSK was more concerned with the content rather than context of science. This second strand of STS scholarship produced a more thoroughly constructivist account of science and technology (which was nonetheless also present in the studies of power and interest in policy and institutions). And while rival theoretical approaches were contested, and heated debates ensued over nuanced distinctions as well as clear oppositions, this stridently constructivist program of scholarship produced the distinctive theoretical contributions of STS scholarship that have influenced scholarship across the social sciences: an intensively researched and theorized account of the social construction of knowledge and expertise, and the identification of things as well as persons as active agents in the networks of interactions that constitute the social. This distinctive posthumanist perspective emerged directly from the unique research site of STS scholars: from the close observation of scientists at work in their laboratories. The extensions and conceptualization of processes and tools of social construction developed from close study across diverse fields, such as economic markets, banks, weapons, and design as well as scientific laboratories.

STS STUDIES OF THE INSTITUTIONALIZATION, RECEPTION, AND APPROPRIATION OF SCIENCE AND TECHNOLOGY

Although it had long been clear that science and technology impact society, an impact that was already documented in historical scholarship and economic development, STS explored the ways in which social forces constitute the organization and dissemination of science, but also the content and substance of scientific knowledge itself.

Merton's four norms of scientific institutions claimed that science is socially influenced, although without going so far as to suggest that the content of truth-claims is sociological in nature, as sociologists of scientific knowledge later would. Merton also weaved Marxian arguments regarding the determination of belief systems by class structure into his theory. Merton's question was partly pragmatic in nature: he sought to identify the variables that affect the development of science, the goal of which was "the extension of certified knowledge" (1973 [1942] 226). Merton's norms (disinterest, universality, communism, and organized skepticism), parallel those of the Protestant ethic and owe a debt to Weber in this respect, and are embedded in institutional values internalized by scientists. However, Merton claimed that these institutional norms clashed with the value placed upon scientific authorship, credit regimes, and funding, creating a pathogenic culture in which phenomena such as plagiarism and fabrication of data are endemic (cf. Silbey and Ewick 2002). Writing in the years leading up to World War II, Merton was acutely aware of the external political influences that can shape scientific practice, "the ways in which logical and nonlogical processes converge to modify or curtail scientific activity" (1973 [1942] 255). However, Merton believed these instances to be the exceptions that prove the rule, as political interests usually run counter to the scientific norms Merton set forth. Recent developments in the intellectual property regime have, however, transformed the basic norms of contemporary science such that it would be difficult to claim disinterest or communism as institutional constraints.

As STS developed in the early 1960s and 1970s, it was animated less by the theoretical issues driving Merton in sociology specifically and the theoretical debates in the social sciences generally than by more immediate policy concerns where the role of science and technology seemed to be both a product and a driving force. These early policy concerns developed into a flourishing industry on scientific and technological controversies (e.g. Nelkin 1979, 1982; Nelkin and Pollack 1981). Such work exposes the divergent theoretical assumptions, rival experimental designs, and contrary evidentiary interpretations, at the same time displaying the communally developed procedures for reaching closure on debate to restore continuity and consensus (Hagstrom 1965; Collins and Pinch 1993, 1998).

Although these institutional and policy topics were present in the pre-STS work, science and technology studies developed not only a more nuanced but also a more critical stance toward science and technology than had prevailed in the earlier, pre-1960s disciplinary accounts of autonomous, progressive scientific development. STS contributed its critical dimension by revealing and unpacking the embedded, often unreflective, claims of scientific expertise in law and elsewhere. Emerging simultaneously within periods of intense public skepticism of the roles of science and technology in the anti-Vietnam War movement in the United States in the 1960s and 1970s, and the growing anti-nuclear and environmental movements in the United Kingdom and Europe in the 1980s, the constructivist position that social forces constitute not only the context but also the content of science developed from roots in sociology and anthropology and spread from there. At the same time, researchers explored the ways in which such expert authority is constructed and legitimated in and through government policies and programs (Hilgartner 2000; Wynne 1987). STS scholars also study public and private systems of risk analysis in such diverse fields as weapons, environmental management, and financial markets (Gusterson 2004; MacKenzie 1990, 2001, 2006; Masco 2006). Some, not all, of this research adopts a distinctly progressive, democratic stance, worrying about the consequences of concentrated expertise and public exclusion from critical decisions and the public responsibilities of science (Collins and Evans 2002; DeVries 2007). Perhaps this was an outgrowth of movements such as Science for the People that emerged as organized opposition to the American war in Vietnam but continue to this day in studies concerning such issues as genetically modified foods, the explosion in the use and marketing of pharmaceuticals, as well as global warming and world-wide environmental degradation, unplanned growth, resource depletion, and inequality. Much feminist scholarship on sex and gender also emerged from grassroots activism, pioneered for example in groups such as the Boston Women's Health Collective, which produced an informed, gender-sensitive, and critical account of women's health and sexuality, *Our Bodies, Ourselves*, in 1973, now in its twelfth edition, and translated into 20 languages and Braille. Although some of this early literature was quite essentialist, arguing for fundamental differences from nature, not social organization, critical reactions generated some of the more important and longer-lasting theoretical advances, for example in the work of Marilyn Strathern (1980) and Donna Haraway (1991; cf. Merchant 1990; Tuana 1989).

Considerable lines of research in this general rubric follow the Mertonian lead, focusing on science institutions and funding, science education and public understandings of science, and technological innovation, planning, and assessment. Closely related are studies of the role of science and science advising in government (e.g. Jasanoff 1990; Mukerji 1989) and the role of scientific evidence in law (Cole 2001; Jasanoff 1995; Smith and Wynne 1989). Since the 1980s, when American law changed markedly as a result of the Bay–Dole Act, allowing the results of publicly funded research to be patented and licensed, the institutional and distributional issues associated with technology licensing and transfer have been the subject of extensive research (Owen-Smith 2005).

A corollary of research on the public understanding of science (PUS) and social movements is the question of how social groups organize and define themselves around scientific facts, a phenomenon anthropologist of science Paul Rabinow terms "biosociality" – that is, a mode of sociality in which "nature will be modeled on culture understood as practice; it will be known and remade through technique, nature will finally become artificial, just as culture becomes natural" (1992: 10). Examples of social movements developing around scientific information include groups of people sharing a genetic illness (Taussig, Rapp, and Heath 2003). Still more recently, science studies scholars have turned towards questions of environmental risk and global inequalities, synthesizing Ulrich Beck's work on the dynamics of environmental and technological risk in a period of reflexive modernization with social movement theory. For example, Kim Fortun's *Advocacy after Bhopal* analyzes protest in the global South, and Adriana Petryna's *Life Exposed* adapts Rabinow's biosociality to argue that "biocitizenship" is a means by which people call upon their shared disordered biology in order to claim government resources and medical care. Using science to make policy, law, and property constitutes a thick strand of STS scholarship.

Recognition of the historical embeddedness of science drew scholars away from philosophical questions regarding how scientific knowledge is logically generated and verified, and towards questions of the material practices that embody the *work* of doing science. This historical social constructivist orientation probably claims more than some in the field would admit. It has been the source of shared interests as well as extended controversy among science and technology scholars and between the field and the practitioners under study: scientists, engineers, and policymakers.

PRODUCTION OF SCIENTIFIC KNOWLEDGE: ELUSIVE BOUNDARIES AND POSTHUMANIST SOCIAL SCIENCE

While STS scholarship is marked by a multitude of varying approaches and schools of thought, one theoretical aspect has unified much of the research – that is, the question of the ontology of scientific things and the relations of diverse heterogeneous people, animals, machines, and things to one another. Whether taking the name of "assemblage" (Callon), "network" (Latour), "cyborg" (Haraway), "parliament of things" (Latour), "capillary" (Foucault), "the body multiple" (Mol 2002), or "rhizome" (Deleuze), the emergent properties of the Rube Goldbergesque complex systems that refuse encapsulation within the boundaries that distinguish what is interior or exterior to science, agential or passive, living or inert, intentional or otherwise, have been of prime importance to scholars of science. Indeed, recognizing how diverse elements become "black-boxed" as things and determining what kinds of knowledge are deployed and what powers assembled in this process of "entification" is where science studies both draws upon and makes its distinctive contribution to social theory at large. It begins from the "Strong Programme" exploring the construction of social scientific knowledge and leads to recent publications in posthumanist social science.

In defining what became known as the Edinburgh school's Strong Programme of the sociology of scientific knowledge, David Bloor listed four central tenets: (1) SSK is concerned with the conditions that cause certain knowledge claims; (2) SSK should not prejudice research by observing and treating statements regarded as true differently than those that are regarded as false; (3) SSK should explain different belief systems symmetrically; and (4) SSK should reflexively apply these methods to itself. Specifically rejecting Merton's distinction that science constituted a unique mode of producing knowledge, SSK scholars, in effect, pursued a rigorous constructivist sociology of knowledge, subjecting science to the same intensive examination that Mannheim had applied to social or cultural knowledge. In doing so, however, SSK erased a distinction between knowledge of things and knowledge of persons that Mannheim believed was essential to understanding not the uniqueness of science but the uniqueness of human, sentient life, and reintroduced a different flavor of scientism within the sociology of science. "Where Mannheim and his mentors and colleagues distinguished between *Verstehen* [understanding] and *Erklärung* [explanation], Bloor . . . called for studies which are simply "causal" and "empirical" (Kaiser 1998: 76).

Producing an accurate analysis of the construction of scientific facts required a new methodology with which to examine scientific activity. Beginning in the 1970s, scholars approached scientific culture as a field of social practice like any other, and hence subject to the same tools of investigation and analysis as had been used by anthropologists and sociologists in other social fields (Callon 1986; Clarke and Fujimura 1992; Collins 1985, 2004; Dumit 2004; Franklin 2007; Gieryn 1999; Knorr-Cetina 1981; Landecker 2007; Latour and Woolgar 1986; Lynch 1985, 1993; Pickering 1984, 1995; Rheinberger 1997; Traweek 1988). Although the research methods were not new and much of the theoretical apparatus with which anthropologists and sociologists undertook closely observed ethnographic studies of laboratory practices, processes of scientific discovery, and technological invention were also not new, some vigorously touted the attention to subjects closer to home as an innovation. As we have been suggesting throughout, science studies built on nearly a century of social constructivist theorizing and empirical research about the widest range of activities. What was new was subjecting scientists, and later engineers in work groups, to the same scrutiny and in-depth analysis of social organization, culture, and epistemology that anthropologists had long applied to small-scale, often pre-industrial societies and tribes and sociologists had applied to street gangs, police, and factory workers. These early forays into laboratory studies self-consciously appropriated the ethnographic voice in analyzing scientific activity, producing rich descriptions of the unarticulated and often tacit understandings that made science and scientists. In the preface to Karin Knorr-Cetina's *The Manufacture of Knowledge*, Rom Harré describes laboratory studies: "Suppose that instead of approaching the scientific community with Marx or even Goffman in hand, one were to adopt the stance of the anthropologist coming into contact with a strange tribe. . . . Laboratories are looked upon with the innocent eye of the traveler in exotic lands" (Knorr-Cetina 1981: vii–viii).

These studies critiqued, and also built on, Merton's research that had identified functional, normative requisites for scientific communities as well as Kuhn's (1996 [1962]) account of the paradigmatic development of scientific theories. While both Merton and Kuhn had described the structures of normal science, for example dialectical developments among theory, experimentation, and career advancement, the laboratory studies added to the mix insights from critical theory, ethnomethodology, and symbolic interaction, to pay particularly close attention to the cumulative consequences of micro-transactions, discursive strategies, and forms of representation within the production of a particular scientific fact or practice. These same perspectives and research methods were also adopted to study technological innovation, engineers, and designers (Downey 1998; Forsythe 2001; Gusterson 1996; Helmreich 1998; Henderson 1999; Pinch and Trocco 2002). These closely observed studies of scientific and engineering practice have also led to extensive research on processes of cognition and categorization (Bowker and Star 1999).

Much of this work was influenced by Garfinkel's *Studies in Ethnomethodology*, in which he argued that "the objective reality of social facts" is an "ongoing accomplishment of the converted activities of daily life" that must be studied by closely examining the ad hoc activities and utterances of daily life (1967: vii). Scholars of science like Gaston Bachelard drew upon Garfinkel's work in calling for a focus upon scientific projects rather than scientific objects, where a "project" is the activity of giving body to reason. Gilbert and Mulkay similarly applied an ethnomethodological discourse analysis to science, arguing that scientific worlds were constituted by "an indefinite series of linguistic potentialities" (1984: 10). In this way, they demonstrated that science is not a distinct realm of social action, but is like other social settings, rife with conflict, compromise, pragmatic adjustments, and power, as well as taken-for-granted habits that make social settings transparent and familiar to socially competent members but alien and uninterpretable to non-member outsiders.

In *The Manufacture of Knowledge: An Essay on the Constructivist and Contextual Nature of Science* (1981) Knorr-Cetina explicitly adopted the literary devices of ethnography to frame her study of a food science lab in Berkeley, in which she examined how facts are fabricated within the context of social life. Rather than taking a hard-line constructivist position, she argued that culture imposes the constraints and "the system of reference which makes the objectification of reality possible" (1981: 2). Further, "the experimenter is a *causal agent* of the sequence of events created" (1981: 3), all experimentation is a process of production, and facts are fabricated by social consensus and experimenters' "expectation-based tinkering." The scientific facts produced in this manner, Knorr-Cetina argued, are geared towards reaching previously predicted solutions rather than solving open-ended problems, and are marked by analogical reasoning and the manipulation of scientific concepts through analogy and metaphor. In order to understand such processes, Knorr-Cetina adopted a position of "methodological relativism" that emphasized letting one's subjects speak. Instead of referring to scientific cultures or social groups, Knorr-Cetina described the objects of her research as "variable transscientific fields" – opportunity-directed networks of scientists connected through resource relationships, resources being either materials and tools necessary for experimentation or the raw material of ideas that can be converted into success through the consensus of a scientist's peers. In her later *Epistemic Cultures: How the Sciences Make Knowledge* (1999) Knorr-Cetina revised the focus of her analysis, not examining the construction of knowledge as she and other early laboratory ethnographers had, but rather the way the machineries of knowledge construction are themselves constructed. She compared high-energy physics and molecular biology labs as knowledge cultures in order to expose the "knowledge machineries of contemporary sciences." Rather than looking at the kinds of things found in laboratories, she attended to the unique relations between things that are brought together in laboratories.

By the 1980s it was well understood, and in some scholarly networks taken for granted, that science is in this regard the same as all other human activities, a socially constructed phenomenon: the product of collectively organized human labor and decisionmaking. "Facts do not fall out of the sky, they are not 'given' to us directly, we do not come to them by means of revelation . . . [W]ork is embodied in the fact, just as the collective toil of the multitude of workers in Rodin's workshop is embodied in *The Thinker*. This is what it means to say that a fact is socially constructed" (Restivo 2005: xiii). This does not mean that any statement can secure the status of scientific fact; social construction is not a recipe for cognitive solipsism or moral relativism. Nor does it mean that scientific facts are completely arbitrary accidents. It means only that scientific facts are contingent: the ways in which a fact is produced – the choice of topic, location of research, the constraints of resources, the accumulation of empirical evidence, the transparency of methods – are part of the constitution or construction of the fact.

Collins coined the term "experimenters' regress" to refer to the impossibility of definitively proving the results of an experiment by replicating those results. Collins argues that agreement regarding the results of experiments is arrived at socially, as scientists reach a consensus founded upon "shared perception" and "the forms of life or taken-for-granted practices – ways of going on – in which they are embedded" (1985: 9, 18). Such consensual agreement breaks the logical short-circuit of infinite regress by using "tacit knowledge" (Polanyi 1997) which allows practitioners to separate relevant and meaningful information from data that can be qualified as insignificant or artifactual. Collins pointed out that all experiments have a certain amount of interpretive flexibility built into them – as well as a dose of uncertainty – because (1) the results of an experiment are predicated upon faith in the equipment used in the experiment; (2) the conclusion rests upon belief that enough data have been gathered in order to adequately prove a theory; and (3) belief that the data are not an artifact of experimental noise. Pickering (1984) also claimed that scientific narratives obscure the fact that scientists agree only *retrospectively* upon the validity of a theory (cf. Collins and Pinch 1993, 1998).

Ian Hacking connected this social constructivist work emerging in the 1980s with the earlier philosophy of science. He responded to Carnap's, Popper's, and Kuhn's theories of so-called "mummified" science by also drawing attention to what scientists *do* rather than how they *think*. In so doing, he articulated the relation of theory and experiment – "We represent in order to intervene, and we intervene in the light of representations" (1983: 31). To address the persistent issues of the relationships among observable sense data, statements, meanings, induction across observations, and generalizations, Hacking distinguished several different types of realism, differentiating between the realism of concepts and the realism of things. Further, he elaborated upon Kuhn's claim that different scientific paradigms are incommensurable by pointing to three different forms of incommensurability – topic, dissociation, and meaning incommensurability. Topic incommensurability refers to when different paradigms take different types of questions to be theoretically relevant. Dissociation refers to the way in which different types of phenomena are classed into sets that reflect upon certain types of questions – that is, what kinds of phenomena can be used in tandem to reach an inductive account of a principle. Meaning incommensurability, the most radical incommensurability, refers to when the terms of one paradigm cannot be explained or accounted for in the terms of another. Hacking identified three sticking points that characterize the debate between adherents and detractors of social constructivism as it was developing in STS scholarship: contingency (constructivists believe that there is no one accurate system that is inevitable for producing a successful science: "a research program that does not incorporate anything equivalent to the standard model, but which is as progressive as contemporary high energy physics" [Hacking 1999: 70]); metaphysics (classifications are convenient ways to represent the world, but not determined by an objective reality); and stability (constructivists provide external conditions for the stability of a concept, whereas non-constructivists offer internal explanations). Contingency does not imply randomness – Hacking conceded that "scientists who do not simply quite have to *accommodate* themselves to that resistance [of the world]" (1999: 71) and that the fit between theory, phenomenology, schematic model, and apparatus is a robust one (1999: 72). Thus, constructivism, according to these conditions, claims that X is not predetermined, although that which can be counted as X is specified by resistance and robustness.

Thus while some of the early work focused on the contextual shaping of the content of science and technology, STS as a mature field rejected the notion of a natural or fixed boundary between science and its context. Considerations of organization, resources, and human capacity seemed obvious with respect to technological innovation, but in the traditional disciplines had often been relegated to the boundaries of science or the social conditions of its making. What became known through Gieryn's work (1999) as "boundary work" – the discourses and practices of institutional legitimacy and exclusion – became a central focus of STS research tracking the human transactions – symbolic and material – that shaped scientific facts as well as membership in scientific communities. They attended to the ways in which science is internally defined as a privileged site of knowledge production, focusing their attention on the indistinguishability of science from non-science. For example, Daston and Park (2001) dismiss of distinctions between medieval and early modern periods and attendant distinctions of pre-scientific from scientific inquiry, and feminist scholars claim that feminine science has historically been devalued as mere "art" (Hubbard 1990). Others looked at activities not heretofore categorized as science by contemporary scientists, such as Newton and Boyle's alchemical interests and the relationship of these to the works that are taken to have made the scientific revolution (Dobbs 1975; Newman and Principe 2002). No longer do scholars regard it as appropriate to isolate the elements of scientists' work that have over time proven useful and scientifically productive, discarding what modern science has rejected as aberrational or simply wrong.

Similarly, any hard and fast distinction between basic science and applied technology became difficult to sustain, once the work practices of scientists and engineers were closely observed. The advance of modern physics, for example, is described as a productive collaboration between theory, instrumentation, and experiment in Peter Galison's *Image and Logic* (1997). Galison breaks with both logical positivism and antipositivism by arguing that physics communities are heterogeneous and intercalated with one another within "trading zones," areas of cultural contact in which scientists deploy pidgins with which they are able to converse across sub-disciplinary lines. Finally, any hard and fixed division between the disciplinary approaches to the production or reception of science began to merge in important studies. Steven Shapin and Simon Schaffer's influential book *Leviathan and the Air-Pump* (1985) encouraged scholars to move among the historical, anthropological, and sociological approaches to the study of science and technology.

Recent studies of elusive boundaries between science and non-science have focused on the ways in which non-scientists participate in the construction of scientific knowledge. Steven Epstein (1996), for example, described the ways in which gay rights activists became expert analysts of the existing medical knowledge concerning AIDS when the epidemic first took hold, and eventually became co-producers of new knowledge, especially the treatment protocols and drug trials. Emily Martin's (1987) research responded to critiques of both the science and pseudoscience of gender and reproductive medicine while exploring the production and appropriation of scientific knowledge and lay models of scientific information. The scholarly work on reproductive medicine and technology, like the work on AIDS, followed upon grassroots activism that exposed the limitations, and often ideological or biased assumptions, of the then conventional science in these areas.

In the attempts to produce fuller, more comprehensive and complex, accounts of science, its methods and its subject matter, scholars have also looked far beyond the borders of Europe and the US to understand, for example, the ways in which mathematical equations are understood in some African cultures (Verran 2001), or to investigate more carefully postcolonial science (Abu El-Haj 2001; Mitchell 1991; Ong and Collier 2005; Prakash 1999; Redfield 2000; Tsing 2005). These studies have emphasized how scientific knowledge is produced and disseminated in service of the state, how colonial resources and lay knowledge have been exploited to further scientific and technological growth in the metropol (Hayden 2003; Helmreich 2007), and how Otherness and the exotic have been constructed by scientific projects embedded in colonial legacies (Jasanoff 2005; Reardon 2004; Schiebinger 1993).

This burgeoning increase in empirical observation of the practice of science has produced two notable contributions: the work of the "Strong Programme" of SSK which we have already mentioned and actor network theory (ANT), to which we turn now. Latour's ANT posits that scientific facts are *things* in motion that must be followed in order to understand how scientists circulate scientific texts and inscriptions – "immutable mobiles" – as a means of gathering support for their theories by enrolling the support of colleagues (see CHAPTER 7). According to Latourian theory, facts and machines in the making are underdetermined and are collectively constructed by actors and actants, where an actant is an agent that cannot speak, and thus must be represented by a spokesperson. Central to ANT is the claim that the settlement of controversy is the cause of natural facts, not the result of them, and similarly that the settlement of scientific controversies causes, and is not the result of, social stability. Central to the production of facts, as Latour argues, is the process by which scientific facts come to be accepted as *facts* – that is, the way in which supporters are enrolled and actor networks are extended by trials of strength until the cost of dissent becomes too high (Latour 1987). Scientific facts are produced under constraints that vary historically and culturally; thus scientific inquiry is both enabled and constrained by what is already known, by technological capacity and the material resources that are available, and human capacity for work, imagination, collaboration, and communication. Those constraints shape the content of the science as well as the process of producing that content. The contingency of scientific facts implied by social constructivism is potentially prescriptive: if scientific facts are produced in particular contexts and are shaped by social factors, then they are contestable (see CHAPTER 14). As Hacking put it in *The Social Construction of What?*, to claim that something is socially constructed is to claim that it is not inevitable, and hence it is possible to say that "X is quite bad as it is" and "We would be much better off if X were done away with, or at least radically transformed" (1999: 6).

In the development of ANT, Latour and Callon profoundly influenced the course of science studies by arguing that objects – things rather than persons or animate beings – are *agential*, operating in concert with humans within extended heterogeneous networks of objects and persons. The analysis of the scientific fact as a constructed thing is extended to the full range of obdurate materiality. Latour made no fundamental distinctions between people and things, treating their influence upon scientific action as symmetrical, in this sense extending SSK's injunction to treat all belief systems and truth claims as symmetrical to the treatment of all phenomena symmetrically. Alongside Latour and Callon, Haraway also promoted what would eventually be considered a posthuman sociology that identifies and maps distributed agency. The very title of Haraway's book, *Simians, Cyborgs and Women* (1991), highlights her interest in the ways in which different forms of agency, capacity, and effectiveness circulate in practices and accounts of technoscience. Writing specifically against Latour and Callon, however, Collins and Yearley (1992) pointed out that, despite claims to the contrary, the relation of human and nonhuman actors is asymmetrical in ANT. Although Latour and Callon may have symmetrically attributed agency to inanimate matter, as they claimed in their studies of scallops and door closers, critics focused on the differential interpretive apparatus required for theorizing the action of persons and the action of things. If the "French school" insisted on the symmetrical treatment of persons and things, critics claimed, they would be unable to distinguish, even if they did not wish to valorize, the true from the false, and would fall into the "relativist's regress." "Symmetry of treatment between the true and the false requires a human-center universe" Collins and Yearley (1992: 303) wrote.

This turn towards the agency of things has been embraced by posthumanist theory, both within science studies and more broadly. Three ideas are combined variously by different authors in posthumanist theory: the hybrid assemblage of social and material elements in our world; the agency (Latour 2005) or "performativity and power" (Pickering 2005) of the material world, and finally, the resistances enacted by social and material phenomena in their interplay with each other. Within science studies, posthumanist theory is particularly noticeable in analyses the human–machine interface from the point of view of instrument design as well as the role of technology, for example computers, in human relations and development (Stone 1995; Suchman 2006; Turkle 1985). Other research focuses on human relations with animals or nature in general (for example, Haraway 1989; Latour 2004). Work on human–animal relations followed two intellectual trajectories: first, a thread of laboratory studies that examines the role of model organisms in the production of scientific knowledge (Creager 2002; Kohler 1994; Rader 2004), and second, feminist science studies that interrogated the relationships of scientists to animals, particularly in reference to how animals stand in for humans in scientific narrative (Haraway 1989), a research agenda that gained momentum following a series of legal decisions establishing that biological materials were patentable, alienable, and commodifiable technologies (Diamond *v.* Chakrabarty; Moore *v.* The Board of Regents of the University of California). In essence, this thread of STS scholarship marries in-depth technical knowledge of particular scientific fields or pieces of technology with examinations of the public and private uses for business, management, government, and interpersonal relations.

CONCLUSION

Over the decades, STS has produced a set of useful concepts that together constitute something much more than Mannheim's sociology of knowledge: black boxes, the Matthew principle, trading zones, boundary objects and boundary work, experimenter's regress, epistemological symmetry, and actants are now part of the general sociological repertoire for describing, and explaining, the processes of social construction.

Most recently, science studies generally have become concerned with how theories developed to study science can be made relevant to the rest of the social sciences, to any and all claims of knowledge, whether scientific, social, or political. STS has become a generalized study of expertise. Partly, this interest has arisen from the ugly battles of the science wars, in which STS scholars were attacked for critiquing scientific knowledge to the point of vertiginous relativism if not outright solipsism. In part, however, is it simply a logical extension of the unrelenting reflexivity of the Strong Programme of SSK, in which all beliefs and all knowledge claims should be subject to symmetrical, impartial examination.

However, unrelieved skepticism about the construction of knowledge has had (what should have been sociologically expected) unintended political consequences. The science wars – between scientists and STS scholars – may be over, but this issue has a newfound critical importance in contemporary political debates. For example, in political debates surrounding climate change, many science studies scholars were disturbed to realize that their own critical tools were used to question scientific facts and to reopen black boxes. In the case of current debates over climate change, the tools of STS have not been deployed in order to point towards the contingency and underdetermination of social circumstances, but invoked by global-warming deniers to delay any political or material response to compelling empirical evidence of climate change. Other politically driven right-wing groups have also adapted the constructivist argument to suggest that "intelligent design" of the universe is as appropriate an account as natural selection and Darwinian evolution. Thus, as one scholar confessed, his worst fears came true. Mobiling the rhetorical staples of SSK, British STS scholar Steven Fuller testified in the Dover, PA (USA) trial that "intelligent design" deserved time in science classes equal to that devoted to evolution; neither has determinant nor otherwise compelling status as more legitimate science.

Such developments have prompted a new round of debates among science studies scholars, echoing the field's origins. Renewed concerns about the implications for democracy of the complexity and inaccessibility of scientific knowledge, and yet its increasing importance for our collective survival, are producing what Collins and Evans (2002) call the third wave of science studies. STS scholars have joined the age-old discussions among philosophers, political scientists, and sociologists generally about politics: "How we shall live together in the polis?" (DeVries 2007; Latour 2005). The discussion for STS is not just about science; it never was. However, a renewed empirical consensus seems to be emerging. As Latour reiterates in "Why Has Critique Run out of Steam?" (2004), the goal of science studies was "never to get *away* from facts but *closer* to them," to "renew empiricism."

Notes

We are very grateful for the thoughtful comments and suggestions by Douglas Goodman, Stefan Helmreich, and David Kaiser that have saved us from many an embarrassing error. Any remaining inadequacies are our responsibility alone.

SCIENCE AND TECHNOLOGY STUDIES 467

1   For an excellent and thorough analysis of the genealogy of the sociology of scientific
    knowledge from Mannheim through Merton to Barnes and Bloor whom we will discuss
    below, see Kaiser 1998.
2   Journals include, for example, *Social Studies of Science* for science studies generally, *Isis*
    for the history of science, *Science Technology and Human Values* covering contemporary
    science, policy and culture, *History and Technology*, *Science in Context*, *Minerva*, *Osiris*,
    Technology and Culture, *Studies in History and Philosophy of Science*, and a wide range
    of specialized and regional publications such as *Metascience*, *Science Studies*, *Knowledge
    and Technology in Society*, *Public Understandings of Science*, *History of Science*, *Philoso-
    phy of Science*, *British Journal of the Philosophy of Science*, *British Journal of the History
    of Science*, *Science for the People*, and *Science Technology* and *Société*. Professional
    associations include, for example, Society for the Social Studies of Science, Society for
    the History of Technology, ICOHETEC (International Committee for the History of
    Technology), HSS (History of Science Society), and IASTS (International Association for
    Science, Technology and Society). A list of departments offering undergraduate and
    advanced degrees in STS can be found at <http://web.mit.edu/hasts/about/index.html>.

Bibliography

Abu El-Haj, N. (2001) *Facts on the Ground: Archaeological Practice and Territorial Self-
    Fashioning in Israeli Society*. Chicago: University of Chicago Press.
Ayer, A. J. (1936) *Language, Truth and Logic*. London: Gollancz.
Barnes, B., Bloor, D., and Henry, J. (1996) *Scientific Knowledge: A Sociological Analysis*.
    Chicago: University of Chicago Press.
Beck, U. (1992) *Risk Society: Towards a New Modernity*. Newbury Park: Sage
    Publications.
Biagoli, M. (ed.) (1999) *The Science Studies Reader*. New York: Routledge.
Bloor, D. (1976) *Knowledge and Social Imagery*. Chicago: University of Chicago
    Press.
Boston Women's Health Book Collective (2005) *Our Bodies, Ourselves: A New Edition for
    a New Era*. New York: Touchstone.
Bowker, G. C., and Star, S. L. (1999) *Sorting Things Out: Classification and its Consequences*.
    Cambridge, MA: MIT Press.
Callon, M. (1986) "Some Elements of a Sociology of Translation: Domestication of the Scal-
    lops and the Fishermen of St. Brieuc Bay," in J. Law (ed.), *Power, Action, and Belief: A
    New Sociology of Knowledge*. London: Routledge & Kegan Paul.
Chorover S. (1979) *From Genesis to Genocide: The Meaning of Human Nature and the
    Power of Behavior Control*. Cambridge, MA: MIT Press.
Clarke A., and Fujimura J. (1992) *The Right Tools for the Job: At Work in Twentieth Century
    Life Sciences*. Princeton: Princeton University Press.
Cole, S. (2001) *Suspect Identities: A History of Fingerprinting and Criminal Identification*.
    Cambridge, MA: Harvard University Press.
Collins, H. M. (1985) *Changing Order: Replication and Induction in Scientific Practice*.
    Beverly Hills: Sage Publications.
Collins, H. M. (2004) *Gravity's Shadow: The Search for Gravitational Waves*. Chicago:
    University of Chicago Press.
Collins, H. M., and Evans, R. (2002) "The Third Wave of Science Studies: Studies of Expertise
    and Experience." *Social Studies of Science* 32(2): 235–96.

Collins, H. M., and Pinch, T. (1993) *The Golem: What Everyone Should Know about Science*. Cambridge: Cambridge University Press.

Collins, H. M., and Pinch, T. (1998) *The Golem at Large: What Everyone Should Know About Technology*. Cambridge: Cambridge University Press.

Collins, H. M., and Yearley, S. (1992) "Epistemological Chicken" and "Journey Into Space," in A. Pickering (ed.), *Science as Practice and Culture*. Chicago: University of Chicago Press.

Comte, A. (1896) *The Positive Philosophy of Auguste Comte*, trans. H. Martineau. London: Bell.

Creager, A. N. H. (2002) *The Life of a Virus: Tobacco Mosaic Virus as an Experimental Model, 1930–1965*. Chicago: University of Chicago Press.

Daston, L., and Park K. (2001) *Wonders and the Order of Nature, 1150–1750*. New York: Zone Books.

DeVries, G. (2007) "What Is Political in Sub-Politics: How Aristotle Might Help STS." *Social Studies of Science* 37(5): 781–809.

Dobbs, B. J. T. (1975) *The Foundations of Newton's Alchemy*. Cambridge: Cambridge University Press.

Downey, G. L. (1998) *The Machine in Me: An Anthropologist Sits among Computer Engineers*. New York: Routledge.

Dumit, J. (2004) *Picturing Personhood: Brain Scans and Biomedical Identity*. Princeton: Princeton University Press.

Durkheim, É. (1950) *The Rules of Sociological Method*. New York: The Free Press.

Edge, D. (1995) "Reinventing the Wheel," in S. Jasanoff, G. Markle, J. Petersen, and T. Pinch (eds.), *Handbook of Science and Technology Studies*. Thousand Oaks: Sage.

Engelhardt, H. T., and Caplan, A. L. (eds.) (1987) *Scientific Controversies: Case Studies in the Resolution and Closure of Disputes in Science and Technology*. Cambridge: Cambridge University Press.

Epstein, S. (1996) *Impure Science: AIDS, Activism, and the Politics of Knowledge*. Berkeley: University of California Press.

Fausto-Sterling, A. (1992) *Myths of Gender: Biological Theories about Women and Men*. New York: Basic Books.

Fausto-Sterling, A. (2000) *Sexing the Body: Gender Politics and the Construction of Sexuality*. New York: Basic Books.

Fischer, M. (2007) "Four Genealogies for a Recombinant Anthropology of Science and Technology." *Cultural Anthropology* 22(4): 539–615.

Forsythe, D. (2001) *Studying Those who Study Us: An Anthropologist in the World of Artificial Intelligence*. Stanford: Stanford University Press.

Fortun, K. (2001) *Advocacy after Bhopal: Environmental, Disaster, New Global Orders*. Chicago: University of Chicago Press.

Franklin, S. (2007) *Dolly Mixtures: The Remaking of Genealogy*. Durham NC: Duke University Press.

Galison, P. (1997) *Image and Logic: A Material Culture of Microphysics*. Chicago: University of Chicago Press.

Garfinkel, H. (1967) *Studies in Ethnomethodology*. Englewood Cliffs, NJ: Prentice Hall.

Gieryn, T. F. (1999) *Cultural Boundaries of Science: Credibility on the Line*. Chicago: University of Chicago Press.

Gilbert, G. N., and Mulkay, M. (1984) *Opening Pandora's Box: A Sociological Analysis of Scientists' Discourse*. Cambridge: Cambridge University Press.

Golinksi, J. (1998) *Making Natural Knowledge: Constructivism and the History of Science.* Cambridge: Cambridge University Press.

Gould, S. J. (1981) *Mismeasure of Man.* New York: Norton Publishers.

Gould, S. J. (1996) *Mismeasure of Man,* rev. edn. New York: Norton Publishers.

Gusterson, H. (1996) *Nuclear Rites: A Weapons Laboratory at the End of the Cold War.* Berkeley: University of California Press.

Gusterson, H. (2004) *People of the Bomb: Portraits of America's Nuclear Complex.* Minneapolis: University of Minnesota Press.

Hackett, E. J., Amsterdamski, O., Lynch, M., and Wajcman, J. (2007) *The Handbook of Science and Technology Studies,* 3rd edn. Cambridge, MA: MIT Press.

Hacking, I. (1983) *Representing and Intervening: Introductory Topics in the Philosophy of Natural Science.* Cambridge: Cambridge University Press.

Hacking, I. (1999) *The Social Construction of What?* Cambridge, MA: Harvard University Press.

Hagstrom, W. O. (1965) *The Scientific Community.* New York: Basic Books.

Hammonds, E. (forthcoming) *The Logic of Difference: A History of Race in Science and Medicine in the United States.* Chapel Hill: University of North Carolina Press.

Haraway, D. J. (1989) *Primate Visions: Gender, Race, and Nature in the World of Modern Science.* New York: Routledge.

Haraway, D. J. (1991) *Simians, Cyborgs, and Women: The Reinvention of Nature.* New York: Routledge.

Haraway, D. J. (1994) "A Game of Cat's Cradle: Science Studies, Feminist Theory, Cultural Studies." *Configurations* 1: 59–71.

Haraway, D. J. (1997) *Modest_Witness@Second_Millennium.FemaleMan_Meets_Onco-Mouse: Feminism and Technoscience.* New York: Routledge.

Haraway, D. J. (2003) *The Companion Species Manifesto: Dogs, People, and Significant Otherness.* Chicago: Prickly Paradigm.

Harding, S. (1993) *The Racial Economy of Science: Toward a Democratic Future.* Bloomington: Indiana University Press.

Hayden, C. (2003) *When Nature Goes Public: The Making and Unmaking of Bioprospecting in Mexico.* Princeton: Princeton University Press.

Hayles, N. K. (1999) *How We Became Posthuman: Virtual Bodies in Cybernetics, Literature, and Informatics.* Chicago: University of Chicago Press.

Helmreich, S. (1998) *Silicon Second Nature: Culturing Artificial Life in a Digital World.* Berkeley: University of California Press.

Helmreich, S. (2007) *Alien Ocean: An Anthropology of Marine Microbiology and the Limits of Life.* Berkeley: University of California Press.

Henderson, K. (1999) *On Line and on Paper: Visual Representations, Visual Culture, and Computer Graphics in Design Engineering.* Cambridge, MA: MIT Press.

Hess, D. (1997) *Science Studies: An Advanced Introduction.* New York: New York University Press.

Hilgartner, S. (2000) *Science on Stage: Expert Advice as Public Drama.* Stanford: Stanford University Press.

Hollinger, D. (1983) "The Defense of Democracy and Robert K. Merton's Formulation of the Scientific Ethos." *Knowledge and Society: Studies in the Sociology of Culture Past and Present* 42: 1–15.

Hubbard, R. (1990) *The Politics of Women's Biology.* New Brunswick: Rutgers University Press.

Jasanoff, S. (1990) *The Fifth Branch: Science Advisers as Policymakers.* Cambridge, MA: Harvard University Press.

Jasanoff, S. (1995) *Science at the Bar: Law, Science, and Technology in America.* Cambridge, MA: Harvard University Press.

Jasanoff, S. (2005) *Designs on Nature.* Princeton: Princeton University Press.

Jasanoff, S., Markle, G., Petersen, J., and Pinch, T. (eds.) (2002) *Handbook of Science and Technology Studies,* 2nd edn. London: Sage.

Kaiser, D. (1998) "A Mannheim for All Seasons: Bloor, Merton, and the Roots of the Sociology of Scientific Knowledge." *Science in Context* 11(1): 51–87.

Kaiser, D. (2005) *Drawing Theories Apart: The Dispersion of Feynman Diagrams in Postwar Physics.* Chicago: University of Chicago Press.

Knorr-Cetina, K. (1981) *The Manufacture of Knowledge: An Essay on the Constructivist and Contextual Nature of Science.* Oxford: Pergamon Press.

Knorr-Cetina, K. (1999) *Epistemic Cultures: How the Sciences Make Knowledge.* Cambridge, MA: Harvard University Press.

Kohler, R. E. (1994) *Lords of the Fly: Drosophila Genetics and the Experimental Life.* Chicago: University of Chicago Press.

Kuhn, T. S. (1996) *The Structure of Scientific Revolutions.* Chicago: University of Chicago Press.

Landecker H. (2007) *Culturing Life: How Cells Became Technologies.* Cambridge, MA: Harvard University Press.

Latour, B. (1987) *Science in Action: How to Follow Scientists and Engineers through Society.* Cambridge, MA: Harvard University Press.

Latour, B. (2004) *Politics of Nature: How to Bring the Sciences into Democracy.* Cambridge, MA: Harvard University Press.

Latour, B. (2005) *Reassembling the Social: An Introduction to Actor-Network Theory.* New York: Oxford University Press.

Latour, B., and Woolgar, S. (1986) *Laboratory Life: The Construction of Scientific Facts.* Princeton: Princeton University Press.

Lewontin, R. (1991) *Biology as Ideology: The Doctrine of DNA.* New York: Harper Books.

Lewontin R., Rose, S., and Kamin, L. (1984) *Not In Our Genes.* New York: Pantheon Books.

Lynch, M. (1985) *Art and Artifact in Laboratory Science.* London: Routledge & Kegan Paul.

Lynch, M. (1993) *Scientific Practice and Ordinary Action.* New York: Cambridge University Press.

MacKenzie, D. (1990) *Inventing Accuracy: A Historical Sociology of Nuclear Missile Guidance.* Cambridge, MA: MIT Press.

MacKenzie, D. (2001) *Mechanizing Proof: Computing, Risk, and Trust.* Cambridge, MA: MIT Press.

MacKenzie, D. (2006) *An Engine, Not a Camera: How Financial Models Shape Markets.* Cambridge, MA: MIT Press.

MacKenzie, D., and Spinardi, G. (1995) "Tacit Knowledge, Weapons Design, and the Uninvention of Nuclear Weapons." *The American Journal of Sociology* 101(1): 44–99.

Mannheim, K. (1936 [1929]) *Ideology and Utopia: An Introduction to the Sociology of Knowledge.* New York: Harcourt, Brace.

Martin, E. (1987) *The Woman in the Body: A Cultural Analysis of Reproduction*. Boston: Beacon Press.

Masco, J. P. (2006) *The Nuclear Borderlands: The Manhattan Project in Post-Cold War New Mexico*. Princeton: Princeton University Press.

Merchant, C. (1990) *Death of Nature: Women, Ecology, and the Scientific Revolution*. New York: Harper One Books.

Merton, R. K. (1937) "The Sociology of Knowledge." *Isis* 27: 493–503.

Merton, R. K. (1968 [1941, 1957]) "Karl Mannheim and the Sociology of Knowledge," repr. in *Social Theory and Social Structure*. New York: The Free Press.

Merton, R. K. (1973 [1942]) "The Normative Structure of Science," in *The Sociology of Science: Theoretical and Empirical Investigation*. Chicago: University of Chicago Press.

Mindell, D. A. (2002) *Between Human and Machine: Feedback, Control, and Computing Before Cybernetics*. Baltimore, Johns Hopkins University Press.

Mitchell, T. (1991) *Colonizing Egypt*. Berkeley: University of California Press.

Mol, A. (2002) *The Body Multiple: Ontology in Medical Practice*. Durham, NC: Duke University Press.

Mukerji, C. (1989) *A Fragile Power: Scientists and the State*. Princeton: Princeton University Press.

Nelkin, D. (1979) *Controversy: Politics of Technical Decisions*. Newbury Park: Sage.

Nelkin, D. (1982) *The Creation Controversy: Science or Scripture in the Schools*. New York: Norton.

Nelkin, D., and Pollak, M. (1981) *The Atom Besieged: Extraparliamentary Dissent in France and Germany*. Cambridge, MA: MIT Press.

Newman, W., and Principe, L. (2002) *Alchemy Tried in the Fire: Starkey, Boyle and the Fate of Helmontian Chemistry*. Chicago: University of Chicago Press.

Ong, A., and Collier, S. J. (eds.) (2005) *Global Assemblages: Technology, Politics, and Ethics as Anthropological Problems*. Oxford: Blackwell.

Owen-Smith, J. (2005) "Dockets, Deals, and Sagas." *Social Studies of Science* 35(1): 69–97.

Petryna, A. (2002) *Life Exposed: Biological Citizens after Chernobyl*. Princeton: Princeton University Press.

Pickering, A. (1984) *Constructing Quarks: A Sociological History of Particle Physics*. Chicago: University of Chicago Press.

Pickering, A. (1995) *The Mangle of Practice: Time, Agency, and Science*. Chicago: University of Chicago Press.

Pickering, A. (2005) "Decentering Sociology: Synthetic Dyes and Social Theory." *Perspectives on Science* 13(3): 352–405.

Pinch, T., and Trocco, F. (2002) *Analog Days: The Invention and Impact of the Moog Synthesizer*. Cambridge, MA: Harvard University Press.

Polanyi, M. (1997) *Personal Knowledge: Towards a Post-Critical Philosophy*. New York: Routledge.

Prakash, G. (1999) *Another Reason: Science and the Imagination of Modern India*. Princeton: Princeton University Press.

Principe, L. (1998) *The Aspiring Adept: Robert Boyle and his Alchemical Quest*. Princeton: Princeton University Press.

Proctor, R. (1991) *Value-Free Science? Purity and Power in Modern Knowledge*. Cambridge: MA: Harvard University Press.

Rabinow, P. (1992) "Studies in the Anthropology of Reason." *Anthropology Today* 8(5): 10.

Rabinow, P. (1996) *Making PCR: A Story of Biotechnology*. Chicago: University of Chicago Press.

Rader, K. A. (2004) *Making Mice: Standardizing Animals for American Biomedical Research, 1900–1955*. Princeton: Princeton University Press.

Reardon, J. (2004) *Race to the Finish: Identity and Governance in an Age of Genomics*. Princeton: Princeton University Press.

Redfield, P. (2000) *Space in the Tropics: From Convicts to Rockets in French Guiana*. Berkeley: University of California Press.

Restivo, S. (ed.) (2005) *Science, Technology, and Society: An Encyclopedia*. New York: Oxford University Press.

Rheinberger H. J. (1997) *Toward A History of Epistemic Things: Synthesizing Proteins in the Test Tube*. Stanford: Stanford University Press.

Ronell, A. (1989) *The Telephone Book: Technology, Schizophrenia, Electric Speech*. Lincoln: University of Nebraska Press.

Rouse, J. (1987) *Knowledge and Power: Toward a Political Philosophy of Science*. Ithaca, NY: Cornell University Press.

Rouse, J. (1992) "What Are Cultural Studies of Scientific Knowledge?" *Configurations* 1(1): 57–94.

Schiebinger, L. (1993) *Nature's Body: Gender in the Making of Modern Science*. Boston: Beacon Press.

Shapin, S. (1993) "Discipline and Bounding: the History and Sociology of Science as Seen Through the Internalism-Externalism Debate." *History of Science* 30: 333–69.

Shapin, S., and Schaffer, S. (1985) *Leviathan and the Air Pump*. Princeton: Princeton University Press.

Silbey, S. S., and Ewick, P. (2002) "The Structure of Legality: The Cultural Contradictions of Social Institutions," in R. A. Kagan, M. Krygier, and K. Winston (eds.), *Legality and Community: On the Intellectual Legacy of Philip Selznick*. Berkeley: University of California Press.

Sismondo, S. (2004) *An Introduction to Science and Technology Studies*. Oxford: Blackwell.

Smith, R., and Wynne, B. (eds.) (1989) *Expert Evidence: Interpreting Science in the Law*. London: Routledge/Chapman & Hall.

Stone, A. R. (1995) *The War of Desire and Technology at the Close of the Mechanical Age*. Cambridge, MA: MIT Press.

Strathern, M. (1980) "No Nature, No Culture: The Hagen Case," in C. MacCormack and M. Strathern (eds.), *Nature, Culture, Gender*. Cambridge: Cambridge University Press.

Suchman, L. (2006) *Human and Machine Reconfigurations: Plans and Situated Actions*. Cambridge: Cambridge University Press.

Taussig, K., Rapp, R. L., and Heath, D. (2003) "Flexible Eugenics: Technologies of Self in the Age of Eugenics," in A. Goodman, D. Heath, and M. S. Lindee (eds.), *Genetic Nature/Culture: Anthropology and Science Beyond the Two Culture Divide*. Berkeley: University of California Press.

Traweek, S. (1988) *Beamtimes and Lifetimes: The World of High Energy Physicists*. Cambridge, MA: Harvard University Press.

Traweek, S. (1993) "An Introduction to Cultural, Gender, and Social Studies of Science and Technology." *Journal of Culture, Medicine, and Psychiatry* 17: 3–25.

Tsing, A. (2005) *Friction: An Ethnography of Global Connection*. Princeton: Princeton University Press.

Tuana, N. (ed.) (1989) *Feminism and Science*. Bloomington: Indiana University Press.

Turkle, S. (1985) *The Second Self: Computers and the Human Spirit*. New York: Simon & Schuster.

Verran, H. (2001) *Science and an African Logic*. Chicago: University of Chicago Press.

Wynne, B. (1987) *Risk Management and Hazardous Waste: Implementation and the Dialectics of Credibility*. London: Springer.

Part V
New Developments

24

Mobilities and Social Theory

John Urry

"A self *does not amount to much, but no self is an island; each exists in a fabric of relations that is now more complex and mobile than ever before*" (Lyotard 1984: 15)

"*Transportation is civilisation*" (Ezra Pound 1973 [1917]: 169)

THE MOBILITIES PARADIGM

It sometimes seems that all the world is on the move. International students, the early retired, terrorists, members of diasporas, holidaymakers, businesspeople, slaves, sports stars, asylum seekers, refugees, backpackers, commuters, young mobile professionals, prostitutes – these and many others seem to find the contemporary world is their oyster or at least their destiny. Criss-crossing the globe are the routeways of these many groups intermittently encountering one another in transportation and communication hubs, searching out in real and electronic databases the next coach, message, plane, back of lorry, text, bus, lift, ferry, train, car, website, wifi hot spot, and so on. The scale of this traveling is immense (see Urry 2007). It is predicted that by 2010 there will be at least 1 billion legal international arrivals each year (compared with 25 million in 1950); there are 4 million air passengers each day; at any one time 360,000 passengers are in flight *above* the US, equivalent to a substantial city; 31 million refugees roam the globe (Papastergiadis 1999: 10, 41, 54); and there were 552 million cars in 1998 with a projected 730 million in 2020, equivalent to one for every 8.6 people (Geffen, Dooley, and Kim 2003). In 1800 people in the US traveled 50 meters a day – they now travel 50 kilometers a day (Buchanan 2002: 121). Today world citizens move 23 billion kilometers; by 2050 it is predicted that that figure will have increased fourfold to 106 billion (Schafer and Victor 2000: 171).

However, people do not spend more time traveling, since this has remained constant at around one hour or so per day (Lyons and Urry 2005). But people are traveling further and faster, if not more often or spending more time actually "on the road." And given the spread of various communications such as post, fax, the internet, fixed-line phones, mobiles, mobile computing, and so on, whose uses have all increased in recent decades, it is striking that so far people do still physically travel. Such movement shows little sign of *substantially* abating in the longer term even with September 11, SARS, Bali, Madrid and London bombings, and other global catastrophes. Being physically mobile has become, for the rich and even for some poor, a "way of life" across the globe.

Materials too are on the move, often carried by these moving bodies whether openly, clandestinely, or inadvertently. The "cosmopolitanization" of taste means that consumers in the "North" expect fresh materials from around the world "air-freighted" to their table, while consumers in the "South" often find roundabout ways to access consumer goods from the North. And more generally there are massive flows of illegal if valuable materials, drugs, guns, cigarettes, alcohol, and counterfeit and pirated products.

This movement of people and objects is hugely significant for the global environment, with transport accounting for one-third of total carbon dioxide emissions (Geffen, Dooley and Kim 2003). Transport is the fastest-growing source of greenhouse emissions, and with the predicted growth of car and lorry travel within China and elsewhere throughout the world, the rapid growth of air travel and transport, and the political movement especially in the US critiquing the thesis of global climate change, there has been little likelihood of this growth abating. Many other "environmental" consequences follow from the growth of mass mobilities: reduced air quality; increased noise, smell, and visual intrusion; ozone depletion; social fragmentation; and medical consequences of "accidental" deaths and injuries, asthma, and obesity (Whitelegg and Haq 2003).

The internet has simultaneously grown incredibly rapidly, faster than any previous technology and with huge impacts throughout much of the world. There are 1 billion internet users. Also since 2001 there are world-wide more mobile phones than landline phones (Katz and Aakhus 2002a). The overall volume of international telephone calls increased at least tenfold between 1982 and 2001 (Vertovec 2004: 223). Virtual communications and mobile telephony are calling into being new ways of interacting and communicating within and across societies, especially with some less well-developed societies jumping directly to mobile rather than landline telephony.

These converging mobile technologies appear to be transforming many aspects of economic and social life that are in some sense on the "move" or away from "home." In a mobile world there are extensive and intricate connections between physical travel and modes of communication, and these form new fluidities and are often difficult to stabilize. Physical changes appear to be "dematerializing" connections, as people, machines, images, information, power, money, ideas, and dangers are "on the move," making and remaking connections at often rapid speed around the world (see Urry 2007, for more detail throughout).

Indeed issues of movement, of too little movement for some or too much for others or of the wrong sort or at the wrong time, are central to many people's lives and to the operations of many public, private, and non-governmental organizations. Thus social life presupposes people, images, ideas, and objects being at least from time to time on the move. It is an empirical question as to how important such movement is within different societies or types of society. Contemporary societies demonstrate more movement for more people across longer distances albeit occurring for shorter time periods. Further, there are more diverse forms of such movement. Also, movement is increasingly deemed as a right, as in the UN Declaration of Universal Rights or the constitution of the European Union. And those who, for whatever reason, are denied such movement suffer multiple forms of exclusion. There is an ideology of movement and distinct forms of "capital" acquired by those on the move.

Various theorists as well as more empirical analysts are now mobilizing a "mobility turn," a different way of thinking through the character of economic, social, and political relationships. There is we might say a "mobility" structure of feeling in the air, with Simmel and Benjamin, Deleuze and Lefebvre, de Certeau and Erving Goffman proving important guides. Such a turn is spreading in and through the social sciences, mobilizing analyses that have been historically static, fixed, and concerned with predominantly a-spatial "social structures." The mobility turn is postdisciplinary. Elsewhere I develop a new cross or postdisciplinary mobilities paradigm (Hannam, Sheller and Urry 2006; Sheller and Urry 2006; Urry 2007). It is argued that thinking through a mobilities "lens" provides a distinctively different social science productive of different theories, methods, questions, and solutions.

So the aim in this chapter is both to make the substantive claim that there are multiple kinds of movement and that much social science has inadequately examined them, *and* that there is a putative new paradigm which involves a postdisciplinary, productive way of doing social science, especially in the new century where mobility issues would seem to be center-stage.

A-MOBILE SOCIAL SCIENCE

Initially, then we can note that much social science has been "a-mobile." First, there has been *neglect* of movement and communications and the forms in which they are economically, politically, and socially organized. Thus although such activities (such as holidaymaking, walking, car driving, phoning, flying) are often personally and culturally significant within people's lives, they have been mostly ignored by social science. Along with others I have sought to draw such topics into the viewfinder of social science, especially the analysis of holidaymaking, leisurely travel, and the "productive" experiences of different forms of movement (Lyons and Urry 2005; Urry 2002).

Second, there has been the *minimization* of the significance of these forms of movement for the nature of work, schooling, family life, politics, and protest, that is, within crucially important social institutions. And yet for example families depend upon patterns of regular visiting, schools are chosen in terms of catchment areas, work patterns depends on the way congestion structures commuting flows, new industries depend upon new migrants, protest movements depend upon marches and co-present demonstrations. These patterns of movement structure how these social institutions and activities develop and change, something minimized in conventional "structural" analyses.

Third, social science mostly focuses upon the patterns in which human subjects directly interact together and ignores the underlying physical or material infrastructures that orchestrate and underlie economic, political, and social patterns. Almost all mobilities presuppose large-scale immobile infrastructures that make possible the socialities of everyday life. These "immobile" infrastructures include paths, railway tracks, public roads, telegraph lines, water pipes, telephone exchanges, pylons, sewerage systems, gas pipes, airports, radio and TV aerials, mobile phone masts, satellites, underground cables, and so on (Graham and Marvin 2001). Intersecting with these infrastructures are the social solidarities of class, gender, ethnicity, nation, and age orchestrating diverse mobilities (see Ray 2002), including both enforced fixity within "enclaves" (Turner 2007) as well as coerced movement (Marfleet 2006).

Overall the term "mobile" or "mobility" is used in four main ways (see Jain 2002). First, there is the use of mobile to mean something that moves or is *capable* of movement, as with the mobile (portable) phone but also with the mobile person, home, hospital, kitchen, and so on. Mobility is a property of things and of people. Many technologies in the contemporary era appear to have set in motion new ways of people being temporarily mobile, including physical prostheses that enable the "disabled immobile" to acquire some means of movement. Mostly the term mobile here is a positive category, except in the various critiques of what has been termed "hypermobility" (Adams 1999).

Second, there is the sense of mobile as a *mob*, a rabble or an unruly crowd. The mob is seen as disorderly precisely because it is mobile, not fully fixed within boundaries and therefore needs to be tracked and socially regulated. The contemporary world appears to be generating many significant new mobs or multitudes, including smart mobs that generate for their governance, new and extensive physical and/or electronic systems of counting, regulation and fixing within known places or specified borders (Hardt and Negri 2000; Rheingold 2002; Turner 2007).

Third, there is the sense of mobility deployed in mainstream sociology/social science. This is upward or downward *social* mobility. It is presumed that there is relatively clear cut *vertical* hierarchy of positions and that people can be located by comparison with their parents' position or with their own starting position within such hierarchies. There is debate as to whether or not contemporary societies have increased the circulation of people up and down such hierarchies, making the modern world more or less mobile. Some argue that extra circulation only results from changes in the number of top positions and not in increased movement between them (Goldthorpe 1980).

Fourth, there is mobility as migration or other kinds of semi-permanent geographical movement. This is a horizontal sense of being "on the move," that refers to moving country or continent often in search of a "better life" or to escape from drought, persecution, war, starvation, and so on. Although it is thought that contemporary societies entail much mobility in this sense, especially through diasporic travel (Cohen 1997), previous cultures also presupposed considerable movement, such as from Europe to the dominated countries of their various empires or later to North America.

This chapter investigates all these senses of "mobility." Such a generic "mobilities" includes various kinds and temporalities of physical movement, ranging from standing, lounging, walking, climbing, dancing, to those enhanced by technologies, of bikes, buses, cars, trains, ships, planes, wheelchairs, crutches (see Cresswell 2006; Kellerman 2006; Thomsen, Nielsen, and Gudmundsson 2005; Urry 2007 for recent book-length treatments).

Movements examined range from the daily, weekly, yearly, and over people's lifetimes. Also included are the movement of images and information on multiple media, as well as virtual movement as communications are effected one-to-one, one-to-many, and many-to-many through networked and embedded computers. A mobilities turn also involves examining how the transporting of people and the communicating of messages, information, and images may overlap, coincide, and converge through digitized flows. And the ways in which physical movement pertains to upward and downward social mobility are also central to a mobilities analysis. Moving between places physically or virtually can be a source of status and power, an expression of the rights to movement either temporarily or permanently. And where movement is coerced it may generate social deprivation and exclusion.

The classical sociological tradition did not entirely neglect such issues, but only Simmel really put the organization and consequences of mobilities within social life center-stage in his analysis. Accordingly I turn to Georg Simmel, the one "classical" sociologist who attempted to develop a mobilities paradigm though analyses of proximity, distance, and movement within the modern city (Jensen 2006: 146). In subsequent sections I examine important other contributions in developing a mobilities paradigm.

SIMMEL AND MOBILITIES

Simmel notes the exceptional human achievement involved in creating a "path" between two particular places. No matter how often people have gone backwards and forwards between the places and "subjectively" connected them in their mind, it is "only in visibly *impressing* the path into the surface of the earth that the places were objectively connected" (Simmel 1997: 171; emphasis added). This permanent "connection" between places is derived from the "will to connection" which is a shaper of things and of relations. Animals by contrast cannot accomplish such a "miracle of the road," an even more developed "impressing . . . into the surface of the earth" having the effect of "freezing movement in a solid structure" (1997: 171).

And this freezing, this achievement of connection, reaches its zenith with a bridge that "symbolizes the extension of our volitional sphere over space" (Simmel 1997: 171). Only for humans are the banks of the river not just apart but separated and thus potentially bridgeable. And like Marx's analysis of the "architect" (as opposed to the bee) humans are able to "see" these connections in their mind's eye as separated *and* as therefore needing connection. Simmel summarizes the power of human imagination, of "conception": "if we did not first connect them in our practical thoughts, in our needs and in our fantasy, then the concept of separation would have no meaning" (1997: 171).

Such a bridge can moreover become part of "nature," picturesque, as it accomplishes the connection between places. For the eye the bridge stands in a close and fortuitous relationship to the banks. Such a freezing of movement can seem like a natural "unity," with high aesthetic value, almost an improvement upon "nature" since it "naturally" appears to connect the banks.

So what of movement? Simmel distinguishes between various socio-spatial patterns, including nomadism, wandering, a royal tour, diasporic travel, the court's travel, migration, and adventure. What is distinct is the "form of sociation . . . in the case of a wandering group in contrast to a spatially fixed one" (Simmel 1997: 160). And these variations stem from the "temporal duration" implicated in the period "away." Time structures the "nuancing of the course of a gathering" – but this is no simple and direct relationship. Sometimes a short time encounter can lead to the conveying of secrets through the role of the temporary "stranger," while on other occasions spending a long time together is necessary for mutual adaptation and trust to develop.

Simmel also emphasizes how physical or bodily travel is interconnected with other mobilities. He hypothesizes that there was more travel by scholars and merchants in the Middle Ages than there was at the beginning of the twentieth century. This is because in the latter period there were "letters and books, bank accounts and branch offices, through mechanical reproduction of the same model and through photography" (Simmel 1997: 165). In the Middle Ages all this information "had to be brought about through people traveling" from place to place since there were few other "systems" to move ideas, information and especially money (1997: 167). And yet that traveling was almost always full of "dangers and difficulties," especially since there were relatively few "expert systems" that would mitigate the risks of such physical travel (1997: 167). Indeed there were also many itinerant poor, the vagabonds, whose lives were based upon a "restlessness and mobility" and which generated various "fluid associations" such as bands of "wandering minstrels" characterized by the "impulse for a continuous change of scene, the ability and desire to 'disappear'" (1997: 168).

Simmel had much to say about the contemporary city where new modes of movement and restlessness are widespread. The metropolitan type of personality consists in "the *intensification of nervous stimulation* which results from the swift and uninterrupted change of outer and inner stimuli" (Simmel 1997: 175). The modern city involves the "unexpectedness of onrushing impressions . . . With each crossing of the street, with the tempo and multiplicity of economic, occupational and social life," he says that the city sets up a "deep contrast with small town and rural life with reference to the sensory foundations of psychic life" (1997: 175; and see Simmel 1990).

And because of the richness and diverse sets of onrushing stimuli in the metropolis, people are forced to develop an attitude of reserve and insensitivity to feeling. Otherwise most would not be able to cope with overwhelming experiences generated by a high density and movement of population. Onrushing stimulations produce a blasé attitude, the incapacity to react to new sensations with appropriate energy. The movement of the city, as well as the rapid movement of money, generates reserve and indifference (Jensen 2006: 148–9).

Thus Simmel provides an early examination, paralleling Marx and Engels in *The Manifesto of the Communist Party*, of the effects of "modern" patterns of mobility upon social life (Marx and Engels 1952; see also Berman 1983; Simmel 1997). Simmel analyzes the fragmentation and diversity of modern life and shows that motion, the diversity of stimuli, and the visual appropriations of place are centrally important to new modern urban experiences.

Moreover, because of money with "all its colourlessness and indifference" (Simmel 1997: 178; see also 1990) and its twin, the modern city, a new precision comes to be necessary in social life. Agreements and arrangements need to demonstrate unambiguousness in timing and location. Life in the mobile, onrushing city presupposes punctuality, and this is reflected by the "universal diffusion of pocket watches" (Simmel 1997: 177). This was as symbolic of the "modern" as the ubiquitous mobile phone is today. Simmel argues that the "relationships and affairs of the typical metropolitan usually are so varied and complex that without the strictest punctuality in promises and services the whole structure would break down into an inextricable chaos" (1997: 177). This necessity for punctuality: "is brought about by the aggregation of so many people with such differentiated interests who must integrate their relations and activities into a highly complex organism" (1997: 177).

So the forming of a complex system of relationships means that meetings and activities have to be punctual, timetabled, rational, a system or "structure of the highest impersonality" often involving much distance-keeping politeness (Simmel 1997: 178; Toiskallio 2002: 171). This "system-ness" of mobility results in the individual becoming "a mere cog in an enormous organization of things and powers"; as a result "life is made infinitely easy for the personality in that stimulations, interests, uses of time and consciousness are offered to it from all sides" (Simmel 1997: 184). Simmel tellingly notes how as a consequence "they carry the person as if in a stream, and one needs hardly to swim for oneself" (1997: 184).

But simultaneously modern city life produces people each with a "highly personal subjectivity," a tendency to be "different," of standing out in a striking manner and thereby seeking attention, a "culture of narcissism" (Lasch 1980; Simmel 1997: 178). People gain self-esteem through being aware of how they are perceived by others. But because of the scale of mobility in the metropolis, there is a "brevity and scarcity of inter-human contacts" (Simmel 1997: 183). Compared with the small-scale community, the modern city gives room to the individual and to the peculiarities of their inner and outer development. It is the spatial form of modern urban life that permits the unique development of individuals who socially interact with an exceptionally wide range of contacts. People seek to distinguish themselves; they try to be different through adornment and fashion encountering each other in brief moments of proximity.

Simmel places particular emphasis upon the eye as a "unique sociological achievement" (1997: 111) that is the "most direct and purest interaction that exists" (1997: 111). People cannot avoid taking through the eye without at the same time giving. The eye produces "the most complete reciprocity" of person to person, face to face (1997: 112). Such face-to-face co-presence is key to the obligations to, and consequences of, travel. Boden and Molotch summarize how "Copresent interaction remains, just as Georg Simmel long ago observed, the fundamental mode of human intercourse and socialization, a 'primordial site for sociality'" (1994: 258).

Simmel also examines the attractions of the "adventure" in shaping the desire to be elsewhere; such "adventures" occur "outside the usual continuity of this life"

(1997: 222). Because life has become "easy" in the city, so it is outside, in places of adventure, where the body might come *to* life, it is a "body in motion" that finds its way, being natural, knowing nature, saving oneself "naturally." The adventure thus enables the body to escape the blasé attitude, to be rejuvenated during moments of bodily arousal in motion.

More generally Simmel sets himself against analyses that seek to explain social phenomena in terms of individual acts. Important social phenomena are not the consequence of combinations of a lower order. He is anti-reductionist, being concerned with an array of emergent social forms, the elementary substance of social life (Lash 2005: 11). Simmel's approach speaks of how "things find their meaning in relation to each other, and the mutuality of the relationships in which they are involved constitutes what and how they are" (Simmel 1990: 128–9).

Some elements of Simmel's ideas were developed within the Chicago School which in the first half of this century provided a range of post-Simmelian mobility studies especially concerned with the itinerant lives of hoboes, gangs, prostitutes, migrants, and so on (see e.g. Park 1970). However, this development was cut short in its tracks as a range of structural or static theories took over within sociology, including structural functionalism, positivist analysis of "variables," structural Marxism, and so on. Meanwhile the study of mobilities turned into the professional examination of "transport" including "transport geography," and to a lesser extent of "tourism," that were taken to be differentiated and specific domains that should be researched far away from the provocative promptings of Simmel's essays and analyses.

In the next sections I describe an eclectic range of other "mobility" theories and programs of research in order to develop Simmel's sketch for a mobilities paradigm. This paradigm has waited one hundred years to get out of the garage, we might say.

SEDENTARISM

I begin somewhat surprisingly with sedentarist thinking derived from Heideggerian notions. For Heidegger dwelling means to reside or to stay, to dwell at peace, to be content or at home within a place. To build (*bauen*) involved cherishing and protecting, tilling soil and cultivating vines. Such building involved care and was habitual. Heidegger wants to ensure how building and dwelling can be combined once again, calling this "letting dwell" (1993: 361; Zimmerman 1990: 151).

Such dwelling involves a staying *with* things which are bodily ready to hand. Thus Heidegger argues against the separation of man [*sic*] and space, as though they stand on opposite sides. Rather to speak of men [*sic*] is to speak of those who already dwell through moving through space: "To say that mortals *are* is to say that *in dwelling* they persist through spaces by virtue of their stay among things and locales. And only because mortals pervade, persist through, spaces by their very essence are they able to go through spaces" (Heidegger 1993: 359). But people only go through spaces in ways which sustain them through the relationships which are established "with near and remote locales and things" (1993: 359). When one goes to open the door of a room one is already part of that room. A person is not a separate "encapsulated body" since such a person already pervades the space of the room they are about to enter. Only because of the form of dwelling is it possible to go through that particular door. To dwell we might say is always to be moving and sensing, both within and beyond.

Heidegger, like Simmel, discusses the significance of bridges. They do not connect banks that are in a sense already "there." The banks only emerge as a consequence of a bridge that now crosses the stream. A bridge causes the banks to lie across from each other. This has the effect that surrounding land on either side of the stream is brought into closer juxtaposition. Heidegger argues that the bridge functions as an actant since it "brings stream and bank and land into each other's neighbourhood. The bridge *gathers* the earth as landscape around the stream" (1993: 354).

Furthermore, a new bridge reorganizes how people dwell/move within that area. Bridges initiate new social patterns, forming a locale or connecting different parts of a town, or the town with the country, or the town with "the network of long-distance traffic, paced and calculated for maximum yield" (Heidegger 1993: 354). A bridge is ready on call, waiting for slow movement across it, the "lingering" ways of people to and fro across the bridge, moving from bank to bank. Tourist places are waiting also, on call for inspection by a tourist group said to be ordered there by the vacation industry (Heidegger 1993).

Ingold analogously writes how "landscape is constituted as an enduring record of – and testimony to – the lives and works of past generations who have dwelt within it, and in so doing, have left there something of themselves" (1993: 152). Landscape is thus neither nature nor culture, neither mind nor matter. It is the world as known to those who have dwelt in that place, those who currently dwell there, those who will dwell there, and those whose practical activities take them though its many sites and journey along its multiple paths. It is, Ingold argues, the "task-scape" of any environment that produces the social character of a landscape. Paths especially demonstrate the accumulated imprint of the countless journeys made as people go about their everyday business. The network of paths shows the sedi-mented activity of a community stretching over generations; it is the taskscape made visible (Ingold 1993: 167). People imagine themselves treading the same paths as earlier generations as the path gets impressed into the ground. And thus the redirec-tion of a path, or its elimination with a new road, will often be viewed as vandalism against that community and its collective memories and forms of dwelling/moving in and through a given place (and see Ingold 2004).

NOMADISM

Almost the opposite set of ideas is provided by metaphors and theories of fluidity and nomadism (Bauman 2000; Cresswell 2002: 15–18). Many writers have devel-oped metaphors of sea, river, flux, waves, liquidity, the vagabond, the pilgrim, and nomadism. Such metaphors often draw upon Derrida, who says: "*Différance* is incompatible with the static, synchronic, taxonomic, ahistoric motifs in the concept of *structure*" (1987: 27).

Deleuze and Guattari elaborate on the implications of nomads, external to each state (1986: 49–53). Nomads characterize societies of deterritorialization, constituted by lines of flight rather than by points or nodes. They maintain that: "the nomad has no points, paths or land . . . If the nomad can be called the Deterritorialized *par excellence*, it is precisely because there is no reterritorialization *afterwards* as with the migrant" (1986: 52). More generally here, this neo-vitalism emphasizes process and change, as the core of social life (see Lash 2005). There is no stasis, only processes of creation and transformation. There is nothing before movement; movement expresses how things are.

Other mobile metaphors are those of the vagabond and the tourist (Bauman 1993). The vagabond is a pilgrim without a destination, a nomad without an itinerary; while the tourist "pay[s] for their freedom; the right to disregard native concerns and feelings, the right to spin their own web of meanings . . . The world is the tourist's oyster . . . to be lived pleasurably – and thus given meaning" (Bauman 1993: 241). Both vagabonds and tourists move through other people's spaces, they involve the separation of physical closeness from any sense of moral proximity and they set standards for happiness (Bauman 1993: 243). More generally, Bauman argues that there is a shift from modernity as heavy and solid to one that is light and liquid and where speed of movement of people, money, images, and information is paramount (2000; the strange death of Concorde partly shows the limits of this claim).

A further nomadic metaphor is the "motel" (Morris 1988). The motel has no real lobby, it is tied into the network of highways, it functions to relay people rather than to provide settings for coherent human subjects, it is consecrated to circulation and movement, and it demolishes the sense of place and locale. Motels "memorialize only movement, speed, and perpetual circulation" (Morris 1988: 3); they "can never be a true *place*" and one is only distinguished from another in "a high-speed, *empiricist* flash" (Morris 1988: 5). The motel, like the airport transit lounge, represents neither arrival nor departure but the "pause" (Morris 1988: 41; Augé 1995).

Wolff and others criticize the masculinist character of many of these nomadic and travel metaphors since they suggest that there is ungrounded and unbounded movement (see the critique in Skeggs 2004). But clearly different social categories have very different access to being "on the road" both literally and metaphorically. Jokinen and Veijola show that certain male metaphors can be rewritten or coded differently (1997). If these male metaphors are so rewritten, as say, paparazzi, homeless drunk, sex tourist, and womanizer, then they lose such positive valuation. Jokinen and Veijola also propose female metaphors of movement, including those of the prostitute, the babysitter, and the au pair (1997).

MATERIALS ON THE MOVE

There was a "spatial turn" in the social sciences during the 1980s. This involved theory and research that demonstrated that social relations are spatially organized and such spatial structuring makes a significant difference to social relations (see Gregory and Urry 1995). Massey proclaimed that "space matters" to social life (1994). Now space is increasingly viewed as made up of moving elements with various "power-geometries." Most relevant here is the way that spaces are viewed as comprised of various materials, of objects and environments, that are intermittently in motion. These materials are assembled and reassembled in changing configurations and rearticulated meanings (Cresswell 2002).

Studies of travel, migration, and belonging show how cultural objects are on the move and how they may hold their meaning as they move and are moved around. There are different kinds of objects and they variably hold or lose their value as they move from place to place. Objects variably mobilize place and they are involved in the reconstitution of belonging and memory (Lury 1997; Molotch 2003).

Analyses here often draw upon science and technology studies which are often concerned with "transport," with how the laws of science sometimes but contingently work similarly across the globe through the effective movement of scientific procedures, methods, and findings. Machines and machinations travel (Law and Mol 2001: 611). Science and technology studies show how humans are intricately networked *with* machines, and also with software, texts, objects, databases, and so on. Law thus goes on to argue much more generally that "what we call the social is materially heterogeneous: talk, bodies, texts, machines, architectures, all of these and many more are implicated in and perform the social" (1994: 2). Such hybrids are on occasions tightly coupled with complex, enduring, and predictable connections between peoples, objects, and technologies, and these may move scientific findings across multiple and distant spaces and times (Law 1994: 24). A particular scientific theory and set of findings may form an "immutable mobile" where relative distance is a function of the relations between the heterogeneous components comprising that actor network (Latour 1999; Law and Hassard 1999). The invariant outcome of a network may be delivered so as to overcome regional boundaries. Things can be made *close* through networked relations.

Mobilities involve heterogeneous "hybrid geographies" of humans-and-machines that contingently enable people and materials to move and to hold their shape as they move across various networks (Whatmore 2002). Dant develops the hybrid of the "driver-car" that is neither the car nor the driver but the specific hybrid or intermittently moving combination of the two (2004). There are many other mobile hybrids, including the "leisure-walker," the "train-passenger," the "cycle-rider" and so on (as set out in Urry 2007).

MIGRATIONS AND DIASPORAS

Multiple mobilities have been central to much historical development and are not simply "new." Thus over many centuries there were complex trading and travel routes that constituted what we now call the Mediterranean world (Braudel 1992). The ships, sea routes, and interconnectivity of the slave and post-slave trade engendered what Gilroy terms the "Black Atlantic" (1993). And the complex mobilities of diasporas and transnational migrants are key to examining many contemporary postcolonial relationships. There is a "diasporization" of communities in the contemporary era (Cohen 1997).

But although these are not new, the mobile character of such processes is now much more evident. Analyses of migration, diasporas, and more fluid citizenships are central to critiques of the bounded and static categories of nation, ethnicity, community, and state present in much social science (Brah 1996; Joseph 1999; Ong

1999; Ong and Nonini 1997). Various works theorize the multiple, overlapping, and turbulent processes of migration, dislocation, displacement, disjuncture, and dialogism. These massive contemporary migrations, often with oscillatory flows between unexpected locations, have been described as a series of turbulent waves, with a hierarchy of eddies and vortices, with globalism being a virus that stimulates resistance, and with the migration system's "cascading" moves away from any state of equilibrium (Papastergiadis 1999: 102–4, 121).

For example, the fluid diaspora of the 32 million or so Latinos now living in the US is the largest ethnic group in Los Angeles, forming a city within a city, and they will soon outnumber whites living in California (Davis 2000). There are wide-ranging processes of "cultural syncretism that may become a transformative template for the whole society" as the US becomes Latinized (Davis 2000: 15). Much of this syncretism stems from such "transnationalized communities" moving between Mexico, a "nomadic" country, and the US "like quantum particles in two places at once" (Davis 2000: 77).

In studies of such turbulence around the world, analyses of the global level are intertwined both with more "local" concerns about everyday transportation and material cultures, as well as with the "technologies" of information and communication technologies and the emerging infrastructures of mobility and surveillance (see Clifford 1997; Sheller 2003). These studies of far-flung communities also bring out why and how members of such diasporic communities, although increasingly using the internet and mobile telephony, do meet on occasions face to face, in other words with the necessity of travel and meetings to reconstitute friendship or business networks or a family life lived at a distance (see Miller and Slater 2000, on Trinidad).

Also increasingly significant within the contemporary world are many forms of forced migration (see Marfleet 2006). Such migrants originate in zones of economic and political crisis in the most vulnerable parts of the developing world. Their mobility is engendered by the instability of economic, social, and environmental structures and especially the weakness of local states. Migrants mainly originate from "wild zones" that the globalizing world engenders, and especially from a "culture of terror" and from sites overwhelmed by the early consequences of "global heating" (Lovelock 2006). As Ascherson writes, "the subjects of history, once the settled farmer and citizens, have now become the migrants, the refugees, the *Gastarbeiter*, the asylum seekers, the urban homeless" (cited in Papastergiadis 1999: 1). And once people are forced to migrate, they then encounter the legal and social systems of the developed world, which sets up many restrictions and limitations upon their migration and upon their capacity to stay. And their journeys are often extraordinarily long and complex, involving multiple relationships often of an exploitative character, various transit points especially in major cities and different modes of transport, some of which are notoriously unsafe (Marfleet 2006: ch. 10).

PROXIMITIES AND PLEASURES

Patterns of movement involve intermittent face-to-face proximities with other people (friends, kin, workmates, colleagues, networks), with other places (beaches, cities, river valleys, mountains, lakes) and with events (conferences, meetings, Olympics, festivals, exhibitions: Urry 2002, 2003). These face-to-face proximities produce a strong obligation to travel in order to experience the person, place, or event and to be in their presence (but see de Botton 2002 on the contrary delights of armchair travel).

Especially significant are occasioned intermittent face-to-face conversations and meetings that "have" to occur within certain places at certain moments. Such inter- mittently occurring meetings seem obligatory for the sustaining of family, friendship, work groups, businesses, and leisure organizations (Goffman 1963, 1971a, 1971b, 1972). At the same time there are periods of distance and solitude in between these intermittent moments of co-presence.

Such mobilities often also entail distinct social spaces or nodes where these face- to-face encounters take place, such as stations, hotels, motorways, resorts, airports, corners, malls, subway stations, buses, public squares, leisure complexes, cosmo- politan cities, beaches, galleries, roadside parks, and so on (Amin and Thrift 2002). These are places of intermittent movement where specific groups come together, normally now involving the use of phones, mobiles, laptops, SMS messaging, wire- less communications, and so on, often to make arrangements "on the move." Some of these "meetings" consist of "underground" social gatherings or "smart mobs" (Rheingold 2002), while other groups involve moving through relatively smooth corridors linking different nodes, as with business class air travel, fast lanes, express checkouts, business lounges, and so on (see Lassen 2006 on the smooth corridors of aeromobility).

In particular, places are also experienced through various senses. Various theories of romanticism, the sublime, the picturesque, and the performative are necessary to account for why certain groups feel a burning desire to be by a given lake, up a mountain, on that beach. These are distinctly visceral desires and they mobilize huge numbers of people regularly to travel and move around particular sites, so effecting the tourist gaze (Urry 2002).

Moreover, different modes of travel involve different embodied performances, they are forms of material and sociable dwelling-in-motion, places of and for various occasioned activities. Different means of transport provide contrasting experiences, performances, and affordances (Gibson 1986). Thus the railway in the late nine- teenth century provided new ways of moving, socializing and seeing the swiftly passing landscape (Schivelbusch 1986). Recent analyses show how the car is "dwelt in" or corporeally inhabited and experienced through a combination of senses (Featherstone, Thrift and Urry 2004). These sensuous geographies of the car are not so much located within individual bodies but extend to familial spaces, neigh- borhoods, regions, and national cultures through various sensuous dispositions (Sheller 2004).

Various technologies are organized around and are part of movement. The iconic Sony Walkman was described as virtually an extension of the skin, molded like much else in modern consumer culture to the body and designed for movement (Du Gay et al. 1997: 23–4). Indeed there are many activities possible while on the move, some of which presuppose new mobile technologies. These include talking face to face and on mobile phones, glancing at the scenery, texting, working, listening to music (Walkman/iPod), using computers, information-gathering, and being connected through maintaining a moving presence with others also on the move (Lyons, Jain and Holley 2007).

SYSTEMS

Human beings are nothing without objects organized into various systems (see Graham and Marvin 2001). The systems come first and serve to augment the otherwise rather thin powers of individual human subjects. Those subjects are brought together and serve to develop significant powers only because of the systems that implicate them, and especially significant are those systems that move them, or their ideas, or information or various objects. There are various points to note about such mobility systems: they are organized around the processes that circulate people, objects, and information at various spatial ranges and speeds; these various mobility systems and routeways often linger over time with a powerful spatial fixity; and such mobility systems are based on increasingly expert and alienating forms of knowledge. There are interdependent systems of "immobile" material worlds, and especially exceptionally immobile platforms (transmitters, roads, garages, stations, aerials, airports, docks), and they structure mobility experiences through forming *complex* adaptive systems. These systems, almost all now software-based, ensure and make it seem unexceptional that products can be purchased, meetings will happen, components will arrive at the factory, planes will be waiting, messages will get through, money will arrive, and so on. These systems make repetitive or iterative actions possible and mostly happen without much cognitive thought (Thrift 2004). They produce regular and repetitive "spaces of anticipation" distributing economies, peoples, activities across the world.

In the modern world automobility is by far the most powerful of such mobility systems (Featherstone, Thrift and Urry 2004), while other such systems include the pedestrian system, the rail system, and aeromobility. Historically earlier systems include the road system of the Roman empire, the medieval horse system after the invention of the stirrup, and the cycle system in twentieth-century China. Historically most societies have been characterized by one major mobility system that is in an evolving and adaptive relationship with that society's economy, through the production and consumption of goods and services and the attraction and circulation of the labor force and consumers. Such mobility systems are also in adaptive and co-evolving relationships with each other, so that some such systems expand and multiply while others may over time shrink in terms of their range and impact. Such systems provide the environment within which each other system functions.

Further, the richer the society the greater the range of mobility systems that will be present and the more complex the intersections between such systems. These mobility systems have the effect of producing substantial inequalities between places and between people in terms of their location and access to these mobility systems. All societies presuppose multiple mobilities for people to be effective participants. Such access is unequally distributed but the structuring of this inequality depends *inter alia* on the economics of production and consumption of the objects relevant to mobility, the nature of civil society, the geographical distribution of people and activities, and the particular mobility systems in play and their forms of interdependence. We might say that unforced "movement" is power, that is, to be able to move (or to be able voluntarily to stay still) is for individuals and groups a major source of advantage and conceptually independent of economic and cultural advantage. High access to mobility depends upon access to more powerful mobility systems and where there is not confinement to mobility systems reducing in scale and significance.

These systems have the effect of spreading connections that become less based upon predictable co-presence and more upon relatively far-flung networks of at least partially weak ties. Thus the apparently different domains of work, family, and social life each become more networked – and in a way more similar to each other (see Larsen, Urry and Axhausen 2006). Moreover, networks within these domains increasingly overlap so movement between and across them becomes significant. Weak ties spread from domain to domain, especially with the growth of network capital that dramatically enhances the power of some nodes, and overall generate social inequalities that increasingly seem to depend upon relative levels of access to the array of resources necessary for networking, what I term "network capital" (Urry 2007).

And as people are moving about so information about them as human subjects is forcibly left behind in countless traces. Much of what was once "private" and carried close or on the person as body now exists outside of that body and outside the "self." Or, the self, we can say, is hugely distributed across various databases spread through time-space. There has been an irreversible shifting of the social world towards the "database-ization" of everyday life on the move (Information Commissioner 2006).

CONCLUSION

In this chapter I set out a range of social theoretical ideas that relate to the new mobilities paradigm. Especially significant are the varied writings of Simmel. However, there was little further development during much of the twentieth century. But in the past decade or so an array of new initiatives in both theory and methods has begun to make possible the mobilities paradigm. I have set out the contributions of sedentarist and nomadic theories, analyses of moving materials, the study of migrations and diasporas, the significance of "proximity" and "pleasure" and the nature of systems (see Urry 2007: ch. 2 on some methodological implications of the paradigm).

This paradigm is not just substantively different, in that it remedies the academic neglect of various movements of people, objects, information, and ideas. It is transformative of social science, authorizing an alternative theoretical and methodological landscape. It enables the "social world" to be theorized as a wide array of economic, social, and political practices, infrastructures, and ideologies that all involve, entail, or curtail various kinds of movement of people, or ideas, or information or objects. And in so doing this paradigm brings to the fore theories, methods, and exemplars of research that so far have been mostly out of sight. The term "mobilities" refers to this broad project of establishing a "movement-driven" social science in which movement, potential movement, and blocked movement are all conceptualized as constitutive of economic, social, and political relations (see many of the papers in the new journal *Mobilities*).

And in making the subterranean visible it redraws many ways in which social science has been practiced, especially as organized within distinct "regions" or "fortresses" of policed, bounded, and antagonistic "disciplines." I use the term subterranean to indicate how this paradigm is not being generated *de novo*. There are various paradigmatic fragments found in multiple archives that rest uneasily within their current disciplinary fortresses. The new paradigm is seeking to release these fragments from their cage and enable them to fly, confronting and engaging with other "angels" in flight, as Serres (1995) might fancifully express it.

Bibliography

Adams, J. (1999) *The Social Implications of Hypermobility*. OECD Project on Environmentally Sustainable Transport. Paris: OECD.

Amin, A., and Thrift, N. (2002) *Cities. Reimagining the Urban*. Cambridge: Polity.

Augé, M. (1995) *Non-Places*. London: Verso.

Bauman, Z. (1993) *Postmodern Ethics*. London: Routledge.

Bauman, Z. (2000) *Liquid Modernity*. Cambridge: Polity.

Berman, M. (1983) *All That Is Solid Melts into Air*. London: Verso.

Boden, D., and Molotch, H. (1994) "The Compulsion to Proximity," in R. Friedland and D. Boden (eds.), *Nowhere: Space, Time and Modernity*. Berkeley: University of California Press.

Brah, A. (1996) *Cartographies of Diaspora: Contesting Identities*. London: Routledge.

Braudel, F. (1992) *The Mediterranean and the Mediterranean World in the Age of Philip II*. London: BCA.

Buchanan, M. (2002) *Nexus: Small Worlds and the Groundbreaking Science of Networks*. London: W. W. Norton.

Clifford, J. (1997) *Routes: Travel and Translation in the Late Twentieth Century*. Cambridge, MA: Harvard University Press.

Cohen, R. (1997) *Global Diasporas*. London: UCL Press.

Cresswell, T. (2002) "Introduction: Theorizing Place," in G. Verstraete and G. Cresswell (eds.), *Mobilizing Place, Placing Mobility*. Amsterdam: Rodopi.

Cresswell, T. (2006) *On the Move*. London: Routledge.

Dant, T. (2004) "The Driver-Car." *Theory, Culture and Society* 21: 61–80.

Davis, M. (2000) *Magical Urbanism*. London: Verso.

De Botton, A. (2002) *The Art of Travel*. New York: Pantheon Books.

Deleuze, G., and Guattari, F. (1986) *Nomadology*. New York: Semiotext(e).

Derrida, J. (1987) *Positions*. London: Athlone Press.

Du Gay, P., Hall, S., Janes, L., Mackay, H., and Negus, K. (1997) *Doing Cultural Studies: The Story of the Sony Walkman*. London: Sage.

Featherstone, M., Thrift, N., and Urry, J. (eds.) (2004) "Automobilities." *Theory, Culture and Society* 21: 1–284.

Geffen, C., Dooley, J., and Kim, S. (2003) "Global Climate Change and the Transportation Sector: An Update on Issues and Mitigation Options." Paper presented to the 9th Diesel Engine Emission Reduction Conference, USA.

Gibson, J. J. (1986) *The Ecological Approach to Visual Perception*. Boston: Houghton Mifflin.

Gilroy, P. (1993) *The Black Atlantic: Modernity and Double Consciousness*. London: Verso.

Goffman, E. (1963) *Behaviour in Public Places*. New York: The Free Press.

Goffman, E. (1971a) *The Presentation of Self in Everyday Life*. Harmondsworth: Penguin.

Goffman, E. (1971b) *Relations in Public*. Harmondsworth: Penguin.

Goffman, E. (1972) *Interaction Ritual*. Harmondsworth: Penguin.

Goldthorpe, J. H. (1980) *Social Mobility and Class Structure in Modern Britain*. Oxford: Clarendon Press.

Graham, S., and Marvin, S. (2001) *Splintering Urbanism: Network Infrastructures, Technological Mobilities and the Urban Condition*. London: Routledge.

Gregory, D., and Urry, J. (eds.) (1985) *Social Relations and Spatial Structures*. London: Macmillan.

Hannam, K., Sheller, M., and Urry, J. (2006) "Editorial: Mobilities, Immobilities and Moorings." *Mobilities* 1: 1–22.

Hardt, M., and Negri, A. (2000) *Empire*. Cambridge, MA: Harvard University Press.

Heidegger, M. (1993) *Basic Writings*, ed. D. Farrell Krell. London: Routledge.

Information Commissioner (2006) A *Report on the Surveillance Society*. London: The Surveillance Network.

Ingold, T. (1993) "The Temporality of the Landscape." *World Archaeology* 25: 152–74.

Ingold, T. (2000) *The Perception the Environment: Essays on Livelihood, Dwelling and Skill*. London: Routledge.

Ingold, T. (2004) "Culture on the Ground." *Journal of Material Culture* 9: 315–40.

Jain, S. (2002) "Urban Errands." *Journal of Consumer Culture* 2: 385–404.

Jensen, O. (2006) " 'Facework,' Flow and the City: Simmel, Goffman, and Mobility in the Contemporary City" *Mobilities* 1: 143–65.

Jokinen, E., and Veijola, S. (1997) "The Disoriented Tourist: The Figuration of the Tourist in Contemporary Cultural Critique." in C. Rojek and J. Urry (eds.), *Touring Cultures*. London: Routledge.

Joseph, M. (1999) *Nomadic Identities: The Performance of Citizenship*. Minneapolis: University of Minnesota Press.

Katz, J., and Aakhus, M. (2002a) "Introduction: Framing the Issues," in J. Katz and M. Aakhus (eds.), *Perpetual Contact: Mobile Communication, Private Talk, Public Performance*. Cambridge: Cambridge University Press.

Katz, J., and Aakhus, M. (eds.) (2002b) *Perpetual Contact*. Cambridge: Cambridge University Press.

Kellerman, A. (2006) *Personal Mobilities*. London: Routledge.

Larsen, J., Urry, J., and Axhausen, K. (2006) *Mobilities, Networks, Geographies*. Aldershot: Ashgate.

Lasch, C. (1980) *The Culture of Narcissism*. London: Sphere.

Lash, S. (2005) " 'Lebenssoziologie': Georg Simmel in the Information Age." *Theory, Culture and Society* 22: 1–23.

Lassen, C. (2006) "Rethinking Central Concepts of Work and Travel in the 'Age of Aeromobility.' " *Environment and Planning A* 38: 301–12.

Latour, B. (1999) "On Recalling ANT," in J. Law and J. Hassard (eds.), *Actor Network Theory and After*. Oxford: Blackwell/Sociological Review.

Law, J. (1994) *Organizing Modernity*. Oxford: Basil Blackwell.

Law, J., and Hassard, J. (eds.) (1999) *Actor Network Theory and After*. Oxford: Blackwell/ Sociological Review.

Law, J., and Mol, A. (2001) "Situating Technoscience: An Inquiry into Spatialities," *Environment and Planning D: Society and Space* 19: 609–21.

Lovelock, J. (2006) *The Revenge of Gaia*. London: Allen Lane.

Lury, C. (1997) "The Objects of Travel," in C. Rojek and J. Urry (eds.), *Touring Cultures: Transformations of Travel and Theory*. London: Routledge.

Lyons, G., Jain, J., and Holley, D. (2007) "The Use of Travel Time by Rail Passengers." *Transportation Research A* 41: 107–20.

Lyons, G., and Urry, J. (2005) "Travel Time Use in the Information Age." *Transportation Research A* 39: 257–76.

Lyotard, J.-F. (1984) *The Postmodern Condition*. Manchester: Manchester University Press.

Marfleet, P. (2006) *Refugees in a Global Era*. Basingstoke: Palgrave Macmillan.

Marx, K., and Engels, F. (1952 [1848]) *The Manifesto of the Communist Party*. Moscow: Foreign Languages.

Massey, D. (1994) *Space, Class and Gender*. Cambridge: Polity.

Miller, D., and Slater, D. (2000) *The Internet*. Oxford: Berg.

Molotch, H. (2003) *Where Stuff Comes From: How Toasters, Toilets, Cars, Computers, and Many Other Things Come To Be as They Are*. New York: Routledge.

Morris, M. (1988) "At Henry Parkes Motel." *Cultural Studies*, 2: 1–47.

Ong, A. (1999) *Flexible Citizenship: The Cultural Logics of Transnationality*. Durham, NC: Duke University Press.

Ong, A., and Nonini, D. (eds.) (1997) *Ungrounded Empires: The Cultural Politics of Modern Chinese Transnationalism*. New York: Routledge.

Papastergiadis, N. (1999) *The Turbulence of Migration: Globalization, Deterritorialization and Hybridity*. Cambridge: Polity.

Park, R. E. (1970 [1925]) "The Mind of the Hobo: Reflections Upon the Relation Between Mentality and Locomotion," in R. Park, E. Burgess, and R. McKenzie (eds.), *The City*. Chicago: University of Chicago Press.

Pound, E. (1973 [1917]) *Selected Prose, 1909–1965*. London: Faber & Faber.

Ray, L. (2002) "Crossing Borders? Sociology, Globalization and Immobility." *Sociological Research Online* 7: 1–18.

Rheingold, H. (2002) *Smart Mobs: The Next Social Revolution*. Cambridge, MA: Basic Books.

Schafer, A., and Victor, D. (2000) "The Future Mobility of the World Population." *Transportation Research A* 34: 171–205.

Schivelbusch, W. (1986) *The Railway Journey: Trains and Travel in the Nineteenth Century*. Oxford: Blackwell.

Serres, M. (1995) *Angels: A Modern Myth*. Paris: Flammarion.

Sheller, M. (2003) *Consuming the Caribbean*. London: Routledge.

Sheller, M. (2004) "Automotive Emotions: Feeling the Car." *Theory, Culture and Society* 21: 221–42.

Sheller, M., and Urry, J. (eds.) (2006) "The New Mobilities Paradigm." *Environment and Planning A* 38: 207–26.

Simmel, G. (1990) *The Philosophy of Money*. London: Routledge.

Simmel, G. (1997) *Simmel on Culture*, ed. D. Frisby and M. Featherstone. London: Sage.

Skeggs, B. (2004) *Class, Self, Culture*. London: Routledge.

Thomas, C. (2002) *Academic Study into the Social Effects of UK Air Travel*. London: Freedom-to-Fly.

Thomsen, T., Nielsen, L., and Gudmundsson, H. (eds.) (2005) *Social Perspectives on Mobility*. London: Ashgate.

Thrift, N. (2004) "Movement-Space: The Changing Domain of Thinking Resulting from the Development of New Kinds of Spatial Awareness." *Economy and Society* 33: 582–604.

Toiskallio, K. (2002) "The Impersonal Flâneur: Navigation Styles of Social Agents in Urban Traffic." *Space and Culture* 5: 169–84.

Turner, B. S. (2007) "Enclave Society: Towards a Sociology of the Immobility Regime." *European Journal of Social Theory* 10(2): 287–303.

Urry, J. (2002) *The Tourist Gaze*, 2nd edn. London: Sage.

Urry, J. (2003) "Social Networks, Travel and Talk." *British Journal of Sociology* 54: 155–75.

Urry, J. (2007) *Mobilities*. Cambridge: Polity.

Vertovec, S. (2004) "Cheap Calls: The Social Glue of Migrant Transnationalism." *Global Networks* 4: 219–24.

Whatmore, S. (2002) *Hybrid Geographies: Natures, Cultures, Spaces*. London: Sage.

Whitelegg, J., and Haq, G. (eds.) (2003) *The Earthscan Reader in World Transport Policy and Practice*. London: Earthscan.

Zimmerman, M. (1990) *Heidegger's Confrontation with Modernity*. Bloomington: Indiana University Press.

25

Sociological Theory and Human Rights: Two Logics, One World

Judith Blau and Alberto Moncada

Human rights, as South African jurist Albie Sachs put it, include both the right to be the same as everyone else and the right to be different from everyone else (An-Na'im 2002: 1). That is, all humans have equal rights to freedom, security, and peace, and all humans have equal rights to their own identity, personality, and culture. In their origins human rights are ancient, but the most important milestone in their advance was December 10, 1948, when the UN General Assembly adopted and proclaimed the Universal Declaration of Human Rights (UDHR; UN 1948). However, it has only been in the last approximately two decades that what is called the "human rights revolution" gathered momentum to sweep the globe, connect communities, transform locales, and shape laws and constitutions. Human rights can be thought of as a logic and language that unites people world-wide, peasant farmers and slum dwellers, nomads and factory workers, miners and fishermen. What has made this practically possible is the widespread diffusion of electronic communications and media, a shared vision that is rests on the principles enshrined in the UDHR, but also, as we will describe, a new consciousness that we all share one planet. Human rights is also a logic that stands in opposition to global capitalism.

The same communications technologies that spur the human rights revolution also transformed the character and intensity of capitalism. Global capitalism is driven by a logic and set of practices that can be described as follows: (1) investors can transfer funds instantaneously from tax havens to banks to multinationals, which imperils and destabilizes burgeoning economies; (2) producers transfer operations from one place to another with lightning speed, creating massive unemployment; (3) commodities are marketed globally without recognition of fragile economies; (4) agribusiness buys up immense tracts of land, displacing peasant farmers and harming ecosystems; and (5) unregulated trade imperils local producers by undercutting them. The ideology of neoliberalism holds that "the social good will be maximized by maximizing the reach and frequency of market transactions, and it seeks to bring all human action into the domain of the market" (Harvey

2005: 3). Thus poised on one side is the logic of neoliberalism and on the other, the logic of human rights.

For many in the world today, this is the logic of accumulation and exploitation versus the logic of humanity and human rights. There are many puzzles, not least of which is the extraordinary ease with which the logic of human rights has found its way into barrios, urban slums, peasant villages, and fishing communities. One reason is that there has been a dramatic increase in the numbers of nongovernmental organizations (NGOs) that advocate human rights. They have dense interconnections through their networks and some have consultative status with the UN or their own governments. Another reason is that all humans have the same needs and therefore relate to the same human rights. A global consciousness is, however, new. People have discovered that everyone shares the same planet and that all share what Peter Singer calls, *One World*: "now people living on opposite sides of the world are linked in ways previously unimaginable" (Singer 2002: 9).

THE TWO LOGICS

Human rights might be understood as resting on two pillars. One is human equality: as stated in the Universal Declaration of Human Rights: "All human beings are born free and equal in dignity and rights. They are endowed with reason and conscience and should act towards one another in a spirit of brotherhood" (UN 1948). Another is that universal rights include the rights to differences that follow from recognition of diversity as highlighted in the Universal Declaration on Cultural Diversity: "The defence of cultural diversity is an ethical imperative, inseparable from respect for human dignity" (UNESCO 2001).

Together these two statements are the foundations of international human rights doctrine and law, empowering people to seek recognition of their rights, and they are the driving force behind the global human rights movement. They also help to shape inquiry on a variety of topics of special interest to social scientists, and to name a few: global civil society (Köhler 1998), development (Uvin 2004), international peace (Galtung 1994), ethics and mutual recognition (Turner 2006a). We will elaborate, but it is important to indicate here that human rights challenge Western, especially American, social thought that rests on such principles as individualism and competition that are at odds with human rights principles, which favor cooperation and egalitarian relations. Human rights are also compatible with more participatory forms of democracy than representative democracy allows, and as states embrace human rights they introduce welfare protections for their citizens.

At the international level, and sometimes at the national level, human rights law covers many areas, with specific prohibition on harmful acts, such as rape, trafficking in persons, and housing evictions, and also encompasses standards, such as laws for occupational safety, decent jobs, health care, and the affirmative rights of race and cultural minorities, women, and protections for people who are vulnerable, such as children and the elderly. In sum, the logic of human rights draws from the universally shared conception of humanity, the essence of which is equality and uniqueness.

The logic of human rights stands in stark opposition to neoliberalism, which puts market freedoms ahead of human welfare, and profits ahead of society. In defense of free and unimpeded markets, Margaret Thatcher famously declared in 1987, "There is no such thing as society." Sociologists were appalled. Since then, under the banner of market fundamentalism (neoliberalism, or the Washington Consensus) the World Trade Organization (WTO), the International Monetary Fund (IMF), and the World Bank have pursued policies that have increased poverty, slowed growth rates in Third World countries, ripped apart societies, and contributed to environmental disasters, while a tiny number have amassed enormous wealth (for example see Brysk 2005; Khor 2001). Thatcher's statement helps to clarify the contrasting logics, between, on the one hand, of markets and the accumulation of wealth, and, on the other hand, of society and social forms in which human rights are embedded.

THE COMPREHENSIVE SCOPE OF HUMAN RIGHTS

After 1948, when the General Assembly of the UN adopted the Universal Declaration of Human Rights, there was some interest in human rights among scholars, but for the most part human rights were situated in the domain of groups with practical objectives, such as Amnesty International (founded in the UK in 1961) and Human Rights Watch (founded as Helsinki Watch in 1978). Not entirely, but to a great extent, the Cold War had the effect of bifurcating rights: the Soviet Union defended socioeconomic rights and the US and its allies, civil and political rights. Political scientists (e.g. Donnelly 1989) first took up human rights after the end of the Cold War, but sociologists were slow to do so. Among the very earliest sociologists to write about human rights was Bryan S. Turner (1993), and since then sociologists' interest in the field has grown, as we explain below. Although human rights are inherently multidisciplinary, sociology is especially suited to the study of human rights because regardless of whether human rights deal with health, housing, civil rights, non-discriminatory rights, or anything else, they are expressed and realized interpersonally and socially, that is, in communities and societies.

FOUR PARADOXES

One way of describing the scope of human rights is to consider the implications of four paradoxes. One, already suggested, is that human rights are both *universal and particularistic*. That is, everyone, regardless of their nationality, gender, race, ethnicity, religion, or sexual orientation, have identical rights to equality of personhood, to dignity, and to economic and social security. It is also the case that every human being has the right to their own unique identity, personality, and cultural traditions (Recep 2005).

A second paradox arises from the fact that persons are citizens of nation-states and as such have certain protected *territorial rights* – in particular, civil and political rights – and under the United Nations human rights framework everyone also has universal, unconditional, and *deterritorialized rights*, including economic and social rights. (To be sure, the state is accountable for ensuring these rights, but regional and international governments are beginning to hold states themselves accountable for protecting the rights of their citizens.) Additionally, migrants, asylum seekers, refugees, and stateless persons have transnational rights that states may not readily recognize. A cruel reality is that many states do not recognize people's universal rights, confounded by the fact that multinationals and financiers recognize no borders, whereas human populations are mostly trapped in their country of birth.

The third paradox arises from the fact that "rights holders" are "rights agents" – that is, people possess rights and simultaneously have obligations and responsibilities. In recognition of this link between "holders" and "agents" human rights doctrine and practice highlight "solidarity," "reciprocity," and "deontology." The fourth paradox is that some rights can only be secured and enjoyed collectively, such as clear air, transparent governance, and democracy, which underscores the links between rights, reciprocity, and collective responsibilities and also the connections between human rights and common goods, especially the environment.

The core assumptions of human rights have far-reaching consequences, and are the point of departure for a broad range of queries, including in the following areas: collective or public goods (Kaul et al. 2003); women's rights (Epstein 2007); world poverty (Pogge 2005); environmental sustainability (Page and Redclift 2002); participatory democracy (Gould 2004; Green 1999); fair trade (Aaronson and Zimmerman 2006); cultural rights (Chiriboga 2006); corporate responsibility (Monshipouri, Welch, and Kennedy 2003); transnational citizenship (Basok and Ilcan 2006; Shafir and Brysk 2006); cultural rights (An-Na'im 2002; Jovanović 2005); worker rights (Gross 2003); global governance (Monbiot 2003); food (Maxwell and Slater 2004); and international peace (Coicaud, Doyle, and Gardner 2003). Human rights are therefore comprehensive in their implications. They are also comprehensive in their scope. Michael Ignatieff writes, "human rights has gone global by going local, imbedding itself in the soil of cultures and worldviews" (2001: 7).

HUMAN RIGHTS AS AN INTERNATIONAL FRAMEWORK

Human rights, both as concept and as a set of practical objectives, are hardly new, and can be found in all religious traditions, ancient and modern, as well as in all philosophical traditions, including in the writings of Plato, Abu Al-Farabi, St. Thomas Aquinas, and Enlightenment philosophers (Ishay 2004; Lauren 2003). What we know now as civil and political rights, at least in the formal sense, evolved beginning in the thirteenth century as natural law (the natural equal rights of all human beings) in English common law and under King Magnus in Norway. These principles were unequivocally affirmed in the 1776 US Declaration of Independence and the 1789 French Declaration of the Rights of Man and of the Citizen. The next significant steps in the evolution of human rights came with the abolition of the slave trade in 1803–8, the emancipation of slaves in the US in 1865, and then finally the abolition of slavery altogether, in Brazil in 1888.

The horror and trauma of the Holocaust spurred the member states of the newly created United Nations to negotiate and sign the Universal Declaration of Human Rights. It is an extraordinary document, revolutionary in its implications, and at the time of its adoption, and still today, no state can meet its standards. It is also a bold document. The Preamble asserts it is the "common standard of achievement for all peoples and all nations," and to that end every individual and every organ of every society must keep the Declaration "constantly in mind" (UN 1948).

Although drawing on old and distinguished traditions, the UDHR uniquely clarifies what human rights are, how they are related to one another, how states must hold them, and why securing human rights for everyone is essential for world peace, security, and human happiness. The UDHR encompasses those rights that evolved in the West with state formation, namely civil and political rights, but also economic rights (the right to work, labor protections, social protection, and an adequate standard of living), social rights (education, the rights of the elderly, medical care, and the right to leisure), and cultural rights (to enjoy community traditions), and the rights of all to benefit from advances in science.

The UDHR is, however, a statement of principles, not law, and the original plan was to promulgate a treaty that would encompass all the provisions of the UDHR, along with enforcement mechanisms. Owing to the opposition of the United States, this did not happen, and instead the UDHR was divided into two treaties: the International Covenant for Civil and Political Rights (CCPR) and the International Covenant for Economic, Social, and Cultural Rights (CESCR). Each was ratified and went into force in 1976. Whereas most countries ratified both, the US only ratified the CCPR and included as a reservation that it would not recognize the Treaty Body that is responsible for monitoring and compliance.

The US has continued to be the spoiler; it has ratified few international human rights treaties that protect workers' rights (under the auspices of the International Labour Organization [ILO]), and has not ratified treaties on the rights of women, the rights of the child, migrant rights, and abolition of the death penalty (see Blau and Moncada 2005; Pubantz 2005). Besides, the US has not ratified any of the seven human rights treaties promulgated by the Organization of American States (OAS), has ratified fewer ILO treaties (conventions) than practically any other country, and rarely ratifies environmental treaties under the aegis of the UN Environmental Agency, including the Kyoto Protocol for Climate Change. In fact, the US is not really a party to any international human rights agreement (including those promulgated by the UN, the United Nations Educational, Scientific, and Educational Organization [UNESCO], ILO, and OAS) because the US always includes as a reservation to every human rights treaty that it does ratify the phrase that it is "not self-executing" (Henkin 1990).

The governments of all the major regions – the Americas, Asia, Africa, the Arab League, and the European Union – have adopted their own human rights charters, and continue to add supplemental treaties, such as ones dealing with the rights of migrants and the rights of indigenous peoples. These charters and treaties are very similar to those encompassed within the UN framework, but the rationale is that proximate countries that share similar histories and circumstances are best able to monitor human rights violations and deal with offenders. Besides these recent human rights charters, the vast majority of the 191 countries that do have constitutions have revised or substantially rewritten their constitutions to include human rights provisions (Blau and Moncada 2006). Our sense is that democratization movements go hand in hand with human rights campaigns and together these mobilize states to rewrite constitutions, but playing a major role in this immense wave of constitutional revision is that states are trying to buffer their populations against the force of globalization.

STATE-BASED HUMAN RIGHTS

In the West, civil, political, and property rights were advanced in successive successful uprisings, movements, and revolutions. Their philosophical underpinnings can be traced in the writings of Thomas Hobbes, Edmund Burke, Jean-Jacques Rousseau, and, most especially, John Locke. In the state of nature, Locke contended, all men are rational and capable of action and creativity. Thus natural rights were derived by Locke from natural law, still a tenet of human rights. His idea that property was a fundamental right, as well as his conception that government rested on the consent of citizens, played, of course, a key role in the US Federalist Papers, the Declaration of Independence, and the US and French Constitutions.

From the late eighteenth century to the final decades of the nineteenth in industrialized countries, the term, "rights" meant civil and political rights for men, and, as we have mentioned earlier, white men. Women's suffrage was not achieved until later, first in New Zealand in 1893, and then in other countries. Economic and social rights were achieved incrementally in the West, and nearly always in response to waves of protest.

Playing an exceedingly important role in advancing the idea of social rights was sociologist T. H. Marshall (1950), who contended that a full citizen possesses civil, political, and social rights, and the state has an obligation to uphold the social rights of its citizens. While this may have seemed obvious to people living in the Soviet Union and China, Marshall legitimized social and economic rights within a Western context and laid the groundwork for the British welfare state. With British Prime Minister Margaret Thatcher the nineteenth-century conception that welfare was theft of hard-earned property was resurrected. Besides, corporations were quick to signal to all governments that they would not pay taxes or in other ways support welfare state regimes. States everywhere reduce social expenditures in response to the pressures of globalization (Scholte 2000), jeopardizing precisely those programs that are in line with human rights. Of course there are countervailing forces. A recent important development is the likely possibility that individuals and groups may be able to seek formal remedy in the UN for violation of economic and social rights (Squires, Langford, and Thiele 2005).

THE TWO OPPOSITIONAL LOGICS

In sum, human rights is an ethic of interconnectedness and solidarity and a perspective that relates human needs to rights and to responsibilities (Turner 1993). In an interconnected world, human rights offer a logic that stands in opposition to the logic of neoliberalism, and arguably to the logic of self-interest and private property on which capitalism depends. We will not discuss this latter supposition because the UN considers capitalism as a throughput for many of its development and human rights programs, although UN agencies, especially the United Nations Development

Programme (UNDP), have not hidden their opposition to the neoliberal policies of the IMF, the WTO, and the World Bank. Their policies and practices have, without question, aggravated poverty (New Economics Foundation 2006; UNDP 2003) and economic inequalities (World Institute for Development Economics Research 2006).

To understand how these logics oppose one another, it is useful to examine how they evolved in relation to each other. The epicenter of neoliberalism is the United States, which has the margin of power in international financial institutions, possesses the world's reserve currency, and is the richest country in the world. The US is also the world's superpower, with over 7,000 military bases and a nuclear capability that is many, many times greater than that of all other countries combined. The US uses its considerable power to advance the neoliberal project in ways that are consistent with its own national culture. For example, the US has the only constitution in the world that gives corporations rights of personhood, and is virtually the only constitution in the world that does not encompass people's fundamental rights to economic and social security.

The US does not "own" neoliberalism; rather, neoliberalism is an ideology and set of practices that dominate the contemporary world economy, privileging the economic rights of investors and owners over the rights and welfare of workers, over human populations, over societies, and over the environment (Blau 1993). Where did neoliberalism come from? Margaret Thatcher and Ronald Reagan were the first world leaders to embrace the neoliberal project, thereby abandoning Keynesian economics. Its origins were at the University of Chicago when a group of economists launched what would become "trickle-down economics," or "market fundamentalism," reviving principles of the libertarian nineteenth-century "Manchester School of Economics." In a nutshell, the aim, which they sought to accomplish through the World Bank and the IMF, was to turn around the economies of Third World countries by privatizing their government programs, eliminating trade barriers, and easing restrictions on transnationals. Markets, according to the neoliberal logic, must be free, unencumbered by governments and societies, and unconstrained by national borders (see Stiglitz 2003).

Harvey (2005: 93) writes that, as early as 1982, Keynesian economics had been purged from the corridors of the IMF and the World Bank, and was never an impediment to the WTO, which was established in 1995, completing an ideological triumvirate that together imperiled the economies of the Third World and eliminated job security for the workers in the First World. By around 2004, it was clear that market reforms had led to extremely high levels of indebtedness, the devastation of social services and education, the collapse of indigenous agriculture, and, additionally, populations were worse off as the result of migration, job displacements, and the phenomenal growth of urban slums. There was no doubt that the economies of poor countries were sliding backwards because market reforms had in fact resulted in negative growth (New Economics Foundation 2006; World Commission on the Social Dimension of Globalization 2005; World Institute for Development Economics Research 2006).

Yet neoliberalism confronted an increasingly powerful human rights movement, or as it is sometimes called, "the human rights revolution." It too is global and rests on an entirely different logic. Although, as noted, human rights were first formally codified internationally in 1948, they became global only when they "hit the ground," which is to say became the objective of peoples' movements, infused civil society, and were embraced by trade unions. The internet, which made neoliberalism possible, also became a powerful tool for civil society actors, unions, and movement actors. As has always been the case, the vanguard are the oppressed: peasants, Dalits, slum dwellers, the landless, factory workers, indigenous peoples, and persecuted minorities. They are the world's dispossessed, and comprise nearly two-thirds of the entire world's population (Amin 2003). They organize through NGOs and community-based organizations, which in turn are connected by far-flung networks; they launch campaigns and disruptions; they host blogs; and they demonstrate at trade talks.

To give just two examples, Via Campesina, the international peasant movement, has regional coordinators in all continents and 150 member organizations, and Shack/Slum Dwellers International (SDI) has member organizations in 21 countries. Largely responsible for the global movement against genetically modified (GM) seeds, the food sovereignty movement for peasants, and the "local food movement" in Europe, Via Campesina has been increasingly successful in shaping national policies that benefit local peasants and farmers. Its origins may have been rural, but Via Campesina organizers have become adept at forging links with university research centers and other NGOs, such as Food First.

SDI has been successful at the national level, in advancing housing rights often in partnership with other NGOs, in winning court cases against local and state governments, securing micro-loans from banks for its members, and, internationally, in attracting the support of housing experts, obtaining funding from European governments and NGOs. Both Via Campesina and SDI have consultative status at the UN, and both have been active at the World Social Forum, which has been a powerful force in its own right, attracting labor unions, NGOs, and various movements (see e.g. Wallerstein 2007). The charter of the World Social Forum embraces human rights, and the many hundreds of groups that participate in the annual forum have discovered that what they have in common is human rights (Blau 2007).

To summarize, then, as a counterthrust to neoliberalism, people have launched what Kofi Annan, the former Secretary General of the UN, called "a global revolution." This revolution has been a groundswell, uniting peoples through networks and in large coalitions to advance fundamental rights. The human rights focus of the newly reorganized global workers' union, the International Trade Union Confederation, is indicative of this revolution and how powerful human rights has become a vehicle for solidarity among the world's peoples.

What, then, can be concluded about these oppositional logics? First, human rights defenders and advocates need the support of the United Nations but it is practically constrained by its member states. In particular, the US has been an obstacle to the advance of human rights, both in America and overseas, notwithstanding rhetoric to the contrary, and even then, only a slim majority of countries are reliable and staunch supporters of human rights. Second, poised on one side is the United Nations, along with its specialized agencies, especially the ILO, the World Health Organization, UNESCO, UNDP, and a few other specialized agencies , and posed on the other side are WTO, the IMF, the World Bank, and major investors and CEOs of multinationals. Opponents of neoliberalism are nevertheless increasingly vocal and growing in number. As a report of the British New Economics Foundation (2006) concluded, "the global economy must work for the people."

THE EPISTEMIC RUPTURE

The overriding assumption in Western political theory until very recently was that because political rights were the backbone of the liberal state and its constitution, political rights constituted the sum total of rights (Freeden 1991: 1). That is, even though people in principle have rights rooted in a universal natural law it is the nation-state that in practice confers rights, and the rights it confers are political ones and no more than that. Judiciary systems and legal thought have evolved in the tradition that includes Hobbes, Locke, and Bentham, and this tradition has continued, as we will note below, in the work of such theorists as Rawls and Dworkin. Even T. H. Marshall (1950), whose work on social rights was so pioneering, positioned rights within the context of the state. Even though the 1948 Universal Declaration formulates rights as inalienable (independent of the state), universal (that is, global), and indivisible (including political, economic, social, and cultural rights), realist assumptions about sovereignty dominated political theory about rights through most of the second half of the twentieth century, and to a considerable extent still do. Yet these are unrealistic assumptions in today's world.

To pose the contrast in sharper terms, contemporary human rights rest on assumptions about global solidarity in the face of diminishing natural resources and climate change, collaboration, equality, and substantive freedoms, whereas Western conceptions of rights rest on assumptions of state sovereignty inherited from the realist school of international relations and strong assumptions from Western economic and political liberalism about individualism, meritocracy, competition, and abstract freedoms (see Blau and Moncada 2007).

CONTEMPORARY PHILOSOPHY

It is useful to compare the elements of an individualistic rights-based philosophy with the assumptions of a substantive human rights philosophy, because this helps to clarify why liberal principles rest uneasy within human rights. For this purpose we use Ronald Dworkin, but we could easily have used Isaiah Berlin or John Rawls. Dworkin, in his *Taking Rights Seriously* (1977).

> defends a conception of positive rights that generate entitlements and protect individuals' dignity. In asserting that "rights are trumps," he contends that where a right stands nothing else can interfere. His writings have been useful in advancing legal arguments against discrimination because of his emphasis on equality, but he fails to make a case for substantive rights on which any epistemology of human rights, in our view, must stand.

Dworkin here, but other philosophers as well who defend the rights and freedoms of individual, autonomous persons, such as Isaiah Berlin, Richard Rorty, and John Rawls, have difficulty putting humans into a social context. Liberal rights-based philosophers focus exclusively on the rights and freedoms of individual, autonomous persons, who may be anyone – citizens, foreigners, workers, young, old, black or white. An expanded conception of rights must recognize, in our view, the rights of embodied human beings in pursuit of happiness, fulfillment, and accomplishment, as well as economic and social security. Another criticism of this liberal tradition is that it is agnostic regarding questions bearing on what constitutes the good community or the good society. It is useful to briefly sketch new contributions in ethics, moral philosophy, and political philosophy that may address questions relevant for human rights.

The ethical turn has emerged within poststructuralism, both in philosophy and literary theory, and major contributors have been Emmanuel Lévinas (1981) and Judith Butler (2005). At the center of this thinking has been the ethical significance of recognizing, transcending, and respecting social boundaries, of intersubjectivities, and the problematic nature of alterity. Because this work centers on the importance of empathetic and egalitarian relations, it rejects essentializing the other and clarifies the importance of inter-cultural and inter-group dialog across the great divides of race, sexuality, ethnicity, nation, class, indigeneity, and language.

If the work in ethics is helpful for understanding how to negotiate "betweenness," this work, like social constructionism generally, can verge on relativism, at fundamental odds with the premises of human rights (see CHAPTER 14). Here tenets of moral philosophy are useful because from this vantage point it is possible to query the significance of non-contingent moral claims. On the one hand, questions such as "How can I better appreciate the differences between us?" are ones about ethics, whereas "I value your loyalty" and "I have deontological responsibilities to you, and you to me," are moral assertions. The recent realist (or naturalist) turn in moral philosophy is relevant for human rights because of its insistence on the substantive and empirical underpinnings of social relations and the central role that human needs and human cooperation play. It is claimed by moral realists that egalitarianism is a moral good, and therefore that having social responsibilities is also a moral good, because, just as having food and water are moral goods, having responsibilities to ensure these goods is also moral because these goods verifiably satisfy human needs (Boyd 1988).

Political philosophy more directly engages questions about distributive justice and departs from ethics and moral philosophy in the way it engages questions about the polity and political economy. One of the most ambitious undertakings in this area is Carol C. Gould's *Globalizing Democracy and Human Rights* (2004). In it she poses three challenging questions: (1) How can increasingly globalized political and economic institutions be opened up to democratic participation by all those affected by decisions? (2) How can people's rights be assured to guarantee an adequate standard of living for all? (3) Is there a way to retain cultural and social differentiation at the local level while preventing violations of human rights? In her ambitious and comprehensive analysis, Gould argues that human rights must have priority even over democracy because people who have human rights will inevitably create deep forms of democracy, and what protects them both is pluralization and empowerment. Arguing that a social correlate of empathy is solidarity, she develops a model for the radical decentralization of political and economic power in "caring" communities, somewhat along the lines of philosopher Judith M. Green (1999), and proposes ways of expanding the participation of stakeholders in global decisionmaking.

TOWARD A RIGHTS-BASED SOCIOLOGY

As background, challenging liberal assumptions is sometimes tantamount to embracing the assumptions of a rights-based sociology whether that is the intention or not. For example, Sjoberg, Gill, and Cain (2003) propose rejecting prevailing, assumptions about rational choice, individualism, self-interest, and scientific neutrality to deal more holistically and empathetically with the human experience. Immanuel Wallerstein is more blunt. He argues that the liberal assumptions of Western social science, and Western science, generally – value neutrality, objectivity, universalism, causality, and meritocracy – are used to justify the exercise of power in the modern world (Wallerstein 2006: 77). Any social science project that makes the social scientist the advocate and cheerleader for humans is, in our view, a rights-based social science project.

Social theory that centers on human rights draws from the impulses in similarly themed work in philosophy and political theory that engages questions about freedom and rights, but sociologists more directly engage questions about what sorts of societies, and communities best promote substantive freedoms and human rights. Instead of asking "How best can we explain social behavior and social arrangements?" the human rights epistemology prompts instead questions such as "How best can we enhance the human experience . . . the collective good . . . the rights of disadvantaged minorities . . . pluralism?" and "How can we promote solidarities?" Yet one thing is unquestionably clear and that is that, regardless of the specific realm – political, economic, educational, medical, housing, food and water – human rights are embedded in communities, social relations, and society. Sociologists have abundant opportunities to contribute to the understanding and advance of human rights.

In "Outline of a Theory of Human Rights" Turner (1993) contrasts the conception of Western (liberal) citizenship with the premises of the UDHR that instead rest on ideas of solidarity and the ethic of responsibility and of recognition. He stresses the importance of common vulnerability and human misery throughout the world, proposing the importance of "collective compassion." In his recent book on vulnerability and human rights (2006a; see also Turner 2006b), he further expands on the universal dimension of human rights – stemming from universal frailties – while also stressing the paradox that human rights also include the right to a particular identity, which he clarifies in terms of multiculturalism and an ethic of recognition.

In an elegant analysis, Anthony Woodiwiss (2005) asks the question: Why did the West choose some rights and not others? He traces his answer through the works of European philosophers, Weber, Durkheim, Elias, and Foucault, and in international comparisons including the US, Japan, England, and the European continent. He concludes that the West privileges property rights at the expense of other rights. In a deft account of the intellectual history of the internationalization of human rights discourse, he clarifies the dominant role that the US played in the UN in more or less successfully marginalizing economic, social and cultural rights. Woodiwiss's own position is that the US's position on human rights is increasingly unacceptable, and that globalization has opened up an expansive world discussion on human rights that recognizes the importance of protection, the equal status of civil, political, and social rights, and the rights to development and of indigenous groups.

In contrast to Britain and much of western Europe, social citizenship failed to take hold in the US, in spite of Franklin Delano Roosevelt's ambitions to incorporate into the US Constitution provisions for economic and social rights (see Blau and Moncada 2006). Although stillborn, his proposal was very much along the lines of what would later become the British and European welfare state. The intellectual pioneer was T. H. Marshall (1950), as earlier noted, who contended that by fulfilling the duties of citizenship (employment and military service) citizens were entitled to social rights, including housing, employment, and health care. Marshall's legacy has been considerable, and most highly industrialized countries, except the United States, have social rights provisions. New work that responds to the realities of globalization, however, suggests that Marshall's work needs updating. Murray (2007) proposes that a contemporary conception of social rights must include environmental rights and expanded conceptions of democratic rights and workplace rights.

Some human rights theorists make globalism their central focus, as does Richard A. Falk (2000), who notes that human rights have only recently "come in from the cold," but dramatically so, and arrived on the global scene through far-flung networks of international and national NGOs that transcend nation-states. He goes on to note that most social science thinking is state-centric and that many social scientists have failed to recognize the growing practical significance of human rights. Besides documenting emerging movements for the rights of the marginalized, for humane governance, and for self-determination, Falk also clarifies variation in the area of expressions of human rights, such as the greater community focus found in Islamic and African societies.

After making the point that multiple actors have overlapping responsibilities for upholding human rights, Koen de Feyter (2005) stresses that, although the obligations of states have been recognized, those of economic actors have been neglected. In his view multinationals and businesses must be held accountable for safeguarding human rights. Feyter also highlights, as we have, the importance of civil society actors (NGOs) in advocating and demanding the protection of people's rights. He describes, for example, how in 2001, the Brazilian Movement of Landless Workers held an "international tribunal on the crimes of the *latifundio* [landowners] and on the official policies of human rights violators." The tribunal was chaired by a member of the Inter-American Commission of Human Rights, with prominent intellectuals and representatives of international NGOs serving on the jury. Extra-legal, to be sure, but the tribunal shone a spotlight on human rights abuses, and thereby put pressure on the Brazilian government, which responded by transferring vast land holdings to peasant farmers.

New interest among sociologists in human rights is consistent with the recent "normative turn" in sociology, especially evident in the areas of race, gender, migration, Latino studies, and the sociology of children. Havidán Rodríguez (2004) comes to the sociology of human rights by way of disaster research, and Keri Iyall Smith (2006) does so through indigenous studies. What we are calling the normative turn in sociology was evident at the 2004 meetings of the American Sociological Association, at which Michael Burawoy (2005) underscored in his presidential address the importance of a committed and engaged "public sociology." Elsewhere he makes the connections between public sociology and human rights: "at the heart of sociology must lie a concern for society as such . . . for those social relations through which we recognize each other as humans" (Burawoy 2006: 1). This marks a shift in sociology, away from scientism (the conception of the analyst as a neutral and objective observer) and the idea that relatively autonomous and rational individuals competitively pursue their interests.

REPRESSIVE REGIMES AND HUMANITARIAN CRIMES

There is remarkable similarity in human rights principles, at least formally, across all civilizations. Countries with varied civilizational orientations – Buddhist, Christian, Hindu, and Islamic – all recognize state-based liberal rights, at least in principle, and these include the right to vote, the right to a fair trial, and freedom of speech. Although there is variation in the relative emphasis on communitarian or collective rights or individual rights, virtually all countries embrace in principle civil and political rights. That is, these rights are included in practically all recently revised constitutions (Blau and Moncada 2006). Yet some regimes violate their citizens' rights with impunity: Burma, Chad, China, Egypt, Ethiopia, Iran, North Korea, Russia, Saudi Arabia, Syria, and Zimbabwe. What they have in common are long histories of colonial oppression and occupation, and little or no experience with democracy. These countries brutally violate the civil and political rights of citizens, repress speech and press freedoms, and have unreliable and capricious judiciary systems.

The international community is for all practical purposes prevented by the UN Charter and international customary law from violating national sovereignty for the purpose of protecting populations even when the state is causing them great harm and suffering. Outsiders watch with horror as a state brutally suppresses and sometimes slaughters its own people, and the most the international community can do is to impose boycotts, which is fraught with problems since they can harm the people they are intended to help. The hope, of course, is that internal, home-grown movements will successfully lead to regime change, as was the case in South Africa, the Republic of Korea, and recently in Nepal, and also in democratization movements in Chile, the Czech Republic, Georgia, Ghana, Latvia, and Uruguay. In all contemporary comparisons, it is important to remember that barbaric atrocities were committed by Germany as well as by its satellite states, Austria and Poland, and that Nazi sympathizers ran the governments of Belgium, Denmark, France, the Netherlands, and Norway.

Louise Arbor (2006: 1) distinguishes human rights violations – "actions and omissions that interfere with a person's birthright" – and humanitarian crimes – "so heinous they shock the human conscience." The International Criminal Court, under the Rome Statute (UN 2003), hears four types of case: genocide, crimes against humanity, apartheid, and war crimes. Sociologist John Hagan (2005) draws on Hannah Arendt's *Eichmann in Jerusalem* (1977 [1963]), to illustrate the reasoning behind having an international court, and not simply national courts, to try such heinous crimes.

For Arendt, it was not Eichmann who was singularly guilty but rather the whole of German society, a view that also informed thinking in South Africa, and later in Rwanda and elsewhere, leading to the establishment of Truth and Reconciliation Commissions. These commissions establish courts to hear cases of egregious human rights abuses and they also aim in community trials and hearings to repair the social fabric through a process of atonement and recognition (see Robertson 1999). These commissions and the processes they set in motion should be of great interest to sociologists because they highlight over time social processes and overlapping groups and communities, and they clarify the articulation of social control and social norms within institutions, communities, and the state. Although Arendt contended that all the citizens of an entire nation can be complicit in evil and villainous acts against other human beings, there are many questions left for sociologists as to the societal conditions that make such evil and villainy possible.

CONCLUSIONS

The sociological perspective provides a distinctive vantage point on human rights, complementing the contributions of philosophers, legal scholars, and political scientists because sociologists bring to human rights an understanding of the embodied human condition. Besides political and civil rights, people have rights to housing, food, water, health care, and a decent education, or, in other words, the rights that sociologists understand to be the basis of security. Human rights also include the rights to culture and identity, another area of sociological knowledge. What a human rights perspective brings to sociology is, first, an understanding that these rights are interdependent and advanced together; second, that rights are entitlements; and, third, that human rights are the objective of any political, social, and economic order, and not the means.

The recent normative turn in sociology, along with renewed interest in social realism (evident in qualitative research and ethnography), provides the epistemic grounding for inquiries about human rights. Social theorists now recognize the democratic character of knowledge and the interactive character of theory, knowledge, and praxis. NGOs and, towards this end, human rights advocates can be savvy partners for advancing an understanding and deep appreciation of human rights. The domain of human rights, is broad and expansive, bridging the humanities, law, and the social and natural sciences; indeed, it is a perspective, not simply a field, and one with broad scope and great promise.

Bibliography

Aaronson, S. A., and Zimmerman, J. M. (2006) "Fair Trade? How Oxfam Presented a Systemic Approach to Poverty, Development, Human Rights and Trade." *Human Rights Quarterly* 28, 998–1031.

Amin, S. (2003) "World Poverty, Pauperization and Capital Accumulation." *Monthly Review* 55(5). <http://www.monthlyreview.org/1003amin.htm>.

An-Na'im, A. A. (2002) Introduction, in A. A. An-Na'im (ed.), *Cultural Transformation and Human Rights in Africa*. London: Zed.

Arbour, L. (2006) *Frequently Asked Questions on a Human Rights-Based Approach to Development Cooperation*. Office of the United Nations High Commissioner for Human Rights.

Arendt, H. (1977 [1963]) *Eichmann in Jerusalem: A Report on the Banality of Evil*. Harmondsworth: Penguin.

Basok, T., and Ilcan, S. (2006) "In the Name of Human Rights: Global Organizations and Participating Citizens." *Citizenship Studies* 10, 309–27.

Blau, J. (1993) *Social Contracts and Economic Markets*. New York: Plenum.

Blau, J. (2007) "A Better World is a World with Universal Human Rights." *American Sociological Association Footnotes* March(2): 3.

Blau, J., and Moncada, A. (2005) *Human Rights: Beyond the Liberal Vision*. Lanham, MD: Rowman & Littlefield.

Blau, J., and Moncada, A. (2006) *Justice in the United States: Human Rights and the US Constitution*. Lanham, MD: Rowman & Littlefield.

Blau, J., and Moncada, A. (2007) *Freedoms and Solidarities: In Pursuit of Human Rights*. Lanham, MD: Rowman & Littlefield.

Boyd, R. N. (1988) "How to Be a Moral Realist," in G. Sayre-McCord (ed.), *Essays on Moral Realism*. Ithaca, NY: Cornell University Press.

Brysk, A. (2005) *Human Rights and Private Wrongs*. New York: Routledge.

Burawoy, M. (2005) "For Public Sociology." *American Sociological Review* 70: 4–28.

Burawoy, M. (2006) "Introduction: A Public Sociology for Human Rights," in J. Blau and K. I. Smith (eds.), *Public Sociologies Reader*. Lanham, MD: Rowman & Littlefield.

Butler, J. (2005) *Giving an Account of Oneself*. New York: Fordham University Press.

Chiriboga, Oswaldo Ruiz (2006) "The Right to a Cultural Identity of Indigenous Peoples and National Minorities." *SUR: International Journal on Human Rights* 5: 43–70.

Coicaud, J.-M., Doyle, M. W., and Gardner, A.-M. (2003) *The Globalization of Human Rights*. Tokyo: United Nations University Press.

Donnelly, J. (1989) *Universal Human Rights in Theory and Practice* Ithaca, NY: Cornell University Press.

Dworkin, R. (1977) *Taking Rights Seriously*. Cambridge, MA: Harvard University Press.

Epstein, C. F. (2007) "Great Divides: The Cultural, Cognitive, and Social Bases of the Global Subordination of Women: 2006 Presidential Address," *American Sociological Review* 72: 1–22.

Falk, R. A. (2000) *Human Rights Horizons: The Pursuit of Justice in a Globalizing World*. New York: Routledge.

Feyter, K. de (2005) *Human Rights: Social Justice in the Age of the Market*. London: Zed.

Freeden, M. (1991) *Rights*. Minneapolis: University of Minnesota Press.

Galtung, J. (1994) *Human Rights in Another Key*. Cambridge: Polity.

Gould, C. C. (2004) *Globalizing Democracy and Human Rights*. Cambridge: Cambridge University Press.

Green, J. M. (1999) *Deep Democracy: Community, Diversity and Transformation*. Lanham, MD: Rowman & Littlefield.

Gross, J. A. (ed.) (2003) *Workers' Rights as Human Rights*. Ithaca, NY: Cornell University Press.

Hagan, J. (2005) "Crimes of War and the Force of Law." *Social Forces* 83: 1499–1534.

Harvey, D. (2005) *A Brief History of Neoliberalism*. Oxford: Oxford University Press.

Henkin, L. (1990) *Constitutionalism, Democracy, and Foreign Affairs.* New York: Columbia University Press. <http://www.ohchr.org/english/about/publications/docs/FAQ_en.pdf>.

Ignatieff, M. (2001) *Human Rights as Politics and Idolatry*, ed. A. Gutmann. Princeton: Princeton University Press.

Ishay, M. R. (2004) *The History of Human Rights from Ancient Times to the Globalization Era.* Berkeley: University of California Press.

Jovanović, M. A. (2005) "Recognizing Minority Identities through Collective Rights." *Human Affairs Quarterly* 27: 597–624.

Kaul, I., Conceição, P., Le Goulven, K., and Mendoza, R. U. (2003) *Providing Global Public Good.* New York: Oxford University Press.

Khor, M. (2001) *Rethinking Globalization: Critical Issues and Policy Choices.* London: Zed.

Köhler, M. (1998) "From the National to the Cosmopolitan Public Sphere," in D. Archibugi, D. Held, and M. Köhler (eds.), *Re-imagining Political Community* Stanford: Stanford University Press.

Lauren, P. G. (2003) *The Evolution of International Human Rights.* Philadelphia: University of Pennsylvania Press.

Lévinas, E. (1981) *Otherwise than Being or Beyond Essence*, trans A. Lingis. Dordrecht: Kluwer.

Marshall, T. H. (1950) *Citizenship and Social Class and Other Essays.* Cambridge: Cambridge University Press.

Maxwell, S., and Slater, R. (2004) *Food Policy Old and New.* Oxford: Blackwell.

Monbiot, G. (2003) *Manifesto for a New World Order.* New York: The New Press.

Monshipouri, M., Welch, C. E. Jr., and Kennedy, E. T. (2003) "Multinational Corporations and the Ethics of Global Responsibility." *Human Rights Quarterly* 25: 965–89.

Murray, G. (2007) "Who Is Afraid of T. H. Marshall? or, What Are the Limits of the Liberal Version of Rights?" *Societies without Borders* 2.

New Economics Foundation (2006) "Growth Isn't Working: The Uneven Distribution of Benefits and Costs from Economic Growth." <http://www.neweconomics.org/gen/m1_i1_aboutushome.aspx>.

Page, E. A., and Redclift, M. (eds.) (2002) *Human Security and the Environment.* Cheltenham: Edward Elgar.

Pogge, T. (2005) "World Poverty and Human Rights." *Ethics and International Affairs* 19: 1–8.

Pubantz, J. (2005) "Constructing Reason: Human Rights and the Democratization of the United Nations." *Social Forces* 84: 1291–1302.

Recep, S. (2005) "Sociology of Rights: 'I Am Therefore I Have Rights'. Human Rights in Islam between Universalistic and Communalistic Perspectives." *Muslim World Journal of Human Rights* 2(1). <http://www.bepress.com/mwjhr/vol2/iss1/art11>.

Robertson, G. (1999) *Crimes Against Humanity: The Struggle for Global Justice.* New York: The New Press.

Rodriguez, H. (2004) "A 'Long Walk to Freedom:' Human Rights, Globalization and Social Injustice." *Social Forces* 83: 391–425.

Scholte, J. A. (2000) *Globalization: A Critical Introduction.* New York: Palgrave.

Shafir, G., and Brysk, A. (2006) "The Globalization of Rights: From Citizenship to Human Rights." *Citizenship Studies* 10: 275–87.

Singer, Peter. (2002) *One World: The Ethics of Globalization.* New Haven: Yale University Press.

Sjoberg, G., Gill, E. A., and Cain, L. D. (2003) "Countersystem Analysis and the Construction of Alternative Futures." *Sociological Theory* 21: 210–35.

Smith, K. I. (2006) *The State and Indigenous Movements*. New York: Routledge.

Squires, J., Langford, M., and Thiele, B. (2005) *The Road to a Remedy: Current Issues in the Litigation of Economic, Social and Cultural Rights*. Sydney: Australian Human Rights Centre/Centre on Housing and Evictions.

Stiglitz, J. E. (2003) *Globalization and its Discontents*. New York: W. W. Norton.

Turner, B. S. (1993) "Outline of a General Theory of Human Rights." *Sociology* 27(3): 489–512.

Turner, B. S. (2006a) *Vulnerability and Human Rights: Essays on Human Rights*. University Park: University of Pennsylvania Press.

Turner, B. S. (2006b) "Global Sociology and the Nature of Rights." *Societies without Borders* 1: 41–52.

UN (United Nations) (1948) Universal Declaration of Human Rights. <http://www.unhchr.ch/udhr/lang/eng.htm>.

UN (2003) Rome Statute of the International Criminal Court. <http://www.un.org/law/icc/>.

UNDP (United Nations Development Programme) (2003) *Human Development Report: Millennium Development Goals*. New York: Oxford University Press.

UNESCO (United Nations Educational, Scientific, and Cultural Organization) (2001) Universal Declaration of Cultural Diversity. <http://unesdoc.unesco.org/images/0012/001271/127160m.pdf>.

Uvin, P. (2004) *Human Rights and Development*. Bloomfield, CT: Kumarian Press.

Wallerstein, I. (2006) *European Universalism: The Rhetoric of Power*. New York: The New Press.

Wallerstein, I. (2007) "The World Social Forum: From Defense to Offense." Fernand Braudel Center, Binghamton University: Commentary No. 202, Feb 1, 2007. <http://www.binghamton.edu/fbc/202en.htm>.

Woodiwiss, A. (2005) *Human Rights*. London: Routledge.

World Commission on the Social Dimension of Globalization (2004) *A Fair Globalization: Creating Opportunities for All*. Geneva: International Labour Organization.

World Institute for Development Economics Research (2006) *The World Distribution of Household Wealth*. Available at Global Policy Forum. <http://www.globalpolicy.org/socecon/inequal/income/2006/1206unufull.pdf>.

26

The Sociology of the Body

Bryan S. Turner

INTRODUCTION: THE BIOLOGICAL AND THE SOCIAL

From a conceptual point of view, "the body" may appear to be either outside "the social" or even opposed to it, and hence the body from this standpoint cannot be of interest to sociologists. If we start with a simple distinction between nature and nurture in which sociology concerns itself with the cultural nurturing of individuals as social beings, then once more the body belongs to nature and not to society. This exclusion of the body from the realm of the social can be said to have its origin in Greek thought. For Aristotle, man as *zoon logon ekhon* (a living being capable of speech) rises above the merely biological world of necessity when he creates the *polis* as a site of rational public discourse. If the *polis* is the world of choice, then the biological world of the body is the site of need. Recent philosophical accounts of the biological by writers such as Giorgio Agamben have developed this Aristotelian separation of *bios* and *zoe* or politics and biology to emphasize the distinction between "the [political] forms of life" and "bare life." In part this way of thinking about the separation between biology (the world of natural necessity) and politics (the world of action, judgment and decision) has drawn heavily on Hannah Arendt's observations in *The Human Condition* (1958: 23) that the word "social" is Roman in its origin and has no equivalent in Greek. This legacy from the classical world may also have been further reinforced by Christian thought, especially in the Letters of St. Paul, that the body stands in opposition to the spiritual nature of human beings. In Christian theology, the body is alien to the social world and needs to be controlled and disciplined by piety. This legacy received its critical affirmation in the distinction between mind and body in the philosophy of Descartes, especially in the starting point of Cartesianism: I think, therefore I am.

This legacy may serve to give us some explanation of the apparent absence of the body from the traditional discourse of the social sciences. In this chapter, I attempt to outline why this absence is problematic and why the sociology of the body opens up new possibilities for empirical research and social theory. As a preliminary position, we might start with three short observations. First we can observe that even in Greek thought the separation of thinking and embodiment was not part of Aristotle's philosophy. The idea of human beings as "rational animals" did not for Aristotle express such a divorce since embodiment is not separate from thinking. Contemporary interpretations of Aristotle have argued that, since thinking and embodiment are necessarily united, *legein* (to lay down, to gather, or to pick out) and *noein* (the way of being) "constitute the way in which the human being embodies himself as a whole" (Brogan 2005: 100). Second, the distinction between nature and nurture is in fact open to dispute and interpretation, and they cannot be successfully disconnected. It is not in fact obvious on reflection that the body falls outside of the social. Third, the distinction itself is historically and culturally variable in the sense that one can find periods in human history when nature and nurture are indeed seen to be in opposition, and other cultures and periods in which they are seen to be in harmony. The main drift of this chapter is that in modern societies biological life often appears to be given some priority over the social and the cultural – for example in the popularity of genetic explanations of human behavior and institutions. The idea that criminal behavior is genetically determined or that the criminal is a special biological type are well established notions in positivist criminology (Davie 2005). Because the body in modern society has an uncertain ontological status (as a living organism, as part of nature, or as a system of biological information), we can think of the modern world as a "somatic society" that is a social system in which political and social problems are often expressed through or manifest in the body. For instance the problematic status of young women in the hierarchy of social roles is thought to be expressed through such conditions as anorexia nervosa (Turner 1992).

THE ORIGINS OF THE SOCIOLOGY OF THE BODY

Professional sociology has been slow to accept the development of the sociology of the body as a recognized sub-field within the university undergraduate curriculum. There is no recognized official section of the American Sociological Association on the human body, but the body has, as one might expect, had more intellectual exposure in social anthropology, where it is difficult to undertake ethnographic research on ritual and myth without attending to the body. The anthropological contribution can be readily documented in the work for instance of Mary Douglas, whose *Purity and Danger* (1966) remains one of the most influential theories of the body as classificatory system. Her research on the classification of pollution and taboo through metaphorical references to apertures in the human body – what goes into man does not defile him, but what comes out does – remains the classical text on the categorization of risk. There is a well-established anthropological tradition of research on such topics as dance, tattooing, body symbolism, and somatic classification schemes from the work of Marcel Mauss onwards (Blacking 1977). Anthropologists have made important contributions to the analysis of body decoration (Caplan 2000), to the study of healing and trance in relation to body states (Strathern 1996), and in general to the idea of bodily performance such as in dance as an expression of cultural values (Hahn 2007).

The study of the body is beginning to emerge in sociology because there is a range of problems and issues in modern societies associated with the human body that cannot be easily ignored. For example the political and cultural complexity of the body is a product of changes in medical and biological sciences, and their application to human reproduction. It is also a consequence of social movements such as the disability movement, feminism, and environmentalism. The body as a topic of research is increasingly important in studies of modern sexuality (Richardson and Seidman 2002; Seidman, Fisher, and Meeks 2006). Many of the most pressing moral problems of the modern world are related to changes in the character of human embodiment. The changing nature of aging is one such key issue. With stem cell research, it has been claimed that in principle we can live forever (Appleyard 2007). Furthermore in advanced societies, women in old age can claim an unlimited right to reproduce through assisted reproduction. With the use of drugs (or, metaphorically speaking, "mental steroids") to enhance brain cells, it is theoretically possible to manufacture an intellectual elite. These are some of the political and ethical issues relating to the human body that modern society needs to address and which sociology cannot ignore.

The sociology of the body developed initially in British sociology at the beginning of the 1980s (Turner 1984). This specifically British context in the emergence of the sociology of the body was a consequence of the relatively strong development of medical sociology in Britain, especially through the journal *Sociology of Health and Illness*. In addition, continental philosophy and French social theory probably had a more significant impact on British than on American sociology. Michel Foucault and Pierre Bourdieu were especially influential in this regard, but it is also evident that French feminist theory played an important role (Evans and Lee 2002; James and Hockey 2007). The work of Jean-Luc Nancy has been important in continental philosophy, where he developed the perspective of Maurice Merleau-Ponty in his analysis of touch, the body, and spirituality (James 2006). Sociological studies of the body were also interested in the impact of consumerism on the representation of the body in urban societies (Featherstone 1982), in gender differentiation through bodily practices, and in the "mask of aging" (Featherstone and Hepworth 1991). The journal *Body & Society* was founded in 1995.

Although initially these developments were somewhat confined to British sociology, there has subsequently been an expanding global interest with *Five Bodies* (O'Neill 1985), *Le Gouvernement des corps* (Fassin and Memmi 2004), and with *Soziologie des Korpers* (Gugutzer 2004). In addition, the study of the body is distinctively multidisciplinary in orientation, with major contributions from history, religious studies, philosophy, and archaeology. In this context, one can identify a number of influential works such as Richard Sennett's *Flesh and Stone* (1994), Thomas Laqueur's *Making Sex* (1990), J. J. Brumberg's *Fasting Girls* (1988), and Jean-Luc Nancy's *The Ground of the Image* (2005).

One can of course find earlier sociological roots to the study of the body in various sociologists, as illustrated by Erving Goffman in *The Presentation of Self in Everyday Life* (1959) and on the stigmatized body (1964), or by Norbert Elias on the civilizing process (1978). The study of the body has drawn upon a heterogeneous range of theoretical sources from Michel Foucault's *History of Sexuality* (1979), and, through the work of Peter Berger and Thomas Luckmann

(1967), it has drawn upon the philosophical anthropology of Arnold Gehlen (1980). It is possible to identify an intellectual history that includes Karl Marx's Paris manuscripts, where he developed the notions of *praxis*, species-being, technology, and alienation that were subsequently to prove influential in critical theories (Markus 1978). Sociology has drawn significantly from modern philosophy At least one linking theme here is the impact of Friedrich Nietzsche, Martin Heidegger, and broadly "continental philosophy" in terms of the creation of a social ontology. Finally, the sociology of the body can be seen as an aspect of a broader philosophical criticism of the legacy of Cartesian rationalism by the Frankfurt School, existentialism, and phenomenology.

CONCEPTUAL DISTINCTIONS: WHAT IS THE BODY?

If sociology involves the study of social action and interaction, then we need to provide a convincing description of the actor. The contention of the sociology of the body is simply that in commonsense terms the social actor is embodied. In conjunction with this claim, there is by implication the notion that the conventional sociology of action, in not taking embodiment seriously, has an implicit cognitive bias, privileging mental willing (choice and decisionmaking) over embodied practices. In these terms the sociology of the body involves the study of the embodied nature of the social actor, social action, and social exchange, the cultural representations of the human body, the social nature of performance (in dance, games, sport, and so forth), and the reproduction of the body and populations in the social structure. In intellectual terms, the sociology of the body is an attempt to offer a critical sociological reflection on the separation of mind and body that has been characteristic of Western philosophy since the time of René Descartes (1591–1650).

Recent sociological theory has been significantly influenced by feminism, cultural anthropology, and postmodern philosophy, and hence sociologists have been concerned to understand how the naturalness of the body is socially constructed as a social fact. For example, sociologists have questioned the notion that right-handedness is produced by left- and right-sidedness in the brain by arguing that the superiority of right-sidedness in human societies is a cultural convention that is reinforced by socialization. As a result, the sociology of the body has had a critical edge in medical sociology, disability studies, and radical feminism, where activists have used sociology to deconstruct the dominant, hegemonic interpretations of the body as an unchanging aspect of nature or as a machine or simply an organism. Sociologists have generally criticized the claim that the body is simply a natural phenomenon and that this form of naturalism tends to support existing relations of power and authority, especially in a patriarchal system. In a postmodern framework, the sociology of the body shades off into queer theory, lesbian and gay studies, film theory, dance studies, radical feminism, and postmodernism (Halberstam and Livingston 1995). In all of these areas, the work of Judith Butler (1990, 1993) on the theory of identity construction through language, interpellation, and performativity has been deeply influential. These radical theories in general emphasize the fluidity and volatility of the gendered body in challenging existing social boundaries. Feminist writers thus conceptualize the (female) body as "leaky" (Shildrick 1997) or "volatile" (Grosz 1994). For reasons that will become clear shortly, I do not think these forms of constructionism are entirely satisfactory and I shall attempt to develop a modified form of constructionism as the basis for future research. One aspect of this alternative position is to make a distinction between performance and representation.

It is important to distinguish between the body and embodiment. The former topic includes cultural analyses of how the body is represented in society and how it functions as a symbolic system. Studies of embodiment focus by contrast on practice and performance. For example, the body of the king was often taken to be a symbolic representation of the sovereignty of the state, and by contrast the study of courtly rituals might focus on embodiment such as the actual bodily practices of court officials around the monarch. In medieval Christianity, the spirituality of the pope was represented through the purity of his body and the notion that popes were destined to enjoy long lives on this corrupt earth (Paravicini-Bagliani 2000). This distinction between symbolic cultures and performance is a useful if not significant conceptual distinction in sociology. This distinction can also be associated with the division between various forms of structuralism, on the one hand, and phenomenology, on the other.

THEORETICAL PERSPECTIVES

In the light of this discussion, one can identify four theoretical traditions in the sociology of the body. The first demonstrates that the body is not a natural phenomenon but is a social construct. This argument is normally deployed to criticize an assumption about "essentialism" – for example that anatomy is an essential aspect of the division between men and women. The second perspective explores how the body is a representation of the social relations of power. The point of research in this tradition is to read the body as a text that represents power relations in society. In a third orientation, sociology examines the phenomenology of the "lived body," that is, the experience of embodiment in the everyday world. Finally, sociology, in this case much influenced by anthropology, looks at bodily performance of acquired practices or techniques.

The notion that the body is socially constructed has been the dominant perspective of modern sociology and it is closely associated with radical social movements, which typically employ constructionism as a critical tool to deny that the body is simply a natural object (Radley 1995) (see CHAPTER 14). For example, feminist theory has examined the social construction of the body and rejected the notion of an essential or natural body. Simone de Beauvoir, in *The Second Sex* (1972a), argued famously that women are not born but become women through social and psychological processes that construct them as essentially female. Her work inaugurated a research tradition concentrating on the social production of differences in gender and sexuality. The basic contribution of feminist theories of the body has been to disturb and disrupt the hegemonic view that the differences between male and female (bodies) in the everyday world can be take for granted, as if they were facts of nature. In a similar fashion, de Beauvoir (1972b) wrote critically about age to show that age categories are deeply problematic and that we cannot take age as unambiguously a natural or chronological status. Feminism in the 1970s was intellectually important in establishing the difference between biologically determined sex and the social construction of gender roles and sexual identities. Empirical research has subsequently explored how the social and political subordination of women is orchestrated through various medical categories that define psychological depression and physical illness. Critical research in medical sociology, such as Susan Bordo's *Unbearable Weight* (1993), examined anorexia nervosa, obesity, and eating disorders. There have also been important historical studies of anorexia (Brumberg 1988), while the popular literature was influenced by Susan Orbach's *Fat Is a Feminist Issue* (1985).

Sociological research on the body in popular culture has explored how women's bodies are literally constructed as consumer or sexual objects, for example through the application of medical technology (Davis 2002; Negrin 2002). Cosmetic surgery involves the actual reconstruction of the body in order to produce desirable social and aesthetic effects. While cosmetic surgery is now simply routine, the negative effects of such surgery have come to public attention through sensational cases such as the death of Lolo Ferrari, whose 18 operations created what were reputed to be the largest female breasts in the world. There are other notorious celebrity cases such as that of Jocelyne Wildenstein, who has reconstructed her face to resemble a leopard (Pitts 2003). Similarly Orlan's surgical performances were designed to expose and to challenge the alliance between medicine, market, and aesthetics in a consumer society where the human (typically female) body is being simultaneously physically and socially reconstructed. More recently, the notion of the constructed body has become especially significant in political advocacy by disability groups. Influenced by sociological theory, disability activists argue that "disability" is not physical impairment, but fundamentally a loss of social rights (Barnes, Mercer, and Shakespeare 1999).

Within this constructionist perspective, there has also been considerable sociological interest in the social implications of machine–body fusions, or cyborgs (Featherstone and Burrows 1995). There is a well-known association between technology and masculinity. In popular culture, Robocop was at one stage the ultimate cyborg in the merging of machine and organism, but he also illustrated very traditional gender themes about power and sexuality. While the technology of *Robocop* now looks antiquated by comparison with the sophisticated computerized world of *Terminator*, *Star Wars*, and *Matrix*, this perspective on man as *homo faber* remains a vivid myth representing Man as the maker and builder, whose hands are potent tools and weapons. These pervasive urban myths elevate a particular form of masculinity, thereby denying the potential of alternative relations between the body and technology (Wajcman 1991). In recent social theory, feminists have sought to confront the conventional relationship between women and technology, and to explore the potential benefits for women of reproductive technologies, but also to consider the general emancipatory implications of technologies (Haraway 1991). The new information technology and the possibility of virtual reality and cyberspace have all attracted great interest. Computer simulations and networks create the possibilities of new experiences of disembodiment, re-embodiment, and emotional attachment. All of these technological developments threaten to transform conventional assumptions about the nature of social relationships.

Technological constructionism, as opposed to social constructionism as an implicit theoretical framework, can also be said to include the political statements of the artistic performances by Stelarc and Orlan. In a series of controversial artistic events, Stelarc demonstrated the interconnections between the body, technology, and the environment to promote the idea of the end of the body as a natural phenomenon (Fleming 2002). In the case of Orlan's career, the surgical reconstructions of her face are intended to be performances in which she ironically calls into question the transformation of women's bodies by cosmetic surgery. By transforming surgery into a public drama, she has critically exposed the exploitative relationship between the cosmetics industry, the medical establishment, and gender stereotypes. Her public performances literally show that medical technology can socially and physically reconstruct her body. Here we see the body being used as a site upon which a performance occurs delivering a powerful political statement (Featherstone 2000). Orlan's surgery displays the power of medical technology, while also calling technology into question as part of the commercial apparatus of a consumer society. Although this technological dimension is an underdeveloped aspect of the theory of social constructionism, I include this example here in order to make a clear contrast with more deterministic theories of the cultural production of the body.

Secondly, the body is often understood as a cultural representation of social organization and power relations. This approach has become a common aspect of art criticism and history (Adler and Pointon 1993), and has been fundamental to social anthropology. The human body has been a persistent metaphor for social and political relations throughout human history. Social functions have been historically represented through different parts of the body. For instance, we refer to "the head of state" and "the head of the corporation" to talk about organizational power and leadership, while the heart has been a rich metaphor for life, imagination, and emotions. It has been understood as the house of the soul and the book of life, and the "tables of the heart" provided a perspective into the whole of nature (Doueihi 1977). Similarly, the hand defines people and objects that are beautiful (handsome) or useful (handy) or damaged and incomplete (handicap). Following the work of Michel Foucault, historical research has demonstrated how representations of the body are expressions of relations of power, particularly between men and women. One classic illustration has been the historical argument that anatomical maps of the human body varied between societies in terms of the dominant discourse of gender (Petersen 1998).

Social anthropologists have also shown how disturbances are typically grasped in the metaphors by which we understand mental and physical health. Bodily metaphors have been important in moral debate about these social disruptions. The division between good and evil has drawn heavily on bodily metaphors; what is seen as sinister is related to left-handedness, the illegitimate side, the awkward side (Hertz 1960). Our sense of social order is spoken of in terms of the balance or imbalance of the body. In the eighteenth century, as doctors turned to mathematics to construct a Newtonian geography of the body, the idea of hydraulic pumps was used to express such phenomena as human digestion and blood circulation. The therapeutic bleeding of patients by knife or leech was thought to assist these hydraulic mechanisms, and to relieve morbid pressures on the minds of the disturbed.

Severe political disruptions in society were often imagined in terms of poor social digestion. The idea that political unrest produced disorder in the gut was reflected in the master metaphor of the government of the body. Ideas about dietary management were translated into notions about the need for fiscal constraint, reduction in government expenditure, and downsizing of public functions. In the discourse of modern management theory, a lean and mean corporation requires a healthy management team.

Thirdly, the notion of the "lived body" was developed by the French philosopher Maurice Merleau-Ponty in *Phenomenology of Perception* (1982). In creating the phenomenology of the everyday world, he was concerned to understand human consciousness, perception and intentionality (see CHAPTER 11). Applying Edmund Husserl's phenomenology of intentional consciousness to everyday phenomena from the perspective of corporeal existence, Merleau-Ponty wanted to describe the lived world without the use of the conventional dualism between subject and object. Hence, he was critical of the legacy of Cartesianism, namely Descartes's *cogito ergo sum* ("I think, therefore I am"). Cartesianism had consecrated the dualism between mind and body which had become an essential presupposition of Western science. In developing the idea of the "body-subject" that is always situated in a specific social reality, he dismissed behavioral and mechanistic approaches, arguing that the body is constitutive of our being in the world. Perception cannot therefore be treated as merely a disembodied consciousness. This perspective, which was later developed in philosophy by Jean-Luc Nancy, has important implications for how sociologists think about "the social actor." Research inspired by this idea of the lived body and lived experience has been important in demonstrating the intimate connections between body, experience, and identity. In medical sociology studies of traumatic experiences resulting from disease or accident have shown how damage to the body transforms the self-image and notions of identity. Sociological research has concentrated on how damaged embodiment can have major implications for self-understanding and how shared narratives of trauma can be valuable in sustaining an adequate sense of self-worth (Becker 1997). Research on violence and torture has also drawn upon the sociology of the body to understand how the everyday environment (of tools and domestic appliances) can be used to undermine the ontological security of people (Scarry 1985).

Finally, we can also examine how human beings are embodied and how they acquire corporeal practices that are necessary for walking, dancing, shaking hands, and other everyday activities. Influenced by Marcel Mauss (1979) and his concept of "body techniques," anthropologists have attempted to describe how people learn to manage their bodies according to social norms. Children for instance have to learn how to sit properly at table and boys learn how to throw in ways that differentiate them from girls. This anthropological legacy suggests that we should think about embodiment as an ensemble of practices. These assumptions about practice and embodiment have been developed by Pierre Bourdieu in terms of a set of influential concepts. Following Aristotle's discussion of practice and virtue, "hexis" refers to deportment (gait, gesture, or posture) by which people carry and socially present themselves. "Habitus" refers to the dispositions through which tastes or preferences are manifest. Habitus is literally the habitual way of doing things. Bourdieu has employed these terms to study the everyday habitus of social classes in France in *Distinction* (1984). The body is invested with symbolic capital whereby it becomes a corporeal expression of the hierarchies of social power. The body is permanently cultivated and represented by the aesthetic preferences of different social classes whereby, in French culture for example, mountaineering and tennis require the flexible, slim, and pliant bodies of the middle and upper classes, whereas the working-class sports of wrestling and weightlifting produce an entirely different body and habitus. Bourdieu's work, which is important in identifying the significance of embodiment and practice in the notions of hexis and habitus, has been influential in studies of habitus from boxing (Wacquant 1995) to classical ballet (Turner and Wainwright 2003), and in studies of female piety in Islam (Mahmood 2005).

Social theory and empirical work inspired by the legacy of Bourdieu are currently the most promising framework for developing sociological perspectives on the body. Whereas the work of Foucault was probably the most important influence on the study of the body in the 1980s, Bourdieu's intellectual legacy has become increasingly significant in the development of the sociology of the body in the 1990s and beyond (Wacquant 2004). While *Distinction* (1984) played an important role in the evolution of sociological research on the working class, sociology has yet to incorporate fully the insights of *Pascalian Meditations* (2000) for an understanding of reflexive embodiment. Both the potential and limitations of Bourdieu can be illustrated by an examination of one neglected area in sociology, namely performance. The need for an understanding of embodiment and lived experience is crucial in approaching the performing arts, but also for the study of sport. Dance has an aesthetic immediacy, which cannot be captured by discourse analysis. This commentary brings out the important difference between the body as text and representation and the body as embodiment and practice. Thus choreography is in one sense the text of the dance, but performance takes place outside the strict directions of the choreographic work. Dance is a theoretically interesting topic because it demonstrates the analytical limitations of cultural interpretations of the body as text, and directs our attention to the phenomenology of performance.

In concluding this section, I propose to simplify this fourfold division of recent theoretical perspectives by reducing its complexity to two fundamental but distinctive theoretical options. There is either the cultural decoding of the body as a system of meaning that has a definite structure existing separately from the intentions and conceptions of individuals, or there is the phenomenological study of embodiment that attempts to understand human practices that are organized around the life course (of birth, maturation, reproduction, and death). Bourdieu's sociology offers one possible solution to this persistent tension between representation and practice. The notions of habitus, practice, and bodily knowledge offer useful research concepts for looking simultaneously at how status difference is inscribed on the body and how we experience the world through our bodies, which are involuntarily ranked in terms of their cultural capital (Bourdieu 1977, 2000). This reconciliation of these traditions can be assisted by distinguishing between the idea of the body as representation and embodiment as practice and experience. In my own work, I have argued elsewhere that these theoretical conflicts between representation and practice can be resolved by sharply distinguishing between "the body" as a cultural system in which bodies are produced as carriers of powerful symbolic realities and

BRYAN S. TURNER

"embodiment" as the practices that are necessary to function in the everyday world (Turner and Rojek 2001).

EMBODIMENT AND HUMAN MOVEMENT

We can illustrate the issues about embodiment by further considering the question of human movement in dance. As a "natural language," dance occurs in a myriad of forms and with multiple cultural functions. In traditional societies dance takes place in specific ritualized tradition, for example as a war dance. These traditional performances often occur in stylized or ritualized settings such as a court. There is typically an important relationship between the training of the body, the norms of civility, and the political power of the court. For example, Javanese dance required precise, formalized movements, and performances were evaluated in terms of their exact adherence to formal rules that had to be mastered with considerable care and diligence. In classical Japanese dance, or *nihon buyo*, the rules that determine the use of fans have to be acquired in such a manner that there is no division between body and mind, because the performer perfectly embodies the performance (Hahn 2007). These rules determined that certain postures would be repeated according to their ritualistic significance. The dexterity and training of the performer produced an authentic aesthetic experience, and not one whose aura could be diminished by its rule-bound reproducibility. Training produced a natural, apparently spontaneous flow of the body according to specific rules and codes.

While Bourdieu offers a set of concepts that are highly relevant to the study of dance, perhaps the most interesting critical response to Bourdieu's sociology came from Richard Shusterman in *Pragmatist Aesthetics* (1992) and *Surface & Depth* (2002). Shusterman makes an important contribution to aesthetic theory by examining the relationship between the pragmatist legacy of John Dewey and Bourdieu's cultural sociology. In his emphasis on the body in relation to aesthetics, Shusterman establishes the important point that Bourdieu's analysis of the cultural field is exclusively concerned with the audible (musical taste) and the visual (conventional works of art). Performance is not adequately addressed by Bourdieu despite the centrality of a theory of practice to his sociology as a whole. Shusterman argues that Bourdieu's sociology of the aesthetic is implicitly parallel to Theodor Adorno's critique of popular culture. Visual culture – such as a Baroque painting – or literary culture – such as a Shakespearian sonnet – have more cultural capital than a dance, which is necessarily impermanent. For example, Shusterman, who has been interested in rap music as a critique of American society, does not regard rap as simply an expression of inauthentic popular culture. He claims that Bourdieu failed to provide an adequate sociology of experience, particularly aesthetic experience, and that Bourdieu's reluctance to treat the experience (of movement) seriously is associated with the fact that appreciation of rap falls outside the cultural arena of privilege accorded to intellectual self-consciousness and reflection. Reliance on such intellectual introspection will not help us penetrate to "the deeper, unconscious, socially structured strata of the self that help shape individual consciousness" (Shusterman 2002: 224). Despite Bourdieu's own protests to the contrary, Shusterman (2002: 221) claims that Bourdieu failed to deal with lived experience, especially an ephemeral experience of a dance gesture – "No sympathetic attention is given to the phenomenologi-cal dimension of lived experience, its power of meaningful, qualitative immediacy, and its potential for the transformation of attitudes and habits." While Shusterman takes rap as a powerful instance of these aesthetic presuppositions, dance in general provides as it were a litmus test of the scope of traditional aesthetic theory, in which the Kantian legacy of disinterested, rational judgment is still hegemonic.

This focus on dance can help us also to consider the current status of the sociol-ogy of the body, mainly because the promise and limitations of social studies of the body are replicated in dance studies. My principal criticisms of the existing sociol-ogy of the body are firstly that it has become too self-consciously theoretical, and hence it is often divorced from actual empirical research. While theories relating for example to the social construction of the body proliferate, there are few important, genuinely creative ethnographies of embodiment. Secondly, both the sociology of the body and contemporary dance studies, insofar as they have been influenced by postmodern perspectives, by concentrating on the body as a cultural text, have often neglected, somewhat paradoxically, the issue of human performance. Dance brings into sharp focus the important issue that the aesthetics of the body cannot be under-stood without attention to performance, and postmodern readings of the body as text have obscured not illuminated this basic point. Let us put Shusterman's argu-ment in a slightly different framework (Turner and Wainwright 2003). Sociologists, including Bourdieu, have neglected the issue of the body-in-movement. Specifically there is really no development of the sociology of dance – although there is a respect-able field of anthropological research. This absence comes out in Shusterman's observation that our taste for popular music is often displayed by movement – tapping feet, swaying hips, clicking fingers, or shaking heads. By contrast, apprecia-tion of classical music is often shown by the absence of any such bodily movements.

A RESEARCH AGENDA: REPRODUCTION AND LONGEVITY

The study of the body has a promising research future, but it is also in danger of becoming repetitive and conventional rather than innovative. One major research area for this sub-field is to explore the transformation of the body by modern science and technology. Reproductive technologies and the new social gerontology provide two good examples (Turner 2004). This aspect of the sociology of the body has been particularly influenced by the social philosophy of Foucault. His approach has proved to be useful because he described a conceptually important division between the study of the individual body and the study of populations. In the first area of the "anatomo-politics of the human body," Foucault (1979: 139) examined how various forms of discipline have regulated individuals, and in the second he referred to the "bio-politics of the population" (1979: 139), involving the regulatory controls of populations. Anatomo-politics is concerned with the micro-politics of identity, concentrating on the sexuality, reproduction, and life histories of individuals. The clinical inspection of individuals has become a routine part of the anatomo-politics of society, whereas the bio-politics of populations employed demography and epi-demiology to manage whole populations. While the anatomo-politics of medicine involves the discipline of individuals, the bio-politics of society achieves a surveillance and regulation of populations. Foucault's study of the body was thus organized around the notions of discipline and regulatory controls which collectively constitute a system of "governmentality."

This paradigm is helpful in understanding developments in contemporary biological sciences and their application to individuals and populations. The social consequences of cloning, genetics, and new reproductive technologies are already revolutionary, and the social conflicts emerging from these scientific innovations for state policies, politics, and law will be profound (see CHAPTER 17). There is an obviously important area of comparative and legal research on state responses to genetic research and patent policy. These developments raise new questions about the legal ownership of the human body in modern societies. These ethical and political issues are already significant in the area of organ transplants and reproduction, and the legal and social problems associated with these scientific developments will became more intense as new medical procedures become feasible and affordable. Medical technology and microbiology hold out the promise (for example through the Human Genome Project, cloning, transplants, "wonder drugs," and microsurgery) of human freedom from aging, disability, and disease. These medical possibilities have given rise to utopian visions of a world wholly free from disease and disability – a new mirage of health. It is clear that the human body will come to stand in an entirely new relationship to self and society as a result of these technological developments.

These social changes raise important legal issues for the ownership and use of the human body. For example, we might assume that in a liberal society people should be free to sell parts of their bodies for commercial gain. While we might believe that selling one's hair for commercial gain would be trivial, selling a kidney is clearly more serious. These changes create further opportunities for the development of a global medical system of governance in which medicine may exercise an expanded power over life and death. Few national governments have as yet attempted to regulate this global medical system through legislation.

The emergence of a new eugenics is implicitly embedded in the emergence of these new biotechnologies, which are forcing modern states to develop science policies that will address the new challenge, for example of asexual reproduction. At one level, eugenics is simply any strategy to improve human reproduction. The term "eu-genesis" refers, according to the *Oxford English Dictionary*, to "the quality of breeding well and freely," while "eugenic" or "the production of fine offspring" appeared first in 1833. The eugenics of the 1930s that were associated with authoritarian regimes have been widely condemned as an attack on human dignity. We might say that if fascist eugenics involved compulsory state policies, post-war eugenics were thought to be individualistic and discretionary. The new eugenics allegedly enhances human choice and liberates us from the determinism of our genetic inheritance. However, any policy that influences reproduction can be described as "eugenic." For example, handing out free contraceptives and giving contraceptive advice to schoolchildren constitute eugenic practices. Fascist eugenics involved a policy of public regulation of breeding and, in modern times, the one-child family policy of the Chinese Communist Party has involved a draconian attempt to control population growth.

The sex act is still regarded in the liberal tradition as a private matter, and historically states and their legislatures have been reluctant to regard reproductive activity as a matter of public concern unless such activity took place with children. However, new reproductive technologies have major consequences for the public domain, and in general the new biotechnology holds out the prospect of a posthuman future; therefore eugenics can no longer be left entirely to individuals making private decisions about their reproductive goals and the biological futures of their children. Although states have in the past attempted to control the spread of sexually transmitted diseases among the military, and have waged educational campaigns to promote the use of condoms, democratic states have been reluctant to control directly the spread of AIDS through the use of criminal law. The separation of private sex acts from reproduction by technology does complicate the legal issue. There are few contemporary societies in which individuals (heterosexual, gay, or lesbian) have an unlimited right to reproduce by whatever technological means possible regardless of the future implications for social identities and relationships. Nevertheless, reproductive technology has advanced rapidly, and in principle we can expect these technologies to change the conditions under which reproduction takes place. These technologies have profound implications therefore for how bodies are reproduced and who owns them. In Foucault's terms therefore, eugenics is probably the original case of governmentality.

IMMORTAL BODIES

In terms of medical science research is unclear what causes aging (Turner 2007). Of course, medical interest in the human aging process goes back to writers such as Luigi Cornaro (1464–1566), who in his *Discourses on the Temperate Life* (1558) argued that his own longevity was a result of temperance, exercise, and diet. The body's finite supply of vital spirits could be soberly husbanded by diet and exercise. His discourses, which were translated in 1903, had an impact on American temperance ideas, and can be regarded as the earliest defense of a low-calorie diet. George Cheyne (1671–1743) took a similar view of the relationship between diet, healthy living, and social order in his *The Natural Method of Cureing the Diseases of the Body* (1742). While diet can help prolongevity, the idea that human aging is inevitable has been a fundamental presupposition of scientific gerontology ever since. If aging is an inevitable process of cellular degeneration, then the question about life extension does not arise, apart from mere fanciful speculation.

More recently, however, considerable attention has been given to whether medical science could successfully reverse or at least delay this aging process. Between the 1960s and 1980s the view put forward by biologists was that normal cells had a "replicative senescence," because normal tissues can only divide a finite number of times before becoming quiescent. Cells were observed *in vitro* in a process of natural senescence, but eventually experiments *in vivo* established an important distinction between normal and pathological cells in terms of their cellular division. Pathological cells appeared paradoxically to have no necessary limitation on replication, and therefore "immortalization" was seen to be the defining feature of a pathological cell line. Biologists concluded that finite cell division meant that the aging of the whole organism was inevitable. Basic cellular research confirmed the view that human life had an intrinsic predetermined limit around 120 years of age, and that it was through pathological developments that some cells might out-survive the otherwise inescapable senescence of cellular life. The longevity of individuals was determined primarily by cellular senescence.

This conventional framework was eventually challenged by the discovery that human embryonic cells were capable of continuous division in laboratory conditions and showed no sign of any inevitable replicative crisis. Stem cells were now seen to be capable of indefinite division, and hence were "immortalized." The cultivation of these cells as an experimental form of life has disrupted existing presuppositions about the boundaries between the normal and the pathological, and therefore between survival and extinction. Stem cell research has begun to open up an arena within which the body has reserves of renewable tissue, suggesting thereby that the limits of biological growth are not fixed immutably. The body has a surplus of stem cells capable of survival beyond the death of the organism. With these developments in micro-biogerontology, the capacity of regenerative medicine to expand the limits of life becomes a plausible prospect, creating new opportunities for what we might call "health capitalism," that is, the possibility of new markets in regenerative medicine.

The human consequences of these changes will be rapid and radical, but little systematic thought has been given to the social and political consequences of extended longevity. Although it is mere speculation, this new pattern of aging will produce a range of major socio-economic problems (Dumas and Turner 2007). Growing world inequality between the rejuvenated North and the naturally aging South would further exacerbate existing social conflicts between deprived social groups and wealthy aging populations. There may well be a failure of the labor market to cope with the increasing number of human survivors, and there would be parallel crises in housing markets and in pension schemes. The current crisis in the global pensions industry is perhaps an indication of a deeper crisis around the resources necessary to sustain the increasing longevity of the world population. The inability of the food supply to keep up with population expansion would increase economic dependency on genetically modified food if global warming reduces the amount of available arable land. The rapid transformation of family structures would continue as the elderly survived in greater numbers, presumably taking on new partners and reproducing children in new households through unlimited serial monogamy.

The theological notion of an afterlife would probably disappear, since most survivors would literally experience eternal life or at least indefinite life on earth. It is reasonable to assume that, while medical sciences could reduce mortality, there would at least in the short term be an increase in morbidity as chronic illness and geriatric diseases increased. Living forever would mean in practice living forever in a morbid condition, increasingly dependent on medical technology. One answer to the question "Could we live forever?" would be that, while we might experience prolonged survival, it might not constitute living as a meaningful experience. With mere survival, there would be increasing psychological problems such as depression, ennui, and despair as surviving populations experienced new levels of boredom through the endless repetition of their lives, resulting periodically in episodes of collective hysteria, chronic boredom, and anguish. The problem of "killing time" for survivors with ancient bodies would present individuals with an unprecedented existential crisis (Raposa 1999).

CONCLUSION: THE BODY, SELF, AND SOCIETY

A critical response to this discussion of reproduction and aging might plausibly ask: what have these developments got to do with the body as such? The answer is that, if one takes the notion of embodiment seriously, then self and body are merely two sides of the same ontological coin, and hence these scientific developments have profound implications for selfhood and modernity. Reproductive technology and new patterns of aging resulting from technologies of prolongevity are thus relevant to the sociology of the body, because these examples point to an important field of research, namely the changing relationships between embodiment, selfhood, and social relations. New technologies suggest that humans might acquire different types of embodiment, and will have as a consequence to develop different ways of relating to and thinking about the body. Anthropological research has discovered that radical surgery involving organ transplants forces people to rethink their relationship to the inside of their bodies. In popular imagination, a transplant is subjectively rather like having another person inside one's body. In short, these areas of research are relevant to the sociology of the body because they raise in a new way a traditional debate about the relationship between the body, self, and society. If traditional sociology could be described as the study of self and society as a version of the macro and micro distinction, then we might argue that the sociology of the body suggests that in fact three concepts – body, self, and society – can be broadly regarded as defining the intellectual field occupied by sociology.

There are three components of the self. Most importantly, there is reflection. To be a self, we must be able to reflect upon our identities, our actions, and our relationship with others. In order to recall our own biographical narrative we must have consciousness, language, and memory. Selfhood, whatever else it involves, must presuppose a capacity for continuous self-assessment and oversight of behavior. Secondly, the self is not an independent, free-floating consciousness, because the self is also defined by its relationship to human embodiment. Recognition of the self depends not simply on memory and consciousness, but also on its peculiar physical characteristics. We can reflect on our bodies as objects, but my hand does not have the same type of objectivity to me as the hammer it holds. In short, while the conscious self is a reflective agent, the body is not just an object that is external to that subjectivity, but participates in an embodied agency towards the everyday world. The final dimension of this scheme is the notion of the self as a product of or situated within a dense network of social relationships. The self in the Western tradition has not been invariably captured in the isolated figure of Robinson Crusoe, but has been interpreted as a social being that cannot survive without a social world. We are embedded in social networks. while specific aspects of the self are typically emphasized by philosophers, theories of the self have in practice to address all three aspects (Seigel 2005).

Sociology has characteristically defined the self as simply the product of social processes (such as socialization) and social relationships (such as the looking-glass self). Émile Durkheim is the classical representative of this tradition, but the idea of social determinism was also present in Erving Goffman's notion of the self as merely a script that has to be delivered within a dramaturgical setting (Goffman 1959). This interpretation of sociology is, however, too simplistic. Like the Western philosophical tradition as a whole, sociology has struggled conceptually with the contradictions between action, structure, and the reflective self. Theoretical solutions to this traditional quandary are too numerous to mention, but the sociology of the body suggests that any solution to the structure and agency dilemma must take seriously the embodiment of the reflective self.

We might plausibly argue that the idea of the reflective self was a dominant theme of the Enlightenment and was given its classic statement in Kant's definition of Enlightenment as freedom from infantile tutelage. In Kant's treatment of reason he argues that in practice we must presuppose our freedom from empirical determinism, if we are to justify our sense of moral responsibility and obligation (Ward 1972). At a later stage, the Romantic reaction to Kantian rationalism placed greater emphasis on individuality, subjectivity, and embodiment. This Romanticism was famously illustrated by Goethe, who in some respects launched the cult of mobility, youth, and inwardness, resulting in the full-blown *Bildungsroman* of nineteenth-century European culture (Moretti 1987). With industrialization and the development of the idea of "the social" in industrial society, sociology emerged to define the individual as a product of social forces. This image of the passive self was characteristic of sociology in the middle of the twentieth century, in which theories of mass society, the managerial revolution, and the other-directed self limited the capacity of the individual to act independently. The individual, who was now passive rather than reflective and active, was analyzed notoriously in William H. Whyte's *The Organization Man* (1956). In this conclusion, I want to propose speculatively that the corporeal self may become the dominant theme of modern society, because the scientific revolutions in information science, micro-biology, and genetics have created a new language of genetic determinism in which both the social self of mass society and the reflective self of the Enlightenment are challenged by technological notions of embodiment and reflexivity. For example, the idea of the "criminal gene" or the "divorce gene" means that we can, on scientific grounds, avoid any recognition of individual reflexivity and responsibility in favor of genetic determinism. Individuals are thought, at least within the popular press, to be driven by whatever combination of genes they happen to have fortuitously inherited at birth. Our selves are not determined by a moral education but are an outcome of genetic contingency.

The rise of the sociology of the body can be seen in part as a response to these manifold social changes, including reproductive technologies, health consumerism, and genetic science. In response to these social changes, a variety of sociological perspectives on the body have emerged. It is unlikely and quite possibly undesirable that any single theoretical synthesis will finally emerge out of this heterogeneous ensemble of perspectives. The creative tension between interpreting the body as cultural representation and interpreting embodiment as lived experience will continue to produce innovative and creative approaches. There are, as I have attempted to demonstrate, new issues on the horizon which sociologists will need to examine, such as the posthuman body, cybernetics, genetic modification, the life-extension project, and artificial bodies (Fukuyama 2002). The wealth, diversity, and quality of this research indicates that the sociology of the body is not simply a passing theoretical fashion but an important and vibrant aspect of contemporary sociology.

Bibliography

Adler, K., and Poinyon, M. (eds.) (1993) *The Body Imaged: The Human Form and Visual Cultures since the Renaissance*. Cambridge: Cambridge University Press.

Appleyard, B. (2007) *How to Live Forever or Die Trying*. London: Simon & Schuster.

Arendt, H. (1958) *The Human Condition*. Chicago: University of Chicago Press.

Barnes, C., Mercer, G., and Shakespeare, T. (1999) *Exploring Disability: A Sociological Introduction*. Cambridge: Polity.

Beauvoir, S. de (1972a) *The Second Sex*. Harmondsworth: Penguin.

Beauvoir, S. de (1972b) *Old Age*. London: Andre Deutsch/Weidenfeld & Nicolson.

Becker, G. (1997) *Disrupted Lives: How People Create Meaning in a Chaotic World*. Berkeley: University of California Press.

Blacking, J. (ed.) (1977) *The Anthropology of the Body*. London: Academic Press.

Bordo, S. (1993) *Unbearable Weight: Feminism, Western Culture and the Body*. Berkeley: University of California Press.

Bourdieu, P. (1977) *Outline of a Theory of Practice*. Cambridge: Cambridge University Press.

Bourdieu, P. (1984) *Distinction: A Social Critique of the Judgement of Taste*. London: Routledge & Kegan Paul.

Bourdieu, P. (2000) *Pascalian Meditations*. Cambridge: Polity.

Brogan, W. A. (2005) *Heidegger and Aristotle: The Twofoldness of Being*. Albany: State University of New York Press.

Brumberg, J. J. (1988) *Fasting Girls: The Emergence of Anorexia Nervosa as a Modern Disease*. Cambridge, MA: Harvard University Press.

Butler, J. (1990) *Gender Trouble: Feminism and the Subversion of Identity*. London: Routledge.

Butler, J. (1993) *Bodies that Matter: On the Discursive Limits of "Sex."* London: Routledge.

Caplan, J. (ed.) (2000) *Written on the Body: The Tattoo in European and American History*. London: Reaktion Books.

Davie, N. (2005) *Tracing the Criminal: The Rise of Scientific Criminology in Britain 1860–1918*. Oxford: Bardwell.

Davis, K. (2002) "'A Dubious Equality': Men, Women and Cosmetic Surgery." *Body & Society* 8(1): 49–65.

Doueihi, M. (1997) *A Perverse History of the Human Heart*. Cambridge, MA: Harvard University Press.

Dubos, R. (1959) *Mirage of Health: Utopias, Progress and Biological Change*. London: George Allen & Unwin.

Dumas, A., and Turner, B. S. (2007) "The Life-Extension Project: A Sociological Critique." *Health Sociological Review* 16(1): 5–17.

Elias, N. (1978) *The Civilising Process*. Oxford: Blackwell.

Evans, M., and Lee, E. (eds.) (2002) *Real Bodies*. Houndmills: Palgrave.

Fassin, D., and Memmi, D. (eds.) (2004) *Le Gouvernement des corps*. Paris: Éditions de l'École des Hautes Études en Sciences Sociales.

Featherstone, M. (1982) "The Body in Consumer Culture." *Theory Culture & Society* 1(2): 18–33.

Featherstone, M. (ed.) (2000) *Body Modification*. London: Sage.

Featherstone, M., and Burrows, R. (1995) *Cyberspace, Cyberbodies, Cyberpunk*. London: Sage.

Featherstone, M., and Hepworth, M. (1991) "The Mask of Ageing and the Postmodern Life Course," in M. Featherstone, M. Hepworth, and B. S. Turner (eds.), *The Body: Social Process and Cultural Theory*. London: Sage.

Featherstone, M., Hepworth, M., and Turner, B. S. (1991) (eds.) *The Body: Social Processes and Cultural Theory*. London: Sage.

Fleming, C. (2002) "Performance as Guerrilla Ontology: The Case of Stelarc." *Body & Society* 8(3): 95–109.

Foucault, M. (1979) *The History of Sexuality*. London: Tavistock.

Fukuyama, F. (2002) *Our Posthuman Future: Consequences of the Biotechnology Revolution*. New York: Farrar, Straus & Giroux.

Gehlen, A. (1980) *Man in the Age of Technology*. New York: Columbia.

Goffman, E. (1959) *The Presentation of Self in Everyday Life*. Garden City, NY: Doubleday Anchor.

Goffman, E. (1964) *Stigma: Notes on the Management of a Spoiled Identity*. Englewood Cliffs, NJ: Prentice Hall.

Grosz, E. (1994) *Volatile Bodies: Towards a Corporeal Feminism*. London: Routledge.

Gugutzer, R. (2004) *Soziologie des Korpers*. Bielefeld: Transcript.

Hahn, T. (2007) *Sensational Knowledge: Embodying Culture through Japanese Dance*. Middletown, CT: Wesleyan University Press.

Halberstam, J., and Livingston, I. (eds.) (1995) *Posthuman Bodies*. Bloomington and Indianapolis: Indiana University Press.

Haraway, D. (1991) *Simians, Cyborgs and Women: The Reinvention of Nature*. London: Free Association Books.

Hertz, R. (1960) *Death and the Right Hand*. London: Cohen & West.

James, A., and Hockey, J. (2007) *Embodying Health Identities*. Houndmills: Palgrave.

James, I. (2006) *An Introduction to the Philosophy of Jean-Luc Nancy*. Stanford: Stanford University Press.

Laqueur, T. (1990) *Making Sex: Body and Gender from the Greeks to Freud*. Cambridge, MA: Harvard University Press.

Mahmood, S. (2005) *Politics of Piety: The Islamic Revival and the Feminist Subject*. Princeton: Princeton University Press.

Markus, G. (1978) *Marxism and Anthropology*. Assen: Van Gorcum.

Mauss, M. (1979) "Body Techniques," in *Sociology and Psychology: Essays*. London: Routledge.

Merleau-Ponty, M. (1982) *Phenomenology of Perception*. London: Routledge & Kegan Paul.

Moretti, F. (1987) *The Way of the World: The Bildungsroman in European Culture*. London: Verso.

Nancy, J.-L. (2005) *The Ground of the Image*. New York: Fordham University Press.

Negrin, L. (2002) "Cosmetic Surgery and the Eclipse of Identity." *Body & Society* 8(4): 21–42.

O'Neill, J. (1985) *Five Bodies: The Human Shape of Modern Society*. Ithaca, NY: Cornell University Press.

Orbach, S. (1985) *Fat is a Feminist Issue*. London: Faber & Faber.

Paravicini-Bagliani, A. (2000) *The Pope's Body*. Chicago: University of Chicago Press.

Petersen, A. (1998) "Sexing the Body: Representations of Sex Differences in Gray's *Anatomy*, 1858 to the Present." *Body & Society* 4(1): 1–15.

Pitts, V. (2003) *In the Flesh: The Cultural Politics of Body Modification*. London: Palgrave.

Radley, A. (1995) "The Elusory Body and Social Constructionist Theory." *Body & Society* 1(2): 3–23.

Raposa, M. L. (1999) *Boredom and the Religious Imagination*. Charlottesville: University of Virginia Press.

Richardson, D., and Seidman, S. (eds.) (2002) *Handbook of Lesbian & Gay Studies*. London: Sage.

Scarry, E. (1985) *The Body in Pain: The Making and Unmaking of the World*. Oxford: Oxford University Press.

Seidman, S., Fischer, N., and Meeks, C. (eds.) (2006) *Handbook of the New Sexuality Studies*. London: Routledge.

Seigel, J. (2005) *The Idea of the Self: Thought and Experience in Western Europe since the Seventeenth Century*. Cambridge: Cambridge University Press.

Sennet, R. (1994) *Flesh and Stone: The Body and the City in Western Civilization*. New York: Norton.

Shepherd, S. (2004) "Lolo's Breasts, Cyborgism, and a Wooden Christ," in H. Thomas and J. Ahmed (eds.), *Cultural Bodies: Ethnography and Theory*. Oxford: Blackwell.

Shildrick, M. (1997) *Leaky Bodies and Boundaries: Feminism, Postmodernism and (Bio)ethics*. London: Routledge.

Shilling, C. (1993) *The Body and Social Theory*. London: Sage.

Shusterman, R. (1992) *Pragmatist Aesthetics: Living Beauty, Rethinking Art*. Oxford: Blackwell.

Shusterman, R. (1999) *Bourdieu: A Critical Reader*. Oxford: Blackwell.

Shusterman, R. (2000) *Performing Live: Aesthetic Alternatives for the Ends of Art*. Ithaca, NY: Cornell University Press.

Shusterman, R. (2002) *Surface & Depth: Dialectics of Criticism and Culture*. Ithaca, NY: Cornell University Press.

Strathern, A. J. (1996) *Body Thoughts*. Ann Arbor: University of Michigan Press.

Turner, B. S. (1984) *The Body & Society. Explorations in Social Theory*. Oxford: Blackwell.

Turner, B. S. (1992) *Regulating Bodies: Essays in Medical Sociology*. London: Routledge.

Turner, B. S. (2000) Preface to the Second Edition, in *The Blackwell Companion to Social Theory*. Oxford: Blackwell.

Turner, B. S. (2003) "Biology, Vulnerability and Politics," in S. J. Williams, L. Birke, and G. A. Bendelow (eds.), *Debating Biology: Sociological Reflections on Health, Medicine and Society*. London: Routledge.

Turner, B. S. (2004) *The New Medical Sociology*. New York: Norton.

Turner, B. S. (2007) "Culture, Technologies and Bodies: The Technological Utopia of Living Forever," in C. Shilling (ed.), *Embodying Sociology Retrospect, Progress and Prospects*. Oxford: Blackwell.

Turner, B. S., and Rojek, C. (2001) *Society & Culture: Principles of Scarcity and Solidarity*. London: Routledge.

Turner, B. S., and Wainwright, S. (2003) "Corps de Ballet: The Case of the Injured Ballet Dancer." *Sociology of Health & Illness* 25(4): 269–88.

Wacquant, L. J. D. (1995) "Pugs at Work: Bodily Capital and Bodily Labour among Professional Boxers." *Body & Society* 1: 65–93.

Wacquant, L. J. D. (2004) "Lire 'Le Capital' de Pierre Bourdieu," in L. Pinto, G. Sapiro, and P. Champagne (eds.), *Pierre Bourdieu, sociologue*. Paris: Fayard.

Wajcman, J. (1991) *Feminism Confronts Technology*. Oxford: Blackwell.

Ward, K. (1972) *The Development of Kant's Ethics*. Oxford: Blackwell.

Whyte, W. H. (1956) *The Organization Man*. New York: Simon & Schuster.

27

Cosmopolitanism and Social Theory

DANIEL CHERNILO

The relationship between cosmopolitanism and social theory cannot be reconstructed directly. What we commonly refer to as the leading figures in the history of social theory – Marx, Weber, Durkheim, Simmel, Parsons – did not write much, if at all, on cosmopolitanism. True, in the *Communist Manifesto* Marx and Engels (1976) used the term loosely as an adjective to describe the new kind of cultural artifacts with world-wide orientation that were being created in capitalism. Thus, although they spoke of "cosmopolitan" literature and science – the German term they used there was *Weltbürgertum* – this hardly amounts to a systematic treatment or valuation of it as an idea. More poignantly, in his lectures on political sociology Émile Durkheim (1992) used the notion of *cosmopolitanisme* to recover Kant's idea of perpetual peace as he tried to reconcile the old natural law cosmopolitan credo with the nascent force of nationalism just before World War I. But again in this case the highly politicized meaning Durkheim gave to the concept does not warrant, at least without further ado, depicting his sociological viewpoint as cosmopolitan. This chapter therefore begins with a note of caution. The assessment of the connections between cosmopolitan thinking and social theory cannot replicate the paths followed by those who have reconstructed how social theory relates to a number of alternative social and intellectual trends: the rise of capitalism (Giddens 1971) and the critiques of the Enlightenment (Hawthorn 1987), liberalism (Seidman 1983), Romanticism (Nisbet 1967), and nationalism (Chernilo 2007a). Rather, we need first to identify the defining elements of cosmopolitanism as an intellectual tradition and only then can we attempt to move on and assess the extent to which they are compatible with the modern social theory's main features.

This chapter's starting point is that such a connection between cosmopolitanism and social theory can be found in and is based on a *claim to universalism*. First and foremost, this means that they both equally work under the normative presuppositions of the *fundamental unity of the human species* and the *ultimate equality of all human beings*. All forms of gender, ethnic, cultural, national, and religious differences must be theorized as something internal to the substantive unity of humanity; the very existence of such differences is taken as the expression of the ultimate equality of all human beings. My argument here is, then, that this *cosmopolitan layout* underlies, over the past two centuries, the work of the most salient social theorists not only in their normative standpoints but also in their concepts and methods. In other words, for classical cosmopolitanism and modern social theory alike, humanity can only be meaningfully comprehended if treated as a single subject. So, even if it would be wholly inappropriate to see sociology as the social scientific incarnation of a cosmopolitan program that had developed mostly at a philosophical level, I would nonetheless like to argue that social theory is highly compatible with a cosmopolitan outlook because of the claim to universalism they both share.

There are, of course, important differences in the way in which the old tradition of cosmopolitan thinking, which goes back to Greek Stoic philosophy (d'Entrèves 1970: 22–36; Harris 1927; Rommen 1998: 3–29), and modern social theory, understand and justify this claim to universalism. The precise delimitation of these differences lies beyond the scope of this chapter, but let me at least summarily state the most important ones in relation to the forthcoming discussion. The first has to do with the fact that, whereas a universalistic idea of the unity of humankind was already at the center of all ancient empires' world-views (Voegelin 1962), in modern social theory we are in the presence of a *claim* to such universalism. I shall demonstrate below that social theory requires the two presuppositions I introduced above – the fundamental unity of humankind and the ultimate equality of all human beings – but in modernity sociologists can no longer argue that they have found the definitive answers to these questions. They have to believe in, and have to work with, these notions of unity and equality but cannot to establish them dogmatically in any particular and definitive way. Rather, social theory uses this claim to universalism as a regulative ideal, a standard to strive for even though it is known in advance that it will never be fully accomplished (Emmet 1994; Kant 1973). This leads, secondly, to the recognition that, whereas the old cosmopolitan tradition states its universalism on the basis of metaphysical presuppositions, such an ultimate orderly cosmos based upon a divine natural law (Toulmin 1990), or, as Immanuel Kant himself (1999) would still have it, as a teleological law of providence, modern social theory makes use of this universalistic claim as something to be internally granted. In modernity, a cosmopolitan viewpoint cannot be imposed from above – or the outside – on human beings themselves. The claim that a certain ultimate unity underwrites all kinds of social relations and ways of life needs to be demonstrated with arguments that are indeed theoretically consistent and empirically sound, but its ultimate tribunal is the fact that they are potentially acceptable to human beings themselves. Finally, social theory's cosmopolitanism is established upon the notion that it is only in modernity that human beings can realize the fact that whole globe is actually becoming a single place. Social theory emerged alongside, as much as it helped give form to, the view that the rise of modernity created the possibility of the historical actualization of the ancient ideal of a single humanity. It is only in modernity that humanity as such becomes responsible for the creation of the institutional framework within which its own ultimate unity can be effectively realized.

Modern social theory's cosmopolitanism does not in this sense refer directly or primarily to the politics of world citizenship and the legal constitution of humanity as a world-wide political community. Its cosmopolitan orientation is more sociological in scope as it seeks to find further *empirical* support and *historical* evidence for the *normative* claim of humanity's ultimate unity. Rather, I should like to argue throughout that the constant refinement of social theory's conceptual tools and methodological devices is geared towards the universalistic conceptualization of social life as a way of recognizing and coming to terms with all the sociocultural variation to be found in modernity. In speaking of modern social theory's cosmopolitan layout, therefore, I refer to a deep philosophical commitment that must be out there in operation regardless of whether it is explicitly recognized. Social theory's long-term research agenda – the understanding of the rise and main features of modern social life in a way that it is theoretically sophisticated, methodologically sound, and empirically cross-cultural – depends upon its consistency with cosmopolitanism's normative universalism. In what follows, I seek to demonstrate these theses by reassessing the work of key social theorists during three phases in the history of social theory.

PHASE 1. CLASSICAL SOCIAL THEORY: MODERNITY AS A WORLD PHENOMENON

We commence with the founding figures of modern social theory because the picture we draw from the agenda of these early thinkers is bound to leave a mark on the way in which we assess social theory's current state, features and challenges. Classical social theory emerged, by the late nineteenth century, as an intellectual program focused on trying to understand and conceptualize the nature of a whole new set of social relations – capitalism, the modern state, national democracy, the socialist revolution – which was having an impact all across the globe. Represented in the conventional figures of Karl Marx, Georg Simmel, Max Weber, and Émile Durkheim, classical social theory still inhabited at least partly the tradition of the Enlightenment and therefore it partially embraced the natural law foundations of earlier forms of normative universalism (Chernilo 2007b). My argument here is that these writers wanted to retain the orientation behind previous forms of normative universalism but needed this universalism to work under two new conditions. One, it had to be sustained without such natural law metaphysical presuppositions as God's ultimate responsibility for earthly affairs or the natural *telos* of a law of providence. Two, it had to be able to incorporate an increasing amount of sociocultural diversity within an ever wider universalistic framework. There was the need to allow for ethical disagreement and empirical variation without, in the same move, discarding the possibility of universalism altogether.

Classical social theory's commitment to the universalistic core of earlier forms of natural law thinking thus needed a subtler claim to universalism; that is, it could no longer deploy cosmopolitanism's previous normative project uncritically. If we now try to formalize the way in which they actually did this, we may say that the general commitment towards universalism remained but that it became differentiated into normative, conceptual, and methodological dimensions. *Normatively*, classical social theory advanced the view that modern society exists only as it progressively encompasses the whole globe and all human beings. *Conceptually*, social theorists were after the delimitation of what was the truly social element that constitutes modern social relations. And *methodologically*, they sought to establish the right procedures with which to guide and justify the results of their empirical research in different historical and cultural settings. Separate work needed to be done within each of these three realms because, although they could still in principle converge, they no longer did so automatically or necessarily. Classical social theory remained committed to such general presuppositions as the fundamental unity of the human species and the ultimate equality of all human beings but, as the older religious and secular answers were no longer held to be valid, they had to renew the justifications of these earlier forms of normative universalism. The specific way in which each of the classic writers of sociology did so, and the extent to which they were consistent in their attempts, may be assessed as more or less successful, but the cosmopolitan layout behind their proposals needs to be acknowledged and accounted for.

In terms of their conceptualization of modernity as a world phenomenon, classical social theorists tried to answer the key question of the extent to which a geographically particular set of historically circumscribed processes had led to the rise of a number of evolutionary tendencies that were having a universalistic impact all over the world. The European origins of modernity did not prevent them from recognizing its inextricably world-wide impact and universalistic vocation. In other words, they were simultaneously interested in the local origins, national organization, and global vocation of modernity. Indeed, it has been demonstrated that the kind of science the classical figures of social theory were about to establish was more a science of the social in general than the science of any particular national society (Turner 2006a). Thus, whereas Marx (1973) attributed to *labor* the key human capacity of transforming nature and in the process transforming human beings themselves, Weber (1949, 1976) stressed that *meaning* was involved in all kinds of social actions; Simmel's (1909) notion of *sociation* underlined the formative moment of interaction and Durkheim (1964) conceived of *social facts* as external and exercising normative coercion. Their reflections on the rise and main characteristics of the European nation-state are made in the context of a world, literally the whole planet, which was now taken as a single place. All these writers tried to conceive of analytical devices that could define what is "the social" element in modern social relations as abstractly and generally as possible (Chernilo 2007a; Frisby and Sayer 1986; Outhwaite 2006).

Their cross-cultural thrust is also expressed in their methodological reflections. We wholly miss the critical impetus behind Marx's monumental effort if we argue that his explanation of the generation and appropriation of surplus value in capitalism holds valid for Belgian but not for Venezuelan workers. Weber's repeated dictum that "one need not to be Caesar in order to understand Caesar" is pointless if, because I was born in Chile in the late twentieth century, it is assumed I will never be able to understand *sociologically* British rule in India or the rationale behind the suicide bombers in Iraq or Palestine. And despite a certain naivety in his use of official statistics, can we simply say that there is no resemblance between Durkheim's methodological reflections on statistically construed comparisons between suicide rates and, say, guidelines on the prevention of eating disorders by the World Health Organization? Surely, the point here is not to uncritically defend these methodological answers as flawless and honor the letter of these works as sacred texts. These writers' own application of their procedures may be judged as inconsistent, and even the proposals themselves might not have lived up to the high cognitive exigencies that were their very *raison d'être*. But the opposite postmodern view of totally disregarding their work because it is "dated" and "Eurocentric" offers no better way of dealing with the complex problems we now face in our own time.

The cosmopolitan layout they were implicitly establishing remains valid as general research program: we refine our key concepts and methodological rules to make the knowledge they help producing comparable data across different cultural settings and historical periods. In so doing, we try to avoid conflating any one particular feature with an ahistorical universal, a one-off occurrence for a general pattern, or a limited set of trends for the definitive march of progress. Only a broad cosmopolitan layout is able to uphold *simultaneously* the global impact of modernity and the view that all human beings are conceived of as part of the same human species. It was nothing short of the whole globe that was being dramatically transformed in modernity, and this globe was to be regarded as a single place inhabited by one and the same human species. If nothing else, this is one of modernity's main accomplishments: it made human beings themselves aware of their fundamental unity for the first time. Or to put it differently, even if one were to concede that classical sociologists were theorizing under Eurocentric assumptions in relation to economic underdevelopment and the lack of political self-rule (Larraín 1989; Muthu 2003), these restrictions were for them never thought of as essentially constitutive or ultimately insurmountable. Rather the opposite: these differences were most often explained as part of a historical process which had long-term structural causes, and these were indeed trends that the agents themselves could overcome. Their normative starting point as critical heirs of the natural law tradition is also the normative corollary of their empirical work: despite all differences, humankind is effectively one and could justly be theorized only as such. Their conceptualization of modernity's global reach requires the normative assumption of a universalistic conception of humanity, and this in turn reinforces, via conceptual and methodological arguments, its cosmopolitan layout. The emergence of modern society is thus understood as humanity itself being able to forge its destiny at last. Even if modernity is not conceptualized as a self-conscious and intended development, modern social theory's cosmopolitan layout now differs from previous notions of human nature because it is seen for the first time as an evolutionary accomplishment of humanity's own history.

PHASE 2. MODERNIST SOCIAL THEORY: SOCIAL SYSTEM AND INDUSTRIAL SOCIETY

The period of modernist social theory encompasses roughly from the outbreak of World War II till the end of the 1970s. The cosmopolitan credentials of the empirical sociology and social theory being developed during this period are possibly harder to find than those of the previous generation; not least because the institutional growth of sociology now took place under sustained state auspices. This phase's research agenda developed around issues such as troop morale, the enhancement of economic productivity, and nationwide public policies that were indeed themes the state itself found most worthy of research funding. Furthermore, the trend toward decolonization that marked this period world-wide led to an approach in which nationalization, industrialization, and modernization were all taken as synonymous with the strengthening of state control over civil society, internally, and with the state's absolute sovereignty, externally. As in the case of classical social theory, moreover, the sociologists of this generation used the term cosmopolitanism only rarely – if at all. But the approach which proved helpful in the previous section may also be of use here: the question is less whether the word "cosmopolitanism" is or is not found in this period's writings and more whether the concepts, methods, and normative standpoints being now advanced by leading social theorists are compatible with the claim to universalism that constitutes social theory's cosmo-politan layout.

My thesis in this section is that the two notions that became most widely accepted within social theory during this period also fulfill the universalistic criterion we put forward above: *social system* and *industrial society*. I am aware of the fact that to argue that these two concepts could be seen not only as compatible with, but as key representatives of, a cosmopolitan layout in modernist social theory is not pre-cisely a conventional interpretation. Rather the opposite, they have been broadly taken as the expression of sociology's obsession with the nation-state during this time (Giddens 1973; Smith 1979). But I believe my case gains plausibility if we see that both concepts became the two most salient analytical tools of this period pre-cisely because they were envisaged and deployed with a highly universalistic orienta-tion (Chernilo 2007a). At the conceptual level, a technical conception of the social system was the most important innovation during this period. The concept of system had of course already made its way into sociological analysis, via the work of Herbert Spencer, in the late nineteenth century, but it was only now, above all with the work of Talcott Parsons, that a coherent and abstract concept of social system became part and parcel of the sociological lexicon. For its part, the most important of this period's epochal diagnoses seems to have been that of the industrial society. The notion of industrial society was not only thought of as applicable to different sociocultural settings but it was also designed to pay special attention to the way in which modern social life was being materially reproduced. Beyond Parsons (1963), who also wrote often enough on industrial society, the concept plays a central role in the work of a number of leading sociologist at the time such as Raymond Aron (1967), Reinhard Bendix (1964), and Barrington Moore (1967). As it is Aron the writer who made the biggest effort in fully unfolding the notion ana-lytically, it is on the basis of his work that industrial society's cosmopolitan layout will be assessed here.

Parsons (1977) defines social systems as systems of interaction. He chooses the notion of system because it is the most abstract analytical tool with which to define not only a scientific object of inquiry but also the dimensions to be studied within that object. Through the concept of social system a unit of analysis becomes clearly defined so that the sociologist can compare different but analogous units. At the most abstract level, Parsons (1967) distinguishes four "evolutionary universals" – adaptation, differentiation, inclusion, and value generalization – that are the mecha-nisms through which social relations change in the long term. The argument is that all forms of social relations must resolve these four key functional problems. At the most abstract definition of society, this means that there is one specialized language – a generalized symbolic medium of exchange – for each of its four sub-systems and that these media control the internal operations within each sub-system as well as the exchanges between them (Chernilo 2002). Parsons delineates thus: (A) adaptation problems in the way in which society achieves the material resources it needs for its survival (an economy whose medium is money); (G) goal attainment problems to decide society's priorities (a polity that operates with political power); (I) integrative problems that threaten society's internal fairness (a community that is based on influence); and (L) internal consistency problems owing to its own multiple normative orientations (fiduciary institutions such as schools, universities, and churches that require the development of value-commitments). In this connection, Parsons's (1971) notion of society refers to the *nation-state* as much as it refers to a notion of *modern society* that, geographically, oscillates from "the West" to "the whole world" and, normatively, hints towards a cosmopolitan international order (Chernilo 2007a, 2008). His theorization of modernity takes its particular location and origins as given but seeks to explain it in terms of its truly universalistic vocation and world-wide impact as represented in such principles as individual freedom, collective self-determination, social welfare, and the rule of law. And the cosmopolitan layout of Parsons's social theory is also apparent in his thesis that one and the same analytical scheme is to be deployed for the study of all kinds of social relations – from face-to-face interactions to truly global processes. Indeed, Parsons's (1978) own late application of the AGIL scheme to what he referred to as the "paradigm of the human condition" is nothing but the application of this theoretical model to the idea of *humanity* itself: (A) the physico-chemical system; (G) the human organic system; (I) the action system; and (L) the telic system. The same level of abstraction that made Parsonian social theory prone to criticism is in this case the guarantee of the universalistic commitment of its knowledge claims: his whole theoretical framework necessarily requires the presupposition of the fundamental unity of human species.

The concept of industrial society was, for its part, devised for representing the stage of development of social relations in the mid-twentieth century. Thus, at the very beginning of his *18 Lectures on Industrial Society*, Raymond Aron (1967: 3) explicitly states that industrial society is an analytical concept that should not be mistaken for any specific form of sociopolitical arrangement: "no one national society is *the* industrial society as such, and all the industrial societies together do not compose *one* industrial society." The concept of industrial society is therefore an analytical device that is nowhere to be found in its pure form but which should nonetheless help us understand modernity's predominant type of social relations. It refers more to a framework for the understanding of the reproduction of social life in general and less to any particular sociopolitical unit. This highly universalistic orientation of industrial society can be further recognized if we take another of its features into account. The notion of industrial society tried to grasp those issues in which "socialist" and "capitalist" regimes mirrored each other and, by the same token, the concept was also expected to highlight those elements in which the "industrial world" – both socialist and capitalist – differed from the developing or non-industrial one. The underlying presupposition behind this use of industrial society is that, even if taking into account all kinds of ethnic, geographical, and indeed political differences, the whole globe needed to be assessed against the highest level of economic output that humanity *as such* had so far achieved.

In other words, the claim seems to be that no essential division within the human species can be used to account for disparities in socioeconomic development. On the one side, the argument is that humanity had reached a certain stage of economic development (industrialization) and that there were two equally modern ways of arriving at that stage: capitalism and socialism. On the other side, the fact that only certain groups of human beings had actually reached that stage, and were actually profiting from industrialism's benefits, had to be explained via historical and structural merits rather than on the basis of national personalities, cultural essences, or racial traits. Indeed, mainstream social theory was then highly enthusiastic about the fact that all states and peoples could modernize and become industrialized if only the right measures were devised and the right policies correctly put in place on the ground. No historical, cultural, or ethnic difference in the way in which technology is adapted to local settings was able to deny the fact that the human species is only one: "The dialectic of universality is the mainspring of the march of history" (Aron 1972: 306). And social theory's key intellectual challenge was thus no other than the "move from a national to a human frame of reference" (Aron 1972: 200). The universalistic impact of the world's technological unification under the auspices of industrialism becomes the infrastructure upon which a deeper recognition of humanity's unity could be achieved.

PHASE 3. CONTEMPORARY SOCIAL THEORY: TOWARDS AN EXPLICIT COSMOPOLITAN APPROACH

After the end of the 1990s' uncritical celebration of globalization we are now in a position to advance more sober accounts of those empirical trends that have indeed made the world a smaller place. Thanks to the efforts of globalization studies, though, cosmopolitanism has increasingly become an explicit feature of contemporary social theory in a way that was not the case in the past. Take as an indication of this the fact that since the year 2000 there have been at least three special issues of important scholarly journals devoted solely to cosmopolitanism: *Theory, Culture & Society* (19(1–2), 2002), edited by Mike Featherstone, the *British Journal of Sociology* (57(1), 2006), edited by Ulrich Beck and Natan Sznaider, and the *European Journal of Social Theory* (10(1), 2007), edited by Robert Fine and Vivienne Boon. In all three periodicals we find not only a number of theoretical approaches to cosmopolitanism but also the empirical application of an emergent cosmopolitan perspective to issues like migration, humanitarian military interventions, and the memory of traumatic events such as the Holocaust. It is thus no exaggeration to assert that the claim to universalism underlying the relationship between social theory and cosmopolitanism has taken an exciting new turn. I believe we can distinguish four major versions of cosmopolitanism in contemporary social sciences and these I shall briefly review in what follows: Niklas Luhmann's notion of *world society*, Ulrich Beck's *methodological cosmopolitanism*, Jürgen Habermas's *postnational constellation*, and Robert Fine and Bryan S. Turner's *cosmopolitan social theory*.[1]

A radical follower of Parsons's systemic approach, Luhmann is the only writer of this last group who does not make consistent use of the term cosmopolitanism. A reason for this may well be his skepticism towards concepts with a heavy normative orientation. For him, this kind of notion puts too much of a metaphysical load into social theory's already complex task of explicating the social. In the case of cosmopolitanism, Luhmann may have argued that its natural law presupposition – for instance, the ontologically burdened idea of a single human species – is precisely the kind of philosophical dead weight that is neither plausible nor necessary in sociology. As a vetted intellectual tradition, cosmopolitanism may be seen as part of the old way of European thinking from which he was trying to break away. Having said this, Luhmann's (1977) forceful attempt to decouple the notion of society from the historical formation of the nation-state, and his argument that the idea of society must be linked to the notion of "world society," equally point in a direction that is widely compatible with cosmopolitanism (Chernilo and Mascareño 2005). Luhmann's notion of world society is twofold. Its *world* aspect points to the self-referential, all-inclusive, and endless nature of the social as composed only by meaningful communications (Luhmann 1995: 69). The idea of the world here knows of no other limits than those thus far achieved by the ever-growing expansion of communication processes. And the *society* element refers to communication as the only element that is able to encompass all the features that make society an emergent reality: social life understood as continuous, improbable, and meaningful. It is only with the rise of modernity, Luhmann argues, that the idea of society can effectively be associated with the notion of world society because modernity marks the threshold that creates a world-wide communicative system which cannot help but turn the world into a single place.

The second cosmopolitan perspective within contemporary social sciences is that of Ulrich Beck (2000, 2006). I have commented elsewhere on the main features of Beck's conception of the nation-state (Chernilo 2006), so I can now concentrate on his contribution to the explicit incorporation of cosmopolitanism into the mainstream of European sociology. Beck's main proposition is that if earlier, rather philosophical, approaches to cosmopolitanism saw it as an active and purposive task, a new social scientific cosmopolitanism is needed because of what he calls the "cosmopolitanization of reality . . . a process of *compulsory* choice or a *side effect* of unconscious decisions" (Beck 2004: 134). Cosmopolitanism has transcended the terrain of normative political philosophy and landed in the everyday life of individuals for better and worse. Empirical sociologists need to realize that older assumptions based on a nation-state perspective no longer make sense in helping us comprehend and act upon world-wide risks such as climate change, international terrorism, and the AIDS epidemic. Beck's principal contribution lies at the methodological level – thus his proposal of methodological cosmopolitanism – because the kind of shift he is after can help improve the social relevance and public vocation of the social sciences. Both as a social scientific observer and as a citizen-actor, he argues that the task is to encourage the transition from an uncritical cosmopolitan condition – that is poorly understood and uncritically accepted – to a cosmopolitan moment – that can be reflexively conceptualized and intelligently worked upon (Beck and Sznaider 2006: 6).

The third cosmopolitan perspective to be reviewed here is that of Jürgen Habermas. His interest in cosmopolitanism over the past decade is consistent with the universalistic fundamentals of his earlier philosophical and sociological work, but here I can only devote attention to three features of his cosmopolitan perspective (Fine and Smith 2003). First, Habermas's (1998) incorporation of cosmopolitanism consciously relates itself to Immanuel Kant's writing on the subject. By making explicit the original connection between cosmopolitanism and the rise of modernity, Habermas differentiates his position from those of Luhmann and Beck who, as we have just reviewed, see that it is precisely those trends which mark a rupture with the recent past that make cosmopolitanism relevant in the present. Second, Habermas (2001) also follows Kant in the idea that a cosmopolitan world order cannot be founded on any grandiose idea of a world state but rather on a voluntary federation of nations. Habermas agrees with Kant in the idea that the design of a cosmopolitan order must be federal or multilayered, that is, it implies the recognition of local, national, international, and global fields of action. Although his own labeling of this current period as a "postnational constellation" is misleading, as it seems to hint towards an alleged decline of the nation-state, Habermas's argument is in fact that cosmopolitan law complements rather than overrides or supersedes previous and geographically more restrictive legal orders (Held 1995). Finally, Habermas breaks with Kant's metaphysical justification of cosmopolitanism as a "law of providence." There is a sense of logical necessity in Kant's cosmopolitan law because it is inscribed in the very nature of modern legal relations. In the same way as individuals resign part of their liberty to enter into a civil association that protects their rights, Kant believes that states must also enter into a kind of voluntary association and thus replace their state of permanent warfare for one of perpetual peace. Habermas's postmetaphysical view of cosmopolitanism, for its part, is based on the idea of the free and rational agreement of all those who are potentially involved – citizens, denizens, foreigners, and refugees alike. His cosmopolitan perspective can only be accredited from within; it is never imposed from above as a law of nature or historical progress but has to be the result of an inclusive process of deliberation. The claim to universalism underwriting the notion of human rights is appealing for him precisely because it works both as a moral norm and as a state-enforced positive law (Habermas 2006).

I have called the final position I would like to review in this chapter *cosmopolitan social theory* not only because it explicitly points beyond disciplinary boundaries restrictively defined but also because it is concerned above all with cosmopolitanism as a *way of thinking about the present*. I will concentrate here on two scholars who have been most consistent on the importance of cosmopolitanism for understanding our current world and age – Bryan S. Turner and Robert Fine – although other voices could well have been considered (Calhoun 2002; Delanty 2006). Bryan Turner (1990) pioneered the view of the history of social theory being advanced in this chapter as he demonstrated almost two decades ago that, right from its inception, social theory has been simultaneously concerned with the national and global arenas. More recently, as I have already pointed out, he reassessed the work of classical social theorists as broadly compatible with a cosmopolitan perspective (Turner 2006a). In my view, Turner has contributed decidedly to the sociological debate on cosmopolitanism on two grounds. On the one hand, the theme of human frailty – "our propensity to morbidity and inevitable mortality" – underlies his *bodily* justification of human rights. He thus points beyond the claim that rights can only be granted by the state and begins to develop a notion of "rights enjoyed by humans *qua* humans" (Turner 1993). On the other hand, Turner is concerned with the question of rebutting the kind of "cultural relativism" that promotes what he calls "epistemological disinterest" – the kind of intellectual position that "cannot support political and legal judgements about ethics and politics" (Turner 2006b). He has moved a step further in the defense of the universalistic core of cosmopolitanism because in addition to human rights we are in need of "a corresponding set of cosmopolitan obligations and virtues" such as "*irony* . . . to achieve some emotional distance from our local culture; *reflexivity* with respect to other cultural values; *care for other cultures* . . . and an *ecumenical commitment to dialogue*" (Turner 2001: 134, 150). These virtues may, for instance, allow participants in inter-faith dialogs to de-essentialize each other's positions. Turner's "methodological irony" points to the recognition of internal contradictions within one's own worldview and allows for skepticism towards one's own values.

Robert Fine has, for almost a decade now, also been engaged in the reconstruction and renovation of cosmopolitan thinking. He has devoted attention to a number of issues that are at the center of contemporary cosmopolitan thinking, such as the question of crimes against humanity (Fine 2000), the history of modern cosmopolitan thinking (Fine 2003a), the cult of the new in recent cosmopolitan literature (Fine 2003b), humanitarian military interventions (Fine 2006a), and cosmopolitanism as an empirical research agenda (Fine 2006b). His interest in cosmopolitanism derives from his long-term engagement with the canon of social theory in relation to the tradition of natural law theory (Fine 2001, 2002) and he argues that, although natural law theory is not the most popular subject in current social theory, the explication of the connections between both traditions may actually reinvigorate current cosmopolitan thinking (Fine 2007). His methodological approach to the history of social theory can be described as a systematic *critique* of the way in which social theory claims to have "jumped over" natural law whereas in fact, more often than not, it mirrors the tradition it seeks to overcome. He has demonstrated the continuities between Kant's cosmopolitanism and the tradition of natural law theorizing – "Grotius, Pufendorf and the rest" – which Kant himself thought he had moved beyond. Fine relocates cosmopolitanism within the *development* of critical theory and reveals the pivotal role played by Hegel and Marx not so much in criticizing Kant but rather in serving as a bridge between the Kantian reconstruction of natural law and cosmopolitan social theory. This is the reason why Fine's cosmopolitan social theory centers on cosmopolitan law as a contradictory social form of right. Cosmopolitanism is not the apex of modernity, the synthetic moment within which all previous struggles of modernity will necessarily dissolve. Rather, as with all forms of rights, cosmopolitan law is bound to clash with other legal forms, is open to conflictive interpretations, and can indeed be cynically misused. Cosmopolitanism should then be seen as a permanent act of normative judgment rather than as an already established number of principles and rules. It is no teleological law of nature but a way in which concrete human beings battle for equal recognition and treatment in the face of all their differences.

CONCLUSION: COSMOPOLITANISM'S UNIVERSALISM
AND ITS CRITICS

Cosmopolitanism has proved no simple topic for those interested in the past of social theory. Current social theory cannot ignore it either if it wishes to remain connected with some of the most important social trends of our own time. Regardless of whether social theorists have referred to cosmopolitanism explicitly, my proposition in this chapter is that a claim to universalism is the tie that binds cosmopolitanism and the tradition of modern social theory. In addition to the old natural law propositions of the *fundamental unity of the human species* and the *ultimate equality of all human beings*, modern social theory adds the view that modernity creates the structural conditions and institutional framework for realizing *humanity's own fundamental unity for the first time*. All three propositions constitute therefore what I have called here modern social theory's cosmopolitan layout. This chapter has thus attempted to discover the presence of cosmopolitanism within past and present social theory, to describe its most salient features and indeed to convince of its current appealing. I have tried to unfold this claim to universalism for the three periods of classical, modernist and contemporary social theory and to demonstrate that for all three phases a certain canon can be recovered and made compatible with cosmopolitanism's key normative and conceptual commitments. Social theory, both past and present, has kept the cosmopolitan torch alight because it requires, and in turn reinforces, this kind of cosmopolitan layout. A subsidiary argument running through this piece is that social theory has on the whole rejected nationalistic or racial explanations and viewpoints. Rather the opposite, social theory seems to require a wider and broader outlook in which differences in economic and political development are attributed to structural causes which are never referred back to an essentialist understanding of ethnicity, religion, culture or nationality. Social theory's claim to universalism pushes its explanations beyond both the ethnographic description that merely mimics the participant's viewpoint and eternal general laws based on self-consciously metaphysical presuppositions.

The universalistic orientation of cosmopolitanism has however proved highly contentious within social theory and the social sciences at large. For instance, Mike Featherstone's (2002) largely friendly assessment of cosmopolitanism queries whether its western roots make its universalistic aspirations untenable. This comment begs though the question of whether it makes sense to label the classical tradition of Greek philosophy as Western – what would exactly mean to say that Plato and Cicero belong to "the West?" More importantly it misses the point that at the center of social theory's cosmopolitanism there is a *claim* to universalism so that the geographical origins of an intellectual tradition are far less important than its ultimate self-regulating orientation towards an ever widening and more robust conception of the human species. And if we now look at the critiques to modern cosmopolitanism and trace them back to Kant's self-conscious use of the term towards the end of the eighteenth century, we also witness the fierce resistance these proposals have encountered ever since. I should then like to close this chapter with a brief assessment of these criticisms and the problems they raise – for cosmopolitan thinking as much as for the critics themselves.

In nineteenth-century anthropology, for example, cosmopolitanism's universalism was already being strongly resisted. This rejection was based either on the self-transparent superiority of the white colonizer or on a highly uncritical defense of the native's viewpoint – the alleged supremacy of empire's civilizing mission against the myth of the noble savage. In either version, the same claim was made, that the power difference underwriting the imperial encounter just dooms the very attempt at finding the common ground around which human beings can recognize each other's *differences* as constitutive of their fundamental *equality*. Cosmopolitanism then becomes, if not a fantastic dream, a wholly untenable position for all practical purposes. Indeed, this mode of conceiving things has permeated into important sections of the social sciences and humanities, as the problems raised by these "thick" descriptions did not fade away during the twentieth century. It is as though social scientific thinking remained trapped in the imperial web of ideas and institutional practices so that all attempts at correcting the shortcomings of these universalistic propositions only worsened the case they tried to defend (Said 2003). Identity politics theorists, as much as romantics of civil society, have kept defending a view of "the local," "the particular," "the non-Western," "the native," and "the authentic" that still regards the universalistic orientation behind cosmopolitanism as decisively misguided and politically dangerous.

It is in this context that twentieth-century feminist critics have not been short of arguments for resisting the driving force behind these universalistic statements and thus adding their own vindication of "the female" to the list above (Nicholson 1990). Cosmopolitanism would thereby be rejected because it contributes to the reproduction and even the reinforcement of masculine domination and prejudices: human equality means, for all relevant purposes, male equality. Similarly, the postmodern critique of metanarratives – progress, liberal democracy, communism – sought to uncover the metaphysical and natural law presuppositions and illusions that still remained within social theory. This rejection of metaphysics lies at the center of the postmodern theorists' attack on social scientific thinking, and cosmopolitanism's universalistic orientation makes it an easy target indeed. The argument here runs that, as the heirs of the Enlightenment's belief in reason, early as much as recent forms of cosmopolitan thought would reproduce not so much the insights as the shortcomings of that eighteenth-century philosophical movement. In that sense, postmodern critics certainly share the view that cosmopolitanism is unable to overcome the power difference underwriting all forms of intercultural, racial, gender, or class relations. But to this charge they add that it is cosmopolitanism's metaphysical baggage – i.e. precisely its claim to universalism – that creates the ultimate impasse. They hold that cosmopolitanism's universalism fails *in practice* because the institutions that were established upon its ideals have been unable to correct or even to curb the injustices against which they were first devised. But above all they quarrel against it *in theory* because cosmopolitanism simply cannot provide sufficient support for its fundamental propositions on the ultimate unity of the human species and equality of all human beings. Insofar as plurality, diversity, and fragmentation seem to have won the popular vote, universalistic normative statements become little more than old Enlightenment metaphysical dead weight that is still contaminating contemporary social theory.

These different criticisms have certain traits in common. They point to the imperfections, deficiencies, and incompleteness that have accompanied the cosmopolitan program, in both theory and practice, right from its inception. And they also seem to agree on the fact that cosmopolitanism is not merely intellectual self-deception but, far more intensely, they treat it as an ideological weapon that the powers that be are always happy to use hypocritically to legitimize their domination and undercut normative grounds for resistance. As those of us who remain advocates for cosmopolitanism's universalism would be simply unwilling to learn from past failures, these critics' point effectively comes down to the fact that idiocy, if not dishonesty, is at the center of cosmopolitanism's current revival. Against this, I believe we can here return to Kant's own ambivalent assessment of the French Revolution and the universalistic ideals it upheld but could not actually establish. Kant surely assessed the revolution as a dramatic event marked by lost opportunities and forsaken promises, but this did not lead him to throw out the baby with the bathwater and abandon universalistic ideals altogether. On the institutional side, the failures in the implementation of universalistic ideals only make apparent that there are no angels inhabiting this earth of ours; there are only human beings who can be greedy as well as altruistic. Errors, and even the cynical use of universalistic principles, are the expression of the gap between ideals and reality but they do not prove that the institutional strategies established upon these universalistic ideals were a wrong path to follow. On the theoretical side, the lesson seems to be that even though any of the metaphysical presuppositions underlying cosmopolitanism can be refuted, we do not forsake the project of trying to find a better and more convincing way of grounding it. Modern social theory's cosmopolitanism requires no specific conception of human nature but a perennial search for ever more inclusive ways of grounding its universalism; it requires no definitive kind of universalism but a claim to it. Cosmopolitanism's universalism must be thought of as a regulative ideal rather than as a fixed set of contents.

Cosmopolitanism's universalism does not seek to ignore or override particular ways of life; rather the opposite, it expects to defend and promote them. If genocide has been recognized as "the supreme crime against humanity" it is precisely because "it aims at the destruction of human variety, of the many and diverse ways of being human" (Benhabib 2004: 128). The critics' position ultimately becomes untenable because they fail to grasp that their recognition and protection of particular ways of life requires a wider conception of humanity's ultimate unity. For their claim on authenticity and locality to be *effectively* communicated to, translated for, and understood by anyone outside the particular instance, critics need to appeal to a higher and more general moral order within which human beings treat one another as individuals who belong to the same species. Cosmopolitanism's claim to universalism cannot be dishonored without falling into the "performative contradiction" of undermining the very position of equality the critics must presuppose to launch their argumentative attacks and get their case heard. Otherwise, the critics are left in a normative vacuum in which either total indifference among persons and groups (postmodern fatigue as much as utilitarian selfishness) or the brute application of the law of the strongest prevails (Schmittian *Realpolitik*). Or, as Margaret Archer (2000: 32) put it with her usual sharpness: "if resistance is to have a locus, then it needs to be predicated upon a self which has been violated, knows it and can do something about it." We can try to avoid this normative morass, however, via the reintroduction of cosmopolitanism's claim to universalism, but the critics can now only do so through the back door; they have to advance surreptitiously, rather than justify upfront, the universalistic common ground that is needed for a normative argument to have any real purchase. They are unable to recognize, and indeed unwilling to accept, that their vindication of the local, the particular, and the female does require a claim to universalism. Their attempts end up, then, begging the ultimate normative question posed by cosmopolitanism: where can normative grounds be founded if not in a strongly universalistic belief in the ultimate unity of the human species?

Notes

I should like to thank Robert Fine for his comments to this article and indeed his unrelenting support for over seven years now. I am also grateful to Bryan Turner for his invitation to contribute to this *Companion* and his helpful editorial suggestions, and, last but not least, to Aldo Mascareño for his insightful criticisms and generous ideas. Material help for the realization of this article has been provided by the Chilean Council for Science and Technology (Grant Numbers 107082, 1080213).

1 I cannot discuss here contemporary accounts that are closer to political philosophy than to social theory. A word seems needed, however, on recent attempts at linking republicanism and cosmopolitanism (Benhabib 2004, 2007; Bohman 2004). On the basis of Hannah Arendt's (1958, 1992) classic accounts of totalitarianism and crimes against humanity, this strand of cosmopolitan thought emphasizes that such cosmopolitan norms as human rights need to be attached to the granting of membership rights to all human beings within the framework of an idea of humanity now constituted as a universalistic political community. They hint towards a notion of humanity which refers both to the fundamental legal status of all human beings and to their belonging to a – still in the making – universalistic political community.

Bibliography

Archer, M. (2000) *Being Human: The Problem of Agency.* Cambridge: Cambridge University Press.

Arendt, H. (1958) *The Origins of Totalitarianism.* New York: Meridian Books.

Arendt, H. (1992) *Eichmann in Jerusalem.* London: Penguin.

Aron, R. (1967) *18 Lectures on Industrial Society.* London: Weidenfeld & Nicolson.

Aron, R. (1972) *Progress and Disillusion.* Harmondsworth: Penguin.

Beck, U. (2000) *What is Globalization?* Cambridge: Polity.

Beck, U. (2004) "Cosmopolitan Realism: On the Distinction Between Cosmopolitanism in Philosophy and the Social Sciences." *Global Networks* 4(2): 131–56.

Beck, U. (2006) *Cosmopolitan Vision.* Cambridge: Polity.

Beck, U., and Sznaider, N. (2006) "Unpacking Cosmopolitanism for the Social Sciences: A Research Agenda." *British Journal of Sociology* 57(1): 1–23.

Bendix, R. (1964) *Nation-Building and Citizenship.* New York: John Wiley.

Benhabib, S. (2004) "Reclaiming Universalism: Negotiating Republican Self-Determination and Cosmopolitan Norms." *The Tanner Lectures on Human Values.* <http://www.tannerlectures.utah.edu/lectures/volume25/benhabib_2005.pdf>, last accessed Aug. 20, 2007.

Benhabib, S. (2007) "Twilight of Sovereignty or the Emergence of Cosmopolitan Norms? Rethinking Citizenship in Volatile Times." *Citizenship Studies* 11(1): 19–36.

Bohman, J. (2004) "Republican Cosmopolitanism." *Journal of Political Philosophy* 12(3): 336–52.

Calhoun, C. (2002) "The Class Consciousness of Frequent Travellers: Towards a Critique of Actually Existing Cosmopolitanism," in S. Vertovec and R. Cohen (eds.), *Conceiving Cosmopolitanism*. Oxford: Oxford University Press.

Chernilo, D. (2002) "The Theorization of Social Co-Ordinations in Differentiated Societies: The Theory of Generalized Symbolic Media in Parsons, Luhmann and Habermas." *British Journal of Sociology* 53(3): 431–49.

Chernilo, D. (2006) "Social Theory's Methodological Nationalism: Myth and Reality." *European Journal of Social Theory* 9(1): 5–22.

Chernilo, D. (2007a) *A Social Theory of the Nation-State: The Political Forms of Modernity Beyond Methodological Nationalism*. London: Routledge.

Chernilo, D. (2007b) "A Quest for Universalism: Reassessing the Nature of Classical Social Theory's Cosmopolitanism." *European Journal of Social Theory* 10(1): 17–35.

Chernilo, D. (2008) "Talcott Parsons' Sociology of the Nation-State," in C. Hart (ed.), *Talcott Parsons: Theories, Developments and Applications. Essays Examining the Relevance of Parsonian Theory in the 21st Century*. Midrash Publishing.

Chernilo, D., and Mascareño, A. (2005) "Universalismo, particularismo y sociedad mundial: Obstáculos y perspectivas de la sociología en América Latina." *Persona y Sociedad* 19(3): 17–45.

Delanty, G. (2006) "The Cosmopolitan Imagination: Critical Cosmopolitanism and Social Theory." *British Journal of Sociology* 57(1): 25–47.

d'Entrèves, A. (1970) *Natural Law*. London: Hutchinson.

Durkheim, É. (1964) *The Rules of Sociological Method*. New York: The Free Press.

Durkheim, É. (1992) *Professional Ethics and Civic Morals*. London: Routledge & Kegan Paul.

Emmet, D. (1994) *The Role of the Unrealisable: A Study in Regulative Ideals*. New York: St. Martin's Press.

Featherstone, M. (2002) "Cosmopolis: An Introduction." *Theory, Culture & Society* 19(1–2): 1–16.

Fine, R. (2000) "Crimes against Humanity: Hannah Arendt and the Nuremberg Trials." *European Journal of Social Theory* 3(3): 293–311.

Fine, R. (2001) *Political Investigations: Hegel, Marx, Arendt*. London: Routledge.

Fine, R. (2002) *Democracy and the Rule of Law*. New Jersey: The Blackburn Press.

Fine, R. (2003a) "Kant's Theory of Cosmopolitanism and Hegel's Critique." *Philosophy and Social Criticism* 29(6): 609–30.

Fine, R. (2003b) "Taking the 'ism' out of Cosmopolitanism: An Essay in Reconstruction." *European Journal of Social Theory* 6(4): 451–70.

Fine, R. (2006a) "Cosmopolitanism and Violence: Difficulties of Judgement." *British Journal of Sociology* 57(1): 49–67.

Fine R. (2006b) "Cosmopolitanism: A Social Science Research Agenda," in G. Delanty (ed.), *Handbook of European Social Theory*. London: Routledge.

Fine, R. (2007) *Cosmopolitanism*. London: Routledge.

Fine, R., and Smith, W. (2003) "Jürgen Habermas's Theory of Cosmopolitanism." *Constellations* 10(4): 469–87.

Frisby, D., and Sayer, D. (1986) *Society*. London: Ellis Horwood/Tavistock.

Giddens, A. (1971) *Capitalism and Modern Social Theory*. Cambridge: Cambridge University Press.

Giddens, A. (1973) *The Class Structure of the Advanced Societies*. London: Hutchinson.

Habermas, J. (1998) *The Inclusion of the Other*. Cambridge, MA: MIT Press.

Habermas. J. (2001) *The Postnational Constellation*. Cambridge: Polity.

Habermas, J. (2006) *The Divided West*. Cambridge: Polity.

Harris, H. (1927) "The Greek Origins of the Idea of Cosmopolitanism." *International Journal of Ethics* 38(1): 1–10.

Hawthorn, G. (1987) *Enlightenment and Despair*. Cambridge: Cambridge University Press.

Held, D. (1995) *Democracy and the Global Order*. Cambridge: Polity.

Kant, I. (1973) *Critique of Pure Reason*. London: Macmillan.

Kant, I. (1999) *Political Writings*. Cambridge: Cambridge University Press.

Larraín, J. (1989) *Theories of Development: Capitalism, Colonialism and Dependency*. Cambridge: Polity.

Luhmann, N. (1977) "Generalized Media and the Problem of Contingency," in J. Loubser, R. Baum, A. Effrat, and V. Lidz (eds.), *Explorations in the General Theory In Social Science: Essays in Honor of Talcott Parsons*. New York: The Free Press.

Luhmann, N. (1995) *Social Systems*. Stanford: Stanford University Press.

Marx, K. (1973) *Grundrisse*. London: Penguin.

Marx, K., and Engels, F. (1976) "Manifesto of the Communist Party," in K. Marx and F. Engels, *Collected Works*, vol. 6. London: Lawrence & Wishart.

Moore, B. (1967) *Social Origins of Dictatorship and Democracy*. London: Allen Lane/Penguin.

Muthu, S. (2003) *Enlightenment Against Empire*. Princeton: Princeton University Press.

Nicholson, L. (ed.) (1990) *Feminism/Postmodernism*. New York: Routledge.

Nisbet, R. (1967) *The Sociological Tradition*. London: Heinemann.

Outhwaite, W. (2006) *The Future of Society*. Oxford: Blackwell.

Parsons, T. (1963) "Some Principal Characteristics of Industrial Societies," in *Structure and Process in Modern Societies*. New York: The Free Press.

Parsons, T. (1967) *Sociological Theory and Modern Society*. New York: The Free Press.

Parsons, T. (1971) *The System of Modern Societies*. Englewood Cliffs, NJ: Prentice Hall.

Parsons, T. (1977) *Social Systems and the Evolution of Action Theory*. New York: The Free Press.

Parsons, T. (1978) *Action Theory and the Human Condition*. New York: The Free Press.

Rommen, H. (1998) *The Natural Law: A Study in Legal and Social History and Philosophy*. Indianapolis: The Liberty Fund.

Said, E. (2003) *Orientalism*. London: Penguin.

Seidman, S. (1983) *Liberalism and the Origins of European Social Theory*. Oxford: Blackwell.

Simmel, G. (1909) "The Problem of Sociology." *American Journal of Sociology* 15(3): 289–320.

Smith, A. D. (1979) *Nationalism in the Twentieth Century*. Oxford: Martin Robertson.

Toulmin, S. (1990) *Cosmopolis: The Hidden Agenda of Modernity*. Chicago: University of Chicago Press.

Turner, B. S. (1990) "The Two Faces of Sociology: Global or National?," in M. Featherstone (ed.), *Global Culture: Nationalism, Globalisation and Modernity*. London: Sage.

Turner, B. S. (1993) "Outline of a Theory of Human Rights." *Sociology* 27(3): 489–512.

Turner, B. S. (2001) "Cosmopolitan Virtue: On Religion in a Global Age." *European Journal of Social Theory* 4(2): 131–52.

Turner, B. S. (2006a) "Classical Sociology and Cosmopolitanism: A Critical Defence of the Social." *British Journal of Sociology* 57(1): 133–55.

Turner, B. S. (2006b) *Vulnerability and Human Rights*. Pennsylvania: Penn State University Press.

Voegelin, E. (1962) "World-Empire and the Unity of Mankind." *International Affairs* 38(2): 170–88.

Weber, M. (1949) *The Methodology of the Social Sciences*. New York: The Free Press.

Weber, M. (1976) *Roscher and Knies*. New York: The Free Press.

28

The Future of Social Theory

Stephen Turner

Social theory, both the term and the subject, preceded the discipline of sociology. Non-academic writers, such as Herbert Spencer (1969 [1851]; 1897 [1876]), and Benjamin Kidd (1894), academics from other fields, such as the economist Simon Patten (1896), as well as socialist thinkers, wrote extensively on the subject. Some of this "social theory" never became part of sociology. But during the first decade of the twentieth century, in the course of the division of the social sciences into disciplines in the United States, social theory had a disciplinary home. Disciplinarization produced a demand for theory writing of a particular kind: for a history with canonical texts, and for systematization, at least for the purposes of teaching a settled subject, and required theorists to pay attention to one another. This led, in the United States, to many surveys both of the history (Barnes 1948; Barnes and Becker 1961 [1938]; Becker 1971; Ellwood 1971) and present (House 2004) of social theory, and to such things as a catalog of sociological concepts logically arranged, by University of Chicago graduate Earle Edward Eubank (1932), to a series of dissertations on founding figures, and to classifications of theory. Eubank, like many Americans, was an admirer of the neo-Kantian influenced system-building of German social theorists and celebrated these "masters of sociology." But the most powerful and influential adaptor of this style was Talcott Parsons (1937).

The division of academic subjects in other national university traditions came much later – indeed, in France sociology was not separated from philosophy until the 1950s, and the different trajectory of European social theory reflected these institutional facts. In Europe, social theory remained more open, more philosophical, and less "scientific." In the United States, the politics of disciplinary competition and the role of the Rockefeller philanthropies led to an emphasis on the idea of sociology as a science (Camic 1995). Parsons, influenced by Harvard writers on science, such as his patron L. J. Henderson (1970 [1941–2]), combined the impulse toward conceptual system construction and systematic surveys of past theory with the aspiration of making sociology a science. Parsons took from Henderson the belief that every science possessed and required a single, unified, conceptual scheme, and he set about providing one through an analysis of what he took to be the most important canonical figures in sociology including Vilfredo Pareto, Émile Durkheim, and especially Max Weber, as well as the economist Alfred Marshall. Parsons's huge undertaking, similar to the many analogous systems provided by his German counterparts in the 1930s that were influenced by the neo-Kantian idea that an organized and hierarchical scheme of concepts was the key to being a science, had little to distinguish it other than his insistence that this was "science" in the sense of natural science. But Parsons had historical luck on his side. His shrewd and relentless politicking at Harvard made him a key figure when Harvard emerged from World War II as the most powerful university in the world.

Sociology in Britain had only a tenuous academic hold at this time and sociology in the rest of Europe, with the exception of France, had been subject to a radical discontinuity as a result of the rise of fascism and Nazism. American university models were widely copied in the re-establishment of the sometimes politically tainted universities of Europe, and a generous system of provision for visiting scholars and students to the United States was established. Sociology was the great beneficiary of this change and of American foundation funding in the social sciences, which was motivated in part by the desire to establish an alternative to communism. As a result, Parsons's ideas became more influential outside the United States than they had ever been within it (where they were often dismissed for their association with Ivy League snobbery, an association well warranted by Parsons's penchant for cultivating and then aggressively backing protégés from the Harvard undergraduate population), and provided a common lingua franca within which the idea of what was now called "sociological theory," or even "theoretical sociology" in Robert Merton's terminology (1967), could be taught and discussed. Influential as Parsons was, there was plenty of other "theory" around: symbolic interactionism, phenomenology, exchange theory, and various forms of Marxism. And to some extent the power of Parsons even served to legitimate these rivals in the eyes of empirical sociology.

In the 1960s sociology grew rapidly in public esteem and student interest. Parsons, and "positivism" or the aspiration to science, was attacked both by critics both within and outside sociology but most virulently by student radicals, and various forms of left sociology, such as critical theory, increased in influence. In the early 1970s the influence of Parsons collapsed. But the debate lingered in Germany, where Niklas Luhmann (1970) produced dozens and dozens of impressive texts in language that relied on Parsons-like systemic ideas and a kind of debate between Luhmann and Jürgen Habermas, the grand figure of the second Frankfurt School. Habermas, in *The Theory of Communicative Action* (1984), produced a systematic alternative to Parsons's similarly sweeping and canon-oriented *Structure of Social Action* (1937). With the revised canon of Marx, Durkheim, Weber, and G. H. Mead, theory was flourishing and becoming more diverse, as movements such as realism in Britain and ethnomethodology staked their claims.

Yet here the story becomes confused. Several important changes occurred more or less simultaneously over the next two decades, which led to theory being displaced from its former role in relation to sociology. The institutional setting is important to understanding this. After a rapid rise in popularity during the 1960s and a turn in the public spotlight along with the student movement of the late 1960s, both sociology and social theory suffered a near-death experience in the 1970s as student interests became more vocational and sociology came to be blamed for the excesses and failures of the welfare state to deliver on its promises to solve problems such as poverty. The ending of the student movement was a world-wide phenomenon, and it had the effect of damping student interest everywhere. In the United States student enrollment in sociology courses dropped dramatically and the number of bachelors degrees granted fell to less than a third of the peak it had reached in the early 1970s.

One immediate effect was that the issues of theory and methodology, such as the debate over positivism, became less central: the audience for these debates had been graduate students finding their intellectual identity rather than mature scholars and research practitioners. But the ongoing estrangement between social theory and sociology had intellectual causes as well. One of the important developments of the 1970s and 1980s was the return to the classics, a process whose general character, well captured by the title "DeParsonizing," had important implications for the character of writing in social theory. The classics that were being rediscovered in their full historical complexity were not "sociologists" in any narrow sense of this word, and not in the narrow sense, for example, of a widely read summary Reinhard Bendix, an influential commentator on Weber, who had written an "intellectual portrait" of Weber which omitted both his "philosophical" methodological writings and his political writings, making Weber into the narrower kind of "sociologist" that Bendix himself was (1960). When Weber's methodological and political writings were "rediscovered" they became central to a new Weber and a raft of new Weber scholarship. Durkheim was of course trained as a philosopher and unintelligible without reference to the philosophical tradition in which he was trained and in which he originally taught. His image as a precursor to the survey research tradition was also revised. The "new" classics were thus interdisciplinary or nondisciplinary and both were more closely akin in their thinking to philosophy and political theory than the older view had depicted them. As the classics were restored to their historical context, however, they became less relevant to sociology as it was then practiced.

The process of revising the image of the classics was bitter and divisive. Adherents of the old scientistic view of theory, such as Randall Collins, and the Parsonians, routinely complained about articles about "what Weber meant" and were hostile to the whole style of scholarship and specialist intellectual habitus that it was associated with. This hostility reflected the subversive nature of the new history of the classics. In the era of Merton/Parsons domination, the systematic, scientific, and classically oriented elements had often been combined in the work of a single scholar. They established the acceptable way of approaching the classics, of treating them as precursors to the Merton/Parsons model of theoretical sociology. Alvin Gouldner (Chriss 1999), a student of Merton, was perhaps a paradigm example of this, but other figures, such as Lewis Coser (1975) and Reinhard Bendix (1960), also fit this pattern. During the 1970s and 1980s many of these figures were engaged in a bitter rearguard action, in which they used their power as editorial advisors to suppress the newer scholarship. This struggle, inevitably, went to the young. Recapturing classics as real historical figures rather than precursors to structural functionalism and survey sociology was a necessary struggle. But the victory was pyrrhic:

the price was the removal of the classic figures from the core of conventional socio-logical discussion and the marginalization of their study.

The second major change involved the idea of culture and cultural sociology. Many former theorists, especially students of the students of Parsons, came to iden-tify themselves as cultural sociologists. This transformation was led by Clifford Geertz, a Parsonian anthropologist, who published an influential collection of essays called *The Interpretation of Culture* (1973) which transformed his previous com-mitment to the Parsonian doctrine into a postmodern notion of "the mind filled with presuppositions" which diminished the role of idea of consensus but expanded the insistence on the omnipresent significance of culture. This built on Parsons's own cultural turn in *The Social System* (1951), in which the social system or society was the subject but culture and especially the modern value commitment were the primary explainer. It is thus not surprising that Parsonians, such as Robert Bellah, hitherto a typical product of the Parsonian career-making machine, reappeared as cultural sociologists in the 1980s and 1990s. It allowed them to get rid of the baggage of Parsons's complex models of "the system," his commitment to "system-atic theory," and his aspiration to science, thus eliminating the controversial ele-ments of his theory.

In this new form, its political significance was inverted. It could be remade as a left doctrine, assimilated to Michel Foucault (1981), Pierre Bourdieu (1977 [1972]), and the powerful but mechanically Marxist writings of cultural studies theorist Stuart Hall (1997; Hall, Morley, and Chen 1996). The Parsonian account explained the remarkable stability, as well as the good things about modern capitalist society in terms of culture, especially the "modern" values. The left account used the same explanation to explain the pervasive false consciousness that produced the stability, and the bad things, of modern capitalist society. The issue of meritocracy is a simple example of this: for Parsons, and in a more subtle way for sociologists like Michael Young (1958), meritocracy was central to modernity, and of course the universalism which Parsons took to be a major value of modern society was also an Enlighten-ment value. The left, which absorbed Carl Schmitt's dictum that "Words, such as state, republic, society, class, as well as sovereignty, constitutional state, absolutism, dictatorship, economic planning, neutral or total state, and so on, are incompre-hensible if one does not know exactly who is to be affected, combated, refuted, or negated by such a term" (1976 [1932]: 30–1), looked at these Enlightenment notions accordingly. Merit was unquestionably a concept that "affected, combated, refuted, or negated." For feminists, it excluded women; for Bourdieu, writing about "distinction" (1977 [1972]), it was enacted in practice in the French educational system as a means of excluding the working class from positions of authority in the system and the state. The processes of internalization of values which were central to Parsons were replaced in Bourdieu by processes of reproduction that assured the continuity of dominance by the dominant (Bourdieu and Passeron 1977).

The cultural turn was also aided by the rise of social constructionism (see CHAPTER 14). Berger and Luhmann's book *The Social Construction of Reality* (1966) was the most cited sociology book of its time. The term was soon applied, contrary to the authors' specific disclaimers, not only to scientific concepts, produc-ing the widely influential "Strong Programmes" in the sociology of knowledge and other related ideas. It quickly spreading to gender studies, leading to Judith Butler's famous formulation about the social construction of gender differences – that everyone is in drag – as well to such areas as disability studies in which the disabled were regarded not so much as disabled but as mislabeled. Finally, it became a commonplace that what died in the last part of the twentieth century was "the social" and that social relations had become mediatized. Media, it was argued should henceforth be the new vehicle and subject of social theory (cf. Gane 2004).

The cultural turn had paradoxical implications for social theory. On the one hand, it expanded the audience for social theory, which now became a staple of literature departments and the humanities as well as central to new fields such as media studies and to changing fields such as communications. On the other hand, the traditional concerns of social theory were replaced and its explanatory structure simplified into a relatively crude and easily parodied model, in which culture was made into an instrumentality of unconscious domination in which the dominated were complicit in their own domination by virtue of accepting or enjoying the ideas and activities that led them to be dominated. This simultaneous expansion of the audience of social theory, its sideward movement into the topics of culture, the carrying through of themes such as social construction into applied disciplines, the widespread employment of ideas derived from critical theory across the social sciences and then philosophy, the contemporary rise of "theory" in literary studies, and the use of ideas like practice and hidden mechanisms of oppression by social movements created a new and quite different space for social theory. This space was often very far removed from disciplinary sociology, and especially from empirical research in sociology, which, especially in the United States, had come to focus on the secondary data analysis and the construction of causal models – something that required minimal "theory."

But sociology itself changed significantly during these two decades in another profound way. A new issue dominated sociology: gender. Schemes for the increased employment of women were imposed on universities in the United States; other countries followed. "Affirmative action" was enthusiastically taken up in sociology, partly by groups which believed themselves (often correctly) to have been excluded from positions of influence, partly by the old guard which saw it as a means of excluding their younger adversaries. The regime was applied most rigidly to social sciences, where there were more women available. In short order, gender issues became essential to sociology, and gender inequality became its central subject. In bookstores the category of sociology in many places was merged with that of women's studies. The women's studies movement and the "Black Studies" movement provided a model of solidaristic relations between academic subjects and social movements that proved to be replicable in relation to other causes. In the United States, the sociology of relations became assimilated to the reality of black studies programs and evolved into an African American-oriented field from which whites were essentially excluded. The pattern was repeated world-wide for other excluded groups, and other social movements, such as gay and lesbian movements, would be given similar treatment. These relations attracted a new group of students to sociology, and created new audiences for sociological writing.

The kind of theory that was attractive to these audiences was the kind that validated the social movements that they were allied to and in particular validated their claims to oppression. In most of the cases these claims were that the ordinary nominally egalitarian procedures of the liberal state were the source of hidden forms of oppression which resulted from such things as the masculinist assumptions inscribed into the law (MacKinnon 1989) or that the nominally egalitarian and race- and gender-blind procedures of the liberal state represented the denial of ethnic values and the imposition of whiteness. Values, such as the value of mothering, which facilitated the relegation of women to the mommy track or to self-exclusion from the job market, were understood in these terms. "Hidden injuries" thinkers such as Sennett (1977), and theorists whose primary focus was oppressive practices such as Foucault, Bourdieu, Dorothy Smith (1990), and Patricia Hill Collins (2000 [1990]), "theorized" these hidden forms of oppression and explained why the oppressed unconsciously conspired in their own oppression. This particular kind of utility, a utility for social movements in their aim of transforming consciousness and recognizing and combating "victimization," established a new relationship between social theory and the now significantly transformed audience of sociology students for whom these victimization narratives were central parts of their personal identity (Glassner and Hertz 2006).

These new usages had obvious continuities with Marxism. As Michael Burawoy put it in his important American Sociology Association presidential address about public sociology (Burawoy 2005), this new kind of relationship with social movements could be understood in terms of Gramsci's idea of the organic intellectual who represented and led, but who was also bound to, the proletariat (1996). But there was also a rupture. The new social movements typically abandoned not only the grand theoretical narrative of Marxism, with its commitment to the idea of the historical mission of the proletariat, but grand theoretical narrative itself, restricting themselves, as Foucault did, to a model of protest and resistance. The effect of this new user relation was to exclude as useless much of what theory had traditionally talked about, while at the same time uncritically taking for granted theoretical notions, such as practice, and various de-Marxified and renamed versions of the notion of false consciousness.

What did this have to do with theory? Although "theorists" in the younger generation took up these authors, commented on them, explicated them, and both endorsed and criticized them, "theory talk" about, and criticism of, these theoretical notions were not of any interest to these users, and not welcomed. A new and quite different kind of theoretical discourse emerged that was, in practice, entirely segregated from "theory talk." Feminist social theorists engaged in extensive and sometimes acrimonious, not to say vituperative, discussions with one another focused on the question of who truly represented the viewpoint of women or how to represent the standpoint of particular oppressed groups of women. Although they creatively extended the ideas of male and white domination, this was not "theory talk," and theories were used uncritically – uncritically except for the central issue of their utility for the cause. For example, the concept of practices, which was the subject of extensive debate and discussion in the 1990s (Schatzki 1996; Schatzki, Knorr-Cetina, and von Savigny 2001), was used by feminists without their participation in, or even acknowledgment of, this debate.

This division between men's and women's spheres of discussion was paralleled by quite different attitudes toward and enactments of theoretical debate. Women complained about being excluded and ignored by theorists, and this was partly true

(Ferree, Khan, and Morimoto 2007). But movement women did not want into the "boys' club" of theory so much as want deference from it for their views. The extensive efforts of theory organizations to include women were frequently rebuffed by women, and were always subject to the difficulty that while women wished to have their theoretical contribution recognized they had no wish to play the game of traditional theory – of allowing themselves to be subjected to searching critique from all directions. This difference in style was enacted in a number of dialogs-of-the-deaf encounters between theorists and feminists in which feminists said they were deeply offended by what was no more, and usually less, than standard kinds of questions and criticisms. The paradoxical character of these demands is on display in the article on gender studies in Craig Calhoun's centennial volume on American sociology. Myra Marx Ferree and her collaborators speak of themselves as feminists being "incensed" and "offended" (Ferree, Khan, and Morimoto 2007: 474) But what produced this reaction was merely innocuous criticism by standard empirical sociologists. Being exposed to the rougher kinds of critical exchanges typical of theory and to what they regarded as a lack of suitable respect and deference by the "boys' club" of theory was simply not acceptable to them, and they did not submit to it. But the deference issue had another side: males were routinely told that they did not have the authority to speak to women's issues. And it was a standard gimmick of feminist presentations for many years to forbid men to speak, or prevent them from speaking until all the women who wished to speak had had their say. Women, in any case, did not have any compelling reason to pay the price of admission to theory discussion. They had an audience apart from the theory audience, an organic relation to a movement, and a strong sense of the legitimacy of their cause. And they also had something that traditional theory after the demise of the student movement lacked: an avidly interested and personally motivated student audience.

The "boys' club" had troubles of its own. The relations between theory and traditional empirical sociology, which had been good during the era of Robert Merton and Paul Lazarsfeld, also degenerated. One of the reasons for this was purely technical. Merton and Lazarsfeld had supported a notion of theory construction in which middle-range theories were the source of hypotheses which could be tested though statistical methods involving 2 by 2 tables, and which required background knowledge (which they understood as theoretical) to assess the "causal" relationships using the elaboration method, namely of partialing the tables, understood as a total relationship by variables that might render the relationship spurious or otherwise change the values through the introduction of "test" variables. Causal modeling, which replaced this method, relied on an absolute minimum of background knowledge, which was understood as knowledge so trivial or uncontested that little or no "theory" was needed, and this minimum was steadily reduced by the creation of new statistical methods to eliminate spurious relationships and detect latent variables (Pearl 2000). This change meant that, during the period in which "theorists" were shifting their attention to the classics, to Foucault, and to culture, the relevance of "theory" of any kind to the practical enterprise of empirical sociology was diminishing.

The role of theory in teaching declined accordingly. The present situation of theory teaching in the United States, though it is more extreme than elsewhere, is one in which little theory is on offer. The chairman of the theory section of the American Sociological Association posed the question of how theory was taught at the leading American sociology departments, and by whom, and published the results of some of this inquiry on the section website, prompting a blog discussion on the section homepage (<http://www.asatheory.org/>). In this discussion it became evident that theory was for the most part no longer taught in leading American sociology departments to the extent that it once had been, that the people teaching theory were in many cases people who did not write or publish in the area of theory. There was a widely held perception that it was better for empirical sociologists rather than "theorists" to teach theory because empirical sociologists were better able to show how theory could be used or could be made useful than theorists.

Theory done by theorists – consisting of things like papers on the subject of what Weber meant – was seen as largely irrelevant to the role theory had in the curriculum: to provide graduate students the means of giving some theoretical content to their empirical studies. The attitudes toward theory of non-theorists who teach these courses is exemplified in one especially explicit syllabus, which collects a variety of quotations illustrating the uselessness of theory for empirical sociology and unintelligibility. The syllabus writer comments that " 'theory' can be defined in practice as what people called 'theorists' do, but is as well or better defined as the guiding ideas used by practicing sociologists to understand the world" (Shrum 2003: 8). The syllabus writer quoted here, Wesley Shrum, adds that "Sociological theorists remain committed to studying each other, rather than the subject of which they signed up: the social world" (Shrum 2003: 9).

Not surprisingly, the opportunities to learn "theorists' theory" diminished quickly. Judith Butler observed in a recent interview that when she was a student at Yale it was possible to get a solid grounding there in classical social theory (2004). She points out that this is no longer the case, though in fact there are more opportunities at Yale than at many other American departments. Thus the estrangement of theorists' theory and sociology has had consequences. The most important of these consequences has been that reproduction, the training of theorists in theorists' theory, has essentially ceased in American sociology. Sociology students still learn some theory in some departments, but the kind of thorough training in a common core of texts that was the normal entry ticket for students interested in theorists' theory in the 1960s and early 1970s now no longer exists. At best, there are highly idiosyncratic treatments of theory in a few sociology departments and a small theory community among the students in those departments. But the training is limited and the sense of a larger community with core confidences and points of reference and common concerns is no longer there within sociology. Nor are theoretical interests thought to be a ticket to a career in sociology. The dearth of production in the area of theory and the retirement of many teachers of theory has meant that there is a certain amount of demand, but the demand is being filled by sociologists whose interest in theory is distinctly secondary. The picture outside the United States is often better, but the pressures and the competition are the same.

So what do these institutional facts mean for the future of social theory? They indicate that the older relation to sociology of a semi-autonomous field of social theory doing theory-talk, and through this providing ideas which can be studied empirically, is no longer viable. This was a relationship that in large part survived because of the centrality of the idea of a scientific sociology based on the model of physics, that is to say a relationship with theorists and empirical researchers engaged in a fruitful dialog in pursuit of the common goal of an overarching empirical science. This goal no longer motivates anyone but an eccentric faction of American sociologists. Inquiry that has theoretical context and is primarily driven by disciplinary concerns does continue – economic sociology is an example. But the primary intellectual impetus to sociological research now comes from the organic relations between sociologists and social movements, which use theoretical ideas, but are driven primarily by particular notions of oppression and injury that are rooted in personal experience and related to policies and programs.

Yet social theory goes on, both within sociology, and, increasingly, outside of it. The same forces that led to the estrangement between social theory and empirical sociology have brought social theory closer to political theory, to such topics as citizenship and such figures as Arendt and Schmitt, for example, and to other bodies of thought, such as pragmatism and cultural studies in the humanities. Despite the displacement of theory from sociology, the subject has matter flourished, in different settings and forms. Durkheim, for example, once freed from Parsons, took his place as a theorist of religion and culture: a recent volume on "teaching Durkheim" was published by the American Academy for Religion, a religious studies association, and included chapters on the use of Durkheim in the classroom from scholars in various fields – only one of whom was in a sociology department (Godlove 2005). Weber became part of the canon of political theory (Weber 1994). Indeed, the historical study and interpretation of the classics has flourished over the last few decades to a greater extent than it had when they were tied to the project of scientific sociology. Much of this thinking, for example Chantal Mouffe's Schmittian approach to democratic theory (1985, 1999), is politically engaged. But it is also willing, in ways that "organic" sociology is not, to debate its premises and commitments and to measure itself against past theoretical traditions.

The persistence of social theory and its survival outside of sociology tells its own tale. It shows that the tradition of social theory is deeper and richer than the discipline of sociology on which it depended. Its future, however, is better understood by extrapolating from its pre-disciplinary past, which was also "engaged," open to contestation, and unconcerned about boundaries.

New Challenges and the Persistence of the Old Regime

If we ignore the relationship between social theory and sociology, and ask what the challenges to the social theory tradition are today, four come immediately to mind. In each case they represent competitors to social theory or problems with the relevance of social theory. The most obvious of these challenges arises from the oldest organic relation of social theory, with the left. With the demise of the Soviet Union and the emergence of capitalist-like states from state socialism in eastern Europe, Marxism and Marxist thought has been compelled to rethink itself and to find some theoretical basis for the project of critique (Žižek 2001). Post-Marxist thinkers such as Zygmunt Bauman have proposed such notions as "liquid modernity" to capture the nature of social transformations that made irrelevant the older more mechanistic materialism and its view of the social (2000). As noted, many who think about this transition have turned to the idea of media on the grounds that the space in the determination of human relations formally occupied by the social, that is to say personal relations between people, is now occupied by the media, which mediates relations between people.

The second challenge comes from evolutionary theorizing. The idea that the subject matter of the social was more or less an autonomous subject in which such questions as what is the source of social order and what binds people together could be understood and accounted for in terms of features of the social world itself is subject to a powerful challenge from evolutionary psychologists. They regard the social patterns established by evolution in the genetically reinscribed responses of other primates not only as constraining the answers that can be given to these traditional social theory questions but in large part answering them. Even the evolution of cultural forms, long disregarded as a serious topic in social theory and in anthropology, is now subject to extensive mathematical treatment using evolutionary models (Richerson and Boyd 2006). Social theorists lack the cultural status to set the terms of conventional wisdom on these subjects. The terms are set instead by writers such as Steven Pinker, who has dismissed as false most of the standard objections made by social scientists to the reductive explanation of human culture by reference to consideration sexual selection. Pinker says, for example, that the idea that "throughout history the bride and groom had no say in marriage" (1997: 431–2) and many other social science commonplaces about kinship and social psychology are bunk, and makes universalizing claims about the effects of such things as sexual selection – ignoring the fact that the effects would be quite different if marriages were arranged or greatly constrained by kinship rules, as they have been, Pinker notwithstanding, in much of the world for most of human history.

The third challenge comes from a closely related source, namely cognitive neuroscience. To the extent that aspects of social interaction can be shown to be exhibited in actual brain structures, social theory is compelled to listen. When it is discovered, for example, as it recently was, that altruistic behavior is centered in a certain portion of the brain, theorizing that ignores the phenomenon of altruism or accounts for it entirely in non-altruistic terms, fails to match the "scientific" facts. An extensive body of research in neuroeconomics has now begun which addresses such problems as the neurochemical character of trust, the question of whether punishing free riders is on its own a source of pleasure for the punisher, and so forth (Fehr and Fishbacher 2005; Fehr, Fischbacher, and Kosfeld 2005). This creates a new universe of facts that social theorists need to take account of, facts which stand in a peculiar relationship to the history of social theory.

One important example should make this clear. Early sociological social psychological theorizing was greatly influenced by the idea of imitation, especially in the formulation of Gabriel Tarde (1903). The recent discovery of mirror neurons in human and monkey brains provides an actual neurocognitive mechanism for this social theoretical idea (Hurley and Chater 2005; see also the exchange between Lizardo [2007] and Turner [2007]). And the very possibility of validating our social theoretical distinctions by strapping a subject into an fMRI or some other neuroscientific method radically alters the kind of relation to science social theory can have and the kind of science that social theory can be. On the one hand, it frees social theory from the necessity to, as Noam Chomsky famously put it, "imitate the surface features of the more established sciences" (1967), i.e. to be like physics, and enables social theory to ground its distinctions in an accepted and uncontroversial substrate of scientific facts. The technologies of neuroscience also offer some tantalizing possibilities. If some of these central concepts of social theory, such as authoritarianism or charisma, could be studied in terms of the particular neuro-structures that they involve, social theory would become "scientific" in a more powerful and dramatic way than the kind of imitation science that statistical sociology represents. And if so, it could become allied with and an extension of an acknowledged "real science." On the other hand, it raises the question of whether many traditional social theoretical notions with cognitive implications, such as the idea of collective memory, do in fact correspond to anything in the brain, and forces us to ask whether we should take seriously mental concepts, such as Geertz's "head full of presuppositions," which may fail to correspond to anything discoverable by neuroscience.

A fourth challenge is a bit more familiar in that it is closely related to rational choice thinking of the kind that is highly familiar to those practicing social science. Much rational choice thinking in social science has been addressed to issues that are removed from the classical tradition and classical problems of social theory. This cannot be said of an increasingly important body of applications of rational choice and game theory ideas which is directly concerned with problems of social theory, particularly problems which arise from the social contract tradition and are concerned with the establishment of norms (Bicchieri 2006; Skyrms 2004). This type of thinking is especially associated with Hobbes and tends to use essentially eighteenth-century concepts together with elaborate mathematical arguments to produce conceptually clear formal analyses of problems of convention, norm, and collective order. As this style of techno-ethics has evolved, it has begun to take on additional problems in political philosophy, and curiously enough has begun to assimilate and even rely on empirical work in the social sciences, particularly social psychology (cf. Bicchieri 2006). Ironically, this conceptually very thin kind of social theory has managed to get more out of contemporary empirical social science than social theory itself, which almost never refers to this kind of research.

One reason for this surprising relationship is that some social psychologists have concerned themselves with ethical issues such as distributive justice and to inquire empirically into circumstances which encourage the idea of equity and in which some evidence could be found for a human disposition to equitable solutions to distributional problems. This kind of analysis represents a more subtle challenge to the traditional concerns of social theory, which have typically been more closely bound to the history of Europe and its actual class relations and conflicts. By pitching the problem on a very abstract and unhistorical level, these kinds of social philosophy present themselves as empirically based explanatory accounts relying on a minimum of plausible assumptions which explain actual empirical phenomena in the social world and answer fundamental questions traditionally associated with social theory. This style of thinking has a high level of prestige and American analytic philosophy is extensively studied in European philosophical circles influenced by analytic philosophy, and proceeds in close relation to certain branches of economics.

A fifth challenge is more global. Understanding the world – the project the critics of social theory think has been abandoned by "theorist's theory," today means more than just making itself useful for empirical sociology. It means, at a minimum, contributing to an understanding of such topics as the peaceful collapse of Soviet communism, the environmental challenge, the Asian challenge to Western domination (especially the rise of China), and the US reaction to the security threats.[1] It must be said that these topics are almost entirely absent from empirical sociology and cultural sociology: so much for their engagement with reality. The tradition of social theory, however, was concerned with such issues, and Weber, and notably even Durkheim, remain inspirations for the discussion of issues of war and peace today (cf. Wendt 1999).

But there are obstacles to social theory making original contributions to such questions. One is the political center of social theory. Social theory has anti-liberalism in its genes: Comte was a critic of liberalism, and his successors, such as Durkheim, were as well – right down to Bourdieu and Foucault. German social theory in general was anti-liberal, with the ambiguous exception of Weber himself. The social movements with which sociologists have allied themselves in recent decades – the resistance paradigm discussed earlier – have typically been based on hostility to the market, to globalization, and even to free discussion and cultural production – which cultural studies treats as a form of corporatized false consciousness. In consequence, for many sociologists, "society" has come to mean resistance by the local and the marginal, and a rejection of "seeing like a state," which is associated with masculinist assumptions about power, patriarchy, and whiteness.

The realities of globalization, the problems of the environment, the collapse of the Soviet Union, and so forth, however, are bound up with the successes of liberalism. To get back to the "reality" that "theorists' theory" has supposedly abandoned, it is these anti-liberal assumptions – the now conventional assumptions of much standard sociology as well as of much social theory – that must be interrogated. The idea that resistance and solidarity is a sign of political virtue and is also the special business of sociology is fundamental to the Burawoy model of public sociology. But resistance to globalization and liberalism is also almost always self-interested resistance to economic processes which dissolve privilege. And among the most extreme and, in global terms, inegalitarian forms of privilege that are threatened by these processes are the privileges of citizenship in European states, states which preserve the advantages of their citizens by excluding poor countries and their citizens from their markets and economies. Understanding any of this within the limits of the resistance paradigm is pointless, and the focus on resistance obscures the larger processes. Weber did better because he adopted a "standpoint" that the resistance paradigm devalues. Weber's follower Raymond Aron explained the standpoint well when he said "I was always inclined to ask myself what I could do in the place of those in power" (1990: 30). In asking this question one acknowledges the discipline of reality in a way that the resistance paradigm rejects as ideological and unprogressive. But the resistance paradigm is no longer entitled to the notions of "ideology" and "progress." Indeed, it is the product of the failure of the grand narrative of Marxism that enshrined these notions in social theory.

Is social theory up to the challenge of dealing with the liberalized world? The process has already begun, though it is not without difficulties. The rise of citizenship studies, though rooted in T. H. Marshall's classic essay, is an example: citizenship is a normative and legal concept that is part of the liberal conception of the state, but it also has a critical edge (cf. B. Turner 1986). The study of the public sphere (Alexander 2006; Calhoun 1992), though it is rooted in Habermas's Marxist critique of liberal public as sham (Habermas 1992), nevertheless acknowledges the centrality of the problem of the public sphere and public discussion to understanding modern politics, and avoids reducing the public realm to its extra-political determinants, such as class, as Marxist critiques formerly did.

CONCLUSION: HOPE AND SKEPTICISM

Ulrich Beck says that the core ideas of the tradition of social theory are "zombie concepts" (2004: 152), mindlessly persisting and of no relevance to the present, and he calls for a conceptual revolution: not so much new social theory extending the past as a complete replacement for it. If skeptics like Beck are right, there is no point to extrapolating from the pre-disciplinary past of social theory: social theory as hitherto known is simply dead. If the skeptics like Shrum are right, the end of its role in relation to sociology would be the end of its purpose. But the skeptics are wrong. It is telling that on the commentary pages of the *Financial Times*, a newspaper read most assiduously by the international elite, Weber is routinely invoked – far more frequently than empirical sociology is, and more often than the kind of "public sociology" that aspires to influencing public opinion. The audience of the *Financial Times* is interested in understanding the world and subject to the discipline evoked by Aron. The fact that century-old texts help them do it is evidence enough that the concepts of classical social theory, far from being Zombies, are often as useful as ever, and that the needs remain. Social theory is changing in the face of its challenges. But it needs to change much more.

Note

1   I am indebted to Jan Pakulski for suggesting this list.

Bibliography

Alexander, J. (2006) *The Civil Sphere*. New York: Oxford University Press.

Aron, R. (1990) *Memoirs: Fifty Years of Political Reflection*, trans. G. Holoch. New York: Holmes & Meier.

Barnes, H. E. (ed.) (1948) *An Introduction to the History of Sociology*. Chicago: University of Chicago Press.

Barnes, H. E., and Becker, H. (1961 [1938]) *Social Thought from Lore to Science*, 3rd edn. New York: Dover Publications.

Bauman, Z. (2000) *Liquid Modernity*. Cambridge: Polity.

Beck, U. (2004) "The Cosmopolitan Turn," in N. Gane (ed.), *The Future of Social Theory*. London: Continuum.

Becker, E. (1971) *The Lost Science of Man*. New York: G. Braziller.

Bendix, R. (1960) *Max Weber: An Intellectual Portrait*. Garden City, NY: Doubleday.

Berger, P. L., and Luhmann, T. (1966) *The Social Construction of Reality: A Treatise in the Sociology of Knowledge*. Garden City, NY: Doubleday.

Bicchieri, C. (2006) *The Grammar of Society: The Nature and Dynamics of Social Norms*. Cambridge: Cambridge University Press.

Bourdieu, P. (1977 [1972]) *Outline of a Theory of Practice*, trans. R. Nice. Cambridge: Cambridge University Press.

Bourdieu, P., and Passeron, J.-C. (1977) *Reproduction in Education, Society and Culture*, trans. R. Nice. London: Sage.

Burawoy, M. (2005) "For Public Sociology." Address to the American Sociological Association, San Francisco, Aug. 15, 2004. *American Sociological Review* 70(1): 4–28. <http://www2.asanet.org/pubs/2004PresidentialAddressASR.pdf>.

Butler, J. (2004) "Reanimating the Social," in N. Gane (ed.), *The Future of Social Theory*. London: Continuum.

Calhoun, C. (ed.) (1992) *Habermas and the Public Sphere*. Cambridge, MA: MIT Press.

Camic, C. (1995) "Three Departments in Search of a Discipline: Localism and Interdisciplinary Interaction in American Sociology, 1890–1940." *Social Research* 62(4): 1003–33.

Chomsky, N. (1967) "The Responsibility of Intellectuals." *The New York Review of Books* 8(3). <http://www.nybooks.com/articles/12172>, accessed 7/30/2007.

Chriss, James J. (1999) *Alvin Gouldner: Sociologist and Outlaw Marxist*. Aldershot: Ashgate.

Collins, P. Hill (2000 [1990]) *Black Feminist Thought: Knowledge, Consciousness, and the Politics of Empowerment*, rev. edn. New York: Routledge.

Connell, R. W. (1997) "Why Is Classical Theory Classical?" *American Journal of Sociology* 102(6): 1511–57.

Coser, L. A. (1975) *The Idea of Social Structure: Papers in Honor of Robert K. Merton*. New York: Harcourt Brace Jovanovich.

Ellwood, C. (1971) *The Story of Social Philosophy*. Freeport, NY: Books for Libraries Press.

Eubank, E. E. (1932) *The Concepts of Sociology: A Treatise Presenting a Suggested Organization of Sociological Theory in Terms of its Major Concepts*. New York: D. C. Heath.

Fehr, E., and Fischbacher, U. (2005) "Altruists with Green Beards." *Analyse & Krytik* 27: 73–84.

Fehr, E., Fischbacher, U., and Kosfeld, M. (2005) "Neuroeconomic Foundations of Trust and Social Preferences." *Centre for Economic Policy Research Discussion Papers* 5127. <http://ideas.repec.org/p/cpr/ceprdp/5127.html>, accessed May 15, 2007.

Ferree, M., Marx, R., Kahn, S., and Morimoto, S. A. (2007) "Assessing the Feminist Revolution: The Presence and Absence of Gender in Theory and Practice," in C. Calhoun (ed.), *Sociology in America: A History*. Chicago: University of Chicago Press.

Foucault, M. (1981) *Power/Knowledge: Selected Interviews and Other Writings, 1972–1977*, ed. and trans. C. Gordon. New York: Pantheon Books.

Gane, N. (ed.) (2004) *The Future of Social Theory*. London: Continuum.

Geertz, C. (1973) *The Interpretation of Cultures: Selected Essays*. New York: Basic Books.

Giddens, A. (1984) *The Constitution of Society: Outline of the Theory of Structuration*. Berkeley: University of California Press.

Glassner, B., and Hertz, R. (eds.) (2006) *Our Studies, Ourselves: Sociologists' Lives and Work*. Oxford: Oxford University Press.

Godlove, T. F. (ed.) (2005) *Teaching Durkheim*. New York: Oxford University Press.

Gramsci, A. (1996) "The Intellectuals (from *Prison Notebooks*)," in R. Kearney and M. Rainwater (eds.), *The Continental Philosophy Reader*. London: Routledge.

Habermas, J. (1984) *The Theory of Communicative Action*, trans. T. McCarthy. Boston: Beacon Press.

Habermas, J. (1992) *The Structural Transformation of the Public Sphere*. Cambridge: Polity.

Hall, S. (1997) *Representation: Cultural Representations and Signifying Practices*. London: Sage.

Hall, S., Morley, D., and Chen, K.-H. (1996) *Critical Dialogues in Cultural Studies*. London: Routledge.

Henderson, L. J. (1970 [1941–2]) "Sociology: 23 Lectures, 1941–42," in B. Barber (ed.), *L. J. Henderson on the Social System*. Chicago: University of Chicago Press.

House, J. S. (2004) *A Telescope on Society: Survey Research and Social Science at the University of Michigan and Beyond*. Ann Arbor: University of Michigan Press.

Hurley, S., and Chater, N. (eds.) (2005) *Perspectives on Imitation: From Neuroscience to Social Science*. Cambridge, MA: MIT Press.

Kidd, B. (1894) *Social Evolution*. New York: Macmillan.

Lizardo, O. (2007) " 'Mirror Neurons,' Collective Objects and the Problem of Transmission: Reconsidering Stephen Turner's Critique of Practice Theory." *Journal for the Theory of Social Behaviour* 37: 319–50.

Luhmann, N. (1970) *Soziologische Aufklärung. Aufsätze zur Theorie sozialer Systeme*. Cologne: Westdeutscher Verlag.

MacKinnon, C. (1989) *Toward a Feminist Theory of the State*. Cambridge, MA: Harvard University Press.

Mead, G. H. (1932) *The Philosophy of the Present*. Chicago: University of Chicago Press.

Merton, R. (1967) *On Theoretical Sociology; Five Essays, Old and New*. New York, Free Press.

Merton, R. (1973) *Sociology of Science: Theoretical and Empirical Investigations*, ed. N. Storer. Chicago: University of Chicago Press.

Mouffe, C. (1999) *The Challenge of Carl Schmitt*. London: Verso.

Mouffe, C., and Laclau, E. (1985) *Hegemony and Socialist Strategy: Towards a Radical Democratic Politics*. London: Verso.

Parsons, T. (1937) *The Structure of Social Action*. New York, The Free Press.

Parsons, T. (1951) *The Social System*. New York: The Free Press.

Patten, S. (1896) *The Theory of Social Forces*. Philadelphia: American Academy of Political and Social Science.

Pearl, J. (2000) *Causality: Models, Reasoning, and Inference*. Cambridge: Cambridge University Press.

Pinker, S. (1997) *How the Mind Works*. New York: W. W. Norton.

Richerson, P. J., and Boyd, R. (2006) *Not by Genes Alone: How Culture Transformed Human Evolution*. Chicago: University Of Chicago Press.

Schatzki, T. R. (1996) *Social Practices: A Wittgensteinian Approach to Human Activity and the Social*. Cambridge: Cambridge University Press.

Schatzki, T. R., Knorr-Cetina, K., and von Savigny, E. (eds.) (2001) *The Practice Turn in Contemporary Theory*. London: Routledge.

Schmitt, C. (1976 [1932]) *The Concept of the Political*, trans. G. Schwab. New Brunswick, NJ: Rutgers University Press.

Sennett, R., and J. Cobb (1972) *The Hidden Injuries of Class*. New York: Knopf.

Shrum, W. (2003) "Syllabus for Contemporary Social Theory, Spring 2003." <http://appl003.lsu.edu/artsci/sociologyweb.nsf/$Content/Shrum/$file/SOCL+7131+Shrum.pdf>, accessed July 30, 2007.

Skyrms, B. (2004) *The Stag Hunt and the Evolution of Social Structure*. Cambridge: Cambridge University Press.

Smith, D. (1990) *The Conceptual Practices of Power: A Feminist Sociology of Knowledge*. Boston: Northeastern University Press.

Spencer, H. (1851) *Social Statics: or, The Conditions Essential to Human Happiness Specified, and the First of them Developed*. London: John Chapman.

Spencer, H. (1897 [1876]) *The Principles of Sociology*. New York: Appleton.

Tarde, G. (1903) *The Laws of Imitation*, trans. E. C. Parsons. New York: Henry, Holt.

Turner, B. S. (1986) *Citizenship and Capitalism: The Debate over Reformism*. London: Allen & Unwin.

Turner, S. (2007) "Mirror Neurons and Practices: A Response to Lizardo." *Journal for the Theory of Social Behaviour* 37: 351–71.

Weber, M. (1994) *Political Writings*, ed. P. Lassman and R. Speirs. Cambridge: Cambridge University Press.

Wendt, A. (1999) *Social Theory of International Politics*. Cambridge: Cambridge University Press.

Young, M. F. D. (1971) *Knowledge and Control: New Directions for the Sociology of Education*. London: Collier Macmillan.

Žižek, S. (2001) *Did Somebody Say Totalitarianism?* London: Verso.

Index

Simmel, Georg (*cont'd*)
  and tragedy of culture, 28, 29
  and *Wechselwirkung* (interaction), 85
Simon, Herbert, 366
simplification, 147
simulation, of reality, 258–9
Singer, Peter, 497
Singleton, Vicky, 152
situational-interactional dimension, 90, 95,
    99
Sjoberg, Gideon, Gill, Elizabeth A., and
    Cain, Leonard D., 506
Skeggs, Beverley, 245
skepticism, 466, 543, 563
  critical, 253–5, 258, 262, 385
  organized, 454, 457
  public, 457
skills, 93–4
Skinner, David, 352–3
Sklair, Leslie, 329–30
Skocpol, Theda, 393, 395, 396, 404, 405
skulls, human, measuring, 343
slavery, 127, 245, 246, 325, 327, 487
  abolition, 499
  global, 6
slums, urban, 502, 503
Smart, Barry, 254
Smelser, Neil, 393, 404, 415
  see also Parsons, Talcott, and Smelser,
    Neil
Smith, Adam, 190–1, 209, 394
Smith, Anthony, 397, 398
Smith, Dennis, 396
Smith, Dorothy, 284, 556
Smith, Keri Iyall, 507
Smith, Neil, 330
smoking
  and cancer, 293
  effects, 125
social, the, 260, 487, 528, 536, 555, 560
  changes in nature of, 252
  and cultural, 95
  end of, 274
  and feminist theory, 249
  key aspects, 251
  and non-social, 112
  notion of, 74, 75, 111
  simulation of, 259
  and technical, 147–8
social, as non-Greek word, 513

social action, 2, 8, 43, 138, 292, 385, 516
  cultural dimension, 122
  and emotion, 207
  integration of, 88
  structural theory of, 132
  theories of, 83–101
  unintended consequences of, 2, 8, 108,
    121
  and *Verstehen*, 66
  Weber on, 283
social actor, 516, 520
social agents, 138
social analysis, 388
social arrangements, 260
social being, 83, 84
social change, 429, 436, 438, 441
  and history, 391
  and population, 430–1
  transformative, 47
social class *see* class, social
social configurations, effects of change in,
    251–2
social construction, 466, 555
  of technology (SCOT), 455
social constructionism, 281–95, 343–4,
    350, 461, 505, 519, 554
  dilemma of, 289, 294
  origins of, 282–7
  as possible threat to social sciences, 251
  virtues of, 282
social constructivism, 460, 462, 464
social contract, 138, 310, 561
social control, 32, 71, 115
social coordination mechanisms, 122
social critics, 111
social determinism, 528
social drama, 383
social dynamics, 24
social economics, 361
social engineering, 254, 352
social exchange, 516
social groups, 453
social history of technology (SHOT), 455
social institutions, 227–9, 343
  and biotechnology, 350
social integration, 41, 44–5, 392, 412, 413
social interaction, 47, 49–52, 114, 224,
    225, 283, 290
  Berger and Luckmann and, 227
  determination of, 344